Praise for the first edition of *The Linux Cookbook*

"This is the book that will bring back your love of computing."—VANCOUVER WASHINGTON LINUX USERS GROUP

"Having this book on your desk is probably the next best thing to having your own personal guru."—UNIXREVIEW.COM

"Beginners will find this book invaluable. . . . There is plenty of good information to be had in these pages . . ."—SLASHDOT

"It's by far the most entertaining UNIX book I've ever read, and the only one I could recommend without reservations to people who already have basic UNIX skills."—FRESHMEAT

"If you plan on running any distribution of Linux—this book needs to be on your desk."—TECHWEEKTV

"[*The Linux Cookbook*] is the most practical daily use Linux book I've seen so far—highly recommended for anyone getting started with Linux."—PCUNIX

"If you own a Linux system you'll find this book indispensable."—NETSURFER DIGEST

"[With this book] I can face the Linux command line without fear."—SKIPPING DOT NET

"This book has given me the knowledge to get the most out of Linux. I am now more productive with Linux and understand it better because of this book."—RAVEN MATRIX

"An excellent reference."—CHOICE MAGAZINE, a publication of the AMERICAN LIBRARY ASSOCIATION, upon designating the first edition of *The Linux Cookbook* an OUTSTANDING ACADEMIC TITLE in January, 2003.

The Linux Cookbook

Tips and Techniques for Everyday Use

Michael Stutz

2ND EDITION

COMPLETELY REVISED AND EXPANDED

**NO STARCH
PRESS**

San Francisco

Printed in the United States of America
1 2 3 4 5 6 7 8 9 10–04 03 02 01

Publisher: William Pollock
Managing Editor: Karol Jurado
Cover Design: Octopod Studios
Book Design: Michael Stutz
Technical Reviewer: John Mark Walker
Copyeditor: Andy Carroll
Proofreader: Mary Johnson

For information on book distribution or translations, please contact No Starch Press, Inc. directly:

No Starch Press, Inc.
555 De Haro Street, Suite 250, San Francisco, CA 94107
phone: 415-863-9900; fax: 415-863-9950; info@nostarch.com; www.nostarch.com

Library of Congress Cataloging-in-Publication Data

```
Stutz, Michael.
   Linux cookbook : tips and techniques for everyday use / Michael
Stutz.-- 2nd ed.
       p. cm.
Includes index.
   ISBN 1-59327-031-3
   1. Linux. 2.  Operating systems (Computers)  I. Title.
   QA76.76.O63 S788 2004
   005.4'32--dc22
```
                                                              2003021940

Brief Contents

Table of Contents

11.   Grammar and Reference 275

12.   Analyzing Text 293

13. Formatting Text 305

APPENDICES 697

Appendix A.   Administrative Issues 699

Preface to the Second, Revised Edition

This is a book about using computers to get your work done in the best and most efficient manner possible. As with a culinary cookbook, it gives tested recipes for the successful preparation or accomplishment of particular things. In the preface to the first edition of this book, I explained it like this:

> I know that Linux isn't difficult to use, especially when compared with other software and operating systems, but what was needed was a guide to show people how to use it to get things done: "Oh, you want to do *that*? Here, type this."

> That explains the premise of the book—it's a hands-on guide to getting things done on a Linux system, designed for the everyday user who is not necessarily a computer programmer.

This new, revised edition of the *Cookbook* remains all of that and more. Its coverage has been expanded, and every recipe has been refined.

Once again, it only got there with the assistance of some individuals whom it is now my pleasure to thank—foremost being those at No Starch Press: publisher William Pollock; Karol Jurado, under whose editorship this book was prepared; John Mark Walker, for his technical review of the manuscript; and, for helpful assistance that speeded production, Hillel Heinstein, Riley Hoffman, and Leigh Sacks. On behalf of the Press, Andy Carroll and Mary Johnson contributed valuable corrections and comments.

I also thank the following individuals for their critical comments and suggestions: Ralph Amissah, Jiri Baum, Simon Bellwood, Conny Brunnkvist, Ed Casas, John R. Daily, Herbert Martin Dietze, Eric Engberg, David Fabiani, Nelson Correa de Toledo Ferraz, John Gilmore, Sven Grewe, V.T. Jones, Donald E. Knuth, Rüdiger Kuhlmann, Adrian Lanning, Jonathan Nichol, Miroslaw Osys, Fernando Perez, Alex Radsky, Mark Rahner, Rinaldo Rasa, Roel Schroeven, Ken Stewart, Frank Wallingford, Rich Warren, and Albert Witteveen.

Finally, I am happy to thank the usual suspects for their encouragement and general presence: Jack Angelotta, Bradford W. Byron, Aldo P. Magi, Steven Snedker, Mr. & Mrs. Walter V. Stutz, and—most of all—Marie R. Stutz.

The Linux Cookbook was printed in its first edition three years ago, and it was conceived four years before that. Life moves on. And in its appearance, the Linux system too is always changing; this outer shell moves with the fashions of the season, it ages and becomes obsolete, and it fades away into the mists of time, while the inner core does not.

The core melds, picks up new features, refines or discards others, but somehow it lingers and remains. In that sense it is the only part worth dwelling on. In the 1970s, typing `ls` from a hardware terminal to list the files in a directory worked much the same as it does today on Linux. This inner core is the language of UNIX, and it is the foundation upon which the entire system is laid.

It has always been my desire to clearly and completely teach that foundation in the *Cookbook*, and I hope that the product you now hold may be of more worth, and resonate longer, than something that only chases after the sleek contours and momentary luster of the latest and already fading outer shell, while leaving so much of the inner magic still a mystery.

And so here it is: A new edition that gives, to the reader, a book whose substance is improved, its horizons broadened—and to the author, a chance to do a second take, to trim and burnish, to attempt refinement of a work once labored on. I hope you likewise find the journey sufficiently rewarding.

MICHAEL STUTZ
JUNE 2004

I. WORKING WITH LINUX

## CHAPTER 1

Introduction

Before we start "cooking," we'll get some preliminaries out of the way in this first chapter, which explains both how the book is organized and the conventions that are used throughout it. It also shows you where to begin if you're new to Linux, and how to get more help, should you need it. It concludes with a short background history of the software that is the subject of the book.

The rest of the book is all recipes, which are categorized by the tasks they perform or the objects they work on—such as text, files, images, and so forth. This first part of the book explains the general techniques and methods for working with Linux—including how to get the system ready for use, how to run commands on the system, which commands every Linux user knows, and how to use the interfaces that come with Linux.

1.1 Recipes

Recipes are methods for accomplishing a particular task on Linux. Recipes are organized into chapters, which deal with one specific kind of task, such as Viewing Text or Editing Images. Chapters are often concluded with a table of hints identifying more applications or tools pertinent to the subject of that chapter.

1.1.1 Recipe Numbers

Each recipe is referenced by its *recipe number*, which is constructed as follows: the first figure in the recipe number always corresponds to the the chapter number, and the second figure to the section or category of the recipe. So if Chapter 3 is The Shell, then Recipe 3.5 is the fifth recipe on shells.

Sometimes a recipe number will contain a third figure. This is for subjects that are so broad as to have more than one recipe that fits it. Recipe 3.5 [Using Shell Variables], page 77, for example, is on the subject of using command history in the shell, and is divided further into more recipes; Recipe 3.5.3 [Displaying the Contents of a Variable], page 79, is the third recipe on shell variables.

This numbering system is adopted from Buwei Yang Chao's *How To Cook and Eat In Chinese* (John Day, 1945), one of the culinary cookbooks that served as initial inspiration for this book. I am told that her system shares a commonality with Chinese dictionaries and with the Chinese language itself.

1.1.2 Preparation of Recipes

Each recipe describes a method for completing a specific task on the system, and these tasks require at least one software program. The software programs or files a recipe calls for in its preparation are its *ingredients*.

You might not have all of these programs installed on your system and ready for use, so recipes commence with a listing of the programs it uses and the packages or URLs where you can find them.

Ingredients that most everyone is sure to have on hand are omitted from this listing. For example, the `ls` tool for listing files in a directory will be available on all systems, so its listing is always omitted.

The rule of measure for determining whether an ingredient is listed or not comes from the Debian distribution, which classifies packages in varying levels of importance, from the "Required" packages that all systems absolutely must have in order to run, to "Optional" and "Extra" packages that you only install if you want them. If it's "Required" or "Important" to Debian, then it's a very common program no matter what your distribution, and I don't need to list it.

1.1.3 Format of Recipes

Recipes are structured in the following way:
  1. Recipe number and title of the recipe.
  2. General description of recipe and, optionally, the number of suggested methods of preparation.
  3. If a recipe has more than one suggested method to get the same results, the method number will be given here and the remaining elements of the recipe will be repeated for each method, each preceded by its method number.
  4. Special ingredients, if any.

     The package name(s) and URLs where the software can be obtained are listed here.

     Packages are listed in the two preeminent Linux formats: DEB and RPM; chances are your distribution uses one of them. The DEB format originated with Debian and is also used by a few others, while RPM began with Red Hat and has since been adopted several major distributions.

     To find the package for your hardware platform and distribution version, look for this package base name in your Linux distribution CD-ROMs or archive. You can also search for them online: DEB packages are available at Debian's package site [http://packages.debian.org/], and RPM packages can be searched for at the online RPM Database [http://rpmfind.net/].

For example, if XFree86 is listed for the RPM package, the actual package file name for your particular RPM-based system might be XFree86-VGA16-3.3.6-29.sparc.rpm which, according to its entry for XFree86 in the aforementioned RPM Database, is the latest XFree86 package file for use with VGA16 video cards on the SPARC platform.

The sources and binaries for these programs are usually available unpackaged, too; the location from where they can be retrieved on the World Wide Web is listed, if available. Use these sources for distributions that use neither package format (Slackware is the prime example), or for those odd but occasional cases where a DEB or RPM doesn't exist for some program. (Sometimes, the home page will contain the sources in one or both of these package formats anyway.)

But Web sites, of course, are transient; if you cannot find the source package for a program at its given URL, you can always obtain the sources from Debian's package site [http://packages.debian.org/], where each package has its own page containing a link with a .tar.gz archive of its sources.

5. Special preparation or setup, if any. If you must be the superuser or require special privileges to run the command, this is noted here. When a configurable program is described, the standard setup as provided by the Debian distribution is assumed, unless otherwise specified here.

6. "Cooking" method proper.

7. Remarks concerning the results and use.

8. At least one example of the method in a specific context, set off from the text by an arrow. If the example takes several steps to perform, these steps are then enumerated. Where multiple examples are given, each is set off from the text by a bullet.

9. Variations on the standard preparation, with additional examples.

10. Extra commands or actions you might want to do next. Some programs take a number of options that modify the way they work. Sometimes, various options that a tool takes are listed in a table. These lists are not always exhaustive; rather, they contain the most popular or useful options, or those options that are relevant to the discussion at hand. Consult the online manual page of a particular tool for the complete listing (see Recipe 2.8.4 [Reading a Page from the System Manual], page 46).

11. Special notes of caution or interest.

12. Sources of further information.

Not all of these items will be present in every recipe.

1.2 Typographical Conventions

The display of computer interaction presents a special problem in a written work. What follows are the typographical conventions used in this book.

The names of files or directories appear in a monospaced typewriter face, as `file`; commands appear in the same face, as `command`, and strings of text are typeset like "`some text.`" Options, application modes, menu items, function names, and variable names are all set in this same typewriter face.

The names of documents or users in some recipes may not always reference actual documents or users on your system, but are examples that demonstrate the general principles involved. So when I show how to print a file called `resume`, you might not necessarily have a file with that name on your system, but you should understand from it how to print a file.

⇒ The text that introduces an example is offset from the text with an arrow, like this.

- If there are multiple examples, then each individual example is bulleted like this.

- When several discrete steps are necessary, they are enumerated.

Text you are intended to type is written in a slanted typewriter face *like this*. When you are meant to press a specific key on the keyboard, its conventional name is given displayed in a key box. For example, (Q) represents pressing the "Q" key on the keyboard, and (RET) denotes pressing the "Return" key on the keyboard for typing a newline.[1]

So where I say, "To do this, type:" and then give a sample command line, the text you actually type is presented *like this* and the text that is output by the system is presented `like this`. Keys you are to press, as opposed to characters you literally type, are given as a key box.

⇒ For example, typing an uppercase "F" is denoted by *F*, and typing a lowercase "f" by *f*, while just pressing the "F" key (regardless of case) is denoted by (F).

---

[1] This key is labeled "Enter" on some keyboards, while still others have only an arrow going downward and then pointing to the left, like the old carriage return of typewriters.

In examples where keys are meant to be pressed and held down together, the keys are connected together with hyphens; the hyphens are not meant to be literally pressed. For example, pressing the ⟨CTRL⟩, ⟨ALT⟩, and ⟨DEL⟩ keys, and holding them down at the same time, is a combination that has meaning in some operating systems (including Linux, where this keystroke shuts down the system and reboots the computer); it is represented in the text like this:

⟨CTRL⟩-⟨ALT⟩-⟨DEL⟩

In the same way, keys that are meant to be pressed one after another are separated by a space; the space is not to be literally typed. So for a keystroke like this:

⟨RET⟩ ⟨RET⟩

you would press the carriage return key, and then press the carriage return key again, but do not type a space between them. The same goes for text followed by a key—for example, a physical space appears in the book between commands and the final ⟨RET⟩ that ends a command line, and it should not be literally typed (although there is often no consequence for actually typing this space). Where explicitly pressing the space bar is called for, that key is represented in examples as ⟨SPACEBAR⟩.

There are also some special keys that we should talk about.

Excepting a few special three-key combinations, the ⟨CTRL⟩ ("Control") key is always used in combination with one other key. First, the ⟨CTRL⟩ key is pressed, and, while it is still depressed, the second key is pressed; then, both keys are released. This is a *control-key combination*. Control keys have special meanings that are applicable in most programs. For example, the "Control-C" combination, depressing the ⟨CTRL⟩ key and then pressing ⟨C⟩, is the "cancel" command, which cancels or breaks out of whatever command is running.

There are three ways these control key combinations are denoted in writing. The traditional way is with a caret (^) followed by the capital letter of the second key in the combination. For example, to represent "Control-C" in this way, one would write ^C. This is called *hat notation*.

The second way is to use C- (to represent the ⟨CTRL⟩ key) followed by the lowercase letter of the second key. So to represent the "Control-C" key combination in this manner, one would write C-c. This notation is used by the GNU Project, and is written this way in GNU documentation, so I call it *GNU notation*.

The third way to represent control-key combinations is to show a literal ⟨CTRL⟩ key followed by a hyphen and the second key to press. So "Control-C" would be written as ⟨CTRL⟩-⟨C⟩. I call this *key notation*, and it is the notation used throughout this book.

To type one of these combinations, press and hold ⟨CTRL⟩, press the second key, and then release both keys.

⇒ For example, to type "Control-D," which may be written as ^D, C-d or ⟨CTRL⟩-⟨D⟩, press and hold ⟨CTRL⟩, type the ⟨D⟩ key, and then release both keys.

In some applications, the ⟨META⟩ key is used in the same way as ⟨CTRL⟩. GNU Project programs and documentation denote ⟨META⟩ key combinations by *M-x*, where *x* is the second key in the combination. Most keyboards today don't have a ⟨META⟩ key, of course; where you see reference to this key, just use the ⟨ALT⟩ key. Throughout this book, I'll write these combinations in key notation with ⟨ALT⟩ instead of ⟨META⟩, since the former key is most often the actual key in use.

⇒ So to type *M-c*, press and hold ⟨ALT⟩, press the ⟨C⟩ key, and then release both keys.

You can often get the same effect by pressing and releasing ⟨ESC⟩, and then pressing the second key. Do this if your keyboard doesn't have an ⟨ALT⟩ key, or if your ⟨ALT⟩ isn't set up as the ⟨META⟩ key.[2]

⇒ To type *M-c* without using ⟨ALT⟩, press and release ⟨ESC⟩, and then press and release the ⟨C⟩ key.

Both ⟨CTRL⟩ and ⟨ALT⟩ sequences are not case-sensitive; that is, pressing a capital *C* to make the last example is the same as pressing the lowercase *c* (although *c* is certainly easier to type, if Caps Lock is off). In GNU notation, the *C-* or *M-* prefix is always given as an uppercase letter, and the key that follows is always given as a lowercase letter. The convention for hat notation is to always use an uppercase letter for the control key.

Furthermore, some programs take commands that are a combination of key combinations and sequences, and so the hyphen and space representations can be combined. For instance, if a command is to press and hold ⟨CTRL⟩, press ⟨X⟩ and release both keys, and then type a lowercase letter "q," it will be denoted in the text like so:

⟨CTRL⟩-⟨X⟩ q

---

[2] If your keyboard has a Windows key, then it, and not ⟨ALT⟩, may be set up as the ⟨META⟩ key. You will have to experiment to see which combination works on your system.

Sometimes, a terminal screen is shown to illustrate an interactive session, as in Figure 1-1. A border is also drawn around shell scripts and other program listings that are to be typed in.

In examples where a shell prompt is displayed, the default current working directory is omitted in the prompt, and a "$" is used on its own; when a command outputs text and then exits, the last line of an example contains a "$" character to denote the return to a shell prompt. Don't worry if this sounds strange to you now; all of this "shell" business is explained in Chapter 3 [The Shell], page 53.

```
$ Text that you actually type is displayed in a slanted typewriter
face, like this. If it is a command to be typed at a shell prompt, the
command is preceded by a $ character to indicate the prompt.

Text that denotes program output is displayed in a monospaced typewriter
face, like this. When there is such output, a shell prompt is also given
to denote program completion:

$
```

Figure 1-1. Interactive session in examples.

Borders are not drawn around "one-liner" examples showing commands that return to the shell prompt without giving any output, or commands whose output is not particularly relevant to the example. The returning shell prompt is omitted here, too.

And finally, a remark on quoted punctuation. In the Internet age it has become a trend, away from the American printing convention, to place trailing punctuation outside of the quotation. The argument is that computers cannot recognize the punctuation for what it is, and assume it is part of the literal characters being quoted. We operators don't want to confuse the machine, so we keep this trailing punctuation outside the quotes. First it was adopted in the computer programming languages (not a one, to my knowledge, accepts text written in the American convention), and then in the technical manuals and computer books, and it is now becoming widespread throughout other literature, especially in online publications.

But we human beings understand punctuation, and it is for us that it exists. We should make systems that work *for* us, and print words the way we intend to write them—not bend our own expressions to fit the tooth of a sprocket.

1.3 Who This Book Assumes You Are

There a few assumptions that this book makes about you, the reader, and about your Linux system.

The *Cookbook* assumes that you have at least minimal understanding of your computer—you know that the *hardware* is the machinery itself, and the *software* is the instructions that run on it. You don't have to know how to take your system apart or anything like that, but you ought to know how to operate the mouse, where the power button is on your computer and monitor, how to load paper in your printer, and so forth. If you need help with any of these tasks or concepts, ask your dealer or the party who set up your computer.

This book also assumes that you already have Linux installed and properly set up, and that you have your own user account set up on your system (making a user account is described in Recipe A.6.1 [Making a User Account], page 717; if you need help with installation and setup, please see Recipe 1.6 [If You Need More Help], page 13). No one distribution of Linux is assumed, and any specialties for any one of them in the text are identified as such.

While this book can and should be used by the newcomer to Linux, I like to think that I've presented broad enough coverage of the Linux-based system, and have included enough interesting or obscure material, so that gurus, hackers, and members of the Linux Cabal may find some of it new and useful—and that any such user will not feel ashamed to have a copy of this book on his desk or as part of his library.

And there is another assumtion this book makes that is of importance only to such gurus and old-timers. The Bash shell, as you gurus know, may be thought of as the "default" shell of Linux; because this is so, it is the shell assumed for all examples in this book. So if you have experience with another shell, take note of the differences—you may find examples that do not work in your favorite non-Bash shell (for example, the command `locate *txt` will not work as intended in Csh).

1.4 What This Book Won't Show You

The point of this book is to show people how to use Linux for all of their everyday tasks. That is a broad subject, encompassing a great deal of material. Topics that are outside of that scope do not appear in this book at all; these topics are worth mentioning up front.

This book won't show you how to:

1. **Install Linux.** No book can do that and remain accurate for very long. Books that say that they can tell you how are fibbing. As described later in this chapter, Linux comes in many different "distributions," and each has its own install process. Distributions themselves come in different versions, which change all the time. And then the vagaries of hardware must be added to the equation: Dick will go through a different procedure installing Linux on his Dell PC with USB that came with Windows 2000 pre-installed on it as Jane will installing Linux on her Apple iPOD.

   If you are a computer beginner, and not technically proficient enough to install an operating system and make the requisite hardware adjustments, your best bets are the following:

   a. Purchase a computer with Linux pre-installed.[3]

   b. Have a Linux-savvy friend install it for you.

   c. Take your system to your local Linux User Group (LUG) and have them do it for you while you wait. They frequently run "InstallFests" for such purpose (for a list of LUGs, see list item #4 in Recipe 1.6 [If You Need More Help], page 13).

2. **Use proprietary software.** The very reason I use Linux and recommend it to others is because it's not proprietary, but instead is published in such a way so that anyone can examine the software, share it with others, and adapt it to his needs. I don't use proprietary software at all and don't know the first thing about it. Therefore, there will be no proprietary software in this book.

3. **Use experimental software.** There are thousands of software programs available for Linux, and I cover a good deal of the most popular and important ones. What I omit are the software packages that are currently in a "beta" or some other unstable release not yet intended for the general public.

4. **Secure your system.** The specialized topic of security is sufficiently large to warrant its own book.

5. **Become a system administrator.** The basic tasks of system administration for the home user are described in Appendix A [Administrative Issues], page 699, which is enough to get you going successfully; for more detail than this, you will need a specialized book on the subject. I recommend the *Linux System Administrators' Guide*, which should be available right

---

[3] For a complete list of such dealers, see http://www.linux.org/hardware/.

on your system (for how to access it, see Recipe 2.8.6 [Reading System Documentation and Help Files], page 50).

6. **Administrate a network.** There are too many kinds of networks, and this is most often a technical and not user-based application. The *Linux Network Administrators' Guide* is recommended for this purpose (see Appendix D [References For Further Interest], page 731).

7. **Use Linux in software development.** Program development, compilation, and software project management are out of this book's scope. However, the programmer will find much of the material in this book useful for his task.

8. **Use Linux in other specialized fields.** Everything in this book should be useful to you, whether you are a music composer, biochemist, schoolteacher, secretary, or whatever. However, this book will have no specific sections for "Using Linux for Music Composition," "Using Linux in Biochemistry Research," "Using Linux in the Classroom," or "A Secretary's Guide to Linux," although Linux is used in such fields of endeavor to great success. Reports, papers, Web sites and even books have been written on the use of Linux in innumerable special fields, and its applications in varied fields are growing. In the *Cookbook*, I cover the basics of using Linux as a general tool, regardless of your specific field or interest.

9. **Use a non-Linux system.** Most of the free software described in this book has been ported to other systems, particularly to other flavors of UNIX. The recipes in this book should more or less work on these systems. However, this isn't *The UNIX Cookbook*, and so any peculiarities of non-Linux usage are not addresssed—Linux is always the assumed platform.

1.5 What to Try First

The first four chapters of this book contain all of the introductory matter you need to begin working with Linux. These are the basics. Beginning Linux users should start with the concepts described in these first chapters. Once you've learned how to power up the system and log in, you should look over the chapter on the shell, just enough so that you are familiar with typing at the command prompt; then, skip over to the chapter on the graphical interface called the X Window System, so that you can start X and run programs from there if you like (most distributions today are set up to automatically start out in X).

Once you know your way around X, you should read the chapter on files and directories next, to get a sense of what the system looks like and how to maneuver through it. Then, go on to learn how to view text, and how to edit it in an editor (described in the chapters on viewing text and editing text). After this, explore the rest of the book as your needs and interests dictate.

⇒ To recapitulate, here is what I consider to be the essential material to absorb in order to familiarize yourself with the basic usage of a Linux system:

1. Chapter 1 [Introduction], page 3 (this chapter).

2. Chapter 2 [What Every Linux User Knows], page 27.

3. Chapter 3 [The Shell], page 53 (just looking over the main portions of the first three sections, and ignoring the rest for now).

4. Chapter 4 [The X Window System], page 95 (ignoring the section on configuration for now).

5. Chapter 5 [Files and Directories], page 125.

6. Chapter 9 [Viewing Text], page 211 (mostly the first section on perusing text).

7. Chapter 10 [Editing Text], page 231 (enough to select a text editor and begin using it).

If you have a question about a particular program name, function name, or mode name, look it up in the *program* index ([Program Index], page 739). The other index, listing recipe names, proper names, and the general concepts involved, is called the *concept* index ([Concept Index], page 747).

1.6 If You Need More Help

If you need more help than this book can give, remember that you do have other options. Try these steps for getting help:

1. Chances are good that you are not alone in your question, and that someone else has asked it before; therefore, the compendiums of "Frequently Asked Questions" may have the answer you need. What follows are some of the more popular FAQs for Linux.

   `http://faqs.org/faqs/linux/faq/`   The Linux FAQ.

   `http://tinyurl.com/fqe8`   Linux FAQ for Windows Users.

`http://debian.org/doc/FAQ/`	The Debian FAQ.
`http://rhlufaq.synfin.net/`	The Red Hat Linux User's FAQ.
`http://faqs.org/`	The Internet FAQ Archives; contains hundreds of FAQs on a variety of subjects.

2. The Linux Documentation Project [`http://linuxdoc.org/`] is the center of the most complete and up-to-date Linux-related documentation available; see if there is a document related to the topic you need help with.

3. Usenet newsgroups are often an excellent place to discuss issues with other Linux users, and to get technical help. (Usenet is described in Recipe 34.4 [Reading Usenet], page 679). The following table lists some newsgroups that may be of interest.

`news:comp.os.linux.hardware`	Hardware help and support.
`news:comp.os.linux.help`	General Linux help and support.
`news:comp.os.linux.setup`	Linux installation assistance.
`news:alt.os.linux`	Main Linux "alt" newsgroup for general assistance (branches here include special groups for Red Hat, Mandrake and other distributions).
`news:linux.debian.user`	Help for Debian users.

4. Find the Linux User Group (LUG) nearest you—people involved with LUGs can be great sources of hands-on help, and it can be fun and rewarding to get involved with other Linux and free-software enthusiasts in your local area.

`http://www.ssc.com:8080/glue/`	GLUE ("Groups of Linux Users Everywhere")
`http://lugww.counter.li.org/`	Linux Users Groups World-Wide
`http://www.linux.org/groups/`	Linux User Groups

5. Consider hiring a consultant. This may be a good option if you need work done right away and are willing to pay for it. The *Linux Consultants HOWTO* is a list of consultants around the world who provide various support services for Linux and open source software in general. A copy of it should be installed on your system (see Recipe 2.8.6 [Reading System Documentation and Help Files], page 50). Consultants have various interests and areas of expertise, and they are listed in that document with contact information.

6. Finally, see the list of recommendations in Appendix D [References for Further Interest], page 731, which includes books and Web sites that may be of help.

1.7 Background and History of Linux

In order to understand what Linux is all about, it helps to know a bit about how it all began—the history of Linux goes back well before 1991, when Linus Torvalds famously began work on his free OS. The following is a historical overview, giving a concise background of the software that is the subject of this book. You'll find more information on this topic in the books listed in Appendix D [References For Further Interest], page 731.

This history may explain the longevity of UNIX and why it may be around in some form for time to come—today as Linux, and tomorrow as perhaps something else.

1.7.1 Early Days of UNIX

UNIX, the original ancestor of Linux, is an *operating system*.[4] Or at least it *was* an operating system; the original system known as UNIX proper is not the "UNIX" we know and use today; there are now many "flavors" of UNIX, of which Linux has become the most popular.

A product of the 1960s, UNIX and its related software was invented by Dennis Ritchie, Ken Thompson, Brian W. Kernighan, and other hackers[5] at

---

[4] The set of basic software tools that a computer needs so that you can operate it to any success, including a means to run other programs.

[5] While the term *hacker* has come to refer to a computer vandal or intruder, the original computer meaning concerned a computer programmer or technician who finds obsessive joy in programming and consequently is adept or inventive at it.

Bell Labs in 1969; its name was a play on MULTICS, another operating system of the time.[6]

In the early days of UNIX, any interested party who had the hardware to run it could get a tape of the software from Bell Labs, with printed manuals, for a very nominal charge. (This was before the era of personal computing, and in practice, mostly universities and research laboratories did this.) Local sites played with the software's *source code* (the instructions that formed the software work itself, written in a human-readable language),[7] extending and customizing the software to their needs and liking.

Beginning in the late 1970s, computer scientists at the University of California, Berkeley, a licensee of the UNIX source code, had been making their own improvements and enhancements to the UNIX source during the course of their research, and those improvements included the development of TCP/IP Internet networking. Their work became known as the BSD ("Berkeley Systems Distribution") flavor of UNIX.

The source code of their work was made publicly available under licensing that permitted redistribution, with source or without, provided that Berkeley was credited for its portion of the code. There are many modern variants of the original BSD still actively developed today, and some of them—such as NetBSD, OpenBSD, and Apple's Mac OS X—can run on personal computers.

1.7.2 Genesis of the Free Software Movement

Over the years, UNIX's popularity grew. But after the divestiture of AT&T in 1984, the tapes of the source code that Bell Labs provided became the basis for a proprietary, commercial product: AT&T UNIX. The uppercase word UNIX became a trademark of AT&T (since transferred to other organizations), to identify its particular operating system.[8] It was expensive, and didn't come with the source code that showed how it worked and let you fix, extend, or improve it. Even if you paid extra for a copy of the sources, you couldn't

---

[6] The name UNIX was first written as UNICS, which stood for "Uniplex Information and Computing System."

[7] For a computer to make use of these written works, the source code must be run through a *compiler*, which is a program that uses these writings to output a new file of machine instructions. A software program in compiled form, not readable by man, is called a *binary* or *executable* file. Binaries are the files you use when you run a program on the system.

[8] But today, when people say "UNIX," they usually mean "a UNIX-like operating system," a generalization that includes Linux.

share with your programmer colleagues any of the improvements, fixes, or discoveries you made.

By the early 1980s, proprietary software development, by only-for-profit corporations, was quickly becoming the norm—even at the universities. No longer was software source code considered a work of technical literature to be published for an educated public, but these written works were now kept secret and hidden, and in their compiled forms they were put in boxes to be sold as proprietary, commercial products that your system could execute but that you could never read.

In 1984, while at the Massachusetts Institute of Technology in Cambridge, Massachusetts, hacker Richard Stallman saw his colleagues gradually move to this proprietary development model. But he could not accept the kind of civilization such proprietism would offer: No sharing your findings with your fellow man, no freedom for anyone to take a look "under the hood" of a published work to understand it or to build upon it, and certainly no general advance. There would not even be a way to improve or extend your own copy of such works, or gain insight from the writings of other programmers. The proprietary model would mean the end of computer software as literature.

Instead of following in the direction that most of computing had taken, Stallman decided to start a project to build and assemble a new UNIX-like operating system from scratch, and publish it in written (source code) form. He announced his project on September 27, 1983.[9] This was the GNU Project, whose name stands for itself ("GNU's NOT UNIX").[10]

Stallman had to devise a way to publish these writings so that others could use them to advance the body of source-code literature, but so that no one could use them as the secret instructions for a software "product." He could not place them in the public domain, because then he would forfeit all rights given by copyright law, and could not stop others from using this source code in products where the source code is kept secret.

Licensing was developed as a way to expressly give everyone the right to copy, distribute, and modify his copy of the work, though under certain strict terms and conditions. For the GNU Project, Stallman had the General Public

---

[9] The original announcment can be viewed here:
http://groups.google.com/groups?selm=771%40mit-eddie.UUCP.

[10] No such "official GNU" operating system has yet been released in its entirety, but most people today consider Linux-based free software systems to be the effective realization of Stallman's goals—hence his famous request for people to call the Linux-based system "GNU/Linux" instead.

License, or GNU GPL, devised.[11] It formalized through a legal contrivance what had been the common, unspoken practice in the early days of UNIX: Popularly called a *copyleft*, it permits anyone to copy, distribute, or modify a so-licensed work, provided that all copies are released with the same license, and all changes are documented. Even today it is the most widely used of all such licenses.

This kind of software became known as *free software*. Stallman formed the Free Software Foundation (FSF), a non-profit corporation, to advance this concept and his GNU Project. The FSF also made copies of the GNU software available for sale as it was developed; individuals and businesses may charge for copies of a free software work, but there are never any secret writings—with free software, anyone can read the source code.

1.7.3 The Arrival of Linux

In the early 1990s, as the Internet grew on college campuses, a new generation discovered the small but burgeoning free software movement. Finnish computer science student Linus Torvalds had been hacking on Minix, a miniature UNIX-like operating system for personal computers then used in college operating systems courses.[12] He decided to improve the main software component underlying Minix, called the *kernel*, by writing his own. (The kernel is the central component of any UNIX-like operating system.)

In late 1991, Torvalds published the first version of this kernel on the Internet, calling it "Linux," a play on both Minix and his own name.[13]

When Torvalds published Linux, he used the copyleft software license published by the Free Software Foundation, the GNU GPL. Torvalds also invited contributions from other programmers, and these contributions came—slowly at first, but as the Internet grew, thousands of hackers and programmers from around the globe contributed to his free software project.

This began the exciting period of development that throughout the 1990s made Linux *the* talk of the computing world; the technical press ignored it at first, while old-timers said they'd seen nothing like it since the beginning of the PC revolution many years back—it gave every individual the opportunity

---

[11] Originally the "Emacs Public License" when first published in 1985; the current GNU GPL is on the Web at http://www.gnu.org/copyleft/gpl.txt.

[12] Presumably, they all use Linux now.

[13] This was not the original name, however. Torvalds had originally called it `freax`, for " 'free' + 'freak' + the obligatory '-x' "; while the 1990s were fast becoming the "freaky" alterna decade (at least in fashion), more people seemed to favor "Linux," and the name stuck.

to work, and to make his contribution to the public good. The land was uncharted and the possibilities were abundant. In other words, as expressed by many observers, it made computing *fun* again!

But even as the reputation of Linux rose during this time, it was not always treated seriously by some UNIX folk and other skeptics. This may have been due, in part, to the fact that Linux was running on home computers with off-the-shelf components, whereas UNIX, like any "serious" OS, ran on expensive minicomputers and powerful machinery out of reach of the average person.

Another reason may have been that, as an "official" UNIX, Linux wasn't quite there yet. POSIX (a registered trademark that is pronounced "pahz-icks"), a published standard from the IEEE,[14] gives a specification for the characteristics and features that a basic UNIX operating system should have. When Linux began to meet these technical specifications, and then when it finally became POSIX compliant, the efficacy of Linux as a viable flavor of UNIX could not be denied, and it received acceptance in areas where there had been marked resistance in the past.

Through these relatively few years of development, the Linux software has been immensely extended and improved, so that the Linux-based system of today is a complete, modern operating system that rivals anything else that is currently available, for any price.

1.7.4 Debian, Red Hat, and Other Linux Distributions

It takes more than individual software programs to make something that we can use on our computers—someone has to put it all together. It takes time to assemble the pieces into a cohesive usable collection, test it all, and then keep up to date with the new developments of each piece of software (a small change in any one of which may introduce a new software dependency problem or conflict with the rest). A Linux *distribution* is such an assemblage. You can do it yourself, of course, and "roll your own" distribution—since it's all free software, *anyone* can add to it or remove from it and call the resulting concoction his own. Most people, however, choose to leave the distribution business to the experts.

There are scads of distributions, although not more than a half-dozen make up the bulk of all Linux systems: Debian GNU/Linux, Fedora Linux, Mandrakelinux, Red Hat Enterprise Linux, Slackware Linux, and SuSE. So when people speak of Debian, Fedora, Mandrake, Red Hat, Slackware, SuSE and the

---

[14] The Institute of Electrical and Electronics Engineers, Inc., although everybody just uses the acronym, pronouncing it "I triple E."

like in terms of Linux, they're talking about the specific *distribution* of Linux and related software, as assembled and repackaged by these companies or organizations. The core of the distributions are the same—they're all the Linux kernel, the GNU Project software, and many other free software packages—but each distribution has its own packaging schemes, defaults, and configuration methods. Unless otherwise noted, recipes in this book are general to Linux and are not dependent on a specific distribution.

All of the major distributions today are reputable, and you should have no serious problems with any of them. Each has its loyalists and adherents, while some Linux users like to drift from distro to distro, trying them all. Among the distributions Debian has special qualities worth noting. It is the only one designed and assembled by volunteers in the same open manner that the Linux kernel and most other free software is written; it is also robust (the standard Debian CD-ROM set comes with more software than any other, with 2,500 different software packages), and is entirely committed to free software by design (yes, there are distributions that are not). In Debian's early days, it was referred to as the "hacker's distro" because it could be very difficult for a Linux newbie[15] to install and manage. However, that has changed.

1.7.5 The Penguin

You've surely seen the "Linux penguin" in advertisements and all over the Web. Larry Ewing's penguin drawing (made in the free-software GIMP image editor) has become a guaranteed sighting anywhere that Linux comes up, and is the "official" Linux mascot. Yes, it has a name: Tux.

Figure 1-2. Tux.

Many variations on the standard drawing now exist. Linus Torvalds' favorite is actually distributed right along with the Linux kernel sources now, so if your system has the Linux source code installed (it's kept in `/usr/src/linux`), you can see a copy of his favorite for yourself at

---

[15] Slang for novice, from the English "new boy" at school.

`/usr/src/linux/Documentation/logo.gif`; it'll look something like Figure 1-2.

While it seems like he was always a part of Linux, Tux actually didn't come to be until about 1994. In the earliest days of Linux, the storm petrel was a popular mascot, drawn by Peter Williams. His illustration shows the storm petrel in flight, from a perspective where its left wing appears raised and right wing sharply parallel to the view, so that its body forms an L shape.[16]

1.7.6 Open Source, Free Content, and the Future

The term *open source* was first introduced by some free software advocates in 1998 as a marketing term for free software. They felt that some people unfamiliar with the free software movement—especially the executives at certain large corporations who'd suddenly taken an interest in the more than ten years' worth of work that had been put into this software—might be scared off by the word "free." They were concerned that said industry decision-makers might confuse free software with unrelated concepts such as *freeware*, which is software provided free of charge, but in in executable form only.[17]

The Open Source Initiative (OSI) was founded to promote software that conforms with its public "Open Source Definition," which in turn was derived from the "Debian Free Software Guidelines" (DFSG), originally written by Bruce Perens as a set of software inclusion guidelines for Debian. All free software—including software released under the terms of the GNU General Public License—conforms with this definition.

But some free-software advocates and organizations, including the Free Software Foundation, loudly criticized the term "open source," believing that it obscured the importance of "freedom" in this movement.

However, even "free software" is now much too limited, because the very scope of the "movement" itself is a source of contention and debate. As long ago as 1994, I pointed out that it took more than computer program source code to make a complete and working operating system (non-software elements such as documentation, graphic icons, audio samples, and databases would be necessary).

---

[16] You can still see this logo, on letterhead, by viewing the PostScript file `letter.ps` in the package at `http://www.funet.fi/pub/Linux/doc/logos/logo2u.tar.gz` (see Recipe 17.4.2 [Previewing a PostScript File], page 414).

[17] "Free software" means nothing of the sort, of course; the "free" has always referred to a user's *freedom* to read and use the software's source code, and not the price he paid to obtain it.

In time, groups were formed to advance the free copying and modification of specific types of non-software works, such as audio recordings of pop music. New terms including "open content" and "free content" then became popular to differentiate these new works from free software. Eventually, even software organizations began to recognize the role of non-software works in achieving their stated goals, and some endorsed other kinds of works, like software documentation, as deserving of free licensing.

Today, the surfeit of so many amateur "free" or "open" works, self-published on the Web, shows that many people clearly want to share—but the outcome may not be what they expected. With so many specialized licenses and conflicting methods for "free" publishing, these works all remain incompatible with each other, enclosed in their own separate commons.

Other questions and concerns quickly arise: The goals of license makers are not always identical to those of publishers who use such licenses; the promise of "free" invites careless violation of license terms and conditions by casual users and amateur publishers alike; enforcement is difficult if not impossible; assistance is nonexistent, since the practice occurs outside of traditional publishing; what constitutes the open "source" for different works is heavily debated; and, while the availabilty of works on the Internet is generally transnational, it is unclear whether international law or the laws of sovereign nations apply to these licensed works and their copies and derivatives.

The situation is this. Computers have made it possible for machine-readable works to be published in such a way so that anyone can instantly access copies of these works from anywhere, and then sample from, modify, or distribute these copies free of charge and without harm to the originals (and theoretically preserving all access and authorship credit in some appropriate manner), but this has only been demonstrated by individual self-publishers who have released their works under unique licenses—there is no acknowledged universal standard or commons for such works, and no clear economic model to replace the old publication methods. The future of this practice, and of all the works already so published, is unclear.

1.7.7 UNIX and the Tools Philosophy

The fact that the UNIX computer operating system has survived for more than thirty-five years should tell us something about the temerity of its design considerations. One of these considerations—perhaps its most endearing—is the "tools" philosophy.

A brief discussion of this philosophy will help clarify the role of this book as "cookbook." I will show you how tools are used to run commands on Linux, and how specifying commands for the system to execute is a kind of language.

Most operating systems are designed with a concept of files, come with a set of utility programs for handling these files, and then leave it to the large *applications* to do the interesting work: a word processor, a spreadsheet, a presentation designer, a Web browser. (When a few of these applications recognize each other's file formats or share a common interface, the group of applications is called a "suite.")

Each of these monolithic applications presumably has an "open file" command to read a file from disk and open it in the application; most of them, too, come with commands for searching and replacing text, checking spelling, printing the current document, and so on. The programming code for handling all of these tasks must be included inside each application—taking up extra space both in memory and on disk. This is the anti-UNIX approach.

In the case of proprietary software, all of the actual program source code is kept from the public—so other programmers can't use, build on, or learn from any of it. This kind of closed-source software is presented to the world as a kind of magic trick: If you buy a copy of the program, you may *use* it, but you can never learn how the program actually *works*.[18]

The result of this is that the code to handle essentially the same function inside all of these different applications must be developed by programmers from scratch, separately and independently of the others every time—so the progress of society as a whole is set back by the countless man-hours of time and energy programmers must waste by inefficiently reinventing all the same software functions to perform the same tasks, over and over again.

UNIX-like operating systems don't put so much weight on application programs. Instead, they come with many small programs called *tools*. Each tool is generally capable of performing a very simple, specific task, and performing it well—one tool does nothing but output the file(s) or data passed to it, one tool spools its input to the print queue, one tool sorts the lines of its input, and so on.

Collective sets of tools, designed around a certain field or concept, were called "workbenches" on older UNIX systems; for example, the tools for checking the spelling, writing style, and grammar of text were part of the "Writer's Workbench" package (see Recipe 11.3 [Checking Grammar], page 286). While

---

[18] In fact, under the Digital Millennium Copyright Act (DMCA), signed into law by President Clinton on October 28, 1998, it is a federal crime for you to even *try*.

the idea of "workbenches" is generally not part of the idiom of today's UNIX-based systems, tool collections are often distributed as *toolkits*, and the GNU Project still publishes collections of tools under certain general themes such as the "GNU text utilities" and "GNU file utilities." The invention of new tools and applications to fill new needs has been on the rise along with the increased popularity of Linux-based systems; at the time of this writing, there were a total of 1,631 tools and applications in the two primary program directories (/bin and /usr/bin) on my Linux system.

An important early development in UNIX was the invention of "pipes," a way to pass the output of one tool to the input of another. By knowing what the individual tools do and how they are combined, a user could now build powerful "strings" of commands.

Just as the tensile strength of chrome-nickel steel is greater than the added strength of its components, multiple tools could then be combined to perform a task unpredicted by the function of the individual tools. This is the concept of *synergy*, and it forms the basis of the UNIX tools philosophy.[19]

Here's an example, using two tools. The first tool, called **who**, outputs a list of all the users who are currently logged on to the system (see Recipe 2.6.2 [Listing Who Is on the System], page 39). The second tool is called **wc**, which stands for "word count"; it outputs a count of the number of words (or lines or characters) of the input you give it (see Recipe 12.1 [Counting Text], page 293).

By combining these two tools, giving the output of **who** to the **wc** command, you can build a new command to list the number of users currently on the system, as in Figure 1-2.

```
$ who | wc -l (RET)
        4
$
```

Figure 1-2. Listing the number of users on the system.

The output of **who**, a list of all the users who are on the system right now, is piped—via a "pipeline," specified by the vertical bar—to the input of **wc**, which through use of the **-l** option outputs the number of *lines* of its input.

---

[19] Because of this approach, and because of its licensing that gives access to all, I like to call Linux a "synergetic" operating system, in honor of the late R. Buckminster Fuller, who invented a new mathematical system based on these same principles.

In this example, the numeral 4 is output, indicating that four users are currently logged on to the system.[20]

Another famous pipeline from the days before spell-check tools goes something like Figure 1-3.

This command (typed all on one long line) uses the `tr`, `sort`, and `comm` tools to make a spelling checker—after you type this command, the lines of text you type (until you interrupt it) are converted to a single-column list of lowercase words with two calls of `tr`, are then sorted in alphabetical order while ferreting out all duplicates, and the resultant list is then compared with `/usr/dict/words`, which is the system "dictionary," a list of properly spelled words kept in alphabetical order (see Recipe 11.1 [Spell Checking], page 275).

```
$ tr -cs A-Za-z '\012' | tr A-Z a-z | sort -u |
comm -23 - /usr/dict/words  RET
```

Figure 1-3. An early spelling checker.

The great bulk of this book details various combinations of tools you can use to obtain the desired results for various common tasks. Some tasks will require more than one command sequence; others need the fine, complex motions exercised through the large application programs. You'll find that there's usually one tool or command sequence that works perfectly for a given task, but sometimes a satisfactory or even identical result can be had from different combinations of different tools—especially at the hands of a UNIX expert.[21]

This way of formulating commands to accomplish tasks, so different from the WYSIWYG[22] systems where you "point and click" at graphic icons, is the language of UNIX. In most everyday use, you'll rarely use more than a vocabulary of twenty words (tools) and a few inflections each (their options)—but what can you express with them, and how quickly, in contrast to merely pointing at pictures!

---

[20] Piping the output of `who` to `wc` in this fashion is a classic tools example. A.N. Walker called it "the most quoted pipe in the world"—over twenty years ago! See his book in Appendix D [References for Further Interest], page 731.

[21] Such an expert used to be called a *wizard*; a more colloquial expression is *guru*, and then there's the more generalized (and downright awful) *computer geek* of today.

[22] "What You See Is What You Get."

## CHAPTER 2

What Every Linux User Knows

This chapter concerns those concepts and commands that every Linux user knows—how to start and stop the system, log in and out from it, change your password, see what is happening on the system, and use the system help facilities. Mastering these basic concepts is essential for using Linux with any degree of success.

Some of these recipes make reference to files and directories; these concepts are explained in Chapter 5 [Files and Directories], page 125.

2.1 Controlling Power to the System

These recipes show how to start and stop power to the system—how to turn it on and turn it off. It's more than just pressing the button on the computer chassis; in particular, there is a right way to turn off the system, and doing it wrong can result in losing some of your work. Fortunately, there isn't any black magic involved, as you soon shall see—properly shutting down the system is easy!

2.1.1 Powering Up the System

The first thing you do to begin using the system is start power to it. To power up the system, just turn it on. This is called *booting* (or sometimes *booting up*) the system.

As the Linux kernel boots there will be many messages on the screen. After a while, the system will display a `login:` prompt. You can now log in. See Recipe 2.2.1 [Logging In to the System], page 29.

Some systems are configured to start `xdm` at boot time (see Recipe 4.1.1 [Starting X], page 98). If your system is configured like this, instead of the `login:` prompt, you'll see a graphical screen with a box in the middle containing both `login:` and `Password:` prompts. Type ⟨CTRL⟩-⟨ALT⟩-⟨F1⟩ to switch to the first virtual console, where you can log in to the system in the usual way (see Recipe 2.3 [Using Consoles and Terminals], page 32).

2.1.2 Turning Off the System

You can't just flip the power switch when you are done using the computer, because Linux is constantly writing data to disk. (It also keeps data in memory, even when it may have appeared to have written that data to disk.) Simply

turning off the power could result in the loss or corruption of some of your
work.

There is a special `shutdown` tool the system administrator can use to shut
down the computer, as described in Recipe A.2 [Shutting Down the System],
page 703. But you can always shut down your system from the console,
whether you are logged in or not, by using the special (CTRL)-(ALT)-(DEL)
keystroke (also known as the "three-finger salute," a carry-over from the DOS
days). This keystroke immediately begins the shutdown process, and then
reboots the system. If you cut power to the system before it reboots, you can
shut it down in this way.

⇒ To turn off a single user system even when you are not logged in as the
administrator, type (CTRL)-(ALT)-(DEL) (press and hold these three keys
at once).[1]

When you do this, the system will display some messages to the screen as
it shuts down; when you see the line, "`Rebooting...`," it's safe to flip the
power switch.

NOTES: You don't want to wait *too* long after you see this message; if left
untouched, the system will reboot and you'll be back to the beginning!

2.2 Using Your Account

Linux is a multi-user system, meaning that many users can use one Linux
system simultaneously, from different terminals. So to avoid confusion (and
to maintain a semblance of privacy), each user's workspace must be kept
separate from the others.

Even if a particular Linux system is a stand-alone personal computer with
no other terminals physically connected to it, it can be shared by different
people at different times, so the separation of user workspace is still a valid
issue.

This separation is accomplished by giving each individual user an *account*
on the system. You need an account in order to use the system; with an
account you are issued an individual workspace to use, and a unique *username*
that identifies you to the system and to other users. The username is the name
that the system (and those who use it) will then forever know you by; it's a
single word, in all lowercase letters.

During the installation process, the system administrator should have created an account for you. (The system administrator has a special account

---

[1] If your keyboard has two (ALT) and (CTRL) keys, use the *left* set of these keys.

whose username is `root`; this account has total access to the entire system, so it is often called the *superuser*.)

Until the mid-1990s, it was common for usernames to be the first letter of your first name followed by your entire surname, up to 12 characters total. So, for example, user George Washington would have a username of `gwashington` by this convention; this, however, is not a hard and fast rule, especially on home systems where you may be the only user. Sometimes, a middle initial is added ("`usgrant`"), or sometimes even nicknames or initials are used ("`gipper`," "`jfk`"). But whatever username you pick for yourself, make sure it's one you can live with, and one you can stand being called by both the system and other users (your username also becomes part of your email address, as you'll see in Chapter 32 [Email], page 611).

In addition to your username, you should also have a *password* that you can keep secret so that only you can use your account. Good passwords are strings of text that nobody else is likely to guess, (i.e., not obvious words like "`secret`," or identifying names like "`Ruski`," if that happens to be your pet cat). A good password is one that is so memorable to you that you don't ever have to write it down, but complex enough in construction so that no one else could ever guess it. For example, "`t39sAH`" might be a fine password for someone whose first date was to see the movie *The 39 Steps*, directed by Alfred Hitchcock.

NOTES: While usernames are always in lowercase, passwords are case sensitive; the passwords "Secret," "secret," "SECReT," and "SECRET" are all considered different.

2.2.1 Logging In to the System

To begin a session on a Linux system, you need to *log in*. Do this by entering your username at the `login:` prompt on your terminal, and then entering your password when asked. Once you've entered your username and password, you are logged in to the system. You can then use the system and run commands.

A typical `login:` prompt looks like Figure 2-1.

```
Debian GNU/Linux 3.0 bardo tty1

bardo login:
```

Figure 2-1. Typical Linux `login:` prompt.

The `login:` prompt appears on the terminal after the system boots. If your system is configured to start the X Window System at boot time, you'll be presented with an X login screen instead of the standard login prompt. If that happens, press ⟨CTRL⟩-⟨ALT⟩-⟨F1⟩ to switch to the text login screen; this is explained further in Recipe 2.3 [Using Consoles and Terminals], page 32.

To log in to the system, type your username (followed by ⟨RET⟩) at the `login:` prompt, and then type your password when asked (also followed by ⟨RET⟩). For security purposes, nothing is displayed on the screen when you type your password; if you make a mistake while typing it in, type ⟨CTRL⟩-⟨U⟩ to erase the line of input and start over.

⇒ To log in to the system with a username of "kurt" and a password of "empathy," type:

```
Debian GNU/Linux 3.0 bardo tty1

bardo login: kurt ⟨RET⟩
Password: empathy ⟨RET⟩
Linux bardo 2.4.18 #1 Sat Dec 6 16:05:52 EST 2003 i686 unknown

Copyright (C) 1993-1998 Software in the Public Interest, and others

Most of the programs included with the Debian Linux system are freely
redistributable; the exact distribution terms for each program are
described in the individual files in /usr/doc/*/copyright

Debian GNU/Linux comes with ABSOLUTELY NO WARRANTY, to the extent
permitted by applicable law.
Last login: Tue Apr  5 12:03:47 on tty1.
No mail.
~ $
```

As soon as you log in, the system displays the contents of `/etc/motd`, the "Message of the Day" file. The system then displays the time and date of your last login, and reports whether or not you have mail waiting for you (see Chapter 32 [Email], page 611). Finally, the system puts you in a *shell*—the environment in which you interact with the system and give it commands. The default shell on most Linux systems is Bash, and how you use it is discussed in Chapter 3 [The Shell], page 53.

The dollar sign ($) displayed to the left of the cursor is called the *shell prompt*; it means that the system is ready and waiting for input. (You can change this prompt to any text of your liking; to learn how, see Recipe 3.5.6 [Changing the Shell Prompt], page 80.) Many distributions are set up so that the shell prompt includes the name of the current directory by default, which it places to the left of the dollar sign. When you log in, you are in your home directory, which the shell represents as the the tilde character (~). Directories are explained in Chapter 5 [Files and Directories], page 125.

NOTES: Every Linux system has its own name, called the system's *hostname*; a Linux system is sometimes called a *host*, and it identifies itself with its hostname at the `login:` prompt. It's important to name your system; like a username for a user account, a hostname gives a name to the system you are using (and it becomes especially important when putting the system on a network). The system administrator usually names the system when it is being initially configured (the hostname can always be changed later; its name is kept in the file `/etc/hostname`).

Like usernames, hostnames are single words in all lowercase letters. People usually give their systems a name they like, such as `darkstar` or `shiva`. In the preceding examples, "`bardo`" is the hostname of this particular Linux system, which happens to be running the Debian distribution.

The name of the terminal you are connecting from is displayed just after the hostname. In this example, the terminal is `tty1`, which means that this is the first terminal on this particular system. (Incidentally, "tty" is short for "teletype," which historically was the kind of terminal hardware that most UNIX-based systems used by default.)

2.2.2 Logging Out of the System

Logging out of the system frees the terminal you were using—and ensures that nobody can access your account from that terminal.

To end your session on the system, type `logout` at the shell prompt. This command logs you out of the system, and a new `login:` prompt appears on the terminal.

What works equally well as typing the `logout` command is to just type ⟨CTRL⟩-⟨D⟩ (hold down ⟨CTRL⟩ and press ⟨D⟩). You don't even have to type ⟨RET⟩ afterwards. Many users prefer this quick shortcut.

⇒ To log out of the system, type:

```
$ logout (RET)


Debian GNU/Linux 3.0 bardo tty1

bardo login:
```

NOTES: If you are the only person using your system and have just ended a session by logging out, you might want to power down the system. See Recipe 2.1.2 [Turning Off the System], page 27, earlier in this chapter.

2.3 Using Consoles and Terminals

A Linux *terminal* is a device for entering input and getting output from the system. It can be a physical device with a keyboard and display,[2] connected to the system over network or serial line, or it can be a software program running on a computer to mimic such a terminal, called a *terminal emulator*. There are many terminal emulators available, especially for the graphical X Window System (see Recipe 4.5 [Getting a Terminal Window in X], page 109).

When you access a Linux system with the keyboard and monitor that are directly connected to it, using the built-in Linux facilities for emulating a text terminal device, you are said to be using the *console* terminal.

Linux systems feature *virtual consoles*, which act as individual consoles that can run their own login sessions simultaneously, but are accessed from the same physical console terminal. Most Linux systems are configured to have seven virtual consoles by default (up to sixty-three are currently possible). When you are at the console terminal, you can switch between virtual consoles at any time, and you can log in and use the system from several virtual consoles at once. Virtual consoles are sometimes also called *virtual terminals*.

The following recipes explain the basic ways to operate virtual consoles, and terminals in general.

---

[2] Hardware built especially for this function are called *dumb terminals* because they have no computing power of their own, but are just input and output facilities for interacting with the actual computer they are connected to.

2.3.1 Getting the Virtual Console Number

When you are not logged in, the number of the current virtual console is displayed on the console screen. When you are logged in and in the shell, use `fgconsole` to determine which virtual console you are in. It outputs the number of the current virtual console.

⇒ To see which virtual console you are in, type:

```
$ fgconsole ⟨RET⟩
3
$
```

In this example, `fgconsole` outputted the numeral 3, indicating that the user is in the third virtual console.

NOTES: If you try running `fgconsole` from a terminal emulator in the X Window System, you'll see that it won't output a number because you're not running it from a virtual console.

2.3.2 Switching Between Consoles

There are two methods to switch to a different virtual console; one uses a special keystroke, and the other is a command.

METHOD #1

To switch to a different virtual console, press and hold ⟨ALT⟩ plus the function key whose number corresponds to the number of the console you would like to switch to.

⇒ To switch to the fourth virtual console, press ⟨ALT⟩-⟨F4⟩.

This command switches to the fourth virtual console, denoted by "`tty4`":

```
Debian GNU/Linux 3.0 bardo tty4

bardo login:
```

You can also cycle through the different virtual consoles with the left and right arrow keys. To switch to the next-lowest virtual console (or wrap around to the highest virtual console, if you're at the first virtual console), press ⟨ALT⟩-⟨←⟩. To switch to the next-highest virtual console, press ⟨ALT⟩-⟨→⟩.

⇒ To switch from the fourth to the third virtual console, press:

⟨ALT⟩-⟨←⟩

This keystroke switches to the third virtual console, tty3:

```
Debian GNU/Linux 3.0 bardo tty3

bardo login:
```

To switch back to the console you were last at, press ⟨ALT⟩-⟨PrtScrn⟩.

The seventh virtual console is reserved for the X Window System. If X is installed, this virtual terminal will never show a login: prompt, but when you are using X, this is where your X session appears. If your system is configured to start X immediately, this virtual console will show an X login screen.

You can switch to a virtual console from the X Window System using ⟨CTRL⟩ in conjunction with the usual ⟨ALT⟩ and function keys. This is the only console manipulation keystroke that works in X.

⇒ To switch from X to the first virtual console, press:

⟨CTRL⟩-⟨ALT⟩-⟨F1⟩

METHOD #2

Use chvt to change to a different virtual console. It takes as an argument the number to change to.

⇒ To change to the seventh virtual console, type:

$ *chvt 7* ⟨RET⟩

NOTES: This method is useful for putting in scripts.

2.3.3 Scrolling Text in the Console

When you are logged in at a virtual console, new lines of text appear at the bottom of the console screen, while older lines of text scroll off the top of the screen. Use ⟨SHIFT⟩ with ⟨PgUp⟩ or ⟨PgDn⟩ to scroll backward ("up") or forward ("down") through scrolled text.

⇒ Here are two ways to use this.

- To view lines of text that have scrolled off the top of the screen, press ⟨SHIFT⟩-⟨PgUp⟩ to scroll backward through it.
- Once you have scrolled back, press ⟨SHIFT⟩-⟨PgDn⟩ to scroll *forward* through the text toward the more recent text.

The amount of text you can scroll back through depends on system memory.

NOTES: This technique is for scrolling through text displayed in your shell session (see Chapter 3 [The Shell], page 53). It does not work for scrolling through text in a tool or application in the console. In other words, you can't use this technique to scroll through text that is displayed by a tool for perusing text files. To scroll through text in an application, use its own facilities for scrolling, if it has any.

2.3.4 Clearing the Terminal Screen

There are two methods to clear the terminal screen.

METHOD #1

Type `clear` to clear the screen of the terminal you are working in. The screen will be redrawn with a new command line on the top line, and all other contents on the screen will be erased.

⇒ To clear the terminal screen, type:

       $ `clear` ⟨RET⟩

This works in the console as well as in a terminal emulator in X. You can put this command in scripts.

METHOD #2

To clear the terminal screen and redraw the current command line at the top, type ⟨CTRL⟩-⟨L⟩.

Unlike `clear`, which is a complete command you input at the command line, you can type ⟨CTRL⟩-⟨L⟩ anywhere on a command line that contains something else you're typing—it redraws the current command line you are at, complete with everything on it, at the top of the screen.

⇒ To clear the terminal screen and redraw the current command line at the top of the screen, type:

       ⟨CTRL⟩-⟨L⟩

NOTES: This keystroke works in the Bash shell, which is the subject of the next chapter.

2.3.5 Resetting the Terminal Screen

To reset the terminal screen to its default settings, use **reset**. This is good for when the contents of a binary file are accidentally displayed to the screen, after which only garbage characters are printed when you type. Other times, the terminal will simply stop clearing characters properly. This will fix it.

When this happens, type *reset* and then hit ⟨RET⟩, even though you will not be able to read what you're typing on the screen. This works both in the console, and in terminals running in X.

⇒ To reset your terminal, type:

    $ *reset* ⟨RET⟩

NOTES: You can practice this so you know what it looks like when it really happens. Do this by sending the output of a binary file to the terminal screen—type `cat /bin/ls` and see what it does to the terminal; then type *reset* to reset it.

2.4 Running a Command

A *tool* is a software program that performs a certain function—usually a specialized, simple task. For example, the **hostname** tool outputs the system's hostname, and the **who** tool outputs a listing of the users who are currently logged in. An *application* is a larger, usually interactive, program for completing a broader kind of task—think of image editors and word processors.

A tool or application may take any number of *options* (sometimes called "flags"), which specify a change in its default behavior. It may also take *arguments*, which specify a file or some other text to operate on. Arguments are usually specified after any options.

The term *command* refers to the name of a tool or application, along with any specified options and arguments. Since typing the name of a tool itself is often sufficient to accomplish a desired task, tools alone are often called commands.

Commands are case-sensitive; the names of tools and applications are usually in all lowercase letters.

To run (or "execute") a tool or application without giving any options or arguments, type its name at a shell prompt, followed by ⟨RET⟩.

⇒ To run the **hostname** tool, type:

```
$ hostname ⟨RET⟩
camelot
$
```

The hostname of the system in the example is **camelot**.

Options always begin with a hyphen character (-), which is usually followed by one alphanumeric character. To include an option in a command, follow the name of the tool or application with the option. Always separate the tool name, each option, and each argument from one another with a space character.

Long-style options (sometimes called "GNU-style" options) begin with two hyphen characters (--) and are usually one English word.

Sometimes an option itself may take an argument. For example, **hostname** has an **-F** option, for specifying a file name to read the hostname from; it takes as an argument the name of the file that **hostname** should read from.

⇒ To run **hostname** and specify that the file **host.info** is the file to read from, type:

```
$ hostname -F host.info ⟨RET⟩
```

2.4.1 Displaying a Tool's Available Options

To get a list of available options and other help for a tool, use the **--help** (long-style) or **-h** option.[3] It usually outputs some information about a tool's usage, and lists its available options.

⇒ To list the available options for the **hostname** tool, type:

```
$ hostname --help ⟨RET⟩
```

Sometimes the list of available options fills much more than a screen, so you may want to pipe the output through **less** for perusal (see Recipe 9.1 [Perusing Text], page 211). Press ⟨Q⟩ to stop perusal.

⇒ To peruse the available options for the **lynx** tool, type:

```
$ lynx -? | less ⟨RET⟩
```

---

[3] Some tools have neither option, in which case you should try the -? option.

2.4.2 Displaying the Version of a Tool

Sometimes it is useful to know which version of a command you have on your system. If an option or feature does not work as expected, it could be because the command you have installed is an older version.

Use the `--version` (long-style) or the `-v` option to output the version number of a particular tool.

⇒ To output the version of the `hostname` tool, type:

```
$ hostname --version ⟨RET⟩
hostname 2.10
$
```

This command outputs the text "`hostname 2.10`," indicating that this is version 2.10 of the `hostname` tool.

2.5 Changing Your Password

To change your password, use the `passwd` tool. It prompts you for your current password and a new password to replace it with. For security purposes, neither the old nor the new password is displayed on the screen as you type it. To make sure that you type the new password correctly, `passwd` prompts you for your new password twice. You must type it exactly the same way both times, or `passwd` will not change your password.

⇒ To change your password, type:

```
$ passwd ⟨RET⟩
Changing password for kurt
Old password: your current password ⟨RET⟩
Enter the new password (minimum of 5, maximum of 8 characters)
Please use a combination of upper and lower case letters and numbers.
New password: your new password ⟨RET⟩
Re-enter new password: your new password ⟨RET⟩
Password changed.
$
```

NOTES: Passwords can contain uppercase and lowercase letters, the digits 0 through 9, and punctuation marks; they should be between five and eight characters long. See Recipe 2.2 [Using Your Account], page 28, for suggestions on choosing a good password.

2.6 Listing User Activity

The recipes in this section describe some of the simple commands for finding out who you are currently sharing the system with and what they are doing.

2.6.1 Displaying Your Username

Use `whoami` to output the username of the user that is logged in at your terminal. This is not as inutile a command as one might first think—if you're at a shared terminal, it's useful to determine whether or not it is your account that you're messing in, and for those with multiple accounts on a system, it's useful to see which of them you're currently logged in with.

⇒ To output your username, type:

```
$ whoami (RET)
will
$
```

In this example, the username of the user logged in at this terminal is "`will`."

2.6.2 Listing Who Is on the System

Use `who` to output a list of all the users currently logged in to the system. It outputs a minimum of three columns, listing the username, terminal location, and time of login for all users on the system. A fourth column is displayed if a user is using the X Window System; it lists the window location of the user's session (see Chapter 4 [The X Window System], page 95).

⇒ To see who is currently logged in, type:

```
$ who (RET)
murky     tty1          Oct 20 20:09
dave      tty2          Oct 21 14:37
kurt      tty3          Oct 21 15:04
kurt      ttyp1         Oct 21 15:04 (:0.0)
$
```

The output in this example shows that the user murky is logged in on tty1 (the first virtual console on the system), and has been on since 20:09 on 20 October. The user dave is logged in on tty2 (the second virtual console), and has been on since 14:37 on 21 October. The user kurt is logged in twice—on tty3 (the third virtual console), and on ttyp1, which is an X session with a window location of (:0.0).

NOTES: This command is for listing the users on the local system; to list the users connected to a different system on the network, or to see more detailed personal information that a user may have made public, see Recipe 34.5.1 [Checking Whether a User Is Online], page 683.

2.6.3 Listing Who Is on and What They're Doing

The w tool is similar to who, but it displays more detail. It outputs a header line that contains information about the current system status, including the current time, the amount of time the system has been up and running, and the number of users on the system. It then outputs a list of users currently logged in to the system, giving eight columns of information for each. These columns include username, terminal location, X session (if any), the time of login, the amount of time the user has been idle, and what command the user is running. (It also gives two columns showing the amount of time the system's CPU has spent on all of the user's current jobs (JCPU) and foreground processes (PCPU); processes are discussed in Recipe 2.7 [Listing Processes], page 41, and jobs in Recipe 3.3 [Managing Jobs], page 70.)

⇒ To see who is currently logged in and what they are doing, type:

```
$ w ⟨RET⟩
  5:27pm  up 17:53, 4 users, load average: 0.12, 0.06, 0.01
USER     TTY      FROM           LOGIN    IDLE   JCPU    PCPU   WHAT
murky    tty1              Oct 20 20:09   17:22m  0.32s   0.32s  -bash
dave     tty2                     14:37   13.00s  2:35    0.07s  less foo
kurt     tty3                     15:04   1:00m   0.41s   0.09s  startx
kurt     ttyp1    :0.0            15:04   0:00s  21.65s  20.96s  emacs
$
```

In this example, the command's output shows that the current system time is 5:27 p.m., the system has been up for 17 hours and 53 minutes, and there are four users currently logged in: murky is logged in at tty1, has been idle for 17 hours and 22 minutes, and is at a Bash shell prompt; dave is logged in at tty2, has been idle for 13 seconds, and is using less to peruse a file named `foo` (see Recipe 9.1 [Perusing Text], page 211); and `kurt` is logged in at two terminals—`tty3` and `ttyp1`, which is an X session. He ran the `startx` command on `tty3` to start his X session, and within his X session, he is currently using Emacs.

2.6.4 Listing the Last Time a User Logged In

Use `last` to find out who has recently used the system, which terminals they used, and when they logged in and out.

⇒ To output a list of recent system use, type:

    `$ last` ⟨RET⟩

To find out when a particular user last logged in to the system, give the username as an argument.

⇒ To find out when user `james` last logged in, type:

    `$ last james` ⟨RET⟩

NOTES: The `last` tool gets its data from the system file `/var/log/wtmp`; the last line of output tells how far this file goes back. Sometimes, the output will go back for several weeks or more.

2.7 Listing Processes

When you run a command, you are starting a *process* on the system, which is a program that is currently executing. Every process is given a unique number, called its *process* ID, or PID.

You can list the processes that are running on the system at any one time; use `ps` to do so.

By default, `ps` outputs five columns of information about each process: process ID; the name of the terminal from which the process was started; the current status of the process (including "S" for *sleeping*, meaning that it is on hold at the moment, "R" meaning that it is running, and "Z" meaning that it is a *zombie* process, or a process that has already died); the total amount of time the CPU has spent on the process since the process began; and finally, the name of the command being run.

The following recipes describe popular uses of `ps`; there will be more about controlling the processes you run in the next chapter.

2.7.1 Listing Your Current Processes

Type *ps* with no arguments to list the processes you have running in your current shell session.

⇒ To list the processes in your current shell session, type:

```
$ ps ⟨RET⟩
  PID TTY    STAT    TIME COMMAND
  193   1    S       0:01 -bash
  204   1    S       0:00 ps
$
```

In this example, `ps` shows that two processes are running: the `bash` and `ps` commands.

2.7.2 Listing All of a User's Processes

To list all the processes of a specific user, use `ps` and give the username as an argument to the `-u` option. While you can't snoop on the actual activities of other users, you can list the commands they are running at a given moment.

⇒ To list all the processes that user `harry` has running on the system, type:

```
$ ps -u harry ⟨RET⟩
```

NOTES: This command is useful for listing all of your own processes, running across all terminals and shell sessions; give your *own* username as an argument.

2.7.3 Listing All Processes on the System

For listing all of the processes running on the system, there are two methods to know.

METHOD #1

To get a list of all processes being run by all users on the system, use `ps` with the `aux` options.

⇒ To list all of the processes and give their usernames, type:

```
$ ps aux ⟨RET⟩
```

NOTES: There could be a lot of output—even single-user Linux systems typically have forty or more processes running at one time—so you may want to pipe the output of this command through `less` for perusal (see Recipe 9.1 [Perusing Text], page 211).

METHOD #2

Use `top` to show a chart of all processes on the system, sorted by their demands on the system resources. The display is continually updated with current process information; press ⟨Q⟩ to stop the display and exit the program. This tool also displays the information about system runtime and memory that can be output with the `uptime` and `free` commands.

⇒ To see a continually updated display of the current system processes, type:

    $ top ⟨RET⟩

2.7.4 Listing Processes by Name or Number

To list processes whose output contains a name or other specific text you want to match, list all processes and pipe the output to `grep`. This is useful when you want to see which users are running a particular program or command.

⇒ Here are two ways to use this.

- To list all the processes whose commands contain the string "`sbin`," type:

      $ ps aux | grep sbin ⟨RET⟩

- To list any processes whose process IDs contain a 13, type:

      $ ps aux | grep 13 ⟨RET⟩

To list the process (if any) that corresponds to a particular process ID, give that PID as an argument to the `-p` option.

⇒ To list the process whose PID is 344, type:

    $ ps -p 344 ⟨RET⟩

2.8 Using the Help Facilities

Linux systems come with a lot of help facilities, including complete manuals in etext form. In fact, the foremost trouble with Linux documentation isn't that there is not enough of it, but that you have to sift through the mounds of it, trying to find the precise information you're looking for!

I describe the various help facilities in the following sections; their relative usefulness for the particular kind of information you're looking for is noted.

If you find that you need more help, don't panic—other options are available. They're described in Recipe 1.6 [If You Need More Help], page 13.

2.8.1 Finding the Right Tool for the Job

There are a few methods for finding tools by keyword. The first is the common method and the last two are used by more intermediate users (in other words, *every* Linux user doesn't know them).

METHOD #1

When you know what a particular tool or application *does* but you can't remember its name, the first thing to do is use `apropos`. This tool takes a keyword as an argument, and it outputs a list of installed software whose one-line descriptions contain that keyword. It searches for the given text in the names and short descriptions in the system manual, and it outputs a list of the tools that match. This is also useful for finding software on your system related to, say, "audio" or "sound" or "sort" or some other such general concepts.

⇒ To output a list of programs that pertain to consoles, type:

   $ apropos console ⟨RET⟩

NOTES: The `apropos` tool matches lines that contain the keyword you give exactly as typed, anywhere in the line. A search for the keyword "`consoles`" might not list all the programs that a search for the keyword "`console`" would yield; a search on "`con`" matches even more. Therefore, it's better to try singular forms, and then refine your terms if you need to. The trick to getting good results from `apropos` is to know just which keywords are apt to be used in the descriptions of the thing you're looking for.

The `apropos` tool is an alias for `man` with the `-k` option (see Recipe 2.8.4 [Reading a Page from the System Manual], page 46).

METHOD #2

Dpkg
  DEB: dpkg

On Debian systems, yet another way to find installed software by keyword is to use `dpkg`, the Debian package tool. Use the `-l` option to list all of the installed packages, which are each output on a line of its own with its package name and a brief description.

You can output a list of packages that match a keyword by piping the output to `grep`. Use the `-i` option with `grep` to match keywords regardless of case (`grep` is discussed in Chapter 14 [Searching Text], page 333).

Additionally, you can directly peruse the file **/var/lib/dpkg/available** with `less` (see Recipe 9.1 [Perusing Text], page 211); this file lists all available packages and gives a description of them.

⇒ Here are three ways to use this.

- To list all of the DEB packages installed on the system, type:

  $ *dpkg -l* ⟨RET⟩

- To list all of the DEB packages installed on the system whose name contains the text "`edit`," regardless of case, type:

  $ *dpkg -l | grep -i edit* ⟨RET⟩

- To peruse descriptions of all DEB packages that are currently available, type:

  $ *less /var/lib/dpkg/available* ⟨RET⟩

NOTES: For more information on using `dpkg`, see Recipe A.4 [Managing DEB Packages], page 709.

METHOD #3

On RPM-based systems such as Fedora and Red Hat Enterprise Linux, you can find installed software by keyword using `rpm`, the package management tool. Give the `-qa` option to output the names of all packages installed on the system. To find specific packages, pipe the output to `grep` with the `-i` option and a pattern to match (see Recipe 14.1 [Searching Text for a Word], page 333). Pipe this to `less` for perusal.

⇒ Here are some ways to use this.

- To peruse a list of all RPM packages installed on the system, type:

  $ *rpm -qa | less* ⟨RET⟩

- To list all packages whose name or description includes the word "`edit`," regardless of case, type:

  $ *rpm -qa | grep -i edit* ⟨RET⟩

- To list all of the RPM packages installed on the system whose name contains the text "`1.2`," type:

  $ *rpm -qa | grep "1\.2"* ⟨RET⟩

NOTES: For more information on using `rpm`, see Recipe A.5 [Managing RPM Packages], page 714.

2.8.2 Getting a Description of a Program

Use `whatis` to get a one-line description of a program. Give as an argument the name of the tool or application you want described.

⇒ To get a description of the `who` tool, type:

    $ whatis who ⟨RET⟩

NOTES: The `whatis` tool gets its descriptions from the *manual page* of a given program; manual pages are described later in this section, in Recipe 2.8.4 [Reading a Page from the System Manual], page 46.

2.8.3 Listing the Usage of a Tool

Many tools have a long-style option, `--help`, that outputs usage information about the tool, including the options and arguments the tool takes.

⇒ To list the possible options for `whoami`, type:

```
$ whoami --help ⟨RET⟩
Usage: whoami [OPTION]...
Print the user name associated with the current effective user id.
Same as id -un.

  --help      display this help and exit
  --version   output version information and exit

Report bugs to <bug-sh-utils@gnu.org>.
$
```

This command outputs some usage information about the `whoami` tool, including a short description and a list of possible options.

NOTES: Not all tools take the `--help` option; some tools take a `-h` or `-?` option instead, which performs the same function.

2.8.4 Reading a Page from the System Manual

In the olden days, the hardcopy reference manual that came with most UNIX systems also existed electronically on the system itself; each software program that came with the system had its own *manual page* (often called a "man page") that described it. This is still true on Linux-based systems today, except they usually don't come with a hardcopy manual.

Use the **man** tool to view a page in the system manual. As an argument to **man**, give the name of the program whose manual page you want to view (so to view the manual page for **man**, you would type *man man*).

⇒ To view the manual page for **w**, type:

$ *man w* ⟨RET⟩

This command displays the manual page for **w**, as in Figure 2-2.

```
W(1)                    Linux Programmer's Manual                    W(1)

NAME
        w - Show who is logged on and what they are doing.

SYNOPSIS
        w - [husfV] [user]

DESCRIPTION
        w displays  information  about the users currently on the
        machine, and their processes.  The header shows,  in  this
        order,   the  current  time,  how long the system has been
        running, how many users are currently logged on,  and  the
        system load averages for the past 1, 5, and 15 minutes.

        The  following  entries  are displayed for each user: login
        name, the tty name, the  remote  host,  login  time,  idle
        time,  JCPU,  PCPU,  and the command line of their current
        process.

        The JCPU time is the time used by all  processes  attached
Manual page w(1) line 1
```

Figure 2-2. Reading a **man** *page.*

Use the up and down arrow keys to move through the text. Press ⟨Q⟩ to stop viewing the manual page and exit **man**. Since **man** uses **less** to display the text, you can use any of the **less** keyboard commands to peruse the manual page (see Recipe 9.1 [Perusing Text], page 211).

NOTES: Despite its name, a manual page does not always contain the complete documentation for a program; it's more like a quick reference card. It usually has a short description of the program, and lists the options and arguments it takes; some manual pages also include an example or a list of related commands. (Sometimes, commands have very complete, extensive manual pages, but more often, their complete documentation is found either in other help files that come with it or in its Info documentation; these are the subjects of the following two recipes.)

To prepare a `man` page for printing, see Recipe 25.3.4 [Preparing a Manual Page for Printing], page 522.

2.8.5 Reading an Info Manual

The GNU Info System is an online hypertext reference system for documentation prepared in the Info format. This documentation tends to be more complete than a typical `man` page, and often, the Info documentation for a given software package will be an entire book or manual. All of the manuals published by the Free Software Foundation are released in Info format; these manuals contain the same text (*sans* illustrations) as the paper manuals that you can purchase directly from the Free Software Foundation.

There are different ways to peruse the Info documentation: You can use the standalone `info` tool, read Info files in the Emacs editor (see Recipe 10.1 [Using Emacs], page 232), or use one of the other tools designed for this purpose. Additionally, tools exist for converting Info documentation to HTML, which you can read in a Web browser (see Recipe 5.10 [Browsing Files and Directories], page 157).

To read the Info manual for a tool or application with the `info` tool, give its name as an argument. With no arguments, `info` opens your system's "Top" Info menu, which lists all of the manuals that are installed on the system.

⇒ To view all of the Info manuals on the system, type:

> `$ info `⟨RET⟩

This command starts `info` at the system's "Top" menu, which shows some of the `info` key commands and displays a list of available manuals, as in Figure 2-3.

Use the arrow keys to move through each "page" of information, called an Info *node*. Nodes are arranged hierarchically. Every Info document has a "Top" node, which is like the frontmatter and table of contents of a printed book; it usually contains the name of the document and an Info *menu* with links to its various chapters. A chapter node will contain a menu with links for its sections and so on. Links to other nodes may also appear in the text of any node, as cross references.

Links look the same in both menu items and cross references: an asterisk (*), the name of the node it links to, and either one or two colon characters (: or ::). To follow a link to the node it points to, move the cursor over any part of the node name in the link and press ⟨RET⟩.

```
File: dir,      Node: Top,      This is the top of the INFO tree

  This (the Directory node) gives a menu of major topics.
  Typing "q" exits, "?" lists all Info commands, "d" returns here,
  "h" gives a primer for first-timers,
  "mEmacs<Return>" visits the Emacs manual, etc.

  In Emacs, you can click mouse button 2 on a menu item or cross reference
  to select it.

* Menu:

Texinfo documentation system
* Info: (info).                Documentation browsing system.
* Texinfo: (texinfo).          The GNU documentation format.
* install-info: (texinfo)Invoking install-info. Updating info/dir entries.
* texi2dvi: (texinfo)Format with texi2dvi.     Printing Texinfo documentation.
* texindex: (texinfo)Format with tex/texindex. Sorting Texinfo index files.
* makeinfo: (texinfo)makeinfo Preferred.        Translate Texinfo source.
-----Info: (dir)Top, 211 lines --Top-------------------------------------------
Welcome to Info version 2.18. "C-h" for help, "m" for menu item.
```

Figure 2-3. Reading an Info node.

Press ⟨H⟩ to run a tutorial that describes how to use `info`. Press ⟨Q⟩ to stop reading the documentation and exit the program. You can press these buttons at any time you are in `info`.

To read Info documentation for a particular tool or application, give its name as an argument to `info`; if no Info manual exists for that tool, `info` displays the `man` page for that tool instead.

⇒ To read the Info documentation for the `tar` tool, type:

    $ info tar ⟨RET⟩

This command opens a copy of *The GNU tar Manual* in `info`.

To read the contents of a file written in Info format, give the name of the file to read with the `-f` option. This is useful for reading an Info file that you have obtained elsewhere, and that is not in the `/usr/info` directory with the rest of the installed Info files. Info can automatically recognize and expand Info files that are compressed and have a `.gz` file name extension (see Recipe 8.4 [Compressed Files], page 196).

⇒ To read an Info file in the current directory named `faq.info`, type:

    $ info -f faq.info ⟨RET⟩

This command starts `info` and opens the Info file `faq.info`, beginning at the top node in the file.

To read a specific *node* in an Info file, give the name of the node to display in quotes as an argument to the -n option.

⇒ To read `faq.info`, an Info file in the current directory, beginning with the node `Text`, type:

    $ info -n 'Text' -f faq.info ⟨RET⟩

NOTES: You can also read Info documentation directly from the Emacs editor; type ⟨CTRL⟩-⟨H⟩ i while in Emacs to start the Emacs Info reader, and then use the same commands as in the stand-alone `info` tool (see Recipe 10.1.1 [Getting Acquainted with Emacs], page 232).

The Emacs "incremental" search command, ⟨CTRL⟩-⟨S⟩, also works in `info`; it's a very fast, efficient way to search for a word or phrase in an entire Info text (like this entire book); see Recipe 14.9.1 [Searching Incrementally in Emacs], page 352.

Some people use Info for everything; on Linux systems, Info is set up to display a tool's `man` page in Info, if the tool lacks Info documentation. So if a `foofoo` tool doesn't have any Info manual, typing `info foofoo` will give you its `man` page.

2.8.6 Reading System Documentation and Help Files

The Linux Documentation Project HOWTOs
  DEB: doc-linux-html
       doc-linux-text
  RPM: howto
  WWW: http://tldp.org/

The /usr/doc directory is for miscellaneous documentation: HOWTOs, FAQs, distribution-specific documentation files, and the documentation that comes with commands.[4] (To learn more about files and directories, see Chapter 5 [Files and Directories], page 125.) To peruse any of these files, use `less`, described in full in Recipe 9.1 [Perusing Text], page 211.

When a software package is installed, any additional documentation files it might have beyond a manual page and Info manual are placed here, in a

---

[4] On some systems, /usr/doc is superseded by the /usr/share/doc directory; still others have both. So if a file is not where it should be, try looking in /usr/share/doc/. For example, the user dictionary is famously at /usr/dict/words. In some distributions now, it has been moved to /usr/share/dict/words, but if you want to restore it to the classical location, you (as the superuser) can create a symbolic link from the former to the latter (see Recipe 5.7 [Giving a File More Than One Name], page 152).

subdirectory with the name of that package. For example, additional documentation for the `hostname` package is in `/usr/doc/hostname`, and documentation for the `passwd` package is in `/usr/doc/passwd`. Most packages have a file called `README` that usually contains relevant information. Often this file is compressed as `README.gz`, in which case you can use `zless` instead of `less`.

The Linux Documentation Project (LDP) has overseen the creation of more than 100 HOWTO files, each of which covers a particular aspect of the installation or use of Linux-based systems.

The LDP HOWTOs are compressed text files stored in the `/usr/doc/HOWTO` directory; to view them, use `zless`. The file `/usr/doc/HOWTO/HOWTO-Index.gz` contains an annotated index of all the HOWTO documents installed on the system.[5]

The `/usr/doc/FAQ` directory contains a number of FAQ ("Frequently Asked Questions") files on various subjects.

Finally, some distributions also keep a directory in `/usr/doc` for their own documentation; Debian, for example, uses `/usr/doc/debian` for documentation relating to that distribution: the files that make up the Debian FAQ are in the `/usr/doc/debian/FAQ` directory, available in both HTML format, which you can view in a Web browser (see Recipe 5.10 [Browsing Files and Directories], page 157), and as a compressed text file, which you can view in `zless`.

⇒ Here are two ways to use this.

- To view the HTML version of the Debian FAQ in the `lynx` Web browser, type:

  ```
  $ lynx /usr/doc/debian/FAQ/debian-faq.html (RET)
  ```

- To view the compressed text version of the Debian FAQ in `zless`, type:

  ```
  $ zless /usr/doc/debian/FAQ/debian-faq.txt.gz (RET)
  ```

NOTES: It's often very useful to use a Web browser to browse through the documentation files in these directories—see Recipe 5.10 [Browsing Files and Directories], page 157.

---

[5] LDP documents are available in other formats as well, including HTML and DVI.

## CHAPTER 3

The Shell

The subject of this chapter is the *shell*, the program that reads your command input and runs the specified commands. It gets its name because it gives a covering that protects you from the outer environment of the system, like the hard protective encasements of the soft mollusks of the sea. The shell is the intermediary between you and the system, and all interaction is done through it; it is both your working environment and your interface. You are said to be "in" a shell from the very moment you've successfully logged in to the system, until right when you log out.

The "$" character preceding the cursor is called the *shell prompt*; it tells you that the system is ready and waiting for input. On Debian systems, the default shell prompt also includes the name of the current directory (see Chapter 5 [Files and Directories], page 125). A tilde character (~) denotes your home directory, which is where you'll find yourself when you log in.

For example, a typical user's shell prompt, when in his home directory, might look like Figure 3-1.

```
~ $
```

Figure 3-1. A Bash shell promt.

If your shell prompt shows a pound sign (#) instead of a "$," this means that you're logged in with the superuser, or `root`, account. Beware: The `root` account has complete control over the system; one wrong keystroke and you might accidentally break it something awful. You need to have a different user account for yourself, which you use for your regular activities (see Recipe A.6.1 [Making a User Account], page 717).

You may sometimes hear the shell called the "command shell," because you run commands through it, but the shell isn't just a prompt where you run other programs—it is also a programming language. Its built-in facilities for writing programs is very powerful. In this chapter, I will show you the basics to get you started, but you should know that many books have been written on shell programming.

There are many shells available for Linux. Some may look similar to each other, but they can behave quite differently. We're going to cover the Bash shell, which is the most commonly used shell on Linux systems and is almost always the default Linux shell. (Its name stands for "Bourne again shell"—a pun on the name of Steve Bourne, who was author of the traditional UNIX shell, the Bourne shell.)

A list of other recommended shells is given at Recipe 3.9.5 [Using Other Shells], page 92. For more information on using Bash beyond what this chapter provides, consult the Info documentation for `bash` (see Recipe 2.8.5 [Reading an Info Manual], page 48).

3.1 Typing at the Command Line

In Recipe 2.4 [Running a Command], page 36, you learned how to run commands by typing them in at the shell prompt. The line where you type in a command at a shell prompt is called the *command line* (it's also called the *input line*). The process of writing a command on the command line is called *command line editing*.

The following sections describe some important features of command line editing, such as quoting special characters and strings, letting the shell complete your typing, re-running commands, and running multiple commands.

NOTES: For more information on Bash's command line editing features, consult the Info documentation for `bash` (see Recipe 2.8.5 [Reading an Info Manual], page 48).

3.1.1 Using Basic Command Line Editing Keys

There are special keystrokes for moving about the input line and editing the line you are typing; the following table describes them.

Typing Commands

`text`	Insert *text* at the point where the cursor is; any text already existing to the right of the cursor is shifted further right to accommodate the new text.
⟨RET⟩	Send the command line to Bash for execution (in other words, it runs the command typed at the shell prompt). You don't have to be at the far right end of the command line to type ⟨RET⟩; you can type it when the cursor is anywhere on the command line.

Cutting and Pasting

⟨BKSP⟩ *or* ⟨CTRL⟩-⟨H⟩	Delete the character to the left of the cursor.

(continued)
Cutting and Pasting

⟨DEL⟩ *or* ⟨CTRL⟩-⟨D⟩   Delete the character the cursor is underneath.

⟨CTRL⟩-⟨K⟩   Kill, or "cut," all text on the input line, from the
                              character the cursor is underneath to the end of the
                              line.

⟨CTRL⟩-⟨U⟩   Kill everything on the input line to the left of the
                              cursor.

⟨CTRL⟩-⟨Y⟩   Yank, or "paste," the text that was last killed. Text
                              is inserted where the cursor is.

Movement

⟨CTRL⟩-⟨A⟩   ·   Move the cursor to the beginning of the input line.

⟨CTRL⟩-⟨E⟩   Move the cursor to the end of the input line.

⟨→⟩ *or* ⟨CTRL⟩-⟨F⟩   Move the cursor to the right ("forward") one char-
                              acter.

⟨←⟩ *or* ⟨CTRL⟩-⟨B⟩   Move the cursor to the left ("backward") one char-
                              acter.

⟨ALT⟩-⟨F⟩   Move the cursor forward one *word*.

⟨ALT⟩-⟨B⟩   Move the cursor backward one *word*.

⟨CTRL⟩-⟨L⟩   Clear the terminal screen, redrawing the current in-
                              put line at the top.

NOTES: These keyboard commands are the same as those used by the Emacs
editor (see Recipe 10.1 [Using Emacs], page 232). Many other Emacs keyboard
commands also work on the command line (see Recipe 10.1.3 [Using Basic
Emacs Editing Keys], page 237). And, for Vi aficionados, it is possible to
configure Bash to recognize Vi-style bindings instead (see Recipe 3.7.3 [Using
Shell Startup Files], page 86).

3.1.2 Typing a Control Character

Control characters can be typed on the input line by using ⟨CTRL⟩-⟨V⟩, the
shell's verbatim insert function, followed by the control character you want.

⇒ To insert a formfeed character ("Control-L") at the current location in the input line, type:

    ⟨CTRL⟩-⟨V⟩ ⟨CTRL⟩-⟨L⟩

3.1.3 Quoting Reserved Characters

Some characters are *reserved* and have special meaning to the shell on their own, such as the dollar sign ($), single quote ('), double quote ("), exclamation point (!), backslash (\), and the newline (⟨RET⟩) which sends what you have typed on the command line to the shell for execution. Before you can pass one of these characters as an argument to a command, you must *quote* it.

There are various ways to quote characters. Each is good for certain purposes, so you should know the differences between them. Sometimes the various methods of quotation are combined in the same argument (see the last example of Method #3 below).

To demonstrate quotation, the examples that follow will use **echo**, a simple tool that displays any text given to it as an argument (technically, this command echoes its arguments to the standard output—see Recipe 3.2 [Redirecting Input and Output], page 67).

METHOD #1

To quote a reserved character, precede it with a backslash (\). The backslash is Bash's *escape character*; a character that immediately follows it will be interpreted literally, and not for any reserved meaning. The one exception to this rule is a newline character (see Recipe 3.1.12 [Typing a Long Line], page 66).

⇒ Here are some ways to use this.

- To echo the string "Isn't this nice?," type:

```
$ echo Isn\'t this nice? ⟨RET⟩
Isn't this nice?
$
```

- To echo the string ""It isn't nice!"," type:

```
$ echo \"It isn\'t nice\!\" (RET)
"It isn't nice!"
$
```

- To echo the string "$HOSTNAME is nice!," type:

```
$ echo \$HOSTNAME is nice\! (RET)
$HOSTNAME is nice!
$
```

- To echo the string ""$HOSTNAME" is nice!," where $HOSTNAME is a shell variable to be expanded, type:

```
$ echo \"$HOSTNAME\" is nice\! (RET)
"lucky" is nice!
$
```

The last two examples use the special Bash variable HOSTNAME, whose value is always the name of the current host (see Recipe 3.5 [Using Shell Variables], page 77). First, the text "$HOSTNAME" is displayed because its "$" is escaped, and then second, the $HOSTNAME variable is expanded to the value it contains. In this example, the system's hostname is lucky.

NOTES: For only one reserved character, this is the simplest quoting method; while you certainly can quote any complex quotation this way, it is cumbersome to add all the backslashes.

When passing a phrase to a command that takes multiple arguments, you will have to escape spaces, too. So the phrase in the first example becomes "Isn'\t\ this\ nice?"

METHOD #2

Quote a literal phrase by enclosing it in single quote characters ('). All characters inside the quotes are taken literally, and not for any reserved meaning—so there's no way to expand variables in single-quoted text. You can even quote newlines with this method. The only character you can't pass in single quotes is a single quote itself.

⇒ Here are some ways to use this.

- To echo a backslash character, type:

```
$ echo '\' RET
\
$
```

- To echo the string "* ! " /," type:

```
$ echo '* ! " /' RET
* ! " /
$
```

- To echo the string ""`$HOSTNAME`"
  `is nice!`," where there is a newline character after the second double quote character, type:

```
$ echo '"$HOSTNAME" RET
> is nice!' RET
"$HOSTNAME"
is nice!
$
```

NOTES: This second method is one of the simpler methods of quoting.

METHOD #3

Quote a phrase by enclosing it in double quote characters (") to retain the special meaning of *some* characters: the dollar sign ($), backtick (`` ` ``), exclamation point (!), and backslash (\).

This means that: Variables are expanded to their values (see Recipe 3.5 [Using Shell Variables], page 77), command output may be specified (see Recipe 3.1.11 [Specifying the Output of a Command as an Argument], page 65), command history may be referenced (see Recipe 3.4 [Using Your Command History], page 74), and single characters may be escaped, as described in Method #1 above.

You can pass single quote and newline characters; to pass double quotes, dollar signs, backticks, or backslashes, escape them first with a backslash (\). Pass an exclamation point by escaping it outside of the double quotes.

⇒ Here are some ways to use this.

- To echo "Isn't it great?," type:

```
$ echo "Isn't it great?" ⟨RET⟩
Isn't it great?
$
```

- To echo "Isn't $HOSTNAME it?," type:

```
$ echo "Isn't \$HOSTNAME it?" ⟨RET⟩
Isn't $HOSTNAME it?
$
```

- To echo "Isn't this $HOSTNAME?," where $HOSTNAME is a shell variable to be expanded, type:

```
$ echo "Isn't this $HOSTNAME?" ⟨RET⟩
Isn't this lucky?
$
```

- To echo "Wow!
This isn't "$HOSTNAME"!," where there is a newline character after the first exclamation point, type:

```
$ echo "Wow"\! ⟨RET⟩
> This isn't \"\$HOSTNAME\""\! ⟨RET⟩
Wow!
This isn't "$HOSTNAME"!
$
```

In the second-last example, the system's hostname is lucky. In the second and the last examples, the text "$HOSTNAME" is quoted literally and is not expanded as a variable; by omitting the backslash directly preceding the dollar sign, the shell will expand the variable.

NOTES: You can sometimes get away with quoting an exclamation point in double quotes, but because it's reserved for referencing your Bash command history, using it in the wrong context can have unexpected results. Unless you're only using the single quotes method, it's safest to escape an exclamation point outside of the double quotes.

METHOD #4

To pass special characters as a string, give them as $'*string*', where *string* is the string of characters to be passed. This is called "ANSI-C style" quoting.

Special backslash escape sequences for certain characters are commonly included in a string, as listed in the following table.

\a	Alert (rings the system bell).
\b	Backspace.
\e	Escape.
\f	Form feed.
\n	Newline.
\r	Carriage return.
\t	Horizontal tab.
\v	Vertical tab.
\\	Backslash.
NNN	Character whose ASCII code is *NNN* in octal (base 8).

⇒ Here are some ways to use this.

- To echo the string "Hello" followed by two newline characters, type:

```
$ echo Hello$'\n\n' (RET)
Hello


$
```

- To echo a pilcrow sign character (octal character code 266), type:

```
$ echo $'\266' ⟨RET⟩
¶
$
```

- To append a newline character and a pilcrow sign character (octal character code 266) to the file **draft**, type:

```
$ echo $'\n\266' >> draft ⟨RET⟩
```

3.1.4 Letting the Shell Complete What You Type

Completion is when Bash does its best to finish your typing for you. To use it, press ⟨TAB⟩ on the input line, and the shell will *complete* the word to the left of the cursor to the best of its ability. Completion is one of those things that, once you begin to use it, you will wonder how you ever managed to get by without it.

Completion works on both file names and command names, depending on the context of the cursor when you press the ⟨TAB⟩ key.

When there is more than a single way to complete a word, the shell will beep[1] to alert you so; pressing ⟨TAB⟩ again will display the possible options, and then redraw your command line. If the options are many, the shell will ask you at that point whether you would really like them all displayed.

⇒ To use completion to specify the **/usr/lib/emacs/20.7/i386-debian-linux-gnu/** directory as an argument to the **ls** command, type:

```
$ ls /usr/lib/⟨TAB⟩  rings the bell  ⟨TAB⟩
Display all 767 possibilities? (y or n)n
$ ls /usr/lib/e⟨TAB⟩  rings the bell  ⟨TAB⟩
elm-me+     emacs      emacsen-common      entity-map
$ ls /usr/lib/em⟨TAB⟩  rings the bell
$ ls /usr/lib/emacs⟨TAB⟩  rings the bell
$ ls /usr/lib/emacs⟨TAB⟩
emacs    emacsen-common
$ ls /usr/lib/emacs/⟨TAB⟩20.7/⟨TAB⟩i386-debian-linux-gnu/
```

---

[1] The UNIX way of saying this is that the command "rings the system bell."

Notice how by typing only the letter "e" followed by ⟨TAB⟩ twice brings up a series of files, while "em" is completed to "emacs," because all options in this directory beginning with the letters "em" complete to at least that word. The final two ⟨TAB⟩ completions were made without ringing the bell, meaning that the completions made were the only possibilities.

NOTES: Many applications also support command and/or file name completion; the most famous example of this is the Emacs text editor (see Recipe 10.1 [Using Emacs], page 232).

3.1.5 Undoing a Mistake at the Command Line

If you want to undo what you just typed on the input line, type ⟨CTRL⟩-⟨_⟩. If you have been backspacing over things, the shell will remember what you erased and will put it back on the input line. You can use this undo command more than once in a row to return the line to even earlier conditions. If you just typed a short line, then this command will erase it entirely.

You can also erase everything to the left of the cursor by typing ⟨CTRL⟩-⟨U⟩.

Finally, you can *transpose* characters: use ⟨CTRL⟩-⟨T⟩ to transpose the two *characters* before the cursor, and use ⟨ALT⟩-⟨T⟩ to transpose the two *words* before the cursor. This is useful for correcting typos.

⇒ To transpose the letters "m" and "o" just before the cursor, type:

    $ echo frmo⟨CTRL⟩-⟨T⟩

This operation fixes the misspelled "frmo" with "from," and so the input line looks like this:

    $ echo from

⇒ To transpose the words "bash" and "man," type:

    $ bash man⟨ALT⟩-⟨T⟩

This operation correctly forms the command to view the bash manual page:

    $ man bash

3.1.6 Repeating the Last Command You Typed

Type ⟨↑⟩ to put the last command you typed back on the input line. You can then type ⟨RET⟩ to run the command again, or you can edit the command first.

⇒ To repeat the last command entered, type:

$ ⟨↑⟩ ⟨RET⟩

By typing ⟨↑⟩ more than once, you can go back to earlier commands you've typed; this is a function of your command *history*, explained further in Recipe 3.4 [Using Your Command History], page 74.

NOTES: You can also search through your command history to repeat a command you typed earlier; See Recipe 3.4.2 [Searching Through Your Command History], page 75.

3.1.7 Running a List of Commands

There are two methods: One specifies the commands at the command line, and the other gets its list from a file.

METHOD #1

To run more than one command on the input line, type each command in the order you want them to run, separating each command from the next with a semicolon (;). This is sometimes a quick way to run several non-interactive commands in sequence.

⇒ Here are two ways to use this.

- To clear the screen and then log out of the system, type:

  $ clear; logout ⟨RET⟩

- To run the **hostname** command three times, type:

```
$ hostname; hostname; hostname ⟨RET⟩
figaro
figaro
figaro
$
```

NOTES: There are many useful things you can do when combining commands in this way. One popular use of this technique is to run **sleep** first and then some other command next, to run that second command on a delay. This is good for making screen shots in some other window (see Recipe 19.1.1 [Taking a Screen Shot in X], page 441).

METHOD #2

You can also run a list of commands by putting them in a file, one per line. Use the special ".". command, and give the name of the file as an argument. This runs, in the current shell, all of the commands that are in the file.

⇒ To run the commands in the file `~/lists/nightly`, type:

   `$ . ~/lists/nightly` ⟨RET⟩

NOTES: This method is good for running many commands with long arguments. For example, you might want to run a tool that takes a URL as an argument, and you have a long series of such URLs to run it on. Use a text editor to copy the URLs into a file, one on each line, and then insert the name of the tool at the beginning of each line.

The built-in `source` command is a synonym for the period; the act of running commands from a file with this method is often called "sourcing" a file.

3.1.8 Running One Command and Then Another

Just as you can string commands together with a semicolon to run them all in a list, you can also specify that a command should run *only* if the previous command ran successfully. To do this, use the special `&&` control operator to separate the commands. If the first command is successful, the second command is run; if the first command is not successful—that is, if the command does not exist, or if it returns an error or any exit status other than zero—the second command is not run.

⇒ Here are two ways to use this.

- To run `foo`, and then run `bar` only if `foo` exists and successfully ran, type:

   `$ foo && bar` ⟨RET⟩

- To search the file `operations` for the word "`planning`" regardless of case, and then peruse `operations` only if that word was found in it, type:

   `$ grep -i planning operations && less operations` ⟨RET⟩

3.1.9 Running One Command or Another

To specify that one *or* another command be run, use the special control operator `||` to separate the two commands. If the first command exists, the shell will run it and ignore the second command; if the first command doesn't exist, returns an error, or otherwise returns with a non-zero exit status, the shell will run the second command.

⇒ To run either **w** or **who**, type:

    $ *w || who* (RET)

In this example, if **w** exists and runs without errors, the shell will run it and exit; otherwise, it will run **who**.

3.1.10 Automatically Answering a Command Prompt

It is sometimes desirable to answer an interactive command without having to interact with the command directly. Use **yes** to do this; by default, it outputs "y" followed by a newline character until it is killed. If you have a command that asks for verification any number of times, and you want to automate the answering process, you can pipe the output of **yes** to it.

⇒ To run a command **barfoo** and automatically answer y to all of its prompts, type:

    $ *yes | barfoo* (RET)

To output something instead of "y," specify it as an argument. To specify a certain number of times to output, pipe **yes** through **head** with the number to output as an option.

⇒ Here are two ways to use this.

- To use **mv** to move all of the files ending in **.sample** in the current directory to a directory called **live**, but answer no to overwriting any existing files, type:

      $ *yes n | mv *.sample live* (RET)

- To run a command **farboo** and automatically answer five prompts with your username, type:

      $ *yes `whoami` | head -5 | farboo* (RET)

3.1.11 Specifying the Output of a Command as an Argument

You can have the shell replace a given command with its output. This is called *command substitution* and is useful for specifying that the output of some command should be used as an argument for some other command.

There are two ways to do it, as described in the following methods.

NOTES: You can nest substitutions, putting one substitution inside another one.

METHOD #1

To substitute a command's output, give the command enclosed in parentheses and preceded by a dollar sign (**$**).

⇒ To locate any files on the system containing your username somewhere in its name, type:

> $ *locate $(whoami)* ⟨RET⟩

METHOD #2

To substitute a command's output, give the command enclosed in backtick characters (`` ` ``).

⇒ To locate any files on the system containing your username somewhere in its name, type:

> $ *locate `whoami`* ⟨RET⟩

NOTES: This is the old-fashioned way of doing it. The backticks enclosing any nested substitutions must be each preceded with backslash characters (\); also use backslash to specify dollar sign or literal backslash characters.

3.1.12 Typing a Long Line

When you are typing a long command and you want to keep the appearance neat on the screen, use a backslash (\) followed by a newline (⟨RET⟩) to stop the current line at that point, and continue it on the beginning of the next line on the screen.

The shell will precede the new line with a special ">" prompt, so you know that this line is a continuation from the previous line. Both the backslash and the newline will be ignored by the shell, as if the text of the beginning line and the line that follows were seamlessly connected as one long line.

It doesn't matter where in a line you break, and you can extend over as many lines as you like with this method.

⇒ Here are two ways to use this.

- To echo the string "`verylongword`" while typing it out over two screen lines, type:

```
$ echo ver\ (RET)
> ylongword (RET)
verylongword
$
```

- To echo the string "`verylongword`" while typing it out over four screen lines, type:

```
$ ech\ (RET)
> o verylo\ (RET)
> ngwor\ (RET)
> d (RET)
verylongword
$
```

NOTES: It may not always look as tidy, but you can type a long command without using this technique.

3.2 Redirecting Input and Output

The shell moves text in designated "streams." The *standard output* is where the shell streams the text output of commands—the screen on your terminal, by default. The *standard input*, typically the keyboard, is where you input data for commands. When a command reads the standard input, it usually keeps reading text until you type (CTRL)-(D) on a new line by itself.

When a command runs and exits with an error, the error message is usually output to your screen, but it is a separate stream called the *standard error*.

You redirect these streams—to a file, or even another command—with *redirection*. The following sections describe the shell redirection operators that you can use to redirect them.

3.2.1 Redirecting Input to a File

To redirect standard input (sometimes called "stdin"), use the < operator. To do so, follow a command with < and the name of the file it should take

input from. For example, instead of giving a list of keywords as arguments to
`apropos` (see Recipe 2.8.1 [Finding the Right Tool for the Job], page 44), you
can redirect standard input to a file containing a list of keywords to use.

⇒ To redirect standard input for `apropos` to a file named `keywords`, type:

```
$ apropos < keywords ⟨RET⟩
```

3.2.2 Redirecting Output to a File

There are two operators for redirecting standard output (or "stdout") to a
file. The `>` operator overwrites a file with output if the file already exists,
whereas the `>>` operator will append output to the file. If the specified file
does not exist, either operator will create it.

To use either operator, follow a command with the operator and the name
of the file the output should be written to.

⇒ Here are two ways to use this.

- To redirect standard output of the command *apropos shell bash*
  to the file `command.suggestions`, overwriting this file if it already
  exists, type:

  ```
  $ apropos shell bash > command.suggestions ⟨RET⟩
  ```

- To append the standard output of *apropos shells* to an existing
  file `command.suggestions`, type:

  ```
  $ apropos shells >> command.suggestions ⟨RET⟩
  ```

3.2.3 Redirecting Error Messages to a File

To redirect the standard error stream (sometimes referred to as "stderr"), use
the `2>` operator. Follow a command with this operator and the name of the
file the error stream should be written to.

⇒ To redirect the standard error of *apropos shell bash* to the file
`command.error`, type:

```
$ apropos shell bash 2> command.error ⟨RET⟩
```

As with redirecting the standard output, there are two variations; `2>>`
works just like `2>` but it appends the standard error to a file, if the file already
exists.

⇒ To append the standard error of *apropos shells* to an existing file
`command.error`, type:

```
$ apropos shells 2>> command.error ⟨RET⟩
```

To redirect *both* standard output and standard error to the same file, use `&>` instead of the stdout and stderr operators.

⇒ To redirect the standard output *and* the standard error of `apropos shells` to a file named `commands`, type:

```
$ apropos shells &> commands (RET)
```

NOTES: The `&>` operator overwrites pre-existing files; there is no `&>>` operator for appending both stdin and stderr in such cases.

3.2.4 Redirecting Output to Another Command's Input

Piping is when you connect the standard output of one command to the standard input of another. You do this by specifying the two commands in order, separated by a vertical bar character (`|`, sometimes called a "pipe"). Commands built in this fashion are called *pipelines*.

Pipes are often used with a *filter*, which is any tool that takes its input, changes it in some way, and sends the result to the standard output. You can connect filters and tools together with pipelines, pushing each one's output onward to the input of the next. The pipe is so powerful as a means of applying and combining filters that we might have a whole chapter on "filtering text"; as it is, filters that change the formatting of text have their own special chapter, and other filters are described elsewhere throughout the book.

It's often useful to pipe commands that display a lot of text output to `less`, a tool for perusing text (see Recipe 9.1 [Perusing Text], page 211).

⇒ To pipe the output of **apropos bash shell shells** to `less`, type:

```
$ apropos bash shell shells | less (RET)
```

This redirects the standard output of the command **apropos bash shell shells** to the standard input of the command **less**, which displays it on the screen for perusal.

3.2.5 Redirecting Output to More than One Place

Use `tee` to redirect standard output to more than one place. `tee` was named after those T-shaped plumbing connections that do the same thing with pipes. When you use `tee` at the end of a pipeline, it redirects its input to both the standard output and the file name you give as an argument.

⇒ To write a copy of the output of **apropos** *bash* *shell* *shells* to a file
   called **shell.commands**, and peruse the output with **less** at the same
   time, type:

   `$ apropos bash shell shells | tee shell.commands | less` (RET)

Use the **-a** option to *append* to the file, and not overwrite any existing
data.

To redirect to multiple files, string multiple **tee** commands together.

⇒ To write a copy of the output of **apropos** *bash* *shell* *shells* to a file
   called **shell.commands**, append a copy of the output to a file named
   command.suggestions, and peruse the output with **less** at the same
   time, type (all on one line):

   `$ apropos bash shell shells | tee shell.commands | tee -a`
   `command.suggestions | less` (RET)

3.2.6 Redirecting Something to Nowhere

The file **/dev/null** is a special device file called the *null device*. It contains
nothing; think of it as a vast bottomless pit whose depths you can never reach
or see. If you try to display its contents, you'll get nothing, and what you
send there will disappear into nothing and you will never get it back.

This is actually useful! Redirect anything to **/dev/null** that you don't
want to see—the standard error, for example. You can also do the opposite, and write the contents of **/dev/null** to something, which is good for
commands that ask for some kind of optional input and you want to run it
without giving any such input at all.

⇒ To run the command **errant** and direct any error messages to **/dev/null**,
   type:

   `$ errant 2> /dev/null` (RET)

NOTES: "Sending to **/dev/null**" is a common phrase. Now you know what
it means when people do this. Some people call it the "bit bucket." Now you
know that, too.

3.3 Managing Jobs

The processes you have running in a particular shell are called your *jobs*.
You can have more than one job running from a shell at once; jobs that are
reading standard input and writing standard output are the *foreground* jobs,
while any other jobs are said to be running in the *background*.

The shell assigns each job a unique *job number*. You can use it as an argument to specify the job to commands. Do this by preceding the job number with a percent sign (%).

To find the job number of a job you have running, list your jobs (see Recipe 3.3.4 [Listing Your Jobs], page 73).

The following sections describe the various commands for managing jobs.

3.3.1 Suspending a Job

Type ⟨CTRL⟩-⟨Z⟩ to suspend or stop the foreground job—useful for when you want to do something else in the shell and return to the current job later. The job stops until you either bring it back to the foreground or make it run in the background (see Recipe 3.3.3 [Putting a Job in the Foreground], page 73 and see Recipe 3.3.2 [Putting a Job in the Background], page 72).

For example, if you are reading a document in `info`, typing ⟨CTRL⟩-⟨Z⟩ will suspend the `info` program and return you to a shell prompt where you can do something else (see Recipe 2.8.5 [Reading an Info Manual], page 48). The shell outputs a line giving the job number (in brackets) of the suspended job, the text "`Stopped`" to indicate that the job has stopped, and the command line itself, as shown here:

```
[1]+  Stopped                 info -f manual.info
```

In this example, the job number is 1 and the command that has stopped is "`info -f manual.info`." The + character next to the job number indicates that this is the most recent job.

If you have any stopped jobs when you log out, the shell will tell you this instead of logging you out, as in Figure 3-2.

```
$ logout ⟨RET⟩
There are stopped jobs.
$
```

Figure 3-2. Stopped jobs when logging out.

At this point, you can list your jobs (see Recipe 3.3.4 [Listing Your Jobs], page 73), stop any jobs you have running (see Recipe 3.3.5 [Stopping a Job], page 73), and then log out.

3.3.2 Putting a Job in the Background

New jobs run in the foreground unless you specify otherwise. To run a job in the background, end the input line with an ampersand (&). This is useful for running non-interactive programs that perform a lot of calculations.

⇒ To run the command *apropos shell > shell-commands* as a background job, type:

```
$ apropos shell > shell-commands & ⟨RET⟩
[1] 6575
$
```

The shell outputs the job number (in this case, 1) and process ID (in this case, 6575), and then returns to a shell prompt. When the background job finishes, the shell will list the job number, the command, and the text "**Done**," indicating that the job has completed successfully:

    [1]+ Done   apropos shell >shell-commands

To move a job from the foreground to the background, first suspend it (see Recipe 3.3.1 [Suspending a Job], page 71) and then type *bg* (for "background").

⇒ For example, to start the command *apropos shell > shell-commands* in the foreground, suspend it, and then specify that it finish in the background, you would type:

```
$ apropos shell > shell-commands ⟨RET⟩
⟨CTRL⟩-⟨Z⟩

[1]+  Stopped                  apropos shell >shell-commands
$ bg ⟨RET⟩
[1]+ apropos shell &
$
```

If you have suspended multiple jobs, specify the job to be put in the background by giving its job number as an argument.

⇒ To run job 4 in the background, type:

    $ bg %4 ⟨RET⟩

NOTES: Running a job in the background is sometimes called "backgrounding" or "amping off" a job.

3.3.3 Putting a Job in the Foreground

Type *fg* to move a background job to the foreground. By default, *fg* works on the most recent background job.

⇒ To bring the most recent background job to the foreground, type:

    $ fg ⟨RET⟩

To move a specific job to the foreground when you have multiple jobs in the background, specify the job number as an option to *fg*.

⇒ To bring job 3 to the foreground, type:

    $ fg %3 ⟨RET⟩

3.3.4 Listing Your Jobs

To list the jobs running in the current shell, type *jobs*.

⇒ To list your jobs, type:

```
$ jobs ⟨RET⟩
[1]-  Stopped              apropos shell >shell-commands
[2]+  Stopped              apropos bash >bash-commands
$
```

This example shows two jobs—*apropos shell > shell-commands* and *apropos bash > bash-commands*. The + character next to a job number indicates that it's the most recent job, and the − character indicates that it's the job *previous* to the most recent job. If you have no current jobs, *jobs* returns nothing.

To list all of the *processes* you have running on the system, use **ps** instead of **jobs**—see Recipe 2.7 [Listing Processes], page 41.

3.3.5 Stopping a Job

Typing ⟨CTRL⟩-⟨C⟩ interrupts the foreground job before it completes, exiting the program.

⇒ To run the `cat` tool and then interrupt it while it is running in the foreground, type:

```
$ cat ⟨RET⟩
⟨CTRL⟩-⟨C⟩ ⟨RET⟩
$
```

Use `kill` to interrupt (or "kill") a background job, specifying the job number as an argument.

⇒ To kill job number 2, type:

```
$ kill %2 ⟨RET⟩
```

3.4 Using Your Command History

Your command *history* is the sequential list of commands you have already typed in both current and previous shell sessions. The commands in this history list are called *events*.

By default, Bash remembers the last 500 events, but this number is configurable (see Recipe 3.7.3 [Using Shell Startup Files], page 86).

Your command history is stored in a text file in your home directory called `.bash_history`; you can view this file or edit it as you would any other text file.

Two very useful abilities that having a command history gives you is to repeat the last command you typed, and (as explained earlier in this chapter) to do an incremental backwards search through your history.

The following sections explain how to view your history and specify events from it on the command line. For more information on command history, consult the Info documentation for `bash` (see Recipe 2.8.5 [Reading an Info Manual], page 48).

3.4.1 Viewing Your Command History

Use `history` to view your command history. It outputs a list of all events in your `.bash_history`, one per line, beginning the oldest event. Events are preceded with their event number and two space characters.

⇒ To view your command history, type:

```
$ history ⟨RET⟩
1 who
2 apropos shell >shell-commands
3 apropos bash >bash-commands
4 history
$
```

This command shows the contents of your command history file, listing one command per line, each prefaced by its *event number*. Use an event number to specify that event in your history (see Recipe 3.4.3 [Specifying a Command from Your History], page 76).

If your history is a long one, this list will scroll off the screen, in which case you may want to pipe the output to **less** in order to peruse it. It's also common to search for a past command by piping the output to **grep** (see Recipe 3.2.4 [Redirecting Output to Another Command's Input], page 69, and Recipe 14.1 [Searching Text for a Word], page 333).

⇒ To search your history for the text "**apropos**," type:

```
$ history | grep apropos ⟨RET⟩
2 apropos shell >shell-commands
3 apropos bash >bash-commands
5 history | grep apropos
$
```

This command will show the events from your history containing the text "**apropos**." (The last line of output is the command you just typed.)

3.4.2 Searching Through Your Command History

There are two methods for searching through your history.

METHOD #1

You can use the Bash reverse-incremental search feature, ⟨CTRL⟩-⟨R⟩, to *search*, in reverse, through your command history. You'll find this useful if you remember typing a command line with "**foo**" in it recently, and you wish to repeat the command without having to retype it. Type ⟨CTRL⟩-⟨R⟩ followed by the text *foo*, and the last command you typed containing "foo" appears on the input line.

Like the Emacs command of the same name (see Recipe 14.9.1 [Searching Incrementally in Emacs], page 352), this is called an *incremental* search because it builds the search string in character increments as you type. Typing the string "cat" will search for (and display) the last input line containing a "c," then "ca," and finally "cat," as you type the individual characters of the search string. Typing ⟨CTRL⟩-⟨R⟩ again retrieves the next previous command line that has a match for the search string.

⇒ Here are two ways to use this.

- To put the last command you entered containing the string "grep" back on the input line, type:

  ```
  $ ⟨CTRL⟩-⟨R⟩
  (reverse-i-search)`': grep
  ```

- To put the third-to-last command you entered containing the string "grep" back on the input line, type:

  ```
  $ ⟨CTRL⟩-⟨R⟩
  (reverse-i-search)`': grep
  ⟨CTRL⟩-⟨R⟩ ⟨CTRL⟩-⟨R⟩
  ```

NOTES: When a command is displayed on the input line, type ⟨RET⟩ to run it. You can also edit the command line as usual.

METHOD #2

You can also pipe your history through **grep** to output lines that match a pattern (see Recipe 14.2 [Searching Text for a Phrase], page 334). This does not put anything on the input line, but will give all the matches at once. You might also want to pipe this output to a text pager such as **less** so you can peruse it (see Recipe 9.1 [Perusing Text], page 211).

⇒ To peruse all the lines in your command history containing the text "newfile," type:

```
$ history | grep newfile | less ⟨RET⟩
```

3.4.3 Specifying a Command from Your History

You can specify a past event from your history on the input line in order to run it again.

The simplest way to specify a history event is to use the up and down arrow keys at the shell prompt to browse your history. The up arrow key

(⇧) takes you back through past events, and the down arrow key (⇩) moves you forward to more recent events. When a history event is on the input line, you can edit it as normal, and type ⟨RET⟩ to run it as a command; it will then become the newest event in your history.

⇒ To specify the second-to-last command in your history, type:

$ ⇧ ⇧

To specify a history event by its event number, enter an exclamation point (!, sometimes called "bang") followed by the event number. (Get the event number by viewing your history; see Recipe 3.4.1 [Viewing Your Command History], page 74).

⇒ To run history event number 1, type:

$ *!1* ⟨RET⟩

NOTES: The special event number "!" is the last event, so typing *! !* is another way to run the last command you typed.

3.5 Using Shell Variables

A shell *variable* is a symbol that stores a value and has a unique name. When its name is referenced, the value it contains is given. Variables are case sensitive, so `NAME`, `Name`, and `name` are all different variables.

You can assign your own variables, but there are also many special built-in variables that have special meaning for the shell. One is `HOME`, which contains the name of your home directory. Variables are often used by scripts and programs on the system.

For example, a convention is to use the `EDITOR` variable to hold the name of your preferred text editor; programs that launch an editor often check to see if this variable is set, and run that editor.

Variables are quite useful when used in shell scripts, which are described later in this chapter.

The following recipes explain how to use variables, and show some of the things you can do with some of Bash's special built-in variables. For a complete list of these built-ins, consult the `bash` manual page (see Recipe 2.8.4 [Reading a Page from the System Manual], page 46).

3.5.1 Assigning a Variable

To assign a new variable, type its name followed by an equals sign (=) and the quoted string that should become the variable's value. Be sure not to type any space characters on either side of the equals sign.

⇒ To make a new variable called **NAME** and give it a value of "**Mary Jones**," type:

     $ *NAME='Mary Jones'* ⟨RET⟩

    Values themselves may contain variables, which are then expanded when the variable is assigned. You can use any quoting method to give the value, and you can specify the output of a command (see Recipe 3.1.11 [Specifying the Output of a Command as an Argument], page 65).

⇒ Here are two ways to use this.

- To give a variable called **NAME** a value of the contents of the **FIRSTNAME** and **LASTNAME** variables, with a space between them, type:

     $ *NAME="$FIRSTNAME $LASTNAME"* ⟨RET⟩

- To give a variable called **NAME** a value of the output of the **whoami** command, type:

     $ *NAME=`whoami`* ⟨RET⟩

    To change the contents of an existing variable, just give its name as the variable to use.

⇒ To assign a new value to an existing variable called **NAME**, type:

     $ *NAME="whoami"* ⟨RET⟩

    This command assigns the value "**whoami**" to the variable **NAME**.

3.5.2 Referencing a Variable

Reference a variable in a command by preceding its name with a dollar sign ($). When the command is executed, the shell will first substitute the variable word (and the dollar sign) with the value stored in that variable word. This process is called *expansion*.

⇒ To execute the value of the **NAME** variable as a command, type:

```
$ $NAME ⟨RET⟩
mary
$
```

If the value of the the `NAME` variable is "`whoami`," referencing it as a command will run the `whoami` tool (see Recipe 2.6.1 [Displaying Your Username], page 39). In this example, that's what happened, and the username is `mary`.

3.5.3 Displaying the Contents of a Variable

When you want to look at the contents of a variable, use `echo` and reference the variable as an argument.

⇒ To display the contents of the variable `NAME`, type:

```
$ echo $NAME ⟨RET⟩
whoami
$
```

In this example, the variable `NAME` is shown to contain the string "`whoami`."

When you want to output other characters immediately after the name of a variable, enclose the variable name in curly braces (`{}`), with the dollar sign on the outside and immediately preceding it.

⇒ To display the contents of the variable `NAME` followed by the string "now," type:

```
$ echo ${NAME}now ⟨RET⟩
whoaminow
$
```

Without the curly braces, it would have looked to the shell as though you were referencing a variable called `NAMEnow`.

3.5.4 Removing a Variable

There are two things about a variable you can remove: its contents, and the variable itself. To remove the *contents* of an existing variable, assign it a new value but give nothing for its contents. The variable will still exist, but it will be assigned the null string (sometimes called the "empty string," because its value is nothing).

⇒ To give a variable called `NAME` the value of the null string, type:

```
$ NAME=⟨RET⟩
```

To remove a variable itself, regardless of the value it contains, use **unset** and give the name of the variable.

⇒ To remove a variable called **NAME**, type:

> `$ unset NAME` ⟨RET⟩

3.5.5 Listing Variables

Use **set** with no options to display all of the variables in your current shell and the values they contain.

⇒ To list all of the variables in your current shell, type:

> `$ set` ⟨RET⟩

3.5.6 Changing the Shell Prompt

The special variable **PS1** is used for the text of the shell prompt. To change the text of the shell prompt, change the contents of this variable.

⇒ To change your shell prompt to "**Your wish is my command: ,**" type:

```
$ PS1="Your wish is my command: " ⟨RET⟩
Your wish is my command:
```

Since the replacement text has spaces in it, I've quoted it (see Recipe 3.1.3 [Quoting Reserved Characters], page 56).

You can put special characters in the prompt variable in order to output special text. For example, the characters "\w" in the value of **PS1** will list the current working directory at that place in the shell prompt text.

⇒ To change your prompt to the default Bash prompt—the current working directory followed by a "**$**" character—type:

```
$ PS1='\w $ ' ⟨RET⟩
~ $
```

The following table lists some special characters and their text output at the shell prompt.

\a	An alert or "bell" character, which rings the system bell (you can ring it yourself by typing (CTRL)–(G)).
\d	The current date.
\h	The hostname of the system.
\n	A newline character.
\t	The current system time, in 24-hour format.
\@	The current system time, in 12-hour a.m./p.m. format.
\w	The current working directory.
\u	Your username.
\!	The history number of this command.

You can combine any number of these special characters with regular characters when creating a value for PS1.

⇒ To change the prompt to the current date followed by a space character, the hostname of the system in parentheses, and a greater-than character, type:

```
$ PS1='\d (\h)>' (RET)
14 Dec 1999 (ithaca)>
```

In this example, the system's hostname is ithaca.

3.5.7 Adding to Your Path

To add or remove a directory in your path, use a text editor to change the shell variable PATH as it's defined in the .bashrc file in your home directory (see Chapter 10 [Editing Text], page 231).

For example, suppose the line that defines the PATH variable in your .bashrc file looks like this:

```
PATH="/usr/bin:/bin:/usr/bin/X11:/usr/games"
```

You can add the directory /home/nancy/bin to this path, by editing the line like so:

```
PATH="/usr/bin:/bin:/usr/bin/X11:/usr/games:/home/nancy/bin"
```

NOTES: See very the beginning of Chapter 5 [Files and Directories], page 125, for a complete description of directories and the path.

3.5.8 Controlling How the Shell Checks Your Mail

When new mail arrives for you, the shell will notify you of this before it gives you a new shell prompt. The interval between checks, in seconds, is kept in the MAILCHECK variable. The default value is 60.

⇒ Here are two ways to use this.

- To have the shell check for mail every five minutes, type:

    $ MAILCHECK=300 ⟨RET⟩

- To have the shell check for mail every hour, type:

    $ MAILCHECK=3600 ⟨RET⟩

The MAIL variable contains the full pathname to your system mail file, usually a directory in /var/spool/mail/ whose name is the same as your username. This is where your incoming mail arrives on the system, and it is the file that the shell checks to see if you have mail. When new messages are written to this file, the shell will tell you, before giving you another input line, that you have mail waiting. To turn off mail call, set MAIL to nothing.

⇒ To turn off mail call in the shell, type:

    $ MAIL= ⟨RET⟩

3.5.9 Seeing How Long Your Shell Has Been Running

The special variable SECONDS contains the current number of seconds that the shell has been running.

⇒ To see how many seconds the current shell has been running, type:

    $ echo $SECONDS ⟨RET⟩

NOTES: To find out how long the shell has been running in minutes, hours, or some other unit of time, you can convert the number of seconds output with units (see Recipe 29.5.1 [Converting an Amount between Units of Measurement], page 567).

3.6 Using Alias Words

An *alias* is a word that represents some other command or commands—perhaps the name of a tool, a long command line, or whatever you like. Aliases are useful for creating short command names for lengthy and frequently used commands.

Once you see how an alias works, you might be tempted to make an alias for everything. However, there are differences between aliases and scripts (discussed in the next section) that you should know.

With an alias, the command you run will show up in your shell history instead of the alias name you use to call it, whereas with a shell script, only the name of the script will appear and not the commands in the script. Only you can run an alias; a script, if it is put in a public **bin** directory, can be run by everyone on the system.

Aliases are best for calling a tool, with or without options or arguments, by another name. How to do that is shown below.

3.6.1 Calling a Command by Some Other Name

Use **alias** to assign an alias for a command; follow it with the name of the alias, an equals sign (=), and the quoted string that the alias word should represent.

⇒ To make "bye" an alias for the **exit** command, type:

    `$ alias bye="exit"` ⟨RET⟩

This command makes "bye" an alias for the **exit** tool in the current shell, so typing *bye* would then run **exit**.

You can also include options and arguments in an alias. When you do, be sure to enclose the entire alias in double quotes.

⇒ To make "ls" an alias for the command to list a directory in color on terminals that allow color display, type:

    `$ alias ls="ls --color=auto"` ⟨RET⟩

This command makes "ls" an alias for the **ls** file listing tool with its **--color=auto** option specified, which sets color when the output is directed to a terminal that is capable of displaying it.

This is a common alias, and many Linux systems come preconfigured with it in the default `.bashrc` file. It's also common to make "l" an alias for **ls** with the **-l** option (see Recipe 5.3.3 [Listing File Attributes], page 136).

When you have this alias defined you can still pass other options to **ls** just by specifying them; so typing *ls -l* in this case will execute **ls --color=auto -l** as the actual command.

Aliases are always expanded before the shell looks on your path, so to run a tool or program whose name is also an alias, give the full path name of

the program to run (see Chapter 5 [Files and Directories], page 125, for more
about the path).

⇒ To run the actual `ls` tool with the `-l` option when "`ls`" is already defined
   as an alias for something, type:

       $ /bin/ls -l ⟨RET⟩

NOTES: When you define an alias, it only works in the current shell. To make
an alias work every time you run a shell, put it in your `.bashrc` startup file,
which is a hidden file in your home directory.

3.6.2 Listing Aliases

To list the aliases currently defined in your shell, simply use **alias** without
any arguments.

⇒ To list all aliases currently defined, type:

       $ alias ⟨RET⟩

3.6.3 Removing an Alias

To remove an alias, use **unalias** and give the name of the alias to remove as
an argument. It is removed for the duration of the shell session, unless you
make the word an alias again.

⇒ To remove the alias for "`ls`," type:

       $ unalias ls ⟨RET⟩

NOTES: If you set an alias in your `.bashrc` or `.bash_profile` file, this will
remove it—but only for the current shell. To remove such an alias from all
future sessions, edit the file where it is defined, and remove that particular
alias line.

3.7 Using Shell Scripts

You know that the shell has a programming language; some of the commands
that make up the Bash programming language are the ones I have been dis-
cussing in this chapter. A shell program is simply a sequence of commands
for the shell to execute; a *shell script* is a text file that contains one. Scripts
are also executable, so you can run them by typing their name as a command
(see Recipe 6.3.6 [Making a File Executable], page 170).

   The following recipes show how you make and run them, and how you can
run special scripts automatically when you start or stop running a shell.

3.7.1 Making a Shell Script

Since shell scripts are text files, you use a text editor to make one (see Chapter 10 [Editing Text], page 231); then, make the file executable so that it can be run. Scripts written for Bash all contain a first line written in one of two ways:

```
#!/bin/bash
```

or

```
#!/bin/sh
```

The pound sign and exclamation point (`#!`) in both examples indicates to the shell that the file contains commands to be executed; the full path name that follows tells the shell which program to execute the commands with—this can be the name of a shell, PERL, SED, AWK, or some other command language.

The first example tells Bash that the file is to be executed by the **bash** program itself (the executable file **/bin/bash**) and not some other program.

The second example tells Bash that the file is to be executed by **/bin/sh**, which on modern systems is another name for the **bash** executable.[2] **sh** used to be the old Bourne shell, which Bash replaced. Bash can run any Bourne shell script, and you'll find that many people still write **/bin/sh** in their Bash scripts.

⇒ To make a Bash shell script named **hello** that just outputs the text "**Hello, world**" to the standard output, do the following:

1. Use a text editor to put the following in a file named **hello**:

```
#!/bin/sh
echo Hello, world
```

2. Use **chmod** to make the file executable:

   `$ chmod a+x hello` (RET)

3.7.2 Running a Shell Script

You run (or "execute") a shell script by giving its file name as a command, just as you would any other program. The file must have executable permission

---

[2] Technically, **/bin/sh** is a symbolic link to **/bin/bash**, done for purposes of backwards-compatibility with older scripts (see Recipe 5.7 [Giving a File More Than One Name], page 152).

set (see Recipe 6.3.6 [Making a File Executable], page 170). Scripts can take arguments, just like other kinds of programs.

If a script is stored in a directory that's on your path (see Recipe 3.5.7 [Adding to Your Path], page 81), just type the name of the script to run it. Otherwise, give the path name of the script, either full or relative, to run it (full and relative path names are discussed in Chapter 5 [Files and Directories], page 125).

⇒ Here are some ways to use this.

- To run a script called **hello** that is kept in a directory on your path, type:

     $ *hello* (RET)

- To run a script called **hello** that is kept in the current directory but isn't on your path, type:

     $ *./hello* (RET)

- To run a script called **hello** that is kept in the directory `~/input/files/new`, type:

     $ *~/input/files/new/hello* (RET)

NOTES: To keep things neat, and to avoid having to call scripts by full path names, you should consider keeping them in your own directory for binaries, as described in Recipe C.1 [Using a Directory for Personal Binaries], page 727.

3.7.3 Using Shell Startup Files

Whenever you log in, log out, or start a new shell, the Bash shell looks for special script files in your home directory and runs the commands they contain. These are called *startup files* because they are automatically run when you start (or stop) a shell.

When you log in, Bash first checks to see if the file **/etc/profile** exists, and if so, it executes the commands in this file. This is a generic, system-wide startup file that is run for all users; only the system administrator can add, delete, or change commands in this file. Next, Bash reads and executes the commands in **.bash_profile**, a "hidden" file in your home directory (see Recipe 5.3.4 [Listing Hidden Files], page 138). Thus, to make a command run every time you log in, add the command to this file.

For all new shells you start after you've logged in (that is, for all but the "login shell"), Bash reads and executes the commands in the **.bashrc** file in your home directory. Commands in this file run whenever a new shell is started *except* for the login shell.

```
# "Comment" lines in shell scripts begin with a # character.
# They are not executed by Bash, but exist so that you may
# document your file.

# You can insert blank lines in your file to increase
# readability; Bash will not mind.

# Generate a welcome message when you log in.
figlet 'Good day, '$USER'!'

# Now run the commands in .bashrc
if [ -f ~/.bashrc ]; then . ~/.bashrc; fi
```

Figure 3-3. A simple `.bash_profile`.

```
# Alias to make color directory listings the default.
alias ls="ls --color=auto"

# Alias make "l" give a verbose directory listing.
alias l="ls -l"

# Set a custom path.
PATH="/usr/local/bin:/usr/bin:/bin:/usr/bin/X11:~/bin:."

# Set a custom shell prompt.
PS1="[\w] $ "

# Set Vi-style editing mode as the default.
set -o vi

# Make a long history list and history file.
HISTSIZE=20000
HISTFILESIZE=20000

# Check mail every ten minutes.
MAILCHECK=600

# Export the path and prompt variables for all
# variables you define.
export HISTSIZE HISTFILESIZE MAILCHECK PATH PS1
```

Figure 3-4. A simple `.bashrc`.

There are separate configuration files for login and all other shells so that you can put specific customizations in your `.bash_profile` that only run when you first log in to the system. To avoid having to put commands in both files when you want to run the same ones for all shells, append the following to the end of your `.bash_profile` file:

```
if [ -f ~/.bashrc ]; then . ~/.bashrc; fi
```

This makes Bash run the `.bashrc` file in your home directory when you log in. In this way, you can put *all* of your customizations in your `.bashrc` file, and they will be run *both* at log in and for all subsequent shells. Any customizations before this line in `.bash_profile` run only when you log in.

For example, a simple `.bash_profile` might look like Figure 3-3, and a simple `.bashrc` file, in turn, might look like Figure 3-4.

The `.bash_profile` in Figure 3-3 prints a welcome message with the `figlet` text font tool (see Recipe 16.4.1 [Outputting Horizontal Text Fonts], page 401), and then runs the user's `.bashrc` file.

The `.bashrc` in Figure 3-4 sets a few useful command aliases and uses a custom path and shell prompt whenever a new shell is run.

When you log out, Bash reads and executes the commands in the `.bash_logout` file in your home directory, if it exists. To run commands when you log out, put them in this file.

⇒ To clear the screen every time you log out, your `.bash_logout` should contain the following line:

```
clear
```

This executes the `clear` command, which clears the screen of the current terminal.

NOTES: Some distributions come with default shell startup files filled with all kinds of interesting things. Debian users might want to look at the example startup files in `/usr/share/doc/bash/examples/startup-files`.

3.8 Making a Typescript of a Shell Session

Use `script` to create a typescript, or "capture log," of a shell session—it writes a verbatim copy of your session to a file, including commands you type and their output. This is useful to record all of your moves when you are doing something big on the system—like installing or upgrading some software, or changing a configuration. As even its manual page notes, programming instructors often request a "script" of students' moves for compiling and running a program when they turn in assignments.

The first and last lines of the file show the beginning and ending time and date of the capture session. To stop recording the typescript, type *exit* at a shell prompt. By default, typescripts are saved to a file called `typescript` in the current directory; specify the file name as an argument.

⇒ To create a typescript of a shell session and save it to the file log.19990525, type:

```
$ script log.19990525 (RET)
Script started, output file is log.19990525
$ hostname (RET)
erie
$ apropos bash > bash.commands (RET)
$ exit (RET)
exit
Script done, output file is log.19990525
$
```

In this example, the typescript records a shell session consisting of two commands (**hostname** and **apropos**) to a file called `log.19990525`. The typescript looks like Figure 3-5.

```
Script started on Tue May 25 14:21:52 1999
$ hostname
erie
$ apropos bash > bash.commands
$ exit
exit

Script done on Tue May 25 14:22:30 1999
```

Figure 3-5. A typescript of a shell session.

NOTES: You won't be happy with the output if you record a session with an interactive program such as Emacs or Vi. This is because such programs control the display; all of their screen-manipulating sequences will be saved to the typescript, where they will appear as junk characters to human eyes.

It's possible, but usually not desirable, to run `script` from within another `script` session. This usually happens when you've forgotten that you are running it, and you run it again inside the current typescript, even multiple times. As a result, you may end up with multiple sessions "nested" inside each other like a set of Russian dolls.

3.9 Running Shells

It is sometimes desirable to start another shell. Do this if you are running one kind of shell and you want to run another, or if you want to change some shell settings before you run a command and then return to the previous settings when you are done.

The following recipes deal with the running of shells.

3.9.1 Starting a Shell

There are different methods for starting a shell. One runs the shell inside your current shell, and the other *replaces* your current shell with the new shell.

METHOD #1

To start another shell and return to your current shell later, just run the new shell by giving the name of its command (the command to run Bash, for example, is bash).

This will suspend your current shell and run the new shell; when you exit the new shell, you will return to your old shell.

⇒ To run a new Bash shell, type:

```
$ bash ⟨RET⟩
```

METHOD #2

To run a shell *in place of* your current shell, use **exec**. Give as an argument the name of the command of the new shell you want to run. This stops your current shell and replaces it with the new shell. If you run this command from a login shell, then when you exit the new shell, you will be logged out.

⇒ To run Csh in place of your current shell, type:

```
$ exec csh ⟨RET⟩
```

NOTES: You can use **exec** to run any command in place of the current shell, not just another shell.

3.9.2 Exiting a Shell

Use **exit** to exit the current shell. This command is a Bash "built-in."

⇒ To exit the current shell, type:

$ *exit* ⟨RET⟩

You can also type ⟨CTRL⟩-⟨D⟩ at the shell prompt, which works as a shortcut to the **exit** command.

⇒ To exit the current shell, type:

$ ⟨CTRL⟩-⟨D⟩

NOTES: Exiting your login shell will log you out of the system (see Recipe 2.2.2 [Logging Out of the System], page 31).

3.9.3 Getting the Name of Your Current Shell

Here is a trick for displaying the name of the shell you are currently in. The special shell variable 0 (zero) is always assigned the value of the name of the shell or script that is currently running (see Recipe 3.5 [Using Shell Variables], page 77). So at a shell prompt, the value of 0 is the name of the current shell— use **echo** to show its value to determine what kind of shell you are currently in.

⇒ To see which shell you are currently in, type:

```
$ echo $0 ⟨RET⟩
ksh
$
```

In this example, **ksh** is the current shell.

NOTES: This will output the name of the current shell in most shells, but there are rare exceptions. With the shell-like **tclsh** and **wish** programs, this will output the following error message: "**can't read "0": no such variable.**"

3.9.4 Changing Your Default Shell

Use **chsh** to change your default login shell. When you run it, **chsh** asks you for your password (for security reasons), and then asks what shell you'd like your login shell to be replaced with. Your answer must be a shell that's installed on the system.[3] If you have second thoughts, just hit ⟨RET⟩ when it asks—then, your login shell will not be changed.

⇒ To change your default shell to **pdmenu**, type:

```
$ chsh ⟨RET⟩
Password: sesame ⟨RET⟩
Changing the login shell for suzie
Enter the new value, or press return for the default
        Login Shell [/bin/bash]: pdmenu ⟨RET⟩

$
```

In this example, the user **suzie** with a password of "**sesame**" changed her login shell to **pdmenu**, a shell described in the next recipe.

3.9.5 Using Other Shells

Everything in this chapter has been about Bash, which is "the Linux shell" if there ever was one—more Linux systems come with Bash as the default than any other shell. But there are many shells and, like text editors and distributions, everyone has his favorite that can do it all. You have many to choose from, and they all work differently, and have their own charms (and annoyances).

Most regular users won't have any reason to run anything other than Bash, but if you are a programmer or are coming to Linux from some other UNIX background, you might already have a favorite shell.

This table describes some of the alternatives.

Ash	NetBSD's **ash** (the "Almquist shell") is smaller than Bash and has features similar to the original Bourne shell. Useful for Linux-on-a-floppy and small installations. DEB: ash RPM: ash WWW: http://sources.isc.org/utils/shell/ash.txt

---

[3] A list is kept at /etc/shells.

Csh	The interface of the "sea shell" is like the C programming language and, having originated on the BSD flavor of UNIX, is popular on those systems. DEB: `csh` RPM: `tcsh` WWW: `http://tcshrc.sourceforge.net/`
Esh	The "easy shell" is a small shell that uses a Lisp-like syntax as the primary means of interface. DEB: `esh` RPM: `esh` WWW: `http://olympus.het.brown.edu/doc/esh/esh.html`
Eshell	A complete Emacs command shell, using Emacs Lisp as the interface. DEB: `eshell` WWW: `http://www.emacswiki.org/johnw/EmacsShell.html`
Lsh	Inspired by old PC command interpreters, this is a shell for novices who have had DOS experience but are new to UNIX. DEB: `lsh`
Psh	A shell that uses the syntax and features of the PERL programming language. DEB: `psh` RPM: `psh` WWW: `http://sourceforge.net/projects/psh/`
Pdksh	AT&T's Korn shell, named after its author David Korn, brought together the features of Csh and the original shell; Pdksh is a public domain implementation of this old UNIX standby. DEB: `pdksh` RPM: `pdksh` WWW: `http://web.cs.mun.ca/~michael/pdksh/`

Pdmenu
     This is a full-screen text menuing system, in color, intended as a way for inexperienced users to select and run programs.
DEB: `pdmenu`
RPM: `pdmenu`
WWW: `http://kitenet.net/programs/pdmenu/`

rc
     Based on the AT&T Plan 9 shell, this is a fast shell with a syntax similar to the C programming language.
DEB: `rc`
WWW: `http://www.star.le.ac.uk/~tjg/rc/`

Tcsh
     The TENEX C shell is an enhanced version of Csh.
DEB: `tcsh`
RPM: `tsch`
WWW: `http://www.tcsh.org/`

Zsh
     Similar to the Korn shell, but with features like spelling correction and scripting enhancements.
DEB: `zsh`
RPM: `zsh`
WWW: `http://www.zsh.org/`

## CHAPTER 4

The X Window System

XFree86
  DEB: `xserver-common`
  RPM: `XFree86`
  WWW: `http://www.xfree86.org/`

The X Window System, commonly called "X,"[1] is a graphical windowing interface that comes with all popular Linux distributions. X is available for many UNIX-based operating systems; the version of X that runs on Linux systems with x86-based CPUs is called "XFree86." The current version of X is 11, Revision 6—or "X11R6."

All the command line tools and most of the applications that you can run in the console can run in X; numerous applications written specifically for X are also available.

Usually, you run X from the console, but there are other ways to do it. When you are running X on your system, it is possible to run some graphical program from a remote system, and have it display on your screen; there are also special terminals designed for X and wired into the main system. With just a keyboard mouse and monitor but no processing power, these are like dumb terminals (see Recipe 2.3 [Using Consoles and Terminals], page 32), but they are designed for accessing the X Window System, and are called *X terminals*.

This chapter shows you how to get around in X: how to start it and stop it, run programs within it, manipulate windows, and customize X to your liking. See *The Linux XFree86 HOWTO* for information on installing X (see Recipe 2.8.6 [Reading System Documentation and Help Files], page 50).

4.1 Running X

When you start X, you should see a mouse pointer appear on the screen as a large, black "X." If your X is configured to start any tools or applications, they should each start and appear in individual windows. A very plain and simple X session might look like Figure 4-1.

The *root window* is the background behind all of the other windows. It is usually set to a color, but you can change it (see Recipe 4.7.3 [Changing the

---

[1] Sometimes you might catch it being called "X Windows," but this term is technically incorrect.

Root Window Parameters], page 118). Each program or application in X runs
in its own window. Each window has a decorative border around some or all
of its sides, called the *window border*; L-shaped corners, called *frames*; a top
window bar, called the *title bar*, which displays the name of the window; and
several title bar buttons on the left and right sides of the title bar (described
in Recipe 4.3 [Manipulating X Client Windows], page 105). Depending on the
window manager and its settings, any of these elements may be invisible.

Figure 4-1. A simple X session.

The entire visible work area, including the root window and any other
windows, is called the *desktop*. The box in the lower right-hand corner, called
the *pager*, allows you to move about a large desktop (see Recipe 4.4 [Moving
Around the Desktop], page 108).

A *window manager* is a program that controls the way windows look and
are displayed—the window dressing, as it were—and can provide some additional menu or program-management capabilities. The window manager
starts as soon as you run X. There are many different window managers to
choose from, each with a variety of features and capabilities; part of the fun of
starting to use Linux is trying them all out to find a favorite. See Recipe 4.7.5
[Using Other Window Managers], page 120, for a list of some of the more
popular or interesting ones.

Window managers typically allow you to customize the colors and borders that are used to display a window, as well as the type and location of buttons that appear on the window (see Recipe 4.2 [Running a Program in X], page 101). For example, in the image above, the clock itself is the `oclock` program, while the title bar above it is drawn by the FVWM2 window manager. With the AfterStep window manager, the title bar would look a little different, as in Figure 4-2.

Figure 4-2. An `oclock` in AfterStep.

There are many window managers you can choose from, all different; instead of describing only one, or describing all of them only superficially, this chapter explains the *basics* of X, the fundamentals that everyone must know to use X regardless of his particular setup, and that are common to all window managers.

In recent years, *desktop environments* have also become popular. These are application suites that run on top of the window manager (and X), with the purpose of giving your X session a standardized "look and feel"; these suites normally come with a few basic tools, such as clocks and file managers. The two principal desktops are GNOME (the GNU Project's "GNU Network Object Model Environment") and KDE (the "K Desktop Environment").[2]

If you have a recent Linux distribution and chose the default install, chances are good that you have either GNOME or KDE installed, with something like Window Maker or FVWM2 assigned as the default window manager. (While you can have more than one window manager installed on your system, you can only run one at a time.)

---

[2] Desktops are designed to be an intuitive and "user friendly" interface to X, so in this book I explain the fundamentals of using X itself; learn more about these desktop environments from their Web sites: `http://gnome.org/` and `http://kde.org/`.

4.1.1 Starting X

There are two principal ways to start X. How you start it on your system will depend on whether or not the X Display Manager is installed.

METHOD #1

Xdm
  DEB: xdm
  RPM: xdm
  WWW: http://www.xfree86.org/

If the X Display Manager, xdm, is installed, use it to manage your X session. Systems that have it installed are typically configured to go to the seventh virtual console when the system boots, so you'll see a graphical xdm login screen right away. Some distributions customize this login screen—for example, Fedora shows a "Fedora Core" logo and draws a box underneath it for entering your username.

You can log in directly to an X session from this screen, typing your username and password in the appropriate boxes.

When xdm is running but the system is not configured to go to the seventh virtual console at boot time, switch to it so you can log in to an X session.

⇒ To switch to the seventh virtual console, type:
        ⟨ALT⟩-⟨F7⟩

METHOD #2

On systems not running xdm, the virtual console reserved for X will be blank, until you start X yourself by running startx in another virtual console. Messages from startx, including any error messages, are displayed in the console you run it in, while X itself will run in the seventh virtual console.

⇒ Here are two ways to use this.

  • To start X yourself from another virtual console, type:
        $ startx ⟨RET⟩

  • To run startx and redirect both its standard output and standard error to a log file, type:
        $ startx &> ~/startx.log ⟨RET⟩

Both of these examples start X on the seventh virtual console, regardless of which console you are at when you run the command—your console automatically switches to X on the seventh console. You can always switch to another console during your X session (see Recipe 2.3 [Using Consoles and Terminals], page 32). The second example writes any error messages or output of `startx` to a file called `startx.log` in your home directory.

When you start X, you can specify the *color depth* to use, which is the number of bits used to render possible colors for each pixel on the display.[3] It is specified in terms of power to two; therefore, 8-bit color means a pixel can be 2^8 or any one of 256 possible colors, 16-bit color gives 65,536 possible colors (2^{16}), and with 24-bit color (2^{24}), pixels can be any one of 16,777,216 colors (1-bit color, then, is exactly two colors). Color depth is limited by display hardware. Depending on your system's configuration and graphics card, X may start with a default color depth anywhere from 8-bit to 24-bit. You can specify another color depth by using `startx` with the special `-bpp` option; follow it with a number indicating the color depth to use, and precede the option with two hyphen characters (`--`), which tells `startx` to pass the options that follow it to the X server itself.

⇒ To start X from a virtual console and specify 24-bit color depth, type:

    $ startx -- -bpp 24 ⟨RET⟩

NOTES: If your system runs `xdm`, you can always switch to the seventh virtual console (or whichever console `xdm` is running on), and then log in at the `xdm` login screen.

4.1.2 Stopping X

There are a few methods for stopping X.

METHOD #1

The normal way to end an X session is to do it through your window manager. Most window managers have an `Exit X` menu option or something similar that you can select with the mouse; others have keystroke commands for exiting X.

---

[3] A *bit* is the computer's smallest unit of information, and can be either a binary 0 or 1; *pixels* are the individual colored dots that make up your display screen.

⇒ Here are some ways to use this.

- To end your X session if you are running the FVWM2 window manager, do the following:
    1. Click the left mouse button anywhere in the root window to pull up the start menu.
    2. Choose `Really quit?` from the `Exit Fvwm` submenu.

- To end your X session if you are running the AfterStep window manager, do the following:
    1. Click the left mouse button anywhere in the root window to pull up the start menu.
    2. Choose `Exit?` from the `Quit` submenu.
    3. Click `Logout`.

- To end your X session if you are running the Ion window manager, do the following:
    1. Press ⟨F12⟩.
    2. Answer "y" in the Ion mode line:

       `Exit Ion (y/n)? y` ⟨RET⟩

If you started your X session with `startx`, these commands will return you to a shell prompt in the virtual console where the command was typed. If, on the other hand, you started your X session by logging in to `xdm` on the seventh virtual console, you will be logged out of the X session and the `xdm` login screen will appear; you can then switch to another virtual console or log in to X again.

METHOD #2

To exit X immediately and terminate all X processes, press the ⟨CTRL⟩-⟨ALT⟩-⟨BKSP⟩ combination (if your keyboard has two ⟨ALT⟩ and ⟨CTRL⟩ keys, use the left ones). You'll lose any unsaved application data, but this is useful when you cannot exit your X session normally—in the case of a system freeze or other problem.

⇒ To exit X immediately, type:

⟨CTRL⟩-⟨ALT⟩-⟨BKSP⟩

4.2 Running a Program in X

Programs running in an X session are called X *clients*. (The X Window System itself is called the X *server*). To run a program in X, you start it as an X client—either by selecting it from a menu, or by typing the command to run in an `xterm` shell window (see Recipe 4.5 [Running a Shell in X], page 109), as follows.

METHOD #1

Most window managers have a "start menu" of some kind; it's usually accessed by clicking the left mouse button anywhere on the root window. To run an X client from the start menu, click the left mouse button to select the client's name from the submenus.

⇒ To start a square-shaped, analog-face clock from the start menu, do the following:

1. Click the left mouse button on the root window to make the menu appear.

2. Click the left mouse button through the application menus and onto `Xclock (analog)`.

This starts the `xclock` client, specifying the option that displays an analog face, as in Figure 4-3.

Figure 4-3. An analog `xclock`.

METHOD #2

You can also start a client by running it from a shell window—useful for starting a client that isn't on the menu, or for when you want to specify options or arguments. When you run an X client from a shell window, the client opens in its own window, but runs as a foreground job in that shell; to use the shell window while the client is running, run the client in the background (see Recipe 3.3.2 [Putting a Job in the Background], page 72).

⇒ To run a digital clock from a shell window, type:

```
$ xclock -digital & ⟨RET⟩
```

This command runs `xclock` in the background from a shell window; the `digital` option specifies a digital clock.

The following sections explain how to specify certain command line options common to most X clients, such as window layout, colors, and fonts.

4.2.1 Specifying X Window Size and Location

Specify a window's size and location by giving its *window geometry* with the `geometry` option. Four fields control the width and height of the windows, and the window's distance ("offset") from the edge of the screen. It is specified in the form:

```
-geometry WIDTHxHEIGHT+XOFF+YOFF
```

The values in these four fields are usually given in pixels, although some applications measure `WIDTH` and `HEIGHT` in characters. While you must give these values in order, you can omit either pair. For example, to specify just the size of the window, give values for `WIDTH` and `HEIGHT` only.

⇒ Here are some ways to use this.

- To start a small `xclock`, 48 pixels wide and 48 pixels high, type:

  ```
  $ xclock -geometry 48x48 ⟨RET⟩
  ```

- To start a large `xclock`, 480 pixels wide and 500 pixels high, type:

  ```
  $ xclock -geometry 480x500 ⟨RET⟩
  ```

- To start an `xclock` with a width of 48 pixels and the default height, type:

  ```
  $ xclock -geometry 48 ⟨RET⟩
  ```

- To start an `xclock` with a height of 48 pixels and the default width, type:

  ```
  $ xclock -geometry x48 ⟨RET⟩
  ```

You can give positive or negative numbers for the `XOFF` and `YOFF` fields. Positive `XOFF` values specify a position from the left of the screen; negative values specify a position from the right. If `YOFF` is positive, it specifies a position from the top of the screen; if negative, it specifies a position from the bottom of the screen. When giving these offsets, you must specify values for both XOFF and YOFF.

To place the window in one of the four corners of the desktop, use zeroes for the appropriate XOFF and YOFF values, as follows:

+0+0   Upper left-hand corner.

+0-0   Lower left-hand corner.

-0+0   Upper right-hand corner.

-0-0   Lower right-hand corner.

⇒ To start a default size xclock in the lower left-hand corner, type:

> $ xclock -geometry +0-0 ⟨RET⟩

Or, to put it all together, you can specify the size and location of a window with one geometry line that includes all four values.

⇒ To start an xclock with a width of 120 pixels, a height of 100 pixels, an x-offset of 250 pixels from the right side of the screen, and a y-offset of 25 pixels from the top of the screen, type:

> $ xclock -geometry 120x100-250+25 ⟨RET⟩

Use the -iconic option to start a client as an icon, so that it appears as an icon as soon as it is run. The client will start, but it will be displayed as a small icon until you click on it (see Recipe 4.3.5 [Deiconifying an X Window], page 107).

⇒ To start an xclock as an icon, but that will open in the upper right-hand corner when you maximize it, type:

> $ xclock -geometry -0+0 -iconic ⟨RET⟩

4.2.2 Specifying X Window Colors

The window colors available in your X session depend on your display hardware and the X server that is running. The xcolors tool will show all colors available on your X server and the names used to specify them. (Color names are not case-sensitive.)

⇒ To list the available colors, type:

> $ xcolors ⟨RET⟩

Press ⟨Q⟩ to exit xcolors.

To specify a color to use for the window background, window border, and text or graphics in the window itself, give the color name as an argument to the appropriate option: -bg for background color, -bd for window border color, and -fg for foreground color.

⇒ To start an xclock with a light blue window background, type:

    $ xclock -bg lightblue ⟨RET⟩

You can specify any combination of these attributes.

⇒ To start an xclock with a sea green window background and a turquoise window foreground, type:

    $ xclock -bg seagreen -fg turquoise ⟨RET⟩

NOTES: The -bordercolor, -background, and -foreground options are synonymous with -bd, -bg, and -fg.

4.2.3 Specifying X Window Font

To specify a font for use in a window, use the -fn option followed by the X font name to use. (To get an X font name, use xfontsel; see Recipe 16.1 [Using X Fonts], page 395).

⇒ To start an xclock with a digital display, and specify that it use a 17-point Helvetica font for text, type:

    $ xclock -digital -fn -*-helvetica-*-r-*-*-17-*-*-*-*-*-* ⟨RET⟩

This command starts an xclock that looks like Figure 4-4.

Thu Jan 25 11:15:23 2001

Figure 4-4. A digital xclock with Helvetica type.

NOTES: If you specify the font for a shell window, you can resize it after it's running, as described in Recipe 16.1.4 [Resizing the Xterm Font], page 398.

The -font option is synonymous with -fn.

4.2.4 Specifying X Window Border Width

To specify the width of the border of an X client, use -bw followed by the desired width, in pixels.

⇒ To start an xclock with a border width of 30 pixels, type:

    $ xclock -bw 30 ⟨RET⟩

NOTES: The -borderwidth option is synonymous with -bw.

4.2.5 Specifying X Window Title

To specify your own title for a client, use `-title` and follow it with a quoted string for the window title. If you use a long title, you might have to specify the client width to make sure the window is long enough.

⇒ Here are two ways to use this.

- To start an `xclock` with a title of "Time," type:

  ```
  $ xclock -title "Time" ⟨RET⟩
  ```

- To start an `xclock` 225 pixels wide with a title of "As Time Goes By," type:

  ```
  $ xclock -title "As Time Goes By" -geometry 225 ⟨RET⟩
  ```

4.2.6 Specifying Attributes in an X Window

You can specify certain special attributes when an X client is already running in a window.

X applications often have up to three special menus with options for changing certain attributes. To see these menus, press and hold ⟨CTRL⟩ and then click one of the three mouse buttons somewhere in the client's window. (If you have a mouse with only two buttons, click both buttons simultaneously to emulate the middle button.)

⇒ To display an X client's third menu, press and hold ⟨CTRL⟩, move the mouse pointer to somewhere in the X client's window, and click the third mouse button.

4.3 Manipulating X Client Windows

Only one X client can accept keyboard and mouse input at a time, and that client is called the *active client*. To make a client active, move the mouse over the client's window. When a client is the active client, it is said to be "in focus." Depending on the window manager, the shape of the mouse pointer may change, or the window border and title bar of the active client may be different (a common default is steel blue for the active client color and gray for all other windows).

Each window has its own set of controls to manipulate that window. These controls differ slightly between various window managers. Here's how to perform basic window operations with the mouse.

4.3.1 Moving an X Window

Move X client windows by dragging the title bar with the mouse.

⇒ To move an X window, do the following:

1. Click and hold the left mouse button on the window's title bar.
2. Drag its *window outline* to the desired position.
3. Release the left mouse button.

4.3.2 Resizing an X Window

Resize X client windows by dragging any of its frames.

⇒ To resize an X window, do the following:

1. Click and hold the left mouse button on any one of the window's four frames.
2. Move the mouse to shrink or grow the window outline as desired.
3. Release the left mouse button.

4.3.3 Maximizing an X Window

Sometimes you may want to resize an X client window so that the window is as large as it can be, often filling the entire screen. This is called *maximizing* a window.

⇒ The way to maximize a window depends on your window manager; usually one or more of the following methods work:

- Double-click the left mouse button on the title bar (on a maximized window, this sometimes has the effect of returning the window to its smaller original size).
- Click the left mouse button on a square box button on the title bar.
- Click either the middle or right mouse button anywhere on the root window to pull up a menu whose options include "maximize"; select that option and then click on the title bar of the client window to maximize.

NOTES: If the idea of maximizing all your X client windows appeals to you, I suggest looking at Ion, a window manager with no real concept of "windows" at all, but only clients running maximized to full-screen size (see Recipe 4.7.5 [Using Other Window Managers], page 120).

4.3.4 Minimizing an X Window

You can *minimize* an X client window, so that it disappears and an icon representing the running program is placed on the desktop, with the window's "_" button, usually in the upper right-hand corner of the title bar. This is also called *iconifying* a window.

⇒ To minimize an X window, click the left mouse button on the window's "_" button.

NOTES: Some window managers may have slightly different variations on this method, but the basic principle will be the same.

4.3.5 Deiconifying an X Window

Bringing a window back once it has been minimized is called *deiconifying* a window. The icon that represents the window will disappear as the window returns to its prior size and position.

⇒ The way to deiconify a window depends on your window manager, but usually one or more of the following methods work:

- Double-click the left mouse button on the icon.
- Double-click the left mouse button on the icon name that is written underneath it.
- Click either the middle or right mouse button anywhere on the root window to pull up a menu whose options include any of the X client windows in your session; select the name of the client to deiconify.

4.3.6 Getting Information About an X Window

Use `xwininfo` to output information on a client window. This is useful for getting values you'd like to specify for a command—it lists the selected window's geometry, colors, border width, color depth, and other values. Run it in a terminal window (see Recipe 4.5 [Getting a Terminal Window in X], page 109).

⇒ To get information about a client window, do the following:

1. Run `xwininfo` in a terminal window:

```
$ xwininfo ⟨RET⟩

xwininfo: Please select the window about which you
          would like information by clicking the
          mouse in that window.
```

2. Click the left mouse button anywhere in the window you'd like information on.

This command outputs, in the terminal window you typed it in, a list of information on the client window you selected with the mouse.

4.3.7 Destroying an X Window

When you quit or exit an X client, the window is no longer displayed. You can also *destroy* a window in X, where the client running in that window is terminated and the window is no longer displayed.

To destroy a window, click the left mouse button on the "X" button in the upper right-hand corner of the title bar. This is useful for when the program running in the window has stopped responding, and you can't quit it normally.

4.4 Moving Around the Desktop

Many window managers (including AfterStep and FVWM2) allow you to use a *virtual desktop*, which lets you use more screen space than your monitor can display at one time. A virtual desktop can be larger than the display, in which case you can scroll though it with the mouse. The view that fills the display is called the *viewport*. When you move the mouse off the screen in a direction where the current (virtual) desktop extends, the view scrolls in that direction. Virtual desktops are useful for running many clients full screen at once, each in its own separate desktop.

Some configurations disallow scrolling between desktops; in that case, switch between them with a *pager*, which shows a miniature view of your virtual desktop, and allows you to switch between desktops. It is a *sticky window* (it "sticks to the glass" above all other windows), and is always in the lower right-hand corner of your screen, even when you scroll across a virtual desktop. Both your current desktop and active X client are highlighted in the pager.

The default FVWM2 virtual desktop size is nine desktops in a 3x3 grid, as in Figure 4-5.

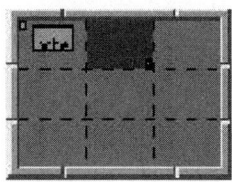

Figure 4-5. An **fvwm2** *pager.*

In the preceding illustration, the current desktop is the second one in the top row. The first desktop contains two X client windows—a small one and a large one—but there are no windows in any other desktops (including the current one).

To switch to another desktop, click the left mouse button on its corresponding view in the pager, or use a keyboard shortcut if your window manager provides one.

⇒ In FVWM2, the default keys for switching between desktops are ⟨ALT⟩ in conjunction with the arrow keys; in AfterStep, use the ⟨CTRL⟩ key in place of ⟨ALT⟩.

- To switch to the desktop to the left of the current one while running FVWM2, type ⟨ALT⟩-⟨←⟩.

- To switch to the desktop directly to the left of the current one while running AfterStep, type ⟨CTRL⟩-⟨←⟩.

4.5 Getting a Terminal Window in X

Xterm
  DEB: xterm
  RPM: xterm
  WWW: http://dickey.his.com/xterm/

A *terminal emulator* lets you run a shell in an X client window. The standard terminal emulator for X on Linux systems is **xterm**, which emulates the DEC

VT102/220 and Tektronix 4014 video terminals.[4] You can run commands in an **xterm** window just as you would in a virtual console; a shell in an **xterm** acts the same as a shell in a virtual console (see Chapter 3 [The Shell], page 53).

You can use all of the standard X client options with **xterm** (see Recipe 4.2 [Running a Program in X], page 101), but it also has many options of its own, which are described in the next recipe.

⇒ To open a new window with a shell, setting the text font to Lucida Sans Typewriter face at a body size of 18 pixels, type:

> $ xterm -fn lucidasanstypewriter-18 ⟨RET⟩

This example requires that you already have a terminal emulator running, with a shell prompt you can type from. If you don't have one, then you will have to start an **xterm** by selecting it from an application menu, as provided through your window manager.

⇒ To open a new window with a shell when using the Ion window manager, setting the text font to Lucida Sans Typewriter face at a body size of 18 pixels, type:

> ⟨F3⟩
> Run: xterm -fn lucidasanstypewriter-18 ⟨RET⟩

You can cut and paste text from an **xterm** to another X client (see Recipe 10.3 [Manipulating Selections of Text], page 253).

To scroll through text that has scrolled past the top of the screen, type ⟨SHIFT⟩-⟨PgUp⟩. The number of lines you can scroll back to depends on the value of the scrollback buffer, specified with the **-sl** option; its default value is 64.

4.5.1 Changing the Default X Terminal Behavior

There are many command line options for controlling **xterm**'s emulation characteristics; the following table lists some of them.

Note that these options are a little idiosyncratic; sometimes a – option turns a thing on, while other times the + option does. Default behavior is noted, although some Linux distributions might change these defaults.

---

[4] To see what the original hardware looks like, see the following:
http://www.cs.utk.edu/~shuford/terminal/dec.html and
http://www.cs.utk.edu/~shuford/terminal/various.html#tek.

+ah	Always highlights the cursor, even when the window is no longer in focus.
-ah	When the window is not in focus, makes the cursor hollow (the default).
-aw	Turns on auto-wraparound, so that text reaching past the right margin is wrapped over to the next line (the default).
+aw	Turns off auto-wraparound; text reaching past the right margin is deleted in such a way so that the last character of a line is printed as the last character before the margin.
-b *pixels*	Specifies the size, in pixels, of the inner border (the default is two).
-bdc	Turns off display of bold characters in color, rather than in bold (the default).
+bdc	Displays bold characters in color.
-cm	Disables recognition of ANSI control sequences.
+cm	Enables recognition of ANSI control sequences (the default).
-cr *color*	Specifies the color to be used for the text cursor.
-fb *font*	Specifies the font used for bold text (the default is to overstrike the normal text font.) The value you give must have the same height and width used for normal text.
-hc *color*	Sets the color used in the background of highlighted or selected text (the default is to use a reverse of the normal text colors).
-j	Turns on *jump scrolling*, where quick-flowing text is scrolled by jumping past many lines at once instead of scrolling every line on the screen; recommended for increasing speed when going through a lot of text (the default).

`+j`	Turns off jump scrolling.
`-leftbar`	Places the scrollbar along the left margin of the window (the default), if also enabled with the `-sb` option.
`-ls`	Uses a login shell for the shell (i.e., for Bash users, this means that the `.bash_profile` is run on startup; this is the default).
`+ls`	Specifies not to use a login shell—uses a normal subshell instead (i.e., for Bash users, this means that the `.bash_profile` is not run).
`-mb`	Turns on a *margin bell*, which rings when the cursor approaches the right margin.
`+mb`	Turns off the margin bell (the default).
`-mc` *milliseconds*	Specifies the time, in milliseconds, between multiple clicks when selecting text.
`-ms` *color*	Specifies the color for the X mouse pointer, when it's in the `xterm` window (this is sometimes called the *pointer cursor*; the value defaults to the foreground color).
`-nb` *color*	Specifies the number of characters, from the right margin, at which point the margin bell should ring, if used (the default is ten).
`-nul`	Enables the display of underlining (the default).
`+nul`	Disables the display of underlining.
`-pc`	Enables PC-style bold colors (brighter color values; the default).
`+pc`	Disables PC-style bold colors.
`-rightbar`	Place the scrollbar along the right margin of the window, if also enabled with the `-sb` option.

`-rw`	Allows for reverse-wraparound, where the cursor may back up from one line to the right margin of the previous one, when editing long command lines (the default).
`+rw`	Does not allow reverse-wraparound.
`-sb`	Enables a scrollbar so that lines scrolled off the top of the window can be viewed by scrolling back on the bar.
`+sb`	Disables the scrollbar (the default).
`-sk`	Specifies that when a key is pressed when using the scrollbar to view previous text, the window display moves forward to the current input line (the default).
`+sk`	Specifies that when a key is pressed when using the scrollbar to view previous text, the window display does not move forward to the current input line.
`-sl` *number*	Specifies the number of lines that scroll off the top of the screen that should be saved, for viewing with the scrollbar.
`-ulc`	Specifies that underlined characters should not be displayed in color (the default).
`+ulc`	Specifies that underlined characters should be displayed in color instead of being underlined.
`-vb`	Specifies that a *visual* bell is to be used rather than an audible one (the window is quickly flashed).
`+vb`	Disables any visual bell (the default).

There are even more options than this; consult the `xterm` `man` page for a complete listing (see Recipe 2.8.4 [Reading a Page from the System Manual], page 46).

4.5.2 Running a Command in an X Window

The `xterm` tools will run a shell by default, but you can use it to run any interactive terminal program instead; do this with the `-e` option, and give

the name of the command to run as an argument. An `xterm` will open with
that command, and it will run in its own window; when that command exits,
the `xterm` window will close. This is handy for when you just want to run a
particular command in its own window, but don't need a shell.

⇒ To run `bc` in its own X window, type:

   $ xterm -e bc ⟨RET⟩

When you exit the command, the shell will exit and the window will close.
You can also pass arguments to the command.

⇒ To run `lynx` with the URL `file:/usr/local/`, type:

   $ xterm -e lynx file:/usr/local/ ⟨RET⟩

In this example, `lynx` opens the given URL in its own window, and will
remain until you either kill the window or exit `lynx`.

NOTES: If calling `xterm` with other options, the `-e` option must be the last
option specified in the command line.

4.5.3 Using Other Terminal Emulators

While `xterm` is the standard Linux terminal emulator, it is certainly not the
only one; there are plenty to choose from, all with special features. The
following table lists some of the better ones.

AfterStep XVT	This color VT102 terminal emulator was made to work with the AfterStep window manager, but can also be used with others; has many special effects such as tinting and shading, yet is smaller than `xterm`—and uses less swap space, too. DEB: aterm RPM: aterm WWW: http://aterm.sourceforge.net/
Enlightened Terminal Emulator	This color VT102 terminal emulator was made to work with the Enlightenment window manager, but can also be used with others; supports themes and has many features to control its appearance. DEB: eterm RPM: Eterm WWW: http://www.eterm.org/

Konsole
: This graphical terminal emulator for KDE allows you to run multiple terminals in a single window.
DEB: konsole
RPM: konsole
WWW: http://konsole.kde.org/

Multi Gnome Terminal
: This graphical terminal emulator for GNOME features enhancements inspired by Konsole, that allow for multiple terminals in a single window.
DEB: multi-gnome-terminal
RPM: multi-gnome-terminal
WWW: http://multignometerm.sourceforge.net/

Multi Lingual TERMinal
: As the name implies, this terminal emulator supports various foreign language encodings.
DEB: mlterm
RPM: mlterm
WWW: http://mlterm.sourceforge.net/

PowerShell
: This color terminal emulator allows multiple terminals in the same window that you can switch between by clicking on "tab" buttons.
DEB: powershell
RPM: powershell
WWW: http://powershell.sourceforge.net/

ouR XVT
: Known to everyone by its command name, rxvt, this is a color VT102 terminal emulator designed to be a xterm replacement, and is smaller and less memory-intensive as the latter, but with less emulation options and configurability.
DEB: rxvt
RPM: rxvt
WWW: http://sourceforge.net/projects/rxvt/

Unicode
: This is xterm with Unicode support.
DEB: xterm
RPM: xterm
WWW: http://dickey.his.com/xterm/

Wterm   This is based on ouR XVT, but optimized for the Window
               Maker window manager. Its features include tranparency, tint-
               ing, and background images.
               DEB: `wterm`
               RPM: `wterm`
               WWW: `http://largo.windowmaker.org/files.php#wterm`

4.6 Magnifying a Portion of the X Desktop

Use `xmag` to magnify a portion of the X desktop. It will open a new window
displaying part of the desktop you select, magnified to a larger size.

When it runs, the X pointer will change to an upper left-hand corner tab.
There are two ways to select the region of the desktop to magnify: Clicking the
left mouse button once, anywhere on the screen, magnifies a region beginning
with where you click as the upper left-hand corner. You can also select a
specific region to magnify—do this by pressing and holding the middle mouse
button at the upper left-hand corner and dragging the pointer to the lower
right-hand corner of the region you want magnified.

⇒ Here are two ways to use this.

- To magnify a region of the desktop, do the following:
  1. Start `xmag`:

     `$ xmag` (RET)

  2. Click the middle mouse button in the upper left-hand corner of
     the region to magnify.
  3. Move the pointer to the lower right-hand corner of the region,
     and then release the middle mouse button.

- To run `xmag` on a three-second delay, to give you time to change to
  another desktop window before it runs, type:

  `$ sleep 3; xmag` (RET)

Click `Close` or type (Q) to exit the program and close the magnified window.

4.7 Configuring X

There are some aspects of X that people usually want to configure right away.
This section discusses some of the most popular, including changing the video
mode, automatically running clients at startup, and choosing a window manager. You'll find more information on this subject in both *The X Window*

User HOWTO and *The Configuration HOWTO* (for how to read them, see Recipe 2.8.6 [Reading System Documentation and Help Files], page 50).

4.7.1 Switching Between Video Modes

A *video mode* is a display resolution, given in pixels indicating the horizontal and vertical values, such as 640x480. An X server can switch between the video modes allowed by your hardware and set up by the administrator; it is not uncommon for a machine running X to offer several video modes, so that 640x480, 800x600, and 1024x768 display resolutions are possible.

To switch to another video mode, use the ⟨+⟩ and ⟨−⟩ keys on the numeric keypad with the left ⟨CTRL⟩ and ⟨ALT⟩ keys. The ⟨+⟩ key switches to the next mode with a lower resolution, and the ⟨−⟩ key switches to the next mode with a higher resolution.

⇒ Here are two ways to use this.

- To switch to the next-lowest video mode, type:

  ⟨CTRL⟩-⟨ALT⟩-⟨+⟩

- To switch to the next-highest video mode, type:

  ⟨CTRL⟩-⟨ALT⟩-⟨−⟩

To cycle through all available modes, type either of these key combinations repeatedly.

NOTES: For more information on video modes, see *The XFree86 Video Timings HOWTO* (see Recipe 2.8.6 [Reading System Documentation and Help Files], page 50).

4.7.2 Running X Clients Automatically

The `.xsession` file, a hidden file in your home directory, specifies the clients that are automatically run when your X session first starts ("hidden" files are explained in Chapter 5 [Files and Directories], page 125). It is just a shell script, usually containing a list of clients to run. You can edit your `.xsession` file in a text editor, and if this file doesn't exist, you can create it.

Clients start in the order in which they are listed, and the last line should specify the window manager to use. The example `.xsession` file in Figure 4-6 starts an `aterm` with a black background, white text, brown cursor, and no scrollbar, puts an `asclock` in the upper left-hand corner (AfterStep's clock inspired by the NeXTSTEP "tear-off" calendar clock), starts the Emacs text editor, opening the file `~/TODO` into a buffer of its own, and then starts the AfterStep window manager.

All clients start as background jobs, with the exception of the window manager on the last line, because when this file runs, the X session is running in the foreground (see Recipe 3.3 [Managing Jobs], page 70). Always put an ampersand (&) character at the end of any command line you put in your .xsession file, except for the line giving the window manager on the last line.

```
#! /bin/sh
#
# A sample .xsession file.

aterm +sb -bg black -fg white -cr brown &
asclock -geometry +0+0 &
emacs ~/TODO &
exec /usr/bin/afterstep
```

Figure 4-6. A sample .xsession file.

4.7.3 Changing the Root Window Parameters

By default, the root window background is painted gray with a woven pattern. To draw these patterns, X tiles the root window with a *bitmap*, which is a black-and-white image stored in a special file format. X comes with some bitmaps installed in the /usr/X11R6/include/bitmaps/ directory; the default bitmap file is root_weave (you can make your own patterns with the bitmap tool; see Recipe 18.4 [Using Other Image Editors], page 435).

Use xsetroot to change the color and bitmap pattern in the root window.

To change the color, use the -solid option, and give the name of the color to use as an argument. (Use xcolors to get a list of possible color names, as described in Recipe 4.2.2 [Specifying X Window Colors], page 103.)

⇒ To change the root window color to blue violet, type:

  $ xsetroot -solid blueviolet ⟨RET⟩

To change the root window pattern, use the -bitmap option, and give the name of the bitmap file to use.

⇒ To tile the root window with a star pattern, type:

  $ xsetroot -bitmap /usr/X11R6/include/bitmaps/star ⟨RET⟩

When specifying a pattern, use the -fg and -bg options to specify the foreground and background colors.

⇒ To tile the root window with a light slate gray star pattern on a black background, type (all on one line):

```
$ xsetroot -fg slategray2 -bg black -bitmap
/usr/X11R6/include/bitmaps/star (RET)
```

Use **xsetroot** with the special **-gray** option to change the root window to a shade of gray designed to be easy on the eyes, with no pattern.

⇒ To make the root window a gray color with no pattern, type:

```
$ xsetroot -gray (RET)
```

NOTES: You can also put an image in the root window (although this consumes memory that could be spared for a memory-hogging Web browser instead; but see Recipe 17.1.2 [Putting an Image in the Root Window], page 410, for how to do it).

4.7.4 Controlling the System Bell in X

X has a utility for controlling user preferences called **xset**, which you use to control various aspects of the system—for instance, you can use it to control screen-saver times, the way LED lights are set, keyclick volume level, and so forth.

To turn off ringing of the system bell, use **xset** and give **off** as an argument to the **b** option.

⇒ To turn off the system bell in X, type:

```
$ xset b off (RET)
```

You can turn the bell back on with the **on** argument.

You can control the volume, pitch, and duration of the bell by giving three numbers as arguments to the **b** option: The first is the volume as a percentage of its maximum value, the second is the pitch in Hertz, and the third is the duration in milliseconds. Running **xset** with the **b** option and no arguments returns the bell to its defaults.

⇒ Here are two ways to use this.

- To set the bell for 75 percent of its maximum volume, ringing at 440 Hz for one second, type:

```
$ xset 75 440 1000 (RET)
```

- To return the system bell to its default values, type:

```
$ xset b (RET)
```

NOTES: To make an `xset` setting permanent, affecting every X session you run, you will want to put the command in your `.xsession` file (see Recipe 4.7.2 [Running X Clients Automatically], page 117).

When you start a terminal emulator, you can use the `-vb` option to turn off the audible bell in just that terminal window (see Recipe 4.5.1 [Changing the Default X Terminal Behavior], page 110).

4.7.5 Using Other Window Managers

Yes, there are many window managers to choose from. Some people like the flash of Enlightenment, running with KDE or GNOME, while others prefer the spartan WM2 or anti-windowing approach of Ion, or a window manager that emulates some other OS environment—the choice is yours.

The following table describes some of the more popular window managers currently available.

9wm	9wm is a simple window manager inspired by the window manager in AT&T's Plan 9 operating system—it does not use title bars or icons. It should appeal to those who like the Wily text editor (see Recipe 10.8 [Using Other Text Editors], page 263). Incidentally, the Plan 9 OS was named after the 1959 film *Plan 9 from Outer Space*, directed by Edward D. Wood, Jr. DEB: 9wm RPM: 9wm WWW: http://www.plig.org/xwinman/archive/9wm/
Afterstep	AfterStep is inspired by the look and feel of the NeXTSTEP interface. DEB: afterstep RPM: AfterStep WWW: http://www.afterstep.org/
BlackBox	BlackBox is a fast, lightweight window manager with a contempoary look and feel. DEB: blackbox RPM: blackbox WWW: http://blackboxwm.sourceforge.net/

Enlightenment   Enlightenment is a graphics-intensive window manager that
                     uses desktop "themes" for decorating the various controls of
                     the X session.
                     DEB: `enlightenment`
                     RPM: `enlightenment`
                     WWW: `http://www.enlightenment.org/`

Fluxbox   Fluxbox is based on BlackBox, adding new features includ-
                     ing window tabs, keyboard shortcuts, and an icon bar.
                     DEB: `fluxbox`
                     RPM: `fluxbox`
                     WWW: `http://www.plig.org/xwinman/fluxbox.html`

FVWM95   FVWM95 makes X look like a certain proprietary "desktop"
                     OS from circa 1995.
                     DEB: `fvwm95`
                     WWW: `ftp://ftp.plig.org/pub/fvwm95/`

Ion   Designed to be navigable by the keyboard, keeping applica-
                     tions and client windows in full-screen frames, Ion is becom-
                     ing a favorite for those who value speed and efficiency and
                     don't particularly care for windowing systems in general.
                     DEB: `ion`
                     RPM: `ion`
                     WWW: `http://modeemi.cs.tut.fi/~tuomov/ion/`

TWM   The Tab Window Manager is an older, simple window man-
                     ager that is available on almost every system. (It's also
                     sometimes called Tom's Window Manager, after its primary
                     author, Tom LaStrange.)
                     DEB: `twm`
                     RPM: `twm`
                     WWW: `http://www.plig.org/xwinman/vtwm.html`

WM2   WM2 is a minimalist, configuration-free window manager.
                     DEB: `wm2`
                     RPM: `wm2`
                     WWW: `http://www.all-day-breakfast.com/wm2/`

Window Maker   The window manager of choice for the GNU Project, Win-
                  dow Maker is configurable through easy menus, and is often
                  compared to NeXTSTEP.
                  DEB: `wmaker`
                       `wmaker-data`
                  RPM: `wmaker`
                  WWW: `http://www.windowmaker.org/`

To try one of these window managers out, select it from the application
menu as given by the current window manager. This will exit your window
manager and start the new one. If you find one you like and wish to make it the
default, edit your `.xsession` file so that its last line contains **exec** followed by
the full path name of the window manager to use (see Recipe 4.7.2 [Running
X Clients Automatically], page 117).

⇒ To make AfterStep your default window manager, put the following as
   the last line in your `.xsession` file:

       `exec /usr/bin/X11/afterstep`

NOTES: Some window managers (such as TWM and WM2) do not have application menus, so if you run such a window manager you won't be able to
easily switch to another during that session—you'll have to exit X and start
it again.

II. FILES

## CHAPTER 5

Files and Directories

This chapter discusses the basic tools for manipulating files and directories—tools that are among the most essential on a Linux system.

A *file* is a collection of data that is stored on disk and that can be manipulated as a single unit by its name.

A *directory* is a file that acts as a folder for other files. A directory can also contain other directories (called *subdirectories* in this context); a directory that contains another directory is called the *parent* directory of the *child* directory it contains.

You might think of a regular file as a folder in a file cabinet drawer. The folder has a name, it holds the information that is put into it, and that information can be rearranged; you can recall the file at any time, and you can destroy it. The drawers of the the file cabinet then would be directories, and every file must be kept in one.

There the metaphor ends. The folders can be copied identically, and phantom folders can exist whose contents point to the contents of one of your real folders, so that when you look inside the phantom you are looking in the contents of a folder somewhere else. You can have as many directories as you like, and unlike physical file cabinets, you can have drawers *inside* other drawers, which in turn can have their own drawers on and on. In fact, there is a "master" drawer, the root directory, which contains inside it all other drawers—each drawer *must* in turn be kept inside some other drawer.

It is also helpful to think of the directories on a system like a tree with all its branches, because directories form a branching hierarchy—and the tree metaphor is used frequently to describe them: a *directory tree* includes a directory and all of its files, including the contents of all subdirectories. (Each directory is a "branch" in the "tree.") A slash character alone (/) is the name of the *root directory* at the base of the directory tree hierarchy; think of it as forming the roots and trunk from which all other files or directories are supported and from which they all inevitably branch out.

An abridged version of the root directory tree is shown in Figure 5-1.

To represent a directory's place in the file hierarchy, specify all of the directories between it and the root directory, using a slash (/) as the delimiter to separate directories. So the directory `dict` as it appears in the preceding illustration would be represented as `/usr/dict`.

Each user has a branch in the /home directory for his own files, called his *home directory*. The hierarchy in the previous illustration has two home directories: joe and jon, both subdirectories of /home.

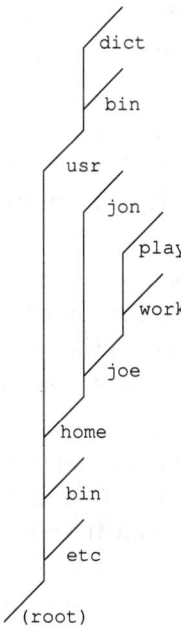

Figure 5-1. The root directory tree.

When you are in a shell, you are always in some directory on the system, and that directory is called the *current working directory*. When you first log in to the system, your home directory is the current working directory.

Whenever specifying a file name as an argument to a tool or application, you can give the slash-delimited *path name* relative to the current working directory. For example, if /home/joe is the current working directory, you can use "work" to specify the directory /home/joe/work, and "work/schedule" to specify schedule, a file in the /home/joe/work directory.

Every directory has two special files whose names consist of one and two periods: .. refers to the parent of the current working directory, and . refers to the current working directory itself. If the current working directory is /home/joe, you can use . to specify /home/joe and .. to specify /home. Furthermore, you can specify the /home/jon directory as ../jon.

Another way to specify a file name is to specify a slash-delimited list of all of the directory branches from the root directory (/) all the way down to the file you want to specify. This unique, specific path from the root directory to a file is called the file's *full path name*. (When referring to a file that is not a directory, this is sometimes called the *absolute file name*).

You can specify any file or directory on the system by giving its full path name. A file can have the same name as other files in different directories on the system, but no two files or directories can share a full path name. For example, user `joe` can have a file `schedule` in his `/home/joe/work` directory and a file `schedule` in his `/home/joe/play` directory. While both files have the same name (`schedule`), they are contained in different directories, so each has a unique full path name—`/home/joe/work/schedule` and `/home/joe/play/schedule`.

However, you don't have to type the full path name of a tool or application in order to start it. The shell keeps a list of directories, called the *path*, where it searches for programs. If a program is "in your path," which means that it is in one of these directories, you can run it simply by typing its name.

By default, the path includes `/bin` and `/usr/bin`. For example, the `who` command is in the `/usr/bin` directory, so its full path name is `/usr/bin/who`. Since the `/usr/bin` directory is in the path, you can type `who` to run `/usr/bin/who`, no matter what the current working directory is.

The following table describes some of the standard directories on Linux systems.

`/`	The ancestor of all directories on the system; all other directories are subdirectories of this directory, either directly or through other subdirectories.
`/bin`	Essential tools and other programs (or *binaries*).
`/dev`	Files representing the system's various hardware *devices*. For example, you use the file `/dev/cdrom` to access the CD-ROM drive.
`/etc`	Miscellaneous system configuration files, startup files, *et cetera*.
`/home`	The *home* directories for all of the system's users.
`/lib`	Essential system *library* files used by tools in `/bin`.
`/proc`	Files that give information about current system *processes*.

/root	The superuser's home directory, whose username is root. (In the past, the home directory for the superuser was simply /; later, /root was adopted for this purpose to reduce clutter in /.)
/sbin	Essential system administrator tools, or *system binaries*.
/tmp	*Temporary* files.
/usr	Subdirectories with files related to *user* tools and applications.
/usr/X11R6	Files relating to the X Window System, including those programs (in /usr/X11R6/bin) that run only under X.
/usr/bin	Tools and applications for users.
/usr/dict	*Dictionaries* and word lists (slowly being outmoded by /usr/share/dict).
/usr/doc	Miscellaneous system *documentation*.
/usr/games	*Games* and amusements.
/usr/info	Files for the GNU *Info* hypertext system (see Recipe 2.8.5 [Reading an Info Manual], page 48).
/usr/lib	*Libraries* used by tools in /usr/bin.
/usr/local	*Local* files—files unique to the individual system—including local documentation (in /usr/local/doc) and programs (in /usr/local/bin).
/usr/man	The online *manuals*, which are read with the man command (see Recipe 2.8.4 [Reading a Page from the System Manual], page 46).
/usr/share	Data for installed applications that is architecture-independent and can be *shared* between systems. A number of subdirectories with equivalents in /usr also appear here, including /usr/share/doc, /usr/share/info, and /usr/share/icons.

`/usr/src`	Program *source* code for software compiled on the system.
`/usr/tmp`	Another directory for *temporary* files.
`/var`	*Variable* data files, such as spool queues and log files.

For more information on the directory structure of Linux-based systems, see the Filesystem Hierarchy Standard [`http://www.pathname.com/fhs/`].

On Debian systems, you can also view this information in the compressed files in the `/usr/doc/debian-policy/fsstnd/` directory (see Recipe 9.1 [Perusing Text], page 211).

5.1 Naming Files and Directories

File names can consist of any combination of upper- and lowercase letters, numbers, periods (`.`), hyphens (`-`), and underscores (`_`).[1] File names are also case-sensitive—`foo`, `Foo`, and `FOO` are all different file names, and they can all exist at the same time in a directory (files of identical name cannot). By convention, file names are almost always all lowercase letters.

Linux does not force you to use file extensions, but it is convenient and useful to give files proper extensions, since they will help you to identify file types at a glance.

There is no special requirement for extensions; the dot is just an old convention—you could use any system you like for any of your files:

```
Penny_Parker-20031103.letter
```

Files don't have to have any extensions at all, like `myfile`, and you can have files with multiple extensions, too, like `long.file.with.many.extensions`. A JPEG-format image file, for example, does not have to have a `.jpg` or `.jpeg` extension, and program files do not need a special extension to make them work.

Extensions are particularly useful if you're sending files to users on other computers, particularly systems that require extensions—send a file in Microsoft Word format to a Windows user without giving it a `.doc` extension first, and you're likely to be told the file doesn't work.

---

[1] Technically, there *are* other characters that you can use—but doing so may get you into trouble later on.

The file name before any file extensions, but without the path, is called the *base file name*. For example, the base file name of /home/lisa/house.jpeg is house, without the dot or trailing jpeg, and without the path.

For a list of commonly used file extensions and their meanings, see Appendix B [Conventional File Name Extensions], page 723.

The following sections show how to make new files. To rename an existing file, just move it to a file with the new name—see Recipe 5.5 [Moving Files and Directories], page 144.

5.1.1 Making an Empty File

You may sometimes want to create a new, empty file as a kind of "placeholder." To do so, give the name that you want to use for the file as an argument to touch.

⇒ Here are some ways to use this.

- To create the file a_fresh_start in the current directory, type:

      $ touch a_fresh_start ⟨RET⟩

- To create the file another_empty_file in the work/completed subdirectory of the current directory, type:

      $ touch work/completed/another_empty_file ⟨RET⟩

This tool "touches" the files you give as arguments. If a file does not exist, it creates it; if the file already exists, it changes the modification timestamp on the file to the current date and time, just as if you had used the file.

NOTES: Often, you make a file when you edit it, such as with a text or image or sound editor; in that case, you don't need to make the file first.

5.1.2 Making a Directory

Use mkdir ("make directory") to make a new directory, giving the path name of the new directory as an argument. Directory names follow the same conventions as other files—that is, no spaces, slashes, or other unusual characters are recommended.

⇒ Here are some ways to use this.

- To make a new directory called work in the current working directory, type:

      $ mkdir work ⟨RET⟩

- To make a new directory called work in the /tmp directory, type:

      $ mkdir /tmp/work ⟨RET⟩

5.1.3 Making a Directory Tree

Use `mkdir` with the `-p` option to make a subdirectory and any of its parents that do not already exist. This is useful when you want to make a fairly complex directory tree from scratch and don't want to have to make each directory individually.

⇒ To make the `work/completed/2001` directory—a subdirectory of the `completed` directory, which in turn is a subdirectory of the `work` directory in the current directory, type:

$ `mkdir -p work/completed/2001` ⟨RET⟩

This makes a 2001 subdirectory in the directory called `completed`, which in turn is in a directory called `work` in the current directory; if the `completed` or the `work` directories do not already exist, they are made as well. If you know that `work` and `completed` both exist, the previous command works fine without the `-p` option.

5.1.4 Using a File with Spaces in Its Name

While a space character is not forbidden in naming files, it does make them difficult to use. Sometimes you might get one made on a system running MacOS, where space characters are common in file names. If a directory or file has a space in its name, there are two methods for specifying the name on the command line.

To reference a file with a space character in its name, quote the name (see Recipe 3.1.3 [Quoting Reserved Characters], page 56). The following methods are variations on this.

METHOD #1

To use a file with space in its name, enclose the file in single-quote characters (`'`).

⇒ To list the contents of the directory named **Top Secret**, type:

$ `ls 'Top Secret'` ⟨RET⟩

You can also use double quote characters (`"`) to quote; if a file name contains one kind of quote in its name, use the other.

⇒ To list the contents of the directory named **McHale's Restuarant**, type:

$ `ls "McHale's Restaurant"` ⟨RET⟩

METHOD #2

To use a file with space characters in its name, precede each space character with a backslash character (\).

⇒ To change to the directory named `Newspaper Photo Archive`, type:

    $ cd Newspaper\ Photo\ Archive ⟨RET⟩

Use the backslash to precede other special characters, including quotes.

⇒ To remove a file named `A "tough" one`, type:

    $ rm -i A\ \"tough\"\ one ⟨RET⟩

In this example, `rm` was called with the `-i` option, which removes files interactively, asking for confirmation before each remove takes place (see Recipe 5.6.2 [Removing Files Interactively], page 150).

NOTES: If you don't want spaces in a file, but you would like the words in its name to be separated, you might change the spaces in the file name to underscore characters (_). This is a common UNIX convention.

5.2 Changing Directories

Use `cd` to change the current working directory; give as an argument the relative or full path name of the directory to change to.

⇒ Here are some ways to use this.

- To change the current working directory to `work`, a subdirectory in the current directory, type:

      $ cd work ⟨RET⟩

- To change to the current directory's parent directory, type:

      $ cd .. ⟨RET⟩

- To change the current working directory to `/usr/doc`, type:

      $ cd /usr/doc ⟨RET⟩

The following recipes show special ways of using `cd`.

5.2.1 Changing to Your Home Directory

With no arguments, `cd` makes your home directory the current working directory.

⇒ To make your home directory the current working directory, type:

    $ cd ⟨RET⟩

5.2.2 Changing to the Last Directory You Visited

To return to the last directory you were in, use cd and give – as the directory name. For example, if you are in the /home/mrs/work/samples directory, and you use cd to change to some other directory, then at any point while you are in this other directory you can type *cd* – to return the current working directory to /home/mrs/work/samples.

⇒ To return to the directory you were last in, type:

> $ *cd* – ⟨RET⟩

5.2.3 Getting the Name of the Current Directory

Most people have their shell prompt set up to display the name of the current directory; this is the default setup in most Linux distributions. But you can always get the name of the current directory with pwd ("print working directory"), which lists the full path name of the current working directory.

⇒ To output the name of the current working directory, type:

```
$ pwd ⟨RET⟩
/home/mrs
$
```

In this example, pwd output the text /home/mrs, indicating that the current working directory is /home/mrs.

5.3 Listing Directories

Use ls to *list* the contents of a directory. It takes as arguments the names of the directories to list. With no arguments, ls lists the contents of the current working directory.

⇒ Here are some ways to use this.

- To list the contents of the current working directory, type:

```
$ ls ⟨RET⟩
apple    cherry   orange
$
```

- To list the contents of `work`, a subdirectory in the current directory, type:

    `$ ls work` $\langle$RET$\rangle$

- To list the contents of the `/usr/doc` directory, type:

    `$ ls /usr/doc` $\langle$RET$\rangle$

In the first example, the current working directory contains three files: `apple`, `cherry`, and `orange`.

The following subsections describe some commonly used options for controlling which files `ls` lists, and what information about those files `ls` outputs. You can combine these options to get their combined effects; the order in which the options are specified does not matter. There are even more options than what is given here; the Info documentation for `ls` is worth perusing. It is one of the most often used file commands on UNIX-based systems.

NOTES: There are a few other common ways to list the contents of directories. One that is common when in X, and when you want to peruse image files in those directories, is to use Mozilla or some other Web browser as a local file browser. Use the prefix[2] `file:/` to view local files. Alone, it opens a directory listing of the root directory; `file:/home/joe` opens a directory listing of user `joe`'s home directory, `file:/usr/local/src` opens the local source code directory, and so on. Directory listings will be rendered in HTML on the fly in almost all browsers, so you can click on subdirectories to traverse to them, and click on files to open them in the browser. This and other methods for browsing files are described in Recipe 5.10 [Browsing Files and Directories], page 157.

5.3.1 Listing Directories in Color

Use `ls` with the `--color` option to list the directory contents in color; files appear in different colors depending on their content. Some of the default color settings include displaying directory names in blue, text files in white, executable files in green, and links in turquoise.

⇒ To list the files in the root directory in color, type:

    `$ ls --color /` $\langle$RET$\rangle$

This command lists the root directory in color, as in Figure 5-2. (While this illustration is black and white, the actual directory listing is in color.)

---

[2] Called a URN, or "Uniform Resource Name."

```
$ ls --color /
System.map      etc             man             usr
System.old      floppy          mnt             var
bin             home            proc            vmlinuz
boot            initrd          root            vmlinuz.old
cdrom           lib             sbin
dev             lost+found      tmp
$
```

Figure 5-2. A color directory listing.

NOTES: Many systems are set up to use this flag by default, so that using `ls` with no options will list in color. If yours isn't set up this way, and you'd like it to be, you can always make `ls` a shell alias word for `ls --color` in your `.bashrc` startup file (see Recipe 3.6.1 [Calling a Command by Some Other Name], page 83 and see Recipe 3.7.3 [Using Shell Startup Files], page 86).

5.3.2 Listing File Types

To display the file type along with the name of a file, use `ls` with the `-F` option. With this option set, regular files are displayed as usual, and `ls` appends an indicator of the following type to other files:

/	File is a directory.
*	File is executable.
@	File is a symbolic link (see Recipe 5.7 [Giving a File More Than One Name], page 152).
|	File is a FIFO (also called a *named pipe*), a special file that processes use for reading from and writing to.
=	File is a *socket*, a special file that provides a connecting point through which processes may communicate.

⇒ To list the contents of the directory so that directories, executables, and
special files are distinguished from all other files, type:

```
$ ls -F (RET)
repeat* test1    test2    words/
$
```

In this example, the current directory contains an executable file named
repeat, a directory named **words**, and some other regular files named **test1**
and **test2**.

5.3.3 Listing File Attributes

Use **ls** with the **-l** ("long") option to output a more extensive directory
listing—one that contains each file's size in bytes, last modification time, file
type, ownership, and permissions (see Recipe 6.2 [File Ownership], page 166).

⇒ To output a verbose listing of the **/usr/share/doc/bash** directory, type:

```
$ ls -l /usr/share/doc/bash (RET)
```

This command outputs a verbose listing of the files in
/usr/share/doc/bash, as in Figure 5-3.

```
~ $ ls -l /usr/share/doc/xterm/
total 592
-rw-r--r--   1 root    root      2416 Nov 25  2001 README.Debian
-rw-r--r--   1 root    root     44893 Apr 16  2002 changelog.Debian.gz
-rw-r--r--   1 root    root     49519 Nov 25  2001 copyright
-rw-r--r--   1 root    root    138631 Apr 16  2002 ctlseqs.ps.gz
-rw-r--r--   1 root    root     13187 Apr 16  2002 ctlseqs.txt.gz
-rw-r--r--   1 root    root     87114 Nov 25  2001 xterm.faq.html
-rw-r--r--   1 root    root     27060 Apr 16  2002 xterm.faq.text.gz
-rw-r--r--   1 root    root    198385 Apr 16  2002 xterm.log.html
-rw-r--r--   1 root    root      3611 Apr 16  2002 xterm.termcap.gz
-rw-r--r--   1 root    root      7626 Apr 16  2002 xterm.terminfo.gz
~ $
```

Figure 5-3. A verbose directory listing.

The first line of output gives the total amount of disk space, in 1024-byte
blocks, that the files take up (in this example, 144). Each subsequent line
displays several columns of information about one file.

The first column displays the file's type and permissions. The first character in this column specifies the file type; the hyphen (-) is the default and
means that the file is a regular file. Directories are denoted by **d**, and symbolic links (see Recipe 5.7 [Giving a File More Than One Name], page 152)
are denoted by **l**. The remaining nine characters of the first column show the
file permissions (see Recipe 6.3 [Controlling Access to Files], page 167). The

second column lists the number of hard links to the file. The third and fourth columns give the names of the user and group that the file belongs to. The fifth column gives the size of the file in bytes, the sixth column gives the date of last modification, and the last column gives the file name.

Other options change the defaults for the long-style output.

To change the modification date from the abbreviated month, day, and then year output to show the full time and date (like the default of `date`, as described in see Recipe 27.1 [Displaying the Date and Time], page 537), use the special `--full-time` option.

⇒ To output a verbose listing of the `/usr/share/doc/bash` directory, giving the full time and date of last modification, type:

$ *ls -1 --full-time /usr/share/doc/bash* (RET)

This command outputs a verbose listing of the files in the `/usr/share/doc/bash` directory, showing the full time and date of last modification, as in Figure 5-4.

```
$ ls -1 --full-time /usr/share/doc/xterm/
total 592
-rw-r--r--    1 root     root          2416 Sun Nov 25 17:52:43 2001 README.Debian
-rw-r--r--    1 root     root         44893 Tue Apr 16 07:39:49 2002 changelog.Debian.gz
-rw-r--r--    1 root     root         49519 Sun Nov 25 17:52:42 2001 copyright
-rw-r--r--    1 root     root        138631 Tue Apr 16 08:23:58 2002 ctlseqs.ps.gz
-rw-r--r--    1 root     root         13187 Tue Apr 16 08:23:58 2002 ctlseqs.txt.gz
-rw-r--r--    1 root     root         87114 Sun Nov 25 17:52:42 2001 xterm.faq.html
-rw-r--r--    1 root     root         27060 Tue Apr 16 08:22:08 2002 xterm.faq.text.gz
-rw-r--r--    1 root     root        198385 Tue Apr 16 07:41:27 2002 xterm.log.html
-rw-r--r--    1 root     root          3611 Tue Apr 16 08:22:59 2002 xterm.termcap.gz
-rw-r--r--    1 root     root          7626 Tue Apr 16 08:22:59 2002 xterm.terminfo.gz
~ $ 
```

Figure 5-4. A verbose directory with modification time.

```
~ $ ls -lh /usr/share/doc/bash
total 184k
-rw-r--r--    1 root     root           41k Apr  8  2002 CHANGES.gz
-rw-r--r--    1 root     root          3.5k Apr  8  2002 COMPAT.gz
-rw-r--r--    1 root     root           23k Apr  8  2002 FAQ.gz
-rw-r--r--    1 root     root          2.9k Apr  8  2002 INTRO.gz
-rw-r--r--    1 root     root           11k Apr  8  2002 NEWS.gz
-rw-r--r--    1 root     root          2.2k Apr  8  2002 POSIX.NOTES.gz
-rw-r--r--    1 root     root          2.2k Apr  8  2002 README.Debian.gz
-rw-r--r--    1 root     root           674 Apr  8  2002 README.abs-guide.gz
-rw-r--r--    1 root     root          2.9k Apr  8  2002 README.bash_completion.gz
-rw-r--r--    1 root     root           12k Apr  8  2002 changelog.Debian.gz
-rw-r--r--    1 root     root           16k Apr  8  2002 changelog.bash_completion.gz
-rw-r--r--    1 root     root           30k Apr  8  2002 changelog.gz
-rw-r--r--    1 root     root          1.7k Apr  8  2002 copyright
drwxr-xr-x   10 root     root          4.0k Apr 28 07:07 examples
-rw-r--r--    1 root     root           268 Apr  8  2002 inputrc.arrows.gz
~ $ 
```

Figure 5-5. A verbose directory with human-readable numbers.

To specify that the numbers in the output should be in a "human readable" form, instead of in blocks, use the `-h` option. When combined with `-1`, this will give the total amount of disk space and size of each file in bytes, kilobytes (followed by a `k`), or megabytes (followed by an `M`).

⇒ To output a verbose listing of the **/usr/share/doc/bash** directory, giving all numbers in a human readable form, type:

$ *ls -lh /usr/share/doc/bash* (RET)

This command outputs a verbose listing of the files in the **/usr/share/doc/bash** directory, giving all numbers in a human readable form, as in Figure 5-5.

5.3.4 Listing Hidden Files

By default, ls does not output files that begin with a period character (.). To reduce clutter, many applications "hide" configuration files in your home directory by giving them names that begin with a period; these are called *dot files*, or sometimes "hidden" files. As mentioned earlier, every directory has two special dot files: .., the parent directory, and ., the directory itself.

To list *all* contents of a directory, including these dot files, use the **-a** option.

⇒ To list all files in the current directory, type:

$ *ls -a* (RET)

Use the **-A** option to list *almost* all files in the directory: it lists all files, including dot files—with the exception of the .. and . directory files.

⇒ To list all files in the current directory except for .. and ., type:

$ *ls -A* (RET)

5.3.5 Listing Directories in Columns

Use the **-1** option to list a directory in a single column. Files will be listed one to a line. This is good for cut and pasting.

⇒ To list the contents of **/usr/bin** in a single column, type:

$ *ls -1 /usr/bin* (RET)

When output from ls is piped to anywhere but the terminal, ls uses this single-column format.

Normally, ls lists files in columns going vertically—first the leftmost column will be filled, and then the next column, all the way over toward the right side of the screen. Use **-x** to make the columns list *horizontally* instead—so that the first line across is filled with file names first, and then the next line, until all files are listed.

⇒ To list the contents of **/usr/bin** in columns printed horizontally, type:

> $ *ls -x /usr/bin* ⟨RET⟩

Use the **-m** option to output files not in columns at all, but in a single horizontal line, separated by commas.

⇒ To output the contents of /usr/bin in a single line, with file names separated by commas, type:

> $ *ls -m /usr/bin* ⟨RET⟩

5.3.6 Listing Files in Sorted Order

By default, the file listing output by **ls** is sorted alphabetically, in character order—that is, files are listed from smallest to largest ASCII code (see Recipe 9.3.7 [Viewing a Character Set], page 228), so that, for example, files beginning with uppercase letters are listed before files with lowercase letters. There are several options for controlling the way the output is sorted; some of them are given below.

METHOD #1

To sort files by size, use the **-S** option. Files are sorted with the largest first.

⇒ To list all of the files in the **/usr/bin** directory sorted by size, with the largest first, type:

> $ *ls -S /usr/bin* ⟨RET⟩

METHOD #2

Use the **-t** option with **ls** to sort a directory listing by *time*, so that the files are listed according to when they were last modified, with the most recently modified listed first.

⇒ To list all of the files in the **/usr/tmp** directory sorted by their modification time, with the mostly recently modified files first, type:

> $ *ls -t /usr/tmp* ⟨RET⟩

METHOD #3

To sort files by their extension, use the **-X** option. Files with no extension are listed first.

⇒ To list all files in the current directory, sorted by extension, type:

> $ *ls -X* ⟨RET⟩

METHOD #4

Use -v to give a *version sort*, where instead of sorting by character, the file names are sorted by the way they are numbered, so that file-2 will come between file-1 and file-10, and not after the two files as it would in a normal character sort. This is useful for sorting files whose names are numbered in some way, such as by versions, indices, or date.

⇒ To list all of the files in the current directory ending in .jpeg and sorted by version, type:

    $ ls -v *.jpeg (RET)

METHOD #5

Use -r to *reverse* the order of the sorted output. This works with all other sort options.

⇒ Here are some ways to use this.

- To list files in the current directory from highest ASCII character value to lowest, type:

    $ ls -r (RET)

- To list all of the files in the /usr/bin directory sorted by their size, with smallest files first, type:

    $ ls -Sr /usr/bin (RET)

- To list all of the files in the current directory sorted by modification date, with the most recently modified files last, type:

    $ ls -tr (RET)

METHOD #6

Use the -U option to turn off all sorting and output files in *unsorted* order—the order they appear on the disk.

⇒ To output all files in the current directory in the order they appear on the disk, type:

    $ ls -U (RET)

5.3.7 Listing Subdirectories

Normally when you list the contents of a directory, any subdirectories are just listed by their name—their contents are not listed. To list the contents of all subdirectories a directory may contain, use the -R option. This lists the contents of a directory *recursively*, outputting a listing of that directory and the contents of all of its subdirectories.

⇒ To output a recursive directory listing of the current directory, type:

```
$ ls -R (RET)
play    work

play:
notes

work:
notes
$
```

In this example, the current working directory contains two subdirectories, `work` and `play`, and no other files. Each subdirectory contains a file called `notes`.

⇒ To list all of the files on the system, type:

   `$ ls -R / (RET)`

This command recursively lists the contents of the root directory, `/`, and all of its subdirectories. It is common to combine this with the attribute option, `-l`, to output a verbose listing of all the files on the system:

   `$ ls -lR / (RET)`

NOTES: You can't list the contents of some directories on the system if you don't have permission to do so (see Recipe 6.3 [Controlling Access to Files], page 167).

5.4 Copying Files and Directories

Use `cp` ("copy") to copy files. It takes two arguments: the *source file*, which is the existing file to copy, and the *target file*, which is the file name for the new copy. The `cp` command then makes an identical copy of the source file, giving it the specified target name. If a file with the target name already exists, `cp` overwrites it. It does not alter the source file.

⇒ To copy the file `my-copy` to the file `neighbor-copy`, type:

   `$ cp my-copy neighbor-copy (RET)`

This command creates a new file called **neighbor-copy** that is identical to
my-copy in every respect except for its name, owner, group, and timestamp—
the new file has a timestamp that shows the time when it was copied. The
file **my-copy** is not altered.

Use the **-v** ("verbose") option to list files as they are copied. This is useful
for large copies, where a lot of files are being copied, so you can monitor the
progress.

⇒ To copy all the files in the ~/workgroup/final directory to the
~/workgroup/backup directory, specifying verbose output so each file is
listed as it is copied, type:

    $ *cp -v ~/workgroup/final/* ~/workgroup/backup* (RET)

5.4.1 Copying Files with Their Attributes

When you copy a file, the attributes such as timestamp and file ownership
will differ between the original and the copy. Use **cp** with the **-p** option to
preserve all of the attributes of the original, whenever possible, including its
timestamp, owner, group, and permissions.

⇒ To copy the file **my-copy** to the file **neighbor-copy**, preserving all of the
attributes of the source file in the target file, type:

    $ *cp -p my-copy neighbor-copy* (RET)

This command copies the file **my-copy** to a new file called **neighbor-copy**
that is identical to **my-copy** in every respect except for its name.

While **-p** does not copy any subdirectories a directory may contain, you
can use the **-a** ("archive") option instead, which preserves attributes whenever possible but also copies any subdirectories as well as symbolic links (see
Recipe 5.7 [Giving a File More than One Name], page 152). This is good for
making archival backups of one directory tree to another.

⇒ To make an archival copy of the contents of **/cdrom** to the current directory, type:

    $ *cp -a /cdrom .* (RET)

This command makes a copy of **/cdrom**, including any subdirectories it
may contain, to the current directory. Original file attributes are preserved in
the copy.

NOTES: A *snapshot* is a copy of a directory tree that shows what it looked
like at a particular time. Snapshots are usually made in software development
projects upon each release—to "take a snapshot of the current version" means
to make an archival copy of the directory tree containing the sources.

To make a snapshot of a directory tree, use `cp` with the `-a` option as just described.

5.4.2 Copying Subdirectories

To copy a directory along with the files and subdirectories it contains, use the `-R` option—it makes a *recursive* copy of the specified directory and its entire contents.

⇒ To copy the directory `public_html` and all of its files and subdirectories to a new directory called `private_html`, type:

> `$ cp -R public_html private_html` (RET)

The `-R` option does not copy files that are symbolic links (see Recipe 5.7 [Giving a File More Than One Name], page 152), and it does not retain all original permissions. To recursively copy a directory, including links, and retain all of its permissions, use the `-a` ("archive") option. This is useful for making a backup copy of a large directory tree.

⇒ To make an archive copy of the directory tree `public_html` to the directory `private_html`, type:

> `$ cp -a public_html private_html` (RET)

5.4.3 Copying Files by a Unique Parent Directory

Sometimes it is desirable to copy or rename a group of files, all of which have a common name, so that the new names match the unique parent directory that each original has. To do this, use `basename` to get the name each unique path for the `cp` command. Loop through all the files, running this command line on each of them, with Bash's built-in `for` construct (see the Bash Info documentation for more information on this built-in).

For example, suppose you have in your home directory a directory named `photographs`, and in it you have a number of subdirectories, each named with a unique number, and each one containing many directories, including one named `src`, as in Figure 5-6.

Suppose you only want to copy the `src` directories and their contents, but want the names of these copied directories to be the preceding unique paths before `src` (01, 02, and so on). Use `basename` to pass the unique paths to `cp`.

```
~/photographs/01/
~/photographs/01/640x480
~/photographs/01/320x280
~/photographs/01/src
~/photographs/02
~/photographs/02/640x480
~/photographs/02/320x280
~/photographs/02/src
~/photographs/03
~/photographs/03/640x480
~/photographs/03/320x280
~/photographs/03/src
... continued ...
```

Figure 5-6. Subdirectories with a unique parent.

⇒ To copy all `src` directories to the `/mnt` directory, giving each of the files the unique name of their parent directory in `~/photographs`, type:

```
$ for i in ~/photographs/* (RET)
> { (RET)
> cp -a $i/src /mnt`basename $i` (RET)
> } (RET)
$
```

This command copies all of the `src` directories in `~/photographs`, giving them the uniqe names of their parents—so that `~/photographs/01/src` becomes `/mnt/01`, `~/photographs/02/src` becomes `/mnt/02`, and so on.

You can use the semicolon character (`;`) to run this all on one command line as a single command (see Recipe 3.1.7 [Running a List of Commands], page 63). The following command is equivalent to the preceding example:

```
for i in ~/photographs/*; { cp -a $i/src /mnt`basename $i`; }
```

NOTES: To *rename* files by this method, use `mv` instead of `cp` (see Recipe 5.5 [Moving Files and Directories], page 144).

5.5 Moving Files and Directories

Use the `mv` ("move") tool to move, or rename, a file or directory to a different location. It takes two arguments: the name of the file or directory to move followed by the path name to move it to. If you move a file to a directory that contains a file of the same name, the file is overwritten.

⇒ To move the file **notes** in the current working directory to **../play**, type:

    $ `mv notes ../play` (RET)

This command moves the file **notes** in the current directory to **play**, a subdirectory of the current working directory's parent. If a file **notes** already exists in **play**, that file is overwritten. If the subdirectory **play** does not exist, this command moves the file **notes** from the current directory to its parent directory, renaming the file **play**.

To move a file or directory that is not in the current directory, give its full path name as an argument.

⇒ To move the file **/usr/tmp/notes** to the current working directory, type:

    $ `mv /usr/tmp/notes .` (RET)

This command moves the file **/usr/tmp/notes** to the current working directory.

To move a directory, give the path name of the directory you want to move and the path name to move it to as arguments.

⇒ To move the directory **work** in the current working directory to **play**, type:

    $ `mv work play` (RET)

This command moves the directory **work** in the current directory to the directory **play**. If the directory **play** already exists, **mv** puts **work** inside **play**—it does not overwrite directories.

Renaming a file is the same as moving it; just specify as arguments the file to rename followed by the new file name.

⇒ To rename the file **notes** to **notes.old**, type:

    $ `mv notes notes.old` (RET)

The following recipes describe other ways to move and rename files.

5.5.1 Changing File Names to Lowercase

There are two good methods to change uppercase letters in file names to lowercase letters.

METHOD #1

Use the **rename** tool, which comes as a part of the PERL programming language, to rename groups of files. It takes two arguments: a quoted PERL expression describing the change to make, and the files to make the change on. If a file already exists, **rename** will output a warning and will not rename the file, but other files will be renamed.

To use **rename** to change uppercase letters in file names to lowercase, use **tr/A-Z/a-z/** as the expression.

⇒ To change the file names of all of the files in the current directory to lowercase letters, type:

```
$ rename 'tr/A-Z/a-z/' * (RET)
```

You can specify which files to work on, and you can specify that only certain parts of a filename are to be changed.

⇒ Here are some ways to use this.

- To rename all of the files in the current directory ending with .MP3 to files of the same names in lowercase letters, type:

```
$ rename 'tr/A-Z/a-z/' *.MP3 (RET)
```

- To rename all of the files in the current directory ending with .MP3 to files of the same names with extensions in lowercase letters, type:

```
$ rename 's/.MP3/.mp3/' *.MP3 (RET)
```

In the first example, a file with a name like **Music-Recording.MP3** or **ANOTHER-MUSIC-RECORDING.MP3** would be renamed to **music-recording.mp3** and **another-music-recording.mp3**, while in the second example, these files would be renamed to **Music-Recording.mp3** and **ANOTHER-MUSIC-RECORDING.mp3**.

METHOD #2

To change the uppercase letters in a group of file names to lowercase, use **mv** with the **-i** option to move the files interactively, deriving lowercase file names by piping the old names through the **tr** filter (see Recipe 13.4 [Transposing Characters in Text], page 316). Loop through all the files in the first extension, running this command line on each of them, with Bash's built-in **for** construct (see the **bash** Info documentation for more information on this built-in).

⇒ To rename all of the files in the current directory to all lowercase letters, type:

```
$ for i in * (RET)
> { (RET)
> mv -i $i `echo $i | tr '[A-Z]' '[a-z]'` (RET)
> } (RET)
$
```

You can use the semicolon character (;) to run this all on one command line as a single command. The following command is equivalent to the preceding example:

```
for i in *; { mv -i $i `echo $i | tr '[A-Z]' '[a-z]'`; }
```

The -i option is used with mv because otherwise this command may inadvertently remove files—if, for example, you have files named CAT, Cat, and cat, this command without the -i will remove two of them.

Furthermore, for files that are not affected by the transformation to lowercase (for example, a file named dog), this command will do nothing, and a message will be output indicating that the original file name and the new file name are the same.

⇒ To lowercase all of the file names in the current directory that have a .JPG extension, type:

```
$ for i in *.JPG; { mv -i $i `echo $i | tr '[A-Z]' '[a-z]'`; } (RET)
```

You can use tr to perform any number of transformations on a group of files, such as translating all lowercase letters to uppercase, or deleting certain characters.

⇒ Here are some ways to use this.

- To uppercase all of the file names in the current directory that have a .jpg extension, type (all on one line):

```
$ for i in *.jpg; { mv -i $i `echo $i |
tr '[a-z]' '[A-Z]'`; } (RET)
```

- To rename all of the files in the current directory that have 386 somewhere in their names, and delete the 386 from the name, type:

```
$ for i in *386*; { mv -i $i `echo $i | tr -d '386'`; } (RET)
```

5.5.2 Renaming Multiple Files with the Same Extension

There are three reliable methods for taking a group of files that have the same extension, and renaming them all with some other extension. The first two methods are the same as used in the preceding recipe.

METHOD #1

Use the **rename** tool, which comes as a part of the PERL programming language. It takes two arguments: a quoted PERL expression describing the change to make, and the files to make the change on.

⇒ To rename all the files in the current directory ending in .JPG to files
ending in .jpeg, type:

```
$ rename 's/.JPG/.jpeg/' *.JPG (RET)
```

METHOD #2

Use mv to move the files, deriving the new file names with the **basename** tool.
Loop through all of the files, running this command line on each of them,
with Bash's built-in **for** construct (see the **bash** Info documentation for more
information on this built-in).

⇒ To rename all the files in the current directory then end in .JPG to files
that end end in .jpeg, type:

```
$ for i in *.JPG (RET)
> { (RET)
> mv -i $i `basename $i JPG`jpeg (RET)
> } (RET)
$
```

You can use the semicolon character (;) to run these commands on one
command line. The following command is equivalent to the previous example:

```
for i in *.JPG; { mv -i $i `basename $i JPG`jpeg; }
```

METHOD #3

To rename a group of files from one extension to another, use mv with a **for**
loop, as with Method #2, but instead of using **basename**, specify the new
extension with the Bash shell parameter expansion feature.[3]

⇒ To rename all of the .jpg files in the current directory, so that they all
have a .jpeg file name extension instead, type:

```
$ for i in .jpg (RET)
> { (RET)
> mv $i "${i%.jpg}.jpeg" (RET)
> } (RET)
$
```

---

[3] For more information on this feature, consult the Info documentation for **bash** (see
Recipe 2.8.5 [Reading an Info Manual], page 48).

NOTES: Renaming multiple files at once is a common request.

5.6 Removing Files and Directories

Use **rm** ("remove") to delete a file and remove it from the system. Give the name of the file to remove as an argument.

⇒ To remove the file **notes** in the current working directory, type:

> $ rm notes ⟨RET⟩

To remove a directory and all of the files and subdirectories it contains, use the **-R** ("recursive") option.

⇒ To remove the directory **waste** and all of its contents, type:

> $ rm -R waste ⟨RET⟩

To remove an empty directory, use **rmdir**; it removes the empty directories you specify. If you specify a directory that contains files or subdirectories, **rmdir** reports an error.

⇒ To remove the directory **empty**, type:

> $ rmdir empty ⟨RET⟩

5.6.1 Removing a File with a Strange Name

Files with strange characters in their names (such as white space, control characters, and beginning hyphens) pose a problem when you want to remove them. There are a few solutions to this problem.

METHOD #1

One way is to use tab completion to complete the name of the file (see Recipe 3.1.4 [Letting the Shell Complete What You Type], page 61). This works when the name of the file you want to remove has enough characters to uniquely identify it so that completion can work.

⇒ To use tab completion to remove the file **No Way** in the current directory, type:

> $ rm No⟨TAB⟩ Way ⟨RET⟩

In this example, once ⟨TAB⟩ was typed, the shell filled in the rest of the file name (" Way").

METHOD #2

When a file name begins with a control character or other strange character, you can specify the file name with a file name pattern that uniquely identifies it (see Recipe 5.8 [Specifying File Names with Patterns], page 153, for tips on building file name patterns). Use the -i option to verify the deletion first.

⇒ To delete the file ^Acat in a directory that also contains the files cat and dog, type:

```
$ rm -i ?cat (RET)
rm: remove `^Acat'? y (RET)
$
```

In the preceding example, the expansion pattern "?cat" matches the file ^Acat and no other files in the directory. The -i option was used because, in some cases, no unique pattern can be made for a file—for example, if this directory also contained a file called 1cat, the preceding rm command in the example would also attempt to remove it; with the -i option, you can answer *n* to it.

METHOD #3

The two previous methods won't work with a file that begins with a hyphen character, because rm interprets such a file name as an option; to remove a file like that, use the -- option—it specifies that what follows are arguments and not options.

⇒ To remove the file -cat from the current directory, type:

```
$ rm -- -cat (RET)
```

5.6.2 Removing Files Interactively

Once a file is removed, it is permanently deleted and there is no command you can use to restore it; you cannot "undelete" it. (However, if you can unmount the filesystem that contained the file immediately after you delete the file, a wizard might be able to help reconstruct the lost file by using **grep** to search the filesystem device file.)

A safer way to remove files is to use rm with the -i option, which specifies that rm run in *interactive* mode, where it will ask you to confirm the deletion of each file.

⇒ To interactively remove the files in the ~/tmp directory, type:

    $ rm -i ~/tmp ⟨RET⟩

In the preceding example, rm will prompt for confirmation before deleting any file in ~/tmp.

You might consider making an alias word for rm with the -i option, such as del, and get in the habit of using this word in place of rm (see Recipe 3.6.1 [Calling a Command by Some Other Name], page 83).

You can get the same effect as an alias by making the following two-line shell script, which you might write to a file called del and put in your personal bin directory (see Recipe A.3.4 [Installing a Shell Script], page 708, and Recipe C.1 [Using a Directory for Personal Binaries], page 727):

```
#!/bin/sh
/bin/rm -i $*
```

NOTES: Question 3.6 in the UNIX FAQ[4] discusses this issue and gives a shell script called can that you can use in place of rm—it puts files in a "trashcan" directory instead of removing them; you then periodically empty out the trashcan with rm.

5.6.3 Removing Files without Verification

If a file is write-protected, rm will always ask you to verify its removal first, should you try to remove it. When you have a lot of files to remove, this is cumbersome. In this case, use yes to pipe an automatic "y" answer to rm with the -R option (see Recipe 3.1.10 [Automatically Answering a Command Prompt], page 65).

⇒ To remove the scrap directory and all its contents, including any write-protected files, type:

    $ yes | rm -R scrap ⟨RET⟩

NOTES: This is a dangerous operation! This command will permanently remove all files and directories you give it, so be certain you want them removed before you run it!

---

[4] See the file /usr/doc/FAQ/unix-faq-part3, or on the Web:
http://www.faqs.org/faqs/unix-faq/faq/.

5.7 Giving a File More Than One Name

Links are special files that point to other files; when you act on a file that is
a link, you act on the file it points to. There are two kinds of links: symbolic
links and hard links.

A *symbolic link* (sometimes called a "symlink" or "soft link") passes most
operations—such as reading and writing—to the file it points to. Symlinks are
identified in file listings with an "l" in the first character of the first column,
and, by default, are output as cyan in color listings.

If you remove a symlink, you remove only the symlink itself, and *not* the
original file. However, if you remove the original file, and replace it with some
other file, the symbolic link will point to the contents of the new file. You can
make a symlink of a directory, and you can make symlinks across filesystems
(see Chapter 24 [Disk Storage], page 501).

A *hard link* is another name for an existing file, and is indistinguishable
from the file it is linked from. If you alter a file, any hard links to it are also
altered; and conversely, altering any hard link will also alter the original file
plus any other hard links it may have. So if you make a hard link from file
`foo` to file `bar`, and then alter the file `bar`, file `foo` is equally altered.

So where a symlink points to the file it links to, a hard link is another
instance of the file. If you change the original file, all of the hard links are also
changed. If you change any of the hard links, the original file and all other
hard links are all changed. But if you *remove* the original file, any hard links
will still contain the contents that the original did.

Unlike symlinks, you cannot make a hard link to a directory, and you
cannot make a hard link across filesystems.

Each file on the system has at least one hard link, which is the original
file name itself. Directories always have at least *two* hard links—the directory
name itself (which appears in its parent directory) and the special file . inside
the directory. Likewise, when you make a new subdirectory, the parent directory gains a new hard link for the special file .. inside the new subdirectory.

If you remove a hard link, you will not remove the file it is linked to, nor
any other hard links that point to it; conversely, you will not remove any of a
file's hard links by removing the file itself.

METHOD #1

Use `ln` ("link") to make a link to a file. Give as arguments the name of the
existing file to link to and the name to use for the link. By default, `ln` makes
hard links.

⇒ To create a hard link from **seattle** to **emerald-city**, type:

    $ ln seattle emerald-city (RET)

This command makes a hard link from an existing file, **seattle**, to a new file, **emerald-city**. You can read and edit the **emerald-city** file just as you would **seattle**; any changes you make to **emerald-city** are also written to **seattle** (and vice versa). But if you remove the **emerald-city** file, the **seattle** file is *not* removed (and vice versa).

METHOD #2

To create a symbolic link, use **ln** with the **-s** option.

⇒ To create a symbolic link from **seattle** to **emerald-city**, type:

    $ ln -s seattle emerald-city (RET)

This command makes a symbolic link from an existing file, **seattle**, to a new file, **emerald-city**. If you remove the file **emerald-city**, the file **seattle** will *not* be removed, but removing the **seattle** file, on the other hand, will make **emerald-city** a broken link until some other file named **seattle** exists in its place again—at which point **emerald-city** will point to that new file.

NOTES: This recipe might also be called "Linking a File to Another."

5.8 Specifying File Names with Patterns

When you specify the name of a file or files in a command, you are giving a *file specification*, which is often written as *filespec* for short.

These filespecs don't need to be the literal names of specific files. The shell provides a powerful way to construct patterns, called file name *expansions*, that specify a group of pathnames and files. Specifying files in this manner is called *globbing* in UNIX parlance.

You can use these patterns when specifying file and directory names as arguments to any tool or application; the shell expands (or "globs") your pattern to the names of the files that fit the pattern, and it passes that expansion to the tool or application. A given pattern is a *glob expression*.

The following table lists the various file-expansion characters and describes their meaning in forming glob expressions.

*	The asterisk matches a series of zero or more characters, and is sometimes called the "wildcard" character. For example, "*" alone expands to all file names in the given directory, "a*" expands to all file names that consist of an "a" character followed by zero or more characters, and "a*b" expands to all file names that begin with an "a" character and end with a "b" character, with any (or no) characters in between.
?	The question mark matches exactly one character. Therefore, "?" alone expands to all file names with exactly one character, "??" expands to all file names with exactly *two* characters, and "a?" expands to all file names that begin with an "a" character and have exactly one character following it.
{*string1,string2,...*}	Curly brackets group a comma-delimited set of strings, all of which are to be matched. So "{a,b}c" expands to "ac" and "bc."
[*list*]	Square brackets match one character in *list*. For example, "[ab]" matches exactly two file names: "a" and "b." The pattern "c[io]" matches "ci" and "co," but no other file names.
~	The tilde character expands to your home directory (the value of the HOME variable; see Recipe 3.5 [Using Shell Variables], page 77). For example, if your username were mary and your home directory were therefore /home/mary, then ~ would expand to /home/mary. You can follow the tilde with a path to specify a file in your home directory—for example, ~/work would expand to /home/mary/work.

Brackets also have special meaning when used in conjunction with other characters, as described in the following table.

-	A hyphen as part of a bracketed *list* denotes a *range* of characters to match—so "[a-m]" matches any of the lowercase letters from "a" through "m." To match a literal hyphen character, use it as the first or last character in the list. For example, "a[-b]c" matches two files: a-c and abc.
!	Put an exclamation point at the beginning of a bracketed list to match all characters *except* those listed. For example, "a[!b]c" matches all files that begin with an "a" character, end with a "c" character, and have any one character (*except* a "b" character) in between; it matches the files aac, a-c, adc, and so on.

You can combine these special expansion characters in any combination, and you can specify more than one pattern as multiple arguments.

⇒ The following examples show file expansion in action, using commands described earlier in this chapter.

- To list all files in the **/usr/bin** directory that have the text "**tex**" anywhere in their name, type:

   `$ ls /usr/bin/*tex*` (RET)

- To copy all files whose names end with .txt, .text, .doc, or .info to the **doc** subdirectory, type:

   `$ cp *.txt,text,doc,info doc` (RET)

- To output a verbose listing of all files whose names end with a three-character extension, sorting the list so that newer files are listed first, type:

   `$ ls -lt *.???` (RET)

- To move all files in the **/usr/tmp** directory whose names consist of the text "**song**" followed by an integer from 0 to 9 and a .cdda extension, placing them in a directory **music** in your home directory, type:

   `$ mv /usr/tmp/song[0-9].cdda ~/music` (RET)

- To remove all files in the current working directory that begin with a hyphen and have the text "out" somewhere else in their file name, type:

  $ rm -- -*out* (RET)

- To concatenate all files whose names consist of an "a" character followed by two or more characters, type:

  $ cat a??* (RET)

5.9 Listing Directory Tree Graphs

Tree
  DEB: tree
  RPM: tree
  WWW: ftp://mama.indstate.edu/linux/tree/

Use **tree** to output an ASCII text tree graph of a given directory tree.

⇒ To output a tree graph of the current directory and all its subdirectories, type:

```
$ tree (RET)
.
|-- projects
|   |-- current
|   `-- old
|       |-- 1
|       `-- 2
`-- trip
    `-- schedule.txt

4 directories, 3 files
$
```

In the preceding example, a tree graph is drawn showing the current directory, which contains the two directories **projects** and **trip**; the **projects** directory in turn contains the directories **current** and **old**.

To output a tree graph of a specific directory tree, give the name of that directory tree as an argument.

⇒ To output a tree graph of your home directory and all its subdirectories, type:

    $ tree ~ ⟨RET⟩

To output a graph of a directory tree containing directory names only, use the **-d** option. This is useful for outputting a directory tree of the entire system, or for getting a picture of a particular directory tree.

⇒ Here are some ways to use this.

- To output a tree graph of the entire system to the file **tree**, type:

    $ tree -d / > tree ⟨RET⟩

- To peruse a tree graph of the **/usr/local** directory tree, type:

    $ tree -d /usr/local | less ⟨RET⟩

NOTES: Another tool for outputting directory trees is described in Recipe 24.2 [Listing a File's Disk Usage], page 502.

5.10 Browsing Files and Directories

There are several methods for browsing the files on your system. Here are three I recommend.

METHOD #1

Midnight Commander
  DEB: mc-common
      mc
  RPM: mc
  WWW: http://www.ibiblio.org/mc/

The easiest method for browsing files on your system is to use a "file manager" tool that was made for that purpose. There are at least a few on Linux, aside from the file managers that are part of GNOME and KDE[5]; the most popular stand-alone file manager is probably the venerable "Midnight Commander."

Type mc to run it. Give as an argument the name of a directory to browse, either relative to the current directory or with its full path name. If you give none, mc will use the current working directory.

⇒ To browse the **/usr/local/** directory with the Midnight Commander, type:

    $ mc /usr/local ⟨RET⟩

---

[5] Nautilus and Konqueror, respectively.

When browsing a directory, `mc` gives two display windows, called *directory panels*. Use the mouse to access the pull-down menus on the top menu bar. The function keys provide help and other menus; they are listed at the very bottom of the screen. Above them is a Bash command line, which you can use just as you normally do in the shell. Type (F10) to exit `mc` and return to the shell where you ran it.

An illustration of what the Midnight Commander looks like when browsing the root directory of a typical system is given in Figure 5-7.

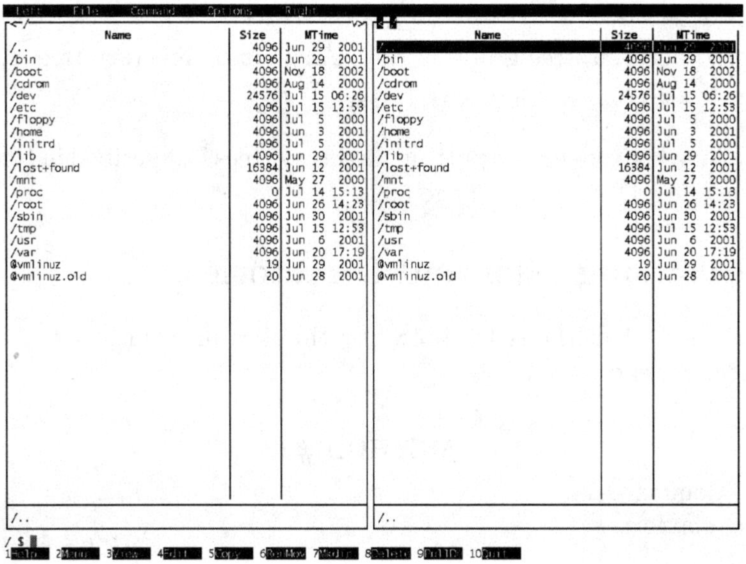

Figure 5-7. Browsing local files with the Midnight Commander.

METHOD #2

Lynx
  DEB: lynx
  RPM: lynx
  WWW: http://lynx.browser.org/

You can view and peruse local files in a Web browser, such as the text-only browser `lynx` or the graphical Mozilla browser for X.

The `lynx` tool is very good for browsing files on the system—give the name of the directory to browse as an argument, and `lynx` will display a listing of available files and directories in that directory.

You can use the cursor keys to browse and press ⟨RET⟩ on a subdirectory to traverse to that directory.[6] You can use `lynx` to display plain text files, compressed text files, and files written in HTML; it's useful for browsing system documentation in the **/usr/doc** and **/usr/share/doc** directories, where many software packages come with help files and manuals written in HTML.

Use the **-localhost** option to disable any URLs that point to remote hosts.

⇒ Here are two ways to use this.

- To browse the system documentation files in the **/usr/doc** directory, disabling all links to other hosts, type:

  `$ lynx -localhost /usr/doc` ⟨RET⟩

- To browse the files and subdirectories in the current directory, type:

  `$ lynx .` ⟨RET⟩

An illustration of what Lynx looks like when browsing the root directory of a typical system is given in Figure 5-8.

```
Current directory is /

drwxr-xr-x    2 root     root      4096 Jun 29  2001 bin/
drwxr-xr-x    2 root     root      4096 Nov 18  2002 boot/
dr-xr-xr-x   10 root     root      4096 Aug 14  2000 dev/
drwxr-xr-x    5 root     root     24576 Jul 15 06:26 etc/
drwxr-xr-x   62 root     root      4096 Jul 15 12:53 home/
drwxr-xr-x    2 root     root      4096 Jul  5  2000 floppy/
drwxrwsr-x    4 root     staff     4096 Jun  3  2001 home/
drwxr-xr-x    2 root     root      4096 Jul  5  2000 initrd/
drwxr-xr-x    5 root     root      4096 Jun 29  2001 lib/
drwxr-xr-x    2 root     root     16384 Jun 12  2001 lost+found/
drwxr-xr-x    2 root     root      4096 May 27  2000 mnt/
dr-xr-xr-x   60 root     root         0 Jul 14 15:13 proc/
drwxr-xr-x    9 root     root      4096 Jun 26 14:23 root/
drwxr-xr-x    2 root     root      4096 Jun 30  2001 sbin/
drwxrwxrwt    5 root     root      4096 Jul 15 12:59 tmp/
drwxr-xr-x   16 root     root      4096 Jun  6  2001 usr/
drwxr-xr-x   15 root     root      4096 Jun 20 17:19 var/
lrwxrwxrwx    1 root     root        19 Jun 29  2001 vmlinuz -> /boot/vmlinuz-2.4.5
lrwxrwxrwx    1 root     root        20 Jun 28  2001 vmlinuz.old -> /boot/vmlinuz-2.2.17

Commands: Use arrow keys to move, '?' for help, 'q' to quit, '<-' to go back.
  Arrow keys: Up and Down to move.  Right to follow a link; Left to go back.
  C)reate D)ownload E)dit F)ull menu M)odify R)emove T)ag U)pload
```

Figure 5-8. Browsing local files with Lynx.

NOTES: See Recipe 33.2 [Using Lynx], page 643, for more about using Lynx.

---

[6] In X, you can also use the mouse; see Recipe 33.2.8 [Using Lynx with a Mouse], page 648.

METHOD #3

Mozilla
 DEB: mozilla-browser
 RPM: mozilla
 WWW: http://www.mozilla.org/

Use Mozilla to browse files much as with Lynx as described in Method #2,
giving a full path name as an argument.

⇒ To browse the system documentation files in the **/usr/share/doc** directory in Mozilla, type the following in Mozilla's **Location** window, or give
  it as an argument to **mozilla**:

      /usr/share/doc

An illustration of what Mozilla looks like when browsing the root directory
of a typical system is given in Figure 5-9.

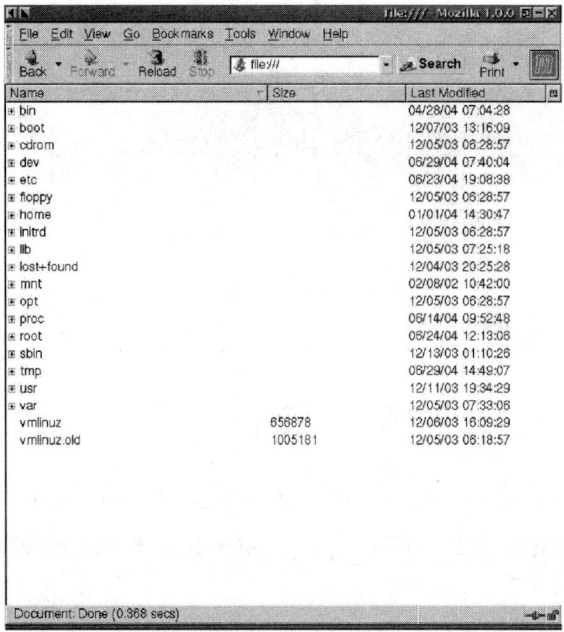

Figure 5-9. Browsing local files with Mozilla.

NOTES: Other Web browsers work in this way, too. For other recommended browsers to use, see the table in Recipe 33.11 [Using Other Web Browsers], page 667.

## CHAPTER 6

Sharing Files

Groups, file ownership, and access permissions are Linux features that enable users to share files with one another. But this topic is important to know even if you don't plan on ever sharing files with other users on the system; these are concepts that will help you understand how file access and security work in Linux, and enable you to control the way a file may be accessed. By changing the access permissions to files, files can be placed into a state so that they can't be modified, copied, or even viewed by certain users—including you!

6.1 Working in Groups

A *group* is a set of users, created to share files and to facilitate collaboration. All groups have a unique name, and are assigned a unique group ID, called a GID. Each member of a group can work with the group's files and make new files that belong to the group. The system administrator can add new groups and give users membership to the different groups, according to the users' organizational needs. For example, a system used by the crew of a ship might have special groups such as `galley`, `deck`, `bridge`, and `crew`; the user `captain` might be a member of all the groups, but user `steward` might be a member of only the `galley` and `crew` groups.

On a Linux system, you're always a member of at least one group: your *login group*. Its name is the same as your username, and you are its only member.[1]

The following recipes show how to list groups and their members.

6.1.1 Listing Available Groups

The list of all groups that are available on the system is kept in the file `/etc/group`, which is called the *user group file*. This is a text file containing a list of groups, one per line, with fields delimited by a colon character (`:`): group name, encrypted password (systems today employ what is called *shadow passwords*, which means that the actual encrypted password is kept elsewhere, and an "x" character appears here as a placeholder), GID, and a comma-separated list of all users who are members of the group.

To list the available groups on the system, list the contents of this file.

---

[1] This is the default on some systems, including the Debian distribution, but is not standard across all distributions; in such matters, this chapter will assume the Debian behavior.

⇒ To list the contents of the file **/etc/group**, type:

```
$ cat /etc/group (RET)
```

This command uses the **cat** tool to output the entire contents of the file (see Recipe 9.2 [Displaying Text], page 216), listing all fields. Use **cut** to output only certain fields (see Recipe 13.7.4 [Removing Columns from Text], page 324).

⇒ To output a list of all group names on the system, type:

```
$ cut -d : -f1 /etc/group (RET)
```

NOTES: For more information about the user group file, consult the **group man** page.

6.1.2 Listing the Groups a User Belongs To

To list a user's group memberships, use the **groups** tool. Give any number of usernames as arguments, and **groups** will output a line for each containing a list of all of the groups the user is a member of, preceded by the username and a colon character (:). With no arguments, **groups** lists your own group memberships.

⇒ To list your group memberships, type:

```
$ groups (RET)
steward galley crew
$
```

In this example, three groups are output: **steward** (the user's login group), **galley**, and **crew**.

⇒ To list the group memberships of user **marlow**, type:

```
$ groups marlow (RET)
marlow : marlow
$
```

In this example, the command outputs the given username, **marlow**, followed by the name of one group, **marlow**, indicating that user **marlow** belongs to only one group: his login group.

6.1.3 Listing the Members of a Group

There are two methods for listing the members of a particular group.

METHOD #1

Members
 DEB: `members`

Use the `members` tool to list the members of a particular group. Give the name of the particular group as an argument.

⇒ To output a list of the members of the `galley` group, type:

```
$ members galley (RET)
captain steward pete
$
```

In this example, three usernames are output, indicating that these three users are the members of the `galley` group.

NOTES: The `members` tool is not yet widely available outside of the Debian distribution; if you can't locate a copy, you can always install the sources from the Debian package (see Recipe 1.1.2 [Preparation of Recipes], page 4).

METHOD #2

On systems without `members` conveniently installed, the members of a particular group may be listed by using `grep` in conjunction with `cut`. First, use `grep` to output the line in `/etc/group` whose first field matches the particular group name, and pipe the output to `cut` to output only the last field, containing the list of users who belong to that group.

⇒ To list all members of the `crew` group, type:

```
$ grep ^crew: /etc/group | cut -d : -f 4 (RET)
```

NOTES: For more information on `grep` and `cut`, see Recipe 14.1 [Searching Text for a Word], page 333 and Recipe 13.7.4 [Removing Columns from Text], page 324, respectively.

6.2 Owning Files

Every file belongs to both a user and a group—usually to the user who created it and to the group the user was working in at the time (which is almost always the user's login group). File ownership determines the type of access users have to particular files (see Recipe 6.3 [Controlling Access to Files], page 167).

6.2.1 Determining the Ownership of a File

To find out which user and group own a particular file, use `ls` with the `-l` option to list the file's attributes (see Recipe 5.3.3 [Listing File Attributes], page 136). The name of the user who owns the file appears in the third column of the output, and the name of the group that owns the file appears in the fourth column.

For example, suppose the verbose listing for a file called **cruise** looks like this:

```
-rwxrw-r--  1 captain   crew      8,420 Jan 12 21:42 cruise
```

The user who owns this file is **captain**, and the group that owns it is **crew**.

NOTES: When you create a file, it normally belongs to you and to your login group, but you can change its ownership, as described in the next recipe. You normally own all of the files in your home directory.

6.2.2 Changing the Ownership of a File

You can't give away a file to another user, but other users can make copies of a file that belongs to you, provided they have read permission for that file (see Recipe 6.3 [Controlling Access to Files], page 167). When you make a copy of another user's file, you own the copy.

You can also change the group ownership of any file you own. To do this, use `chgrp`; it takes as arguments the name of the group to transfer ownership to and the names of the files to work on. You must be a member of the group you want to give ownership to.

⇒ To change the group ownership of file **cruise** to **bridge**, type:

```
$ chgrp bridge cruise RET
```

This command transfers group ownership of **cruise** to **bridge**; the file's group access permissions (as shown in the following recipe) now apply to the members of the **bridge** group.

Use the `-R` option to *recursively* change the group ownership of directories and all of their contents.

⇒ To give group ownership of the **maps** directory and all the files it contains
to the **bridge** group, type:

    $ *chgrp -R bridge maps* ⟨RET⟩

6.3 Controlling Access to Files

Each file has a set of *permissions* that specify what type of access that different
users have to the file. There are three kinds of permissions: read, write,
and execute. You need *read* permission for a file to read its contents, *write*
permission to write changes to or remove the file, and *execute* permission to
run the file as a program.

Normally, users have write permission only for files in their own home
directories. Only the superuser has write permission for the files in important
directories, such as **/bin** and **/etc**—so as a regular user, you never have to
worry about accidentally writing to or removing an important system file.

Permissions work differently for directories than for other kinds of files.
Read permission for a directory means that you can see the files in the directory; write permission lets you create, move, or remove files in the directory; and execute permission lets you use the directory name in a path (see
Chapter 5 [Files and Directories], page 125).

If you have read permission but not execute permission for a directory, you
can only read the names of files in that directory—you can't read their other
attributes, examine their contents, write to them, or execute them. With
execute but not read permission for a directory, you can read, write to, or
execute any file in the directory, provided that you know its name and that
you have the appropriate permissions for that file.

Each file has separate permissions for three categories of users: the user
who owns the file, all other members of the group that owns the file, and all
other users on the system. If you are a member of the group that owns a file,
the file's group permissions apply to you (unless you are the owner of the file,
in which case the user permissions apply to you).

When you create a new file, it has a default set of permissions—usually
read and write for the user, and read for the group and all other users. (On
some systems, the default permissions are read and write for both the user
and group, and read for all other users.)

The file access permissions for a file are collectively called its *access mode*.
The following sections describe how to list and change file access modes, including how to set the most commonly used access modes.

NOTES: The superuser, `root`, can always access any file on the system, regardless of its access permissions.

For more information on file permissions and access modes, see the `fileutils` Info documentation (see Recipe 2.8.5 [Reading an Info Manual], page 48).

6.3.1 Listing the Permissions of a File

To list a file's access permissions, use `ls` with the `-l` option (see Recipe 5.3.3 [Listing File Attributes], page 136). File access permissions appear in the first column of the output, after the character for file type.

For example, consider the verbose listing of the file `cruise`:

```
-rwxrw-r--     1 captain    crew        8,420 Jan 12 21:42 cruise
```

The first character ("`-`") is the file type; the next three characters ("`rwx`") specify permissions for the user who owns the file; and the next three ("`rw-`") specify permissions for all members of the group that owns the file *except* for the user who owns it. The last three characters in the column ("`r--`") specify permissions for all other users on the system.

All three permissions sections have the same format, indicating, from left to right, read, write, and execute permission with "`r`," "`w`," and "`x`" characters. A hyphen (`-`) in place of one of these letters indicates that permission is not given.

In this example, the listing indicates that the user who owns the file, `captain`, has read, write, and execute permission, and the group that owns the file, `crew`, has read and write permission. All other users on the system have only read permission.

6.3.2 Changing the Permissions of a File

To change the access mode of any file you own, use the `chmod` ("change mode") tool. It takes two arguments: an *operation*, which specifies the permissions to grant or revoke for certain users, and the names of the files to work on.

To build an operation, first specify the category or categories of users as a combination of the following characters:

u   The user who owns the file.

g   All other members of the file's group.

o   All other users on the system.

a   All users on the system; this is the same as **ugo**.

Follow this with the operator denoting the action to take:

+   Add permissions to the user's existing permissions.

-                          Remove permissions from the user's existing permissions.

=   Make these the *only* permissions the user has for this file.

Finally, specify the permissions themselves with a special character:

r   Set read permission.

w   Set write permission.

x   Set execute permission.

For example, use **u+w** to add write permission to the existing permissions for the user who owns the file, and use **a+rw** to add both read and write permissions to the existing permissions of all users. (You could also use **ugo+rw** instead of **a+rw**.)

6.3.3 Write-Protecting a File

If you revoke users' write permissions for a file, they can no longer write to or remove the file. This effectively "write-protects" a file, preventing accidental changes to it. A write-protected file is sometimes called a "read-only" file.

To write-protect a file so that no users other than yourself can write to it, use **chmod** with **go-w** as the operation.

⇒ To write-protect the file **cruise** so that no other users can change it, type:

      $ *chmod go-w cruise* (RET)

6.3.4 Making a File Private

To make a file private from all other users on the system, use **chmod** with **go=** as the operation. This revokes all **group** and **other** access permissions.

⇒ To make the file **cruise** private from all users but yourself, type:

      $ *chmod go= cruise* (RET)

6.3.5 Making a File Public

To allow anyone with an account on the system to read and make changes to a file, use chmod with a+rw as the operation. This grants read and write permission to all users, making the file "public." When a file has read permission set for all users, it is called *world readable*, and when a file has write permission set for all users, it is called *world writable*.

⇒ To make the file `cruise` both world readable and world writable, type:

        $ chmod a+rw cruise ⟨RET⟩

6.3.6 Making a File Executable

An *executable file* is a file that you can run as a program. To change the permissions of a file so that all users can run it as a program, use chmod with a+x as the operation.

⇒ To give execute permission to all users for the file `myscript`, type:

        $ chmod a+x myscript ⟨RET⟩

NOTES: Often, shell scripts that you obtain or write yourself do not have execute permission set, and you'll have to do this yourself.

## CHAPTER 7

Finding Files

Sometimes you may want to locate files on the system that match given criteria, such as a particular name or file size. This chapter will show you how to find a file when you know only part of the file name, and how to find a file whose name matches a given pattern. You will also learn how to list files and directories by size and how to find the locations of commands.

These are not searches for matching the *contents* of files. That kind of activity is described in Chapter 14 [Searching Text], page 333. A method of searching the contents of files you find is given in Recipe 7.2.7 [Running Commands on the Files You Find], page 178.

For more information on finding files, consult the **find** Info documentation (see Recipe 2.8.5 [Reading an Info Manual], page 48).

7.1 Finding All Files That Match a Pattern

The simplest way to find files is with GNU **locate**. Use it when you want to list all files on the system whose full path names match a particular pattern—for example, all files containing a particular string somewhere in the full path name, or all files ending with some extension. The **locate** tool outputs a list of all files on the system that match the pattern you give as an argument, listing each with its full path name and each on a line by itself.

When specifying a pattern, you can use any of the file name expansion characters (see Recipe 5.8 [Specifying File Names with Patterns], page 153).

⇒ Here are some ways to use this.

- To find all the files on the system that have the text **audio** anywhere in their full path name, type:

    $ *locate audio* (RET)

- To find all the files on the system whose file names end with a .c extension, type:

    $ *locate *.c* (RET)

- To find all hidden "dot files" on the system, type:

    $ *locate /.* (RET)

Sometimes, a **locate** search will generate a lot of output. Pipe the output to **less** to peruse it (see Recipe 9.1 [Perusing Text], page 211).

⇒ To peruse a list of all `.cfg` files on the system, type:

     $ *locate .cfg | less* (RET)

NOTES: Searches are case-sensitive. Thus, a search for `*history*` will match `~/.bash_history` and `/usr/local/history_data/README`, but not `~/History_of_a_nation`.

7.2 Finding Files in a Directory Tree

Use `find` to find specific files in a particular directory tree, outputting their full path names to the standard output, one per line. First specify the name of the directory tree to search, then give as options the criteria to match, and if desired, the action to perform on the found files. (Unlike most other tools, you must specify the directory tree argument *before* any other options.)

You can specify multiple search criteria in one command, and you can format the output in various ways. The following sections include recipes for the most commonly used `find` commands; see the Info documentation for a complete treatment of the `find` tool's many options.

Numeric arguments to the options described in the following recipes take one of three forms: When the number is preceded by a plus sign (`+`), it matches all files *greater* than the given number; when preceded by a hyphen or minus sign (`-`), it matches all files *less* than the given number; and with neither prefix, it matches all files whose number is *exactly* as specified.

7.2.1 Finding Files in a Directory Tree by Name

To find files in a directory tree by name, use `find`, first giving the name of the directory tree to search through, and then the `-name` option followed by the name you want to find.

⇒ To list all files on the system whose file name is **top**, type:

     $ *find / -name top* (RET)

This command will search all directories on the system to which you have access; if you don't have `execute` permission for a directory, `find` will report that permission is denied to search the directory.

The `-name` option is case-sensitive; use the similar `-iname` option to find a name regardless of case.

⇒ To list all files on the system whose file name is **top**, regardless of case, type:

     $ *find / -iname top* (RET)

This command would match any files whose name consisted of the letters top, regardless of case—including Top, top, and TOP.

Use file expansion characters (see Recipe 5.8 [Specifying File Names with Patterns], page 153) to find files whose names match a pattern. Give these file name patterns between single quotes.

⇒ Here are some ways to use this.

- To list all files on the system whose names begin with the characters top, type:

  $ *find / -name 'top*'* ⟨RET⟩

- To list all files whose names begin with the three characters top followed by exactly three more characters, type:

  $ *find / -name 'top???'* ⟨RET⟩

- To list all files whose names begin with the three characters top followed by five or more characters, type:

  $ *find / -name 'top?????*'* ⟨RET⟩

- To list all files in your home directory tree that end in .tex, regardless of case, type:

  $ *find ~ -iname '*.tex'* ⟨RET⟩

- To list all files in the /usr/share directory tree that end with .jpg or .jpeg, regardless of case, type:[1]

  $ *find /usr/share -iname '*.jp*g'* ⟨RET⟩

- To list all files in the /usr/share directory tree with the text farm somewhere in their name, type:

  $ *find /usr/share -name '*farm*'* ⟨RET⟩

Use -regex in place of -name to search for files whose full or relative path names match a *regular expression*, a pattern describing a set of strings (see Recipe 14.3 [Matching Patterns of Text], page 335).

⇒ Here are two ways to use this.

- To list all files in the current directory tree whose relative path names have either the string net or comm anywhere in them, type:

  $ *find . -regex '.*\(net\|comm\).*'* ⟨RET⟩

---

[1] This pattern also matches files that contain any other character or characters in place of the "e"—for example, .jpog or .jp123g. To match files ending *only* with .jpg or .jpeg, use the -regex or -iregex search that is described next.

- To list all files in the **/usr/share** directory tree that end *only* with
  .jpg or **.jpeg**, regardless of case, type:

    `$ find /usr/share -iregex '.*\.\(jpg\|jpeg\)'` ⟨RET⟩

The **-regex** option matches the whole path name, relative to the directory
tree you specify, and not just file names; for this reason, the regexps in the
previous examples began with ".*," so that characters making up the path
were matched first. To only match file names in a search for a word or phrase,
exclude the forward slash character (/) after the string you're searching for,
and exclude directory names with **\! -type d** (see Recipe 7.4.5 [Finding the
Number of Files in a Listing], page 184).

⇒ To list all files in the current directory tree whose names have either the
string **net** or **comm** anywhere in their file names, type:

    `$ find . -regex '.*\(net\|comm\).[^/]*' \! -type d` ⟨RET⟩

7.2.2 Finding Files in a Directory Tree by Size

To find files of a certain size, use the **-size** option, following it with the file
size to match. The default unit is 512-byte blocks; follow the size with "k" to
denote kilobytes or "b" to denote bytes.

⇒ Here are some ways to use this.

- To list all files in the **/usr/local** directory tree that are greater than
  10,000 kilobytes in size, type:

    `$ find /usr/local -size +10000k` ⟨RET⟩

- To list all files in your home directory tree less than 300 bytes in size,
  type:

    `$ find ˜ -size -300b` ⟨RET⟩

- To list all files on the system whose size is exactly 42 512-byte blocks,
  type:

    `$ find / -size 42` ⟨RET⟩

Use the **-empty** option to find empty files—files whose size is 0 bytes. This
is useful for finding files that you might not need, and can remove.

⇒ To find all empty files in your home directory tree, type:

    `$ find ˜ -empty` ⟨RET⟩

NOTES: To find the largest or smallest files in a given directory, output a
sorted listing of that directory (see Recipe 7.4 [Finding Files in Directory
Listings], page 183).

7.2.3 Finding Files in a Directory Tree by Access Time

To find files that were last accessed during a specified time, use `find` with any of the `-amin`, `-anewer`, or `-atime` options. The argument you give with `-amin` specifies the number of minutes ago that the file was accessed; you can also find files that were accessed more recently than the file name given as an argument to `-anewer` was modified. Finally, `-atime` specifies the number of 24-hour periods ago when the file was last accessed.

⇒ Here are some ways to use this.

- To find all files in your home directory tree that were last accessed one hour ago, type:

      $ find ~ -amin 60 ⟨RET⟩

- To find all files in your home directory tree that were last accessed within the past sixty minutes, type:

      $ find ~ -amin -60 ⟨RET⟩

- To find all files in the `/usr/share` directory tree that were last accessed twenty-four hours ago, type:

      $ find /usr/share -atime 1 ⟨RET⟩

- To find all files in the `/usr/share` directory tree that were last accessed more recently than the file `~/template` was modified, type:

      $ find /usr/share -anewer ~/template ⟨RET⟩

Include the `-daystart` option to measure time from the beginning of the current day, instead of 24 hours ago. This option must precede the time expression it works on.

⇒ To find all files in the `/usr/share` directory tree that were last accessed two days ago, type:

      $ find /usr/share -daystart -atime 2 ⟨RET⟩

7.2.4 Finding Files in a Directory Tree by Change Time

To find files whose status last changed at a specified time (that is, its permissions and not its contents), use `find` with the `-ctime`, `-cmin`, or `-cnewer` options; the argument you give with `-ctime` specifies the number of 24-hour periods, and with `-cmin` it specifies the number of minutes. A file name given as an argument to `-anewer` specifies files whose status have changed more recently than this particular file was modified.

⇒ Here are some ways to use this.

- To find all files in your home directory tree whose status has changed within the last ten minutes, type:

  `$ find ~ -cmin -10` (RET)

- To find all the files on the system whose status has changed more recently than the file **/etc/inittab** was modified, type:

  `$ find / -cnewer /etc/inittab` (RET)

- To find all files in the current directory tree whose status last changed exactly twenty-four hours ago, type:

  `$ find . -ctime 1` (RET)

- To find all files in the current directory tree whose status has changed within the last twenty-four hours, type:

  `$ find . -ctime -1` (RET)

Include the **-daystart** option to measure time from the beginning of the current day, instead of 24 hours ago. This option must precede the time expression it works on.

⇒ To find all files in the current directory tree whose status last changed a week ago, type:

  `$ find . -daystart -ctime 7` (RET)

7.2.5 Finding Files in a Directory Tree by Modification Time

To find files last modified at a specified time, use **find** with the **-mtime** or **-mmin** options; the argument you give with **-mtime** specifies the number of 24-hour periods, and with **-mmin** it specifies the number of minutes.

⇒ Here are some ways to use this.

- To list all the files in the current directory tree whose contents have been modified within the last ten minutes, type:

  `$ find . -mmin -10` (RET)

- To list the files in the **/usr/local** directory tree that were modified exactly 24 hours ago, type:

  `$ find /usr/local -mtime 1` (RET)

- To list the files in the **/usr** directory tree that were modified exactly five minutes ago, type:

  `$ find /usr -mmin 5` (RET)

- To list the files in the `/usr/local` directory tree that were modified within the past 24 hours, type:

    $ *find /usr/local -mtime -1* ⟨RET⟩

- To list the files in the `/usr` directory tree that were modified within the past five minutes, type:

    $ *find /usr -mmin -5* ⟨RET⟩

Include the **-daystart** option to measure time from the beginning of the current day, instead of 24 hours ago. This option must precede the time expression it works on.

⇒ Here are some ways to use this.

- To list all of the files in your home directory tree that were modified yesterday, type:

    $ *find ~ -daystart -mtime 1* ⟨RET⟩

- To list all of the files in the `/usr` directory tree that were modified one year or longer ago, type:

    $ *find /usr -daystart -mtime +365* ⟨RET⟩

- To list all of the files in your home directory tree that were modified from two to four days ago, type:

    $ *find ~ -daystart -daystart -mtime +2 -mtime -4* ⟨RET⟩

In the preceding example, the combined options **-mtime +2** and **-mtime -4**, each prefaced by the **-daystart** option, matched files that were modified between two and four days ago.

To find files newer than a given file, give the name of that file as an argument to the **-newer** option.

⇒ To find files in the `/etc` directory tree that are newer than the file `/etc/motd`, type:

    $ *find /etc -newer /etc/motd* ⟨RET⟩

To find files newer than a given date, use the trick described in the **find** Info documentation: Create a temporary file in `/tmp` with **touch** whose timestamp is set to the date you want to search for, and then specify that temporary file as the argument to **-newer**.

⇒ To list all files in your home directory tree that were modified after May 4 of the current year, type:

    $ *touch -t 05040000 /tmp/timestamp* ⟨RET⟩
    $ *find ~ -newer /tmp/timestamp* ⟨RET⟩

In this example, a temporary file called /tmp/timestamp is written; after the search, you can remove it (see Recipe 5.6 [Removing Files and Directories], page 149).

NOTES: You can also find files that were last accessed a number of days after they were modified by giving that number as an argument to the -used option. This is useful for finding files that get little use—files matching -used +100, say, were accessed 100 or more days after they were last modified.

7.2.6 Finding Files in a Directory Tree by Owner

To find files owned by a particular user, give the username to search for as an argument to the -user option.

⇒ To list all files in the /usr/local/fonts directory tree owned by the user warwick, type:

> `$ find /usr/local/fonts -user warwick` ⟨RET⟩

The -group option is similar, but it matches group ownership instead of user ownership.

⇒ To list all files in the /dev directory tree owned by the audio group, type:

> `$ find /dev -group audio` ⟨RET⟩

7.2.7 Running Commands on the Files You Find

You can also use find to execute a command you specify on each found file, by giving the command as an argument to the -exec option. If you use the string "'{}'" in the command, this string is replaced with the file name of the current found file when the command executes. Mark the end of the command with a semicolon character enclosed in single quotes (;).

⇒ To find all files in the ~/html/ directory tree with an .html extension, and then output lines from these files that contain the string "organic," type (all on one line):

> `$ find ~/html/ -name '*.html' -exec grep organic '{}'`
> `';'` ⟨RET⟩

In this example, the command grep organic *file* is executed for each file that find finds, with *file* being the name of each file in turn.

To have find pause and confirm execution for each file it finds, use -ok instead of -exec.

⇒ To remove files from your home directory tree that were accessed more than one year after they were last modified, pausing to confirm before each removal, type:

```
$ find ~ -used +365 -ok rm '{}' ';' ⟨RET⟩
```

7.2.8 Finding Files by Multiple Criteria

You can combine many of **find**'s options to find files that match multiple criteria.

⇒ Here are two ways to use this.

- To list files in your home directory tree whose names begin with the string **top**, and that are newer than the file **/etc/motd**, type:

```
$ find ~ -name 'top*' -newer /etc/motd ⟨RET⟩
```

- To compress all the files in your home directory tree that are two megabytes or larger, and that are not already compressed with **gzip** (having a **.gz** file name extension), type (all on one line):

```
$ find ~ -size +2000000c -regex '.*[^gz]' -exec
gzip '{}' ';' ⟨RET⟩
```

As all options are combinable, you can use multiple calls of the same option. So you can combine several of the same time options to get a range of times, for instance.

⇒ To find all files in your home directory whose contents were modified today, but at least 120 minutes ago, type:

```
$ find ~ -daystart -mtime 0 -mmin +120 ⟨RET⟩
```

Use the special **-o** option (the OR operator), to separate two options when either of them are to be matched. For example, you can use it with multiple **-name** options to find different file names in the same directory tree.

⇒ To find all files ending in **.ps**, **.pdf**, or **.dvi** in the current directory tree, type (all on one line):

```
$ find . -name '*.ps' -o -name '*.pdf' -o -name
'*.dvi' ⟨RET⟩
```

The following tables describe some of the many options you can use with **find**. The first table lists and describes **find**'s general options for specifying its behavior.

-daystart	Use the beginning of today rather than 24 hours previous for time criteria.
-depth	Search the subdirectories before each directory.
-maxdepth *levels*	Specifies the maximum number of directory levels to descend in the specified directory tree.
-mount *or* -xdev	Do not descend directories that have another disk mounted on them.

The following table lists and describes find's options for specifying which files to find.

Specify the numeric arguments to these options in one of three ways: preceded by a plus sign (+) to match values equal to or greater than the given argument; preceded by a hyphen or minus sign (-) to match values equal to or less than the given argument; or list the number alone to match exactly that value.

-amin *minutes*	Time in minutes since the file was last accessed.
-anewer *file*	File was accessed more recently than *file*.
-atime *days*	Time in days since the file was last accessed.
-cmin *minutes*	Time in minutes since the file was last changed.
-cnewer *file*	File was changed more recently than *file*.
-ctime *days*	Days since the file was last changed.
-empty	File is empty.
-group *group*	Name of the group that owns file.
-iname *pattern*	Case-insensitive file name pattern to match ("report" matches the files Report, report, REPORT, etc.).
-ipath *pattern*	Full path name of file matches the pattern *pattern*, regardless of case ("./r*rt" matches ./records/report and ./Record-Labels/ART.
-iregex *regexp*	Path name of file, relative to specified directory tree, matches the regular expression *regexp*, regardless of case ("t?p" matches TIP and top).

-links *links*	Number of links to the file (see Recipe 5.7 [Giving a File More Than One Name], page 152).
-mmin *minutes*	Number of minutes since the file's data was last changed.
-mtime *days*	Number of days since the file's data was last changed.
-name *pattern*	Base name of the file matches the pattern *pattern*.
-newer *file*	File was modified more recently than *file*.
-path *pattern*	Full path name of file matches the pattern *pattern* ("./r*rt" matches ./records/report).
-perm *access mode*	File's permissions are exactly *access mode* (see Recipe 6.3 [Controlling Access to Files], page 167).
-regex *regexp*	Path name of file, relative to specified directory tree, matches the regular expression *regexp*.
-size *size*	File uses *size* space, in 512-byte blocks. Append *size* with "b" for bytes or "k" for kilobytes.
-type *type*	File is type *type*, where *type* can be "d" for directory, "f" for regular file, or "l" for symbolic link.
-user *user*	File is owned by *user*.

The following table lists and describes **find**'s options for specifying what to do with the files it finds.

-exec *commands*	Specifies commands, separated by semicolons, to be executed on matching files. To specify the current file name as an argument to a command, use "'{}'."
-ok *commands*	Like **-exec**, but prompts for confirmation before executing *commands*.
-print	Outputs the name of found files to the standard output, each followed by a newline character so that each is displayed on a line of its own (the default).

-printf *format*   Use "C-style" output (the same as used by the
                          printf function in the C programming language),
                          as specified by string *format*.

The following table describes the variables that may be used in the *format*
string used by the -printf option.

\a   Rings the system bell (called the "alarm" on older
                          systems).

\b   Outputs a backspace character.

\f   Outputs a formfeed character.

\n   Outputs a newline character.

\r   Outputs a carriage return.

\t   Outputs a horizontal tab character.

\\   Outputs a backslash character.

%%   Outputs a percent sign character.

%b   Outputs file's size, rounded up in 512-byte blocks.

%f   Outputs base file name.

%h   Outputs the leading directories of file's name.

%k   Outputs file's size, rounded up in 1 K blocks.

%s   Outputs file's size in bytes.

7.3 Finding Directories

To find directories that have a particular name, use find with the -
nameoption, giving the glob expression to match, and also giving the -type
option with the d argument, which specifies that directories are the only files
that should be searched for.

⇒ Here are two ways to use this.

- To find all of the directories in your home directory tree with a name
  of audio, type:

  ```
  $ find ~ -name audio -type d (RET)
  ```

- To find all of the directories in your home directory tree with the string "`audio`" anywhere in their names, type:

  `$ find ~ -name *audio* -type d` (RET)

7.4 Finding Files in Directory Listings

The following recipes show how to find the largest and smallest files and directories in a given directory or tree by listing them by size. They also show how to find the number of files in a given directory.

7.4.1 Finding the Largest Files in a Directory

To find the largest files in a given directory, list its contents using `ls` wtih the `-S` option, which sorts files in descending order by their size (normally, `ls` outputs files sorted alphabetically). Include the `-l` option to output the size and other file attributes.

⇒ To list the files in the current directory, with their attributes, sorted with the largest files first, type:

  `$ ls -lS` (RET)

NOTES: Pipe the output to `less` to peruse it (see Recipe 9.1 [Perusing Text], page 211).

7.4.2 Finding the Smallest Files in a Directory

To list the contents of a directory with the smallest files first, use `ls` with both the `-S` and `-r` options, which *reverses* the sorting order of the listing.

⇒ To list the files in the current directory with their attributes, sorted from smallest to largest, type:

  `$ ls -lSr` (RET)

7.4.3 Finding the Smallest Directories

To output a list of *directories* sorted by their size—the size of all the files they contain—use `du` and `sort`. The `du` tool outputs directories in ascending order with the smallest first; the `-S` option puts the size in kilobytes of each directory in the first column of output. Give the directory tree you want to output as an option, and pipe the output to `sort` with the `-n` option, which sorts the input numerically.

⇒ To output a list of the subdirectories of the current directory tree, sorted in ascending order by size, type:

    $ du -S . | sort -n (RET)

7.4.4 Finding the Largest Directories

Use the **-r** option with **sort** to *reverse* the listing and output the largest directories first.

⇒ Here are some ways to use this.

- To output a list of the subdirectories in the current directory tree, sorted in descending order by size, type:

      $ du -S . | sort -nr (RET)

- To output a list of the subdirectories in the **/usr/local** directory tree, sorted in descending order by size, type:

      $ du -S /usr/local | sort -nr (RET)

7.4.5 Finding the Number of Files in a Listing

To find the number of files in a directory, use **ls** and pipe the output to **wc -l**, which outputs the number of lines in its input (see Recipe 12.1 [Counting Text], page 293).

⇒ To output the number of files in the current directory, type:

```
$ ls | wc -l (RET)
      19
$
```

In this example, the command outputs the numeral "**19**," indicating that there are 19 files in the current directory.

Since **ls** does not list hidden files by default (see Recipe 5.3.4 [Listing Hidden Files], page 138), the preceding command does not count them. Use **ls**'s **-A** option to count dot files as well.

⇒ To count the number of files—including dot files—in the current directory, type:

```
$ ls -A | wc -l (RET)
      81
$
```

This command outputs the numeral "81," indicating that there are 81 files, including hidden files, in the current directory.

To list the number of files in a given directory *tree*, and not just a single directory, use `find` instead of `ls`, giving the special `find` predicate `\! -type d` to exclude the listing (and therefore, the counting) of directories.

⇒ Here are some ways to use this.

- To list the number of files in the **/usr/share** directory tree, type:

  `$ find /usr/share \! -type d | wc -l` ⟨RET⟩

- To list the number of files *and* directories in the **/usr/share** directory tree, type:

  `$ find /usr/share | wc -l` ⟨RET⟩

- To list the number of *directories* in the **/usr/share** directory tree, type:

  `$ find /usr/share \! -type f | wc -l` ⟨RET⟩

7.5 Finding Where a Program Is Located

Use `which` to find the full path name of a tool or application from its base file name; when you give the base file name as an option, `which` outputs the absolute file name of the command that would have run had you typed it. This is useful when you are not sure whether or not a particular command is installed on the system.

⇒ To find out whether the `perl` program is installed on your system, and, if so, where it resides, type:

```
$ which perl ⟨RET⟩
/usr/bin/perl
```

In this example, `which` output "/usr/bin/perl," indicating that the `perl` binary is installed in the **/usr/bin** directory.

NOTES: This is also useful for determining "which" binary would execute, should you type the name, because some systems may have different binaries of the same file name located in different directories. In that case, you can use `which` to find which one would execute.

## CHAPTER 8

Managing Files

File management tools include those for splitting, comparing, and compressing files, making backup archives, and tracking file revisions. Other management tools exist for determining the contents of a file, and for changing its timestamp.

8.1 Getting Information About a File

The following recipes describe ways to get information about a file: how to determine its file type and format, and how to display and change its timestamp.

8.1.1 Determining a File's Type and Format

When we speak of a file's *type*, we are referring to the kind of data it contains, which may include text, executable commands, or some other data; this data is organized in a particular way in the file, and this organization is called its *format*. For example, an image file might contain data in the JPEG image format, or a text file might contain unformatted text in the English language or text formatted in the TEX markup language.

The `file` tool analyzes its input files, indicating their type and—if known—the format of the data they contain. Supply the name of a file as an argument to `file`, and it outputs the name of the file, followed by a description of its format and type.

⇒ To determine the format of the file /usr/doc/HOWTO/README.gz, type:

```
$ file /usr/doc/HOWTO/README.gz ⟨RET⟩
/usr/doc/HOWTO/README.gz: gzip compressed data, deflated, original
filename, last modified: Sun Apr 26 02:51:48 1998, os: Unix
$
```

This command reports that the file /usr/doc/HOWTO/README.gz contains data that has been compressed with the `gzip` tool.

To determine the original format of the data in a compressed file, use the **-z** option.

⇒ To determine the format of the compressed data contained in the file
/usr/doc/HOWTO/README.gz, type:

```
$ file -z /usr/doc/HOWTO/README.gz (RET)
/usr/doc/HOWTO/README.gz: English text (gzip compressed data, deflated,
original filename, last modified: Sun Apr 26 02:51:48 1998, os: Unix)
$
```

This command reports that the data in **/usr/doc/HOWTO/README.gz**, a
compressed file, is English text.

NOTES: Currently, `file` differentiates among more than one hundred different
data formats, including several human languages, many sound and graphics
formats, and executable files for many different operating systems.

For more information on file formats, see Appendix B [Conventional File
Name Extensions], page 723.

8.1.2 Determining a Program's Type

Use `type`, a built-in function of the Bash shell, to determine what type of
command a given program is: an alias word for some other command, a shell
keyword, a built-in function (such as `type` itself), or a regular file (such as
any tool stored in the `/usr/bin` directory). Give the name of the program as
an argument.

This is useful for determining whether or not a particular command is running a tool directly or is running an alias first. For example, the `ls` command
is frequently aliased to `ls --color` so that it runs in color mode by default.

⇒ To see whether the `ls` you type at the shell prompt is an alias or the tool
itself, type:

```
$ type ls (RET)
ls is aliased to `ls --color=auto'
$
```

8.1.3 Listing When a File Was Last Modified

To display the timestamp of a file, use `date` with the `-r` option, and give the name of the file as an argument.

⇒ To display the timestamp of file `/vmlinuz`, type:

    $ date -r /vmlinuz ⟨RET⟩

8.1.4 Changing a File's Modification Time

Use `touch` to change a file's timestamp without modifying its contents. Give the name of the file to be changed as an argument. The default action is to change the timestamp to the current time.

⇒ To change the timestamp of file `pizzicato` to the current date and time, type:

    $ touch pizzicato ⟨RET⟩

To specify a timestamp other than the current system time, use the `-d` option, followed by the date and time that should be used enclosed in quote characters. You can specify just the date, just the time, or both.

⇒ Here are some ways to use this.

- To change the timestamp of file `pizzicato` to May 17, 1990 at 2:16 p.m., type:

      $ touch -d '17 May 1990 14:16' pizzicato ⟨RET⟩

- To change the timestamp of file `pizzicato` to May 17th of the current year, type:

      $ touch -d '17 May' pizzicato ⟨RET⟩

- To change the timestamp of file `pizzicato` to 2:16 p.m. of the current day, type:

      $ touch -d '14:16' pizzicato ⟨RET⟩

NOTES: When only the time is given, the date is set to the current date, and when only the date is given, the time is set to "0:00." When just a year is given, the current day and month is used, and when a day and month but no year is given, the current year is used.

For more information on date input formats, consult the Info documentation for `date` (see Recipe 2.8.5 [Reading an Info Manual], page 48).

8.2 Splitting a File into Smaller Ones

It's sometimes necessary to split one file into a number of smaller files. For example, suppose you have a very large sound file in the near-CD-quality MPEG2, level 3 (MP3) format. Your file, `large.mp3`, is 4,394,422 bytes in size, and you want to transfer it from your desktop to your laptop, but your laptop and desktop are not connected on a network—the only way to transfer files between them is by floppy disk. Because this file is much too large to fit on one floppy, you use `split`.[1]

The `split` tool copies a file, chopping up the copy into separate files of a specified size. It takes as optional arguments the name of the input file (using standard input if none is given) and the file name prefix to use when writing the output files (using "x" if none is given). The output files' names will consist of the file prefix followed by a group of letters: `aa`, `ab`, `ac`, and so on—the default output file names would be `xaa`, `xab`, and so on.

Specify the number of *lines* to put in each output file with the `-l` option, or use the `-b` option to specify the number of *bytes* to put in each output file. To specify the output files' sizes in kilobytes or megabytes, use the `-b` option and append "k" or "m," respectively, to the value you supply. If neither `-l` nor `-b` is used, `split` defaults to using 1,000 lines per output file.

⇒ To split `large.mp3` into separate files of one megabyte each, whose names begin with `large.mp3.`, type:

```
$ split -b1m large.mp3 large.mp3. RET
```

This command creates five new files whose names begin with: `large.mp3.` The first four files are one megabyte in size, while the last file is 200,118 bytes—the remaining portion of the original file. No alteration is made to `large.mp3`.

You could then copy these five files onto four floppies (the last file fits on a floppy with one of the larger files), copy them all to your laptop, and then reconstruct the original file with `cat` (see Recipe 10.6 [Concatenating Text], page 256).

⇒ To reconstruct the original file from the split files, type:

```
$ cat large.mp3.* > large.mp3 RET
$ rm large.mp3.* RET
```

In this example, the `rm` tool is used to delete all of the split files after the original file has been reconstructed.

---

[1] Another method for splitting files is to use GNU `shar`, the shell archiver, which bundles files into archives made especially for transmission by email. It can split and compress files as it archives them.

8.3 Comparing Files

There are a number of tools for comparing the contents of files in different ways; these recipes show how to use some of them. These tools are especially useful for comparing passages of text in files, but that's not the only way you can use them.

8.3.1 Determining Whether Two Files Differ

Use cmp to determine whether or not two text files differ. It takes the names of two files as arguments, and if the files contain the same data, cmp outputs nothing. If, however, the files differ, cmp outputs the byte position and line number in the files where the first difference occurs.

⇒ To determine whether the files master and backup differ, type:

```
$ cmp master backup ⟨RET⟩
```

8.3.2 Determining Whether Two Directories Differ

There are two methods to determine whether two directories are different from each other.

METHOD #1

Midnight Commander
  DEB: mc-common
       mc
  RPM: mc
  WWW: http://www.ibiblio.org/mc/

The most quick and easy way to determine whether two entire directories differ is to use mc, the Midnight Commander. By default, mc draws two directory columns upon starting; select two directories, one in each column, and then compare them with the directory compare command, ⟨CTRL⟩-⟨X⟩ d (press ⟨CTRL⟩-⟨X⟩ and then type d).

There are three ways you can compare files in this manner: the quick method, which just compares file size and date (if files have different contents but identical sizes, they will still show up as not differing); a size-only comparison; and the "thorough" method, which compares all files byte by byte.

⇒ To compare two directories with `mc`, do the following:

1. Use the cursor keys to select the first directory to compare in the current column.

2. Type ⟨TAB⟩ to move to the other column.

3. Use the cursor keys to select the second directory.

4. Type ⟨CTRL⟩-⟨X⟩ *d* to compare the two selected directories, and select which method to use from the pop-up menu.

The number of bytes that differ, in the total number of differing files, is displayed at the bottom of the first column; the number of bytes in the number of files that are the *same* in both directories is displayed at the bottom of the second column.

METHOD #2

The second method is to use `cmp` on all files in each of the directories. Loop through all of the files, running this command on each of them, using the Bash built-in `for` construct (see the `bash` Info documentation for more information on this built-in).

⇒ To compare all of the files in the directory `~/site/current` with all of the files in the directory `~/development/latest`, type:

```
$ for i in ~/site/current/*; { cmp $i ~/development/latest/$i; }
```

NOTES: This `cmp` method only works on directories that contain regular files; if the directories contain subdirectories, this method will fail.

8.3.3 Finding the Differences Between Files

Use `diff` to compare two files and output a *difference report* (sometimes called a "diff") containing the text that *differs* between two files. The difference report is formatted so that other tools (namely, `patch`—see Recipe 8.3.7 [Patching a File with a Difference Report], page 196) can use it to make a file identical to the one it was compared with.

To compare two files and output a difference report, give their names as arguments to `diff`. The difference report is written to the standard output; to save it to a file, redirect standard output.

⇒ Here are some ways to use this.

- To compare the files `manuscript.old` and `manuscript.new`, type:

```
$ diff manuscript.old manuscript.new ⟨RET⟩
```

- To compare the files `manuscript.old` and `manuscript.new`, writing the difference report to a file named `manuscript.diff`, type:

    $ `diff manuscript.old manuscript.new > manuscript.diff` (RET)

The difference report is meant to be used with commands such as `patch`, in order to apply the differences to a file. For more information on `diff` and the format of its output, consult its Info documentation (see Recipe 2.8.5 [Reading an Info Manual], page 48).

To better see the difference between two files, use `sdiff` instead of `diff`; instead of giving a difference report, it outputs the files in two columns, side by side, separated by spaces. Lines that differ in the files are separated by a pipe character (|); lines that appear only in the first file are ended with a less-than sign (<), and lines that appear only in the second file are preceded with a greater-than sign (>).

⇒ To peruse the files `laurel` and `hardy` side by side on the screen, with any differences indicated between columns, type:

    $ `sdiff laurel hardy | less` (RET)

To output the difference between *three* separate files, use `diff3`.

⇒ To output a difference report for files `larry`, `curly`, and `moe`, and output it in a file called `stooges`, type:

    $ `diff3 larry curly moe > stooges` (RET)

8.3.4 Perusing the Differences in a Group of Files

To peruse the differences between two groups of files, use the shell `for` directive to specify the files to compare with `diff`, and pipe the output to `less`.

⇒ To peruse the differences between all the `.news` files in the current directory and their counterparts in the `../archive` directory, type:

```
$ for i in *.news (RET)
> { (RET)
> diff $i ../archive/$i | less (RET)
> } (RET)
```

In this example, the differences between each file in one directory and its counterpart in the other directory are displayed in turn; press (N) to move to the next file, and (P) to move to the previous one.

8.3.5 Finding the Differences Between Directories

You can use diff to compare two directories and all of their contents. This is useful for making a patch of a directory of text files, such as a directory of computer program source code, or a collection of writing. To do this, give the names of the directories to compare as arguments to diff.

To examine the differences between whole directory trees, where each directory may contain subdirectories, use the -r option to search recursively, and use the -N option to have diff write a whole new file in one directory where it doesn't exist (and have it delete whole files where a file exists only in the other directory). Since a directory diff will tend to be large, use the -u option to specify the *unified* patch format, which eliminates some redundancies and is more compact than the normal patch format.

⇒ Here are two ways to use this.

- To make a patch to change the ~/apples directory to match the ~/oranges directory, specifying all files in ~/apples to be changed to their equivalents in ~/oranges, and writing the patch to a file called fruit-patch.diff in the current directory, type:

    $ *diff -N apples oranges > fruit-patch.diff* (RET)

- To make a patch to change the ~/apples directory tree to match the ~/oranges directory tree, specifying all files in ~/apples and its subdirectories to be changed to their equivalents in the ~/oranges tree, and writing the patch to a file in the current directory called fruit-patch.diff in unified format, type:

    $ *diff -r -u -N apples oranges > fruit-patch.diff* (RET)

To apply one of these patches, use patch with the -p1 option, which eliminates leading slashes in filenames. Put the patch file in the directory you want to patch, and run the patch tool from that directory. Use the -s option to work *silently*, omitting any output to the standard output.

⇒ To silently apply the patch file fruit-patch.diff to the ~/apples directory, type:

```
$ mv fruit-patch.diff ~/apples (RET)
$ cd ~/apples (RET)
$ patch -p1 -s < fruit-patch.diff (RET)
```

8.3.6 Finding the Percentage Two Files Differ By

Wdiff
  DEB: `wdiff`
  RPM: `wdiff`
  WWW: http://www.gnu.org/software/wdiff/wdiff.html

The `wdiff` tool is a front-end to `diff`. It finds and displays the differences between words in the two text files you give as arguments. It outputs an annotated version of the second file, showing the changes necessary to make it identical to the first: Word deletions are marked like "`[- this -]`," additions are marked like "`[+ this +]`," and changes are marked like "`{+ this +}`."

⇒ To peruse an annotated copy of the file `story_draft.1`, showing the changes necessary to make it identical to the file `story_draft.2`, type:

> `$ wdiff story_draft.2 story_draft.1 | less` ⟨RET⟩

To forgo the default annotations and instead make annotations good for sending to a *printer*, use the -p option; deleted text is underlined and inserted text is output in bold.

⇒ Here are two ways to use this.

- To print an annotated copy of the file `story_draft.1`, showing the changes necessary to make it identical to the file `story_draft.2`, type:

  > `$ wdiff -p story_draft.2 story_draft.1 | lpr` ⟨RET⟩

- To peruse an annotated copy of the file `story_draft.1`, showing the changes necessary to make it identical to the file `story_draft.2` with underlining and bold lettering, type:

  > `$ wdiff -p story_draft.2 story_draft.1 | less` ⟨RET⟩

Use `wdiff` with the -s option to display a number of *statistics* about the differences: the total number of words; the number of common words and the percentage relative to the total; the number of words deleted or inserted, and the percentage relative to the total; and the number of words changed, and the percentage relative to the total. These statistics are output as two lines at the end, after an annotation of the second file is output.

⇒ Here are two ways to use this.

- To output the differences in words between files `story_draft.1` and `story_draft.2`, showing statistics about the differences, type:

    $ *wdiff -s story_draft.1 story_draft.2* ⟨RET⟩

- To output the two lines of statistics about the differences in words between files `story_draft.1` and `story_draft.2`, type:

    $ *wdiff -s story_draft.1 story_draft.2 | tail -2* ⟨RET⟩

NOTES: The `wdiff` command is not included with all Linux distributions.

8.3.7 Patching a File with a Difference Report

To apply the differences in a difference report to the original file compared in the report, use `patch`. It takes as arguments the name of the file to be patched and the name of the difference report file (or "patchfile"). It then applies the changes specified in the patchfile to the original file. This is especially useful for distributing different versions of a file—small patchfiles may be sent across networks easier than large source files.

⇒ To update the original file `manuscript.old` with the patchfile `manuscript.diff`, type:

    $ *patch manuscript.old manuscript.diff* ⟨RET⟩

8.4 Using File Compression

File compression is useful for storing or transferring large files. When you *compress* a file, you shrink it and save disk space. File compression uses an algorithm to change the data in the file and make it smaller; to use the data that's in a compressed file, you must first *uncompress* it to restore the original data (and original file size).

The `gzip` compression tool has been the popular standard for many years, but recently the newer `bzip2` is seeing increased use. It uses a better compression algorithm—in many cases it can compress files smaller than `gzip` can—but it does this at the expense of taking a little longer to work, in both the compressing and uncompressing processes. Files compressed with `gzip` will uncompress more quickly than files compressed with `bzip2` (but usually, on modern computers, we are talking about a matter of tens of seconds).

The following recipes explain how to compress and uncompress files with both `gzip` and `bzip2`, which work very similarly.

8.4.1 Compressing a File

There are two methods for compressing files. Use `gzip` for speed and compatibility, and use `bzip2` when compression ratio is of the highest importance.

METHOD #1

Use the `gzip` ("GNU zip") tool, giving as arguments the names of any files to compress; it writes compressed versions of the specified files, appends a `.gz` extension to their file names, and then deletes the original files.

⇒ To compress the file **war-and-peace**, type:

    $ gzip war-and-peace (RET)

    This command compresses the file 'codewar-and-peace, putting it in a new file named **war-and-peace.gz**; gzip then deletes the original file, **war-and-peace**.

NOTES: The amount of compression to use can be specified by giving a number in the range from 1 to 9 as an option, with 1 being minimal compression with the fastest compressing speed, and 9 being the best possible compression, at the expense of taking the most amount of time to compress. The default behavior is set to use a value of 6.

    Specifying the ratio used is not necessary during uncompression; files uncompress at the same speed regardless of the data's compression ratio.

    Special options **-fast** and **-best** are synonymous with **-1** and **-9**, respectively.

METHOD #2

Bzip2
  DEB: bzip2
  RPM: bzip2
  WWW: http://sources.redhat.com/bzip2/

Use the `bzip2` tool, giving as arguments the names of any files to compress; it writes compressed versions of the specified files, appends a `.bz2` extension to their file names, and then deletes the original files.

⇒ To compress the file **war-and-peace**, type:

    $ bzip2 war-and-peace (RET)

    This command compresses the file **war-and-peace**, putting it in a new file named **war-and-peace.bz2**; the original file, **war-and-peace**, is then deleted.

8.4.2 Decompressing a File

There are two methods for decompressing a file, depending on the method used to compress it. Files compressed with gzip will have, by default, a .gz file name extension added to the file name, while files compressed with bzip2 will have a default extension of .bz2 added.

METHOD #1

To access the contents of a file compressed with gzip, use gunzip to uncompress (or "decompress") it.

As with gzip, gunzip takes as an argument the name of the file or files to work on. It expands the specified files, writing the output to new files without the .gz extension, and then it deletes the compressed files.

⇒ To expand the file war-and-peace.gz, type:

```
$ gunzip war-and-peace.gz RET
```

This command expands the file war-and-peace.gz and puts it in a new file called war-and-peace; gunzip then deletes the compressed file, war-and-peace.gz.

NOTES: When uncompressing with gunzip, it is not necessary to specify the .gz extension.

You can also view the contents of a file compressed with gzip without uncompressing it first. This is useful when you want to view a compressed file but do not want to write changes to it, and therefore do not need to compress it. Do this either with zless, for gzip-compressed text files (see Recipe 9.1 [Perusing Text], page 211), or with see, which displays text and other files that have been compressed with either gzip or bzip2 style compression (see the following recipe).

METHOD #2

Bzip2
  DEB: bzip2
  RPM: bzip2
  WWW: http://sources.redhat.com/bzip2/

To access the contents of a file compressed with bzip2, use bunzip2 to uncompress it.

As with `bzip2`, `bunzip2` takes as an argument the name of the file or files to work on. It expands the specified files, writing the output to new files without the `.bz2` extension, and then it deletes the compressed files.

⇒ To expand the file `war-and-peace.bz2`, type:

> `$ bunzip2 war-and-peace.bz2` (RET)

This command expands the file `war-and-peace.bz2` and puts it in a new file called `war-and-peace`; `bunzip2` then deletes the compressed file, `war-and-peace.bz2`.

8.4.3 Seeing What's in a Compressed File

Run-mailcap
  DEB: `mime-support`

To see what's in a compressed file without uncompressing the file on disk, use `see`, giving the name of the file as an argument. This is handy when you want to read or look at the contents of a compressed file, but you'd like to keep it compressed after you've looked at it.

`see` can read files compressed by either `gzip` or `bzip2`; if it is a text file, `see` uses `less` to display the file (see Recipe 9.1 [Perusing Text], page 211); if it is a DVI file, `see` shows it with `xdvi`; PostScript, EPS, and PDF files are all viewed in `gv`, if it is installed.

⇒ To view the contents of `full_dossier.pdf.bz2`, type:

> `$ see full_dossier.pdf.bz2` (RET)

NOTES: `see` will not work for compressed images; to view their contents without uncompressing them, use `display`. It can view compressed image file formats (see Recipe 17.1 [Viewing an Image in X], page 407).

The `see` command is not commonly included with some Linux distributions. You can install a copy from the sources on its Debian package page (see Recipe A.4 [Managing DEB Packages], page 709).

8.5 Managing File Archives

An *archive* is a single file that contains a collection of other files, and often directories. Archives are usually used to transfer or make a backup copy of a collection of files and directories—this way, you can work with only one file instead of many. This single file can be easily compressed as explained in the previous section, and the files in the archive retain the structure and permissions of the original files.

Use the `tar` tool to create, list, and extract files from archives.[2] Archives made with `tar` are sometimes called "tar files," "tar archives," or—because all the archived files are rolled into one big file—"tarballs."

The following recipes show how to use `tar` to create an archive, list the contents of an archive, and extract the files from an archive. Two common options used with all three of these operations are `-f` and `-v`: to specify the name of the archive file, use `-f` followed by the file name, and use the `-v` ("verbose") option to have `tar` output the names of files as they are processed. While the `-v` option is not necessary, it lets you observe the progress of your `tar` operation.

NOTES: The name of this tool comes from "tape archive," because it was originally made to write the archives directly to a magnetic tape device. It is still used for this purpose, but today, archives are almost always saved to a file on disk.

For more information about managing archives with `tar`, consult its Info documentation (see Recipe 2.8.5 [Reading an Info Manual], page 48).

8.5.1 Making a File Archive

To create an archive with `tar`, use the `-c` ("create") option and specify the name of the archive file to create with the `-f` option. It's common practice to use a name with a `.tar` extension, such as `my-backup.tar`.

Give as arguments the names of the files to be archived; to create an archive of a directory and all of the files and subdirectories it contains, give the directory's name as an argument.

⇒ To create an archive called `project.tar` from the contents of the `project` directory, type:

    $ tar -cvf project.tar project (RET)

This command creates an archive file called `project.tar` containing the `project` directory and all of its contents. The original `project` directory remains unchanged.

Use the `-z` option to compress the archive as it is being written. This yields the same output as creating an uncompressed archive and then using `gzip` to compress it, but it eliminates the extra step.

---

[2] ZIP archives, popular on other operating systems, are discussed in Recipe 26.7 [Managing ZIP Archives], page 533.

⇒ To create a compressed archive called `project.tar.gz` from the contents of the `project` directory, type:

```
$ tar -zcvf project.tar.gz project ⟨RET⟩
```

This command creates a compressed archive file, `project.tar.gz`, containing the `project` directory and all of its contents. The original `project` directory remains unchanged.

NOTES: When you use the `-z` option, you should specify the archive name with a `.tar.gz` extension and not a `.tar` extension, so the file name shows that the archive is compressed. This is not a requirement, but it serves as a reminder and is the standard practice.

8.5.2 Listing the Contents of an Archive

To list the contents of a `tar` archive without extracting them, use `tar` with the `-t` option.

⇒ To list the contents of an archive called `project.tar`, type:

```
$ tar -tvf project.tar ⟨RET⟩
```

This command lists the contents of the `project.tar` archive. Using the 'code-v option along with the `-t` option causes `tar` to output the permissions and modification time of each file, along with its file name—the same format used by the `ls` command with the `-l` option (see Recipe 5.3.3 [Listing File Attributes], page 136).

Include the `-z` option to list the contents of a compressed archive.

⇒ To list the contents of a compressed archive called `project.tar.gz`, type:

```
$ tar -ztvf project.tar.gz ⟨RET⟩
```

8.5.3 Extracting Files from an Archive

To extract (or *unpack*) the contents of a `tar` archive, use `tar` with the `-x` ("extract") option.

⇒ To extract the contents of an archive called `project.tar`, type:

```
$ tar -xvf project.tar ⟨RET⟩
```

This command extracts the contents of the `project.tar` archive into the current directory.

If an archive is compressed, which usually means it will have a `.tar.gz` or `.tgz` extension, include the `-z` option.

⇒ To extract the contents of a compressed archive called `project.tar.gz`, type:

```
$ tar -zxvf project.tar.gz ⟨RET⟩
```

NOTES: If there are files or subdirectories in the current directory with the same name as any of those in the archive, those files will be overwritten when the archive is extracted. If you don't know what files are included in an archive, consider listing the contents of the archive first as shown in the preceding recipe.

Another reason to list the contents of an archive before extracting them is to determine whether the files in the archive are contained in a directory. If not, and the current directory contains many unrelated files, you might confuse them with the files extracted from the archive.

To extract the files into a directory of their own, make a new directory, move the archive to that directory, and change to that directory, where you can then extract the files from the archive.

8.6 Tracking Revisions to a File

The Revision Control System (RCS) is a set of tools for managing multiple revisions of a single file.

To store a revision of a file so that RCS can keep track of it, you *check in* the file with RCS. This deposits the revision of the file in an RCS *repository*—a file that RCS uses to store all changes to that file. RCS makes a repository file with the same file name as the file you are checking in, but with a `,v` extension appended to the name. For example, checking in the file `foo.text` with RCS creates a repository file called `foo.text,v`.

Each time you want RCS to remember a revision of a file, you run a command to *check in* the file, and RCS writes to that file's RCS repository the *differences* between the file and the last revision on record in the repository.

To access a revision of a file, you *check out* the revision from RCS. The revision is obtained from the file's repository and is written to the current directory.

Although RCS is most often used with text files, you can also use it to keep track of revisions made to other kinds of files, such as image files and sound files.

Another revision control system, Concurrent Versions System (CVS), is used for tracking collections of multiple files whose revisions are made concurrently by multiple authors. While it is not as simple as RCS, it is very popular for managing free software projects on the Internet. For information on using CVS, consult its Info documentation (see Recipe 2.8.5 [Reading an Info Manual], page 48).

8.6.1 Checking In a File Revision

When you have a version of a file that you want to keep track of, use `ci` to check in that file with RCS.

Type *ci* followed by the name of a file to deposit that file into the RCS repository. If the file has never before been checked in, `ci` prompts for a description to use for that file; each subsequent time the file is checked in, `ci` prompts for text to include in the file's revision log (see Recipe 8.6.3 [Viewing a File's Revision Log], page 205). Log messages may contain more than one line of text; type a period (.) on a line by itself to end the entry.

For example, suppose you have a text file `novel` like the one in Figure 8-1.

```
This is a tale about many things, including a long voyage across
America.
```

Figure 8-1. First revision of `novel`.

⇒ To check in the file `novel` with RCS, type:

```
$ ci novel (RET)
novel,v  <--  novel
enter description, terminated with single '.' or
end of file:
NOTE: This is NOT the log message!
>> The Great American Novel. (RET)
>> . (RET)
$
```

This command deposits the file in an RCS repository file called `novel,v`, and the original file, `novel`, is removed. To edit or access the file again, you must check out a revision of the file from RCS to work on (see the next recipe for how to do this).

Whenever you have a new revision that you want to save, use `ci` again to check in the file. This begins the process all over again.

For example, suppose you have checked out the first revision of **novel** and changed the file so that it now looks like Figure 8-2.

> This is a very long tale about a great many things, including my long
> voyage across America, and back home again.

Figure 8-2. A new revision of **novel**.

⇒ To deposit this revision in RCS, type:

```
$ ci novel ⟨RET⟩
novel,v  <-- novel
new revision: 1.2; previous revision: 1.1
enter log message, terminated with single '.' or end of
file:
>> Second draft. ⟨RET⟩
>> . ⟨RET⟩
$
```

If you create a subdirectory called **RCS** (in all uppercase letters) in the current directory, RCS recognizes this specially named directory instead of the current directory as the place to store the **,v** revision files. This helps reduce clutter in your work directory.

If the file you are depositing is a text file, you can have RCS insert a line of text in the file, every time the file is checked out, containing the name of the file, the revision number, the date and time in UTC (Coordinated Universal Time), and the user ID of the author. To do this, put the text "**Id**" at a place in the file where you want this text to be written. You only need to do this once; each time you check the file out, RCS replaces this string in the file with the header text.

For example, this chapter was written to a file, **managing-files.texinfo**, whose revisions were tracked with RCS; the "**Id**" string in this file currently reads:

    $Id: managing-files.texinfo,v 2.12 2004/07/15 21:04:57 m Exp m $

NOTES: You should always make your log message descriptive enough so that later, you won't be confused about what you had done to the file.

8.6.2 Checking Out a File Revision

Use **co** to check out a revision of a file from an RCS repository.

To check out the latest revision of a file that you intend to edit (and to check in later as a new revision), use the `-l` (for "lock") option. Locking a revision in this fashion prevents overlapping changes from being made to the file, should another revision be accidentally checked out before this revision is checked in.

⇒ To check out the latest revision of the file **novel** for editing, type:

> `$ co -l novel` ⟨RET⟩

This command checks out the latest revision of file **novel** from the **novel,v** repository, writing it to a file called **novel** in the current directory. (If a file with that name already exists in the current directory, `co` asks whether or not to overwrite the file.) You can make changes to this file and then check it in as a new revision (see the previous recipe).

You can also check out a version of a file as *read only*, where changes cannot be written to it. Do this to check out a version to view only and not to edit.

To check out the current version of a file for examination, type *co* followed by the name of the file.

⇒ To check out the current revision of file **novel**, but not permit changes to it, type:

> `$ co novel` ⟨RET⟩

This command checks out the latest revision of the file **novel** from the RCS repository **novel,v** (either from the current directory or in a subdirectory named RCS).

To check out a version other than the most recent version, specify the version number to check out with the `-r` option. Again, use the `-l` option to allow the revision to be edited.

⇒ To check out revision 1.14 of file **novel**, type:

> `$ co -l -r1.14 novel` ⟨RET⟩

NOTES: Before checking out an old revision of a file, remember to check in the latest changes first, or they may be lost.

It is possible to make *branching* revisions; otherwise, your old revisions with changes will be checked in as the newest revision on the main "branch" (see the `rcs man` page for more information on branching in `rcs`).

8.6.3 Viewing a File's Revision Log

Use `rlog` to view the RCS revision log for a file—type *rlog* followed by the name of a file to list all of the revisions of that file.

⇒ To view the revision log for file **novel**, type:

```
$ rlog novel ⟨RET⟩

RCS file: novel,v
Working file: novel
head: 1.2
branch:
locks: strict
access list:
symbolic names:
keyword substitution: kv
total revisions: 2;      selected revisions: 2
description:
The Great American Novel.
----------------------------
revision 1.2
date: 1991/06/20 15:31:44;  author: leo;  state: Exp;
  lines: +2 -2
Second draft.
----------------------------
revision 1.1
date: 1991/06/21 19:03:58;  author: leo;  state: Exp;
Initial revision
=========================================================
$
```

This command outputs the revision log for the file **novel**; it lists information about the RCS repository, including its name (**novel,v**) and the name of the actual file (**novel**). It also shows that there are two revisions—the first, which was checked in to RCS on 20 June 1991, and the second, which was checked in to RCS the next day, on 21 June 1991.

8.6.4 Checking In Many Files

There are a few considerations when checking in lots of files at once.

Sometimes you may want to check in a group of files and specify a particular revision number to use. Do this by giving the revision number to use as an argument to the **-r** option. The **ci** command does not take space characters between an option and its argument, so be sure to follow the option immediately with the revision number.

If a file is unchanged, `ci` normally reverts to the last revision; to force a check in, useful for when you want to give a particular revision number to a group of files when some may be unchanged, use the **-f** option.

You can use the Bash **for** directive so that you can check in all of the files at once, and not have to do them individually. Use the -m option to specify a common message to all of them—give the quoted log message as an argument, and again make sure there is no space between the option and the argument.

⇒ To check in all of the `.html` files in the current directory at once, giving each file a log message of "`Updated for new product release`" and a revision number of 3.0, even if the file is unchanged, and then checking out and locking the latest version, type:

```
$ for i in *.html ⟨RET⟩
> { ⟨RET⟩
> ci -f -r3.0 -m"Updated for new product release" $i ⟨RET⟩
> co -l $i ⟨RET⟩
> }
... log messages ...
$
```

You could give the command in the preceding example on one long line, like so:

```
for i in *.html; { ci -f -r3.0 -m"Updated for new product
release" $i; co -l $i; }
```

III. TEXT

## CHAPTER 9

Viewing Text

Dealing with textual matter is the meat of Linux (and of most computing), so there are going to be many chapters about the various aspects of text. This first chapter in this part of the book shows how to *view* text on your display screen.

Text files come in any number of formats, from formatted text in some particular language—such as English or the C programming language—to saved email messages or HTML files. Plain text files don't have to have a `.txt` or `.text` file name extension, although they often do (see Appendix B [Conventional File Name Extensions], page 723).

If you are not sure whether the content of a file is text or not, use `file` to find out, as described in Recipe 8.1.1 [Determining a File's Type and Format], page 187.

A tool that just allows you to view text on the screen, but not edit it, is called a *pager*. When most people view text without editing it, they use `less`, which is described in the following recipes.

There are many ways to view or otherwise output text. For example, you can view text as you browse files and their contents, as described in Recipe 5.10 [Browsing Files and Directories], page 157. When your intention is to edit the text of a file, you should open it in a text editor, as described in Chapter 10 [Editing Text], page 231. The Vi editor comes with a special command, `view`, to open a file in read-only mode with Vi, so that it can only be viewed—you cannot, accidentally or intentionally, make any changes to the file while it is open if you use this command.

Some kinds of files—such as PostScript, DVI, and PDF files—often contain text in them, but they are technically not text files. These are image format files, and I describe methods for viewing them in Recipe 17.4 [Previewing Print Files], page 413.

9.1 Perusing Text

Use `less` to peruse text, viewing it one screen (or "page") at a time. The `less` tool works on either files or standard output—it is popularly used as the last command on a pipeline so that you can page through the text output of some commands. For an example, see Recipe 3.2.4 [Redirecting Output to Another Command's Input], page 69. The following recipes describe various ways to use `less`.

Another tool, `zless`, is identical to `less`, but you use it to view compressed text files; it allows you to read a compressed text file's contents without having to uncompress the file first (see Recipe 8.4 [Using File Compression], page 196). Most of the system documentation in the `/usr/doc` and `/usr/share/doc` directories, for example, consists of compressed text files.

You may, on occasion, be confronted with a reference to a command for paging text, called `more`. It was the standard tool for paging text until it gave way to `less` in the early to mid 1990s; `less` comes with many more options—its most notable advantage being the ability to scroll *backward* through a file—but at the expense of being almost exactly three times the size of `more`. Hence, there are two meanings to the saying, "less is more."

The following table summarizes the most essential keyboard commands for paging through text in `less`. It lists the keystrokes and describes the commands.

Cursor Movement

⟨↑⟩	Scroll back through the text ("up") one line.
⟨↓⟩	Scroll forward through the text ("down") one line.
⟨←⟩ *or* ⟨→⟩	Scroll horizontally (left or right) one tab stop; useful for perusing files that contain long lines.
⟨PgUp⟩ *or* ⟨SPACEBAR⟩	Scroll backward ("up") through the text by one screenful.
⟨PgDn⟩	Scroll forward ("down") through the text by one screenful.
⟨<⟩	Move to the beginning of the file.
⟨>⟩	Move to the end of the file.

Searching Text

⟨/⟩*pattern*	Search forward through the file for lines containing *pattern*.
⟨?⟩*pattern*	Search backward through the file for lines containing *pattern*.

Miscellaneous

(R) or (CTRL)-(L)   Redraw (or "repaint") the screen.

(H)   Display a help screen.

(V)   Open the file in the Vi editor, so you can edit it.
                              (Then, when you write and save it with :wq or just
                              exit with :q, you will be back in less.)

(Q)   Quit viewing the file and exit less.

NOTES: less has many command line options as well as key commands to
be used while running, and there are all kinds of tricks you can do with it—
almost enough for a whole chapter. If this sort of thing interests you, it's
worth reading through the less man page.

9.1.1 Perusing a Text File

To peruse or page through a text file, give the name of the file as an argument
to less.

⇒ To page through the text file README, type:

        $ less README (RET)

This command starts less and displays the file README on the screen.

You can move forward through the document a line at a time by typing
(↓), and you can move forward through the document a screenful at a time
by typing (PgDn). To move backward by a line, type (↑), and type (PgUp) to
move backward by a screenful.

You can also search through the text you are currently perusing—this is
described in Recipe 14.11 [Searching the Text You're Perusing], page 355. To
stop viewing the file and exit less, press (Q).

9.1.2 Perusing Text with a Prompt

When you peruse a text file with less, it displays a default prompt at the
bottom of the screen with the name of the file in inverse video. As soon as
you touch a key, the prompt disappears.

Use the -M option to display a long prompt line, containing the file name,
the current and total lines, and the percentage into the file the current line is
at. This prompt remains as you move through the text.

⇒ To peruse the file **boardreport** with a long prompt, type:

    `$ less -M boardreport` (RET)

NOTES: You can make your own custom prompt, making use of a number of variables that hold information about the file; see the **less man** page for information on how to do this.

9.1.3 Perusing a Text File from the Bottom

Type *F* in **less** to move to the bottom of the text it is displaying, and to have **less** keep reading from its input. This is useful when you are perusing a file that is being written to from some other command, or when you have piped the output of some command to **less**.

When you type *F*, **less** will attempt to keep reading from its input indefinitely, and if any new text appears, **less** will display it. Type (CTRL)-(C) to interrupt this command and have **less** stop reading from the bottom. Normal perusal will resume.

9.1.4 Perusing Raw Text

By default, **less** displays non-printing control characters in hat notation (thus, a (CTRL)-(L) combination in a file is displayed as "^L"), except for control characters used to affect spacing, such as the tab character, which is (CTRL)-(I).

But it is sometimes desirable to display the *raw text*, which is text unprocessed by other methods and unformatted for the screen. Displaying raw text will show any non-printing or control characters, and not give the screen format they represent instead.

So, for example, when the (CTRL)-(L) combination appears in the text, you want a literal formfeed to be shown, and not the representation "^L."

There are two methods to do this.

METHOD #1

To display raw control characters in text, run **less** with the **-r** option. This may, of course, cause any number of problems with screen display, as the raw characters may affect it.

⇒ To peruse the file **live.transcript** and display any raw control characters in it, type:

    `$ less -r live.transcript` (RET)

METHOD #2

To display raw control characters in text, but try to keep the screen appearance, use `less` with the `-R` option. This displays raw control characters, but any disparities that may be caused by the control characters on the screen are controlled, whenever possible.

⇒ To peruse the file `live.transcript` and display any raw control characters in it, but attempt to keep the screen in order, type:

```
$ less -R live.transcript (RET)
```

9.1.5 Perusing Multiple Text Files

There are two methods for perusing multiple text files.

```
Path: senator-bedfellow.mit.edu!faqserv
From: tmatimar@isgtec.com (Ted Timar)
Newsgroups: comp.unix.questions,comp.unix.shell,comp.answers,news.answers
Subject: Unix - Frequently Asked Questions (1/7) [Frequent posting]
Supersedes: <unix-faq/faq/part1_869650053@rtfm.mit.edu>
Followup-To: comp.unix.questions
Date: 31 Jul 1997 07:55:27 GMT
Organization: ISG Technologies, Inc
Lines: 413
Approved: news-answers-request@MIT.Edu
Distribution: world
Expires: 28 Aug 1997 07:55:05 GMT
Message-ID: <unix-faq/faq/part1_870335705@rtfm.mit.edu>
References: <unix-faq/faq/contents_870335705@rtfm.mit.edu>
NNTP-Posting-Host: penguin-lust.mit.edu
X-Last-Updated: 1996/06/11
Originator: faqserv@penguin-lust.MIT.EDU
Xref: senator-bedfellow.mit.edu comp.unix.questions:131651 comp.unix.shell:52166
  comp.answers:27315 news.answers:108512

Archive-name: unix-faq/faq/part1
Version: $Id: part1,v 2.9 1996/06/11 13:07:56 tmatimar Exp $

/usr/doc/FAQ/unix-faq-part1 (file 1 of 7)
```

Figure 9-1. Viewing multiple files in `less`.

METHOD #1

You can specify more than one file to page through with `less`, and you can specify file patterns in order to open all of the files that match that pattern. The files will be displayed in sequence—`less` displays each file in turn, beginning with the first file you specify or the first file that matches the given pattern. To move to the next file, press (N); to move to the previous file, press (P).

⇒ To page through all of the UNIX FAQ files in **/usr/doc/FAQ**, type:

  $ *less /usr/doc/FAQ/unix-faq-part** (RET)

This command starts **less**, which then opens all of the files that match the given pattern **/usr/doc/FAQ/unix-faq-part***, and begins displaying the first one, as in Figure 9-1.

METHOD #2

Another method is to use **cat** to concatenate all the files together, and pipe that output to **less**. There will be no indicator to mark where one file ends and another begins, but you can scroll through the entire text cleanly without pressing buttons to move from file to file.

⇒ To page through all of the UNIX FAQ files in **/usr/doc/FAQ** all at once, type:

  $ *cat /usr/doc/FAQ/unix-faq-part* | less* (RET)

There is no indicator when one file ends and the next begins, but rather, all are treated as one long file in the order given. (In this case, where the wildcard character was used, they are displayed in the order in which the shell expands the "*" to all of their names.)

9.2 Displaying Text

The simplest way to view text is to send it to the standard output. This is useful for displaying part of a text, or for passing part of a text to other tools in a command line.

Many people still use **cat** to view a text file, especially if it is a very small file. To output all of a file's contents on the screen, use **cat** and give the file name as an argument.

⇒ To output the contents of the file **notes**, type:

  $ *cat notes* (RET)

If you have a small text file that you want to look at, you just **cat** it to the screen. It's quick, it gets the job done, you don't have to think about it. But while it is useful for concatenating text (see Recipe 10.6 [Concatenating Text], page 256), it isn't always the best way to peruse or read text—a very large text will scroll off the top of the screen, for example.

Sometimes, simple outputting of text is quite appropriate, such as when you just want to display one line of a file, or when you want to display the first or last part of a file.

This section describes the tools used for such purposes. These tools are best used as filters, often at the end of a pipeline, taking their input from the output of other commands. To display text in a font, first convert it to PostScript and view that (see Recipe 15.2 [Outputting Text to PostScript], page 359).

9.2.1 Displaying Non-Printing Characters

Use `cat` with the `-v` option to output non-printing characters, such as control characters, in such a way that you can see them. With this option, `cat` outputs those characters in *hat notation*, where they are represented by a caret (^) and the letter or other character corresponding to the actual control character (for example, a "Control-G" or bell character would be output as "^G").

⇒ To output the file **translation** with all non-printing characters displayed in hat notation, type:

> `$ cat -v translation` ⟨RET⟩

To visually display the end of each line, use the `-E` option; it specifies that a "$" should be output after the end of each line. This is useful for determining whether lines contain trailing space characters. (You can also use `grep` to output lines containing trailing spaces.)

Also useful is the `-T` option, which outputs tab characters as their literal control character, written in hat notation as "^I."

The `-A` option combines all three of these options—it is the same as specifying `-vET`.

⇒ Here are some ways to use this.

- To output the file **translation** with a "$" character displayed at the end of every line, type:

  > `$ cat -E translation` ⟨RET⟩

- To output the file **translation** with all tab characters written as "^I" instead of literal tabs, type:

  > `$ cat -T translation` ⟨RET⟩

- To output the file **translation** with non-printing characters, including tabs, displayed in hat notation, and with a "$" character displayed at the end of each line, type:

  > `$ cat -A translation` ⟨RET⟩

9.2.2 Displaying the Beginning Part of Text

Use **head** to output the beginning of a text. By default, it outputs the first ten lines of its input.

⇒ To output the first ten lines of file **placement-list**, type:

    $ head placement-list ⟨RET⟩

You can specify as a numeric option the number of lines to output. If you specify more lines than a file contains, **head** just outputs the entire text.

⇒ Here are two ways to use this.

- To output the first line of file **placement-list**, type:

      $ head -1 placement-list ⟨RET⟩

- To output the first 66 lines of file **placement-list**, type:

      $ head -66 placement-list ⟨RET⟩

To output a given number of *characters* (bytes) instead of lines, give the number of characters to output as an argument to the **-c** option.

⇒ To output the first character in the file **placement-list**, type:

    $ head -c1 placement-list ⟨RET⟩

NOTES: An old UNIX tool named **line** just output the first line of its input. This tool does not exist for Linux, but you can make a pretty good imitation with **head** by defining "**line**" as an alias for **head -1** (for more information on making aliases, see Recipe 3.6 [Using Alias Words], page 82).

9.2.3 Displaying the End Part of Text

The **tail** tool works like **head**, but it outputs the last part of its input. Like **head**, it outputs ten lines by default.

⇒ Here are some ways to use this.

- To output the last ten lines of file **placement-list**, type:

      $ tail placement-list ⟨RET⟩

- To output the last 14 lines of file **placement-list**, type:

      $ tail -14 placement-list ⟨RET⟩

- To output the last hundred characters of file **placement-list**, type:

      $ tail -c 100 placement-list ⟨RET⟩

To specify which part of the text to output by its relation to the *beginning* of the text, precede the number with a plus sign (**+**).

⇒ Here are two ways to use this.

- To output the end part of the file `placement-list`, beginning with the third line, type:

    `$ tail +3 placement-list` ⟨RET⟩

- To output the end part of the file `placement-list`, beginning with the hundredth character, type:

    `$ tail -c +100 placement-list` ⟨RET⟩

It is sometimes useful to view the end of a file on a continuing basis; this can be useful for a "growing" file, a file that is being written to by another process. To keep viewing the end of such a file, use `tail` with the `-f` ("follow") option. Type ⟨CTRL⟩-⟨C⟩ to stop viewing the file.

⇒ To follow the end of the file `access_log`, type:

    `$ tail -f access_log` ⟨RET⟩

NOTES: You can achieve the same result with `less`; to do this, type *F* while perusing the text (see Recipe 9.1 [Perusing Text], page 211).

9.2.4 Displaying the Middle Part of Text

There are a few ways to output only a middle portion of a text.

METHOD #1

To output a particular line of a file, use SED (see Recipe 10.5 [Editing Streams of Text], page 255). Give the line number to output followed by `!d` as a quoted argument to `sed`; give the filespec to output from as the second argument.

⇒ To output line 47 of file `placement-list`, type:

    `$ sed '47!d' placement-list` ⟨RET⟩

To output a region of more than one line, give the starting and ending line numbers, separated by a comma.

⇒ To output lines 47 to 108 of file `placement-list`, type:

    `$ sed '47,108!d' placement-list` ⟨RET⟩

METHOD #2

To output the middle part of some text, you can also combine multiple `head` or `tail` commands on a pipeline (see Recipe 3.2.4 [Redirecting Output to Another Command's Input], page 69).

⇒ Here are some ways to use this.

- To output the tenth line in the file **placement-list**, type:

  `$ head placement-list | tail -1` ⟨RET⟩

- To output the fifth and fourth lines from the bottom of file **placement-list**, type:

  `$ tail -5 placement-list | head -2` ⟨RET⟩

- To output the 500th character in **placement-list**, type:

  `$ head -c500 placement-list | tail -c1` ⟨RET⟩

- To output the first character on the fifth line of the file **placement-list**, type:

  `$ head -5 placement-list | tail -1 | head -c1` ⟨RET⟩

In the preceding example, three commands were used: The first five lines of file **placement-list** are passed to **tail**, which outputs the last line in the output (the fifth line in the file); then, the last **head** command outputs the first character in that last line, which achieves the desired result.

9.2.5 Displaying the Text Between Strings

Use SED to select lines of text between strings and output either just that section of text, or all of the lines of text *except* that section. The strings can be words or even regular expressions (see Recipe 14.3 [Matching Patterns of Text], page 335).

Run **sed** with the **-n** option followed by '/*first*/,/*last*/p' to output just the text between the strings *first* and *last*, inclusive. This is useful for outputting, say, just one chapter or section of a text file when you know the text used to begin the sections with.

⇒ To output all the text from file **book-draft** between "**Chapter 3**" and "**Chapter 4**," type:

  `$ sed -n '/Chapter 3/,/Chapter 4/p' book-draft` ⟨RET⟩

To output all of the lines of text *except* those between two patterns, omit the **-n** option.

⇒ To output all the text from file **book-draft**, except that which lies between the text "**Chapter 3**" and "**Chapter 4**," type:

  `$ sed '/Chapter 3/,/Chapter 4/p' book-draft` ⟨RET⟩

NOTES: For more on SED, see Recipe 10.5 [Editing Streams of Text], page 255.

9.2.6 Displaying the Literal Characters of Text

There are tools for displaying literal characters—text formatted so that you can clearly and unambiguously see each character and its position in the file. The following methods show how to use these tools.

METHOD #1

Use od, the "octal dump" tool, with the -c option to show the ASCII characters in some text. This outputs the characters grouped 16 per line, separated by spaces and, when possible, giving backslash escapes for control characters. A column is displayed on the left, containing the *offset* (the number of bytes into the file) of the first character in that line. Use the -A option and give "d" as an argument to output these numbers in decimal and not the default, which is octal.

⇒ Here are some ways to use this.

- To display the literal characters in the file details, grouped 16 per line, with each line prefaced by an offset number, type:

    $ od -Ad -c details ⟨RET⟩

- To output the literal characters in the last line of file details, type:

    $ tail -1 details | od -Ad -c ⟨RET⟩

METHOD #2

You can get the same effect as od with hexdump. Use the -c option, which displays each byte in the file as the character it represents. As with Method #1, 16 characters of the input is displayed on each line, separated by spaces, and a column is written on the left-hand side showing the offset value of the file, except in this case the offset is given in hexadecimal.

⇒ To display the literal characters in the file exam, grouped 16 per line, with each line prefaced by an offset number in hexadecimal, type:

    $ hexdump -c exam ⟨RET⟩

9.2.7 Displaying the Hex Values of Text

All text characters are stored as numeric values on disk (see Recipe 9.3.7 [Viewing a Character Set], page 228). Sometimes you may want to display the values of text characters instead of the characters these values represent. This is good for examining the literal contents of a text file containing non-printing characters, or for displaying the literal characters that make up a binary file.

There are several methods for doing this, each with its own output format. All of them are capable of outputting in hexadecimal (or "hex" for short); these outputs are sometimes called *hex dumps*.

METHOD #1

The `hexdump` filter dumps its input in any one of a number of formats, showing a number of characters from the file per line, and preceded with a number indicating the location in the file of the first character in that line.

To display text in hex, first use the `tr` filter to eliminate carriage returns from the input, and pass this text to `hexdump` with the `-c` option, which displays its input in hexadecimal, with one byte per character. 16 characters of the input are displayed on each line, separated by spaces, and a column is written on the left-hand side showing the offset value of the file, in hexadecimal.

⇒ To peruse the contents of the file `tarpon` in hexadecimal, type:

```
$ tr -d '\r' < tarpon | hexdump -c | less ⟨RET⟩
```

METHOD #2

Use `od`, "octal dump," to make a literal and unambiguous dump of some text. It works as a filter or takes the name of a file as an argument, and can output in octal, hexadecimal, or other formats

Use the `-t` option to specify the format type of the output, and give "x1" as an argument to specify that the display should be in hexadecimal, with one byte per integer (with an argument of "x2," a hex integer is displayed for every *two* bytes of input).

⇒ To peruse the contents of the file `details` in hex, type:

```
$ od -t x1 details | less ⟨RET⟩
```

This command outputs the values of each literal character of the file `details` in hexadecimal, 16 characters per line, separated by spaces. Each line is preceded by an offset value (in octal) indicating the offset in the file of the first character in that line. To change the offset display from octal to decimal, use the `-A` option and give "d" as an argument (or give "x" if you want hex).

To display the printable characters in a new column on the right-hand side of the screen, add a "z" to the end of your argument to the `-t` option. Each line of the column will be prefaced with a greater-than sign (>) and end with a less-than sign (<).

⇒ To peruse the contents of the file **details** in hex, showing the file's printable characters in its own column, type:

> $ *od -t x1z details | less* ⟨RET⟩

METHOD #3

Midnight Commander
  DEB: mc-common
       mc
  RPM: mc
  WWW: http://www.ibiblio.org/mc/

When you view a file in mc, you can toggle the display of hex values. To do
this, type ⟨F3⟩ on a file in the directory listing to view the file, and then type
⟨F4⟩ while viewing the file to toggle between viewing the ASCII characters or
their hex values; type ⟨F10⟩ to exit viewing the file, and type ⟨F10⟩ again to
exit mc.

METHOD #4

To view a hex dump of a buffer in Emacs, use **hexl-mode**.

⇒ To view a hex dump of the current buffer, type:

> ⟨ALT⟩-⟨X⟩ *hexl-mode* ⟨RET⟩

NOTES: This mode is good for viewing and editing binary files in Emacs.

9.3 Viewing Special Types of Text

These are recipes for viewing text formatted in special ways or written in
certain languages.

9.3.1 Viewing HTML-Formatted Text

There are two general methods for viewing HTML-formatted text, depending
on whether you want to view the HTML *source code* (the formatted text itself),
or the *rendered* HTML (the text with the HTML formatting commands applied
to it).

METHOD #1

To view the HTML-formatted text itself, just view it with **less** as with any
text file, as described in Recipe 9.1 [Perusing Text], page 211.

⇒ To view the HTML-formatted text file **homepage.html** as HTML source code, type:

```
$ less homepage.html (RET)
```

METHOD #2

To view an HTML-formatted text file with the HTML formatting applied to the text, open the file in a Web browser as described in Methods #2 and #3 of Recipe 5.10 [Browsing Files and Directories], page 157.

⇒ To view the HTML-formatted text file **homepage.html** as rendered HTML, type:

```
$ mozilla homepage.html (RET)
```

9.3.2 Viewing NROFF-Formatted Text

To view text written in NROFF format, which is intended for use with the TROFF or GROFF text processors, use **man** with the −l option. Give the name of the file to view as an argument (use "−" as the file argument to view the standard input). By default, **man** sends its output to **less** so you can peruse it.

⇒ Here are two ways to use this.

- To view the NROFF file **program.1**, type:

```
$ man -l program.1 (RET)
```

- To convert the NROFF file **program.1** to text, and write that text to a new file **program.txt**, type:

```
$ man -l program.1 > program.txt (RET)
```

In this last example, the new file **program.txt** will contain overstrike characters for boldface text. The original file **program.1** is unaltered.

NOTES: All **man** pages are written in NROFF format, hence the use of that command to view it.

9.3.3 Viewing C Program Source Code

There are at least two methods for viewing C program source code.

METHOD #1

Cutils
 DEB: cutils
 WWW: http://www.sigala.it/sandro/software.html#cutils

Use the `chilight` filter, distributed as part of the Cutils package, to view
C program source code with language highlighting. Given the name of a file
as an argument (or the standard input if the file name is omitted), `chilight`
outputs the C program source code, highlighted in one of a number of formats.
Specify the highlighting format by giving one of the following as an argument
to the `-f` option; the default value is "`tty`."

`ansi_color`	ASCII text with ANSI color.
`ansi_bold`	ASCII text with ANSI bold.
`html_color`	HTML with color highlights.
`html_font`	Monochrome HTML with bold and italic highlights.
`roff`	TROFF input text.
`tty`	ASCII text with overstrikes (the default).

Since ANSI highlights in text consist of non-printing control sequences, to
peruse such output use `less` with the `-R` option (see Recipe 9.1.4 [Perusing
Raw Text], page 214).

⇒ To peruse the C program source code in the file `myprog.c` with colorized
language highlighting, type:

```
$ chilight -f ansi_color myprog.c | less -R (RET)
```

By default, `chilight` sends its output to the standard output. To write to
a file instead, give the file name to write to as an argument to the `-o` option.

⇒ To format the C program source code in the file `myprog.c` as HTML with
color highlighting and write the output to the file `myprog.html`, type:

```
$ chilight -f color_html -o myprog.html myprog.c (RET)
```

METHOD #2

To view C program source code with highlighting, use `enscript` to "pretty-
print" it, as described in Recipe 15.2.4 [Outputting Text with Language High-
lighting], page 365.

This method outputs the text in PostScript, which you then view or print. It also works with many other languages and formats, and not just C—see the table in the aforementioned recipe.

⇒ To display the C program source code in the file `myprog.c` as PostScript with language highlighting, type:

> `$ enscript -Ec -o i myprog.c | gv -` ⟨RET⟩

In this example, the `gv` command was used to display the `enscript` output.

9.3.4 Viewing Lines of Sorted Text

Use `look` to display certain lines of a sorted text file. It performs a fast search on a sorted file, so it is particularly useful for viewing lines from large, sorted lists. Give as arguments the text to match at the beginning of lines, and the name of the file to read from.

⇒ To display all lines of the sorted file `catalog` that begin with the text "DOT," type:

> `$ look DOT catalog` ⟨RET⟩

If the text to match contains spaces, quote it.

⇒ To display all lines of the sorted file `parts-list` that begin with the text "Part No. 42," type:

> `$ look "Part No. 42" parts-list` ⟨RET⟩

NOTES: Without a second argument, `look` uses the system dictionary. This is described in Recipe 11.2.1 [Listing Words That Match a Pattern], page 283.

9.3.5 Viewing Underlined Text

Plain text can be underlined by inserting, after each character to be underlined, a backspace character ("Control-H"), followed by an underscore character (_). When sent to a printer, the printer will first print the original character, then backspace over it and print an underscore beneath it. This type of underlining is called *overstrike-style* underlining, or *backspace underlining* (see Recipe 13.9 [Underlining Text], page 327).

If you use a tool like `cat` to output such text to the standard output, you will see the underscore characters on your display, but not the characters they are meant to underline—the backspace characters will have already erased them. (But if you pipe `cat`'s standard output to a file or some other command, all characters in the original input are retained.)

There are a few methods for viewing text containing backspace underlines in different ways.

METHOD #1

Use `less` to peruse text containing backspace underlines (see Recipe 9.1 [Perusing Text], page 211).

⇒ To peruse the file `term-paper` so that you can view any backspace underlines it contains, type:

```
$ less term-paper RET
```

METHOD #2

Use the `ul` tool to output text containing backspace underlines, so that these underlines are displayed correctly on your terminal.

⇒ To output the file `term-paper` so that you can view underlined text, type:

```
$ ul term-paper RET
```

This command converts any backspace underlines in `term-paper` to character sequences that your terminal can display; thus, if you have `cat` or some other command further on a pipeline, the text will be displayed properly on your screen.

⇒ To output the file `term-paper` with `cat`, showing any underlined text on your terminal, type:

```
$ ul term-paper | cat RET
```

METHOD #3

Use `colcrt` to convert backspace underlining to *dashing* (a row of hyphen characters, like "------") drawn beneath the underlined text.

⇒ To output the file `term-paper`, with all backspace underlining converted to dashing, type:

```
$ colcrt term-paper RET
```

Dashing inserts a new line in the text directly underneath any underlined text, and this is not always desirable. Use the - option to supress underlining entirely, and display any underlined text as plain text.

⇒ To output the file `term-paper`, with all backspace underlining removed, type:

```
$ colcrt - term-paper RET
```

9.3.6 Listing Text in Binary Files

Use **strings** to output any printable text contained in a binary file. Give the name of the file to search as an argument, and all non-text strings are sent to the standard output. Sometimes, filtering the text through **fmt** improves the display.

⇒ Here are some ways to use this.

- To save any text strings in the file **table.com** to the file **table.txt**, type:

  `$ strings table.com > table.txt` ⟨RET⟩

- To peruse any text strings in the file **table.com**, type:

  `$ strings table.com | less` ⟨RET⟩

- To peruse the formatted output of any text strings in the file **table.com**, type:

  `$ strings table.com | fmt | less` ⟨RET⟩

9.3.7 Viewing a Character Set

A *character set* is a specification that shows the numeric coding that represents each character in the set. ASCII, the American Standard Code for Information Interchange, is a character set that was invented in the early 1960s by Robert W. Bemer, and it is still the standard character set used in computing today. Other character sets are also available. The default Linux character set, the ISO 8859-1 ("Latin 1") character set, is a "dialect" of ASCII, containing all of the standard ASCII character set plus an additional 128 characters. These additional characters are sometimes called *extended characters*.

Several character sets have their own manual pages; to view one of these character sets, view its corrsponding manual page (see Recipe 2.8.4 [Reading a Page from the System Manual], page 46).

To view a chart listing all of the valid characters in the ASCII character set and the character codes to use to type them, view the **ascii man** page.

⇒ To view an ASCII character set, type:

  `$ man ascii` ⟨RET⟩

This displays the values of each character in octal, decimal, and hexadecimal, and also displays their escape codes. These values can be useful for quoting special characters.

The **iso_8859_1 man** page contains the entire ISO 8859-1 character set, including all extended characters above the standard 127 ASCII characters.

⇒ To view the ISO 8859-1 character set, type:

```
$ man iso_8859_1 ⟨RET⟩
```

You can use this page to see all of the characters in this character set and how to input them.

NOTES: There's a special way to "quote" these characters in Emacs; this technique is described in Recipe 10.1.4 [Inserting Special Characters in Emacs], page 239.

The `miscfiles` package also contains charts for these character sets, as explained in Recipe 11.4 [Using Word Lists and Reference Files], page 289.

## CHAPTER 10

Editing Text

Editing text is one of the most fundamental activities of computing on Linux-based systems, or most any computer for that matter. We edit text when writing a document, sending email, making a Web page, posting an article for Usenet, programming—and the list goes on.

Most editing of text is done in a *text editor*, which is an application that generally opens a file containing some text and lets you rearrange, insert, delete and otherwise edit that text. People spend a good deal of their computing time editing text with a text editor application.

In this chapter, I give introductions to the two most popular text editors out there. I also cover other essential or handy ways to edit text without an editor, including concatenation, file inclusion, and cutting and pasting with the mouse.

There are a lot of text editors to choose from, but everyone knows there are really only two choices: Emacs and Vi. The majority of editors are found under one of these two main branches; more programs may have been influenced by Emacs than by any other application, and almost every UNIX system in the world has some version of Vi installed. Most users prefer one or the other; rarely is one adept at both. Many tools and applications have special modes in which the keystroke commands of Emacs and Vi are recognized, including the Bash shell (see Chapter 3 [The Shell], page 53).

Sections in this chapter are devoted to both. Newcomers, you'll do well to spend a half-hour with each of these editors, setting aside time to try the built-in tutorials. Then, go with the one that resonates.

Emacs and Vi are not like the kind of program you are likely to be familiar with, and some newcomers might seem baffled at first—but they're really not difficult to use, and the experience pays off greatly. Anyone who has experience with either of them knows that one can do much more, and more quickly, in such an editor than with any "word processors" that are out there on other systems. If you run the tutorial for both Emacs and Vi, you can get a feel for how they work, and see which might be good for you (the ways to run them are explained in Recipe 10.1.2 [Running an Emacs Tutorial], page 237 and Recipe 10.2.2 [Running a Vi Tutorial], page 247) .

Of course, there are other editors, and many have their devout followers; it is worth having a look at what is available. If you are accustomed to some particular editor on some other system, the chances are great that a "clone" of it exists for Linux. For example, there are editors that work similarly to the

EDIT program in DOS, or the old WordStar word processor (there is a special mode in Emacs, `wordstar-mode`, which emulates its key bindings). A list of other recommended editors concludes the chapter.

10.1 Using Emacs

GNU Emacs
  DEB: `emacsen-common`
       `emacs21`
  RPM: `emacs`
  WWW: `http://www.emacs.org/`

To call Emacs but a text editor does not do it justice—it's a large application capable of performing many functions, including reading email and Usenet news, browsing the World Wide Web, and even perfunctory psychoanalysis (for proof, see Recipe 30.7 [Undergoing Psychoanalysis], page 594).

There are two major variants of Emacs, with a number of minor branches and alternates. GNU Emacs is distributed by the FSF as part of its "GNU system," and is the original Emacs. XEmacs (formerly Lucid Emacs) is an alternate version. It offers essentially the same features GNU Emacs does, but also contains its own features for use with the X Window System (it also behaves differently from GNU Emacs in some minor ways).

GNU Emacs and XEmacs are by far the most popular emacsen (as they are referred to in number); other flavors include JED (see Recipe 10.8 [Using Other Text Editors], page 263) and Chet's Emacs (`ce`), developed by a programmer at Case Western Reserve University. GNU Emacs is the flavor of Emacs assumed in the recipes that follow, but in principle they should work with most any Emacs variant.

First is a brief introduction to using Emacs, interspersed with the necessary Emacs jargon; that is followed by recipes that describe how to use some of Emacs's unique editing features.

10.1.1 Getting Acquainted with Emacs

The fastest way to get acquainted with Emacs is to start it and try to do some basic editing.

You start Emacs in the usual way, either by choosing it from the menu supplied by your window manager in X, or by typing its name (in lowercase letters) at a shell prompt. Give the name of any files as arguments to open them in Emacs for editing.

⇒ Here are two ways to do this.

- To start GNU Emacs at a shell prompt, type:

  $ *emacs* ⟨RET⟩

- To start XEmacs at a shell prompt, opening a file named `journal`, type:

  $ *xemacs journal* ⟨RET⟩

Upon startup in X, a typical GNU Emacs window looks like Figure 10-1 (the client window will differ depending on your window manager).

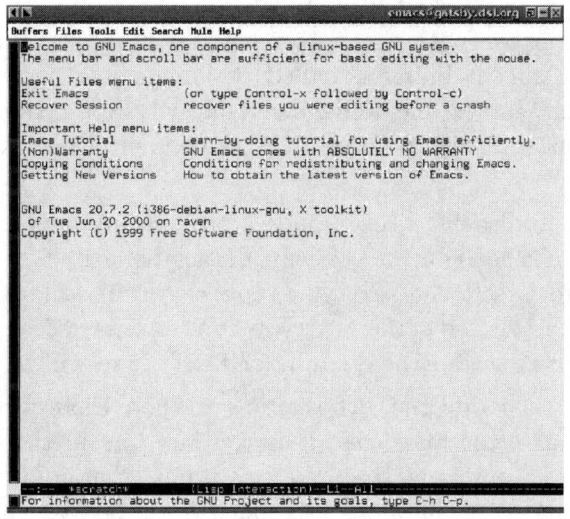

Figure 10-1. Emacs upon startup.

The welcome message appears when Emacs first starts, and it tells you, among other things, how to run a tutorial (which we'll look at in just a minute). The bar running along the entire left-hand side of the window is called the *scroll bar*. The X client window in which an Emacs session is displayed (or the terminal screen, when not running in an X window) is called the *frame*. Notice that there is no border along the sides (if you look closely, you can see that even the side with the scroll bar is lacking a border); that is because many of today's window managers, including the one in the illustration, only draw borders on the top and bottom sides of a window.

The top bar is called the *menu bar*, and you can pull down its menus with the mouse by left-clicking a menu and then dragging it down. When you run Emacs in a terminal, you can't use the mouse to pull down the menus, but you can access and choose the same menu items in a text menu window by typing ⟨F10⟩.[1]

A file or other text open in Emacs is held in its own area called a *buffer*. By default, the current buffer appears in the large area underneath the menu bar. To write text in the buffer, simply type it. The place in the buffer where the cursor sits is called *point*, and is referenced by many Emacs commands.

The filled-in area on the scroll bar represents the text that is displayed in the window in relation to the rest of the buffer. Thus, the scroll bar will be filled completely in a new, small, or empty buffer (as in the illustration), and when you are near the bottom of a very large buffer, only a tiny portion near the bottom of the scroll bar will be filled.

The horizontal bar near the bottom of the Emacs window and directly underneath the current buffer is called the *mode line*; it gives information about the current buffer, including its name, what percentage of the buffer fits on the screen, what line point is on, and whether or not the buffer is saved to a file.

The mode line also lists the modes active in the buffer. Emacs *modes* are general states that control the way Emacs behaves—for example, when `overwrite-mode` is set, the text you type *overwrites* the text at point; in `insert-mode` (the default), the text you type is *inserted* at point. Usually, either `fundamental-mode` (the default) or `text-mode` will be listed.

Just beneath the mode line is the *echo area* where Emacs writes brief status messages, such as error messages; it is the last line in the Emacs window. When you type a command that requires input, that input is requested in this area (and when that happens, the place you type your input, in the echo area, is then called the *minibuffer*). If you look closely, you can see that it has its own scroll bar, too.

Emacs makes extensive use of ⟨CTRL⟩ and ⟨ALT⟩ key combinations. Because Emacs is different in culture from the editors and approach of the Microsoft Windows and Apple MACOS world, it has gotten a rather unfounded reputation in those corners that it is odd and difficult to use. This is not so. The keyboard commands to run its various functions are designed for ease of use and easy recall—once you get used to this concept, you can type these key combinations very quickly.

In Emacs notation, these keypresses are written a certain way. Many commands are begun by typing ⟨CTRL⟩-⟨X⟩, which is written "C-x" (the command to exit Emacs, for example, is ⟨CTRL⟩-⟨X⟩ ⟨CTRL⟩-⟨C⟩, and is written "C-x C-c.")

---

[1] The ⟨F10⟩ key also works in X, where it behaves the same as in a terminal.

Functions are prefaced by ⟨ALT⟩-⟨X⟩, which in Emacs is written as "M-x."[2] You can toggle various modes on or off by functions.

For example, you can make the menu bar appear or disappear by toggling `menu-bar-mode`. Typing ⟨F10⟩ to activate the menu pull-downs works whether `menu-bar-mode` is on or off; if it's off, the menu choices will appear in a new buffer window.

You can run any Emacs function by typing ⟨ALT⟩-⟨X⟩ followed by the function name and pressing ⟨RET⟩.

⇒ To run the `menu-bar-mode` function, thus turning off the top menu bar, type:

    ⟨ALT⟩-⟨X⟩ `menu-bar-mode` ⟨RET⟩

(If the menu bar is already turned off, running this function will turn it back on.)

Type ⟨CTRL⟩-⟨G⟩ in Emacs to quit a function or command that you are typing; if you make a mistake when typing a command, this is useful for canceling and aborting the keyboard input.

The `find-file` function prompts for the name of a file and opens a copy of the file in a new buffer; its keyboard accelerator is ⟨CTRL⟩-⟨X⟩ ⟨CTRL⟩-⟨F⟩ (you can keep ⟨CTRL⟩ depressed while you press and release the ⟨X⟩ and ⟨F⟩ keys).

⇒ To run the `find-file` function, type:

    ⟨ALT⟩-⟨X⟩ `find-file` ⟨RET⟩

This command runs the `find-file` function, which prompts for the name of a file and opens a copy of the file in a new buffer.

Emacs can have more than one buffer open at once. Any file names you give as an argument to `emacs` will open in separate buffers:

    $ `emacs diary etc/todo etc/rolo` ⟨RET⟩

(You can also make new buffers and open files in buffers later, of course.)

Just as functions are prefaced by the ⟨ALT⟩-⟨X⟩ keystroke, many commands are prefaced by the similar ⟨CTRL⟩-⟨X⟩ keystroke, particularly commands that work on buffers, files, or have to do with exiting Emacs.

To switch between buffers, type ⟨CTRL⟩-⟨X⟩ ⟨CTRL⟩-⟨B⟩. Then, give the name of the buffer to switch to, followed by ⟨RET⟩; alternatively, type ⟨RET⟩ without a buffer name to switch to the last buffer you visited. (Viewing a buffer in Emacs is called *visiting* the buffer.)

---

[2] Technically, this refers to the ⟨META⟩ key. Chances are that your keyboard has an ⟨ALT⟩ key and no ⟨META⟩ key, though, in which case you use ⟨ALT⟩ to type it, so I've used ⟨ALT⟩ to notate this key (see Recipe 1.2 [Typographical Conventions], page 6).

⇒ To switch to a buffer called `todo`, type:

⟨CTRL⟩-⟨X⟩ ⟨CTRL⟩-⟨B⟩ *todo* ⟨RET⟩

If a buffer does not exist, Emacs will make a new buffer with the name you give.

When you start Emacs, a special buffer named ***scratch*** exists, which you can use for writing notes and other things you don't want to save; its contents aren't saved, and the next time you run Emacs the ***scratch*** buffer will be empty again.

⇒ To switch to the ***scratch*** buffer, type:

⟨CTRL⟩-⟨X⟩ ⟨CTRL⟩-⟨B⟩ **scratch** ⟨RET⟩

To write some text in the current buffer, just type it. Text you type is inserted at point.

⇒ To insert a line of text at point in the current buffer, type:

This is how to type in Emacs. ⟨RET⟩

Close a buffer by *killing* it with the ⟨CTRL⟩-⟨X⟩ k command. Emacs asks for the name of the buffer to kill in the minibuffer. The default is the current buffer; just pressing ⟨RET⟩ will kill it. If the contents of the buffer is from a file, and the buffer contains unsaved work, Emacs will ask you to confirm killing the buffer. If it's the ***scratch*** buffer or a new buffer whose contents has never been written to a file, C command will kill it without asking.

⇒ To kill ***scratch*** when it's the current buffer, type:

⟨CTRL⟩-⟨X⟩ k ⟨RET⟩
`Kill buffer: (default *scratch*)` ⟨RET⟩

Now that we have run through the essential Emacs terminology, I'll show you how to exit the program.

To *kill* Emacs, use ⟨CTRL⟩-⟨X⟩ ⟨CTRL⟩-⟨C⟩ which also gives you a chance to save any unsaved buffers before Emacs is killed. You can also type ⟨CTRL⟩-⟨Z⟩ to *suspend* Emacs as a background job, so that you can return to it later (see Recipe 3.3.3 [Putting a Job in the Foreground], page 73). In X, ⟨CTRL⟩-⟨Z⟩ does not suspend Emacs but rather it *iconifies* the Emacs window. Deiconify it to bring it back (see Recipe 4.3.5 [Deiconifying an X Window], page 107).

⇒ Here are some ways to use this.

- To kill Emacs, with a chance to save any unsaved buffers first, type:

  ⟨CTRL⟩-⟨X⟩ ⟨CTRL⟩-⟨C⟩ ⟨RET⟩

- To suspend Emacs when you are running it in the console, type:

  ⟨CTRL⟩-⟨Z⟩

- To iconify Emacs when you are running it in X, type:
  $\boxed{\text{CTRL}}$-$\boxed{\text{Z}}$

10.1.2 Running an Emacs Tutorial

Emacs comes with an interactive, self-paced tutorial that teaches you how to use the basics. In my experience, setting aside 25 minutes to go through the tutorial is one of the best things you can do in your computing career. Even if you decide that you don't like Emacs very much, a great many other applications use Emacs-like keyboard commands and heuristics, so familiarizing yourself with them will always pay off. At any time when you are in Emacs you can use the $\boxed{\text{CTRL}}$-$\boxed{\text{H}}$ *t* command to start the tutorial.

⇒ To start the Emacs tutorial, type:
   $\boxed{\text{CTRL}}$-$\boxed{\text{H}}$ *t*

This command opens the tutorial, a special read-only file, into its own buffer.

NOTES: Incidentally, $\boxed{\text{CTRL}}$-$\boxed{\text{H}}$ is the Emacs help key; all help-related commands begin with this key. For example, to read the *Emacs* FAQ, type $\boxed{\text{CTRL}}$-$\boxed{\text{H}}$ *F*, and to run the Info documentation browser (which contains *The* GNU *Emacs Manual*), type $\boxed{\text{CTRL}}$-$\boxed{\text{H}}$ *i*.

10.1.3 Using Basic Emacs Editing Keys

Anything you type in Emacs is called a *key sequence*, and when you type a sequence that is *bound* to a command, it runs that command.

The following table lists basic editing keys and describes their functions. Where two common keystrokes are available for a function, both are given.

Moving Point

$\boxed{\uparrow}$ or $\boxed{\text{CTRL}}$-$\boxed{\text{P}}$	Move point up to the previous line.
$\boxed{\downarrow}$ or $\boxed{\text{CTRL}}$-$\boxed{\text{N}}$	Move point down to the next line.
$\boxed{\leftarrow}$ or $\boxed{\text{CTRL}}$-$\boxed{\text{B}}$	Move point *back* (to the left) through the buffer one character.
$\boxed{\rightarrow}$ or $\boxed{\text{CTRL}}$-$\boxed{\text{F}}$	Move point *forward* (to the right) through the buffer one character.
$\boxed{\text{ALT}}$-$\boxed{\text{F}}$	Move point forward one *word*.

(continued)
Moving Point

⟨ALT⟩–⟨B⟩   Move point backward one *word*.

⟨ALT⟩–⟨↑⟩   Move point back to the next start-of-paragraph.

⟨ALT⟩–⟨↓⟩   Move point forward to the next end-of-paragraph.

⟨PgUp⟩ or ⟨CTRL⟩–⟨V⟩   Move point forward through the buffer one screenful.

⟨PgDn⟩ or ⟨ALT⟩–⟨V⟩   Move point backward through the buffer one screenful.

⟨CTRL⟩–⟨A⟩   Move point to the beginning of the current line.

⟨CTRL⟩–⟨E⟩   Move point to the end of the current line.

⟨CTRL⟩–⟨L⟩   Re-center the text in the Emacs window, placing the line where point is in the middle of the screen.

Inserting and Deleting

⟨INS⟩   Toggle `overwrite-mode`.

⟨CTRL⟩–⟨T⟩   Transpose the character at point with the character to the left of point.

⟨ALT⟩–⟨T⟩   Transpose the *word* at point with the word to the left of point.

⟨BKSP⟩ or ⟨CTRL⟩–⟨H⟩   Delete character to the left of point.

⟨DEL⟩ or ⟨CTRL⟩–⟨D⟩   Delete character to the right of point.

Cutting and Pasting

⟨SHIFT⟩–⟨INS⟩ or ⟨CTRL⟩–⟨Y⟩   Yank text in the kill ring at point (see Recipe 10.3.2 [Pasting Text], page 254).

⟨CTRL⟩–⟨SPACEBAR⟩   Set mark (see Recipe 10.3.1 [Cutting Text], page 254).

⟨CTRL⟩–⟨_⟩   Undo the last action (control-underscore).

⟨CTRL⟩–⟨K⟩   Kill text from point to end of line.

⟨CTRL⟩–⟨W⟩   Kill text from mark to point.

Getting Help

⟨CTRL⟩-⟨H⟩ t   Start the Emacs tutorial.

⟨CTRL⟩-⟨H⟩ k *keystroke*   Describe *keystroke*.

⟨CTRL⟩-⟨H⟩ a *function*   List all Emacs commands related to *function*.
⟨RET⟩

⟨CTRL⟩-⟨H⟩ F   Open a copy of the *Emacs FAQ* in a new buffer.

⟨CTRL⟩-⟨H⟩ i   Start Info.

Command Operations

⟨CTRL⟩-⟨G⟩   Cancel the current command.

⟨CTRL⟩-⟨U⟩ *number*   Repeat the next command or keystroke you type
                               number times.

File Operations

⟨CTRL⟩-⟨X⟩ ⟨CTRL⟩-⟨C⟩   Save all buffers open in Emacs, and then exit the
                               program.

⟨CTRL⟩-⟨X⟩ ⟨CTRL⟩-⟨F⟩   Open *file* in a new buffer for editing. To create a
file ⟨RET⟩   new file that does not yet exist, just specify the file
                               name you want to give it. To browse through your
                               files, type ⟨TAB⟩ instead of a file name.

Special Menus

⟨CTRL⟩-*left-click*   Display a menu of all open buffers, sorted by major
                               mode (works in X only).

⟨SHIFT⟩-*left-click*   Display a font selection menu (works in X only).

10.1.4 Inserting Special Characters in Emacs

There are some characters that you cannot normally type into an Emacs
buffer. For example, in a text file, you can specify a page break by inserting
the formfeed character, ASCII ⟨CTRL⟩-⟨L⟩ or octal code 014; when you print a
file with formfeeds, the current page is ejected at this character and printing
is resumed on a new page.

However, ⟨CTRL⟩-⟨L⟩ has meaning as an Emacs command. To insert a
character like this, use the `quoted-insert` function, ⟨CTRL⟩-⟨Q⟩. It takes
either the literal keystroke of the character you want to insert, or the octal
code of that character. It inserts the character at point.

⇒ Here are two ways to use this.

- To insert a formfeed character at point by specifying its actual keystroke (⟨CTRL⟩-⟨L⟩), type:

  ⟨CTRL⟩-⟨Q⟩ ⟨CTRL⟩-⟨L⟩

- To insert a formfeed character at point by specifying its octal character code, type:

  ⟨CTRL⟩-⟨Q⟩ *014* ⟨RET⟩

The preceding examples both do the same thing: They insert a formfeed character at point.

An interesting use of ⟨CTRL⟩-⟨Q⟩ is to underline text. To do this, insert a literal ⟨CTRL⟩-⟨H⟩ character followed by an underscore (_) after each character you want to underline.

⇒ To underline the character before point, type:

  ⟨CTRL⟩-⟨Q⟩ ⟨CTRL⟩-⟨H⟩ _

You can then use `ul` to output the text to the screen (see Recipe 13.9 [Underlining Text], page 327).

Another kind of special character insert you might want to make is for accented characters and other characters used in various languages.

There are two methods for inserting them in a buffer.

METHOD #1

To insert an accented character, use `iso-accents-mode`. When this mode is active, you can type a special accent character followed by the character to be accented, and the proper accented character will be inserted at point.

The following table shows the special accent characters and the key combinations to use.

Prefix . . .	*Plus This Letter*	*Yields This Result*
"	a	ä
"	e	ë
"	i	ï
"	o	ö
"	u	ü
"	s	ß
'	a	á
'	e	é

(continued)

Prefix . . .	Plus This Letter	Yields This Result
'	i	í
'	o	ó
'	u	ú
`	a	à
`	e	è
`	i	ì
`	o	ò
`	u	ù
~	a	ã
~	c	ç
~	d	đ
~	n	ñ
~	t	t̃
~	u	ũ
~	<	«
~	>	»
~	!	¡
~	?	¿
^	a	â
^	e	ê
^	i	î
^	o	ô
^	u	û
/	a	å
/	e	æ
/	o	ø

⇒ To write the text "`Emacs ist spaß!`" at point in the current buffer, type:

   ⟨ALT⟩-⟨X⟩ `iso-accents-mode` ⟨RET⟩
   `Emacs ist spa"ss!`

In the event that you want to type the literal key combinations that make up an accented character in a buffer where you have `iso-accents-mode` on, type the prefix character twice.

⇒ To type the text "`'o`" (and not the accent character ó) in a buffer while `iso-accents-mode` is on, type:

   `''o`

METHOD #2

To insert accented characters and other special language characters in a buffer without entering `iso-accents-mode`, use ⟨CTRL⟩-⟨X⟩ ⟨8⟩ followed by the special key combination of accent prefix and character, as described in the previous table.

Non-letter characters do not require the accent prefix with this method.

⇒ To write the text "¡Hasta Mañana!" at point in the current buffer, type:

⟨CTRL⟩-⟨X⟩ ⟨8⟩ ⟨!⟩*Hasta Ma*⟨CTRL⟩-⟨X⟩ ⟨8⟩ ⟨~⟩*nana!*

NOTES: When a buffer contains accented characters, it can no longer be saved as plain ASCII text, but must instead be saved as text in the ISO-8859-1 character set (see Recipe 9.3.7 [Viewing a Character Set], page 228). When you save a buffer, Emacs will notify you that it must do this.

Recently, a number of internationalization functions have been added to GNU Emacs. A complete discussion of their use is beyond the scope of this book; for more information on this topic, consult the "International Character Set Support" section of *The GNU Emacs Manual*.

10.1.5 Making Abbreviations in Emacs

An *abbrev* is a word that is an *abbreviation* of a (usually) longer word or phrase. Abbrevs exist as a convenience to you—you can define abbrevs to expand to a long phrase that is inconvenient to type, or you can define a misspelling that you tend to make to expand to its correct spelling. Abbrevs only expand when you have `abbrev-mode` enabled.

⇒ To turn on `abbrev-mode`, type:

⟨ALT⟩-⟨X⟩ *abbrev-mode* ⟨RET⟩

To define an abbrev, type the abbrev you want to use and then type ⟨CTRL⟩-⟨X⟩ *aig*. Emacs will prompt in the minibuffer for the text you want the abbrev to expand to; type that text and then type ⟨RET⟩.

- To define "ww" as an abbrev for "Walla Walla, Washington," do the following:

  1. First, type the abbrev itself:

     ww

  2. Next, specify that this text is to be an abbrev; type:

     ⟨CTRL⟩-⟨X⟩ *aig*

3. Now type the text to expand it to:

`Global expansion for "ww": Walla Walla, Washington` ⟨RET⟩

Now, whenever you type the text "`ww`" followed by a whitespace or punctuation character in the current buffer, that text will expand to the text "`Walla Walla, Washington`."

To save the abbrevs you have defined so that you can use them later, use the **`write-abbrev-file`** function. This saves all of the abbrevs currently defined to a file that you can read in a future Emacs session. (You can also open the file in a buffer and edit the abbrevs if you like.)

⇒ To save the abbrevs you have currently defined to the file `~/.abbrevs`, type:

⟨ALT⟩-⟨X⟩ `write-abbrev-file` ⟨RET⟩ `~/.abbrevs` ⟨RET⟩

Then, in a future Emacs session, you can use the **`read-abbrev-file`** function to define those abbrevs for that session.

⇒ To read the abbrevs from the file `~/.abbrevs`, and define them for the current session, type:

⟨ALT⟩-⟨X⟩ `read-abbrev-file` ⟨RET⟩ `~/.abbrevs` ⟨RET⟩

NOTES: Emacs mode commands are toggles. So to turn off `abbrev-mode` in a buffer, just type ⟨ALT⟩-⟨X⟩ `abbrev-mode` ⟨RET⟩ again. If you turn `abbrev-mode` on in that buffer later on during the Emacs session, the abbrevs will be remembered and will expand again.

10.1.6 Recording and Running Macros in Emacs

A *macro* is like a recording of a sequence of keystrokes—when you run a macro, Emacs executes that key sequence as if you had typed it.

To begin recording a macro, type ⟨CTRL⟩-⟨X⟩ (. Then, everything you type is recorded as the macro until you stop recording by typing ⟨CTRL⟩-⟨X⟩). After you have recorded a macro, you can play it back at any time during the Emacs session by typing ⟨CTRL⟩-⟨X⟩ e. You can precede it with the **`universal-argument`** command, ⟨CTRL⟩-⟨U⟩, to specify a number of times to play it back.

⇒ Here are some ways to use this.

- To record a macro that capitalizes the first word of the current line (⟨ALT⟩-⟨C⟩ capitalizes the word to the right of point) and then advances to the next line, type:

⟨CTRL⟩-⟨X⟩ (⟨CTRL⟩-⟨A⟩ ⟨ALT⟩-⟨C⟩
⟨CTRL⟩-⟨N⟩ ⟨CTRL⟩-⟨X⟩)

- To play the macro back 20 times, type:

  $\langle$CTRL$\rangle$-$\langle$U$\rangle$ *20* $\langle$CTRL$\rangle$-$\langle$X$\rangle$ *e*

NOTES: Macros are fundamental to how Emacs works—in fact, the name Emacs is derived from "Editing MACroS," because the first version of Emacs in 1976 was actually a collection of such macros written for another text editor.

10.1.7 Viewing Multiple Emacs Buffers at Once

You can divide an Emacs frame into multiple *windows*, each displaying its own buffer. This is useful for viewing parts of more than one buffer at the same time. It's also useful when you have a long buffer, and you would like to look at one part of it while you edit another—if you split the frame in two, you can move to the text you want to view in one window, and edit a different part of it in another.

Use $\langle$CTRL$\rangle$-$\langle$X$\rangle$ *2* to split the current frame into two windows, one on top of the other, and use $\langle$CTRL$\rangle$-$\langle$X$\rangle$ *3* to split it vertically, making two windows side-by-side. By default, the current buffer is displayed in both windows, but you can always change the buffer displayed in any window. In X, use the mouse to adjust the size of either window—left-click on the mode line of a window, and drag it to adjust the size of that window.

Switch to different windows by either using the mouse pointer to position point, and then left-clicking, or by typing $\langle$CTRL$\rangle$-$\langle$X$\rangle$ *o*, which switches to another window. This comes in handy when you need to repeatedly kill selections of text from one part of a long file to another: Cut the text in one window, and in the other, yank it into position. When you have many selections to kill and yank, this method saves time.

Use $\langle$CTRL$\rangle$-$\langle$X$\rangle$ *1* to remove the multiple windows and make the frame one single window again.

10.2 Using Vi

Nvi
 DEB: nvi
 RPM: nvi
 WWW: http://www.bostic.com/vi/
 WWW: http://vasc.ri.cmu.edu/old_help/Editors/Vi/

The following recipes work for the Vi editor. Its name, pronounced "vye," or sometimes "vee-eye," is short for *visual*; when it was first invented, it was among the first text editors to visually display the text on the entire screen for interactive editing (other interactive editors of the time typically displayed files line by line).

As with Emacs, there are many variants of Vi; a few of the more popular ones today are Vim and Elvis, both newer implementations that have many more features than the original Vi. This section will assume use of Nvi, a new implementation of the original Vi for BSD that is commonly found on most Linux systems today.

10.2.1 Getting Acquainted with Vi

As with Emacs, the way to get acquainted with Vi is to start it, and try some basic editing.

You start Vi either by choosing it from the menu supplied by your window manager in X, or by typing its name (in lowercase letters) at a shell prompt. Give the name of a file to begin editing a file.

⇒ Here are two ways to do this.

- To start Vi at a shell prompt, type:

      $ vi ⟨RET⟩

- To open a file name `journal` for editing in Vi, type:

      $ vi journal ⟨RET⟩

Vi is a *modal* editor, where the meaning of text you type depends on the current editing mode the editor is in. When you start, Vi is in **command mode**, which means that the text you type is interpreted as literal Vi commands.

A typical Vi session, upon startup in **command mode** with a new file, looks like Figure 10-2.

The cursor is positioned in the upper right-hand corner. Vi fills lines on the screen after the end of the file with the tilde character (~); so when you are in a new file, such as when you start Vi with no arguments, the screen is filled with tildes because there is nothing yet in the file.

The bottom line of the screen is called the *command line*, and is where Vi displays important messages and information about the file you are editing. When Vi starts, the command line displays three things: First, the name of the recovery file used for this file.[3] Second, Vi displays the name of the file

---

[3] Vi uses the `/tmp` directory to store temporary files for all files that you edit; it saves your editing work so that you can recover it in the event of a crash, or if you accidentally exit Vi before you save it.

being edited; in this case, the file doesn't have a name yet, so "**new file**" is written on the command line. The third thing displayed on the command line is the line number of the file that the cursor is on.

/tmp/vi.ruSAjf: new file: line 1

Figure 10-2. Vi upon startup.

⇒ Type ZZ to exit Vi when you are in **command mode**.

- To exit Vi from **command mode**, type:

    ZZ

To begin editing a particular file, give its name as an argument; if you specify a file that doesn't exist, Vi will begin editing a new file, and when you write it to disk, it will be saved with the name you gave it.

⇒ To start Vi and open a file named **planner**, type:

    $ *vi planner* ⟨RET⟩

When in **command mode**, execute a command by typing it. To cancel a command you have begun typing, press ⟨ESC⟩. Some commands, particularly those for writing files, are preceded by a colon character (:); technically, pressing the colon brings you to a new mode, **command line mode**.

To change to *insert mode*, where text you type is inserted in the file you are editing,[4] you can use one of several commands; the i command enters **insert mode** at the point where the cursor is currently located, and allows you to insert text you type at that point. To exit **insert mode** and move to **command mode**, type ⟨ESC⟩.

---

[4] This is also called **input mode**.

⇒ To insert a line of text in Vi and then move to **command mode**, type:

> *i Hello, world.* ⟨RET⟩
> ⟨ESC⟩

This moves from **command mode** to **insert mode**, inserts the text "**Hello, world.**" and a newline character in the current file, where the cursor was, and then brings Vi back to **command mode**.

The command to get help is **:help**, and to get a list of commands and their usage, run the **:viusage** command.

⇒ To get a list of Vi commands and their usage, type:

> *:viusage* ⟨RET⟩

When you open a file in Vi, the content of the file is placed in its own buffer, as with Emacs. Changes are not made to a file on disk until you write them.

To write a buffer to a file, use **:w** and give the name of the file to write to. Use **:wq** instead to write the file to disk and quit, and use **:q!** to abandon all unsaved editing, and quit Vi.

⇒ Here are two ways to use this.

- To write the contents of the buffer to the file **my_practice_file**, and then exit Vi, type:

  > *:wq my_practice_file* ⟨RET⟩

- To abandon any unsaved editing and exit Vi, type:

  > *:q!* ⟨RET⟩

NOTES: You can also type ZZ to write the changes to the current file and exit.

10.2.2 Running a Vi Tutorial

The Vi editor comes with a hands-on, self-paced tutorial that you can run through in under an hour. As with the Emacs tutorial, it's simply a read-only text file that is opened Vi. It's designed to teach you how to use Vi by showing you the various commands and their effects on the text. It's stored as a compressed file in the **/usr/doc/nvi** directory; copy this file to your home directory, uncompress it, and open it with **vi** to start the tutorial.

⇒ To run the `vi` tutorial, type the following from your home directory:

```
$ cp /usr/doc/nvi/vi.beginner.gz .  (RET)
$ gunzip vi.beginner.gz (RET)
$ vi vi.beginner (RET)
```

NOTES: An advanced tutorial is also available in `/usr/doc/nvi`.

The `vim` editor has an interactive tutorial that you run as its own command, `vimtutor`.

10.2.3 Using Basic Vi Editing Keys

Editing keys depend on the mode you are in. When in **insert mode**, any text you type is inserted in the file until you type (ESC) to switch back to **command mode**.

The following table describes commands available when in **command mode**.

Cursor Movement

(CTRL)-(F)	Scroll text down one full screen.
(CTRL)-(B)	Scroll text up one full screen.
(CTRL)-(D)	Scroll text down one half-screen.
(CTRL)-(U)	Scroll text up one half-screen.
(↓) or `j`	Move down one character.
(↑) or `k`	Move up one character.
(←) or `h`	Move to the left one character.
(→) or `l`	Move to the right one character.
H	Move to top of screen.
L	Move to bottom of screen.
w	Move forward one word.
b	Move backward one word.
(	Move forward one sentence.

(continued)
Cursor Movement

)   Move backward one sentence.

*number*G   Go to line *number*. (With no number preceding it, G goes to the last line in the file.)

0   Go to beginning of line cursor is on.

$ Go to end of line cursor is on.

Cutting and Pasting

x   Delete character cursor is on.

dd   Delete line cursor is on.

D   Delete everything from the cursor to the end of the line.

J   Join the line the cursor is on with the line that follows it (i.e., delete the newline character between them).

p   Paste, after the cursor, the last text that was deleted.

P   Paste, before the cursor, the last text that was deleted.

number yy   "Yank" current line. If preceded by a number, then yank that number of lines.

u   Undo last edit made.

.   Redo last edit made.

Searching

/*pattern* (RET)   Search forward for *pattern* (if none given, then search for the next forward occurrence of the last pattern searched for). Searches wrap from end of file to beginning.

?*pattern* (RET)   Search backward for *pattern* (if none given, then search for the next backward occurrence of the last pattern searched for). Searches wrap from beginning of file to end.

Moving to Insert Mode

a	Appends text just after the cursor.
A	Appends text at the end of the line the cursor is on.
i	Inserts text just before the cursor.
I	Inserts text at the beginning of the line that the cursor is on.
o	Opens a new line below the line the cursor is on, and begins inserting text there.
O	Opens a new line *above* the line the cursor is on, and begins inserting text there.
r	Replaces the character the cursor is over with one you type.
R	Replaces existing text with the text you type.
s	Substitutes the character under the cursor with the text you type, deleting that character and inserting text at that point.
S	Substitutes the line the cursor is on with the text you type, deleting that line and inserting text at that point.

Quitting Vi

:q ⟨RET⟩	Quit Vi only if there are no unsaved edits.
:q! ⟨RET⟩	Quit without saving, even if there have been changes to the file.
:w *name* ⟨RET⟩	Write file to disk; if name is given, write it to that file name.
:wq *name* ⟨RET⟩	Write file to disk and quit Vi; if name is given, write it to that file name.
ZZ	Write file and quit Vi.

10.2.4 Inserting Special Characters in Vi

To insert a control character in Vi verbatim as typed, type ⟨CTRL⟩-⟨V⟩ in **input mode** and then type the control character.

⇒ Here are two ways to use this.

- To insert a formfeed character ("Control-L") before the cursor when you are in **command mode**, type:

  i ⟨CTRL⟩-⟨V⟩ ⟨CTRL⟩-⟨L⟩

- To insert a formfeed character ("Control-L") before the cursor when you are already in **input mode**, type:

  ⟨CTRL⟩-⟨V⟩ ⟨CTRL⟩-⟨L⟩

10.2.5 Running a Command in Vi

To run a shell command in Vi, use `:!` while in **command mode**, and follow it with the name of the command. The output is displayed on the screen while your editing session is suspended; press ⟨RET⟩ to go back to the editing session.

⇒ Here are two ways to use this.

- To run the **date** command from Vi while in **command mode**, type:

  `:!date` ⟨RET⟩

- To run the **date** command from Vi while in **input mode**, type:

  ⟨ESC⟩`:!date` ⟨RET⟩

NOTES: After this last example, you can return to **input mode** by typing a command such as **i**.

10.2.6 Inserting Command Output in Vi

You can insert the output of a command into the file you are editing in Vi. To do this, use `:r!` followed by the command. Output is inserted at the point where the cursor is pointing.

⇒ To insert the current date and time in the current file in Vi, at the point where the cursor is, type:

  `:r!date` ⟨RET⟩

10.2.7 Customizing Vi

There are a number of options you can set in Vi; use the **set** command followed by the name of the option to set it. Given alone, **set** lists all of the options that have changed from their defaults, and given with the **all** option, **set** lists all options that are available.

⇒ Here are two ways to use this.

- To show all the options that have been changed from their default behavior, type:

    :set ⟨RET⟩

- To show all available options, type:

    :set all ⟨RET⟩

The following table lists some of the **set** options and describes their actions.

autoindent	Automatically indent new lines.
autowrite	Automatically write files to disk when changing to another file.
beautify	Do not display control characters.
columns=*number*	Set the number of columns (default 80, sometimes larger in X).
flash	Flash the screen instead of ringing the system bell (the default).
leftright	Allow for scrolling to the left and right.
lines=*number*	Set number of lines shown on the screen at once (default is 24, sometimes larger in X).
list	Text is displayed unambiguously, so that tab characters appear as "^I" instead of as eight spaces, and a "$" is given at the end of every line.
nonumber	Lines are not prefaced with line numbers (the default).
number	Lines are prefaced with line numbers.
ruler	Draw a "ruler" on the command line, showing the current line number and column number.

`showmatch`	Note when closing parentheses or curly braces match their opening partner.
`showmode`	Show the name of the current editing mode on the right side of the command line, and display an asterisk (*) when the file has been modified.
`verbose`	Give verbose error messages.

NOTES: For the complete list of options, consult the `vi man` page.

10.3 Manipulating Selections of Text

You can perform "cut and paste" operations on text, in both X and in a terminal.

In X, you can cut and paste text between different windows, including Xterm and Emacs windows. The most recently selected text is called the *X selection*.

In a terminal, you can cut and paste text in the same virtual console or into a different virtual console. To do this, you need to have the **gpm** package installed and set up for your mouse (this is a default on most systems).

The operations described in this section work the same both in X and in virtual consoles. You cannot presently cut and paste text between X and a virtual console.

Three buttons on the mouse are used for cutting and pasting. If you have a two-button mouse, your administrator can set it to emulate three buttons, where you then press the left and right buttons simultaneously to specify the middle button.

Click the left mouse button and drag the mouse over text to select it. You can also double-click the left mouse button on a word to select that word, or triple-click the left mouse button on a line to select that line. Furthermore, you can click the left mouse button at one end of a portion of text you want to select, and then click the right mouse button at the other end to select all of the text between the points.

NOTES: In an `xterm` window, when you're running a tool or application locally in a shell (such as the Lynx Web browser), the left mouse button alone won't work. When this happens, press and hold (SHIFT) while using the mouse to select text.

10.3.1 Cutting Text

You don't have to select text to cut it. At a shell prompt or in Emacs, type ⟨CTRL⟩-⟨K⟩ to cut the text from the cursor to the end of the line.

In Emacs parlance, cutting text is known as *killing* text.

⇒ Emacs has additional commands for killing text:

- When you have selected an area of text with the mouse as described previously, you can type ⟨SHIFT⟩-⟨DEL⟩ to delete it.
- You can also click the left mouse button at one end of an area of text, and then double-click the right mouse button at the other end of the area, to kill the area of text.
- To kill a large portion of text in an Emacs buffer, set the *mark* at one end of the text by moving point to that end and typing ⟨CTRL⟩-⟨SPACEBAR⟩. Then, move point to the other end of the text, and type ⟨CTRL⟩-⟨W⟩ to kill it.

10.3.2 Pasting Text

XPaste
 DEB: xpaste
 RPM: xpaste
 WWW: http://www.seindal.dk/rene/software/xpaste/

To paste the text that was last selected with the mouse, click the middle mouse button at the place you want to paste to. You can also use the keyboard by moving the cursor to where you want to paste and then typing ⟨SHIFT⟩-⟨INS⟩. These commands work both in X and in a terminal.

In X, to display the content of the X selection in its own window, run the **xpaste** X client; its only purpose in life is to display this text in its window.

In Emacs, pasting text is called *yanking* the text. Emacs offers an additional keystroke, ⟨CTRL⟩-⟨Y⟩ ("yank"), to yank the text that was last selected or killed. This key also works in the Bash shell, where it pastes the last text that was killed with ⟨CTRL⟩-⟨K⟩ in that shell session, if any.

10.4 Using a Token

A handy but rarely discussed method for text editing involves the use of a *token*. The token is nothing more than a little piece of text you put somewhere that represents either a place-holder or some other text that is to come later.

The utility of a token is that when you leave that part of the text, you can quickly return to it later by searching for the token string.

The string you use for a token must be something unique that does not appear in the text proper, and yet is something that you can recognize. Use it to bookmark a point in a text you are editing, for when you need to move elsewhere in the text to do some other thing, but have intend to come back to this place later. It's also handy for when you are editing a text and have to keep a space blank for the time being, such as someone's name that you will add later, once it becomes known.

When you want to go back to the place you have marked with the token, just search for the token using the editor's search facilities. (In Vi, you can use the m command to set a named *mark* in the file at the point where the cursor is.)

My favorite token is "tk," the printers' mark. This two-letter combination occurs rarely in English text, and it is very short, so it is a good one to use for such purposes.[5]

Some people use a silly nonsense word that they can remember, and others use "***" or "###" or some other thing.

10.5 Editing Streams of Text

Some of the recipes in this book for filtering text use SED, the "stream editor." It is not a text editor in the usual sense—you don't open a file in SED and interactively edit it; instead, it performs a given list of editing operations on a *stream* of text sent to its standard input stream, and it writes the results to the standard output stream. This is more like a filter than an editor; SED, which has its own programming language, is a useful tool for formatting and searching through text. It is often used as a filter in a pipeline.

The command itself is called sed; it is usually run by giving as arguments a set of SED commands and, optionally, the file specifications to work on. Without filespec, the standard input is read from.

The simplest thing to do with SED is use it as a filter to edit the input stream in some way, and send it to the output. For example, the SED command to search for all instances of some pattern in the input

---

[5] In printing, where this mark has its origin, it stands for "to kum," meaning that the text where this token was put is *to come* at some later time. Writers would intentionally misspell this and other marks on the copy they submitted, so that the typesetters would know that they were instructions to them, and not a literal part of the text to typeset.

stream and replace it with some other pattern in the output stream is "s/*searchpattern*/*replacepattern*/g"; to filter the output of a command, you can quote this command as an argument to `sed` and put it on a pipeline.

⇒ To output a calendar of the current month, with all "1" characters replaced with "l" characters, type:

    $ cal | sed 's/1/l/g' (RET)

This example uses `cal` to display a calendar (see Recipe 27.3.1 [Displaying a Calendar], page 539). The output of `cal` is edited by `sed` and then sent to standard output.

You can also use `sed` to edit the contents of files by giving some filespec as a second argument; the content of the files are sent to standard output with the specified editing changes, and the original files are not altered.

⇒ Here are two ways to use this.

  • To output the contents of the file **remarks**, replacing every instance of the text "**quite pleased**" with "**absolutely delighted**," type (all on one line):

        $ sed 's/quite pleased/absolutely delighted/g'
        remarks (RET)

  • To output the contents of all files in the current directory whose file names end with **remarks**, replacing every instance of the text "**surprised**" and "**nearly shocked**" with "**utterly astounded**," type (all on one line):

        $ sed 's/surprised\|nearly shocked/utterly
        astounded/g' *remarks (RET)

NOTES: See Appendix D [References for Further Interest], page 731, for more information on `sed`.

10.6 Concatenating Text

The `cat` tool gets its name because it con*cat*enates all of the text given to it, outputting the combined result to the standard output. Think of it as a way of chaining some block of text to some other block of text; you can make chains of any length. This is useful for chaining files of text together into new files.

For example, suppose you have two files, **early** and **later**. The file **early** looks like Figure 10-3, and the file **later** looks like Figure 10-4.

⇒ To concatenate these files into a new file, **novels**, type:

```
$ cat early later > novels ⟨RET⟩
```

This command redirects the standard output to a new file, **novels**, whose contents would look like Figure 10-5. The files **early** and **later** are not altered.

```
This Side of Paradise
The Beautiful and Damned
```

*Figure 10-3. The **early** file.*

```
The Great Gatsby
Tender Is the Night
The Love of the Last Tycoon
```

*Figure 10-4. The **later** file.*

```
This Side of Paradise
The Beautiful and Damned
The Great Gatsby
Tender Is the Night
The Love of the Last Tycoon
```

*Figure 10-5. The **novels** file.*

Had you run `cat later early > novels` instead, the files would be concatenated in that reversed order instead, beginning with **later**; so the file **novels** would look like Figure 10-6.

```
The Great Gatsby
Tender Is the Night
The Love of the Last Tycoon
This Side of Paradise
The Beautiful and Damned
```

*Figure 10-6. The **novels** file reversed.*

The following sections give other recipes for concatenating text.

NOTES: You can also use `cat` to concatenate files that are *not* text, but its most popular usage is with text files. Another way to concatenate files of text in an automated way is to use file *inclusion*—see Recipe 10.7 [Including Text from Other Files], page 261.

A similar tool, `zcat`, works on the contents of compressed files.

10.6.1 Writing Text to Files

Sometimes, it's too much trouble to call up a text editor for a particular job— you just want to write a text file with two lines in it, say, or you just want to append one line to a text file. There are good ways of doing these kind of micro-editing jobs without a text editor.

To write a text file without using a text editor, redirect the standard output of `cat` to the file to write. You can then type your text, typing (CTRL)-(D) on a line of its own to end the file. This is useful when you want to quickly create a small text file, but that is about it; usually, you open or create a text file in a text editor, as described in the previous sections in this chapter.

⇒ To make a file, `novels`, with some text in it, type:

```
$ cat > novels (RET)
This Side of Paradise (RET)
The Beautiful and Damned (RET)
The Great Gatsby (RET)
Tender Is the Night (RET)
(CTRL)-(D)
$
```

In this example, the text file **novels** was created and contains four lines of text (the last line with the (CTRL)-(D) is never part of the file).

Typing text like this without an editor will sometimes do in a pinch but, if you make a mistake, there is not much recourse besides starting over—you can type (CTRL)-(U) to erase the current line, and (CTRL)-(C) to abort the whole thing and not write the text to a file at all, but that's about it.

10.6.2 Appending Text to a File

To add text to a text file without opening the file in a text editor, use `cat` with the append operator, `>>`. (Using > instead would overwrite the file.)

⇒ To add a line of text to the bottom of file **novels**, type:

```
$ cat >> novels ⟨RET⟩
The Love of the Last Tycoon ⟨RET⟩
⟨CTRL⟩-⟨D⟩
```

In this example, no files were specified to `cat` for input, so `cat` used the standard input; then, one line of text was typed, and this text was appended to file **novels**, the file used in the previous recipe. So now this file would look like Figure 10-5.

10.6.3 Inserting Text at the Beginning of a File

Inserting text at the *beginning* of a text file without calling up a text editor is a bit trickier than appending text to a file's end—but it *is* possible. There are several methods for doing this.

METHOD #1

The shell script given in Figure 10-7 will insert the lines you give it into the file specified as an argument.

Put it in a file called **ins**, and install it as a shell script (see Recipe A.3.4 [Installing a Shell Script], page 708).

```
#!/bin/sh
/bin/ed $1 <<EOF
0a
`cat -`
.
w
q
EOF
```

Figure 10-7. The ins *file.*

To insert one or more lines of text at the beginning of a file, give the name of the file into which the text should be inserted as an argument to **ins**; **ins** will read lines of text from the standard input and insert them at the beginning of the file. (It works by opening the file in **ed**, a simple line editor.)

Give the EOF—that is, type ⟨CTRL⟩-⟨D⟩ on a line by itself—to signify the end of the lines of text to insert.

⇒ To insert several lines of text at the beginning of the file **novels**, type:

```
$ ins novels ⟨RET⟩
The Novels of F. Scott Fitzgerald ⟨RET⟩
-------------------------------- ⟨RET⟩
⟨CTRL⟩-⟨D⟩
$
```

This command inserts two lines of text at the beginning of **novels**, the file used in the previous examples in this section. This file would now look like Figure 10-8.

```
The Novels of F. Scott Fitzgerald
--------------------------------
This Side of Paradise
The Beautiful and Damned
The Great Gatsby
Tender Is the Night
The Love of the Last Tycoon
```

Figure 10-8. The **novels** *file with a new beginning.*

METHOD #2

To use **cat** to insert text at the beginning of a file, use **cat** to concatenate the standard input and the file; redirect this to a new file name that will contain the file with the inserted text at the beginning.

⇒ To insert several lines of text at the beginning of the file **novels**, type:

```
$ cat - novels > novels.tmp ⟨RET⟩
The Novels of F. Scott Fitzgerald ⟨RET⟩
-------------------------------- ⟨RET⟩
⟨CTRL⟩-⟨D⟩
$
```

This command writes a new file, `novels.tmp`, containing the lines you typed and then the contents of `novels`. To keep the file with this inserted text, move `novels.tmp` to `novels`.

10.7 Including Text from Other Files

M4
  DEB: m4
  RPM: m4
  WWW: http://www.gnu.org/software/m4/m4.html

File *inclusion* is when the content of a file is included at a particular place within some other file, just by specifying the file's name at that place in the other file.

This is useful if you want or need to frequently rearrange divisions or sections of a document, if you need to keep a document in more than one arrangement, or if you have some sections of text that you frequently insert in more than one document. For these situations, you can keep each section in a separate file and build an *include file* that contains the file names of the various sections in the order you want for that file.

To include a file in a text file, specify the file to be included on a line of its own, like this:

    include(*file*)

When you process this file for inclusion, the line with the "**include**" statement is replaced with the contents of the file *file* (whose path is relative to the current directory of the include file).

```
Clam Chowder
Lobster Bisque
Vegetable
```

Figure 10-9. The **soups** *file.*

Use the `m4` tool, the GNU macro processor, to process an include file. It takes as an argument the name of the include file, and it outputs the inclusion to the standard output. You can use redirection to redirect the output to a file.[6]

---

[6] This is a fairly simple use of `m4`; it can do much more, including run commands, manipulate text, and run custom macros. Consult its Info documentation for more (see Recipe 2.8.5 [Reading an Info Manual], page 48).

For example, suppose you have three files: **soups** as in Figure 10-9, **sandwiches** as in Figure 10-10, and **menu** as in Figure 10-11.

```
BLT
Ham on Rye
Roast Beef
```

Figure 10-10. The **sandwiches** *file.*

```
Diner Menu for Today

Soups
-----
include(soups)

Sandwiches
----------
include(sandwiches)
```

Figure 10-11. The **menu** *file.*

```
Diner Menu for Today

Soups
-----
Clam Chowder
Lobster Bisque
Vegetable

Sandwiches
----------
BLT
Ham on Rye
Roast Beef
```

Figure 10-12. The **monday.txt** *file.*

⇒ To process the file and write it to the file **monday.txt**, type:

```
$ m4 menu > monday.txt ⟨RET⟩
```

This command writes a new file, **monday.txt**, as in Figure 10-12.

NOTES: You can write more than one include file that will use your files—and these include files themselves can have inclusions of their own.

10.8 Using Other Text Editors

The following table describes some of the more popular or interesting text editors available for Linux, and includes information about their special traits and characteristics as well as a screen shot.

AEE   The *advanced easy editor* has a pop-up menu interface and is meant
        to be usable with no prior instruction; includes an interface for use
        in X, **xae**.

        DEB: aee
        RPM: aee
        WWW: http://mahon.cwx.net/

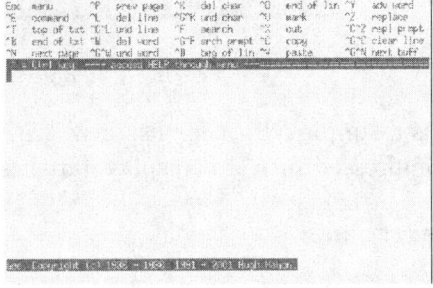

Figure 10-13. Advanced Easy Editor.

Cooledit   Cooledit is a popular, fast text editor for use in X; its features
            include anti-aliased fonts, Unicode support, and extensibility via
            the Python programming language. It's based on the Midnight
            Commander's terminal editor, and it's unique in that it is unlike
            either Emacs or Vi.

            DEB: cooledit
            RPM: cooledit
            WWW: http://cooledit.sourceforge.net/

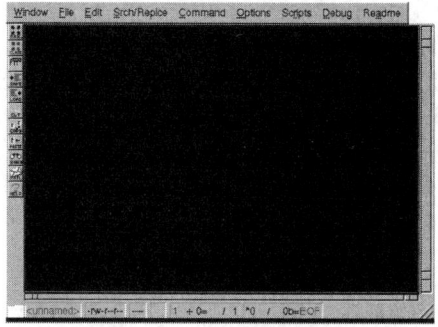

Figure 10-14. Cooledit.

DEdit   DEdit is a simple editor for use in X with GNOME installed. It can
            read compressed files and display Japanese characters.

            DEB: dedit

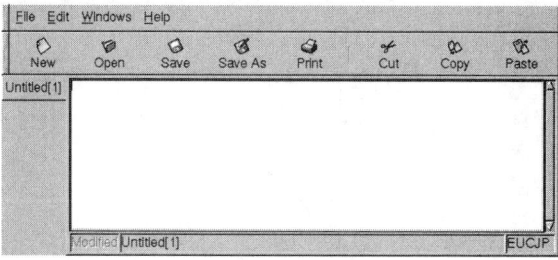

Figure 10-15. DEdit.

E3   A tiny editor (10 KB in size) with available keyboard bindings that
          emulate Emacs, Vi, PICO, Nedit, and WordStar.

          DEB: e3
          RPM: e3
          WWW: http://www.sax.de/~adlibit/

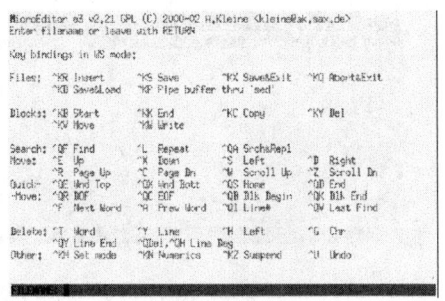

Figure 10-16. E3.

EE   Intended to be an editor that novices can begin using immediately,
          the Easy Editor features pop-up menus and is based on **aee**, de-
          scribed previously.

          DEB: ee
          WWW: http://mahon.cwx.net/

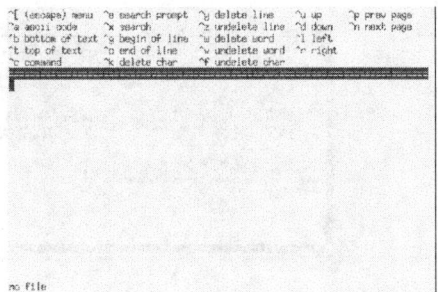

Figure 10-17. Easy Editor.

Elvis   Elvis is a modern implementation of Vi that comes with many new
             features and extensions.

             DEB: `elvis`
             RPM: `elvis`
             WWW: `http://elvis.vi-editor.org/`

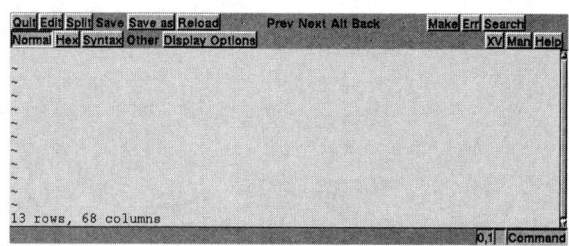

Figure 10-18. Elvis.

Emacs   Emacs is one of the two most popular text editors. A section
             all about it located earlier in this chapter (see Recipe 10.1 [Using
             Emacs], page 232).

             DEB: `emacsen-common`
                  `emacs21`
             RPM: `emacs`
             WWW: `http://www.emacs.org/`

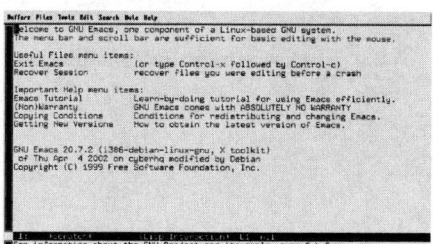

Figure 10-19. Emacs.

Glimmer Intended for use with computer programming languages, it has many features that appeal to programmers.

> DEB: glimmer
> RPM: glimmer
> WWW: http://glimmer.sourceforge.net/

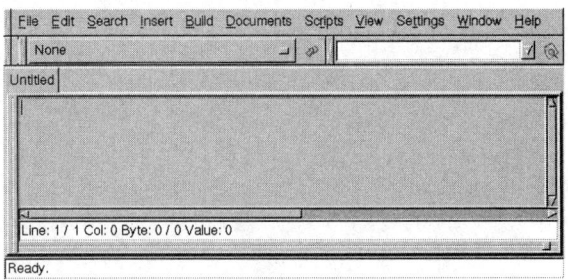

Figure 10-20. Glimmer.

JED John E. Davis's editor offers many of the conveniences of Emacs and is geared specifically toward programmers. Features unique to it include drop-down menus that work in terminals; JED loads quickly, and makes editing files at a shell prompt easy and fast.

> DEB: jed
> RPM: jed
> WWW: http://www.jedsoft.org/jed/

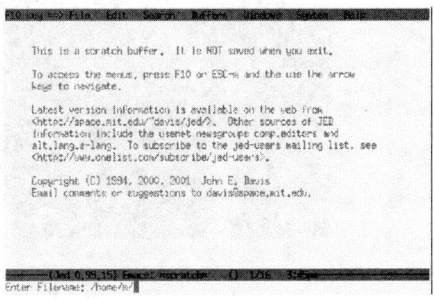

Figure 10-21. JED.

JOE   Joe's Own Editor, `joe`, is a full-screen editor with a look and feel
           reminiscent of the old DOS text editors, such as EDIT.

           DEB: `joe`
           RPM: `joe`
           WWW: `http://sourceforge.net/projects/joe-editor/`

Figure 10-22. Joe's Own Editor.

Le   A multi-lingual editor for use in a terminal, with support for oper-
           ating on rectangular blocks of text.

           DEB: `le`
           RPM: `le`
           WWW: `http://tinyurl.com/23325`

Figure 10-23. Le.

MCedit   This is the full-screen terminal editor that comes with the Midnight
          Commander.

          DEB: mc-common
               mc
          RPM: mc
          WWW: http://www.ibiblio.org/mc/

Figure 10-24. Midnight Commander.

Nano   GNU Nano is a free software editor inspired by PICO, the editor
          that is included with the University of Washington's proprietary
          PINE email program. It's also faster than PICO, and comes with
          more features.

          DEB: nano
          RPM: nano
          WWW: http://www.nano-editor.org/

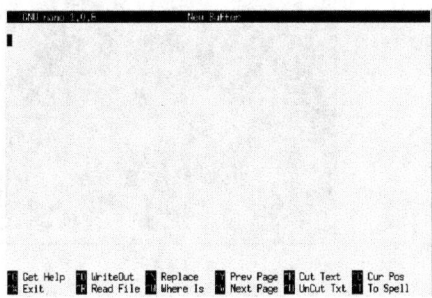

Figure 10-25. Nano.

Ted   Ted is a WYSIWYG, typewriter-like text editor for use in X. It reads and writes RTF files (Microsoft's "Rich Text Format").

DEB: `ted`
RPM: `Ted`
WWW: `http://www.nllgg.nl/Ted/`

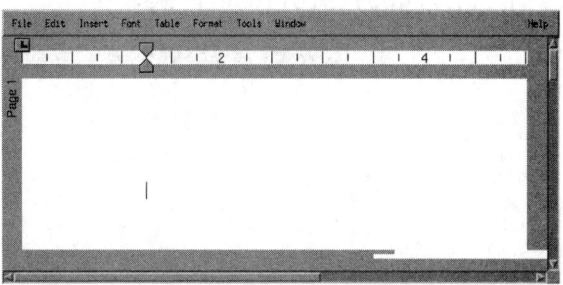

Figure 10-26. Ted.

THE   The Hessling Editor (THE) is a configurable editor that uses the Rexx macro language. It was inspired by the XEDIT editor for VM/CMS and the Kedit editor for DOS.

DEB: `the`
     `the-doc`
RPM: `THE`
WWW: `http://hessling-editor.sourceforge.net/`

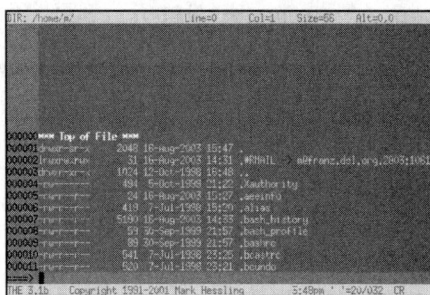

Figure 10-27. The Hessling Editor.

Vi   Vi is a *visual*, or full-screen, editor. It is probably the most popular
            editor on Linux, and on UNIX-based systems in general. Touch
            typists often find its keystroke commands enable very fast editing. A
            section all about it is located earlier in this chapter (see Recipe 10.2
            [Using Vi], page 244).

            DEB: nvi
            RPM: nvi
            WWW: http://www.bostic.com/vi/

Figure 10-28. Vi.

Vim   Like the Elvis editor, Vim ("Vi improved") is a modern implemen-
            tation of Vi; it has more commands and versatility, and new features
            include syntax coloring, scrollbars and menus, mouse support, and
            built-in help.

            DEB: vim
            RPM: vim
            WWW: http://www.vim.org/

Figure 10-29. Vim.

Wily   Wily, an interesting mouse-centric editor, is inspired by the Acme editor from AT&T's Plan 9 experimental operating system. Wily commands consist of various combinations of the three mouse buttons, called *chords*.

DEB: `wily`
WWW: `http://www.cs.yorku.ca/~oz/wily/`

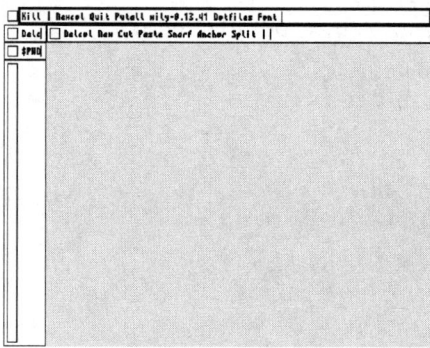

Figure 10-30. Wily.

Xcoral   A mouse-centric text editor for X that uses multiple windows.

DEB: `xcoral`
RPM: `xcoral`
WWW: `http://xcoral.free.fr/`

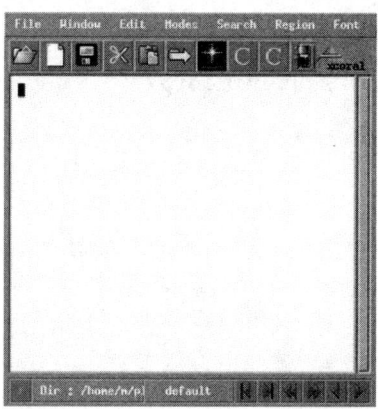

Figure 10-31. Xcoral.

Xedit   Xedit is a simple text editor that comes with, and works in, X. It
           lets you insert, delete, copy, and paste text as well as open and save
           files—the very basics.

           DEB: xbase-clients
           RPM: XFree86
           WWW: http://www.xfree86.org/

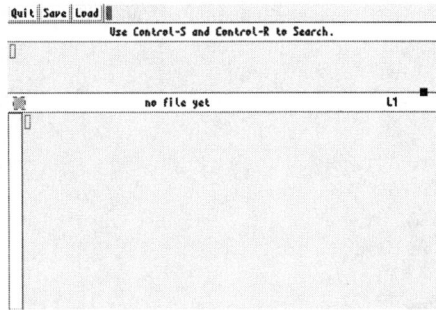

Figure 10-32. Xedit.

XEmacs   XEmacs is a version of Emacs with advanced capabilities for use in
           X, including the ability to display images.

           DEB: emacsen-common
                xemacs21
           RPM: xemacs
           WWW: http://www.xemacs.org/

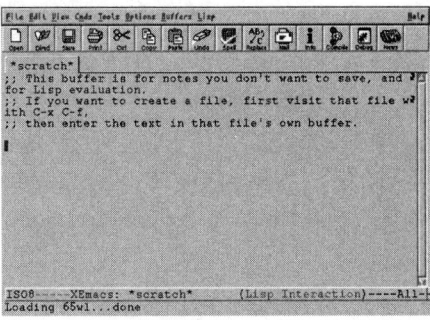

Figure 10-33. XEmacs.

## CHAPTER 11

Grammar and Reference

The tools and resources for writing and editing on Linux-based systems include spell checkers, dictionaries, and reference files. This chapter shows methods for using them.

11.1 Spell Checking

There are several ways to spell-check text and files on Linux; the following recipes show how to find the correct spellings of particular words and how to perform batch, interactive, and Emacs-based spell checks.

The *system dictionary* file, `/usr/dict/words`,[1] is nothing more than a word list (albeit a very large one), sorted in alphabetical order and containing one word per line. Words that are correct regardless of case[2] appear in all lowercase letters, and words that rely on some form of capitalization in order to be correct (such as proper nouns) appear in that form. All of the Linux spelling tools use this text file to check spelling; if a word does not appear in the dictionary file, it is considered to be misspelled.

⇒ To find out how many words come in the user dictionary on your system, type:

```
$ wc -l /usr/dict/words RET
```

NOTES: If you are using the wrong word to begin with, none of the computerized spell-check tools will correct this error—for example, if you have "`there`" when you mean "`their`," the computer cannot catch it (yet!).

11.1.1 Finding the Correct Spelling of a Word

If you're unsure whether or not you're using the correct spelling of a word, use `spell` to find out. `spell` reads from the standard input and outputs any words not found in the system dictionary—so if a word is misspelled, it will be echoed back on the screen after you type it.

---

[1] On an increasing number of systems, this file is being replaced with the newer `/usr/share/dict/words`; administrators should make a symbolic link from this to the shorter, preferred form.

[2] In other words, they are correct whether they appear entirely in lowercase letters, capitalized, or entirely in uppercase letters.

⇒ For example, to check whether the word "occurance" is misspelled, type:

```
$ spell (RET)
occurance (RET)
occurance
(CTRL)-(D)
$
```

In this example, `spell` echoed the word "occurance," meaning that this word was not in the system dictionary and therefore was quite likely a misspelling. Then, (CTRL)-(D) was typed to exit `spell`.

11.1.2 Listing the Misspellings in Text

To output a list of misspelled words in a file, give the name of the file to check as an argument to `spell`. Any misspelled words in the file are output, each on a line of its own and in the order that they appear in the file.

⇒ To spell-check the file `fall-lecture.draft`, type:

```
$ spell fall-lecture.draft (RET)
occurance
willl
occurance
$
```

In this example, three words are output: "occurance," "willl," and "occurance" again, meaning that these three words were found in `fall-lecture.draft`, in that order, and were not in the system dictionary (and so were probably misspelled). Note that the misspelling "occurance" appears twice in the file.

To correct the misspellings, you could then open the file in your preferred text editor and edit it. Later in this section, I'll describe an interactive spell checker that allows you to correct misspellings as they are found. Still another option is to use a text editor with spell-checking facilities built in, such as Emacs.

⇒ To spell-check the file `fall-lecture.draft`, and output any possibly misspelled words to a file `fall-lecture.spelling`, type:

```
$ spell fall-lecture.draft > fall-lecture.spelling (RET)
```

In this example, the standard output redirection operator (>) is used to redirect the output to a file (see Recipe 3.2.2 [Redirecting Output to a File], page 68).

To output an *alphabetical* list of the misspelled words, pipe the output to `sort`; then pipe the sorted output to the `uniq` filter to remove duplicates from the list (`uniq` removes duplicate adjacent lines from its input, outputting the "unique" lines).

⇒ To output a sorted list of the misspelled words that are in the file `fall-lecture.draft`, type:

    $ spell fall-lecture.draft | sort | uniq (RET)

11.1.3 Keeping a Spelling Word List

The stock American English dictionary installed with Linux-based systems includes over 45,000 words. However large that number may seem, a lot of words are invariably left out—including slang, jargon, and some proper names.

You can view the system dictionary as you would any other text file, but users never edit this file to add words to it.[3] Instead, you add new words to your own *personal dictionary*, a file in the same format as the system dictionary, but kept in your home directory as the file `~/.ispell_default`.[4]

A user can have his own personal dictionary; the spelling commands discussed in this chapter automatically use your personal dictionary, if you have one, in addition to the system dictionary.

You build your personal dictionary using the *i* and *u* options of `ispell`, which insert words into your personal dictionary. Use these options either with the stand-alone tool or with the various `ispell` Emacs functions (see Recipe 11.1.4 [Interactive Spell Checking], page 278, and Recipe 11.1.5 [Spell Checking in Emacs], page 280).

⇒ To find out how many words you have in your personal dictionary, type:

    $ wc -l .ispell_default (RET)

NOTES: You can also add (or remove) words by manually editing the file with a text editor, but take care to keep the list in alphabetical order!

---

[3] If a word is reasonably universal, you may, of course, contact the global maintainers of `wenglish` or other appropriate packages, and try to convince them that said word ought to be included.

[4] On newer systems, this file is sometimes replaced by `~/aspell_default`.

Over time, personal dictionaries begin to look very personal, as a reflection of their owners; Gregory Cosmo Haun made a work of conceptual art by photographing the portraits of a dozen users superimposed with listings of their personal dictionaries [http://www.reed.edu/~cosmo/art/DictPort.html].

11.1.4 Interactive Spell Checking

GNU Aspell
  DEB: aspell
  RPM: aspell
  WWW: http://aspell.net/

  or

Ispell
  DEB: ispell
  RPM: ispell
  WWW: http://fmg-www.cs.ucla.edu/geoff/ispell.html

Use `ispell` to spell check a file *interactively*, so that every time a misspelling is found, you're given a chance to replace it then and there.[5]

⇒ To interactively spell-check `fall-lecture.notes`, type:

> `$ ispell fall-lecture.notes` ⟨RET⟩

When you type this, `ispell` begins checking the file. It stops at the first misspelling it finds, as in Figure 11-1.

On the top line of the screen, `ispell` displays the misspelled word, followed by the name of the file. Underneath this is the sentence in which the misspelling appears, with the word in question highlighted. Following this is a list of suggested words, each offset by a number—in this example, `ispell` has only one suggestion: "`lectures`."

To replace a misspelling with a suggested word, type the number that corresponds to the suggested word (in this example, you would type *0* to replace the misspelling with "`lectures`"). You only need to type the number of your selection—a ⟨RET⟩ is not required.

You can also type a correction yourself; this is useful when `ispell` either offers no suggestions, or when it does and the word you want is not one of them. To do this, type *r* (for "replace") and then type the replacement word, followed by ⟨RET⟩.

---

[5] `aspell` is designed to be a drop-in replacement for `ispell`, with greatly improved suggestion algorithms. If your system has `aspell`, use it instead; it otherwise works like `ispell`.

Sometimes, `ispell` will question a word that you may not want to count as a misspelling, such as proper names and the like—words that don't appear in the system dictionary. There are a few things you can do in such cases, as follows.

To accept a misspelled word as correct for the current `ispell` session only, type a; from then on during the current session, this word will be considered correct.

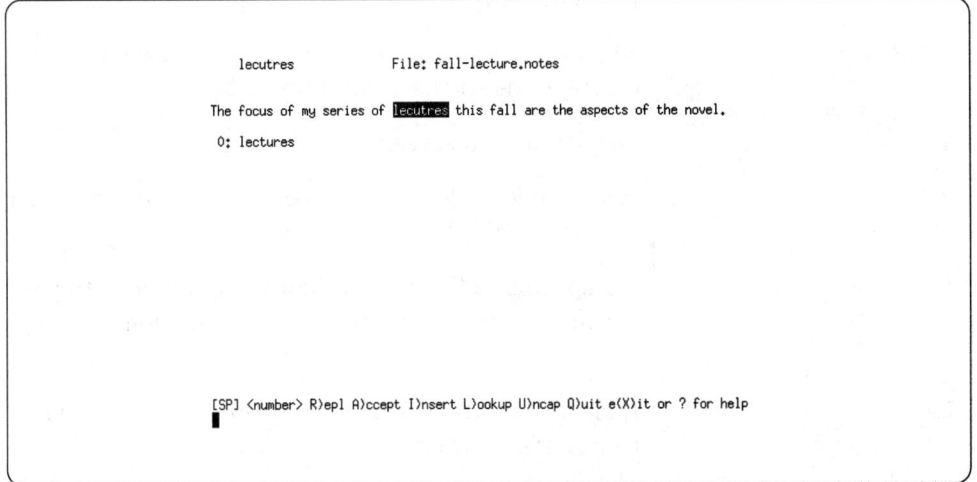

Figure 11-1. A misspelling caught by `ispell`.

If, however, you want `ispell` (and `spell`, and all other tools that access the system dictionary) to remember this word as being correct for this and all future sessions, insert the word in your own personal dictionary. Type u to insert a copy of the word *uncapitalized,* in all lowercase letters—this way, even if the word is capitalized at the beginning of a sentence, the lowercase version of the word is saved. From then on, in the current `ispell` session and in future sessions, this word will be considered correct whether it appears entirely in lowercase letters, capitalized, or entirely in uppercase letters.

When case is important to the spelling—for example, in a word that is a proper name such as "Seattle," or a word with mixed case, such as "DeSalle"—type *i* to insert a copy of the word in your personal dictionary with its case *just as it appears;* this way, words spelled with the same letters but with different cases will be considered misspellings.

When `ispell` finishes spell-checking a file, it saves its changes to the file and then exits. It also makes a copy of the original file, without the changes applied; this file has the same name as the original but with `.bak` added to the end—in our example, the backup file is called **fall-lecture.notes.bak**.

This is useful if you regret the changes you've made and want to restore the file to how it was before you mucked it up—just remove the spell-checked file and then rename the .bak file to its original name.

The following table is a reference to the ispell key commands, listing the keys and describing their actions.

(SPACEBAR)	Accept misspelled word as correct, but only for this particular instance.
number	Replace misspelled word with the suggestion that corresponds to the given number.
?	Display a help screen.
a	Accept misspelled word as correct for the remainder of this ispell session.
i	Accept misspelled word as correct and add it to your private dictionary with the capitalization as it appears.
l	Look up words in the system dictionary according to a pattern you give.
q	Quit checking and restore the file to how it was before this session.
r	Replace misspelled word with a word you type.
u	Accept misspelled word as correct and add it to your private dictionary in all lowercase letters.
x	Save changes made so far, and then stop checking this file.

11.1.5 Spell Checking in Emacs

Emacs has several useful commands for spell-checking. The ispell-word, ispell-region, and ispell-buffer functions, as you might guess from their names, use the ispell command inside Emacs to check portions of the current buffer.[6]

The first command, ispell-word, checks the spelling of the word at point; if there is no word at point, it checks the first word to the left of point. This

---

[6] On many newer systems, aspell is used in ispell's place.

command has a keyboard shortcut, $\langle$ALT$\rangle$-$\langle$\$$\rangle$. The second command, `ispell-region`, checks the spelling of all words in the currently selected region of text. The third command, `ispell-buffer`, checks the spelling of the entire buffer.

⇒ Here are some ways to use this.

- To check the spelling of the word at point, type:

  $\langle$ALT$\rangle$-$\langle$X$\rangle$ `ispell-word` $\langle$RET$\rangle$

- To check the spelling of all words in the currently selected region of text, type:

  $\langle$ALT$\rangle$-$\langle$X$\rangle$ `ispell-region` $\langle$RET$\rangle$

- To check the spelling of all words in the current buffer, type:

  $\langle$ALT$\rangle$-$\langle$X$\rangle$ `ispell-buffer` $\langle$RET$\rangle$

Another useful Emacs spelling feature is `flyspell-mode`. When this mode is set in a buffer, any misspelled words in the buffer are highlighted. This mode is useful when you are writing a first draft, because it lets you catch misspellings as you type them.

⇒ To turn on `flyspell-mode` in a buffer, type:

  $\langle$ALT$\rangle$-$\langle$X$\rangle$ `flyspell-mode` $\langle$RET$\rangle$

NOTES: This mode is a toggle; run it again to turn it off.

To correct a word in `flyspell-mode`, click and release the middle mouse button on the word to pull up a menu of suggestions; you then use the mouse to select the replacement word or add it to your personal dictionary.

If there are words you frequently misspell, you can define abbrevs for them (see Recipe 10.1.5 [Making Abbreviations in Emacs], page 242). Then, when you type the misspelled word, Emacs will automatically replace it with the correct spelling.

Finally, if you prefer the sparse, non-interactive interface of `spell`, you can use the Emacs interfaces to that command instead: `spell-word`, `spell-region`, and `spell-buffer`. When any of these functions find a misspelling, they prompt for a replacement in the minibuffer but do not offer suggestions or provide any of `ispell`'s other features.

11.2 Using Dictionaries

WordNet
 DEB: `wordnet`
      `wordnet-base`
 WWW: `http://www.cogsci.princeton.edu/~wn/`

The term *dictionary* on Linux systems generally refers to one of two things:
the traditional UNIX-style dictionary, which is an alphabetically sorted word
list containing no actual definitions, and the newer database-style dictionary
that contains the headwords as well as their definitions. The latter is the
kind of thing most people mean when they talk about dictionaries. (When
most UNIX folk talk about dictionaries, however, they almost always mean the
former.)

WordNet is a lexical reference system in the form of a database containing
thousands of words arranged in synonym sets. You can search the database
and output the results in text with the **wn** tool or the **wnb** X client (the
"WordNet browser").

Use of the X client is fairly straightforward—type a word in the dialog box
near the top of the screen, followed by ⟨RET⟩, to get its definitions, which are
displayed in the large output window underneath the dialog box.

For example, when you do a search for the definition of the word "**browse**,"
the WordNet browser will look like Figure 11-2.

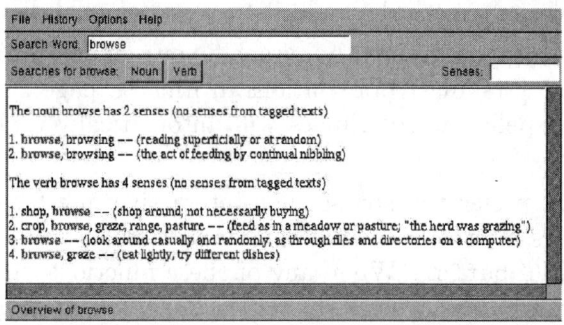

Figure 11-2. The WordNet browser.

Between the dialog box and the output window, there are menus for searching for synonyms and other word senses. A separate menu is given for each
part of speech a word may have; in the preceding example, the word "**browse**"
can be either a noun or a verb, so two menus are shown.

To get a list of all word sense information available for a given word, run **wn** with the word as an argument. This outputs a list of all word sense information available for the word, with each possible sense preceded with the name of the option to use to output it.

⇒ To output a list of word senses available for the word "**browse**," type:

    $ wn browse (RET)

The following sections show how to use **wn** on the command line.

NOTES: For more information on WordNet, consult the **wnintro man** page (see Recipe 2.8.4 [Reading a Page from the System Manual], page 46).

11.2.1 Listing Words That Match a Pattern

There are several ways to search for and output words from the system dictionary.

Use **look** to output a list of words in the system dictionary that begin with a given string—this is useful for finding words that begin with a particular phrase or prefix. Give the string as an argument; it is not case-sensitive.

⇒ To output a list of words from the dictionary that begin with the string "**homew**," type:

    $ look homew (RET)

This command outputs words like "**homeward**" and "**homework**."

Since the system dictionary is an ordinary text file, you can also use **grep** to search it for words that match a given pattern or regular expression (see Recipe 14.3 [Matching Patterns of Text], page 335).

⇒ Here are some ways to use this.

- To list all words in the dictionary that contain the string "**dont**," regardless of case, type:

        $ grep -i dont /usr/dict/words (RET)

- To list all words in the dictionary that end with "**ing**," type:

        $ grep ing^ /usr/dict/words (RET)

- To list all of the words that are composed only of vowels, type:

        $ grep -i '^[aeiou]*$' /usr/dict/words (RET)

To find some words that rhyme with a given word, use **grep** to search **/usr/dict/words** for words ending in the same last few characters as the word they should rhyme with (see Recipe 14.4.2 [Matching Lines Ending with Certain Text], page 343).

⇒ To output a list of words that rhyme with "`friend`," search `/usr/dict/words` for lines ending with "`end`":

```
$ grep 'end$' /usr/dict/words (RET)
```

Finally, to do a search on the WordNet dictionary, use `wn` with one of the `-grep` options. When you give some text to search for as an argument, this command does the equivalent search as `look`, but only the particular kind of word sense you specify is searched: `-grepn` searches nouns, `-grepv` searches verbs, `-grepa` searches adjectives, and `-grepr` searches adverbs. You can combine options to search multiple word senses.

⇒ Here are two ways to use this.

- To search the WordNet dictionary for nouns that begin with "`homew`," type:

```
$ wn homew -grepn (RET)
```

- To search the WordNet dictionary for both nouns and adjectives that begin with "`homew`," type:

```
$ wn homew -grepn -grepa (RET)
```

11.2.2 Listing the Definitions of a Word

To list the definitions of a word, give the word as an argument to `wn`, followed by the `-over` option.

⇒ To list the definitions of the word "`slope`," type:

```
$ wn slope -over (RET)
```

NOTES: If you look up dictionary definitions frequently enough, it is handy to have an alias of "`def`" defined as `wn $1 -over` (see Recipe 3.6.1 [Calling a Command by Some Other Name], page 83).

11.2.3 Listing the Synonyms of a Word

A *synonym* of a word is a different word with a similar meaning that can be used in place of the first word in some context. To output synonyms for a word with `wn`, give the word as an argument, followed by one of the following options: `-synsn` for nouns, `-synsv` for verbs, `-synsa` for adjectives, or `-sysnr` for adverbs.

⇒ Here are two ways to use this.

- To output all of the synonyms for the noun "`break`," type:

```
$ wn break -synsn (RET)
```

- To output all of the synonyms for the verb "`break`," type:

    `$ wn break -synsv` (RET)

11.2.4 Listing the Antonyms of a Word

An *antonym* of a word is a different word that has the opposite meaning of
the first in some context. To output antonyms for a word with **wn**, give the
word as an argument, followed by one the following options: **-antsv** for verbs,
-antsa for adjectives, or **-antsr** for adverbs.

⇒ To output all of the antonyms for the adjective "`sad`," type:

    `$ wn sad -antsa` (RET)

11.2.5 Listing the Hypernyms of a Word

A *hypernym* of a word is a related term whose meaning is more general than
the given word. (For example, the words "`mammal`" and "`animal`" are hypernyms of the word "`cat`.")

To output hypernyms for a word with **wn**, use one of the following options:
-hypen for nouns or **-hypev** for verbs.

⇒ To output all of the hypernyms for the noun "`cat`," type:

    `$ wn cat -hypen` (RET)

11.2.6 Checking Online Dictionaries

Dict
  DEB: dict
  RPM: dict
  WWW: http://www.dict.org/

The DICT Development Group has a number of free dictionaries on its Web site
[`http://www.dict.org/`]. On that page, you can look up words (including
using a thesaurus and other searches) from a dictionary that contains over
300,000 headwords, or you can make a copy of its dictionary for use on your
own system. A `dict` client exists for accessing DICT servers and outputting
definitions locally; this tool is available in the `dict` package.

There are a number of specialized dictionaries available from the DICT
Development Group as well. These dictionaries are plain text files. One such
dictionary is called FILE, *The Free Internet Lexicon and Encyclopedia*. It is
an effort to build a free, open source collection of modern-word, idiom, and

jargon dictionaries. FILE is a volunteer effort and depends on the support of scholars and lexicographers; the DICT pages contain information on how to help contribute to this worthy project.

11.3 Checking Grammar

Diction
 DEB: `diction`
 WWW: `http://www.gnu.org/software/diction/diction.html`

Two venerable UNIX tools for checking writing have recently been made available for Linux-based systems: `style` and `diction`.

Old-timers probably remember these names—the originals came with AT&T UNIX as part of the much-loved "Writer's Workbench" (WWB) suite of tools back in the late 1970s and early 1980s.[7]

AT&T "unbundled" the Writer's Workbench from its UNIX Version 7 product, and as the many flavors of UNIX blossomed over the years, these tools were lost by the wayside—eventually becoming the stuff of UNIX lore.

In 1997, Michael Haardt wrote new Linux versions of these tools from scratch. They support both the English and German languages, and they're now part of the GNU Project.

Two additional commands that were part of the Writer's Workbench have long been standard on Linux: `look` and `spell`, described previously in this chapter.

The following are recipes that use either `diction` or `style`.

11.3.1 Checking Text for Misused Phrases

Use `diction` to check for wordy, trite, clichéd, or misused phrases in a text. It checks for all the kind of expressions William Strunk warned us about in his *Elements of Style* [`http://www.bartleby.com/141/`].

According to *The UNIX Environment* (see Appendix D [References for Further Interest], page 731), the `diction` tool that came with the old Writer's Workbench just *found* the phrases, and a separate command called `suggest` would output suggestions. In the GNU version that works for Linux systems, both functions have been combined in the single `diction` command.

---

[7] There was also a set of tools for formatting text called the "Documenter's Workbench" (DWB), and there was a planned "Reader's Workbench"; today, we can only guess at what that might have been.

In GNU `diction`, the words or phrases are enclosed in brackets "[like this]." If `diction` has any suggested replacements, it gives them preceded by a right arrow, "-> like this."

When checking more than just a screenful of text, you'll want to pipe the output to `less` so that you can peruse it on the screen (see Recipe 9.1 [Perusing Text], page 211), or pipe the output to a file for later examination.

⇒ Here are two ways to use this.

- To check the file `dissertation` for clichés or other misused phrases, type:

      $ *diction dissertation | less* ⟨RET⟩

- To check the file `dissertation` for clichés or other misused phrases, and write the output to a file called `dissertation.diction`, type:

      $ *diction dissertation > dissertation.diction* ⟨RET⟩

If you don't specify a file name, `diction` reads text from the standard input until you type ⟨CTRL⟩-⟨D⟩ on a line by itself. This is especially useful when you want to check a single sentence, as in Figure 11-3.

```
$ diction ⟨RET⟩
Let us ask the question we wish to state. ⟨RET⟩
(stdin):1: Let us [ask the question -> ask]
[we wish to state -> (cliche, avoid)].
⟨CTRL⟩-⟨D⟩
$
```

Figure 11-3. Checking a sentence with `diction`.

To check the text of a Web page, use `lynx` with the `-dump` and `-nolist` options to output the plain text of a given URL, and pipe this output to `diction`. (If you expect there to be a lot of output, add another pipe at the end to `less` so you can peruse it.)

To peruse the URL `http://www.westegg.com/cliche/random.cgi` with markings for possible wordy and misused phrases, type (all on one line):

      $ *lynx -dump -nolist http://www.westegg.com/cliche/random.cgi |*
      diction | less ⟨RET⟩

NOTES: To check text for overused words, use the method described in Recipe 12.2.4 [Counting Word Occurrences in Text], page 299.

11.3.2 Checking Text for Doubled Words

One of the things that `diction` looks for is doubled words—words repeated twice in a row. If it finds such a sequence, it encloses the second member of the doubled pair in brackets, followed by a right arrow and the text "Double word," like "this [<i>this -> Double word.]."

To check a text file for doubled words *only*, and not for any of the other things `diction` checks, use `grep` to find only those lines in `diction`'s output that contain the text "Double word," if any.

⇒ To output all lines containing double words in the file **dissertation**, type:

    $ diction dissertation | grep 'Double word' ⟨RET⟩

11.3.3 Checking Text for Readability

The `style` command analyzes the writing style of a given text. It performs a number of readability tests on the text and outputs their results, and it gives some statistical information about the sentences of the text. Give as an argument the name of the text file to check.

⇒ To check the readability of the file **dissertation**, type:

    $ style dissertation ⟨RET⟩

Like `diction`, `style` reads text from the standard input if no text is given—this is useful for the end of a pipeline, or for checking the writing style of a particular sentence or other text you type.

The sentence characteristics of the text that `style` outputs are as follows:

- Number of characters
- Number of words, their average length, and their average number of syllables
- Number of sentences and average length in words
- Number of short and long sentences
- Number of paragraphs and average length in sentences
- Number of questions and imperatives

The various readability formulas that `style` uses and outputs are as follows:

- Kincaid formula, originally developed for Navy training manuals; a good readability test for technical documentation

- Automated Readability Index (ARI)
- Coleman-Liau formula
- Flesch Reading Ease Score, which gives an approximation of readability from 0 (difficult) to 100 (easy)
- Fog Index, which gives a school-grade reading level
- WSTF Index, a readability indicator for German documents
- Wheeler-Smith Index, Lix formula, and SMOG-Grading tests, all readability indicators that give a school-grade reading level

11.3.4 Checking Text for Difficult Sentences

To output just the "difficult" sentences of a text, use `style` with the `-r` option followed by a number; `style` will output only those sentences whose Automated Readability Index (ARI) is greater than the number you give.[8]

⇒ To output all sentences in the file **dissertation** whose ARI is greater than a value of 20, type:

```
$ style -r 20 dissertation (RET)
```

11.3.5 Checking Text for Long Sentences

Use `style` to output sentences longer than a certain length by giving the number of words as an argument to the `-l` option.

⇒ To output all sentences longer than 14 words in the file **dissertation**, type:

```
$ style -l 14 dissertation (RET)
```

11.4 Using Reference Files

There are reference works and other informative text files that you can install on your system; the following recipes describe some of the more interesting and useful ones that are readily available.

---

[8] To get an idea how the ARI ranks text, see its rankings for various popular Web sites at http://www.readability.info/commonscores.shtml.

11.4.1 Consulting Word Lists and Helpful Files

Miscfiles
 DEB: miscfiles
 WWW: ftp://ftp.gnu.org/pub/gnu/miscfiles/miscfiles-1.1.tar.gz

The GNU Miscfiles collection is a group of text files containing various facts
and reference material, such as common abbreviations, telephone area codes,
and English connective phrases.

   The files are stored in the /usr/share/misc directory, and they are
all compressed; use zless to peruse them (see Recipe 9.1 [Perusing Text],
page 211).

   The following table lists the files as they appear in /usr/share/misc and
describes their contents.

GNU-manifesto.gz	The GNU Manifesto.
abbrevs.talk.gz abbrevs.gen.gz	Collections of common abbreviations used in electronic communication. (This is the place to look to find the secrets of TTYL and LOL.)
airport.gz	List of three-letter city codes for some of the major airports. The city code is useful for querying the National Weather Service computers to get the latest weather report for your region.
ascii.gz	A chart of the ASCII character set.
birthtoken.gz	The traditional stone and flower tokens for each month.
cities.dat.gz	The population, political coordinates (nation, region), and geographic coordinates (latitude, longitude) of many major cities.
inter.phone.gz	International country and city telephone codes.
languages.gz	Two-letter codes for languages, from ISO 639.
latin1.gz	A chart of the extended ASCII character set, also known as the ISO 8859 ("Latin-1") character set.
mailinglists.gz	Description of all the public GNU Project mailing lists.

`na.phone.gz`	North American (+1) telephone area codes.
`operator.gz`	Precedence table for operators in the C programming language.
`postal.codes.gz`	Postal codes for U.S. and Mexican states and Canadian provinces.
`us-constitution.gz`	*The Constitution of the United States of America* and its twenty-seven Amendments (the first ten are the *Bill of Rights*). On Debian systems, this file is placed in a directory named **/usr/share/state**.
`us-declaration.gz`	*The Declaration of Independence of the Thirteen Colonies*. On Debian systems, this file is placed in a directory named **/usr/share/state**.
`rfc-index.txt`	Indexes of Internet standardization Request For Comments (RFC) documents. On Debian systems, this file is placed in **/usr/share/rfc**.
`zipcodes.gz`	U.S. five-digit Zip Codes.

But `miscfiles` is not the only reference package available for Linux; other related packages include the following:

doc-iana	Internet protocol parameter registry documents, as published by the Internet Assigned Numbers Authority. DEB: `doc-iana`
Jargon File	The "Jargon File" is the definitive dictionary of hacker slang, and goes back decades. Might be considered somewhat dated today; is no longer distributed as a single file. DEB: `jargon-text` RPM: `jargon` WWW: `http://www.jargon.org/`
V.E.R.A.	Extensive list of computer acronyms. DEB: `vera` RPM: `vera` WWW: `ftp://ftp.gnu.org/gnu/vera/`

NOTES: The official GNU `miscfiles` distribution also includes the Jargon File and the `/usr/dict/words` dictionary file, which are available in separate packages for Debian, and are removed from the Debian `miscfiles` distribution. On Debian systems, `/usr/dict/words` is part of the standard spelling packages, and the Jargon File comes in the optional `jargon` package and installs in `/usr/share/jargon`.

11.4.2 Translating Common Acronyms

Bsdgames
  DEB: bsdgames
  RPM: bsd-games
  WWW: ftp://metalab.unc.edu/pub/Linux/games/

Use `wtf` to see what an acronym stands for. This is useful for decoding the kind of acronyms commonly used in Usenet chatter and other online chat forums. If it doesn't know the answer, it checks with `whatis` before giving up (see Recipe 2.8.2 [Getting a Description of a Program], page 46), so it will also tell you what any tool or program installed on the system is.

Give the acronym to translate as an argument to `wtf`, optionally preceded by "`is`."

⇒ To translate the acronym "LOL," type:

    $ wtf lol (RET)

Typing `wtf is lol` produces an identical result.

NOTES: While `wtf` is useful for decoding the acronyms of online writing, it doesn't know anything outside of this scope. So it can't tell you, for instance, what LASER stands for (but the WordNet dictionary can—see Recipe 11.2 [Using Dictionaries], page 282), although it will tell you all about how YMMV even when you do RTFB, so you see it is NBD.

Other collections of acronyms are available with the `miscfiles` collection (see Recipe 11.4.1 [Consulting Word Lists and Helpful Files], page 290).

## CHAPTER 12

Analyzing Text

There are many ways to use command line tools to analyze text in various ways, such as finding word frequencies, making word lists from a text, and determining which texts may be similar or otherwise relevant to a given text.

This chapter covers all of these topics. Two important subjects of textual analysis are described elsewhere: the way to determine the *format* of a given text is given in Recipe 8.1.1 [Determining a File's Type and Format], page 187, and for how to compare texts to see if (and optionally where) they differ, see Recipe 8.3 [Comparing Files], page 191.

12.1 Counting Text

Use the "word count" tool, `wc`, to count the characters, words, and lines in text.

Give the name of a file as an argument; if none is given, `wc` works on standard input. By default, `wc` outputs three columns, displaying the counts for lines, words, and characters in the text.

⇒ To output the number of lines, words, and characters in file `outline`, type:

```
$ wc outline  (RET)
```

When you specify more than one file, `wc` lists counts for each of the files and then gives total counts for all of them.

⇒ To output the number of lines, words, and characters for all the files with a `.txt` file name extension in the current directory, type:

```
$ wc -w *.txt  (RET)
```

To only output a combined count for several files, first concatenate the files with `cat`, and then pipe the output to `wc` (for more about concatenating with `cat`, see Recipe 10.6 [Concatenating Text], page 256).

⇒ To output the combined number lines, words, and characters for all the files with a `.txt` file name extension in the current directory, type:

```
$ cat *.txt | wc -w  (RET)
```

Most of the following recipes for counting text use `wc`.

NOTES: You can get a count of how many *different* words are in a text, too— use the method described in Recipe 12.2.3 [Listing Only the Unique Words in Text of a Text], page 298, and pipe the output to `wc`. To count the average *length* of words, sentences, and paragraphs, use `style` (see Recipe 11.3.3 [Checking Text for Readability], page 288).

12.1.1 Counting the Characters in a Text

Use `wc` with the `-c` option to specify that just the number of characters be counted and output.

⇒ To output the number of characters in file `classified.ad`, type:

```
$ wc -c classified.ad RET
```

12.1.2 Counting the Words in a Text

Use `wc` with the `-w` option to specify that just the number of words be counted and output.

⇒ To output the number of words in the file `story`, type:

```
$ wc -w story RET
```

NOTES: This counts the *number of words* in a text; to count the *number of times* a word occurs, see Recipe 12.2 [Listing Words in Text], page 297.

12.1.3 Counting the Lines in a Text

There are two methods; the first uses `wc` to count the lines in an entire text, while the second uses Emacs to count the lines on an individual *page* of a text.

METHOD #1

Use `wc` with the `-l` option to specify that just the number of lines be counted and output.

⇒ To output the number of lines in the file `outline`, type:

```
$ wc -l outline RET
```

METHOD #2

The `count-lines-page` function in Emacs outputs in the minibuffer the number of lines on the current *page* (as delimited by pagebreak characters, if any—see Recipe 13.3 [Paginating Text], page 312), followed by the number of lines in the buffer before the line that point is on, and then the number of lines in the buffer after point.

⇒ To count the number of lines per page in the current buffer in Emacs, type:

⟨CTRL⟩-⟨X⟩ `l`

Emacs outputs the number of lines per page of the current buffer in the echo area.

For example, suppose the output in the minibuffer is this:

`Page has 351 lines (69 + 283)`

This means that the current page contains 351 lines, and point is on line number 70—there are 69 lines before this line and 283 lines after it.

12.1.4 Counting the Occurrences of Something

To find the number of occurrences of a text string or pattern in a file or files, use **grep** to search the file(s) for the text string, and pipe the output to **wc** with the **-l** option.

⇒ Here are two ways to use this.

- To find the number of lines in the file **outline** that contain the string "**chapter**," type:

    `$ grep chapter outline | wc -l` ⟨RET⟩

- To find the number of lines in all of the files with a **.txt** extension in the **/usr/share/doc/** directory tree that contain the string "**chapter**," regardless of case, type:

    `$ grep -r -i chapter /usr/share/doc/ | wc -l` ⟨RET⟩

NOTES: This method is quick and easy, but it will not count more than one occurrence on the same line, and it won't find occurrences that are broken by the end of a line.

For more recipes for searching text, and more about **grep**, see Chapter 14 [Searching Text], page 333.

12.1.5 Counting a Selection of Text

A useful trick for counting how many words are in some text you see displayed in some window or terminal—say, displayed in a Web browser—is to *select* the text (see Recipe 10.3 [Manipulating Selections of Text], page 253), and then count it as follows: run **wc** in another terminal, paste the text selection into this terminal, and then type ⟨CTRL⟩-⟨D⟩ to end the input. It will give a count for the selection.

⇒ Here are two ways to use this.

- To count the number of characters, lines and words in a selection of text in the first virtual console, do the following:

  1. Switch to the second virtual console:

     $\langle\text{ALT}\rangle$-$\langle\text{F2}\rangle$

  2. Log in to this console, and start **wc** at the shell prompt:

     `$ wc` $\langle\text{RET}\rangle$

  3. Switch back to the first virtual console:

     $\langle\text{ALT}\rangle$-$\langle\text{F1}\rangle$

  4. Select the text to be counted by moving the mouse pointer to the beginning of it, pressing and holding the left button and dragging the pointer to the end of the text, and then letting go of the mouse button.

  5. Switch back to the second virtual console:

     $\langle\text{ALT}\rangle$-$\langle\text{F2}\rangle$

  6. Click the middle mouse button.

  7. Type $\langle\text{CTRL}\rangle$-$\langle\text{D}\rangle$ to stop inputting text to **wc**.

- To count the words in a selection of text on a Web page when you are in X, do the following:

  1. Start **wc** in a terminal window:

     `$ wc -w` $\langle\text{RET}\rangle$

  2. Select the text to be counted by moving the mouse pointer to the beginning of it in the browser window, pressing and holding the left button and dragging the pointer to the end of the text, and then letting go of the mouse button.

  3. Move the mouse pointer to where the cursor is in the terminal window, and click the middle mouse button. (If you do not have a three-button mouse, click both the left and right buttons at the same time.)

  4. Type $\langle\text{CTRL}\rangle$-$\langle\text{D}\rangle$ in the terminal window.

12.2 Listing Words in Text

When analyzing text, a "word" can be any grouping of characters that are separated from other words by either blank spaces or newlines. They can be English words, numbers, symbols, and so on.

Making a listing of the words that appear in some text—either a file or standard input—is a simple matter when you use a popular combination of `tr`, `sort`, and `uniq`, all tools for formatting text that are discussed in the next chapter (see Chapter 13 [Formatting Text], page 305).

You can sort these lists alphabetically, remove any duplicate words, and list the frequency each word appears in the original text. These alphabetical word-frequency lists are similar to a *concordance*, which is an index of all the words in a text, along with their contexts.

Since `tr` is a filter, these recipes use redirection to send files to `tr`'s standard input (see Recipe 3.2.1 [Redirecting Input to a File], page 67). The output is usually piped to `less` for perusal. If you want to print or peruse the output of these recipes, I recommend you pipe them to `pr` to paginate the output and place it in columns (see Recipe 13.3 [Paginating Text], page 312). A further refinement is to use `enscript` to print them in a nice font (see Recipe 15.2.1 [Outputting Text in a Font], page 361).

12.2.1 Listing All of the Words in Text

To output a list of all of the words as they appear in some text, use the `tr` filter to translate all horizontal whitespace (such as tab and space characters) to newline characters, and squeeze out blank lines.

⇒ To peruse a list containing all of the words from the text file **book** as they appear in the text, type:

```
$ tr -s '[:blank:]' '\n' < book | less (RET)
```

To remove all of the punctuation from the listed words, pipe the output to another `tr` that deletes it.

⇒ To peruse a list containing all of the words from the text file **book** as they appear in the text, but with punctuation removed, type:

```
$ tr -s '[:blank:]' '\n' < book | tr -d '[:punct:]' | less (RET)
```

Dashes are not removed with punctuation. If the text to filter contains em dashes consisting of two hyphens (--) with no spaces between the words on either side of the dashes, first filter them out by with SED, replacing them with a space character (see Recipe 10.5 [Editing Streams of Text], page 255). Then pass that filtered text to `tr`.

⇒ To peruse a list containing all of the words from the text file **book** as they appear in the text, but with punctuation removed, type (all on one line):

```
$ sed 's/--/ /g' book | tr -s '[:blank:]' '\n' |
tr -d '[:punct:]' | less RET
```

NOTES: If there is any whitespace before the first word in the input, this method inserts a newline character at the beginning of the output. To remove it, add **tail +2** to the end of the pipeline but before you peruse or print it (see Recipe 9.2.3 [Displaying the End Part of Text], page 218).

12.2.2 Listing the Words in Text Sorted Alphabetically

To output a sorted list of the words of some text, use the method as described in the previous recipe and pipe the output to **sort** (see Recipe 13.6 [Sorting Text], page 320).

⇒ Here are two ways to use this.

- To peruse a list containing all of the words from the text file **book** with punctuation removed, sorted alphabetically, type (all on one line):

```
$ tr -s '[:blank:]' '\n' < book | tr -d '[:punct:]'
| sort | less RET
```

- To peruse a list containing all of the words from the text file **book** sorted numerically, type:

```
$ tr -s '[:blank:]' '\n' < book | sort -n | less RET
```

This method is case-sensitive. To sort words regardless of case, first convert all uppercase letters to lowercase by piping to **tr** again before **sort** (see Recipe 13.4.1 [Changing Characters in Text], page 317).

⇒ To peruse a list containing all of the words from the text file **book** with punctuation removed, sorted alphabetically regardless of case, type (all on one line):

```
$ tr -s '[:blank:]' '\n' < book | tr -d '[:punct:]' | tr
'[:upper:]' '[:lower:]' | sort | less RET
```

12.2.3 Listing Only the Unique Words in Text

To list the words in some text, omitting any multiple occurrences of a word, use the method as described in the previous recipe and pipe the output to **uniq** (see Recipe 13.5 [Filtering Out Duplicate Lines of Text], page 319).

⇒ Here are some ways to use this.

- To peruse a list containing all of the words from the text file **book** with punctuation removed, sorted alphabetically with duplicates removed, type (all on one line):

      $ tr -s '[:blank:]' '\n' < book | tr -d '[:punct:]'
      | sort | uniq | less ⟨RET⟩

- To peruse a list containing all of the words from the text file **book** with punctuation removed, sorted alphabetically regardless of case, and with duplicates removed, type (all on one line):

      $ tr -s '[:blank:]' '\n' < book | tr -d '[:punct:]'
      | tr '[:upper:]' '[:lower:]' | sort | uniq | less ⟨RET⟩

- To peruse a list containing all of the words from the text file **book** sorted numerically, but with all duplicates removed, type (all on one line):

      $ tr -s '[:blank:]' '\n' < book | sort -n | uniq |
      less ⟨RET⟩

12.2.4 Counting Word Occurrences in Text

There are two methods of counting word occurrences in text. One outputs a count of each unique word in the input text, and the other outputs a total count of *all* unique words in the input text.

METHOD #1

To get a word-frequency count of words in some text, use the method as described in the previous recipe but give the -c option to **uniq**, which will precede each line with its *count* (the number of times it occurs in the text). Then pipe the output to **sort** with the -n option to sort numerically and -r to reverse the order.

⇒ Here are some ways to use this.

- To peruse a listing of all the words from the text file **book** with punctuation removed, sorted by their frequency, listed with their number of occurrences and beginning with the most frequent, type (all on one line):

      $ tr -s '[:blank:]' '\n' < book | tr -d '[:punct:]'
      | sort | uniq -c | sort -n -r | less ⟨RET⟩

- To peruse a listing of all the words from the text file **book** with punctuation removed, sorted by their frequency regardless of case, listed with their number of occurrences and beginning with the most frequent, type (all on one line):

```
$ tr -s '[:blank:]' '\n' < book | tr -d '[:punct:]'
| tr '[:upper:]' '[:lower:]' | sort | uniq -c |
sort -n -r | less ⟨RET⟩
```

METHOD #2

To get the total number of different words in a text, use the method for listing unique words as described in the previous recipe, and pipe the output to **wc** with the **-l** option. This counts all the lines of its input—which in this case will be the list of unique words, one per line.

⇒ To output a total count of the number of unique words in the text file **book**, type (all on one line):

```
$ tr -s '[:blank:]' '\n' < book | tr -d '[:punct:]' |
sort | uniq | wc -l ⟨RET⟩
```

12.2.5 Counting Selected Word Occurrences in Text

To get a frequency count of only selected words from some text, use Method #1 as described in the previous recipe and pipe the output to **grep**, searching for the particular word or words you want (see Recipe 14.1 [Searching Text for a Word], page 333).

⇒ Here are some ways to do this.

- To list the frequency of the word "**chapter**" as it appears in the text file **book** with punctuation removed, type (all on one line):

```
$ tr -s '[:blank:]' '\n' < book | tr -d '[:punct:]'
| sort | uniq -c | sort -n -r | grep chapter ⟨RET⟩
```

- To list the frequency of the words "**contents**" and "**index**" as they appear in the text file **book** with punctuation removed, type (all on one line):

```
$ tr -s '[:blank:]' '\n' < book | tr -d '[:punct:]'
| sort | uniq -c | sort -n -r | grep
'contents\|index' ⟨RET⟩
```

- To list the frequency of the words ending in "**ing**" as they appear in the text file **book** with punctuation removed, type (all on one line):

```
$ tr -s '[:blank:]' '\n' < book | tr -d '[:punct:]'
| sort | uniq -c | sort -n -r | grep 'ing$' ⟨RET⟩
```

To search on the number of occurrences, `grep` for numbers that occur at the beginning of the line after any number of space characters and followed by a tab character (quote a tab to `grep` as ⟨CTRL⟩-⟨V⟩; see Recipe 3.1.2 [Typing a Control Character], page 55).

⇒ Here are two ways to do this.

- To list the words that occur ten times in the text file **book** with punctuation removed, type (all on one line):

  ```
  $ tr -s '[:blank:]' '\n' < book | tr -d '[:punct:]'
  | sort | uniq -c | sort -n -r | grep '^[ ]*10⟨CTRL⟩-⟨Q⟩
  ⟨CTRL⟩-⟨V⟩' ⟨RET⟩
  ```

- To list the words that occur between eighty and eighty-five times in the text file **book** with punctuation removed, type (all on one line):

  ```
  $ tr -s '[:blank:]' '\n' < book | tr -d '[:punct:]'
  | sort | uniq -c | sort -n -r | grep '^[ ]*8[0-5]
  ⟨CTRL⟩-⟨Q⟩ ⟨CTRL⟩-⟨V⟩' ⟨RET⟩
  ```

12.3 Finding Relevancies in Texts

The following recipes show how to analyze a given text for its similarity or relevance to some other text, either to given keywords or to whole files of text.

You can also use the `diff` family of tools to analyze differences between texts; those tools are especially good for comparing different revisions of the same file (see Recipe 8.3 [Comparing Files], page 191).

12.3.1 Finding Similar or Relevant Text

Compare
WWW: `http://www.english.upenn.edu/~jlynch/Computing/compare.html`

It is sometimes desirable to compare two texts for relevancies—that is, to search for text that is identical or even just *similar*. Jack Lynch's `compare` does this.

Given two files as arguments, `compare` will show lines of text that occur anywhere in both files that are similar to each other, even if these lines contain stylistic or formatting differences. Seventeen common English words, including "the," "a," and "of," are considered *noise words* and are not compared.

By default, `compare` uses a similarity threshold of fifty, on a scale from 0 (whre the two texts contain no similarities at all) to 100 (where the texts consist entirely of exactly identical lines). To specify the threshold value, give a number from 0 to 100 as an option after the two file names.

To ignore exact duplicates, give a fourth option. This can be any value or character, so long as it's there.

⇒ Here are some ways to use this.

- To output a list of any lines in the files **invitations** and **addresses** that are similar to each other, type:

  `$ compare invitations addresses` ⟨RET⟩

- To output a list of any lines in the files **weddings** and **parties** that match with a threshold level of 85 percent similarity, type:

  `$ compare weddings parties 85` ⟨RET⟩

- To output a list of any lines in the files **invitations** and **addresses** that are similar to each other, but not output exact duplicates, type:

  `$ compare invitations addresses 50 1` ⟨RET⟩

NOTES: This tool has many handy uses. Use it whenever you might search for close similarities, but not necessarily identical strings, in two samples of text. For example, comparing catalog or sale lists with collector wish lists; detecting plagiarism and authorship; and comparing reading lists. Its author uses it to find and identify allusions in works of literature.

12.3.2 Listing Relevant Files in Emacs

Remembrance Agent
  DEB: `remembrance-agent`
  RPM: `remem`
  WWW: `http://www.remem.org/`

The purpose of the special **remembrance-agent** mode in Emacs is to analyze the text you type and, in the background, find similar or relevant passages of text within your other files. It then outputs, in a smaller window, a list of suggestions—those files that it has found, which you can open in a new buffer.

When installing **remembrance-agent** mode, you create three databases of files to use when making relevance suggestions; when **remembrance-agent** mode is running, it searches these three databases in parallel, looking for relevant text. You could create, for example, one database of saved email, one of your own writings, and one of saved documents.

⇒ To toggle **remembrance-agent** mode in the current buffer, type:

  ⟨CTRL⟩-⟨C⟩ r t

When `remembrance-agent` is running, suggested buffers will be displayed in the small `*Remembrance*` buffer at the bottom of the screen. To open a suggestion in a new buffer, type ⟨CTRL⟩-⟨C⟩ *r number*, where *number* is the number of the suggestion.

⇒ To open the second suggested file in a new buffer, type:

   ⟨CTRL⟩-⟨C⟩ *r 2*

## CHAPTER 13

Formatting Text

Methods and tools for changing the arrangement or presentation of text are often useful when preparing text for printing. This chapter discusses ways of changing the spacing of text and setting up pages, of underlining and sorting and reversing text, and of numbering lines of text.

Most of these tools are filters (see Recipe 3.2.4 [Redirecting Output to Another Command's Input], page 69).

13.1 Spacing Text

These recipes are for changing the *spacing* of text—the whitespace that exists between words, lines, and paragraphs.

The filters described in this section send output to standard output by default; to save their output to a file, use shell redirection (see Recipe 3.2.2 [Redirecting Output to a File], page 68).

13.1.1 Eliminating Extra Spaces in Text

There are a few methods for doing this. To eliminate extra whitespaces `within` lines of text, use the `fmt` filter; to eliminate extra whitespace *between* lines of text, use `cat`.

METHOD #1

Use `fmt` with the `-u` option to output text with "uniform spacing," where the space between words is reduced to one space character and the space between sentences is reduced to two space characters.

⇒ To output the file **term-paper** with uniform spacing, type:

    $ fmt -u term-paper (RET)

METHOD #2

Use `cat` with the `-s` option to "squeeze" multiple adjacent blank lines into one.

⇒ To output the file **term-paper** with multiple blank lines output as only one blank line, type:

    $ cat -s term-paper (RET)

METHOD #3

You can combine both of these commands to output text with multiple adjacent lines removed *and* with uniform spacing between words. The following example sends the output of the combined commands to **less** so that it can be perused on the screen.

⇒ To peruse the text file **term-paper** with multiple blank lines removed and giving the text uniform spacing between words, type:

```
$ cat -s term-paper | fmt -u | less RET
```

Notice that in this example, both **fmt** and **less** worked on their standard input instead of on a file—the standard output of **cat** (the contents of **term-paper** with extra blank lines squeezed out) was passed to the standard input of **fmt**; its standard output (the space-squeezed **term-paper**, now with uniform spacing) was sent to the standard input of **less**, which displayed it on the screen.

13.1.2 Single-Spacing Text

There are many methods for single-spacing text. These are my favorites.

METHOD #1

To remove all empty lines from text output, use **grep** with the regular expression "." to match any character, and will therefore match any line that isn't empty (see Recipe 14.3 [Matching Patterns of Text], page 335). You can then redirect this output to a file, or pipe it to other commands. The original file is not altered.

⇒ To output all non-empty lines from the file **term-paper**, type:

```
$ grep . term-paper RET
```

This command outputs all lines that are not empty—so lines containing only non-printing characters, such as spaces and tabs, will still be output.

METHOD #2

To remove from the output all empty lines, and all lines that consist of only space characters, use **grep** with "[^]." as the regexp to search for.

⇒ To output only the lines from the file **term-paper** that contain more than just space characters, type:

```
$ grep '[^ ].' term-paper RET
```

NOTES: This regexp will still output lines that contain only tab characters.

METHOD #3

To remove from the output all empty lines, *and* lines that contain only a combination of tab or space characters, use `grep` with "`[^[:space:]].`" as the regexp to search for. It uses the special predefined "`[:space:]`" regexp class, which matches any kind of space character at all, including tabs.

⇒ To output only the lines from the file **term-paper** that contain more than just space or tab characters, type:

    `$ grep '[^[:space:]].' term-paper` (RET)

METHOD #4

If a file is double-spaced, where all even lines are blank, you can remove those lines from the output by using `sed` with the "`n;d`" expression.

⇒ To output only the odd lines from file **term-paper**, type:

    `$ sed 'n;d' term-paper` (RET)

13.1.3 Double-Spacing Text

To double-space text, where one blank line is inserted between each line in the original text, use the `pr` tool with the `-d` option. By default, `pr` paginates text and puts a header at the top of each page with the current date, time, and page number; use the `-t` option to omit this header.

⇒ Here are two ways to use this.

- To double-space the file **term-paper** and write the output to the file **term-paper.print**, type:

    `$ pr -d -t term-paper > term-paper.print` (RET)

- To double-space the file **term-paper** and send the output directly to the printer for printing, type:

    `$ pr -d -t term-paper | lpr` (RET)

NOTES: The `pr` ("print") tool is a text pre-formatter, often used to paginate and otherwise prepare text files for printing; more discussion on the use of this tool is in Recipe 13.3 [Paginating Text], page 312.

13.1.4 Triple-Spacing Text

To triple-space text, where two blank lines are inserted between each line of the original text, use `sed` with the "`G;G`" expression.

⇒ To triple-space the file **term-paper** and write the output to the file **term-paper.print**, type:

$ *sed 'G;G' term-paper > term-paper.print* ⟨RET⟩

The "G" expression appends one blank line to each line of **sed**'s output; using ";" you can specify more than one blank line to append (but you must quote this command, because the semicolon (;) has meaning to the shell—see Recipe 3.1.3 [Quoting Reserved Characters], page 56). You can use multiple "G" characters to output text with more than double or triple spaces.

⇒ To quadruple-space the file **term-paper**, and write the output to the file **term-paper.print**, type:

$ *sed 'G;G;G' term-paper > term-paper.print* ⟨RET⟩

NOTES: SED is described in Recipe 10.5 [Editing Streams of Text], page 255.

13.1.5 Adding Line Breaks to Text

Sometimes a file will not have a line break at the end of each line (this commonly happens during file conversions between operating systems). To add line breaks to a file that does not have them, use the text formatter **fmt**. It outputs text with lines arranged up to a specified width; if no width is specified, it formats text up to a width of 75 characters per line.

⇒ To output the file **term-paper** with lines up to 75 characters long, type:

$ *fmt term-paper* ⟨RET⟩

Use the **-w** option to specify the maximum line width, in characters.

⇒ To output the file **term-paper** with lines up to 80 characters long, type:

$ *fmt -w 80 term-paper* ⟨RET⟩

13.1.6 Adding Margins to Text

Giving text a larger left margin is especially good when you want to print a copy and punch holes in it for use with a three-ring binder.

To output a text file with a larger left margin, use **pr** with the file name as an argument; give the **-t** option (to disable headers and footers), and, as an argument to the **-o** option, give the number of spaces to offset the text. Add the number of spaces to the page width (whose default is 72) and specify this new width as an argument to the **-w** option.

⇒ To output the file **owners-manual** with a 5-space (or 5-*column*) margin to a new file, **owners-manual.pr**, type:

```
$ pr -t -o 5 -w 77 owners-manual > owners-manual.pr RET
```

This command is almost always used for printing, so the output is usually just piped to `lpr` instead of being saved to a file. Many text documents have a width of 80 and not 72 columns; if you are printing such a document and need to keep the 80 columns across the page, specify a new width of 85. If your printer can only print 80 columns of text, specify a width of 80; the text will be reformatted to 75 columns after the 5-column margin.

⇒ Here are two ways to use this.

- To print the file **owners-manual** with a 5-column margin and 80 columns of text, type:

```
$ pr -t -o 5 -w 85 owners-manual | lpr RET
```

- To print the file **owners-manual** with a 5-column margin and 75 columns of text, type:

```
$ pr -t -o 5 -w 80 owners-manual | lpr RET
```

13.1.7 Swapping Tab and Space Characters

Use the **expand** and **unexpand** tools to swap tab characters for space characters, and to swap space characters with tabs, respectively.

Both tools take a file name as an argument and write changes to the standard output; if no files are specified, they work on the standard input.

To convert tab characters to spaces, use **expand**. To convert only the *initial* or leading tabs on each line, give the `-i` option; the default action is to convert *all* tabs.

⇒ Here are two ways to use this.

- To convert all tab characters to spaces in file **list**, and write the output to **list2**, type:

```
$ expand list > list2 RET
```

- To convert only initial tab characters to spaces in file **list**, and write the output to the standard output, type:

```
$ expand -i list RET
```

To convert multiple space characters to tabs, use **unexpand**. By default, it only converts leading spaces into tabs, counting eight space characters for each tab. Use the `-a` option to specify that *all* instances of eight space characters be converted to tabs.

⇒ Here are two ways to use this.

- To convert every eight leading space characters to tabs in file `list2`, and write the output to `list`, type:

    `$ unexpand list2 > list` ⟨RET⟩

- To convert all occurrences of eight space characters to tabs in file `list2`, and write the output to the standard output, type:

    `$ unexpand -a list2` ⟨RET⟩

To specify the number of spaces to convert to a tab, give that number as an argument to the `-t` option.

⇒ To convert every leading space character to a tab character in `list2`, and write the output to the standard output, type:

    `$ unexpand -t 1 list2` ⟨RET⟩

NOTES: You can also use `col` with the `-x` option to turn all tabs in its input to spaces.

13.1.8 Removing or Replacing Newline Characters

The newline character, represented by many commands as the "\n" backslash escape sequence, is the character that terminates every line. Use `tr` to remove it or replace it with something else.

To remove newlines, use the `-d` option and give the newline as the quoted set to delete.

⇒ To take the text in the file **many** and remove any newline characters from it, then write it to a file **single**, type:

    `$ tr -d '\n' < many > single` ⟨RET⟩

To replace the newline character with some other character, use `tr`, giving the newline character as the first quoted set, and the character to replace it with as the second.

⇒ To take the text in the file **many** and replace any newlines with a formfeed, and then send the output to the printer, type:

    `$ tr '\n' '\f' < many | lpr` ⟨RET⟩

13.1.9 Removing Carriage Return Characters

In Linux, as with all unices, lines in a text file end with just a newline character, represented as "\n" (so when you press the ⟨RET⟩ key, it is this character that is typed); in some operating systems, lines end with both a newline character and a carriage return character (represented by "\m"). This shows up as "^M" in a file. Remove them with col.

⇒ To process a file named operating_plan.txt, filtering out any carriage returns from the text, and writing this filtered text to a new file called operating_plan, type:

```
$ col < operating_plan.txt > operating_plan ⟨RET⟩
```

You can then view the literal characters of both the raw and the processed files to see that the carriage returns, displayed as "\r" in the raw file, are gone—see Recipe 9.2.6 [Displaying the Literal Characters of Text], page 221.

13.2 Justifying Text

Probably the best way to justify text is in a text editor. Two that have functions to justify text in all three positions (left, center, and right) are Emacs and Vim.

The following recipes describe command line methods for justifying text in various ways.

13.2.1 Left-Justifying Text

To left-justify text, use sed with "s/^[⟨TAB⟩]*//" as a command option. Given the name of a file as an argument, or piped to the standard input, this SED command outputs the text left-justified.

⇒ To left-justify the text in the file draft.1, writing it to a file draft.2, type:

```
$ sed 's/^[ ⟨CTRL⟩-⟨V⟩ ⟨TAB⟩]*//' draft.1 > draft.2 ⟨RET⟩
```

NOTES: The brackets contain two characters: a space and a tab. In order to pass the literal tab to this command, you do a verbatim insert by first typing ⟨CTRL⟩-⟨V⟩ and then the key you want—in this case, ⟨TAB⟩.

13.2.2 Right-Justifying Text

To right-justify some text, first pass it to col with the -x option to convert any tabs to literal space characters, and then use a SED one-liner.

⇒ To right-justify the text in file new-items, and write it to a new file display-items, type (all on one line):

```
$ col -x < new-items | sed -e :a -e
's/^.\{1,78\}$/ &/;ta' > display-items ⟨RET⟩
```

13.2.3 Center-Justifying Text

Use `fold` to center-justify text, giving the column width as an argument to the `-w` option. You can also use `tr` to remove any linefeeds in the text, and then pipe the output to `fold`.

⇒ Here are some ways to use this.

- To center-justify the text in the file `log` using forty columns, and peruse it on the screen, type:

  `$ fold -w40 log | less` ⟨RET⟩

- To center-justify the text in the file `log` using eighty columns, and write it to a new file called `log2`, type:

  `$ tr -d '\n' < log | fold -w80 > log2` ⟨RET⟩

NOTES: This method breaks words across lines.

13.3 Paginating Text

A page break in a text file is simply a formfeed character ("Control-L," or octal code 014) that you can insert with a text editor at the point in the file where you want one page to end and another to begin. When you send text with a formfeed character to the printer, the current page being printed is ejected and a new page begins—thus, you can paginate a text file by inserting formfeed characters wherever you want a page break to occur.

You can similarly paginate text in a text editor by manually inserting formfeed characters, but there are also tools that do this automatically, inserting formfeeds throughout the text at set increments, optionally processing the file in other ways to give it pages.

The `pr` filter is one such tool. It's a general-purpose page formatter and print-preparation utility. By default, it paginates for a length of 66 lines per page, putting a header and footer on each page. The header contains a line with the date, file name, and current page, with two blank lines before and after it; the footer consists of three blank lines to separate the pages. Thus, 56 lines of input text are on each page by default, and the other lines are the header and footer. Any formfeeds in the text will force a page break at that point, in addition to the regular page breaks just described.

⇒ To print the file `duchess` with the default `pr` preparation, type:

  `$ pr duchess | lpr` ⟨RET⟩

There are many options that you can use to customize the output of text you paginate.

NOTES: It's also common to use `pr` to change the spacing of text (see Recipe 13.1 [Spacing Text], page 305).

13.3.1 Paginating with a Custom Page Length

By default, `pr` outputs pages of 66 lines each. You can specify the page length as an argument to the `-l` option. If you give a value of 10 or less, no headers or footers are printed, and any formfeeds in the file are ignored.

⇒ To paginate the file `listings` with 43-line pages, and write the output to a file called `listings.page`, type:

```
$ pr -f -h "" -l 43 listings > listings.page ⟨RET⟩
```

NOTES: If a page has more lines than a printer can fit on a physical sheet of paper, it will automatically break the text at that line as well as at the places in the text where there are formfeed characters.

13.3.2 Paginating with a Custom Page Width

By default, `pr` outputs text with a width of 72 characters per line. To specify a different width, use `-w` and give the new width as an argument.

⇒ To paginate the text in the file `miscellania` and output it at a width of 80 characters per line, type:

```
$ pr -w 80 miscellania ⟨RET⟩
```

13.3.3 Paginating with Custom Headers

You can change the default `pr` headers, and you can eliminate them entirely.

Use the `-f` option to omit the footer and separate pages of output with the formfeed character. Use the `-h` option to give a new title for the middle part of the header band; quote it as an argument to the option, making sure to keep a space between it and the option. To specify a header with no title, put nothing between the quotes.

⇒ To paginate the file `listings` and write the output to a file called `listings.page`, type:

```
$ pr -f -h "" listings > listings.page ⟨RET⟩
```

Use the `-t` option to omit the header and footer on each page entirely, and use `-T` to omit the header, footer, and any formfeed characters that are in the file.

⇒ To paginate the text in the file **listings** with no headers or footers, but retaining any existing formfeeds, type:

```
$ pr -t listings ⟨RET⟩
```

NOTES: There is currently no **pr** option to place headers on all but the first page, so if you need to format text in this common convention, first use **pr** to output to a file without headers, then use **pr** to output to another file with the headers you want for the remaining pages. Then, use a text editor to combine the first page of the former with the remaining pages of the latter.

13.3.4 Placing Text in Paginated Columns

You can also use **pr** to put text in columns—give the number of columns to output as an argument. Use the **-t** option to omit the printing of the default headers and footers.

⇒ To print the file **news.update** in four columns with no headers or footers, type:

```
$ pr -4 -t news.update | lpr ⟨RET⟩
```

To paginate columns from multiple files, use **-m**. The contents of the files given as arguments are output together, each in its own column.

⇒ To output the text in **col.1**, **col.2**, and **col.3** in paginated columns with no headers, and with pages separated by formfeeds, outputting to a file called **comparisons**, type:

```
$ pr -t -f -m col.1 col.2 col.3 > comparisons ⟨RET⟩
```

Columns are made to fit pages of 72-character line widths; the columns are truncated to fit this size unless you give the **-J** option, which makes columns big enough to fit the text, regardless of line width.

⇒ To print the file **results.data** in six columns and not truncating long lines, type:

```
$ pr -6 -t -J results.data | lpr ⟨RET⟩
```

To fit the columns on a line width that is between 72 and 79 characters, first calculate the character length of an individual column by dividing the line width by the number of columns to use. Format the entire text for that length using **fmt**, giving the column length you calculated as an argument to the **-w** option. Pipe the output of that command to **pr**.

⇒ To print the contents of the file **editorial** in two columns to fit on 72-character lines, type:

```
$ fmt -w 36 editorial | pr -2 | lpr ⟨RET⟩
```

Use the -a option to output in rows (columns running *across* the page) instead of columns running down.

⇒ To output the text in col.1, col.2, and col.3 in paginated columns going across, outputting to a file called comparisons, type:

```
$ pr -a -m col.1 col.2 col.3 > comparisons (RET)
```

13.3.5 Paginating Only Part of Some Text

To paginate only part of the text input, give as an option "+*first*:*last*," where *first* represents the first page to output, and *last* represents the last page. Omit *last* if you want to print from *first* to the end of the text.

⇒ Here are two ways to do this.

- To output to the printer only pages 7 through 14 of the input file sales.feb, type:

```
$ pr +7:14 sales.feb | lpr (RET)
```

- To output to the printer the paginated contents of the file sales.feb, beginning at page 80, and with a header containing the text "DRAFT COPY," type:

```
$ pr +80 -h "DRAFT COPY" sales.feb | lpr (RET)
```

NOTES: You can also use head or tail to display only a certain part of the text, such as an ending or a middle part, and pipe that to pr for pagination (see Recipe 9.2 [Displaying Text], page 216).

13.3.6 Paginating Text with Non-Printing Characters

Two of pr's options control the way that non-printing characters can be represented in the output.

Use -v to output all non-printing characters in *octal backslash* notation, where a backslash is printed, followed by the character's ASCII character code, in octal.

Use -c to output control characters in hat notation, and otherwise output all other non-printing characters in octal backslash.

⇒ Here are two ways to do this.

- To paginate figures with all non-printing characters in octal notation, type:

```
$ pr -v figures (RET)
```

- To paginate `figures` with control characters in hat notation and all non-printing characters in octal notation, type:

    `$ pr -c figures` ⟨RET⟩

13.3.7 Placing Formfeeds in Text

You can place your own formfeeds in some text. Insert them with a text editor that lets you quote special characters, such as Emacs or Vi. Wherever you place a formfeed in the text, a page break will happen when you print it.

It may be useful to convert other characters in some text to formfeeds. This may come up when you are working on a file that you want to print in a certain way. To do this, use SED to convert the character to the ⟨CTRL⟩-⟨L⟩ character.

⇒ To convert three consecutive linefeeds in a file **design** to a single formfeed character, and write the output to a file named **design.paged**, type (all on one line):

    `$ sed -ne '/./{x;/./{s///;s/...*/`⟨CTRL⟩`-`⟨V⟩
    ⟨CTRL⟩`-`⟨L⟩`/;p;s/.*//;}' -e 'x;p;d;}'`
    `-e H design > design.paged` ⟨RET⟩

13.4 Transposing Characters in Text

Use `tr`, the transpose filter, to change some characters of its input text, either deleting them, squeezing duplicate characters, or transposing some specified characters into others. There are no file arguments; `tr` takes its standard input, makes these changes, and then writes the changed text to its standard output—`tr` is the classic text filter (see Recipe 3.2.4 [Redirecting Output to Another Command's Input], page 69).

You specify a *set* to work on as an argument, which is just a quoted list of characters. For example, when using `tr` to delete characters, any characters in the given set is filtered out of its input.

Use a hyphen character (`-`) in a set to denote a *range* of characters—for example, "`A-Z`" means the uppercase letters "`A`" through "`Z`." To give a literal hyphen character, specify it last in the set.

Remember that `tr` only works on characters, and not on strings—so "`cat`" specifies the three letters "`c`," "`a`," and "`t`," not the name of the animal.

Specify control characters or reserved shell characters with backslash notation—but if you do so, be sure to quote the set.

A set can be a *character class*, which is a predefined set of characters, as described in the following table. To specify a character class in a set, use "`[:class:]`," where *class* is the name of the class.

`alnum`	All letters and digits.
`alpha`	All letters.
`blank`	Blank spaces—tab and space characters.
`cntrl`	Control characters.
`digit`	Digits.
`graph`	All printing characters, excepting blank space.
`lower`	All lowercase letters.
`print`	All printing characters, including blank space.
`punct`	Punctuation marks.
`space`	Blank space.
`upper`	All uppercase letters.
`xdigit`	All hexadecimal digits.

There are many examples of `tr` elsewhere in this chapter and throughout this book, and there are many ways `tr` can be used in conjunction with other tools. The following recipes describe its basic functions.

13.4.1 Changing Characters in Text

To change a set of characters in some text to another given set, use `tr` and give the two sets as arguments.

⇒ Here are some ways to use this.

- To output the contents of the file **scanner-copy**, translating all capital "O" characters to zeroes (0) in the output, type:

    $ *tr O 0 < scanner-copy* ⟨RET⟩

- To output the contents of the file **CAPS**, translating all uppercase letters to their lowercase equivalents, type:

    $ *tr A-Z a-z < CAPS* ⟨RET⟩

- To output the contents of the file CAPS, translating all uppercase letters to their lowercase equivalents, type:[1]

    ```
    $ tr [:upper:] [:lower:] < CAPS (RET)
    ```

- To output the contents of the file CAPS, translating all uppercase letters from M to S as hyphen characters, type:

    ```
    $ tr M-S - < CAPS (RET)
    ```

- To output the contents of the file transmission, translating all newline characters to a forward slash character (/) and all "Control-G" characters to an asterisk character (*), type:

    ```
    $ tr "\n\a" "/\*" < transmission (RET)
    ```

13.4.2 Squeezing Duplicate Characters in Text

Use tr with the -s option to *squeeze* repeated characters, where any sequence of repeated characters is replaced by exactly one instance of that character.

⇒ To output the contents of the file moo, with all repeated uppercase and lowercase letters squeezed, type:

    ```
    $ tr -s A-Za-z < moo (RET)
    ```

In this example, only one set is given; any characters in that set that repeat are squeezed into a single instance of the character.

Use two sets to replace a set of repeated characters with some other set.

⇒ To output the contents of the file moo, with all repeated "o" and "O" characters replaced by one instance of "e" or "E," type:

    ```
    $ tr -s oO eE < moo (RET)
    ```

In the preceding example, any repeated characters other than "o" and "O" are untouched, as are any "o" and "O" characters that are *not* repeated.

13.4.3 Deleting Characters in Text

To delete certain characters in some text, use tr with the -d option, and give the set of characters to delete.

⇒ To output the contents of the file CAPS, with all lowercase letters deleted, type:

    ```
    $ tr -d [:lower:] < CAPS (RET)
    ```

---

[1] This example is equivalent to the previous example; one specifies text with a range and another with a character class, but both produce the same result.

13.5 Filtering Out Duplicate Lines of Text

There are two methods for filtering out duplicate lines of text.

METHOD #1

The `uniq` tool outputs only the unique lines of its input—any lines occurring more than once are only output once. The input must be sorted; that is, duplicate lines must be neighboring (see Recipe 13.6 [Sorting Text], page 320).

⇒ To output the contents of the file **options**, with all duplicate lines filtered out, type:

```
$ uniq options RET
```

Use the `-i` option to ignore case when making comparisons.

⇒ To output the contents of the file **options**, with all duplicate lines filtered out, regardless of case, type:

```
$ uniq -i options RET
```

To output *only* the lines that have duplicates, use the `-d` option. To output only the lines that have duplicates, plus every instance of each duplicate line, use `-D` instead.

⇒ Here are two ways to use this.

- To output only the lines in the file **options** that have duplicates, but not the duplicates themselves, type:

```
$ uniq -d options RET
```

- To output all of the lines in the file **options** that have duplicates, and all the duplicates themselves, type:

```
$ uniq -D options RET
```

To output lines preceded by a count telling how many instances exist of that line, use the `-c` option.

⇒ To output all of the lines in the file **options**, each preceded by a count of the number of instances of that line, type:

```
$ uniq -c options RET
```

METHOD #2

To filter out unique lines in some unsorted text, use `sort` with the `-u` option. This sorts the input lines alphabetically and runs `uniq` on them.

⇒ To output only unique lines in the unsorted file **points-of-interest**, type:

```
$ sort -u points-of-interest (RET)
```

NOTES: The **sort** tool is described in the next recipe.

13.6 Sorting Text

You can sort a list, kept in a file or taken from standard input, with **sort**.

By default, it outputs text in ascending alphabetical order; use the **-r** option to reverse the sort and output text in descending alphabetical order.

For example, suppose you have a file, **provinces**, that looks like Figure 13-1.

```
Shantung
Honan
Szechwan
Hunan
Kiangsu
Kwangtung
Fukien
```

*Figure 13-1. The **provinces** file.*

⇒ Here are two ways to use this.

  • To sort the file **provinces** and output all lines in ascending order, type:

```
$ sort provinces (RET)
Fukien
Honan
Hunan
Kiangsu
Kwangtung
Shantung
Szechwan
$
```

- To sort the file **provinces** and output all lines in descending order, type:

```
$ sort -r provinces ⟨RET⟩
Szechwan
Shantung
Kwangtung
Kiangsu
Hunan
Honan
Fukien
$
```

To write the output to a file, give the file name as an argument to the **-o** option.

⇒ To sort the file **provinces** and write all lines in descending order to the file **provinces.sorted**, type:

```
$ sort -r -o provinces.sorted provinces ⟨RET⟩
```

The following recipes show special ways to use **sort**.

13.6.1 Sorting Text Regardless of Spacing

To sort and ignore leading blanks on any lines, use **sort** with the **-b** option.

⇒ To sort the text in file **orders**, ignoring any preceding blank spaces in the sort, type:

```
$ sort -b orders ⟨RET⟩
```

Use the **-i** option to ignore all spaces *and* all non-printing characters.

⇒ To sort the text in file **orders**, ignoring any preceding blank spaces and non-printing characters, type:

```
$ sort -i orders ⟨RET⟩
```

13.6.2 Sorting Text Regardless of Case

To sort text regardless of case, use **sort** with the **-f** option. This option specifies that lowercase letters should be *folded* into their uppercase equivalents for the purpose of sorting, so that differences in case are ignored.

⇒ To sort the text in the file **playlist** regardless of case, type:

```
$ sort -f playlist ⟨RET⟩
```

13.6.3 Sorting Text in Numeric Order

To sort by numeric order instead of by the ASCII value of each character, use
sort with the **-n** option. With this sort, non-numeric text assumes a value of
zero.

⇒ Here are two ways to use this.

- To sort the text in the file **answers** in ascending numeric order, type:

    `$ sort -n answers` ⟨RET⟩

- To sort the text in the file **answers** in descending numeric order,
  type:

    `$ sort -r -n answers` ⟨RET⟩

13.6.4 Sorting Text in Directory Order

To sort lines of text so that only letters, digits, and blanks are sorted, use
the **-d** option. This is sometimes called sorting in "phone directory order,"
because this sort order is the same way names in the telephone book are listed.

⇒ To sort the lines in the file **contacts** in directory order, type:

    `$ sort -d contacts` ⟨RET⟩

13.7 Columnating Text

The following recipes show ways to place text in and out of columns.

For a way to place text in columns when you are paginating that text, see
Recipe 13.3.4 [Placing Text in Paginated Columns], page 314.

13.7.1 Pasting Columns of Text from Separate Files

Use **paste** to paste columns of text together from separate files. Given some
files as arguments, **paste** outputs the contents of each file in separate columns,
so that each line of output consists of one line of input from each file, delimited
by a ⟨TAB⟩ character. Use "**-**" to specify the standard input.

⇒ To paste the contents of **causes** and **effects** together in columns, writing
  to a new file called **table**, type:

    `$ paste causes effects > table` ⟨RET⟩

To specify a different delimiter, give it as an argument to the **-d** option.

⇒ To paste the contents of the files **bases** and **reactants** together in
  columns, separated by a plus sign (**+**), type:

    `$ paste -d "+" bases reactants` ⟨RET⟩

13.7.2 Columnating Text from Separate Files

To combine sorted text from two files based on a similar column (called a *field*), use `join` and give the names of the files as input, using "-" for the standard input.

For each line, `join` outputs the field common to both files (called the *join field*), and then outputs the remaining contents of the line from the first file, and then the remaining contents of the line from the second file. If there is no common field, nothing is output for that line.

⇒ To output the contents of the sorted files `march.stats` and `april.stats`, joining by the first column in each, type:

```
$ join march.stats april.stats RET
```

By default, the first field is used in both files. To specify the field for the first file, use the `-1` option and give the number of the field to use as an argument; to specify the field for the second file, use `-2`.

⇒ To output the contents of the sorted files `march.stats` and `april.stats`, joining by the third column in the first file and the second column in the second file, type:

```
$ join -1 3 -2 2 march.stats april.stats RET
```

13.7.3 Columnating a List

Use `column` to output a list in columns. This is sometimes useful for columnating a list and sending it to a line printer. By default, `column` formats for 80 characters wide (to fit the size of a standard terminal window), writing its input with as many columns as can be made.

⇒ To write the contents of the file `years.list` to a file called `years`, written in columns of lines not longer than 80 characters, type:

```
$ column years.list > years RET
```

Columns are filled before rows. That is, the input lines run down the first column, and then down the next, and so on. To have the input lines fill across the rows instead, use the `-x` option.[2]

---

[2] Some versions have documentation stating the opposite of this effect, but the program works this way in practice.

⇒ To write the contents of the file **years.list** to a file called **years**, written
in columns of lines not longer than 80 characters and filling each row
before advancing to the next, type:

    $ *column -x years.list > years* (RET)

To specify the number of characters to put in each line, give it as an
argument to the **-c** option.

⇒ To columnate the text in the file **YearEnd.Financials** with a line length
of 120 characters, and output it to the printer named **finance**, type:

    $ *column -c120 < YearEnd.Financials | lpr -Pfinance* (RET)

13.7.4 Removing Columns from Text

There are two methods for removing columns. One extracts selected columns,
and the other outputs text with a column or character range extracted from
it. The first is much more versatile and is likely to be the method you will
use most of the time.

METHOD #1

Use **cut** to output selected columns (called *fields*) from text. Give the fields
to output as arguments to the **-f** option. You can specify multiple fields by
delimiting them with commas, and you can specify a range of fields with a
hyphen character (-).

⇒ Here are some ways to use this.

- To output only the first field from the file **bank-statement**, type:

      $ *cut -f1 bank-statement* (RET)

- To output the second and fourth fields from the file **bank-statement**,
type:

      $ *cut -f2,4 bank-statement* (RET)

- To output the first and the third through fifth fields from the file
bank-statement, type:

      $ *cut -f1,3-5 bank-statement* (RET)

Fields are output from lowest to highest, no matter which order you specify
them. If you specify a field out of range for the input text, **cut** outputs a blank
line for each line of input, and if **cut** can find no field at all in an input line,
it outputs the entire line. Use **-s** to suppress the printing of lines that do not
contain the selected field.

By default, **cut** counts fields as delimited by a tab character. To specify
some other delimiter, give it as an argument to the **-d** option.

⇒ To output only the second field from the file **bank-statement**, where fields are delimited by a space character, and suppress output of lines not containing this field, type:

```
$ cut -d " " -f2 bank-statement (RET)
```

Fields are output with the same delimiter used in the input. To specify a different delimiter for the output, give it as an argument to the long-style option **--output-delimiter**.

⇒ To take the third through fifth fields from the file **bank-statement**, where fields are delimited by a space character, and output them delimited by tab characters, type:

```
$ cut -d " " -f3-5 --output-delimiter (CTRL)-(V) (TAB)
  bank-statement (RET)
```

To specify bytes or characters in place of fields, use the **-b** and **-c** options, respectively.

⇒ To output the first, third, fifth, and seventh characters from each line in the file **bank-statement**, type:

```
$ cut -c1,3,5,7 bank-statement (RET)
```

METHOD #2

Use **colrm** to remove columns in text by their character positions. Given a number as an argument, **colrm** will remove all text on each line, beginning at that character position.

⇒ To output only the first two characters on each line of the file **percentages**, type:

```
$ colrm 3 < percentages (RET)
```

If you give an ending column as a second argument, **colrm** removes all columns from the first to the second arguments, inclusive. The columns to the right of the ending column are brought over to join the column preceding the first argument.

⇒ To output the contents of the file **amounts**, removing the tenth through sixtieth characters on each line of text, and writing to a file called **markdown**, type:

```
$ colrm 10 60 < amounts > markdown (RET)
```

13.8 Numbering Lines of Text

There are several ways to put numbers on lines of text. Here are two of the best.

METHOD #1

One way to number text is to use the `nl` ("number lines") tool. Its default action is to write its input (either the file names given as an argument, or the standard input) to the standard output, with an indentation and all non-empty lines preceded with line numbers.

⇒ To peruse the file `report` with each line of the file preceded by line numbers, type:

> `$ nl report | less` (RET)

You can set the numbering style with the `-b` option followed by an argument. The following table lists the possible arguments and describes the numbering style they select.

a	Number all lines.
t	Number only non-blank lines. (This is the default.)
n	Do not number lines.
pregexp	Only number lines that contain the regular expression *regexp* (see Recipe 14.3 [Matching Patterns of Text], page 335).

The default is for line numbers to start with 1 and increment by 1. Set the initial line number by giving an argument to the `-v` option, and set the increment by giving an argument to the `-i` option.

⇒ Here are two ways to use this.

- To output the file `review` with each line of the file preceded by line numbers, starting with the number 2 and counting by 4, type:

  > `$ nl -v 2 -i 4 review` (RET)

- To number only the lines of the file `cantos` that begin with a period (.), starting numbering at 0 and using a numbering increment of 5, and writing the output to `cantos.numbered`, type:

  > `$ nl -i 5 -v 0 -b p'^\.' cantos > cantos.numbered` (RET)

METHOD #2

The other way to number lines is to use `cat` with one of the following two options: The `-n` option numbers each line of its input text, while the `-b` option only numbers non-blank lines.

⇒ Here are two ways to use this.

- To peruse the text file `citations` with each line of the file numbered, type:

      $ cat -n citations | less ⟨RET⟩

- To peruse the text file `citations` with each non-blank line of the file numbered, type:

      $ cat -b citations | less ⟨RET⟩

In the preceding examples, output from `cat` is piped to `less` for perusal; the original file is not altered.

To take an input file, number its lines, and then write the line-numbered version to a new file, send the standard output of the `cat` command to the new file to write.

⇒ To write a line-numbered version of file **report** to file **report.lines**, type:

      $ cat -n report > report.lines ⟨RET⟩

13.9 Underlining Text

In the days of typewriters, text that was meant to be set in an italicized font was denoted by underlining the text with underscore characters. Today, it's common practice to denote an italicized word in plain text by typing an underscore character (`_`) just before and after a word in a text file, like "`_this_`."[3] I call this *etext-style* underlining.[4]

Another method of underlining text is overstrike-style or backspace underlining, where each character to underline is immediately followed by a backspace character ("Control-H") and an underscore character (`_`).

Special ways to view underlined text are described in Recipe 9.3.5 [Viewing Underlined Text], page 226.

---

[3] A method for printing files with this markup is described in Recipe 25.3.5 [Preparing Text for Printing], page 522.

[4] Another variation, though much less popular, is to use forward-slash characters, like "`/this/`."

The following recipes are for placing, converting, or removing these different types of underlines in text.

13.9.1 Placing Underlines in Text

There are different methods of placing underlines in text, depending on whether they are etext-style or overstrike-style underlines.

METHOD #1

To place "`_etext-style_`" underlines in text, you just type an underscore character before and after the text to be underlined. (Another variation is to use the underscore for any space characters *within* the underlined text, "`_just_like_this_`.")

METHOD #2

To place an overstrike-style underline in some text, you need to insert a literal backspace character ("Control-H") immediately after a character you want to underline, and follow that with an underscore character (`_`).

⇒ Here are two ways to use this.

- To write the word "END" with overstrike-style underlines in an Emacs buffer, type (all on one line):

  E⟨CTRL⟩-⟨Q⟩ ⟨CTRL⟩-⟨H⟩_N⟨CTRL⟩-⟨Q⟩
  ⟨CTRL⟩-⟨H⟩_D⟨CTRL⟩-⟨Q⟩ ⟨CTRL⟩-⟨H⟩_

- To write the word "stress" with overstrike-style underlines when you are in **input mode** in Vi, type (all on one line):

  E⟨CTRL⟩-⟨V⟩ ⟨CTRL⟩-⟨H⟩_N⟨CTRL⟩-⟨V⟩
  ⟨CTRL⟩-⟨H⟩_D⟨CTRL⟩-⟨V⟩ ⟨CTRL⟩-⟨H⟩_

NOTES: For more information on inserting control characters in Emacs and Vi, see Recipe 10.1.4 [Inserting Special Characters in Emacs], page 239 and Recipe 10.2.4 [Inserting Special Characters in Vi], page 251, respectively.

13.9.2 Converting Underlines in Text

Text markup languages use different methods for denoting italics; for example, in TeX or LaTeX files, italicized text is often denoted with brackets and the \it command, like "{\it this}." (LaTeX files use the same format, but \emph is often used in place of \it.)

You can convert one form to the other by using the Emacs `replace-regular-expression` function and specifying the text to be replaced as a regexp (see Recipe 14.3 [Regular Expressions—Matching Text Patterns], page 335).

⇒ Here are some ways to use this.

- To replace plaintext-style italics with TEX `\it` commands, type:

  ⟨ALT⟩-⟨X⟩ *replace-regular-expression* ⟨RET⟩
  *_\(([^_]+\)_* ⟨RET⟩
  \{\\it \1} ⟨RET⟩

- To replace TEX-style italics with etext style _underscores_, type:

  ⟨ALT⟩-⟨X⟩ *replace-regular-expression* ⟨RET⟩
  \{\\it \{\(([^\}]+\)\} ⟨RET⟩
  *_\1_* ⟨RET⟩

Both of these examples use the special regexp symbol "`\1`," which matches the same text matched by the first "`\( ... \)`" construct in the previous regexp.

NOTES: For more information on regexp syntax in Emacs, consult its Info documentation (see Recipe 2.8.5 [Reading an Info Manual], page 48).

13.9.3 Removing Underlines from Text

There are two methods to remove underlines from text—the first removes the underlining, and the second removes the characters to be underlined, but not the underlines themselves.

METHOD #1

To remove backspace underlining from text, use `colcrt` with the `-` option, as described in Method #3 of Recipe 9.3.5 [Viewing Underlined Text], page 226.

⇒ To output a file containing backspace underlining called `zim.bibliography`, writing to a new file called `zimbib.txt` with no underlines at all, type:

  $ *colcrt - zim.bibliography > zimbib.txt* ⟨RET⟩

METHOD #2

To remove any text that is marked with underlines and not remove the underlines themselves, send the text to `col` with the `-b` option. This removes all of the characters to be underlined, and the backspace character ("Control-H") that follows each one. The underline characters (`_`) are kept.

⇒ To output the file `zim.bibliography` with all underlined characters removed but all underlines kept, type:

```
$ col -b < zim.bibliography (RET)
```

NOTES: This is also good for removing *overstrikes* from text, where a character such as "X" is used in place of an underline.

13.10 Reversing Text

These recipes show ways to reverse the order of lines of text, and to reverse
the order of characters on each line.

13.10.1 Reversing Lines of Text

The `tac` command is similar to `cat`, but it outputs text in reverse order. That
is, it outputs the last line of its input first, and the first line of its input last.

There is another difference—`tac` works on *records*, sections of text with
separator strings, instead of lines of text. Its default separator string is the
linebreak character, so by default `tac` outputs files in line-for-line reverse
order.

⇒ To output the file `prizes` in line-for-line reverse order, type:

```
$ tac prizes (RET)
```

Specify a different separator with the `-s` option. This is often useful when
specifying non-printing characters, such as formfeeds. To specify such a character, use the ANSI-C method of quoting (see Recipe 3.1.3 [Quoting Reserved
Characters], page 56).

⇒ To output `prizes` in page-for-page reverse order, type:

```
$ tac -s $'\f' prizes (RET)
```

The preceding example uses the formfeed, or page break, character as the
delimiter, so it outputs the file `prizes` in page-for-page reverse order, with
the last page output first.

Use the `-r` option to use a regular expression for the separator string (see
Recipe 14.3 [Regular Expressions—Matching Patterns of Text], page 335).
You can build regular expressions to output text in word-for-word and
character-for-character reverse order:

⇒ Here are two ways to use this.

- To output `prizes` in word-for-word reverse order, type:

```
$ tac -r -s '[^a-zA-z0-9\-]' prizes (RET)
```

- To output **prizes** in character-for-character reverse order, type:

    ```
    $ tac -r -s '.\| (RET)
    ' prizes (RET)
    ```

13.10.2 Reversing the Characters on Lines

To reverse the order of characters on each *line*, use **rev**. It takes as input the name of the file to reverse, and it writes to the standard output. With no options, it reads from standard input.

⇒ To output **prizes** with the characters on each line reversed, type:

    ```
    $ rev prizes (RET)
    ```

Searching Text

It's quite common to search through text for a given sequence of characters (such as a word or phrase), called a *string*, or even for a pattern describing a *set* of such strings; this chapter contains recipes for doing these kind of things.

14.1 Searching Text for a Word

The primary tool used for searching through text is **grep**, whose frog-like name is often used as a verb to describe the process of searching through text, as in "Did you **grep** the list for his name?"[1] It outputs lines of its input that contain a given string or pattern.

The simplest way to search for a word is to give it as the first argument to **grep**; give the name of a file to search as the second argument (**grep** searches standard input by default).

⇒ To output lines in the file **catalog** containing "CD," type:

> $ *grep CD catalog* (RET)

Use the **-i** option to ignore the case when looking for matches.

⇒ To output lines in the file **catalog** containing "cd," regardless of case, type:

> $ *grep -i cd catalog* (RET)

This search matches any lines in **catalog** where the pattern "cd" is found, regardless of case. So it will match lines containing "CD" and "cd," as well as any other variation in case, like "Cd."

However, this search also matches lines containing, say, the word "anecdote," as well as words like "CDROM" or "CDR," because **grep** matches patterns wherever they occur on a line.

To specify that only whole *words* should count as matches, use **grep** with the **-w** option. This ignores matches that occur in the middle of a word. Only entire words will count as a pattern match, which means the pattern's location must match two criteria: One, it must be either at the beginning of the line, or be directly preceded by non-letters and non-digits; and two, it must either be directly followed by non-letters or non-digits, or be at the end of the line.

---

[1] The origin of its name is explained in Recipe 14.3 [Regular Expressions—Matching Patterns of Text], page 335, where its advanced usage is discussed.

⇒ To output lines in the file `catalog` containing the word "CD," type:

    $ grep -w CD catalog ⟨RET⟩

In this example, only lines containing the word "CD" are printed; lines with words such as "CDROM" or "anecdote" are not printed unless they contain the word "CD."[2]

14.2 Searching Text for a Phrase

To search some text for a phrase, specify it in quotes.

⇒ To output lines in the file `catalog` containing the word "Compact Disc," type:

    $ grep 'Compact Disc' catalog ⟨RET⟩

The preceding example outputs all lines in the file `catalog` that contain the exact string "Compact Disc"; it will not match, however, lines containing "compact disc" or any other variation on the case of letters in the search pattern. Use the `-i` option to specify that matches are to be made regardless of case.

⇒ To output lines in the file `catalog` containing the string "compact disc" regardless of the case of the letters, type:

    $ grep -i 'compact disc' catalog ⟨RET⟩

This command outputs lines in the file `catalog` containing any variation on the pattern "compact disc," including "Compact Disc," "COMPACT DISC," and "comPact dIsC."

One thing to keep in mind is that **grep** only matches patterns that appear on a single line, so in the preceding example, if one line in `catalog` ends with the word "compact" and the next begins with "disc," this command will not match either line. There is a way around this with **grep** (see Recipe 14.4.3 [Finding Phrases Regardless of Spacing], page 344), and there is a way to do it in Emacs (see Recipe 14.9.2 [Searching for a Phrase in Emacs], page 353).

A search string may contain tab characters as well as space characters. To type a tab character in a quoted string, first type ⟨CTRL⟩-⟨V⟩ and then type ⟨TAB⟩ (see Recipe 3.1.2 [Typing a Control Character], page 55).

---

[2] However, the word "CD-ROM" would count as a match; **grep** considers the hyphen character to be a word separator, and thus sees "CD-ROM" as two words.

⇒ To output lines in **screenplay** containing the text "**In the beginning**," only when directly preceded by a tab character, type:

> `$ grep '`⟨CTRL⟩`-`⟨V⟩ ⟨TAB⟩`In the beginning' screenplay` ⟨RET⟩

Some special characters have reserved meanings, and to search for them you must specify them in special ways, as described in the next recipe. The period character (.) is one such character. When searching for just strings, though, you can use the **-F** option to specify that the pattern you give is a *fixed string*, with no special characters in it at all.

fgrep is equivalent to **grep** with the **-F** option. It is one of two variations of **grep** assigned to perform a special purpose (the other is discussed below).

⇒ Here are two ways to use this.

- To search the file **screenplay** for the phrase "**the end.**," regardless of case, type:

> `$ grep -F 'the end.' screenplay` ⟨RET⟩

- To search the file **screenplay** for the phrase "**the end.**," regardless of case, type:

> `$ fgrep 'the end.' screenplay` ⟨RET⟩

The results of the two preceding examples are identical.

To search for a string containing double quote characters, use single quotes to quote it, and vice versa. When the text you search for contains both kinds of quote characters, don't quote the string at all, but precede every quote and space character in the string with a backslash character (\).

⇒ Here are some ways to use this.

- To output all lines in the file **screenplay** that contain the string ""**Frankly, Scarlett,**" **he said**," type:

> `$ grep '"Frankly, Scarlett," he said' screenplay` ⟨RET⟩

- To output all lines in the file **screenplay** that contain the string "**I don't give**," type:

> `$ grep "I don't give" screenplay` ⟨RET⟩

- To output all lines in the file **screenplay** that contains the string "**Don't say "Goodbye"**," type:

> `$ grep Don\'t\ say\ \"Goodbye\" screenplay` ⟨RET⟩

14.3 Matching Patterns of Text

In addition to word and phrase searches, you can **grep** for complex text patterns. Called a *regular expression* (or "regexp" for short), this is a text string that specifies a *set* of patterns to match. Regexps are a fundamental concept in the UNIX world, and they are the most powerful way to search for text with a computer.

Technically speaking, the word or phrase patterns described in the previous recipes are regular expressions—just very simple ones. They specify the given word or phrase as the set of patterns to match.

In a regular expression, most characters—including letters and numbers— only represent themselves. For example, the regexp pattern "1" matches the string "1" and nothing else; the pattern "**bee**" matches the string "**bee**" and nothing else. The pattern "" lacks any characters at all and is called the *empty set*; it matches nothing.[3] Each of these are regexps that specify a set of one precise pattern to match.

There are, however, a number of reserved characters, called *metacharacters*, that don't represent themselves in a regular expression. Instead, they have special meanings that are used to build complex patterns. These metacharacters are:

> . * [ ] ^ $ \

To avoid trouble with shell expansion, you should quote regexps that contain any of these metacharacters.

To specify one of these literal characters in a regular expression, precede the character with a "\."[4]

⇒ Here are some ways to use this.

- To output lines in the file `catalog` that contain a literal "$" character, type:

  $ *grep* '\$' *catalog* ⟨RET⟩

- To output lines in the file `catalog` that contain the string "$1.99," type:

  $ *grep* '\$1\.99' *catalog* ⟨RET⟩

- To output lines in the file `catalog` that contain a "\" character, type:

  $ *grep* '\\' *catalog* ⟨RET⟩

---

[3] Since "nothing" can be found in the space between any two characters, the empty set matches every line of its input, which can be useful in some scenarios.

[4] You could also use `fgrep` to search, as described in See Recipe 14.2 [Searching Text for a Phrase], page 334, but then your regexps would have to contain no metacharacters at all.

The following table describes the special meanings of the metacharacters and gives examples of their use.

.	Matches any one character, with the exception of the newline character. For example, "." matches "a," "1," "?," "." (a literal period character), and so forth.
*	Matches the preceding regexp at least zero but as many times as possible. For example, "-*" matches at least "" (the empty set), but preferably "-," "--," "---," "----," "-----," and so forth, continuing the match as much as possible.
[ ]	Encloses a *character set*, and matches any member of the set—for example, "[abc]" matches either "a," "b," or "c." In addition, the hyphen (-) and caret (^) characters have special meanings when used inside brackets:
-	The hyphen specifies a range of characters, ordered according to their ASCII values (see Recipe 9.3.7 [Viewing a Character Set], page 228). For example, "[0-9]" is synonymous with "[0123456789]"; "[A-Za-z]" matches one uppercase or lowercase letter. To include a literal "-" in a list, specify it as the last character in a list: so "[0-9-]" matches either a single digit character or a "-."
^	As the first character of a list, the caret means that any character *except* those in the list should be matched. For example, "[^a]" matches any character except "a," and "[^0-9]" matches any character except a numeric digit.
^	Matches the beginning of the line. So "^a" matches "a" only when it is the first character on a line.
$	Matches the end of the line. So "a$" matches "a" only when it is the last character on a line.

\\	Use "\\" before a metacharacter when you want to specify that literal character. So "\\$" matches a dollar sign character ($), and "\\\\" matches a single backslash character (\\).
	In addition, use \\ to build new extended metacharacters, by using it before a number of other characters:
\\|	Called the *alternation operator*, it matches *either* regexp it is between—use it to join two separate regexps to match either of them. For example, "a\\|b" matches either "a" or "b."
\\+	Matches the preceding regexp as many times as possible, but at least once. So "a\\+" matches one or more adjacent "a" characters, such as "aaa," "aa," and "a."
\\?	Matches the regexp preceding it either zero or one times. So "a\\?" matches either "a," or the empty set—which matches every line.
\\{*number*\\}	Matches the previous regexp (one specified to the left of this construction) that number of times—so "a\\{4\\}" matches "aaaa." Use "\\{*number*,\\}" to match the preceding regexp *number* or more times, "\\{,*number*\\}" to match the preceding regexp zero to *number* times, and "\\{*number1*,*number2*\\}" to match the preceding regexp from *number1* to *number2* times.
\\(*regexp*\\)	Group *regexp* together for an *alternative*, which is useful for combination regexps. For example, while "moo\\?" matches only "mo" or "moo," "\\(moo\\)\\?" matches only "moo" or the empty set.

NOTES: The name "grep" derives from a command in the now-obsolete UNIX ed line editor tool. The ed command for searching *globally* through a file for a *regular expression*, and then *printing* on the screen those lines that contained a match, was *g/re/p*, where *re* was the regular expression you'd use. Eventually, the `grep` command was written to do this search on a file when not using `ed`.[5]

The `grep` variant `egrep`, "extended grep," recognizes all of the extended metacharacters without the preceding "\." You can get the same effect in plain `grep` by using the `-E` option.

The following sections describe some regexp recipes for commonly searched-for patterns.

14.3.1 Matching Lines of a Certain Length

To match lines of a particular length, use that number of "." characters between "^" and "$"—for example, to match all lines that are two characters (or columns) wide, use "`^..$`" as the regexp to search for.

⇒ To output all lines in `/usr/dict/words` that are exactly two characters wide, type:

> `$ grep '^..$' /usr/dict/words` (RET)

For longer lines, where you don't want to have to be counting periods, it is more useful to use a different construct: "`^.\{number\}$`," where *number* is the number of lines to match. Use "," to specify a range of numbers.

⇒ Here are two ways to use this.

- To output all lines in `/usr/dict/words` that are exactly 17 characters wide, type:

  > `$ grep '^.\{17\}$' /usr/dict/words` (RET)

- To output all lines in `/usr/dict/words` that are 25 or more characters wide, type:

  > `$ grep '^.\{25,\}$' /usr/dict/words` (RET)

14.3.2 Matching Lines That Contain Any of Some Regexps

To match lines that contain any of a number of regexps, specify each of the regexps to search for between alternation operators (\|) as the regexp to search for. Lines containing any of the given regexps will be output.

---

[5] The `ed` command is still available on virtually all unices, Linux included, and the old "g/re/p" still works. Perhaps an oft-used function, available only in one application today, might become one of the new tools of tomorrow.

⇒ To output all lines in `playlist` that contain either the pattern "`the sea`" or "`cake`," type:

    $ *grep 'the sea\|cake' playlist* (RET)

This command outputs any lines in "`playlist`" that match the pattern "`the sea`" or "`cake`," including lines matching *both* patterns.

14.3.3 Matching Lines That Contain All of Some Regexps

To output lines that match *all* of a number of regexps, use `grep` to output lines containing the first regexp you want to match, and pipe the output to a `grep` with the second regexp as an argument. Continue adding pipes to `grep` searches for all the regexps you want to search for.

⇒ To output all lines in `playlist` that contain both patterns "`the sea`" and "`cake`," regardless of case, type:

    $ *grep -i 'the sea' playlist | grep -i cake* (RET)

NOTES: To match lines containing some regexps in a particular order, see Recipe 14.3.6 [Using Popular Regexps for Common Situations], below.

14.3.4 Matching Lines That Don't Contain a Regexp

To output all lines in a text that *don't* contain a given pattern, use `grep` with the `-v` option—this option reverses the sense of matching, selecting all non-matching lines.

⇒ Here are two ways to use this.

- To output all lines in `/usr/dict/words` that are not three characters wide, type:

    $ *grep -v '^...$'* (RET)

- To output all lines in `access_log` that do not contain the string "`http`," type:

    $ *grep -v http access_log* (RET)

14.3.5 Matching Lines That Only Contain Certain Characters

To match lines that only contain certain characters, use the regexp "`^[`*characters*`]*$`," where *characters* lists the ones to match.

⇒ To output lines in **/usr/dict/words** that only contain vowels, type:

$ *grep -i '^[aeiou]*$' /usr/dict/words* (RET)

The **-i** option matches characters regardless of case; so, in this example, all vowel characters are matched regardless of case.

14.3.6 Using Popular Regexps for Common Situations

The following table lists sample regexps and describes the lines that they match. Use these regexps as boilerplate when building your own regular expressions for searching text. Remember to type regexps all on one line, and to quote them (see Recipe 3.1.3 [Quoting Reserved Characters], page 56).

To Match ...	Use This Regexp
Any number	[0-9]
Lines *not* containing any number	^[^0-9]*$
At least three uppercase letters together	[A-Z][A-Z][A-Z]
Nine zeroes in a row, anywhere in a line	0\{9\}
Lines exactly four characters long	^....$ *or* ^.\{4\}$
Lines exactly 70 characters long	^.\{70\}$
Lines beginning with an asterisk character	^*
Lines beginning with "tow" and ending with "ing"	^tow.*ing$
Either ".txt" or ".text" on a line	\.te\?xt
"cat" then "gory" in the same word	cat\.\+gory
"cat" then "gory"	cat\.\+\?gory
"cat" except when followed by an "e"	cat[^e]
A "q" not followed by a "u"	q[^u]
"N," "T," and "K," with zero or more characters between each	N.*T.*K
Any ftp://, gopher://, or http:// URLs	\(ftp|gopher|http|\)://.*\..*
A year from 1991 through 1995	199[1-5]

(continued)

To Match ...	Use This Regexp
A year from 1957 through 1969	`\(195[7-9]\)|\(196[0-9]\)`

A date in any one of these formats:
MONTH, DAY YEAR
MON. DAY, YEAR
MON. DAY, 'YY
(Quote in double quotes)
	`[A-Za-z]\{3,10\}\.\?`
	`[0-9]\{1,2\}, \([0-`
	`9]\{4\}|'[0-9]\{2\}\)`

An IP address	`[0-9]\{1,3\}\.[0-`
	`9]\{1,3\}\.[0-`
	`9]\{1,3\}\.[0-9]\{1,3\}`

A Social Security number	`[0-9]\{3\}-\?[0-` `9]\{2\}-\?[0-9]\{4\}`

A United States telephone number	`\(1\+\)\?\(\(\?[0-`
	`9]\{3\}\)\?\)\?\(-`
	`\)\?[0-9]\{3\}\(-`
	`\)\?[0-9]\{4\}`

The following table shows how some of the preceding searches are simplified with `egrep`.

To Match ...	Use This Regexp
Any `ftp://`, `gopher://`, or `http://` URLs	`(ftp|gopher|http|)://\.*.\.*`
A year from 1957 through 1969	`(195[7-9])|(196[0-9])`

A date in any one of these formats:
MONTH, DAY YEAR
MON. DAY, YEAR
MON. DAY, 'YY
(Quote in double quotes)
	`[A-Za-z]{3,10}\.?`
	`[0-9]{1,2}, ([0-`
	`9]{4}|'[0-9]{2})`

(continued)
To Match . . .	*Use This Regexp*
An IP address	`[0-9]{1,3}\.[0-9]{1,3}\.[0-9]{1,3}\.[0-9]{1,3}`
A Social Security number	`[0-9]{3}-?[0-9]{2}-?[0-9]{4}`
A United States telephone number	`(1+)?((?[0-9]{3})?)?(-)?[0-9]{3}(-)?[0-9]{4}`

14.4 Finding Patterns in Certain Places

These recipes describe ways to find patterns only when they appear in particular places—depending on where in the text the pattern is, it may or may not constitute a match.

14.4.1 Matching Lines Beginning with Certain Text

Use "`^`" in a regexp to denote the beginning of a line.

⇒ Here are two ways to use this.

- To output all lines in **/usr/dict/words** beginning with "**pre**," type:

    `$ grep '^pre' /usr/dict/words` (RET)

- To output all lines in the file **book** that begin with the text "**in the beginning**," regardless of case, type:

    `$ grep -i '^in the beginning' book` (RET)

NOTES: These regexps were quoted with single-quote characters; this is because some shells otherwise treat the "`^`" character as a special "metacharacter" (see Recipe 3.1.3 [Quoting Reserved Characters], page 56).

14.4.2 Matching Lines Ending with Certain Text

Use "**$**" as the last character of quoted text to match that text only at the end of a line.

⇒ To output lines in the file **sayings** ending with an exclamation point, type:

    `$ grep '!$' sayings` (RET)

NOTES: To use "**$**" in a regexp to find words that rhyme with a given word, see Recipe 11.2.1 [Listing Words That Match a Pattern], page 283.

14.4.3 Finding Phrases in Text Regardless of Spacing

One way to search for a phrase that might occur with extra spaces between words, or across a line or page break, is to remove all linefeeds and extra spaces from the input, and then **grep** that.

To do this, pipe the input[6] to **tr** with "\r\n:\>\|–" as an argument to the **-d** option (removing all linebreaks from the input); pipe that to the **fmt** filter with the **-u** option (outputting the text with uniform spacing); and pipe that to **grep** with the pattern to search for.

⇒ To search across line breaks for the string "at the same time as" in the file **notes**, type (all on one line):

```
$ cat notes | tr -d '\r\n:\>\|-' | fmt -u | grep
'at the same time as' (RET)
```

NOTES: The Emacs editor has its own special search for doing this—see Recipe 14.9.2 [Searching for a Phrase in Emacs], page 353.

14.4.4 Finding Patterns Only in Certain Positions

To find patterns or strings only at certain positions on a line, use **grep** with the pattern "^.*number*pattern*," where *number* is the number of characters in a line to skip over, and *pattern* is the pattern to search for.

You can use the same pattern with **egrep**—just omit the slashes before the curly braces.

⇒ Here are two ways to use this.

- To find an X at the 50th character on a line in the file **treasure**, type:

```
$ grep '^.\{49\}X' treasure (RET)
```

- To find an X at the 50th character on a line in the file **treasure**, type:

```
$ egrep '^.{49}X' treasure (RET)
```

Both of the preceding examples are equivalent.

---

[6] If the input is a file, use **cat** to do this, as in the example.

14.5 Showing Matches in Context

To search for a pattern that only occurs in a particular context, **grep** for the context in which it should occur, and pipe the output to another **grep** to search for the actual pattern.

For example, this can be useful to search for a given pattern only when it is quoted with a greater-than sign (>) in an email message.

⇒ To list lines from the file **email-archive** that contain the word "**narrative**" only when it is quoted, type:

```
$ grep '^>' email-archive | grep narrative (RET)
```

You can also reverse the order and use the **-v** option to output all lines containing a given pattern that are *not* in a given context.

⇒ To list lines from the file **email-archive** that contain the word "**narrative**," but not when it is quoted, type:

```
$ grep narrative email-archive | grep -v '^>' (RET)
```

The following recipes show how to output matches in various contexts.

14.5.1 Showing Matched Lines in Their Context

It is sometimes useful to see a matched line in its context in the file—that is, to see some of the lines that surround it.

Use the **-C** option with **grep** to output results in *context*—it outputs matched lines with two lines of "context" both before and after each match. To specify the number of context lines output both before and after matched lines, use that number as an option instead of **-C**.

⇒ Here are two ways to use this.

- To search **/usr/dict/words** for lines matching "**tsch**" and output two lines of context before and after each line of output, type:

```
$ grep -C tsch /usr/dict/words (RET)
```

- To search **/usr/dict/words** for lines matching "**tsch**" and output six lines of context before and after each line of output, type:

```
$ grep -6 tsch /usr/dict/words (RET)
```

To output matches and the two lines *before* them, use **-B**; to output matches and the two lines *after* them, use **-A**. Give a numeric value with either of these options to specify that number of context lines instead of the default.

⇒ Here are some ways to use this.

- To search `/usr/dict/words` for lines matching "tsch" and output
  two lines of context *before* each line of output, type:

  `$ grep -B tsch /usr/dict/words` ⟨RET⟩

- To search `/usr/dict/words` for lines matching "tsch" and output
  six lines of context *after* each line of output, type:

  `$ grep -A6 tsch /usr/dict/words` ⟨RET⟩

- To search `/usr/dict/words` for lines matching "tsch" and output
  ten lines of context before and three lines of context after each line
  of output, type:

  `$ grep -B10 -A3 tsch /usr/dict/words` ⟨RET⟩

14.5.2 Highlighting Matches on Their Lines

Highlighting the matches on their lines is useful for learning to make your own
regexps, and for perusing the input text with the matched patterns highlighted
in context. There are a few methods, none of which use **grep** to do the
searching.

METHOD #1

When you search for a regexp in **less**, all matches are highlighted by default.

This is useful for perusing a file containing lines you are searching for, such
as a mail archive or Web log file.

⇒ To highlight the subject lines of all mail messages in the file you are
  perusing in **less**, type:

  `/^Subject:.*$` ⟨RET⟩

NOTES: To highlight seareches in **vim**, type `:set hls` when in **command mode**.

METHOD #2

You can use SED to output lines that match a regexp (see Recipe 10.5 [Edit-
ing Streams of Text], page 255). SED's search and replace functions make it
possible to search for a regexp and surround it with the ANSI escape sequences
necessary to display text in colors. This method works on color terminals.

⇒ To search the file **itinerary** for the pattern "**Paris**," and output the
  contents of the file with that pattern in red, type (all on one line):

  `$ sed 's/Paris/`⟨CTRL⟩-⟨V⟩ ⟨ESC⟩`[31m&`⟨CTRL⟩-⟨V⟩
  ⟨ESC⟩`[37m/g' < itinerary` ⟨RET⟩

The color for the highlighted text is specified by the number in the first escape sequence. In the preceding example, that number is 31 (the second number resets the text color to white, using number 37, for the text following the match). The following table lists available numbers and the colors they set.

30	Black
31	Red
32	Green
33	Yellow
34	Blue
35	Purple
36	Cyan
37	White

NOTES: If you want to pipe the output to a pager for perusal, you should use either **less** with the -R option or use **more**, because control characters by default are not "escaped" in **less** (see Recipe 9.1.4 [Perusing Raw Text], page 214).

14.5.3 Showing Only the Matched Patterns from Input

Showing only the matches, and not the entire lines they are part of, is very useful for collecting patterns from text, for saving to a file or piping to other tools, and for learning regexps. There are two methods of doing this.

METHOD #1

Use **grep** with the -o option to show *only* the matches, and not the entire line containing the match.

⇒ To output all of the IP addresses contained in the file **access.log**, type (all on one line):

```
$ grep -o
'[0-9]\{1,3\}\.[0-9]\{1,3\}\.[0-9]\{1,3\}\.[0-9]\{1,3\}'
access.log (RET)
```

NOTES: This option is new for **grep**, beginning in GNU **grep** version 2.5.

METHOD #2

You can also use SED to output only the matched patterns you search for, and not the lines they are contained in. To do this, run **sed** with the -n

option and the expression "s/.*\\(*PATTERN*\\).*/\\1/p," where *PATTERN*
is the pattern to search for. Finally, give the name of the file to search as an
argument.

⇒ To output the contents of all double quotations (including the quotation
  marks themselves), contained in the file `dialogue`, type:

  `$ sed -n 's/.*\\(".*"\\).*/\1/p' dialogue` (RET)

14.5.4 Showing Which Files Contain Matching Lines

To show which files contain matches for a search, use `grep` with the `-l` option.
It does not output the lines that match the pattern, but only lists the files
that contain matches. This is useful for searching a group of files to see which
ones contain some string or pattern.

⇒ To output a list of all files in the current directory that contain the string
  `RECALL`, type:

  `$ grep -l RECALL *` (RET)

14.6 Keeping a File of Patterns to Search For

You can keep a list of regexps in a file and use `grep` to search text for any of
those patterns. To do this, specify the name of the file containing the regexps
to search for as an argument to the `-f` option.

This can be useful, for example, if you need to search a given text for a
number of words—keep each word on its own line in the regexp file.

⇒ Here are two ways to use this.

  • To output all lines in `/usr/dict/words` containing any of the words
    listed in the file `forbidden-words`, type:

    `$ grep -f forbidden-words /usr/dict/words` (RET)

  • To output all lines in `/usr/dict/words` that do *not* contain any of
    the words listed in `forbidden-words`, regardless of case, type:

    `$ grep -v -i -f forbidden-words /usr/dict/words` (RET)

14.7 Searching More than Plain Text Files

The following recipes are for searching for text in places other than in a plain
text file.

14.7.1 Matching Lines in Many Files

You can use `grep` to search more than just a single file; any file name expansion you specify will be globbed by the shell, and that list of files will be passed to `grep` (see Recipe 5.8 [Specifying File Names with Patterns], page 153).

⇒ Here are two ways to use this.

- To search all files in the current directory for the pattern "**peaches**," type:

  $ *grep peaches* * ⟨RET⟩

- To search all files in the current directory with either "**produce**" or "**inventory**" anywhere in part of their names, type:

  $ *grep peaches *produce,inventory* ⟨RET⟩

When you search multiple files, each match that `grep` outputs is preceded by the name of the file it's in; suppress this with the `-h` option.

⇒ Here are two ways to use this.

- To output lines in all of the files in the current directory containing the word "CD," type:

  $ *grep CD* * ⟨RET⟩

- To output lines in all of the .txt files in the ~/doc directory containing the word "CD," suppressing the listing of file names in the output, type:

  $ *grep -h CD ~/doc/*.txt* ⟨RET⟩

Use the `-r` option to search a given directory *recursively*, searching all subdirectories it contains.

⇒ To output lines containing the word "CD" in all of the .txt files in the ~/doc directory and in all of its subdirectories, type:

  $ *grep -r CD ~/doc/*.txt* ⟨RET⟩

14.7.2 Matching Lines in Compressed Files

Use `zgrep` to search through text in files that are compressed with the `gzip` compression tool. These files usually have a `.gz` file name extension, and they can't be searched or otherwise read by other tools without uncompressing the file first (for more about compressed files, see Recipe 8.4 [Using File Compression], page 196).

The `zgrep` tool works just like `grep`, except it can search through the text of compressed files (it searches uncompressed files, too). It outputs matches

to the given pattern as if you'd searched through normal, uncompressed files.
It leaves the files compressed when it exits.

⇒ Here are some ways to use this.

- To search through the compressed file `README.gz` for the text
  "`Linux`," type:

      $ zgrep Linux README.gz ⟨RET⟩

- To search through all files in the current directory, either compressed
  or uncompressed, for the text "`Linux`," type:

      $ zgrep Linux * ⟨RET⟩

- To recursively search through all files in the current directory tree,
  either compressed or uncompressed, for the text "`Linux`," type:

      $ zgrep -r Linux * ⟨RET⟩

14.7.3 Matching Lines in Web Pages

Depending on the method used, you can match lines in either the *contents* of
a Web page (the text it displays) or in the *source* of the page—its contents
plus HTML formatting codes.

METHOD #1

Lynx
  DEB: lynx
  RPM: lynx
  WWW: http://lynx.browser.org/

You can **grep** the contents of a Web page or other URL by giving the URL to
lynx with the **-dump** and **-nolist** options, and piping the output to **grep**.

⇒ To search the contents of the URL **http://example.com/bingo** for lines
  containing the text "**bango**" or "**bongo**," type (all on one line):

      $ lynx -dump -nolist http://example.com/bingo |
      grep b[ao]ngo ⟨RET⟩

METHOD #2

Wget
  DEB: wget
  RPM: wget
  WWW: http://www.gnu.org/software/wget/wget.html

To grep the actual HTML source of the Web page, use wget and give "-" as an argument to the -O option, piping the output to grep.

⇒ To search the HTML sources of the URL http://example.com/bingo for five sequential digits, type (all on one line):

> $ *wget -O- http://example.com/bingo | grep '[0-9]\{5\}'* (RET)

14.7.4 Matching Lines in Binary Files

The strings tool outputs all of the text strings in a binary file. To search such a file for some text, pipe the output of strings to a grep.

⇒ To output all the lines of text containing the string "http" in the binary file netrun, type:

> $ *strings netrun | grep http* (RET)

14.8 Searching and Replacing Text

There are a few methods for replacing the text you are searching for with some other text. None use grep, because that tool only outputs the matches. You can also search and replace text in most text editors, including Emacs; see Recipe 14.9.4 [Searching and Replacing in Emacs], page 354.

METHOD #1

A quick way to search and replace some text in a file is to use the following one-line perl command:

> perl -pi -e "s/*oldstring*/*newstring*/g;" *filespec* (RET)

In this command, *oldstring* is the string to search for, *newstring* is the string to replace it with, and *filespec* is the name of the file or files to work on. You can use this for more than one file.

⇒ To replace the string "helpless" with the string "helpful" in all files in the current directory that end with a three-character file extension, type:

> $ *perl -pi -e "s/helpless/helpful/g;" *.???* (RET)

METHOD #2

You can use SED to search for and replace text, as described in Recipe 10.5 [Editing Streams of Text], page 255.

⇒ To output the contents of the file `marketing`, replacing the text
  "`television`," capitalized or not, with "`Internet`," type:

    $ *sed 's/[Tt]elevision/Internet/g' marketing* ⟨RET⟩

You can also specify that replacement is to occur only when
lines contain some other text by using the expression "*/other-
text*/s/*searchtext*/*replacetext*/**g**."

⇒ To output the contents of the file `marketing` replacing the text
  "`television`," capitalized or not, with "`Internet`," but only on lines
  that contain a digit character, type:

    $ *sed '/[0-9]/s/[Tt]elevision/Internet/g' marketing* ⟨RET⟩

Finally, to specify that replacement is to occur only when lines
do *not* contain some other text, use `sed` with the expression "*/other-
text*/!s/*searchtext*/*replacetext*/**g**."

⇒ To output the contents of the file `marketing` replacing the text
  "`television`," capitalized or not, with "`Internet`," but not on lines
  that contain the text "`radio`," type:

    $ *sed '/radio/!s/[Tt]elevision/Internet/g' marketing* ⟨RET⟩

14.9 Searching Text in Emacs

The following recipes show ways of searching for text in Emacs—incrementally,
for a word or phrase, or for a pattern—and for searching and then replacing
text.

14.9.1 Searching Incrementally in Emacs

Type ⟨CTRL⟩-⟨S⟩ to use the Emacs incremental search function. It takes text as
input in the minibuffer, and it searches for that text from point toward the end
of the current buffer. Type ⟨CTRL⟩-⟨S⟩ again to search for the next occurrence
of the text you're searching for; this works until no more matches occur. Then
Emacs reports "`Failing I-search`" in the minibuffer; type ⟨CTRL⟩-⟨S⟩ again
to wrap to the beginning of the buffer and continue the search from there.

It gets its name "incremental" because it begins searching immediately
when you start to type text, so it builds a search string in *increments*. For
example, if you want to search for the word "`sunflower`" in the current buffer,
you start to type:

    ⟨CTRL⟩-⟨S⟩ *s*

At that point, Emacs searches forward through the buffer from point to the first "s" character and highlights it. Then, as you type u, it searches forward to the first "su" in the buffer and highlights that (if a "u" appears immediately after the "s" it first stopped at, it stays there and highlights the "s" and the "u"). It continues to do this as long as you type and as long as there is a match in the current buffer. As soon as what you type does not appear in the buffer, Emacs beeps and a message appears in the minibuffer stating that the search has failed.

To search for the next instance of the last string you gave, type ⟨CTRL⟩-⟨S⟩ again; if you keep ⟨CTRL⟩ held down, then every time you press the ⟨S⟩ key Emacs will advance to the next match in the buffer.

This is generally the fastest and most common type of search you will use in Emacs.

You can also do an incremental search through the buffer in *reverse*—that is, from point to the beginning of the buffer—with the `isearch-backward` function, ⟨CTRL⟩-⟨R⟩.

⇒ To search for the text "`moon`" in the current buffer from point in reverse to the beginning of the buffer, type:

> ⟨CTRL⟩-⟨R⟩ *moon*

14.9.2 Searching for a Phrase in Emacs

Like `grep`, the Emacs incremental search only works on lines of text, so it only finds phrases on a single line. If you search for "`hello, world`" with the incremental search, and the text "`hello,`" appears at the end of a line and the text "`world`" appears at the beginning of the next line, it won't find it.

To find a multi-word phrase across line breaks, use the `word-search-forward` function. It searches for a phrase or words regardless of punctuation or spacing.

⇒ To search forward through the current buffer for the phrase "`join me`," type:

> ⟨ALT⟩-⟨X⟩ *word-search-forward* ⟨RET⟩ *join me* ⟨RET⟩

NOTES: The `word-search-backward` function does the same as `word-search-forward`, except it searches *backward* through the buffer, from point to the beginning of the buffer.

14.9.3 Searching for a Regexp in Emacs

Use the `search-forward-regexp` function to search for a regular expression from point to the end of the current buffer.

⇒ To search forward through the current buffer for the regexp "`@.*\.org`," type:

⟨ALT⟩-⟨X⟩ *search-forward-regexp* ⟨RET⟩ @.*\.org ⟨RET⟩

The keyboard accelerator for this command is ⟨ALT⟩-⟨CTRL⟩-⟨S⟩. To repeat the last regexp search you made, type ⟨ALT⟩-⟨CTRL⟩-⟨S⟩ ⟨CTRL⟩-⟨S⟩; then, as long as you have ⟨CTRL⟩ held down, you can keep typing *s* to advance to the next match, just as you would with an incremental search.

NOTES: There is a `search-backward-regexp` function that is identical but searches backward, from point to the top of the buffer.

14.9.4 Searching and Replacing in Emacs

You can also search for and replace text in an Emacs buffer; to do this, use the `replace-regexp` function and give both the expression to search for and the expression to replace it with. Regexps are matched from point to the end of the buffer; to search and replace all occurrences in a buffer, run this function when point is at the beginning of the buffer.

⇒ To replace the text "`day`" with the text "`night`" in the current buffer, type:

```
⟨ALT⟩-⟨X⟩ replace-regexp ⟨RET⟩
Replace regexp: day ⟨RET⟩
Replace regexp day with: night ⟨RET⟩
Replaced 7 occurrences
```

In the preceding example, the regexp "`day`" was found (and replaced by the regexp "`night`") seven times from point to the end of the buffer.

This function is especially useful for replacing control characters with text, or for replacing text with control characters, which you can specify with ⟨CTRL⟩-⟨Q⟩, the `quoted-insert` function (see Recipe 10.1.4 [Inserting Special Characters in Emacs], page 239).

⇒ To replace all the "Control-M" characters in the current buffer with regular linefeeds, type:

```
⟨ALT⟩-⟨X⟩ replace-regexp ⟨RET⟩
Replace regexp: ⟨CTRL⟩-⟨Q⟩ ⟨CTRL⟩-⟨M⟩ ⟨RET⟩
Replace regexp ^M with: ⟨CTRL⟩-⟨Q⟩ 012 ⟨RET⟩ ⟨RET⟩
Replaced 101 occurrences
```

In this example, 101 "Control-M" characters were found (and replaced) from point to the end of the buffer.

14.10 Searching Text in Vi

To search for text in Vi, use the same method for searching text in **less**, which is given in the next recipe.

14.11 Searching the Text You're Perusing

You can search text while you peruse it with **less**. There are two useful commands in **less** for searching through text: / and ?. To search *forward* through the text, type / followed by a regexp to search for; to search *backward* through the text, use ?.

When you do a search, the word or other regexp you search for appears highlighted throughout the text. Typing a / or ? with no search string will search either forward or backward for the previous string or regexp.

⇒ Here are some ways to use this.

- To search forward through the text you are perusing for the word "cat," type:

  /cat ⟨RET⟩

- To search forward for the next instance of "cat," type:

  / ⟨RET⟩

- To search backward for the previous instance of "cat," type:

  ? ⟨RET⟩

- To search backward through the text you are perusing for the regexp "[ch]at," type:

  ?[ch]at ⟨RET⟩

NOTES: In Vi, whose search facility works identically to **less**, the matches are not highlighted by default.

## CHAPTER 15

Typesetting and Word Processing

If you're coming to Linux with a Microsoft Windows or Apple Macintosh background, or from some other non-UNIX computing environment, you are likely used to one approach to "word processing." In these environments, most writing is done in word processors—large programs that offer a vast array of formatting options and that store their output in proprietary file formats. Most people use word processors no matter where the intended output will go (even if it's just a shopping list or secret diary).

Word processors, from complete suites like StarOffice to commercial favorites like WordPerfect, are available for Linux and have been for years. However, the standard personal-computing paradigm known as "word processing" has never really taken off on Linux—or, for that matter, on UNIX-like operating systems in general. With Linux, most writing is done in a text editor, and files are kept in plain text.

As it turns out, this approach is advantageous to the user for many reasons. When you keep a file in plain text, you can use command line tools to format the pages and paragraphs, to add page numbers and headers, check the spelling, style, and usage, to count the lines, words, and characters it contains, to convert it to HTML and other formats, and even to print the text in a font of your choosing—all actions that are described in the recipes in this book. The text can be formatted, analyzed, cut, chopped, sliced, diced, and otherwise processed by the vast array of Linux command line tools that work on text—over 750 in an average installation.

This approach may almost seem primitive at first—especially to those weaned in a computing environment that dictates that all writing must be set in a typeface from the moment of creation—but the word-processing approach can be excessive and time-wasting compared to the facilities that Linux provides for text. You can, if you like, easily view or print plain text in a font—which is what 90 percent of people want to do with a word processor 90 percent of the time, anyway; to do this with a single command, see Recipe 15.2 [Outputting Text to PostScript], page 359.

I contend that word processing is not a forward-thinking direction for the handling of text, especially on Linux systems and especially now that text is not always destined for printed output: Text can end up on a Web page, in an "eBook,"[1] in an email message, or possibly in print. The best common source

---

[1] This is the term now popularly used for files whose content happens to be a book, whether in plain text or some other, often proprietary, format.

for these formats is plain text. Word-processing programs, and the special file formats they generate, are anathema to the generalized, tools-based, and plain-text philosophy of UNIX and Linux (see Recipe 1.7.7 [UNIX and the Tools Philosophy], page 22). "Word processing" itself may be an obsolete idea of the 1980s personal computing environment, and it may no longer be a necessity in the age of the Internet—a medium in which plain text data is fluid and natural, being a native format and accessible on all machines.

If you do need to design a special layout for hardcopy printing, you can *typeset* the text. One could write a book on the subject of Linux typesetting; unfortunately, no such book has yet been written. However, this chapter contains recipes to get you started producing typeset output. These recipes were selected as being the easiest to prepare or most effective for their purpose.

For a list of other popular tools avilable for Linux, including traditional word processors, see Recipe 15.7 [Using Other Word Processors and Type-setting Systems], page 391, and for more information on this subject, I recommend Christopher B. Browne's overview, "Linux Word Processing" [http://www.cbbrowne.com/info/wp.html].

15.1 Selecting the Typesetting System for a Job

Choosing the proper typesetting system to use when you are about to begin a project can be daunting. Each has its own drawbacks and abilities, and to the less experienced, it may not be immediately clear which is most appropriate for a particular document or project.

If you really don't need to typeset a document, then don't bother! Just keep it as a plain text file, and use a text editor to edit it (see Chapter 10 [Editing Text], page 231). Do this for notes, journals, email messages, Web pages, Usenet articles, and so forth. If you ever do need to typeset such a document later, you will still be able to do so. And you can, if you like, view or print plain text in nice fonts (see Recipe 15.2.1 [Outputting Text in a Font], page 361).

Sometimes it is best to write a document in plain text, and when you need to typeset it for some purpose, make a copy of the file and import it into the typesetter or otherwise convert the copy into the typesetting language you want to use.

The following table can help you determine which typesetting system is best for a particular task. There isn't just one way of doing such things, of course—these are only my recommendations. The first column lists the kind of output you want to create, giving examples of the kind of documents, and the second column suggests the typesetting system(s) to use. These systems are described in the remaining sections of this chapter.

Output Format	System to Use
Printed, typeset output *and* electronic HTML or text file [Internet FAQ, white paper, dissertation]	Enscript, LaTeX, Linuxdoc-Tools, Texinfo
Printed, typeset output *and* text file [`man` page, command reference card]	GROFF
Printed, typeset output [Letter or other correspondence, report, book manuscript]	LaTeX, LyX, TeX
Printed, typeset output [Brochure or newsletter with multiple columns and images]	LyX, TeX
Printed, typeset output [Envelope, mailing label, or other specialized document]	TeX
Printed, typeset output *or* text file [Chart or table]	GNUPLOT, Tbl
Printed text output in a font [Grocery list, saved email message, to-do list]	Enscript, AbiWord
Printed, typeset output [Poster, sign]	Enscript, HTML, LyX, TeX
Large printed text output suitable for display [Birthday party banner]	Banner

15.2 Outputting Text to PostScript

Enscript
  DEB: enscript
  RPM: enscript
  WWW: http://www.iki.fi/~mtr/genscript/

The simplest way to typeset plain text is to convert it to PostScript. This is often done to prepare text for printing; the original source text file remains as unformatted text, but the text of the printed output is formatted in basic ways, such as being set in a font. You can also use PostScript previewers such as **gv** or **ghostview** to view it on the screen. Additionally, you can convert the PostScript to PDF or other image formats, like a JPEG image file. In fact, once you make a PostScript file from text input, you can use any of the tools to format this new PostScript file, including rearranging and resizing its pages (see Chapter 20 [PostScript], page 451).

There are several methods for converting text to PostScript output, but the best is to use **enscript**. This is a quick, effective way to make presentable output from plain text. It converts the text file that is specified as an argument into PostScript, making any number of formatting changes in between. It's great for quickly making nice output from a plain text file—you can use it to do things such as output text in a font of your choosing, or paginate text with graphical headers at the top of each page.

By default, **enscript** paginates its input, outputs it in a 10-point Courier font, and puts a simple header at the top of each page containing the file name, date and time, and page number in bold. Use the **-B** option to omit this header.

If you have a PostScript printer connected to your system, **enscript** can be set up to spool its output right to the printer. You can check whether your system is set up this way by looking at the **enscript** configuration file, `/etc/enscript.cfg`. The line

```
DefaultOutputMethod: printer
```

specifies that output is spooled directly to the printer. Changing "**printer**" to "**stdout**" sends the output to the standard output instead.

Even if your default printer does not natively understand PostScript, it may be able to take **enscript** output, anyway. Most Linux installations these days have print filters set up so that PostScript spooled for printing is automatically converted to a format the printer understands. If your system doesn't have this setup for some reason, convert the PostScript to a format recognized by your printer with the **gs** tool, and then print that—see Recipe 20.3 [Converting PostScript], page 459.

⇒ To convert the text file **saved-mail** to PostScript, with default formatting, and spool the output right to the printer, type:

```
$ enscript saved-mail (RET)
```

To select a specific printer to send to, follow the **-d** option with its name.

⇒ To convert the text file **memo** to PostScript, and send it to the printer named **salesroom**, type:

```
$ enscript -dsalesroom memo ⟨RET⟩
```

To write the output to a file instead of spooling it, give the name of the file you want to output as an argument to the **-p** option. This is useful when you don't have a PostScript printer and you need to convert the output first, or for when you just want to make a PostScript image file from some text, or for previewing the output before you print it. In the latter case, you can view it on the display screen with a PostScript viewer application such as **ghostview** (see Recipe 17.4.2 [Previewing a PostScript File], page 414).

⇒ To write the text file **saved-mail** to a PostScript file, **saved-mail.ps**, and then preview it in X, type:

```
$ enscript -p report.ps saved-mail ⟨RET⟩
$ ghostview saved-mail.ps ⟨RET⟩
```

To send it to the standard output, specify "-" as the file; this is good for passing the PostScript along on a pipeline to some other commands, without writing it to a file at all.

⇒ To preview the text file **saved-mail** as a PostScript file in the **gv** viewer, type:

```
$ enscript -p - saved-mail | gv - ⟨RET⟩
```

The following recipes show how to use **enscript** to output text with different effects and properties. You can combine these options, and some of the recipes will demonstrate that.

15.2.1 Outputting Text in a Font

To output text in a particular PostScript font, use **enscript** and give the name of the font you want to use as a quoted argument to the **-f** option.

Specify both the font family and size in points: Give the capitalized name of the font family (with hyphens to indicate spaces between words) followed by the size in points. For example, "**Courier14**" outputs text in the Courier font at 14 points, and "**Times-Roman12.2**" outputs text in the Times Roman font at 12.2 points. Some of the available font names are listed in the file **/usr/share/enscript/afm/font.map**; the **enscript** man page describes how to use additional fonts that might be installed on your system.

⇒ Here are two ways to use this.

- To print the contents of the text file **saved-mail** on a PostScript printer, with text set in the Helvetica font at 12 points, type:

  `$ enscript -B -f "Helvetica12" saved-mail` (RET)

- To make a PostScript file called **saved-mail.ps** containing the contents of the text file **saved-mail**, with text set in the Helvetica font at 12 points, type (all on one line):

  `$ enscript -B -f "Helvetica12" -p saved-mail.ps saved-mail` (RET)

The -B option was used in the preceding examples to omit the output of a header on each page. When headers are used, they're normally output in 10-point Courier Bold; to specify a different font for the text in the header, give its name as an argument to the -F option.

⇒ Here are two ways to use this.

- To print the contents of the text file **saved-mail** to a PostScript printer, with text set in 10-point Times Roman and header text set in 18-point Times Bold, type (all on one line):

  `$ enscript -f "Times-Roman10" -F "Times-Bold18" saved-mail` (RET)

- To make a PostScript file called **saved-mail.ps** containing the contents of the text file **saved-mail**, with text and headers both set in 16-point Palatino Roman, type (all on one line):

  `$ enscript -f "Palatino-Roman16" -F "Palatino-Roman16"`
  `-p saved-mail.ps saved-mail` (RET)

NOTES: A list of available Adobe Type 1 fonts, and the names used to specify them, can be found at **/usr/share/enscript/afm/font.map**.

If you want to output a visual image of a text file, showing the way the text looks as a whole but set at a font too small to read, use a small font size, such as from 1 to 5.

15.2.2 Outputting Text in Custom Pages

You can specify the number of lines per page that **enscript** writes by giving that number as an argument to the -L option.

⇒ To convert the contents of the file **maxims** to PostScript, using a page size of 10 lines and writing to the file **maxims.ps**, type:

  `$ enscript -L10 -p maxims.ps maxims` (RET)

By default, **enscript** wraps long lines over to the next, which does not always look nice. Give the -c option to truncate long lines, or output the text in vertical slices (see Recipe 15.2.8 [Outputting Text in Vertical Slices], page 369).

⇒ To write the file **program.output** to the default printer, with long lines truncated, type:

```
$ enscript -c program.output (RET)
```

Specify the margins with "**--margins=***LEFT*:*RIGHT*:*TOP*:*BOTTOM*," where *LEFT*, *RIGHT*, *TOP*, and *BOTTOM* are the values for the stated margins. These values are given in *PostScript points*, which are 1/72 of an inch. You can omit any of them.

⇒ To print the file **sci.article** to the default printer, with a custom bottom margin of 50 PostScript points, type:

```
$ enscript --margins=:::50 sci.article (RET)
```

You can even print several pages on one page. To specify the number of logical pages to print on every output page, give the number as an argument to the -U option.

⇒ To print the file **tipsheet** to the default printer, with text set in 24-point Times Roman and writing four logical pages to each printed page, type:

```
$ enscript -U4 -f "Times-Roman24" tipsheet (RET)
```

15.2.3 Outputting Text as a Poster or Sign

You can output any text you type directly to the printer (or to a PostScript file) by omitting the name of the input file; **enscript** will read the text on the standard input until you type (CTRL)-(D) on a new line.

This is especially useful as a quick-and-dirty method for printing a sign or poster—to do this, specify a large font for the text, such as Helvetica Bold at 72 points, and omit the display of default headers. Use blank lines to space out the text.

⇒ To print a sign in 72-point Helvetica Bold type to a PostScript printer, type:

```
$ enscript -B -f "Helvetica-Bold72" (RET)
(RET)
(RET)
 CAUTION (RET)
(RET)
(RET)
WET PAINT (RET)
(CTRL)-(D)
```

Use the -j option to draw a border around the page.

⇒ To print a sign in 72-point Helvetica Bold type to a PostScript printer, type:

```
$ enscript -B -j -f "Helvetica-Bold72" (RET)
(RET)
(RET)
  CAUTION (RET)
(RET)
(RET)
  WET PAINT (RET)
(CTRL)-(D)
```

The text in this example was preceded by a few space characters, to set it off from the border.

Because 72-point type is very large, you may want to use the **--word-wrap** option with longer lines of text to wrap lines at word boundaries. You might need this option because at these larger font sizes, you run the risk of making lines that are longer than could fit on the page. You can also use the -r option to print the text in landscape orientation, as described in Recipe 15.2.7 [Outputting Text in Landscape Orientation], page 369.

⇒ To print a sign in 63-point Helvetica Bold across the long side of the page, type:

```
$ enscript -B -r --word-wrap -f "Helvetica-Bold63" ⟨RET⟩
⟨RET⟩
⟨RET⟩
CAUTION -- WET PAINT ⟨RET⟩
⟨CTRL⟩-⟨D⟩
```

NOTES: To make a snazzier or more detailed message or sign, create a file in a text editor and justify the words on each line in the file as you want them to print, with blank lines where necessary. If you're getting that ambitious, it would also be wise to use the -p option once to output to a file, and preview the file before printing it (see Recipe 17.4.2 [Previewing a PostScript File], page 414).

15.2.4 Outputting Text with Language Highlighting

The `enscript` tool currently recognizes the formatting of more than forty languages and formats, from the PERL and C programming languages to HTML, email, and Usenet news articles; `enscript` can highlight portions of the text based on its syntax. In UNIX-speak, this is called *pretty-printing*.

The following table lists the names of some of the language filters that are available at the time of this writing and describes the formats or languages they're used for.

`ada`	Ada95 programming language
`asm`	Assembler listings
`awk`	AWK programming language
`bash`	Bash shell programming language
`c`	C programming language
`changelog`	ChangeLog files
`cpp`	C++ programming language
`csh`	Csh script language

delphi	Delphi programming language
diff	Normal "difference reports" made from `diff`
diffu	Unified "difference reports" made from `diff`
elisp	Emacs Lisp programming language
fortran	FORTRAN 77 programming language
haskell	Haskell programming language
html	HyperText Markup Language (HTML)
idl	IDL (CORBA Interface Definition Language)
java	Java programming language
javascript	Javascript programming language
ksh	Ksh programming language
m4	M4 macro processor programming language
mail	Electronic mail and Usenet news articles
makefile	Rule files for `make`
nroff	Manual pages formatted with NROFF
objc	Objective-C programming language
pascal	Pascal programming language
perl	PERL programming language
postscript	PostScript programming language
python	Python programming language
scheme	Scheme programming language
sh	Bourne shell programming language
skill	Cadence Design Systems Lisp-like language
sql	Sybase 11 SQL
states	Definition files for `states`

synopsys	Synopsys dc shell scripting language
tcl	TCL programming language
tcsh	Tcsh shell script language
vba	Microsoft's Visual Basic for Applications language
verilog	Verilog hardware description language
vhdl	VHSIC Hardware Description Language (VHDL)
vrml	Virtual Reality Modeling Language (VRML97)
zsh	Zsh programming language

To pretty-print a file, give the name of the filter to use as an argument to the **-E** option, without any whitespace between the option and argument.

⇒ Here are some ways to use this.

- To pretty-print the HTML file **index.html**, type:

    $ *enscript -Ehtml index.html* ⟨RET⟩

- To pretty-print an email message saved to the file **important-mail**, and output it with no headers to a file named **important-mail.ps**, type:

    $ *enscript -B -Email -p important-mail.ps important-mail* ⟨RET⟩

- To pretty-print an email message saved to the file **important-mail**, and print it on the default printer with fancy headers, type:

    $ *enscript -G -Email important-mail* ⟨RET⟩

Use the special **--help-pretty-print** option to list the languages supported by the copy of **enscript** you have.

⇒ To peruse a list of currently supported languages, type:

    $ *enscript --help-pretty-print | less* ⟨RET⟩

15.2.5 Outputting Text with an Underlay

You can specify a text *underlay*, which is a kind of printed watermark, to appear on the pages of text. To do this, give the text as an argument to the **-u** option, making sure not to skip any space between the option and the text. If the text is more than a word, quote it.

⇒ To print the file `intelligence.report` with the default `enscript` formatting and an underlay of "TOP SECRET," type:

```
$ enscript -u"TOP SECRET" intelligence.report RET
```

There are a number of options used to specify the properties of the underlay, as described in the following table.

`--ul-angle=`*angle*	Specifies angle, in degrees, of the underlay (default is the arc tangent of two variables: the negative page height and its width).
`--ul-font=`*name*	Specifies font and point size of the underlay (default is Times Roman at 200 points).
`--ul-gray=`*number*	Specifies the value of gray to use in coloring the underlay as a value between 0 and 1 (default is 0.8).
`--ul-position=`*position*	Specifies starting position of underlay, in PostScript coordinates. The X position is given, preceded by either a "+" or "-," followed by the Y position, which is given in the same way (for example, the upper left-hand corner is "+0-0").
`--ul-style=`*style*	Specifies style of text, either "`outline`" where only the character outline is printed (the default) or "`filled`," where characters are filled with gray.

15.2.6 Outputting Text with Fancy Headers

To output text with fancy graphic headers, where the header text is set in
blocks of various shades of gray, use `enscript` with the `-G` option.

⇒ Here are two ways to use this.

- To print the contents of the text file `saved-mail` with fancy headers on a PostScript printer, type:

```
$ enscript -G saved-mail RET
```

- To make a PostScript file called `saved-mail.ps` containing the contents of the text file `saved-mail`, with fancy headers, type:

```
$ enscript -G -p saved-mail.ps saved-mail RET
```

Without the `-G` option, `enscript` outputs text with a plain header in bold
text, printing the file name and the time it was last modified. The `-B` option,
as described earlier, omits all headers.

You can customize the header text by quoting the text you want to use as an argument to the **-b** option. Use the special symbol "**$%**" to specify the current page number in the header text.

⇒ To print the contents of the text file **saved-mail** with a custom header label containing the current page number, type (all on one line):

$ *enscript -b "Page $% of the saved email archive" saved-mail* ⟨RET⟩

NOTES: There is currently no option to place headers on all but the first page, so if you need to format text in this common way, first use **enscript** to output to a file without headers, then use **enscript** to output another file *with* headers, and use **psselect** to combine the first page of the former with the remaining pages of the latter (see Recipe 20.1.2 [Extracting Pages from a PostScript File], page 452).

You can create your own custom fancy headers, too—this is described in the "CUSTOMIZATION" section of the **enscript man** page.

15.2.7 Outputting Text in Landscape Orientation

To output text in *landscape* orientation, where text is rotated 90 degrees counter-clockwise, use the **-r** option.

⇒ To print the contents of the text file **saved-mail** to a PostScript printer, with text set in 28-point Times Roman and in landscape orientation, type:

$ *enscript -f "Times-Roman28" -r saved-mail* ⟨RET⟩

The **-r** option is useful for making horizontal banners by passing output of the **figlet** tool to **enscript** (see Recipe 16.4.1 [Horizontal Text Fonts], page 401).

⇒ To output the text "**Quite a long banner**" in a **figlet** font and write it to the default printer with text set at 18-point Courier and in landscape orientation, type:

$ *figlet "Quite a long banner" | enscript -B -r -f "Courier18"* ⟨RET⟩

15.2.8 Outputting Text in Vertical Slices

When text runs past the right margin, **enscript** wraps it to the next line unless you use the **-c** option to specify that it be truncated at the right margin. You can also specify which vertical region to output; these regions are called *slices*, and each runs the length from the left to the right margin of the page, at which point the next slice of the page begins. Use **--slice=**

followed by a number to specify that slice; slices are numbered beginning with 1.

⇒ To print the second slice from the file `annual-report.txt`, type:

> `$ enscript --slice=2 annual-report.txt` ⟨RET⟩

15.2.9 Outputting Text with Indentation

To indent text you process with `enscript`, give the number of characters to indent as an argument to `-i`, being careful not to leave a space between the option and its argument. To specify a unit other than characters, follow the number by one of the following: "i" for inches, "c" for centimeters, or "p" for PostScript points.

⇒ To print the contents of the file `installment.007` to the default printer, with the `enscript` defaults, and indenting lines by a half an inch, type:

> `$ enscript -i.5i installment.007` ⟨RET⟩

15.2.10 Outputting Multiple Copies of Text

To output multiple copies of text when sending it to the printer with `enscript`, give the number as an argument to the `-#` option. This option doesn't work when sending to a file, but note that `lpr` takes the same option (see Recipe 25.1.2 [Printing Multiple Copies of a Job], page 510).

⇒ To print three copies of the text file `saved-mail` to a PostScript printer with the default `enscript` headers, type:

> `$ enscript -#3 saved-mail` ⟨RET⟩

15.2.11 Outputting Text in Columns

To specify that text should be output in columns, give the number of columns as an argument to the `-columns=` option.

⇒ To send the file `payroll-data` to the default printer with the default `enscript` processing, setting the text in four columns per page, type:

> `$ enscript -columns=4 payroll-data` ⟨RET⟩

If the number of columns is either one or two, you can also give the number itself as an option. Use the `-j` option to place borders around each column.

⇒ To send the file `payroll-data` to the default printer with the default `enscript` processing, setting the text in two columns per page, each with a border drawn around it, type:

> `$ enscript -j -2 payroll-data` ⟨RET⟩

NOTES: You can also place text in paginated columns with `pr`, and then send it to `enscript` (see Recipe 13.3.4 [Placing Text in Paginated Columns], page 314).

15.2.12 Outputting Selected Pages of Text

To specify which pages of a text are output with `enscript`, give the range of page number(s) as an argument to the `-a` option. You can specify individual pages by their numbers, specify a list of pages delinated by commas, and specify a range of pages by giving the first and last page numbers in the range, separated by a hyphen (`-`).

⇒ To print pages 2 through 10 of file `saved-mail` with the default `enscript` headers, type:

```
$ enscript -a2-10 saved-mail (RET)
```

To print just the odd or even pages, use the special "odd" and "even" arguments. This is good for printing double-sided pages: First print the odd-numbered pages, and then feed the output pages back into the printer and print the even-numbered pages.

⇒ Here are two ways to use this.

- To print the odd-numbered pages of the file `saved-mail` with the default headers, type:

```
$ enscript -a odd saved-mail (RET)
```

- To print the even-numbered pages of the file `saved-mail` with the default headers, type:

```
$ enscript -a even saved-mail (RET)
```

15.2.13 Outputting Text Through a Filter

You can pass the input text through an external filter before `enscript` converts it to PostScript. This filter can be a tool or quoted command. Give the filter as an argument to the `-I` option, being sure not to leave a space between the option and its argument.

⇒ To print the file `sensitivity_training` to the default filter, using the default `enscript` settings, but first passing the input text through the `newspeak` filter, type:

```
$ enscript -Inewspeak sensitivity_training (RET)
```

15.3 Using TEX

teTeX
```
DEB: tetex-base
     tetex-bin
     tetex-doc
     tetex-extra
RPM: tetex
WWW: http://www.tug.org/teTeX/
```

The most capable typesetting tool for use on Linux-based systems is the TEX typesetting system and related software. It is the premier computer typesetting system—its output surpasses or rivals all other systems to date. The advanced line and paragraph breaking, hyphenation, kerning, and other font-characteristic policies and algorithms it can perform, and the precision with which it can do them, have yet to be matched in word processors.

The TEX system itself—not a word processor or single program, but a large collection of files and data—is packaged in distributions; teTEX is the TEX distribution designed for Linux.

TEX input documents are plain text files written in the TEX typesetting language, which the TEX tools can process and write to output files for printing or viewing. This approach has great benefits for the writer: The plain text input files can be written with and exchanged between many different computer systems regardless of operating system or editing software, and these input files do not become obsolete or unusable with new versions of the TEX software.

Donald E. Knuth, the world's foremost authority on algorithms, wrote TEX in 1984[2] as a way to typeset his books[3], because he wasn't satisfied with the quality of available systems. Since its first release, many extensions to the TEX formatting language have been made—the most notable being Leslie Lamport's LaTEX, which is a collection of sophisticated macros written in the TEX formatting language, designed to facilitate the typesetting of structured

---

[2] This is the year that Knuth's definitive book on the subject, *The TEXbook*, was published, but the system was technically operational before this time—version 1.0 was released on December 3, 1983, the initial design for the system occurred in 1977, and the first books typeset with early TEX were published by Christmas 1978.

[3] See http://www-cs-faculty.stanford.edu/~knuth/taocp.html.

documents. (LATEX probably gets more day-to-day use than the plain TEX format, but in my experience, each is useful for different situations.)

"TEX" isn't pronounced like the name of a cowboy, nor "LATEX" like a kind of paint: the letters "T," "E," and "X" represent the Greek characters tau, epsilon, and chi (from the Greek *techne*, meaning "art and science"). So the last sound in "TEX" is like the last sound in "Bach," and "LATEX," depending on local dialect, is pronounced either "lay-teck" or "lah-teck." Those who become highly adept at using the system Knuth calls *TEXnicians*.

The collective family of TEX and related programs (including METAFONT; see Recipe 16.5 [Using Other Font Tools], page 403) are sometimes called "TEX and friends," and they are always kept in a directory named `texmf`. For example, the supplementary files included with the bare TEX system are kept in the `/usr/lib/texmf` directory tree.

The following recipes describe how to begin writing input for TEX and how to process these files for viewing and printing. While not everyone wants or even needs to write documents with TEX and LATEX, these formats are widely used—especially on Linux systems—so every Linux user has the potential to encounter one of these files, and ought to know how to process them.

15.3.1 Distinguishing Between TEX and LATEX Files

There are separate commands for processing TEX and LATEX files, and they're not interchangeable, so when you want to process a TEX or LATEX input file, you should first determine its format.

By convention, TEX files always have a `.tex` file name extension. LATEX input files sometimes have a `.latex` or `.ltx` file name extension instead, but not always—one way to tell if a `.tex` file is actually in the LATEX format is to use `grep` to search the file for the text "\document," which every LATEX (and *not* TEX) document will have. So if the search outputs any lines that match, you have a LATEX file. (The regular expression to use with `grep` is "\\document," because backslash characters must be specified with two backslashes.)

⇒ To determine whether the file `smith.tex` is a TEX or LATEX file, type:

```
$ grep '\\document' smith.tex (RET)
\documentclassletter
$
```

In this example, `grep` returned a match, so it's safe to assume that `smith.tex` is a LaTeX file (of the "`letter`" document class) and not a TeX file.

NOTES: For more on regular expressions and searching with `grep`, see Recipe 14.3 [Regular Expressions—Matching Text Patterns], page 335.

15.3.2 Processing a TeX File

Use `tex` to process TeX files. It takes as an argument the name of the TeX source file to process, and it writes an output file in DVI ("DeVice Independent") format, with the same base file name as the source file, but with a `.dvi` extension.

⇒ To process the file `gentle.tex`, type:

> `$ tex gentle.tex` ⟨RET⟩

Once you have produced a DVI output file with this method, you can do any of the following with it:

- Preview it on the screen with `xdvi`; see Recipe 17.4.1 [Previewing a DVI File], page 413.
- Print it with `dvips` or `lpr`; see Recipe 25.2.5 [Printing a DVI File], page 515.
- Convert it to PostScript with `dvips`; see Recipe 25.3.2 [Preparing a DVI File for Printing], page 520; then, you can also convert the PostScript output to PDF or plain text.

15.3.3 Processing a LaTeX File

The `latex` tool works just like `tex`, but it is used to process LaTeX files.

⇒ To process the LaTeX file `lshort.tex`, type:

> `$ latex lshort.tex` ⟨RET⟩

This command writes a DVI output file called `lshort.dvi`.

You may need to run `latex` on a file several times consecutively. LaTeX documents sometimes have indices and cross references, which, because of the way that LaTeX works, take two (and, in rare cases, three or more) runs through `latex` to be fully processed. Should you need to run a file through `latex` more than once in order to generate the proper references, you'll see a message in the `latex` processing output instructing you to process it again.

⇒ To ensure that all of the cross references in `lshort.tex` have been generated properly, run the input file through `latex` once more:

    $ latex lshort.tex ⟨RET⟩

The `lshort.dvi` file will be rewritten with an updated version containing the proper page numbers in the cross reference and index entries. You can then view, print, or convert this DVI file as described in the previous recipe for processing TEX files.

15.3.4 Getting Started with TEX and LATEX

To create a document with TEX or LATEX, you generally use your favorite text editor to write an *input file* containing the text in TEX or LATEX formatting. Then, you process this TEX or LATEX input file to create an *output file* in the DVI format, which you can preview, convert, or print.

It's an old tradition among programmers introducing a programming language to give a simple program that just outputs the text "Hello, world" to the screen; such a program is usually just detailed enough to give those unfamiliar with the language a feel for its basic syntax.

We can do the same with document-processing languages like TEX and LATEX. Figure 15-1 contains the "Hello, world" for a TEX document.

```
Hello, world
\end
```

Figure 15-1. A TEX "Hello, world."

If you processed the input file shown in Figure 15-1 with `tex`, it would output a DVI file that displayed the text "Hello, world" in the default TEX font, on a default page size, and with default margins.

Figure 15-2 contains the same "Hello, world," but for LATEX.

```
\documentclass{article}
\begin{document}
Hello, world
\end{document}
```

Figure 15-2. A LATEX "Hello, world."

Even though the TEX example in Figure 15-1 is much simpler than the LATEX example, LATEX is generally easier to use "fresh out of the box" for writing certain kinds of structured documents—such as correspondence and articles—because it comes with predefined *document classes*, which control the markup for the structural elements the document contains.[4] Plain TeX, on the other hand, is better suited for less casual publishing projects, including custom layouts and specialized documents.

The TeX and LaTeX markup languages are worth a book each, and providing an introduction to their use is well out of the scope of this text. To learn how to write input for them, I suggest two beginning tutorials: Michael Doob's *A Gentle Introduction to TeX*, and Tobias Oetiker's *The Not So Short Introduction to LaTeX*. Both are available on the Web at the URLs listed in Appendix D [References for Further Interest], page 731. These tutorials are each in the format they describe; in order to read them, you must *process* them first, as described in the two previous recipes.

Good LaTeX documentation in HTML format can be found installed on many Linux systems in the /usr/share/texmf/doc/latex/latex2e-html/ directory; browse these files at your leisure (see Recipe 5.10 [Browsing Files and Directories], page 157).

Some other typesetting systems, such as LyX, Linuxdoc-Tools, and Texinfo (all described elsewhere in this chapter), write TeX or LaTeX output, too—so you can use those systems to produce said output without actually learning the TeX and LaTeX input formats. (This book was written in Emacs in Texinfo format, and the typeset output was later generated by TeX.)

NOTES: The Oetiker text consists of several separate LaTeX files in the `lshort` directory; download and save all of these files.

15.3.5 Using TeX and LaTeX Document Templates

Templates for TeX and LaTeX
 WWW: http://dsl.org/comp/templates/

A collection of sample templates for typesetting certain kinds of documents in TeX and LaTeX can be found at the URL listed above. These templates include those for creating letters and correspondence, articles and term papers, envelopes and mailing labels,[5] and fax cover sheets. If you're interested in making typeset output with TeX and LaTeX, these templates are well worth exploring.

---

[4] LyX, being in essence a graphical front-end to LaTeX, uses these same document classes.

[5] In addition, a more advanced LaTeX style for printing many different kinds of shipping and package labels is normally installed at /usr/share/texmf/tex/latex/labels/.

To write a document with a template, insert the contents of the template file into a new file that has a `.tex` or `.ltx` extension, and write your document by making changes to that file. (Use your favorite text editor to do this.)

To make sure that you don't accidentally overwrite the actual template files, you can write-protect them (see Recipe 6.3.3 [Write-Protecting a File], page 169):

$ *chmod a-w template-file-names* ⟨RET⟩

In the templates themselves, the bracketed, uppercase text explains what kind of text belongs there; fill in these lines with your own text and delete the lines you don't need. Then, process your new file with either `latex` or `tex` as appropriate, and you've got a great-looking document!

The following table lists the file names of the TeX templates, and describes their use. Use `tex` to process files you make with these templates (see the preceding recipe).

`fax.tex`	A cover sheet for sending fax messages.
`envelope.tex`	A No. 10 mailing envelope.
`label.tex`	A single mailing label for printing on standard 15-up sheets.

The following table lists the file names of the LaTeX templates, and describes their use.[6] Use `latex` to process files you make with these templates (see Recipe 15.3.3 [Processing a LaTeX File], page 374).

`letter.ltx`	A letter or other correspondence.
`article.ltx`	An article or a research or term paper.
`manuscript.ltx`	A book manuscript.

There are more complex template packages available on the net that you might want to look at:

- The largest listing of LaTeX and TeX templates and style files (and other related software and documentation) on the Internet is the searchable TeX Catalogue Online
  [http://www.ctan.org/tex-archive/help/Catalogue/hier.html].

---

[6] The manuscript template requires that your system has the LaTeX style file called `manuscript.sty` installed; most TeX distributions have this file at `/usr/share/texmf/tex/latex/misc/manuscript.sty`.

- Rob Rutten has assembled a very nice collection of LaTeX templates [http://www.astro.uu.nl/~rutten/rrtex/templates/].

- A collection of plain TeX macros for printing booklets, bulk letters, and outlines worth exploring is the Midnight Macros [http://www.ctan.org/tex-archive/macros/generic/midnight/]

- A set of TeX templates for various kinds of documents, mostly academic and instructional, are available courtesy of the Duke Mathematics Department [http://www.math.duke.edu/computing/tex/templates.html].

15.4 Using LyX

LyX
  DEB: lyx
  RPM: lyx
  WWW: http://www.lyx.org/

LyX is a relative newcomer to the typesetting and word-processing arena, and it is one of the most genuinely fresh ideas in the field: It's a kind of word processor for writing LaTeX input (see Recipe 15.3 [Using TeX], page 372). It is for those who want the benefits of TeX and LaTeX, but want to compose their documents in a word-processor-style application. This means it's a visual, graphic editor for X, but it doesn't emulate the printed output directly on the display screen. In contrast to specifying exactly how each character in the document will look ("make this word Helvetica Bold at 18 points," for example), you specify the *structure* of the text you write ("make this word a chapter heading"). And, in contrast to the WYSIWYG paradigm, its authors call the new approach WYSIWYM—"What You See Is What You *Mean*."

LyX comes with many document *classes* already defined—such as "letter," "article," "report," and "book"—containing definitions for the elements these document types may contain. You can change the look of each element and the look of the document as a whole, and you can change the look of individual selections of text, but with these elements available, it's rarely necessary.

Since LyX uses LaTeX as a back-end to do the actual typesetting, and because LyX is capable of exporting documents to LaTeX input format, you can think of LyX as a way to write LaTeX input files in a GUI without having to know the LaTeX language commands.

However, even those who *do* use LaTeX and related typesetting languages can get some use out of LyX: many people find it quick and easy to create some documents in LyX that are much harder to do in LaTeX, such as multi-column newsletter layouts with illustrations.

You can also import your LaTeX files (and plain text) into LyX for further layout or manipulation.

The following recipes show how to get started using LyX, and where to go to learn more about it.

When editing in LyX, you'll see that it has all of the commands you'd expect from a word processor—for example, some of the commands found on the `Edit` menu include `Cut`, `Copy`, `Paste`, `Find and Replace`, and `Spell Check`.

Here are some of its major features:

- Automatic generation of table of contents, nested lists, and numbering of section headings.

- Easy insertion of PostScript figures and illustrations, which can be rotated, scaled, and captioned.

- WYSIWYG construction of tables.

- Ability to undo and redo any operation or sequence of operations.

- All LyX functions available from both keyboard commands and pull-down menus.

- All keypresses used for commands are configurable.

15.4.1 Getting Started with LyX

LyX runs under X, and you start it in the usual way—either by choosing it from the applications menu provided by your window manager, or by typing `lyx` in an `xterm` window. (For more about starting programs in X, see Recipe 4.2 [Running a Program in X], page 101).

To start a new document from scratch, choose `New` from the `File` menu. You can also make a document from one of the many templates included with LyX, which have the basic layout and settings for particular kind of documents all set up for you—just fill in the elements for your actual document. To make a new document from a template, choose `New from template` from the `File` menu, and then select the name of the template to use.

The following table lists the names of some of the included templates and the kind of documents they're usually used for.

`aapaper.lyx`	Format suitable for papers submitted to *Astronomy and Astrophysics*.
`dinbrief.lyx`	Format for letters typeset according to German conventions.
`docbook_template.lyx`	Format for documents written in the SGML DocBook DTD.
`hollywood.lyx`	Format for movie scripts as they are formatted in the U.S. film industry.
`iletter.lyx`	Format for letters typeset according to Italian conventions.
`latex8.lyx`	Format suitable for article submissions to IEEE conferences.
`letter.lyx`	Basic format for letters and correspondence.
`linuxdoctemplate.lyx`	Format for documents written in the SGML LinuxDoc DTD, as formerly used by the Linux Documentation Project.
`revtex.lyx`	Article format suitable for submission to publications of the American Physical Society (APS), American Institute of Physics (AIP), and Optical Society of America (OSA).
`slides.lyx`	Format for producing slides and transparencies.

To view how the document will look when you print it, choose `View DVI` from the `File` menu. This command starts the `xdvi` tool, which previews the output on the screen. (For more on using `xdvi`, see Recipe 17.4.1 [Previewing a DVI File], page 413).

To print the document, choose `Print` from the `File` menu. You can also export it to LaTeX, PostScript, DVI, or plain text formats; to do this, choose `Export` from the `File` menu and then select the format to export to.

NOTES: If you plan on editing the document again in LyX, be sure to save the actual `.lyx` document file.

15.4.2 Learning More About LyX

The LyX Documentation Project has overseen the creation of a great deal of free documentation for LyX, including hands-on tutorials, user manuals, and example documents.

The LyX Graphical Tour[7] is a Web-based tutorial that shows you how to create and edit a simple LyX file.

LyX has a comprehensive set of built-in manuals, which you can read inside the LyX editor like any LyX document, or you can print them out. All of the manuals are available from the Help menu.

⇒ To run LyX's built-in tutorial, choose Tutorial from the Help menu.

This command opens the LyX tutorial, which you can then read on the screen or print out by selecting Print from the File menu.

The following table lists the names of the available manuals as they appear on the Help menu, and describes what each contains:

Introduction	An introduction to using the LyX manuals, describing their contents and how to view and print them.
Tutorial	A hands-on tutorial to writing documents with LyX.
User's Guide	The main LyX usage manual, describing all of the commonly used commands, options, and features.
Extended Features	"Part II" of the *User's Guide*, describing advanced features such as bibliographies, indices, documents with multiple files, and techniques used in special-case situations, such as fax support, SGML-Tools support, and using version control with LyX documents.
Customization	An explanation of the elements of LyX that can be customized, and how to do so.
Reference Manual	A description of all the menu entries and internal functions.
Known Bugs	A list of bugs. LyX is in active development, and as with any large application, bugs have been found.

---

[7] See http://www.lyx.org/about/lgt-1.0/lgt.html.

LATEX Configuration | An inventory of your LATEX configuration, including the version of LATEX in use, available fonts, available document classes, and other related packages that may be installed on your system. This document is automatically generated by LyX when it is installed on your system.

Finally, LyX includes some example documents in the /usr/X11R6/share/lyx/examples directory. Here's a partial listing of these files with a description of what each contains:

Foils.lyx | Description of how to make *foils*—slides or overhead transparencies—with the FoilTEX package.

ItemizeBullets.lyx | Examples of the various bullet styles for itemized lists.

Literate.lyx | An example of using LyX as a composition environment for "literate programming."

MathLabeling.lyx | Techniques for numbering and labeling equations.

Math_macros.lyx | Explanation of how to make macros in Math mode.

Minipage.lyx | Explanation of how to write two-column bilingual documents.

TableExamples.lyx | Examples of using tables in LyX.

aa_head.lyx
aa_paper.lyx
aas_sample.lyx | Files discussing and showing the use of LyX in the field of astronomy.

amsart-test.lyx
amsbook-test.lyx | Examples of documents written in the format used by the American Mathematical Society.

docbook_example.lyx | Example of a DocBook document.

multicol.lyx | Example of a multi-column format.

scriptone.lyx | Example of a Hollywood script.

15.5 Using GROFF

Groff
  DEB: groff
  RPM: groff
  WWW: http://www.gnu.org/software/groff/groff.html

GNU TROFF (also known as GROFF) is the latest in a line of phototypesetting systems that have been available on UNIX-based systems for years; the original in this line was ROFF ("runoff," meaning that it permitted files to be *run off* to the printer). GROFF is used in the typesetting of **man** pages, but it's possible to use it to typeset many kinds of documents. It produces very high-quality output and has a healthy following of staunch adherents.

Like TEX, GROFF is a typesetting system where input is written in plain text files, using a special formatting language. So GROFF shares the benefits of TEX in this regard—documents written in GROFF a quarter-century ago can still be read on every computer today that reads plain text, and they can be processed on any system that has a GROFF implementation (which, as with TEX, is just about every computer and OS in use today).

The source files you use with **groff** typically have **.ms** or (when the **me** macros are used) **.me** file name extensions.

15.5.1 Processing a GROFF File

Use **groff** to process GROFF source files. Given the name of a source file as an argument, **groff** makes typeset output from it, writing it, by default, in PostScript to the standard output.

⇒ To preview the contents of the GROFF file **doc.ms** in the PostScript reader gv, type:

    $ *groff doc.ms | gv -* ⟨RET⟩

There are several output formats **groff** can write to. To specify a format, give it as an argument to the **-T** option. The following table lists the arguments and describes the formats they specify.

ps	PostScript
dvi	DVI ("DeVice Independent") format
X75	DVI preview in X at 75 dpi (no output file necessary)

X100   DVI preview in X at 100 dpi (no output file neces-
                              sary)

ascii   Plain text

latin1   Plain text in the ISO Latin-1 character set (extended
                              ASCII)

lj4   PCL5 printer format, for HP LaserJet 4 printers and
                              compatibles

html   HTML

By default, **groff** writes to the standard output; to save it to a file, redirect
the output.

⇒ Here are some ways to use this.

- To preview the contents of the GROFF file **doc.ms** in a new X window
  at 100 dpi, type:

    $ *groff -T X100 doc.ms* (RET)

- To process the GROFF file **doc.ms** and send the output to an HP
  LaserJet 4 printer named **frontoffice**, type:

    $ *groff -T lj4 doc.ms | lpr -Pfrontoffice* (RET)

- To display the first 20 lines of the document contained in the GROFF
  file **doc.ms**, ignoring any error messages, type:

    $ *groff -T ascii doc.ms 2> /dev/null | head -20* (RET)

- To mail the contents of the GROFF file **doc.ms** as plain text to the
  email address **home@example.net**, type:

    $ *groff -T ascii doc.ms | mail home@example.net* (RET)

15.5.2 Determining the Command Line Options for a GROFF File

Some GROFF input files require command line options to be passed to **groff**
when you process them. These options set various preprocessing flags and
otherwise control how **groff** will typeset the document.

To determine which command line options should be used with a particular
GROFF file, give the name of the file as an argument to **grog**, the "GROFF
option generator." This tool is part of the GROFF system, and its purpose
is to determine and output the correct **groff** command line to use for a
particular file.

⇒ To see which options should be used with **groff** on the file **meintro.me**, type:

    $ grog meintro.me ⟨RET⟩

15.5.3 Running a GROFF Tutorial

A tutorial on using **groff** is included with its distribution, a compressed **groff** file called **meintro.me.gz** in the **/usr/doc/groff** directory. Since this file is itself a **groff** file, it must be processed by **groff** to get an output file.

⇒ To output the tutorial file included with the **groff** distribution to a DVI file called **intro.dvi**, type (all on one line):

    $ zcat /usr/doc/groff/me-intro.me.gz | groff -me -T
    dvi > intro.dvi ⟨RET⟩

In this example, the uncompressed content of the file was sent to the standard output via **zcat** (see Recipe 10.6 [Concatenating Text], page 256). You can use **xdvi** to preview the resultant DVI output, or **dvips** to print it.

The command options used for this file were determined by **grog** (as described in the previous recipe).

NOTES: Two additional GROFF documentation files included in the same directory are a complete reference manual, **meref.me.gz**, and a guide to making box-and-arrow diagrams with the PIC extension, **pic.ms.gz**.

More recommended resources for learning GROFF can be found in See Appendix D [References for Further Interest], page 731.

15.5.4 Making a Chart or Table

There are facilities in GROFF for making tables and charts of all kinds. Once you learn the minimal formatting commands, it is easy to typeset professional tables. The data for a table is kept in a plain text file with the GROFF commands that specify how to format it; use **tbl** to process such a file. It takes as input a text file with GROFF formatting for a table, and outputs PostScript by default.

Each table is written in its own file, beginning with a **.TS** command ("table start") on the first line. This is followed by the formatting commands used to typeset the table, the data itself, and finally a **.TE** command ("table end") on the last line of the file.

For example, suppose you have a file named **zones**, as in Figure 15-3.

```
.TS
allbox;
c s s
c c c
n n l.
Plant Hardiness Zones
Zone   Min. Temp.    Example Cities
1      Below -50 F   Fairbanks, Alaska; Resolute, Northwest Territories (Canada)
2a     -50 to -45 F  Prudhoe Bay, Alaska; Flin Flon, Manitoba (Canada)
2b     -45 to -40 F  Unalakleet, Alaska; Pinecreek, Minnesota
3a     -40 to -35 F  International Falls, Minnesota; St. Michael, Alaska
3b     -35 to -30 F  Tomahawk, Wisconsin; Sidney, Montana
4a     -30 to -25 F  Minneapolis/St.Paul, Minnesota; Lewistown, Montana
4b     -25 to -20 F  Northwood, Iowa; Nebraska
5a     -20 to -15 F  Des Moines, Iowa; Illinois
5b     -15 to -10 F  Columbia, Missouri; Mansfield, Pennsylvania
6a     -10 to -5 F   St. Louis, Missouri; Lebanon, Pennsylvania
6b     -5 to 0 F     McMinnville, Tennessee; Branson, Missouri
7a     0 to 5 F      Oklahoma City, Oklahoma; South Boston, Virginia
7b     5 to 10 F     Little Rock, Arkansas; Griffin, Georgia
8a     10 to 15 F    Tifton, Georgia; Dallas, Texas
8b     15 to 20 F    Austin, Texas; Gainesville, Florida
9a     20 to 25 F    Houston, Texas; St. Augustine, Florida
9b     25 to 30 F    Brownsville, Texas; Fort Pierce, Florida
10a    30 to 35 F    Naples, Florida; Victorville, California
10b    35 to 40 F    Miami, Florida; Coral Gables, Florida
11     above 40 F    Honolulu, Hawaii; Mazatlan, Mexico
.TE
```

*Figure 15-3. The **zones** file.*

To make a table from such a GROFF input file, use **tbl** and give the name of the file as an argument. This command outputs the raw input text that GROFF uses to typeset the table; to view it or save it to a file, pipe the output to **groff** with the right argument to the **-T** option for the output format you want, as described in Recipe 15.5.1 [Processing a GROFF File], page 383.

⇒ Here are two ways to use this.

- To preview the typeset table made from the file **zones** in a new X window at 100 dpi, type:

  `$ tbl zones | groff -TX100` ⟨RET⟩

- To output the typeset table made from the file **zones** in a PostScript file called **zones.ps**, type:

  `$ tbl zones | groff -Tps > zones.ps` ⟨RET⟩

The previous example text will produce a table that looks like Figure 15-4.

Plant Hardiness Zones		
Zone	Min. Temp.	Example Cities
1	Below -50 F	Fairbanks, Alaska; Resolute, Northwest Territories (Canada)
2a	-50 to -45 F	Prudhoe Bay, Alaska; Flin Flon, Manitoba (Canada)
2b	-45 to -40 F	Unalakleet, Alaska; Pinecreek, Minnesota
3a	-40 to -35 F	International Falls, Minnesota; St. Michael, Alaska
3b	-35 to -30 F	Tomahawk, Wisconsin; Sidney, Montana
4a	-30 to -25 F	Minneapolis/St.Paul, Minnesota; Lewistown, Montana
4b	-25 to -20 F	Northwood, Iowa; Nebraska
5a	-20 to -15 F	Des Moines, Iowa; Illinois
5b	-15 to -10 F	Columbia, Missouri; Mansfield, Pennsylvania
6a	-10 to -5 F	St. Louis, Missouri; Lebanon, Pennsylvania
6b	-5 to 0 F	McMinnville, Tennessee; Branson, Missouri
7a	0 to 5 F	Oklahoma City, Oklahoma; South Boston, Virginia
7b	5 to 10 F	Little Rock, Arkansas; Griffin, Georgia
8a	10 to 15 F	Tifton, Georgia; Dallas, Texas
8b	15 to 20 F	Austin, Texas; Gainesville, Florida
9a	20 to 25 F	Houston, Texas; St. Augustine, Florida
9b	25 to 30 F	Brownsville, Texas; Fort Pierce, Florida
10a	30 to 35 F	Naples, Florida; Victorville, California
10b	35 to 40 F	Miami, Florida; Coral Gables, Florida
11	above 40 F	Honolulu, Hawaii; Mazatlan, Mexico

Figure 15-4. Table made from the **zones** *file.*

Using the `ascii` option with `groff` will output a nice ASCII character table, and the `html` option will output a PNG-format image file plus an HTML file that has an image tag for that file.

NOTES: For more information on using `tbl`, see Appendix D [References for Further Interest], page 731.

You can make nice tables with LaTeX, too. For a good tutorial, consult Chapter 5 of *The LaTeX Environment* (see Appendix D [References for Further Interest], page 731).

15.6 Using SGML

Linuxdoc-Tools
  DEB: `linuxdoc-tools`
       `linuxdoc-tools-info`
       `linuxdoc-tools-latex`
       `linuxdoc-tools-text`
  RPM: `linuxdoc`

Standard Generalized Markup Language, or SGML, is not an actual format, but a specification for writing markup languages; the markup language "formats" themselves are called DTDs ("Document Type Definitions"). When you write a document in an SGML DTD, you write input as a plain text file with markup tags.

The various SGML packages on Linux are currently in a state of transition, and have been for some time.

The original SGML-Tools package (known as LinuxDoc-SGML in another life; then SGMLtools v1) is no longer being developed. However, the newer SGMLtools v2 (a.k.a. "SGMLtools Next Generation" and "SGMLtools '98") was alpha software at the time of this book's first edition, as was SGMLtools-lite, another new subset of SGMLtools. The old Linuxdoc-Tools package with the original (and easy to work with) DTD is still around, and it appears to be getting continued use.[8]

If you want to dive in and get started making documents with the LinuxDoc DTD, it's not hard to do. While the newer DocBook DTD has become very popular for producing technical books and related projects, the LinuxDoc DTD still works fine for smaller documents written by individual authors, such as a multi-part essay, FAQ, or white paper.

With the Linuxdoc-Tools package, you can write documents and generate output in many different kinds of formats—including HTML, plain text, PDF, and PostScript—all from the same plain text input file.

The package gets its name from the old Linux Documentation Project, which used this format in its documentation. In their heyday, the Linux HOWTOs and larger guides were written in LinuxDoc.

The *Linuxdoc-Tools User's Guide* comes installed with the `linuxdoc-tools` package, and it is available in several formats in the `/usr/share/doc/linuxdoc-tools` directory. These files are compressed;

---

[8] If you can't locate a copy, you can always install the sources from the Debian package (see Recipe 1.1 [Format of Recipes], page 3).

if you want to print or convert them, you have to uncompress them first (see Recipe 8.4 [Using File Compression], page 196).

⇒ Here are two ways to use this.

- To peruse the compressed text version of the Linuxdoc-Tools guide, type:

    $ *zless /usr/share/doc/linuxdoc-tools/guide.txt.gz* ⟨RET⟩

- To print a copy of the PostScript version of the Linuxdoc-Tools guide to the default printer, type:

    $ *zcat /usr/share/doc/linuxdoc-tools/guide.ps.gz | lpr* ⟨RET⟩

The following recipes use the Linuxdoc-Tools package and demonstrate its use with documents written in the LinuxDoc DTD.

15.6.1 Writing an SGML Document

A document written in an SGML DTD looks a lot like HTML, which is no coincidence, since HTML is a subset of SGML. A very simple "Hello, world" example in the LinuxDoc DTD might look like Figure 15-5.

```
<!doctype linuxdoc system>
<article>
<title>An Example Document
<author>Ann Author
<date>4 May 2000
<abstract>
This is an example LinuxDoc document.
</abstract>

<sect>Introduction

<p>Hello, world.

</article>
```

Figure 15-5. A LinuxDoc "Hello, world."

NOTES: The Linuxdoc-Tools package also comes with a simple example file, **example.sgml.gz**, which is installed in the **/usr/share/doc/linuxdoc-tools/example** directory.

15.6.2 Checking SGML Document Syntax

To make sure the syntax of an SGML document is correct, use `linuxdoc` and give "check" as the argument to the `-B` option. This outputs any errors it finds in the document that is specified as an argument.

⇒ To check the SGML file `myfile.sgml`, type:

```
$ linuxdoc -B check myfile.sgml RET
```

15.6.3 Generating Output from SGML

Use `linuxdoc` to make typeset output from an SGML source file.

Specify the format of output to generate as an argument to the `-B` option. These commands write a new file with the same base file name as the SGML file you give as an argument, but with the file name extension of their output format.

The following table lists the various format arguments and describes the kind of output they generate.

`html`	Generates HTML files.
`info`	Generates a GNU Info file.
`lyx`	Generates a LyX input file.
`latex`	Generates a LaTeX input file (useful for printing; first process as in Recipe 15.3.3 [Processing a LaTeX File], page 374, and then print the resultant DVI or PostScript output file).
`rtf`	Generates a file in Microsoft's "Rich Text Format."
`txt`	Generates plain text.

⇒ To make a plain text file from `myfile.sgml`, type:

```
$ linuxdoc -B txt myfile.sgml RET
```

This command writes a plain text file called `myfile.txt`.

To make a PostScript or PDF file from an SGML file, first generate a LaTeX input file, run it through `latex` to make a DVI output file, and then process that with `dvips` to make the final output.

⇒ To make a PostScript file from `myfile.sgml`, type:

```
$ linuxdoc -B latex myfile.sgml (RET)
$ latex myfile.latex (RET)
$ dvips -t letter -o myfile.ps myfile.dvi (RET)
$
```

In this example, `linuxdoc` writes a LaTeX input file from the SGML source file, and then the `latex` tool processes the LaTeX file to make DVI output, which is processed with `dvips` to get the final output: a PostScript file called `myfile.ps` with a paper size of "U.S. letter" (8.5 in x 11 in).

To make a PDF file from the PostScript file, you need to take one more step and use `ps2pdf`, part of the `gs` (Ghostscript) package; this converts the PostScript to PDF.

⇒ To make a PDF file from the PostScript file `myfile.ps`, type:

```
$ ps2pdf myfile.ps myfile.pdf (RET)
```

15.7 Using Other Word Processors and Typesetting Systems

The following table describes other suggested word processors and typesetting tools available for Linux.

AbiWord	A graphical, WYSIWYG-style word processor for Linux systems. It can read Microsoft Word files and is reportedly similar to that famous word processor in some ways. DEB: abiword-common RPM: abiword WWW: http://www.abisource.com/
ImPress	Full-featured, WYSIWYG layout and desktop publishing system. DEB: impress RPM: impress WWW: http://www.ntlug.org/~ccox/impress/index.html

LilyPond	A system for typesetting sheet music. DEB: `lilypond` RPM: `lilypond` WWW: `http://lilypond.org/web/`
Maxwell	A graphical word processor for use in X. WWW: `http://sourceforge.net/projects/maxwellwp`
OpenOffice.org	A graphical, window-based "office suite" that includes a word processor called WRITER (along with spreadsheet, presentation, diagram, and database applications). DEB: `openoffice` RPM: `openoffice` WWW: `http://www.openoffice.org/`
PostScript	The PostScript language itself. PostScript is generally considered to be a format generated by software, but some people write straight PostScript! Recipe 15.2 [Outputting Text to PostScript], page 359, has recipes on creating PostScript output from text, including outputting text in a particular font. People have also written PostScript template files for creating all kinds of documents—from desktop calendars to mandalas for meditation. The Debian `cdlabelgen` and `cd-circleprint` packages contain tools for writing labels for compact discs. Also of interest are the following templates for printing label inserts for video and audio tapes; edit the files in a text editor and then view or print them as you would any PostScript file. WWW: `http://www.jwz.org/hacks/audio-tape.ps` WWW: `http://www.jwz.org/hacks/video-tape.ps`
Scribus	A simple layout and desktop publishing system that uses Type 1 fonts. DEB: `scribus` RPM: `scribus` WWW: `http://web2.altmuehlnet.de/fschmid/`

Texinfo

Texinfo is the GNU Project's documentation system, and it is excellent for writing certain kinds of technical manuals. While not extensible enough out-of-the-box for production of serious non-technical publications, it does allow for the inclusion of in-line EPS images and can produce TeX-based, HTML, and Info output. Use it if this matches your needs.
DEB: `tetex-base`
RPM: `texinfo`
WWW: `http://www.gnu.org/software/texinfo/`

Txt2tex

A script that converts plain text to LaTeX.
WWW: `http://www.tex.ac.uk/CTAN/support/txt2tex/`

Using Fonts

A *font* is a collection of characters for displaying text, normally in a common
typeface and with a common size, boldness, and slant.

This chapter discusses the most popular kinds of fonts used on Linux systems: display fonts for use in the X Window System, TeX fonts, fonts for
use in terminals, and the "fonts" often seen in Usenet and email composed
entirely of ASCII characters.

To just print a text file in a font, see Recipe 15.2.1 [Outputting Text in a
Font], page 361.

For more information on fonts and the tools for using them, see the *Font
HOWTO* (see Recipe 2.8.6 [Reading System Documentation and Help Files],
page 50).

16.1 Using X Fonts

You can specify a font as an option to most X clients, so that any text in
the client is displayed in the given font. The way to do this is described in
Recipe 4.2.3 [Specifying X Window Font], page 104.

When you specify a font as an option, you have to give the *X font name*,
which is the exact name used to specify a specific font in X. (An easy way to
get the X font name is described in the first recipe in this section.) X font
names consist of 14 fields, delimited by (and beginning with) a hyphen. All
fields must be specified, and empty fields are permitted:

```
-fndry-fmly-wght-slant-swdth-adstyl-pxlsz
-ptsz-resx-resy-spc-avgwdth-rgstry-encdng
```

The preceding line was split because of its length, but X font names are
always given on one line.

The following table describes the meaning of each field.

fndry	The type foundry that digitized and supplied the font data.
fmly	The name of the typographic style (for example, "courier").

wght	The weight of the font, or its *nominal blackness*, the degree of boldness or thickness of its characters. Values include "heavy," "bold," "medium," "light," and "thin."
slant	The posture of the font, usually "r" (for *roman*, or upright), "i" (*italic*, slanted upward to the right and differing in shape from the roman counterpart), or "o" (*oblique*, slanted but with the shape of the roman counterpart).
swdth	The *proportionate* width of the characters in the font, or its *nominal width*, such as "normal," "condensed," "extended," "narrow," and "wide."
adstyl	Any additional style descriptions the particular font takes, such as "serif" (fonts that have small strokes drawn on the ends of each line in the character) or "sans serif" (fonts that omit serifs).
pxlsz	The height, in pixels, of the type. Also called *body size*.
ptsz	The height, in points, of the type.
resx	The horizontal screen resolution the font was designed for, in dpi ("dots per inch").
resy	The vertical screen resolution the font was designed for, in dpi.
spc	The kind of spacing used by the font (its *escapement class*); either "p" (a *proportional* font containing characters with varied spacing), "m" (a *monospaced* font containing characters with constant spacing), or "c" (a *character cell* font containing characters with constant spacing and constant height).
avgwdth	The average width of the characters used in the font, in 1/10th pixel units.
rgstry	The international standards body, or *registry*, that owns the encoding.

encdng   The registered name of this character set, or its
                            encoding.

NOTES: For more information on using fonts in X, see the *XFree86 Font De-uglification* HOWTO (see Recipe 2.8.6 [Reading System Documentation and Help Files], page 50).

16.1.1 Selecting an X Font Name

X font names can be long and difficult to type; to make it easier, use the **xfontsel** client, an interactive tool for picking X fonts and getting their X font names.

When you start **xfontsel**, it looks like Figure 16-1 (the window frame will differ depending on your window manager).

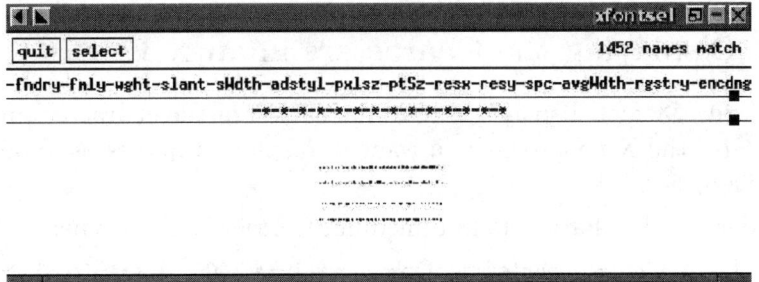

Figure 16-1. Starting **xfontsel**.

The row of buttons are pull-down menus containing options available on your system for each field in the X font name. Use the mouse to select items from each menu, and the X font you have selected is shown in the main window. Above it is written its X font name.

⇒ To make the X font name the X selection, click the mouse on the button labeled **select**.

This example makes the X font name the X selection, which permits you to paste the X font name on a command line or into another window (see Recipe 10.3.2 [Pasting Text], page 254).

16.1.2 Listing Available X Fonts

Use **xlsfonts** to list the X font families, sizes, and weights available on your system. Supply a pattern in quotes as an argument, and it outputs the names of all X fonts installed on the system that match that pattern; by default, it lists all fonts.

⇒ Here are some ways to use this.

- To list all the X fonts on the system, type:

    $ *xlsfonts* ⟨RET⟩

- To list all the X fonts on the system whose names contain the text "rea," type:

    $ *xlsfonts '*rea*'* ⟨RET⟩

- To list all the bold X fonts on the system, type:

    $ *xlsfonts '*bold*'* ⟨RET⟩

NOTES: This is not a way to *display* the characters in a font; for that, use **xfd**, described next. Furthermore, to *browse* through available X fonts, you want to use **xfontsel**, as in the previous recipe.

16.1.3 Displaying the Characters in an X Font

Use the **xfd** ("X font display") tool to display all of the characters in a given X font. Give the X font name you want to display in quotes as an argument to the **-fn** option.

⇒ To display the characters in a medium Courier X font, type:

    $ *xfd -fn '-*-courier-medium-r-normal--*-100-*-*-*-*-iso8859-1'* ⟨RET⟩

16.1.4 Resizing the Xterm Font

See Recipe 4.2.3 [Specifying X Window Font], page 104, for information on specifying the font for X client windows. One of the tools it is most useful to specify a font for is **xterm**, which is usually used to run a shell while in X; many people like to specify which font is used for this window (see Recipe 4.5 [Getting a Terminal Window in X], page 109).

To resize the current font when the **xterm** is running, press and hold ⟨CTRL⟩ and right-click anywhere in the **xterm** window. A menu will appear that gives you the size options, from **Unreadable** and **Tiny** to **Huge**. To resize the font to its original size, choose **Default**.

16.2 Using TeX Fonts

The following recipes pertain to TeX fonts in particular.

16.2.1 Listing Available TeX Fonts

A popular question among new TeX users is how to list all of the TeX fonts installed on the system—most installations come with a lot of them, and it would be helpful to easily list and display them all. Unfortunately, there is no uniform and surefire way to do it. You can use many types of fonts with TeX, and the precise fonts installed will differ from system to system. TeX fonts are typically stored in the `/usr/share/texmf/fonts/` and `/usr/local/share/texmf/fonts/` directory trees.

To get a list of TeX fonts on your system, use `locate` to list files with a `.tfm` extension. These are TeX font metric files. Not all of the TeX fonts have a `.tfm` file, and not all of the `.tfm` files are usable fonts, but you can get a good idea of the TeX fonts installed on your system with this method.

⇒ To list the available `.tfm` fonts on your system, type:

```
$ locate .tfm RET
```

NOTES: You may want to redirect the output to a file, or peruse it with `less` in a terminal window of its own, while you use this output to display samples of the fonts as described in the next recipe.

16.2.2 Viewing a Sample of a TeX Font

The file `/usr/share/texmf/tex/plain/base/testfont.tex`, included with TeX, is a special TeX file you can use to display a sample of any `.tfm` font.

When you process this file, it asks for the name of a font to display. Give the base file name—that is, omit both its path and extension. Then type `\sample` and `\end`, each on lines of their own, TeX commands that first print the sample and then end the TeX file. This command will create a DVI file in the current directory named `textfont.dvi` that contains a sample of the letterset for the given font.

⇒ To view a sample of the `plu10` font, type:

```
$ tex /usr/share/texmf/tex/plain/base/testfont.tex (RET)
This is TeX, Version 3.14159 (Web2C 7.3.1)
(/usr/share/texmf/tex/plain/base/testfont.tex
Name of the font to test = plu10(RET)
Now type a test command (\help for help):)
* \sample (RET)
[1]
* \bye (RET)
[2]
Output written on testfont.dvi (2 pages, 12344 bytes).
Transcript written on testfont.log.
$ xdvi testfont.dvi (RET)
```

16.3 Using Console Fonts

Console fonts are screen fonts for displaying text on the Linux console (and not in the X Window System).

Console fonts are stored in the `/usr/share/consolefonts` directory as compressed files; to install new console fonts, have the system administrator make a `/usr/local/share/consolefonts` directory and put the font files in there.

These recipes show how to set the console font, and how to display a table containing all of the characters in the current font.

16.3.1 Setting the Console Font

Use `consolechars` to set the current console font; give the base file name of a console font as an argument to the `-f` option.

⇒ To set the console font to the `scrawl_w` font, type:

```
$ consolechars -f scrawl_w (RET)
```

Some font files contain more than one height (or size) of the font. If a font contains more than one encoding for different heights, give the height to use as an argument to the `-H` option. (If you try to specify such a font without the height option, `consolechars` will output a list of available sizes.)

Common console font heights include 8 (for 8x8 fonts), 14 (for 8x14 fonts), and 16 (for 8x16 fonts).

⇒ To set the console font to the 8x8 size **sc** font, type:

$ *consolechars -H 8 -f sc* ⟨RET⟩

16.3.2 Displaying the Characters of a Console Font

Use **showcfont** to display all of the characters in the current console font.

⇒ To list all of the characters in the current console font, type:

$ *showcfont* ⟨RET⟩

16.4 Using Text Fonts

Text fonts are fonts created from the arrangement of ASCII characters on the screen; they are often seen in Usenet articles and email messages, included as decorative or title elements in text files, and used for printing simple banners or posters on a printer.

The making of "fonts" (and even pictures) from the arrangement of ASCII characters is known as *ascii art*. The following recipes describe methods of outputting text in these kinds of fonts.

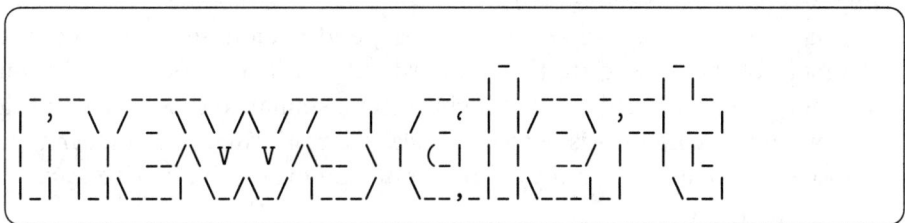

Figure 16-2. Output from figlet.

16.4.1 Outputting Horizontal Text Fonts

Figlet
  DEB: figlet
  RPM: figlet
  WWW: http://www.figlet.org/

The **figlet** filter outputs text in a given text font. Give the text to output as an argument, quoting any text containing shell metacharacters (see Recipe 3.1.3 [Quoting Reserved Characters], page 56).

⇒ To output the text "**news alert**" in the default **figlet** font, type:

$ *figlet news alert* ⟨RET⟩

This command outputs the text in an ASCII text font, as in Figure 16-2.

Fonts for `figlet` are kept in the `/usr/lib/figlet` directory; use the -f option followed by the base name of the font file (without the path or extension) to use that font.

To output the contents of a text file with a `figlet` font, use `cat` to output the contents of a file and pipe the output to `figlet`.

⇒ To output the text of the file `poster` in the figlet `bubble` font, type:

    `$ cat poster | figlet -f bubble` (RET)

NOTES: The `bubble` font is installed at `/usr/lib/figlet/bubble.flf`.

16.4.2 Outputting Text Banners

Bsd-games
  DEB: bsdmainutils
  RPM: bsd-games
  WWW: `ftp://metalab.unc.edu/pub/Linux/games/`

The easiest way to print a long, vertical banner of text on a Linux system is with the old UNIX **banner** tool.

Quote a text message as an argument, and **banner** sends a large, vertical "banner" of the message to the standard output. The message itself is output in a "font" composed of ASCII text characters, similar to those used by `figlet`, except that the message is output vertically for printing, and you can't change the font. To send the output of **banner** to the printer, pipe it to `lpr`.

⇒ Here are two ways to use this.

- To make a banner saying "**Happy Birthday Susan**," type:

    `$ banner 'Happy Birthday Susan'` (RET)

- To print a banner saying "**Happy Birthday Susan**" to the default printer, type:

    `$ banner 'Happy Birthday Susan' | lpr` (RET)

Unfortunately, the breadth of characters that **banner** understands is a bit limited—the following characters can't be used in a **banner** message:

  `< > [ ] \ ^ _ { } | ~`

To make a banner of the contents of a text file, send its contents to **banner** by redirecting standard input (see Recipe 3.2.1 [Redirecting Input to a File], page 67).

To make a banner of the contents of the file **/etc/hostname**, type:

```
$ banner < /etc/hostname (RET)
```

The default width of a banner is 132 text columns; you can specify a different width by specifying the width to use as an argument to the **-w** option. If you give the **-w** option without a number, banner outputs at 80 text columns.

⇒ Here are two ways to use this.

- To make a banner containing the text "**Happy Birthday Susan**" at a width of 23 text columns, type:

```
$ banner -w 23 'Happy Birthday Susan' (RET)
```

- To make a banner containing the text "**Happy Birthday Susan**" at a width of 80 text columns, type:

```
$ banner -w 'Happy Birthday Susan' (RET)
```

NOTES: A method of making a horizontal text banner with `figlet` is described in Recipe 15.2.7 [Outputting Text in Landscape Orientation], page 369.

16.5 Using Other Font Tools

The following table describes some of the other font tools available for Linux.

Console Font Editor	The Linux Console Font Editor (`cse`), an older console font tool for editing font characters on-screen. DEB: `cfe` RPM: `cfe` WWW: `http://lrn.ru/~osgene/`

Debian Font Manager	A tool for configuring fonts on a Debian system.
	DEB: `defoma`
	      `defoma-doc`
	      `psfontmgr`

Fonter	A console font editor. DEB: `fonter` WWW: `ftp://metalab.unc.edu/pub/Linux/apps/misc/`

FontForge	A font editor that recognizes many formats, including PostScript, TrueType, and OpenType. DEB: `fontforge` RPM: `fontforge` WWW: `http://fontforge.sourceforge.net/`
Font Viewer	A tool for viewing Adobe Type 1 and TrueType fonts. DEB: `gfontview` RPM: `gfontview` WWW: `http://gfontview.sourceforge.net/`
Gozer	A tool that renders text given as an argument into an anti-aliased TrueType font. DEB: `gozer` WWW: `http://www.linuxbrit.co.uk/gozer/`

METAFONT	Donald E. Knuth's language for designing fonts and logos (distributed with TEX).
	DEB: `tetex-base`
	    `tetex-bin`
	    `tetex-doc`
	    `tetex-extra`
	RPM: `tetex`
	WWW: `http://www.tug.org/teTeX/`

PkTrace	A tool that converts fonts made with METAFONT into Type 1 fonts. DEB: `pktrace` RPM: `mftrace`

IV. IMAGES

## CHAPTER 17

Viewing Images

There are many tools for viewing images, and as with text, there are both tools for viewing and editing images. This chapter describes some of the best methods for viewing images; the editing of images is discussed in the next chapter. While you can view an image with an image *editor*, it is safer (and faster!) to view with a viewer when you do not intend to edit it.

17.1 Viewing an Image in X

ImageMagick
  DEB: imagemagick
  RPM: ImageMagick
  WWW: http://www.imagemagick.org/

To view an image in X, use `display`, which is part of the ImageMagick suite of tools. It can recognize many image formats, including FlashPix, GIF/GIF87, Group 3 faxes, JPEG, PBM/PNM/PPM, PhotoCD, TGA, TIFF, TransFig, and XBM. It can also view images compressed with `gzip` or `bzip2` without you having to uncompress them, and it also offers rudimentary editing facilities.

   The `display` tool takes as an argument the file name of the image to be viewed, and it displays the image in a new window of its own.

⇒ To view the file `sailboat.jpeg`, type:

   `$ display sailboat.jpeg` (RET)

This command displays the image file in a new window, as in Figure 17-1.

Figure 17-1. An image in `display`*.*

The mouse buttons have special meaning in display. Left-click on the image window to open the display command menu in a new window. The display command menu looks like Figure 17-2.

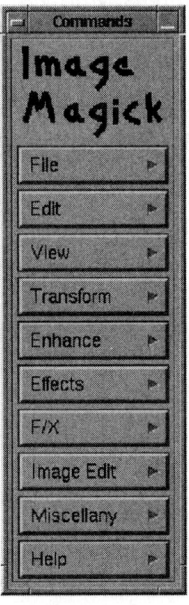

Figure 17-2. The display command menu.

The menu items let you change how the image is displayed (but they don't change the actual image file unless you save your changes to it). You can change the image size, apply effects, and otherwise change or transform the image display. Choose Overview from the Help menu for an explanation of the various commands that are available.

Figure 17-3. Image magnification in display.

Middle-click on the image to open a new window with a magnified view of the image centered where you click. For example, middle-clicking on the previous sailboat image will open a new window that looks like Figure 17-3.

Finally, right-click on the image window for a pop-up menu containing a few of the most frequently-used commands; to choose one of these commands, drag the mouse pointer over the command and release the right button. Commands in the pop-up menu include Quit, which exits display, and Image Info, which displays information about the image file itself, including the number of colors, image depth, and resolution.

The following table describes some of the keyboard commands that can be used when displaying an image in display.

(SPACEBAR)	Display next image specified on the command line.
(BKSP)	Display previous image specified on the command line.
(CTRL)-(Q)	Quit displaying image and exit display.
(CTRL)-(S)	Write image to a file.
<	Halve image size.
>	Double image size.
–	Return image to its original size.
/	Rotate image 90 degrees clockwise.
\	Rotate image 90 degrees counter-clockwise.
?	Open a new window with image information, including resolution, color depth, format, and comments, if any.
h	Toggle a horizontal mirror image.
v	Toggle a vertical mirror image.

The following recipes describe some special uses of display. It can also be used to view images on the Web—see Recipe 33.4 [Viewing an Image from the Web], page 651.

17.1.1 Browsing Image Collections in X

The display tool offers a feature for browsing a collection of images—give "vid:" as the file argument, followed by the file names or pattern to match them in quotes. `display` makes thumbnails of the specified images, and displays them in a new window, which it calls a *visual image directory*.

⇒ Here are two ways to use this.

- To browse through the image files that have a `.gif` extension and are in the `/usr/doc/imagemagick/examples` directory, type:

  $ *display 'vid:/usr/doc/imagemagick/examples/*.gif'* (RET)

- To browse through all image files in the current directory, type:

  $ *display 'vid:*'* (RET)

In the preceding example, only those files with image formats supported by `display` are read and displayed.

NOTES: If the title bar indicates that there is more than one page to the visual image directory, press (SPACEBAR) to advance to the next one (pressing (SPACEBAR) on the last page wraps back to the beginning).

To open an image at its normal size, right-click the image and choose `Load`; the thumbnail will be replaced by its full-size image. To return to the thumbnail directory, press (SPACEBAR).

17.1.2 Putting an Image in the Root Window

One way to put an image in the root window (the background behind all other windows) is to use `display` and give "`root`" as an argument to the `-window` option.

⇒ To put the image `tetra.jpeg` in the root window, type:

  $ *display -window root tetra.jpeg* (RET)

17.2 Browsing Images in a Console

Zgv
  DEB: `zgv`
  RPM: `zgv`
  WWW: `http://freshmeat.net/projects/zgv/`

Use `zgv` to view images in a virtual console (not in X). You can use `zgv` to browse through the filesystem and select images to view, or you can give the names of specific image files to view as arguments. It recognizes many image formats, including GIF, JPEG, PNG, PBM/PNM/PPM, TGA, and PCX; one of its nicest features is that it fills the entire screen with an image.

When you run **zgv** with no options, it displays image icons of any images in the current directory, showing any subdirectories as folder icons. You can also give the name of a directory as an argument in order to browse the images in that directory.

⇒ Here are two ways to use this.

- To browse the images in the current directory, type:

  $ *zgv* ⟨RET⟩

- To browse the images in the **/usr/share/gimp/scripts** directory, type:

  $ *zgv /usr/share/gimp/scripts* ⟨RET⟩

Use the arrow keys to navigate through the file display; the red border around an image or directory icon indicates which image or subdirectory is selected. Type ⟨RET⟩ to view the selected image or to change to the selected directory.

You can manipulate the images you view in a number of ways—zoom the image magnification in and out, change the brightness and color, and even make automatic "slide shows" of images. The following table describes some of **zgv**'s command line options.

`-c`	Toggle image centering. Images are centered on the screen by default; specifying this option turns off centering.
`-i`	Ignore errors due to corrupted files, and display whatever portion of the file is displayable.
`-l`	Start **zgv** in slide-show mode, where it loops through all images specified as arguments, continuously, until you interrupt it.
`-M`	Toggle mouse support. Mouse support is off by default; this option turns it on.
`-r` *integer*	Reread and redisplay every image after every *integer* seconds. Useful for viewing webcam images or other image files that are continuously changing.

17.3 Viewing an Image in a Web Browser

Lynx
  DEB: `lynx`
  RPM: `lynx`
  WWW: `http://lynx.browser.org/`

  or

Mozilla
  DEB: `mozilla-browser`
  RPM: `mozilla`
  WWW: `http://www.mozilla.org/`

Browsers are good for perusing files and directories, and they are equally good at displaying images. You can browse local images in a Web browser running in X just as you would browse any files (see Recipe 5.10 [Browsing Files and Directories], page 157). If you want to view an image file while you are in X, and you have a Web browser running, it can be a quick and easy way to do it.

You can view images in this way using either a graphical browser (such as Mozilla), or in a terminal window with the text-based browser Lynx, in which case the image is displayed in a new window with a "helper" application.[1] Exiting the helper application will bring you back to Lynx.

To view an image file in Mozilla or another graphical Web browser, specify the full path name of the image file in the **Location** field of the browser. To view an image file in Lynx, just give the full or relative path name of the image as an argument, or type *g* while in Lynx to get a prompt where you can then type the full path name.

⇒ Here are some ways to use this.

- To start Mozilla with the file `/usr/share/doc/texmf/pdftex/base/pic.png`, type:

    mozilla /usr/share/doc/texmf/pdftex/base/pic.png (RET)

- To view the file `/usr/share/doc/texmf/pdftex/base/pic.png` in Mozilla, type the following in its **Location** field:

    /usr/share/doc/texmf/pdftex/base/pic.png (RET)

---

[1] The `display` tool is usually the default application set up for viewing images.

- To start Lynx with the file `/usr/share/doc/texmf/pdftex/base/`
  `pic.png`, type:

  lynx /usr/share/doc/texmf/pdftex/base/pic.png (RET)

- To view the file `/usr/share/doc/texmf/pdftex/base/pic.png` in
  Lynx, type:

  ```
  g


  URL to open: /usr/share/doc/texmf/pdftex/base/pic.png  (RET)
  ```

NOTES: The `file:` URL given to Mozilla only has one preceding slash (pointing to the root directory) and not two, as in any `http://` URL.

17.4 Previewing Print Files

The DVI ("DeVice Independent"), PostScript, and PDF ("Portable Document Format") file formats can be generated by a number of applications. They are graphical image formats commonly used for printing; methods for previewing these files on the display screen are discussed in the following recipes.

NOTES: If the file you want to preview is compressed and has either a `.gz` or `.bz2` file name extension, you can still preview it with `see` (see Recipe 8.4.3 [Seeing What's in a Compressed File], page 199).

17.4.1 Previewing a DVI File

Use the `xdvi` tool to preview a DVI file in X. Give the name of the file to preview as an argument. `xdvi` will show how the document will look when printed, and you can view it at different magnifications.

⇒ To preview the file `gentle.dvi`, type:

  $ xdvi gentle.dvi (RET)

To magnify the view of the document, left-click any of the buttons labeled with a percentage, such as **17%**; they magnify the view by that percentage.

⇒ To magnify the view by 33%, left-click the button marked **33%**.

The following table lists the most important keystoke commands to use while previewing with xdvi.

(Q)	Exit xdvi and stop previewing the file.
(N) *or* (F)	Advance *forward* to the next page.
(P) *or* (B)	Move *backward* to the previous page.
(CTRL)-(C)	Same as (Q).
(CTRL)-(D)	Same as (Q).
(SPACEBAR)	Scroll forward down the page, or advance forward to the next page if already near the bottom of the page.
(CTRL)-(L)	Redisplay the current page.
(R)	Re-read the DVI file.

17.4.2 Previewing a PostScript File

Ghostview
  DEB: ghostview
  RPM: ghostview
  WWW: http://www.cs.wisc.edu/~ghost/index.html

   or

GV
  DEB: gv
  RPM: gv
  WWW: http://wwwthep.physik.uni-mainz.de/~plass/gv/

To preview a PostScript or EPS image file in X, use either **ghostview** or **gv**. Both take a file name as an argument, and they preview the contents of the file in a window, starting with its first page.

⇒ To preview the file **/usr/doc/gs/examples/tiger.ps**, type:

   $ *gv /usr/doc/gs/examples/tiger.ps* (RET)

Press (SPACEBAR) to scroll down the page (and then advance to the next one, if there is one), (O) to open a new file, and (Q) to exit.

NOTES: The keys just described work for either **ghostview** or **gv**, but today many people prefer to use the newer **gv**, which was based on **ghostview**, but has a better interface and can preview PDF files, too.

17.4.3 Previewing a PDF File

Xpdf
  DEB: xpdf-common
       xpdf-reader
  RPM: xpdf
  WWW: http://www.foolabs.com/xpdf/

Use **xpdf** to preview a PDF file. Give the name of the PDF file to preview as an argument.

⇒ To preview the PDF file `flyer.pdf`, type:

  $ *xpdf flyer.pdf* ⟨RET⟩

To exit **xpdf**, press ⟨Q⟩; use the two magnifying-glass buttons to zoom the view closer in (+) or further out (-), and click on the left and right arrow buttons to move to the previous and next pages, if any. You can also select text with the mouse by clicking the first mouse button and dragging over the block of text to select; this becomes plain ASCII text in the X selection, which you may paste into another window (like a text editor, for instance, or in an **xterm** shell where you are using **cat** to redirect standard input to a file).

NOTES: You can also use **gv** to preview PDF files (see preceding recipe).

17.5 Browsing PhotoCD Archives

There are two methods for browsing Kodak PhotoCD archives.

METHOD #1

Xpcd
  DEB: xpcd
       xpcd-gimp
  RPM: xpcd
  WWW: http://bytesex.org/xpcd.html

The xpcd tool is an X client for viewing and browsing collections of Kodak PhotoCD images. To browse the images on a Kodak PhotoCD, mount the CD-ROM (see Recipe 24.4.1 [Mounting a Data CD], page 506), and then give the mount point as an argument to xpcd.

⇒ To browse the images on the PhotoCD disc mounted on /cdrom, type:

    $ xpcd /cdrom ⟨RET⟩

The preceding example will open two new windows—a small xpcd command bar window, and a larger window containing thumbnails of all PhotoCD images on the disc.

To open a copy of an image in a new window, left-click its thumbnail image. When you do, xpcd will open the image at the second-smallest PhotoCD resolution, 256x384; to view it at another size, right-click the image and choose the size to view. Once the new window is drawn, you can right-click on this new image to save it as a JPEG, PPM, or TIFF format image.

To view an individual .pcd file with xpcd, give the name of the file as an argument.

⇒ To view the PhotoCD file hawaii-001.pcd, type:

    $ xpcd hawaii-001.pcd ⟨RET⟩

NOTES: While development has been halted on xpcd, it is still a useful viewer, and comes packaged with pcdtoppm, a PhotoCD conversion tool.

See Recipe 19.3 [Extracting PhotoCD images], page 445 for another recipe for extracting PhotoCD images.

METHOD #2

To browse a PhotoCD archive, use display to view the overview.pcd file associated with that archive, which is kept in the top directory of the archive (for how to use display, see Recipe 17.1 [Viewing an Image in X], page 407).

⇒ To browse the images on the PhotoCD disc mounted on /cdrom, type:

    $ display /cdrom/overview.pcd ⟨RET⟩

To view a particular image in a PhotoCD archive, give the file name associated with that image as an argument to display.

⇒ To view the twelfth image on the PhotoCD disc mounted on /cdrom, type:

    $ display /cdrom/images/img0012.pcd ⟨RET⟩

17.6 Viewing an Animation or Slide Show

ImageMagick
  DEB: `imagemagick`
  RPM: `ImageMagick`
  WWW: `http://www.imagemagick.org/`

Use **animate**, part of the ImageMagick suite, to view animations and to view or make slide shows.

To view an animated image file, give the name of the file as an argument.

⇒ To view the animated image `earth.gif`, type:

```
$ animate earth.gif ⟨RET⟩
```

To make a slide show of several images, give the number of hundredths of a second to display each image (the default is 6/100th of a second) as an argument to the **-delay** option, and give the names of all the image files as arguments.

⇒ Here are two ways to use this.

- To display a slide show of all files in the `~/photos/vacation2003/roll1/640` directory, displaying each image for ten seconds before moving to the next, type:

```
$ animate -delay 1000 ~/photos/vacation2003/roll1/640 ⟨RET⟩
```

- To display an animation of four files named **sample.jpg**, **120.tif**, **sampleb.jpg**, and **122.tif**, displaying each image for 1/5th of a second, type:

```
$ animate -delay 20 sample.jpg 120.tif sampleb.jpg 122.tif ⟨RET⟩
```

When **animate** is through displaying all of the given images, it loops back to the beginning. To set the amount of time to pause before starting over, give a second argument to **-delay**, specified as "x*number*," where *number* is the number of seconds to pause before looping again.

⇒ To display a slide show of all the `.jpeg` files in the current directory, displaying each image for the default 6/100ths of a second, and pausing for one second before repeating, type:

```
$ animate -delay x1 *.jpeg ⟨RET⟩
```

Use **-backdrop** to display the animation as a full-screen backdrop.

⇒ To display a full-screen backdrop slide show of all the files in the **our-hawaii-vacation** directory, displaying each image for thirty seconds, and pausing for one minute before repeating all over again, type:

```
$ animate -backdrop -delay 30000x60 our-hawaii-vacation/* RET
```

NOTES: As with all ImageMagick tools, CTRL-Q exits.

To make your own animated image files, use **convert**, which is also part of ImageMagick (see Recipe 18.2 [Converting Image Files], page 432).

17.7 Using Other Image Viewers

The following table lists other tools for viewing images.

Aview
> Displays graphics as "ASCII art." This tool can read any image format supported by the **pbmplus** utility suite, and has fluid zoom in/out, along with all the rendering options you'd expect from a world-class viewer.
> DEB: `aview`
> RPM: `aview`
> WWW: `http://aa-project.sourceforge.net/aview/`

Aatv
> Displays television tuner output in any text terminal as ASCII characters.
> DEB: `aatv`
> WWW: `http://n00n.free.fr/aatv/`

ChBg
> Changes the X background image. Allows for slide shows and other effects.
> DEB: `chbg`
> RPM: `chbg`
> WWW: `http://chbg.sourceforge.net/`

Fbi
> Displays images on Linux framebuffer consoles.
> DEB: `fbi`
> RPM: `fbi`
> WWW: `http://bytesex.org/fbi/`

Fbtv
Displays TV tuner images on Linux framebuffer consoles.
DEB: `fbtv`
RPM: `xawtv`
WWW: `http://bytesex.org/xawtv/`

Feh
Fast image viewer with many features, including the ability to show changing webcam images.
DEB: `feh`
WWW: `http://www.linuxbrit.co.uk/feh/`

Ida
Image viewer, browser, and simple editor, noted for its speed and small size.
DEB: `ida`
WWW: `http://bytesex.org/ida/`

Ogle
Displays DVDs. Includes DVD menu support.
DEB: `ogle`
RPM: `ogle`
WWW: `http://www.dtek.chalmers.se/groups/dvd/`

Quick
Image
Viewer
Displays images in X; specializes in fast load times.
DEB: `qiv`
RPM: `qiv`
WWW: `http://www.klografx.net/qiv/`

ShowImg
Displays images in X with a full-screen mode and many options.
DEB: `showimg`
RPM: `showimg`

Showpicture
Displays images in email attachments; requires `xloadimage` and only works in X.
DEB: `metamail`
RPM: `metamail`
WWW: `http://tinyurl.com/323w7`

VideoLAN
Plays MPEG, MPEG2, and DVD video from a network source.
DEB: `vlc`
RPM: `vlc`
WWW: `http://www.videolan.org/`

Xli
: Displays images in X.
DEB: `xli`
RPM: `xli`
WWW: `http://pantransit.reptiles.org/prog/`

Xloadimage
: Displays images in X; can place images in the root window.
DEB: `xloadimage`
RPM: `xloadimage`
WWW: `http://world.std.com/~jimf/xloadimage.html`

Xwud
: Displays files in the special X Window Dump file format, as created by `xwd`.
DEB: `xbase-clients`
RPM: `XFree86-progs`
WWW: `http://www.xfree86.org/`

## CHAPTER 18

Editing Images

When you take an image file—such as one containing a digitized photograph or a picture drawn with a graphics program—and you make changes to it, you are *editing* an image.

This chapter contains recipes for editing and modifying images, including converting between image file formats. It also gives an overview of other image-related applications you might find useful, including the featuresome GIMP image editor.

18.1 Transforming Images

ImageMagick
  DEB: `imagemagick`
  RPM: `ImageMagick`
  WWW: `http://www.imagemagick.org/`

Many Linux tools can be used to transform or manipulate images in various ways. Described here is the ImageMagick suite of imaging tools, of which the `mogrify` tool is particularly useful for performing fast command line image transforms; use it to change the size of, to rotate, or to reduce the colors in an image.

Figure 18-1. The `phoenix.jpeg` image.

The `mogrify` tool always takes the name of the file to work on as an argument, and it writes its changes to that file. Use a hyphen (-) to specify the standard input, in which case `mogrify` writes its output to the standard output.

I'll use the image `phoenix.jpeg`, shown in Figure 18-1, in the examples that follow to give you an understanding of how to use `mogrify`.

NOTES: You can also perform many of the image transformations described in the following sections interactively with the GIMP (see Recipe 18.3 [Editing Images with the GIMP], page 434); another very useful package for both transforming images and converting between image formats is the **netpbm** suite of utilities (see Recipe 19.2 [Scanning Images], page 443).

Figure 18-2. The `phoenix.jpeg` *image scaled to approximately 480x320pixels.*

18.1.1 Changing the Size of an Image

There are three good methods for resizing an image with `mogrify`, as follows.

NOTES: Images scaled to a larger size will appear blocky or fuzzy.

To *view* an image at a particular scale without modifying the file, use `display`; when you resize its window, you resize the image on the screen only, unless you choose to save it (see Recipe 4.3.2 [Resizing an X Window], page 106).

Figure 18-3. The `phoenix.jpeg` *image scaled to exactly 640x480 pixels.*

METHOD #1

To resize an image but maintain its *aspect ratio*, so that the ratio between the width and height stays the same, use `mogrify` with the `-geometry` option, and give the ideal width and height values, in pixels, as an argument.

⇒ To resize `phoenix.jpeg` to 480x320 pixels, type:

```
$ mogrify -geometry 480x320 phoenix.jpeg RET
```

This command transforms the original `phoenix.jpeg` file to an image sized as close to 480x320 pixels as possible while retaining its original aspect ratio, as in Figure 18-2.

METHOD #2

To resize an image to a particular image size without necessarily preserving its aspect ratio, use `mogrify` with the `-geometry` option, and append the geometry values you give as an argument with a trailing exclamation point (`!`).

⇒ To resize `phoenix.jpeg` to *exactly* 640x480 pixels, regardless of aspect ratio, type:

```
$ mogrify -geometry 640x480! phoenix.jpeg (RET)
```

This command transforms the original `phoenix.jpeg` to an image sized at exactly 640x480 pixels, without attempting to preserve the aspect ratio of the original, as in Figure 18-3.

Figure 18-4. The `phoenix.jpeg` image scaled by percentage.

METHOD #3

You can also scale an image by specifying the width or height by percentage with `mogrify`. To *decrease* by a percentage, give the value followed by a percent sign (`%`). To *increase* by a percentage, give the value plus 100 followed by a percent sign. For example, to increase by 25 percent, give "125%."

⇒ To increase the height of `phoenix.jpeg` by 25 percent and decrease its width by 50 percent, type:

> `$ mogrify -geometry 125%x50% phoenix.jpeg` (RET)

This command transforms the original `phoenix.jpeg` to an image whose height was increased by 25 percent and width increased by 50 percent, as in Figure 18-4.

18.1.2 Rotating an Image

To rotate an image, use `mogrify` with the `-rotate` option followed by the number of degrees to rotate by. If the image width exceeds its height, follow this number with a ">," and if the height exceeds its width, follow it with a "<." (Because both < and > are shell redirection operators, enclose this argument in quotes, omitting either if the image height and width are the same.)

⇒ To rotate `phoenix.jpeg`, whose height exceeds its width, by 90 degrees, type:

> `$ mogrify -rotate '90<' phoenix.jpeg` (RET)

This command transforms the original `phoenix.jpeg` so that it is rotated by 90 degrees, as in Figure 18-5.

Figure 18-5. The `phoenix.jpeg` *image rotated.*

NOTES: After this command, the width of `phoenix.jpeg` now exceeds its height, so to rotate it again use ">" instead of "<."

18.1.3 Adjusting the Colors of an Image

You can use `mogrify` to make a number of adjustments in the color of an image. To reduce the number of colors in an image, use the `-colors` option, followed by the number of colors to use.

⇒ To reduce the colors in `phoenix.jpeg` to two, type:

    $ mogrify -colors 2 phoenix.jpeg (RET)

This command transforms the original `phoenix.jpeg` to a black and white image, as in Figure 18-6.

Figure 18-6. The `phoenix.jpeg` *image in black and white.*

Figure 18-7. The `phoenix.jpeg` *image in dithered black and white.*

Use the `-dither` option to reduce the colors with Floyd-Steinberg error diffusion, a popular algorithm for improving image quality during color reduction.

⇒ To reduce the colors in `phoenix.jpeg` to four and apply Floyd-Steinberg error diffusion, type:

    $ mogrify -colors 4 -dither phoenix.jpeg (RET)

This command transforms the original `phoenix.jpeg` to a dithered black and white image, as in Figure 18-7.

Use the -map option with a second file name as an argument to read the *color map* (the set of colors) from the second image and use them in the first image.

⇒ To change the colors in the file rainbow.jpeg to those used in the file prism.jpeg, type:

$ *mogrify -map prism.jpeg rainbow.jpeg* (RET)

Use the -monochrome option to make a color image black and white.

⇒ To make the color image rainbow.jpeg black and white, type:

$ *mogrify -monochrome rainbow.jpeg* (RET)

If you have a PPM file, use **ppmquant** to *quantize*, or reduce to a specified quantity, the colors in the image—see the **ppmquant man** page for details (see Recipe 2.8.4 [Reading a Page from the System Manual], page 46).

Because of differences in display hardware, the brightness of an image may vary from one computer system to another. For example, images created on a Macintosh usually appear darker on other systems. When you adjust the brightness of an image, it is called *gamma correction*.

To adjust the brightness of an image, give the numeric level of correction to apply as an argument to the -gamma option. Most PC displays have a gamma value of 2.5, while Macintosh displays have a lower gamma value of 1.4.

⇒ To set the gamma correction of the image rainbow.jpeg to .8, type:

$ *mogrify -gamma .8 rainbow.jpeg* (RET)

18.1.4 Annotating an Image

Independent JPEG Group's JPEG software
  DEB: libjpeg-progs
  RPM: libjpeg-progs
  WWW: http://www.ijg.org/

There are a few methods for reading and writing annotations in an image file. This practice is useful for adding a copyright statement to an image or for annotating an image file with a URL. Not all image formats support annotations; JPEG is the most popular.

You won't see the annotation when you view an image; it is added to the image header in the file. You can, however, read image annotations with tools that display information about an image file, such as **display** or the GIMP. Another method for outputting the annotation text is described below.

METHOD #1

Use `wrjpgcom` to write a comment in a JPEG file. Quote the comment as an argument to the `-comment` option, and give the name of the input file as an argument. The default is to write a new JPEG file to the standard output.

⇒ To annotate an image in the file `map.jpeg` with the text "`Map not drawn to full scale`" and write it to a file `warnmap.jpeg`, type (all on one line):

```
$ wrjpgcom -comment "Map not drawn to full scale"
map.jpeg > warnmap.jpeg ⟨RET⟩
```

Use a Bash `for` loop to make the same annotation in a group of files (see the Bash Info documentation for more information on this built-in).

⇒ To annotate all of the `.jpg` files in the current directory with the comment "`Image courtesy Rick Blaine`," writing to a new file with the same base name but a `.jpeg` extension, type:

```
$ for i in *.jpg ⟨RET⟩
> { ⟨RET⟩
> wrjpgcom -comment "Image courtesy Rick Blaine" $i `basename $i
jpg`jpeg ⟨RET⟩
> } ⟨RET⟩
$
```

The previous example could also have been written on a single input line, omitting the `for` loop, as follows:

```
for i in *.jpg; { wrjpgcom -comment "Image courtesy Rick
Blaine" $i `basename $i jpg`jpeg; } ⟨RET⟩
```

METHOD #2

Use `mogrify` with the `-comment` option to annotate image files with a comment. Give the comment in quotes as an argument to the option.

⇒ To annotate the image file `phoenix.jpeg`, type (all on one line):

```
$ mogrify -comment "If you can read this,
you're too close!" phoenix.jpeg ⟨RET⟩
```

METHOD #3

To read annotations in JPEG files, use the `rdjpgcom` tool—it outputs any comments in the JPEG file whose file name is given as an argument.

⇒ To read any comments made in the image file **phoenix.jpeg**, type:

```
$ rdjpgcom phoenix.jpeg (RET)
If you can read this, you're too close!
$
```

18.1.5 Adding Borders to an Image

To draw a border around an image, use `mogrify` with the `-border` option followed by the width and height, in pixels, of the border to use.

⇒ To add a border two pixels wide and four pixels high to **phoenix.jpeg**, type:

```
$ mogrify -border 2x4 phoenix.jpeg (RET)
```

This command transforms the original **phoenix.jpeg** to an image with a 2x4 pixel border, as in Figure 18-8.

Figure 18-8. The `phoenix.jpeg` *image with a border.*

The `-frame` option works like `-border`, but it adds a more decorative border to an image.

⇒ To add a decorative frame eight pixels wide and eight pixels high to **phoenix.jpeg**, type:

```
$ mogrify -frame 8x8 phoenix.jpeg (RET)
```

This command transforms the original `phoenix.jpeg` to an image with an 8x8 decorative frame, as in Figure 18-9.

Figure 18-9. The `phoenix.jpeg` *image with adecorative frame.*

NOTES: The border or frame is added to the outside of the existing image; the image is not cropped or reduced in size to add the border.

18.1.6 Making an Image Montage

To make a montage of several images, use `montage`. It takes as arguments the names of the images to use followed by the name of the output file to write the montage image to.

The montage image is made by scaling all of the input images to fit the largest size possible, up to 120x120 pixels, and tiling these images in rows of five and columns of four.

⇒ To create a montage from the files `owl.jpeg`, `thrush.jpeg`, and `warbler.jpeg` and write it to `ohio-birds.png`, type:

```
$ montage owl.jpeg thrush.jpeg warbler.jpeg ohio-birds.png (RET)
```

NOTES: In this example, three JPEGs were read and output to a PNG file; to specify the format to use in the output, give the appropriate file extension in the output file name.

18.1.7 Combining Images

Use `composite` to combine two images into one new image—give the names of the two source image files and the new file to write to as arguments. Without any options, `composite` makes a new image file by overlaying the smaller of the two images on top of the larger, starting in the top left corner; if both images are the same size, only the second image is visible.

⇒ To combine two images, `ashes.jpeg` and `phoenix.jpeg`, into a new file `picture.jpeg`, type:

```
$ composite ashes.jpeg phoenix.jpeg picture.jpeg (RET)
```

You can specify the percentage by which to blend the two images with the `-dissolve` option. Give the percentage to "dissolve" the first image into the second as an argument to the option.

⇒ To combine the image files `ashes.jpeg` and `phoenix.jpeg` so that the new image contains 70 percent of the first image dissolved into the second, type:

```
$ composite -dissolve 70 ashes.jpeg phoenix.jpeg picture.jpeg (RET)
```

This command combines the two images and writes a new image file, `picture.jpeg`, whose contents contain 70 percent of the first image.

NOTES: Use `-dissolve 50` to blend the two source files equally.

18.1.8 Morphing Two Images Together

Morphing is a computer-imaging method for finding the difference between the shapes in two images; it's often used in special effects to combine aspects of two creatures, such as the faces of a human and an animal.

You can use **convert** to get a morph-like effect with two files by using the `-morph` option. Give as an argument to the option the number of in-between sequence frames to use in the transformation between the two files.

When two input images and an output file are specified, this command takes the difference between corresponding pixels in the two images. The effect is like a "morphed" image.

If you specify a file format that supports animation, such as MIFF, the output will be written to a single animated image file. Otherwise, output is written to a series of files, each with its number in the series appended to its name.

You can also specify the delay to use in displaying each frame of the animated image; to do this, use the `-delay` option and give the time, in hundredths of a second.

⇒ To morph the files `ashes.jpeg` and `phoenix.jpeg`, making a sequence of three images whose names begin with `morph.png`, type:

```
$ convert -morph 3 ashes.jpeg phoenix.jpeg morph.png (RET)
```

This command writes five new PNG-format files: `morph.png.0`, which is identical to `ashes.jpeg`; `morph.png.4`, which is identical to `phoenix.jpeg`; and `morph.png.1`, `morph.png.2`, and `morph.png.3`, which contain transformations between the first and the last images.

⇒ To morph the files `ashes.jpeg` and `phoenix.jpeg`, making a new file called `morph.miff` containing an animated sequence of 25 transformative steps, with each frame in the sequence being displayed for a fifth of a second, type:

```
$ convert -morph 25 -delay 20 ashes.jpeg phoenix.jpeg morph.miff (RET)
```

This command makes a new file, `morph.miff`, which contains an animated sequence of 27 images. Each image in the sequence is displayed for a fifth of a second. When the sequence is finished, it repeats. Use a tool like **animate** to view it (see Recipe 17.6 [Viewing an Animation or Slide Show], page 417).

NOTES: Another tool, **xmorph**, is a special X application for morphing images; see Recipe 18.4 [Using Other Image Editors], page 435.

18.2 Converting Image Files

ImageMagick
  DEB: `imagemagick`
  RPM: `ImageMagick`
  WWW: `http://www.imagemagick.org/`

Use **convert** (also part of the ImageMagick suite of tools described in Recipe 18.1 [Transforming Images], page 421) to convert the file format of an image. Give the name of the file to convert as the first argument and the destination file as the second argument. When you convert a file, the original is not altered.

To specify the file type to convert to, use that file type's standard file extension in the file name of the converted file.

⇒ To convert the JPEG file `phoenix.jpeg` to a PNG image, type:

```
$ convert phoenix.jpeg phoenix.png (RET)
```

This command converts the JPEG image `phoenix.jpeg` to PNG format and writes it to a new file, `phoenix.png`.

When converting a file to JPEG format, be sure to use the `-interlace NONE` option to make sure the resultant JPEG image is non-interlaced—unless, of course, you *want* an interlaced image. An *interlaced* image is drawn in multiple passes, and is often used on the Web where a reader may view the low-resolution image consisting of early passes before the entire image is down-loaded. A *non-interlaced* image is drawn in one single pass.

⇒ To convert the PNM file `pike.pnm` to non-interlaced JPEG, while sharpen-ing the image by 50 percent and adding both a 2x2 border and a copyright comment, type (all on one line):

```
$ convert -interlace NONE -sharpen 50 -border 2x2
-comment 'Copyright 2008 Toby Smith' pike.pnm pike.jpeg (RET)
```

This command writes its output to the file `pike.jpeg`. Notice that the options `-border` and `-comment` were previously described for the `mogrify` tool. Some ImageMagick tools share common options, which is useful if you are making multiple changes to an image file at once; only one tool is needed for the job.

You can convert to and from any of the image formats recognized by Im-ageMagick, including animations. To make an animation, give as arguments the names of the files for the individual frames, in the sequence you want them to appear, and give the name of the new file as the final argument. Formats that support animations include MIFF and GIF.

Use the `-delay` option to specify the delay, in hundredths of a second, between frames.

⇒ To make an animated MIFF file, `driving.miff`, out of all the files `drive1.jpg`, `drive2.jpg`, `drive3.jpg`, `drive4.jpg`, and `drive5.jpg`, with a delay of a fifth of a second between frames, type (all on one line):

```
$ convert -delay 20 drive1.jpg drive2.jpg drive3.jpg
drive4.jpg drive5.jpg driving.miff (RET)
```

NOTES: Some image formats are *lossy*, which means some image information is lost when you convert to it. For example, the JPEG format is a lossy format that is usually used for photographic images. If you convert a file from its source PNM format to JPEG and then back to PNM, the resultant PNM will not be identical to the original source PNM.

To convert image files interactively, open the image in the GIMP, and then choose **Save as** from the **File** menu, and select the file type to use; see the following recipe for more information.

18.3 Using the GIMP

GIMP
   DEB: gimp1.2
       gimp-manual
   RPM: gimp
   WWW: http://www.gimp.org/

If you plan on doing even the slightest or most occasional image editing, such
as applying filters or effects to an image or touching up, resizing, or cropping
digital photographs, you will want to take some time to familiarize yourself
with the GIMP ("GNU Image Manipulation Program").

It is the flagship image editor for Linux-based systems, an all-encompassing
image manipulation program that you can use to paint, draw, create, and edit
images in complex ways. You can also use it to convert image files, retouch
and edit photographic images, and browse collections of images.

The GIMP comes pre-installed with hundreds of tools, filters, fonts, and
other goodies. Here is a partial list of its essential features:

- Contains a full suite of painting tools, including **Brush**, **Pencil**,
  Airbrush, and **Clone**.
- Supports custom brushes and patterns.
- Includes a full suite of image selection, transformation, and manipulation
  tools, including a gradient editor, color blending, and special effects.
- Includes animation support.
- Permits the use of layers and channels.
- Allows for large images, with their size being limited only by available
  disk space.
- Provides high-quality font anti-aliasing.
- Offers full alpha-channel support.
- Supports command scripting.
- Permits multiple undo and redo, limited only by available disk space.
- Allows multiple images to be open simultaneously.
- Supports all popular image file formats, including JPEG, PNG, XPM, TIFF,
  TGA, MPEG, PS, PDF, PCX, and BMP.
- Allows the easy addition of more than 100 plug-ins for new file formats
  and new effect filters.

The GIMP runs under X and is started by running **gimp** or choosing it from your window manager's menu. Give the names of any image files to open as arguments.

⇒ To start the GIMP in the background from a shell prompt, type:

   $ *gimp &* (RET)

When started, any image files you give as arguments are opened in their own windows. The main GIMP panel will open in a window of its own, as in Figure 18-10.

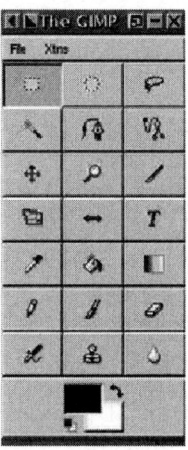

Figure 18-10. The main GIMP *panel.*

NOTES: To learn the basics of using the GIMP, consult *The GIMP User's Manual* and the other documentation and resources available from the GIMP Web site [http://www.gimp.org/]. You can also install the manual on your system; on Debian systems, it comes separately in the **gimp-manual** package.

18.4 Using Other Image Editors

There are all kinds of image-editing applications available for Linux—and there are as many ways to make and edit an image as there are tools to do it with.

The following table lists some other popular tools and applications for making and editing images that you may want to explore. It is not exhaustive.

Aa3d	Generates "ASCII art" stereograms. DEB: aa3d RPM: aa3d WWW: http://aa-project.sourceforge.net/aa3d/
AutoTrace	Converts bitmap images to vector graphics format. DEB: autotrace RPM: autotrace WWW: http://autotrace.sourceforge.net/
Barcode	Makes barcode images; recognizes all of the commercial standards. DEB: barcode RPM: barcode WWW: http://tinyurl.com/36s28
Bitmap	Editor for bitmap files, which are used for icons and tile patterns in the X Window System (see Recipe 4.7.3 [Changing the Root Window Parameters], page 118). DEB: xbase-clients RPM: XFree86-progs WWW: http://www.xfree86.org/
Blender	Hugely popular 3D modeling, rendering, animation and game design software. DEB: blender RPM: blender WWW: http://www.blender.org/
CADUBI	Draws "ASCII art." DEB: cadubi WWW: http://langworth.com/CadubiProject
Drgenius Drgeo	Two related tools for drawing interactive geometric figures. DEB: drgenius RPM: drgenius WWW: http://ofset.sourceforge.net/drgenius/ WWW: http://ofset.sourceforge.net/drgeo/

Dia   Drawing tool for simple charts and diagrams. Exports files
                       to EPS (see Chapter 20 [PostScript], page 451).
                       DEB: dia
                            dia-common
                       RPM: dia
                       WWW: http://www.gnome.org/projects/dia/

Effectv   Processes TV input through various special effects.
                       DEB: effectv

Electric   CAD system for designing images of electric circuits,
                       schematics, and the like.
                       DEB: electric
                       RPM: electric
                       WWW: http://tinyurl.com/3yzbf

Figurine   Vector graphics editor, intended to be easier to pick up than
                       the classic Xfig (listed below), yet remaining compatible
                       with Xfig's file format.
                       DEB: figurine
                       RPM: figurine
                       WWW: http://figurine.sourceforge.net/

Findimagedupes   Performs a "visual diff" on two image files; given a set of
                       files, it finds similar or duplicate images.
                       DEB: findimagedupes
                       WWW: http://www.kudla.org/raindog/perl/

Gnuplot   Robust, non-interactive function-plotting tool. Generates
                       charts and graphs from a data file and a formula (see
                       Recipe 29.8 [Plotting Data], page 575).
                       DEB: gnuplot
                       RPM: gnuplot
                       WWW: http://www.gnuplot.info/

Innovation3d   3D modeling program.
                       DEB: innovation3d
                            innovation3d-plugins
                       WWW: http://innovation3d.sourceforge.net/

Ivtools	Suite of drawing editors, including `idraw`, a vector graphics editor. DEB: `ivtools-bin` RPM: `ivtools` WWW: `http://www.ivtools.org/ivtools/`
Kali	Tool for drawing patterns and tilings, including frieze patterns and infinite or recursive tiles in the spirit of M.C. Escher. DEB: `kali`
Kino	Digital video editor that also has facilities to import from digital movie cameras. DEB: `kino` RPM: `kino` WWW: `http://kino.schirmacher.de/`
LignumCAD	3D CAD system for designing furniture. WWW: `http://tinyurl.com/ysl5o`
Moonlight3d	Formerly the Moonlight Creator, this tool is an X client for modeling, illuminating, and rendering 3D scenes. WWW: `http://moonlight3d.net/`
QCad	Professional 2D CAD system that saves its files in the industry DXF format. DEB: `qcad` RPM: `qcad` WWW: `http://www.ribbonsoft.com/qcad.html`
Sced	Tool for creating 3D scenes. DEB: `sced` RPM: `sced` WWW: `http://tinyurl.com/2g4oy`
Skencil	Full-featued vector drawing program (formerly Sketch) that supports Bézier curves, gradients, blending, and all the other features you would expect from such an application. DEB: `sketch` RPM: `sketch` WWW: `http://sketch.sourceforge.net/`

Sodipodi

Powerful vector drawing program that uses SVG format.
DEB: sodipodi
RPM: sodipodi
WWW: http://sodipodi.sourceforge.net/

Tgif

Interactive 2D drawing tool for X.
DEB: tgif
RPM: tgif
WWW: http://bourbon.usc.edu:8001/tgif/

TKpaint

Tool for drawing figures like those used in graphs, diagrams, and presentations.
DEB: tkpaint
RPM: Tkpaint
WWW: http://mars.netanya.ac.il/~samy/tkpaint.html

Xfig

Venerable application used for drawing figures—complex graphs, floor plans, maps, flow charts, and so forth. It saves files in its own format (giving them a .fig extension by default); the usual thing to do is export to EPS format.
DEB: xfig
RPM: xfig
WWW: http://xfig.org/

Xmorph

Morphs two images together (sometimes referred to as "warping"), making a new image in the process. The input images must be in TrueVision Targa file format, and have the same size, shape, and number of pixels in each file. (For a quick and easy way to morph two images using the ImageMagick suite, see Recipe 18.1.8 [Morphing Two Images Together], page 431.)
DEB: xmorph
WWW: http://xmorph.sourceforge.net/

Xpaint

Simple color "paint" tool that predates the GIMP. It contains all of the basic features that you would expect from an archetypal computer paint program. If you don't need the GIMP's advanced capabilities, consider running the smaller xpaint instead.
DEB: xpaint
RPM: xpaint
WWW: http://sf-xpaint.sourceforge.net/

## CHAPTER 19

Importing Images

While you can always make your own images, you may sometimes want to import and use existing images from other sources. In this chapter, I'll show you how to import images from scanners and Kodak PhotoCD discs. We'll begin with recipes for taking screen shots.

19.1 Taking Screen Shots

A *screen shot* is a picture of all or part of the display screen. The following recipes show you how to take screen shots in X and in the console.

19.1.1 Taking a Screen Shot in X

ImageMagick
 DEB: imagemagick
 RPM: ImageMagick
 WWW: http://www.imagemagick.org/

Use `import`, part of the ImageMagick suite, to take a screen shot in X. `import` can capture the entire screen, a single window, or an arbitrary rectangular area, taking as an argument the name of the file to save to. As with other ImageMagick tools, the image format of the output file depends on the file extension you specify: `.eps` for EPS, `.tiff` for TIFF, `.jpeg` for JPEG, and so on. (For a complete list, see Recipe 18.2 [Converting Image Files], page 432).

After you give the command, the mouse pointer changes to a cross-hairs pointer. You then use the mouse to specify which window to take the shot of, as follows:

- Left-click on a window to capture its contents.
- Left-click on the root window to capture the entire screen.
- Left-click and drag the mouse across an area of the screen to form a rectangular selection outline; release the mouse button to capture the selected area.

When you specify a window, `import` captures only the window's contents; use the `-frame` option to include the window manager frame in the image.

⇒ To capture a particular window, including its window manager frame, and write it to a PNG-format file, do the following:

1. Run `import`:

    ```
    $ import -frame session-1.png ⟨RET⟩
    ```

2. Left-click on the window you want to capture.

In this example, the screen shot is saved to a file called **session-1.png**.

If the window or area you would like to capture is in another X desktop, or is otherwise removed somewhat from the terminal window where you are running the `import` command, you can use `sleep` first to delay the command for a few seconds while you position the mouse pointer.

⇒ To run `import` to make an EPS screen capture in five seconds to a file called **historic_moment.eps**, type:

    ```
    $ sleep 5; import historic_moment.eps ⟨RET⟩
    ```

This command will run `import` five seconds after you type ⟨RET⟩, which should give you time to get the mouse pointer where you want it.

NOTES: The system bell rings once when the screen capture starts, and twice when the captures finishes.

19.1.2 Taking a Screen Shot in a Console

To take screen shots in a virtual console, use `cat` to save the contents of the device file corresponding to that virtual console; these files are in the **/dev** directory and are in the format "**vcs**number," where *number* is the number of the virtual console.

For example, if the target console is the first virtual console (which you would see by typing ⟨ALT⟩-⟨F1⟩), the device to `cat` is **/dev/vcs1**.

⇒ To take a screen shot of the fourth virtual console and save it to a file called **screenshot**, type:

    ```
    $ cat /dev/vcs4 > screenshot ⟨RET⟩
    ```

NOTES: You must have superuser privileges to access these files (see Appendix A [Administrative Issues], page 699).

Take the screen shot from a virtual console other than the one you want to take a shot of; if you try to take it from the same console you want to capture, the command line you give will be included in the shot! (Kind of like having your thumb in front of the lens while taking a photograph.)

Screenshots taken of virtual consoles, as shown in this recipe, are saved as text files; you can't take screen shots of virtual consoles when graphics are displayed.

19.2 Scanning Images

SANE
  DEB: `sane`
  RPM: `sane`
  WWW: `http://www.sane-project.org/`

SANE, "Scanner Access Now Easy," is the de facto Linux scanner interface; use it to scan an image with a scanner and save it to a file.

SANE works with a wide array of scanning hardware, but make sure the scanning hardware you want to use is compatible by checking for it in the Linux Hardware Compatibility HOWTO [`http://en.tldp.org/HOWTO/Hardware-HOWTO/`] and in SANE's own list of supported scanners [`http://www.sane-project.org/sane-backends.html`].

Once you have SANE running, you can scan images with SANE-aware applications like the GIMP (see Recipe 18.3 [Using the GIMP], page 434).

The following recipes describe the use of the command line **scanimage** tool that comes with the SANE package.

NOTES: As the acronym implies, getting a scanner to work on a Linux system hasn't always been smooth going. The SANE interface is completely open, and its developers are making sure that it is generalized enough to be implementable on any hardware or operating system.

19.2.1 Listing Available Scanner Devices

Before you can use a scanner, you need to know its device name. To get this name, use **scanimage** with the **--list-devices** option.

⇒ To list available scanner devices, type:

```
$ scanimage --list-devices RET
device `umax:/dev/sgb' is a UMAX     Astra 1220S     flatbed scanner
$
```

In this example, there's one scanning device on this system, a UMAX brand scanner that can be specified to `scanimage` by giving its device name, `umax:/dev/sgb`, as an argument to the -d option.

To list the available resolutions and options supported by a particular device, use the `--help` option along with the -d option followed by the device name.

⇒ To list available options supported by the device listed in the previous example, type:

> $ *scanimage --help -d 'umax:/dev/sgb'* ⟨RET⟩

NOTES: For all `scanimage` commands, specify the scanner device you want to use by including the -d option with the device name.

19.2.2 Testing a Scanner

To run diagnostic tests on a scanner to make sure that it can be properly read from, use `scanimage` with the `--test` option.

⇒ To test the UMAX scanner listed previously, type:

> $ *scanimage --test -d 'umax:/dev/sgb'* ⟨RET⟩

19.2.3 Scanning an Image

Netpbm
  DEB: `netpbm`
  RPM: `netpbm`
  WWW: `http://netpbm.sourceforge.net/`

Use `scanimage` to scan an image. Most scanners let you specify the x and y values, in pixels, for the image size to scan, starting from the top-left corner of the scanner bed. Give these coordinates as arguments to the -x and -y options. Also, use the `--resolution` option to specify the scan resolution, with the argument given in dpi ("dots per inch"). Common resolution values include 72, 120, 204, 300, and 600 dpi; 72 dpi is the most popular resolution for use on the Web or for viewing on screen, and 204 dpi is often used for images that you want to send on a fax machine.

Scanned output is sent to standard output, so to scan an image to a file, redirect the standard output.

`scanimage` outputs images in the PNM ("portable anymap") formats, so make sure that you have the **netpbm** package (installed on most Linux systems by default); it's a useful collection of tools for converting and manipulating these common formats. The three PNM formats output by **scanimage** are as follows:

PPM	Color images
PBM	Black and white images
PGM	Grayscale images

Use the code–mode option to specify the format of the output, followed by one of the following arguments: "**color**" for color PPM, "**gray**" for PGM grayscale, or "**lineart**" for black and white PBM. Each scanner has a default mode; for most color scanners, the default mode will be "**color**."

⇒ Here are two ways to use this.

- To make a 72 dpi scan of a color image 200 pixels wide and 100 pixels tall, using the UMAX scanner from previous examples, and writing to a file called **scan.ppm**, type (all on one line):

  ```
  $ scanimage -d umax:/dev/sgb --resolution 72 -x 200 -y 100 >
  scan.ppm (RET)
  ```

- To make a 300 dpi scan of a black and white image 180 pixels wide and 225 pixels tall, using the UMAX scanner from previous examples, and writing to a file called **scan.pbm**, type (all on one line):

  ```
  $ scanimage -d umax:/dev/sgb --resolution 300 --mode lineart
  -x 180 -y 225 > scan.pbm (RET)
  ```

NOTES: The command lines in this recipe are split across two lines because they're too long to fit on one, but type these commands on one long line.

Once the image has been scanned and written to a file, you can edit it just as you would any image.

19.3 Extracting PhotoCD Images

Xpcd
  DEB: xpcd
       xpcd-gimp
  RPM: xpcd
  WWW: http://bytesex.org/xpcd.html

There are two methods to extract an image from a Kodak PhotoCD format

file[1] (also known as PCD). If you are browsing the PhotoCD files with the
xpcd tool, then choose an image, extract a copy at the desired resolution, and
save it to a file as described in Recipe 17.5 [Browsing PhotoCD Archives],
page 415.

You can also use pcdtoppm on a PCD file directly to extract an image at
a given resolution and save it to a file in PPM format.[2] Use the -r option to
specify the resolution to extract, given as a numeric argument from 1 (lowest
resolution) to 5 (highest); if this option is omitted, a value of 3 is assumed.
Also give as arguments the name of the PCD file to read from and the name
of the PPM file to write to.

⇒ To extract the highest resolution image from the file sharp.pcd and save
    it to a PNM file named sharp.ppm, type:

```
$ pcdtoppm -r5 sharp.pcd sharp.ppm (RET)
```

19.3.1 Converting a PhotoCD Image

Once you extract a PhotoCD image and write it to a PPM format file, use
convert to convert it to another format and adjust or improve the image (see
Recipe 18.2 [Converting Image Files], page 432).

To improve the image while you convert it to JPEG format, specify no
interlacing with the -interlace option, 50 percent image sharpening with the
-sharpen option, and add an optional border and annotation to the image
with the -border and -comment options.

⇒ To convert the file sharp.ppm to non-interlaced JPEG, sharpen the image,
    add a two-pixel by two-pixel border, and annotate the image, type (all
    on one line):

```
$ convert -interlace NONE -sharpen 50 -border 2x2 -comment
'This is a sharper image' sharp.ppm sharp.jpeg (RET)
```

19.3.2 Removing PhotoCD Haze

GIMP
  DEB: gimp1.2
  RPM: gimp
  WWW: http://www.gimp.org/

---

[1] This is a proprietary scanned-image format from Kodak, and it is currently a standard
     for scanning film images to digital format.
[2] On some systems, the command is hpcdtoppm, not pcdtoppm.

Extracted PhotoCD images are sometimes known to have a kind of "green haze" over them; to remove it, open the image in the GIMP and adjust the color levels with the **Auto Levels** function. This technique works well for improving any scanned or imported image.

⇒ To remove the green haze from a PhotoCD image, do the following:

1. Open the extracted image in the GIMP (see Recipe 18.3 [Using the GIMP], page 434).

2. Click through the **Image** menu to the **Colors** submenu and then to the **Levels** submenu, and choose **Auto Levels**.

3. Click **OK** in the **Levels** window to accept the changes.

19.4 Turning Text into an Image

Sometimes you might like an image file of some text—for example, to use as a header on a Web page. You can always make the text image in an image editor, but there are several other quick and easy ways to go about doing this, such as using **convert**, or **import**, or the **pbmtext** filter, all methods described here. Another tool for making images from plain text is Gozer, mentioned in Recipe 16.5 [Using Other Font Tools], page 403.

METHOD #1

Enscript
  DEB: enscript
  RPM: enscript
  WWW: http://www.iki.fi/~mtr/genscript/

ImageMagick
  DEB: imagemagick
  RPM: ImageMagick
  WWW: http://www.imagemagick.org/

One way to make an image from some text is to convert the text to PostScript (see Recipe 15.2 [Outputting Text to PostScript], page 359), and then use **convert** to convert the PostScript to the image format of your choosing, where you can crop and edit it as desired.

You can use `echo` to send the text to `enscript`, and pipe the output right to `convert`. Use "0x0" as an argument to the `-crop` option to automatically trim this image around the text.

⇒ To make a PNG image of the text "`Amateur Radio History Page`" in the Times Roman Bold font at 42 points, type (all on one line):

```
$ echo "Amateur Radio History Page" | enscript -o - -B -f
"Times-Bold42" | convert -crop 0x0 - arhp.png (RET)
```

This command makes a PNG image file, `arhp.png`, as in Figure 19-1.

Amateur Radio History Page

Figure 19-1. An image made from text.

Use the `-border` and `-bordercolor` options to draw a border (given as an argument to the first option of "*widthxheight*") in any color (given as an argument to the second option).

⇒ To make a PNG image of the text "`Amateur Radio History Page`," in the Times Roman Bold font at 42 points and with a blue border five pixels wide and five pixels high, type (all on one line):

```
$ echo "Amateur Radio History Page" | enscript -o - -B -f
"Times-Bold42" | convert -crop 0x0 -border 5x5
-bordercolor blue - newarhp.png (RET)
```

This command makes a PNG image file, `newarhp.png`, as in Figure 19-2. (While the printed illustration is in black and white, the actual image created from this command has a blue colored border.)

Amateur Radio History Page

Figure 19-2. A bordered image made from text.

NOTES: This method is also good for turning GROFF table output into images.

METHOD #2

If the text is displayed on the screen in X, use `import` to capture it as an image, as described in Recipe 19.1.1 [Taking a Screen Shot in X], page 441.

METHOD #3

To make a bitmap image from some text, use the **pbmtext** filter. It takes any text sent to it as input, and it outputs an image file in PBM format.

⇒ To make a PBM image out of the text "**Recommended Reading**," writing the new file to **header.pbm**, type:

```
$ pbmtext Recommended Reading > header.pbm (RET)
```

This is useful for making image files of large texts, for purposes such as including that text as an illustration. To send a compressed file to **pbmtext**, use **zcat** (otherwise, the **<** redirection operator works fine).

⇒ To make a JPEG image containing the contents of the compressed file **/usr/share/state/us-constitution.gz**, writing to a file named **constitution.jpeg**, type (all on one line):

```
$ zcat /usr/share/state/us-constitution.gz | pbmtext |
convert - constitution.jpeg (RET)
```

19.5 Using Other Image Import Tools

There are many other tools for importing images from various sources. This field is changing all the time, with the introduction of new hardware devices and new tools to import from them. The following table describes some of the tools currently in popular use.

Camediaplay   Downloads images from any digital cameras with Sanyo firmware, including the Olympus Camedia series.
DEB: camediaplay
RPM: camediaplay

Cqcam   Captures images from Color QuickCams.
DEB: cqcam
RPM: cqcam
WWW: http://www.cs.duke.edu/~reynolds/cqcam/

Dvgrab   Captures audio and video from those digital camcorders that use a IEEE1394 link (also known as FireWire), writing the output as an AVI file.
DEB: dvgrab
RPM: dvgrab
WWW: http://kino.schirmacher.de

Fuji   Imports images from (and otherwise manipulates) Fuji digital cameras.
DEB: fujiplay

GOCR   Command line OCR tool that outputs plain text from scanned images.
DEB: gocr
RPM: gocr
WWW: http://jocr.sourceforge.net/

gPhoto   Imports images from digital cameras.
DEB: gphoto
RPM: gphoto
WWW: http://www.gphoto.org/

Grunch   Merges partial scans together to form larger images.
DEB: grunch
WWW: http://www.radagast.org/~dplatt/

Gsumi   Imports black-and-white images from pressure-sensitive input devices, such as drawing tablets.
DEB: gsumi

Pencam   Imports images from digital cameras that use the STV0680B-001 chip.
DEB: pencam
WWW: http://stv0680-usb.sourceforge.net/

Streamer   Captures images from video4linux devices.
DEB: streamer
RPM: xawtv-streamer
WWW: http://bytesex.org/xawtv/

## CHAPTER 20

PostScript

The PostScript programming language, designed and implemented in the early 1980s by John Warnock of Adobe Systems, is used to describe the way a "page" should look. Pages are usually a physical sheet of paper (PostScript is commonly used for sending documents to printer hardware), but they can be any kind of output display.[1] PostScript files are text files containing the PostScript language commands for drawing images to be printed on pages.

Like plain text files, PostScript files are commonly found on the Internet (and are used by commercial printers) because, as with plain text, they can be shared across platforms and hardware without difficulty. The same PostScript file can be output on a high-end display or printed on a low-end printer, to the best of that hardware's capability. PostScript is a compact and elegant format.

While it's possible to write directly in the PostScript language (and some people have become adept at programming PostScript), so many tools and applications convert files to and from PostScript that you don't have to write it yourself. See Recipe 15.2 [Outputting Text to PostScript], page 359, for a way to convert plain text into PostScript.

GNU Ghostscript is a free interpreter of the PostScript language.[2] It comes with **gs**, a tool that is used to convert files from PostScript or PDF to other formats. It's usually used for printing to a non-PostScript printer (see Recipe 25.3.1 [Preparing a PostScript File for Printing], page 518). The **ghostview** tool is used to preview PostScript files on the screen (see Recipe 17.4.2 [Previewing a PostScript File], page 414).

EPS, or Encapsulated PostScript, is a file format that describes the contents of a box within a page. EPS files can be embedded in the page of a PostScript file, and they are therefore commonly used when inserting an illustration into a document (for example, all of the illustrations printed in the *Cookbook* are EPS format files). You can view and print EPS files just as you would PostScript files.

This chapter includes recipes for formatting and manipulating PostScript files. Recipes are separated according to whether they work on the individual, *logical pages* in a PostScript file (the numbered pages in the file that are not

---

[1] PostScript was originally designed for the Apple LaserWriter printer; NeWS was an old UNIX windowing system by Sun Microsystems that used PostScript to draw the display.

[2] It is also an interpreter of Adobe's Portable Document Format (PDF) language.

necessarily the physical pages of output), and those that work on the entire
file as a whole.

Many of the tools used in this chapter come as part of Angus Duggan's
PSUtils ("PostScript Utilities") package. These tools can be used for other
purposes than those described in this chapter; see their respective **man** pages
for more details.

20.1 Manipulating PostScript Pages

These recipes work on individual *pages* of PostScript files, and not the entire
file itself.

20.1.1 Extracting DVI Pages to PostScript

DVIPS
  DEB: `tetex-bin`
  RPM: `tetex-dvips`
  WWW: `http://www.radicaleye.com/dvips.html`

To extract specific pages of a DVI ("DeVice Independent") file to PostScript,
use **dvips** and give the page or hyphenated page range to output with the
`-pp` option.

⇒ To extract only the first page from the file **abstract.dvi** and send the
   PostScript output to the printer, type:

     $ *dvips -pp1 abstract.dvi* (RET)

By default, **dvips** will output to the printer; to save the PostScript output
to a file, specify the file name to be used for output as an argument to the `-o`
option.

⇒ To output as PostScript the pages 137 to 146 of the file **abstract.dvi**,
   and write them to the file **abstract.ps**, type:

     $ *dvips -pp137-146 -o abstract.ps abstract.dvi* (RET)

20.1.2 Extracting Pages from a PostScript File

PSUtils
  DEB: `psutils`
  RPM: `psutils`
  WWW: `http://www.ctan.org/tex-archive/support/psutils/`

Use **psselect** to select pages from a PostScript file; when you give an input file, it outputs a new PostScript file containing the specified pages. Output is sent to the standard output or to a file specified as a second argument.

Give the pages to select as arguments to the -p option; you can list single pages and ranges of pages separated by commas. Give ranges as two numbers separated by a hyphen; thus, "4-6" specifies pages four through six, inclusive. If you omit the first number in a pair, the first page is assumed, and if you omit the last number, the last page is assumed. Pages are written to the new file in the order they are specified.

⇒ Here are some ways to use this.

- To select page 47 from the PostScript file **newsletter.ps** and output it to the file **selection.ps**, type:

    $ *psselect -p47 newsletter.ps selection.ps* ⟨RET⟩

- To select the first ten pages, page 104, pages 23 through 28, and page 2 from the file **newsletter.ps** and write them to the file **selection.ps**, type:

    $ *psselect -p1-10,104,23-28,2 newsletter.ps selection.ps* ⟨RET⟩

- To select page 47 from the PostScript file **newsletter.ps** and output it to the file **selection.ps**, type:

    $ *psselect -p47 newsletter.ps selection.ps* ⟨RET⟩

(In the second example above, page 2 is selected twice—first in the selection of pages 1-10, and then later on its own.)

You can specify reverse ranges, with the higher page listed first in the range, to output pages running backwards from that page toward the lower page. You can also specify pages by their position relative to the last page in the document. Do this by prefixing a number with an underscore (_), which indicates that the given page number is counting backwards toward the first page.

⇒ Here are some ways to use this.

- To select pages 30 to 25 from the PostScript file **newsletter.ps** and output them to the file **selection.ps**, type:

    $ *psselect -p30-25 newsletter.ps selection.ps* ⟨RET⟩

- To select the last page from the PostScript file **newsletter.ps** and output it to the file **end-notes.ps**, type:

    $ *psselect -p_1 newsletter.ps end-notes.ps* ⟨RET⟩

- To select the second-to-last through the tenth-to-last pages from the PostScript file **newsletter.ps** and output them to the file **selection.ps**, type:

  $ *psselect -p_2-_10 newsletter.ps selection.ps* ⟨RET⟩

- To select the second-to-last through the tenth pages from the PostScript file **newsletter.ps** and output them to the file **selection.ps**, type:

  $ *psselect -p_2-10 newsletter.ps selection.ps* ⟨RET⟩

If the file **newsletter.ps** in the last example contained only 12 pages, the example is equivalent to running **psselect** with **-p12-10**.

Use the **-e** option to select all even-numbered pages, and use the **-o** option to select all odd-numbered pages.

⇒ Here are two ways to use this.

- To select all of the even pages in the file **newsletter.ps** and write them to a new file, **even.ps**, type:

  $ *psselect -e newsletter.ps even.ps* ⟨RET⟩

- To select all of the odd pages in the file **newsletter.ps** and write them to a new file, **odd.ps**, type:

  $ *psselect -o newsletter.ps odd.ps* ⟨RET⟩

Use an underscore (_) alone to insert a blank page, and use **-r** to output pages in *reverse* order.

⇒ Here are two ways to use this.

- To select the last ten pages of file **newsletter.ps**, followed by a blank page, followed by the first ten pages, and output them to a new file, **selection.ps**, type:

  $ *psselect -p_1-_10,_,1-10 newsletter.ps selection.ps* ⟨RET⟩

- To select the pages 59, 79, and 99 in the file **newsletter.ps**, and output them in reverse order (with the 99th page first) to a new file, **selection.ps**, type:

  $ *psselect -p59,79,99 -r newsletter.ps selection.ps* ⟨RET⟩

The same result as the last example could have been gotten by omitting the **-r** option and just listing the three pages in the reverse order, like so:

$ *psselect -p99,79,59 newsletter.ps selection.ps* ⟨RET⟩

20.1.3 Combining PostScript Pages

PSUtils
  DEB: psutils
  RPM: psutils
  WWW: http://www.ctan.org/tex-archive/support/psutils/

Use **psnup** to print multiple PostScript pages on a single sheet of paper; give as an option the number of pages to be combined (or put "up") on each sheet.

⇒ To make a new PostScript file, **double.ps**, putting two pages from the file **single.ps** on each page, type:

> $ *psnup -2 single.ps double.ps* ⟨RET⟩

To specify the paper size, give the name of a standard paper size as an argument to the **-p** option: a3, a4, a5, b5, letter, legal, tabloid, statement, executive, folio, quarto, or 10x14. You can also specify any height and width with the **-h** and **-w** options; units can be specified in centimeters (followed by "cm") or inches (followed by "in"). If no size is specified, **psnup** assumes a paper size of a4.

Use the **-l** option when pages are in landscape orientation (rotated 90 degrees counterclockwise from portrait orientation), and **-r** when pages are in seascape orientation (rotated 90 degrees clockwise from portrait orientation).

Pages are placed in "row-major" layout in the output file, where logical pages are placed in rows across the page. Use the **-c** option to specify a "column-major" layout, where logical pages are placed in *columns* down the page. Scale the size of the pages by giving a percentage to multiply the page size by as an argument to the **-s** option; for example, **-s .5** scales pages to 50 percent of their original size.

To draw a border around each page, specify the border's width in points as an argument to the **-d** option (if no width is specified, a value of 1 is assumed).

20.1.4 Arranging PostScript Pages in Signatures

PSUtils
  DEB: psutils
  RPM: psutils
  WWW: http://www.ctan.org/tex-archive/support/psutils/

A *signature* is a group of pages in a document corresponding to sheets of paper folded and bound; these pages are normally not in sequential order in a document (for example, in a document with eight-page signatures, page 8 and page 1 might both be printed on the same sheet of paper).

To rearrange the pages of a PostScript file by signature—usually for printing the file as a book or booklet—use `psbook`. Give as arguments the name of the PostScript file to read from and the name to use for the output file; `psbook` reads the contents of the first, rearranges the pages, and then writes the PostScript output to the second file.

⇒ To rearrange the pages of file `newsletter.ps` into a signature and write it to the file `newsletter.bound.ps`, type:

    `$ psbook newsletter.ps newsletter.bound.ps` ⟨RET⟩

By default, `psbook` uses one signature for the entire file. If the file doesn't contain a multiple of four pages, it adds blank pages to the end.

To specify the size of the signature to use—in other words, the number of pages that will appear on a single piece of paper—give the number as an argument to the `-s` option. Signature size is always a multiple of four.

⇒ To rearrange the pages of file `newsletter.ps` into an eight-sided signature and write it to `newsletter.bound.ps`, type:

    `$ psbook -s8 newsletter.ps newsletter.bound.ps` ⟨RET⟩

20.2 Manipulating PostScript Documents

These recipes work on a PostScript document as a whole.

20.2.1 Resizing a PostScript Document

PSUtils
  DEB: psutils
  RPM: psutils
  WWW: http://www.ctan.org/tex-archive/support/psutils/

Use `psresize` to resize a PostScript document. It takes as arguments the file to resize and the output file to write to; otherwise, it reads from standard input and writes to standard output. If you give the name of an output file, you must also specify the page size to use, written in the same format as with the `psnup` tool: use `-p` or `-h` and `-w` to specify the size of the output file, and use `-P` to specify the size of the input file (see Recipe 20.1.3 [Combining PostScript Pages], page 455).

⇒ To resize the PostScript file `double.ps` to U.S. letter-sized paper, writing output to a new file, `doublet.ps`, type:

> $ *psresize -pletter double.ps doublet.ps* ⟨RET⟩

20.2.2 Combining PostScript Documents

There are two methods worth mentioning for concatenating and merging multiple PostScript files into a single file. One is a more robust solution, and the other is easier to type. I'll begin with the preferred method, which I discovered while combining the PostScript pages of this book.

METHOD #1

Ghostscript
  DEB: `gs-common`
       `gs`
  RPM: `ghostscript`
  WWW: `http://www.cs.wisc.edu/~ghost/`

You can combine many PostScript files into one with **gs**. Use the `-q`, `-dNOPAUSE`, and `-dBATCH` flags so that it works quietly and without pause, and use "pswrite" as the device to write to, giving it as an argument to the `-sDEVICE=` option.[3] Specify the name of the output file with the special `-sOutputFile=` option, and finally, specify the files to combine in the order you want them combined.

⇒ To combine the PostScript files **part1.ps**, **part2.ps**, and **part3.ps** in that order, writing to a new PostScript file **program.ps**, type (all on one line):

> $ *gs -q -dNOPAUSE -dBATCH -sDEVICE=pswrite*
> *-sOutputFile=program.ps part1.ps part2.ps part3.ps* ⟨RET⟩

NOTES: If you plan on doing a lot of this, you can simplify things by making a shell script called **pscat**, as in Figure 20-1 (see Recipe 3.7 [Using Shell Scripts], page 84).

Then, call the script with the name of the file to write to as the first argument, and following that, give the names of the files to combine in the order you wish them to be combined.

---

[3] To work on PDF files instead, use "**pdfwrite**" as the option.

```
#!/bin/sh
gs -q -dNOPAUSE -dBATCH -sDEVICE=pswrite -sOutputFile=$*
```

Figure 20-1. The `pscat` script.

METHOD #2

PSUtils
  DEB: psutils
  RPM: psutils
  WWW: http://www.ctan.org/tex-archive/support/psutils/

Use **psmerge** to combine PostScript files into one. Give the names of the files to be merged as arguments, and **psmerge** outputs them to the standard output in the order given. You can also specify an output file name with the -o option (don't put any spaces between the file name and the option).

⇒ To merge the files slide1.ps, slide2.ps, and slide3.ps into a new PostScript file, slideshow.ps, type:

  $ *psmerge -oslideshow.ps slide1.ps slide2.ps slide3.ps* ⟨RET⟩

NOTES: The **gs** method is really preferable; **psmerge** only works with PostScript files that were made with the same application. For example, **psmerge** would allow you to merge multiple files made with TeX, or multiple files made with Xfig, but not a combination of the two.

20.2.3 Arranging a PostScript Document in a Booklet

PSUtils
  DEB: psutils
  RPM: psutils
  WWW: http://www.ctan.org/tex-archive/support/psutils/

To arrange the pages in a PostScript file to make booklets, rearrange the file in a signature with **psbook**, use **psnup** to arrange the pages (two to a printed page in landscape mode), and then use **pstops** to output first the odd and then the even pages.

The trick to doing this properly is to first determine exactly what you need to do, and then to calculate the proper measurements for use with **pstops**.

⇒ To make a booklet from the file **newsletter.ps**, do the following:

1. Rearrange the pages into a signature:

```
$ psbook newsletter.ps newsletter.signature.ps ⟨RET⟩
```

2. Put the pages two to a page in landscape orientation, at 70 percent of their original size (typed all on one line):

```
$ psnup -l -pletter -2 -s.7 newsletter.signature.ps >
newsletter.2up.ps ⟨RET⟩
```

3. Output the odd pages:

```
$ pstops "2:0(1in,0in)" newsletter.2up.ps > odd.ps ⟨RET⟩
```

4. Output the even pages:

```
$ pstops "2:-1(1in,0in)" newsletter.2up.ps > even.ps ⟨RET⟩
```

Then, to print the booklet, send **odd.ps** to the printer, reload the printed pages in the manual feed tray, and then send **even.ps** to the printer. This prints the odd and even pages on opposite sides of the sheets.

⇒ To make a double-sized booklet on letter-sized paper in landscape orientation from a file using letter-sized portrait orientation, type:

```
$ psbook input.ps > temp1.ps ⟨RET⟩
...processing messages...
$ psnup -l -pletter -2 -s.7 temp1.ps > temp2.ps ⟨RET⟩
...processing messages...
$ pstops "2:0(1in,0in)" temp2.ps > odd.ps ⟨RET⟩
...processing messages...
$ pstops "2:-1(1in,0in)" temp2.ps > even.ps ⟨RET⟩
...processing messages...
$
```

NOTES: If you will be doing a lot of this, you may want to have a look at the ps2book utility, which is a script that aids in making booklets with PSUtils [http://www.kis.uni-freiburg.de/~dobler/utils/ps2book.html].

20.3 Converting PostScript

These recipes show how to convert PostScript files to other formats. See also the recipes for preparing PostScript files for printing, Recipe 25.3.1 [Preparing a PostScript File for Printing], page 518.

20.3.1 Converting PostScript to PDF

Ghostscript
  DEB: gs-common gs
  RPM: ghostscript
  WWW: http://www.cs.wisc.edu/~ghost/

To convert a PostScript file to PDF, use **ps2pdf**, which comes as part of the Ghostscript package. Give as arguments the name of the PostScript file to read from and the name of the PDF file to write to.

⇒ To write a PDF file **sutra.pdf** from the input file **sutra.ps**, type:

> $ *ps2pdf sutra.ps sutra.pdf* ⟨RET⟩

This command writes a new file in PDF format called **sutra.pdf**. The original file, **sutra.ps**, is not altered.

NOTES: To make proper PDF conversions, make sure that you have Ghostscript version 6.01 or higher installed; use the **-v** option with **gs** to output the installed version.

20.3.2 Converting PostScript to Plain Text

Ghostscript
  DEB: gs-common gs
  RPM: ghostscript
  WWW: http://www.cs.wisc.edu/~ghost/

To convert a PostScript file to plain text, use **ps2ascii**, which comes as part of the Ghostscript package. Give as arguments the name of the PostScript file to read from and the name of the text file to write to.

⇒ To make a text file, **sutra.txt**, from the input file **sutra.ps**, type:

> $ *ps2ascii sutra.ps sutra.txt* ⟨RET⟩

This command writes a text file called **sutra.txt**. The original file, **sutra.ps**, is not altered.

V. SOUND

## CHAPTER 21

Playing and Recording Sound

This chapter covers the basic control of the Linux sound system, including how to adjust the audio mixer and how to play and record sound files using basic tools. You can also play and record audio with Snd (see Chapter 23 [Editing Sound Files], page 487) and many other sound applications.

In order to have sound working on your system, you need to have a *sound driver* installed and configured for your sound card. This is the software that controls your sound card, and is in turn part of the Linux sound system.

For some years, the independent ALSA (the "Advanced Linux Sound Architecture") had been the popular choice for sound system among audio aficionados, over the older OSS/Free (Open Sound System) that came with the Linux kernel.

As of the 2.6 kernel, ALSA is now included with Linux. If your version of the Linux kernel is older than that, you will have to have your administrator install ALSA, or just use the older OSS/Free drivers.

Most systems come configured so that you must be the superuser to be able to use sound devices, including audio CDs. If this is the case on your system, ask your administrator to give you access to these devices, typically by adding you to the **audio** group (see Recipe 6.1 [Working in Groups], page 163).

21.1 Adjusting the Audio Controls

ALSA Utilities
  DEB: alsa-utils
  RPM: alsa-utils
  WWW: http://www.alsa-project.org/

A *mixer* program is used to adjust various audio settings such as volume and recording levels, and it is also used for turning on or muting the microphone or other input devices. You must use a mixer to adjust your audio settings before you play or record sound.

Before recording, be sure to mute all channels but your input source—but then don't forget you've got them muted later, when you want to hear sound from them!

ALSA's default mixer is called **amixer**, and the following recipes will show its use. There are other mixers, and some of them are much easier to use than **amixer**. My recommendation is to install **aumix**. See the end of this chapter for other recommendations, including graphical mixers for use in X, in Recipe 21.5 [Using Other Sound Tools], page 474.

21.1.1 Listing the Current Audio Settings

To list all audio input and output devices and their settings, type `amixer` with no options.

Your sound card's components are organized in groups, from the Master group containing the master left and right volume settings, to the individual groups for audio compact discs and digital sound files. (These groups have nothing to do with the file access groups described in Recipe 6.1 [Working in Groups], page 163.)

⇒ To peruse the current mixer settings, type:

```
$ amixer | less (RET)
```

The following table describes some of the important sound groups that `amixer` lists.

`Master`	Master volume settings.
`PCM`	Digital audio for playing sound files; the first channel is group `PCM,0` and the second is `PCM,1`.
`CD`	Audio compact disc player (a cable must be connected from the CD drive to the sound card).
`Synth`	Synthesizer device for MIDI.
`Line`	Sound input device (the jack on the back of the sound card is usually labeled LINE IN).
`MIC`	Microphone device (the jack on the back of the sound card is usually labeled MIC).

To list the settings for only one group, use the **get** option followed by the name of the group you want to list. Group names are case sensitive—so giving `MIC` specifies the microphone group, while `Mic` and `mic` are not valid groups at all.

⇒ Here are two ways to use this.

• To output the microphone settings, type:

```
$ amixer get MIC (RET)
```

• To output the settings of the second PCM device, type:

```
$ amixer get PCM,1 (RET)
```

21.1.2 Changing the Volume Level

To change a mixer setting, give the `amixer set` command as an option, followed by both the group and setting to change as arguments. To change the volume level for a device, give either a numeric value or a percentage for the volume level.

⇒ Here are some ways to use this.

- To set the master volume to 75 percent, type:

    `$ amixer set Master 75%` (RET)

- To set the PCM device volume to 30, type:

    `$ amixer set PCM 30` (RET)

21.1.3 Muting an Audio Device

The special "`mute`" and "`unmute`" arguments are used for muting the volume of a given device. Before you can record something, you must unmute the input device you want to record from. Remember to also mute the microphone after you have finished recording to avoid feedback when you turn up your speakers.

⇒ Here are some ways to use this.

- To unmute the microphone and turn it on for recording, type:

    `$ amixer set MIC unmute capture` (RET)

- To mute the microphone, type:

    `$ amixer set MIC mute` (RET)

- To unmute the master volume and set it to 80 percent volume, type:

    `$ amixer set Master 80% unmute` (RET)

21.1.4 Selecting an Audio Recording Source

To select a device for recording, use `set` followed by the name of the device and the "`capture`" argument, which designates the specified group as the one to capture sound from for recording.

⇒ Here are two ways to use this.

- To select the LINE IN jack as the recording source, type:

    `$ amixer set Line capture` (RET)

- To select the microphone jack as the recording source, type:

    `$ amixer set MIC capture` (RET)

NOTES: You can have only one group selected for capture at a time, and when you select a group as an input source for recording, you are simply turning the microphone or other input on; recording does not occur until you use a recording tool.

21.2 Playing a Sound File

SOund eXchange
  DEB: sox
  RPM: sox
  WWW: http://sox.sourceforge.net/

The **play** tool distributed with "SOund eXchange" (a sound file translation tool) can recognize and play many audio formats, including OGG, WAV, VOC, AU, AIFF, and SND format files, as well as audio CD-format files and various raw binary formats. Just about the only common audio formats it can't handle are MIDI and MP3, which are discussed in the sections to follow. Give the name of a file as an argument to **play**.

⇒ To play the file **sousa.aiff**, type:

    $ *play sousa.aiff* (RET)

NOTES: Before you begin playing sound, make sure you've set the master and PCM volume levels with the mixer (see Recipe 21.1 [Adjusting the Audio Controls], page 463). The most common reason for no sound being produced when you try to play sound is not having the volume turned up!

ALSA comes with **aplay**, a tool for playing sound files that is similar to **play** but does not recognize as many formats.

21.2.1 Playing an Ogg File

Ogg123
  DEB: vorbis-tools
  RPM: vorbis-tools
  WWW: http://www.vorbis.com/

Use **ogg123** to play Ogg Vorbis files, giving the name of the file as an argument.

⇒ To play the file **track1.ogg**, type:

    $ *ogg123 track1.ogg* (RET)

By default, `ogg123` sends to the standard sound device. You can specify a sound device—useful on systems that have more than one device installed—by using the `-d` option, followed by a special argument as described in the following table.

`null`	Null driver, used for testing purposes.
`oss`	Open Sound System (OSS/FREE) driver.
`alsa`	Advanced Linux Sound Architecture (ALSA) driver.
`esd`	Enlightened Sound Daemon driver.
`wav`	WAV format audio output.

⇒ To play the file `archive.ogg` using the OSS driver, type:

    $ ogg123 -d oss archive.ogg ⟨RET⟩

Use the `-k` option to skip part of the beginning of the recording. Give the number of seconds to skip as an argument to the option.

⇒ To play the file `archive.ogg`, beginning exactly one minute into the recording and using the ALSA driver, type:

    $ ogg123 -k 60 -d alsa archive.ogg ⟨RET⟩

To play files in random order, give the `-z` option. This is useful for when you want to shuffle the tracks of an audio archive.

⇒ To play all of the `.ogg` audio files in the `~/audio/incoming` directory, shuffling the order of the tracks, type:

    $ ogg123 -z ~/audio/incoming/*.ogg ⟨RET⟩

21.2.2 Playing Streaming Ogg Audio

To play "streaming" Ogg Vorbis audio, such as an Ogg file accessed directly from the Internet, give the URL of the file as an argument to `ogg123`.

⇒ To play the Ogg stream at `http://auggie.wclv.com/lo.ogg`, type:

    $ ogg123 http://auggie.wclv.com/lo.ogg ⟨RET⟩

21.2.3 Playing a MIDI File

There are two general methods for playing a MIDI file. The method you should
use depends on whether or not your sound card has a built-in MIDI sequencer.

METHOD #1

Playmidi
  DEB: playmidi
  RPM: playmidi
  WWW: http://sourceforge.net/projects/playmidi/

If your sound card has a MIDI sequencer, use **playmidi** to play MIDI files; give
the name of the MIDI file to play as an argument.

⇒ To play the MIDI file **copacabana.mid**, type:

> $ *playmidi copacabana.mid* (RET)

METHOD #2

Playmidi
  DEB: playmidi
  RPM: playmidi
  WWW: http://sourceforge.net/projects/playmidi/

   or

TiMidity++
  DEB: timidity
  RPM: timidity
  WWW: http://www.onicos.com/staff/iz/timidity/

If you have a non-MIDI sound card, you can still play MIDI files by using
timidity, which converts the MIDI format into WAV format, and then plays
it.

⇒ To play the MIDI file **copacabana.mid** on a non-MIDI sound card by converting it to WAV format, type:

> $ *timidity copa-cabana.mid* (RET)

On some systems with non-MIDI sound cards, you can also use **playmidi**
with the **-f** option. This specifies that MIDI output is to be sent to the FM
synthesizer on the sound card, which in turn plays it using FM patches that
come with the **playmidi** distribution.

⇒ To play the MIDI file `copacabana.mid` on a non-MIDI sound card using
FM patches, type:

> `$ playmidi -f copacabana.mid` ⟨RET⟩

21.2.4 Playing a MOD File

MikMod
DEB: `mikmod`
RPM: `mikmod`
WWW: `http://www.tfn.net/~amstpi/mikmod.html`

MOD ("module") files are tracked music files made by music software called
"trackers." Popular trackers include SoundTracker and Impulse Tracker; use
`mikmod` to play audio files made with them. Supported formats include IT,
MOD, MTM, STM, S3M, ULT, UNI, and XM.

⇒ To play the MOD file `demo.it`, type:

> `$ mikmod demo.it` ⟨RET⟩

When `mikmod` is playing, press ⟨F1⟩ to show the help panel, or press ⟨Q⟩ to
exit.

21.2.5 Playing an MP3 File

Mpg321
DEB: `mpg321`
RPM: `mpg321`
WWW: `http://mpg321.sourceforge.net/`

There are many tools for playing MP3 files; some are listed at the end of this
chapter (see Recipe 21.5 [Using Other Sound Tools], page 474).

One such tool is `mpg321`; to use it to play an MP3 file, give the name of the
file as an argument.

⇒ To play the MP3 file `lili-marleen.mp3`, type:

> `$ mpg321 lili-marleen.mp3` ⟨RET⟩

To "buffer" the audio, useful for when the system is running many processes
or otherwise has a lot of activity, give a buffer size, in kilobytes, as an argument
to the `-b` option. The default is 0 (no buffer); if you need this option, use a
size of at least 1024 KB (which is 1 MB), or about six seconds of MP3 audio.

NOTES: The `mpg321` tool is a free software replacement of `mpg123`, another
command line MP3 player that is not free software.

The use of the MP3 format is waning now with the rise of Ogg Vorbis, a format that has better audio quality, smaller files, and most importantly of all is not patented, as the MP3 format is. Even outside the Linux world, where MP3 still enjoys popularity, support for Ogg Vorbis is growing among hardware vendors, radio stations, and audiophiles.

21.2.6 Playing Streaming MP3 Audio

There are several ways to play "streaming" MP3 audio, such as an MP3 file accessed directly from the Internet, or an MPEG audio stream accessible at some URL.

METHOD #1

Mpg321
  DEB: mpg321
  RPM: mpg321
  WWW: http://mpg321.sourceforge.net/

To use mpg321 to play "streaming" MP3 audio from the Web, just give the URL of the MP3 stream as an argument.

⇒ Here are two ways to use this.

- To play http://example.net/broadcast/live.mp3 as an MP3 stream, type:

      $ mpg321 http://example.net/broadcast/live.mp3 (RET)

- To play http://example.net/broadcast/live.mp3 as an MP3 stream with a 2 MB audio buffer, type:

      $ mpg321 -b 2048 http://example.net/broadcast/live.mp3 (RET)

METHOD #2

Splay
  DEB: splay
  RPM: splay
  WWW: http://splay.sourceforge.net/
Wget
  DEB: wget
  RPM: wget
  WWW: http://www.gnu.org/software/wget/wget.html

To play streaming MPEG audio with an MP3 player that doesn't take URLs as an option, first get the stream with **wget** using **-O-** to send it to the standard output, and pipe this output to an MP3 player. Make sure the MP3 player is set to read MPEG audio from standard input—with **splay**, this means giving the special **-M** option to read from standard input and not a file.

⇒ To play the streaming MPEG audio that is broadcast at `http://vox.wclv.com/cgi-bin/swsend/tmp/source3`, type (all on one line):

> ```
> $ wget -O- http://vox.wclv.com/cgi-bin/swsend/tmp/source3 | splay
> -M ⟨RET⟩
> ```

To save a copy of the audio to a file and listen to it while it's being downloaded, just branch the pipeline with **tee** (see Recipe 3.2.5 [Redirecting Output to More than One Place], page 69).

⇒ To to play the streaming MPEG audio that is broadcast at `http://voc.wclv.com/cgi-bin/swsend/tmp/source3`, and save a copy of the audio in a file named `wclv.20051220.mp3`, type (all on one line):

> ```
> $ wget -O- http://voc.wclv.com/cgi-bin/swsend/tmp/source3 | tee
> wclv.20051220.mp3 | splay -M ⟨RET⟩
> ```

NOTES: Often when streaming MPEG audio is offered by a site, a link to a file with an `.m3u` extension will be given as the address to use for listening. This is actually not a link to the streaming audio itself, but to a file that contains the URL to which the actual streaming audio is being broadcast. To use this link, first output the contents of this file to the standard output with **wget** **-O-** followed by the URL, and then select that URL with the mouse so you can paste it in the **wget** command that you pipe to **splay**, as demonstrated above (see also Recipe 10.3 [Manipulating Selections of Text], page 253).

21.3 Displaying Information About a Sound File

Use **file** to get information about most sound files, as described in Recipe 8.1.1 [Determining a File's Type and Format], page 187. It will output the sound file's format and version, and often other details such as sampling rate and whether the recording is monaural or in stereo.

Additionally, methods exist for getting more information about certain kinds of sound files. They follow here.

21.3.1 Displaying Information About an Ogg File

Ogginfo
 DEB: vorbis-tools
 RPM: vorbis-tools
 WWW: http://www.vorbis.com/

Use `ogginfo` to output information about Ogg Vorbis audio files. Give the filespec of the files in question as arguments. For each file, it outputs the file name, title, artist, album, track number, length in total seconds, and play time in minutes and seconds.

⇒ To output information about the Ogg Vorbis audio file **mystery.ogg**, type:

        $ ogginfo mystery.ogg ⟨RET⟩

21.3.2 Displaying Information About an MP3 File

MP3Info
 DEB: mp3info
 RPM: mp3info
 WWW: http://www.ibiblio.org/mp3info/

Use `mp3info` to get information about an MP3 file, including title and artist. Give the name of the file as an argument.

⇒ To output information on the MP3 file **concerto.mp3**, type:

        $ mp3info concerto.mp3 ⟨RET⟩

21.4 Recording a Sound File

SOund eXchange
 DEB: sox
 RPM: sox
 WWW: http://sox.sourceforge.net/

To record sound, first select an input device as a source for recording. Sound cards may have MIC and LINE IN jacks, as well as connections to the CD drive, all of which are sound inputs that can be used as recording sources. When you select a device for capture, your recording will come from this source.

Recording occurs from the currently active input, if any, which must be set with the mixer; unmute it and set its volume level before you begin recording. (Be sure to turn the volume on your speakers all the way off, or you'll get feedback.)

To record audio to a file, use the `rec` tool. It can write many audio file formats, either to a format you specify with the `-t` option, or by determining the format to use based on the file name extension you give the output file (see Appendix B [Conventional File Name Extensions], page 723). Type ⟨CTRL⟩-⟨C⟩ to stop recording.

Give the name of the sound file to record as an argument; if a `.wav` file is specified, it records a simple monaural, low-fidelity sound sample by default.

⇒ To record a simple WAV sample from the microphone and save it to a file called `hello.wav`, type:

```
$ rec hello.wav ⟨RET⟩
```

This command begins an 8,000 Hz, monaural, 8-bit WAV recording to the file `hello.wav`, and it keeps recording until you interrupt it with ⟨CTRL⟩-⟨C⟩. While the default is to make a low-fidelity recording—8,000 Hz, monaural, 8-bit samples—you can specify that a high-fidelity recording be made. (Keep in mind that high-fidelity recordings take up much more disk space.)

To make a stereo recording, use the `-c` option to specify the number of channels, giving 2 as the argument. To make a 16-bit recording, give "`w`" ("wide") as the argument to the `-s` ("sample size") option.

Set the recording sample rate by giving the samples per second to use as an argument to the `-r` option. For CD-quality audio at 44,100 Hz, use `-r 44100`.

Finally, to record a file in a particular format, either give the name of the format as an argument to the `-f` option, or use the traditional file name extension for that format in the output file name (see Appendix B [Conventional File Name Extensions], page 723).

⇒ Here are two ways to use this.

- To make a high-fidelity recording from the microphone and save it to a WAV format file called `goodbye.wav`, type:

  ```
  $ rec -s w -c 2 -r 44100 goodbye.wav ⟨RET⟩
  ```

- To make a sound recording in the CD audio format and write the output to a file called `goodbye.cdr`, type:

  ```
  $ rec goodbye.cdr ⟨RET⟩
  ```

NOTES: When you're not recording sound, keep the inputs muted (see Recipe 21.1.3 [Muting an Audio Device], page 465); this way, you can have a microphone plugged in without having feedback when playing sounds. Also, make sure the volume levels are not set too high or too low when recording; getting the right level for your microphone or other input device may take some initial adjustment.

Like `play`, `rec` is part of the "SOund eXchange" toolkit.

More advanced options exist. Use GramoFile, described in the next recipe, to record high-quality audio with a menu interface.

21.5 Using Other Sound Tools

There are many mixer, playback, and recording tools available. The following table lists some of the better ones.

Aumix	Straightforward audio mixer tool that can be used interactively in a terminal, as well as on the command line and in scripts—use this if you are too frustrated by **amixer**. The standard mixer on many systems. DEB: `aumix` RPM: `aumix` WWW: `http://www.jpj.net/~trevor/aumix.html`
GramoFile	Transfers sound from vinyl records to CD-quality audio files, and can also record from the microphone and other inputs. Especially useful are its processing filters for improving the audio taken off vinyl, filtering out pops, hisses, and other surface noise. GramoFile can automatically detect and split each track on a record side into its own WAV file, a feature that is also good for processing or recording long sessions of spoken word or live music in the same manner. DEB: `gramofile` RPM: `gramofile` WWW: `http://panic.et.tudelft.nl/~costar/gramofile/`
Krecord	Simple WAV file player and recorder for the KDE environment. DEB: `krecord` RPM: `krecord` WWW: `http://bytesex.org/krecord.html`

Splay   Command line MP3 player that can decode and play MPEG-1 layer 1,2,3 and MPEG-2 layer 3 recorded audio. Based on the older Maplay.
DEB: `splay`
RPM: `splay`
WWW: `http://splay.sourceforge.net/`

Xawtv-Tools   Toolkit that includes tools for interactive recording of CD-quality audio in a terminal, dumping the current mixer settings to the standard output, and displaying the structure of RIFF format files (both AVI and WAV).
DEB: `xawtv-tools`
RPM: `xawtv`
WWW: `http://bytesex.org/misc.html`
          `http://bytesex.org/xawtv/`

XMMS   Popular, comprehensive audio player for X, featuring dozens of plug-ins, support for many sound formats (including Ogg and MP3), and "skins" to change its look and feel; it can use FreeAmp themes as well—see listing for **zinf** below. Inspired by Winamp.
DEB: `xmms`
RPM: `xmms`
WWW: `http://www.xmms.org/`

Zinf   Popular audio file player for X that can play Ogg and MP3 formats, and its graphical appearance can be changed with "themes." Formerly known as FreeAmp (the "Free Audio Music Player").
DEB: `zinf`
RPM: `zinf`
WWW: `http://www.zinf.org/`

## CHAPTER 22

Audio Compact Discs

Audio compact discs can be played on systems that have a CD drive[1] and sound card installed. You can control playback of an audio CD in all the ways you can with a traditional CD player, except that on a Linux system you control playback with software tools on the command line. There are also tools for reading the audio data from a CD and writing it to a file (which you can later write to a CD-R disc or convert to Ogg format).

If you get silence when playing audio CDs, make sure that the CD setting is on "REC" in the mixer (this unmutes it).

Tools and techniques for manipulating data CDs are given in Recipe 24.4 [Using Data CDs], page 506.

22.1 Using Audio CDs

CDTOOL
  DEB: `cdtool`
  RPM: `cdtool`
  WWW: `http://www.hitsquad.com/smm/programs/CDTOOL/`

These recipes describe various ways to manipulate audio CDs using the elegant collection of command line tools found in CDTOOL toolkit. All of these tools are actually symbolic links to a single program, `cdtool`; its functionality depends on the name it is run with. Other CD audio tools, including X clients, are listed in Recipe 22.4 [Using Other Audio Compact Disc Tools], page 484.

22.1.1 Playing an Audio CD

Use `cdplay` to play an audio CD in the CD drive; the sound is output through the speakers connected to the LINE OUT jack on your sound card. (You may need to use the audio mixer to adjust the volume level and other settings; see Recipe 21.1 [Adjusting the Audio Controls], page 463.)

⇒ To play an audio CD, type:

    $ *cdplay* (RET)

To begin with a particular track, give the number of the track as an argument.

---

[1] Any drive that is capable of playing audio compact discs—a DVD drive, CD-ROM drive, or CDR or CDRW drive.

⇒ To play an audio CD, beginning with the third track, type:

    $ *cdplay 3* ⟨RET⟩

To *end* with a particular track, give the number of the track as a second argument.

⇒ Here are two ways to use this.

- To play an audio CD, beginning with the first track and ending with the fourth track, type:

      $ *cdplay 1 4* ⟨RET⟩

- To play only the third track of an audio CD, type:

      $ *cdplay 3 3* ⟨RET⟩

To play a special order of selections, combine multiple **cdplay** commands with the Bash semicolon (;) directive (see Recipe 3.1.7 [Running a List of Commands], page 63).

⇒ Here are two ways to use this.

- To play tracks 3 through 7, track 1, and track 12 from the audio **cd** in the CD drive, type:

      $ *cdplay 3 7; cdplay 1 1; cdplay 12 12* ⟨RET⟩

- To play track 1 from the audio **cd** in the CD drive three times, then play the entire CD from the beginning, type:

      $ *cdplay 1 1; cdplay 1 1; cdplay 1 1; cdplay* ⟨RET⟩

22.1.2 Pausing an Audio CD

Use **cdpause** to pause audio CD playback.

⇒ To pause the current CD playback, type:

    $ *cdpause* ⟨RET⟩

Use **cdplay** to start playback at the point where it was paused; to restart the playback from the beginning, use **cdplay** with "x" as an argument.

⇒ Here are two ways to use this.

- To restart a paused CD, type:

      $ *cdplay* ⟨RET⟩

- To restart a paused CD from the beginning, type:

      $ *cdplay x* ⟨RET⟩

22.1.3 Stopping an Audio CD

To stop playback of an audio CD, use `cdstop`.

⇒ To stop the current CD playback, type:

    $ *cdstop* ⟨RET⟩

22.1.4 Shuffling Audio CD Tracks

Use `cdplay` with the "`shuffle`" argument to play the CD tracks in random order.

⇒ To shuffle CD playback, type:

    $ *cdplay shuffle* ⟨RET⟩

22.1.5 Displaying Information About an Audio CD

There are a few methods for displaying information about an audio CD.

METHOD #1

Use `cdinfo` to display information about an audio CD, including its play status and track times. With no options, it outputs the play status: "`play`" if the CD is currently playing; "`paused`" if the CD is currently on pause; "`no-status`" if the CD is not playing; and "`nodisc`" if no disc is in the drive.

⇒ For the current status of the audio CD in the CD drive, type:

    $ *cdinfo* ⟨RET⟩

In addition, `cdinfo` recognizes the following options:

`-a`	Output the absolute disc time.
`-r`	Output the relative track time.
`-s`	Output the play status (the default action).
`-t`	Output the current track.
`-v`	Output all available information: absolute disc time, relative track time, play status, and current track.

METHOD #2

To show the lengths of all tracks on an audio CD in a directory-like format, use `cdir`. This tool will also show titles and artist names, if known, but for this to work, you must set up an audio CD database (see the `cdtool man` page for details—Recipe 2.8.4 [Reading a Page from the System Manual], page 46).

⇒ To show a list of tracks, type:

```
$ cdir (RET)
unknown cd - 43:14 in 8 tracks
  5:15.00  1
  5:50.40  2
  5:29.08  3
  3:50.70  4
  4:17.00  5
  5:56.15  6
  7:13.40  7
  5:19.22  8
$
```

In this example, the CD contains eight tracks, with a total of 43 minutes and 14 seconds of play time.

22.1.6 Ejecting an Audio CD

Use `cdeject` to eject the disc in the CD drive. If the disc is currently playing, play will stop and the disc will eject.

⇒ To eject a CD, type:

    $ cdeject (RET)

NOTES: This command will also eject a data CD, if the data CD is not currently mounted (see Recipe 24.4 [Using Data CDs], page 506).

22.2 Sampling from an Audio C

Cdda2wav
  DEB: cdda2wav
  RPM: cdda2wav
  WWW: http://www.escape.de/users/colossus/cdda2wav.html
    or

Cdparanoia
  DEB cdparanoia
  RPM: cdparanoia
  WWW: http://www.xiph.org/paranoia/

Two tools used for sampling (sometimes called "ripping") data from an audio

CD are `cdda2wav` and `cdparanoia`. Both can sample single tracks or entire disks. `cdda2wav` is the archetypal CD audio-sampling tool for Linux, and it should be used when speed is more important than sound quality. `cdparanoia` does various extra checks for the paranoid, and it should be used when an absolutely perfect copy is necessary (at the expense of speed). `cdda2wav` is perfectly capable of creating a digitally perfect audio sample under normal conditions; `cdparanoia` is useful when your original CD has scratches (its scratch-detection capability can attempt to "hold sync" across the scratch), or when you are using a less-than-optimal-quality CD drive.

With `cdda2wav`, you specify the track number to be retrieved as an argument to the `-t` option; use the `-x` option to specify a CD-quality retrieval, and give the name of the CD device with the `-D` option—unless you have multiple CD drives installed, this is almost certainly going to be `/dev/cdrom`.

By default, files are written as WAV format files; use the `-O` option followed by "cdr" to write the files in CD audio format. CD audio format files are useful for burning an audio CD containing the files as tracks (discussed in the following section), and `.wav` files are useful for converting to Ogg format (see Recipe 23.3.2 [Encoding an Ogg File], page 495). You can convert either format to the other at a later time with `sox`—see Recipe 23.3 [Converting Sound Files], page 493.

⇒ Here are two ways to use this.

- To copy track seven of an audio CD to a CD-quality WAV file in the current directory, type:

      $ cdda2wav -t7 -d0 -x -D /dev/cdrom (RET)

- To copy all tracks on an audio CD to separate CD audio format files, type:

      $ cdda2wav -D /dev/cdrom -x -O cdr -d0 -B (RET)

For more reliable sampling, use `cdparanoia`. Give the *range* of audio tracks to sample as an argument, from the first track to sample to the last; if you give no arguments, it samples the entire disc. Use the `-w` option to specify WAV format output.

⇒ Here are some ways to use this.

- To sample the first through third tracks from a scratched audio CD in the default CD drive using "paranoid" data verification, and write the output as a raw audio-format file in the current directory, type:

      $ cdparanoia 1-3 (RET)

- To sample only the third track of the audio CD using "paranoid" data verification, and write the output to a WAV format file in the current directory, type:

  $ cdparanoia -w 3-3 (RET)

- To sample the entire audio CD using "paranoid" data verification, type:

  $ cdparanoia -w -B (RET)

- To sample the entire audio CD using less-than-maximum "paranoid" data verification, without checking for scratches, and saving each song as a separate raw audio-format file in the current directory, type:

  $ cdparanoia -B -Y -X (RET)

NOTES: Sampling an entire audio CD can use a lot of disk space; most people delete the .cdr or .wav files as soon as they make Oggs or burn an audio CD-R from the data.

22.3 Writing an Audio CD-R

Cdrecord
  DEB: cdrecord
  RPM: cdrecord
  WWW: http://tinyurl.com/2s6a

Use **cdrecord** to write (or "burn") audio files to a blank CD-R disc. You will need a CD-R drive[2] and the audio files must be in CD-DA CD audio format (they usually have a .cdda or .cdr file name extension).

Specify the CD-R drive with the special "**dev**" argument, which is given in this form:

  dev=scsibus, target, lun

where *scsibus* is the number of the SCSI bus (0 for the primary bus), *target* is the SCSI target ID (usually a number from 1 to 6), and *lun* is its LUN number (almost always 0).

Use the **speed** argument to set the speed factor for writing data: give "**speed=2**" to specify double speed or "**speed=4**" to specify quad speed.

Use the **-dummy** option to run with the drive laser turned off, so no actual burning takes place; this is useful when you are first using a CD-R drive and

---

[2] You can also use this tool with a CD-RW drive and write to a CD-RW disc.

need to test your configuration to make sure you've got it right. Another useful option is **-v**, which gives a more *verbose* message output.

Give the names of the audio files to burn, in the order that they should appear on the disc, as arguments to the **-audio** option. The files are written in CD-DA CD audio format, and they should contain 16-bit stereo at 44,100 samples per second (the **.cdr** or x.**cdda** files meet this criterion).

⇒ Here are some ways to use this.

- To burn the file **symphony.cdr** to the disc in the CD-R drive whose target ID is 2 on the primary SCSI bus, type:

  ```
  $ cdrecord dev=0,2,0 -audio symphony.cdr (RET)
  ```

- To burn all the files in the current directory ending with a **.cdr** extension at double speed to the CD-R drive whose target ID is 2 on the primary SCSI bus, and give verbose output, type:

  ```
  $ cdrecord dev=0,2,0 speed=2 -v -audio *.cdr (RET)
  ```

- To run a test burn of the file **symphony.cdr** to the disc in the CD-R drive whose target ID is 6 (LUN 1) on the primary SCSI bus, type:

  ```
  $ cdrecord dev=0,6,1 -dummy -audio symphony.cdr (RET)
  ```

When you use wildcards for files, as in the second example above, the shell expands the files in alphabetical order. To write a group of tracks in a particular order without specifying all of their names as arguments, rename them so that their names begin with numbers corresponding to the order you want to write them in (see Recipe 5.5 [Moving Files and Directories], page 144).

For example, if you have the three files **morning-song.cdr**, **midday-song.cdr**, and **evening-song.cdr**, and you want to write them in that order, rename the files to **01-morning-song.cdr**, **02-midday-song.cdr**, and **03-evening-song.cdr**. Otherwise, if you specify them as *.cdr, the shell will sort their names so that they will be written to CD-R in the order of **evening-song.cdr**, **midday-song.cdr**, and **morning-song.cdr**—exactly the opposite of what was intended!

To write a disc containing both data and audio tracks, first specify the file for the data track (it should contain a filesystem image in either ISO 9660 or Rock Ridge format), and then follow it with the **-audio** option and the names of the audio tracks to use. The resulting CD-R will be both mountable as a data CD and playable on audio CD players (the first track on the disc, the data track, will be skipped when playing the audio).

⇒ To burn the data track **band-info**, plus all the audio tracks in the current directory that have a **.cdda** extension, to the CD-R drive whose target ID is 2 on the primary SCSI bus, type:

```
$ cdrecord dev=0,2,0 band-info -audio *.cdda (RET)
```

NOTES: When writing an audio CD, you should have as few processes running as possible. If **cdrecord** has to pause even momentarily to let the system shuffle other processes, the CD-R could be ruined! For this reason, it is advisable to avoid switching between consoles—or between windows, if running X—during the CD-R burning process.

22.4 Using Other Audio Compact Disc Tools

The following table lists some of the other available tools and applications that work on audio compact discs.

Cdcd	Plays CDs from the command line. DEB: cdcd RPM: cdcd WWW: http://cdcd.undergrid.net/
Cdinfo	Displays information about an audio CD. WWW: http://bytesex.org/misc.html
CDlabelgen	Generates labels and front insert cards for compact discs. DEB: cdlabelgen RPM: cdlabelgen WWW: http://tinyurl.com/3bty3
Cdp	Plays audio CDs in a terminal; it includes both command line and full-screen console modes. RPM: cdp WWW: http://cdp.sourceforge.net/
Groovy CD Player	Plays audio CDs with a panel of display numbers that are so round and "groovy," it instantly appeals to those who think back fondly on 70s popular culture. DEB: groovycd

Player   Console CD player that can read either WorkMan or CDDB
                databases and output PostScript CD audio covers.
                WWW: http://bytesex.org/misc.html

WorkBone   Plays audio CDs in a terminal and allows you to skip forward
                and backward through tracks as they are playing.
                DEB: workbone
                WWW: http://tinyurl.com/2ul7j

WorkMan   Plays audio CDs in X with a graphical interface that mimics the
                front panel of a physical CD player.
                DEB: workman
                RPM: workman
                WWW: http://tinyurl.com/26eof

XCDRoast   Graphical front-end to the cdrecord tool, for use in X.
                DEB: xcdroast
                RPM: xcdroast
                WWW: http://www.xcdroast.org/

## CHAPTER 23

Editing Sound Files

All kinds of tools and applications exist to edit sound files. This chapter describes some of those tools, and gives methods for cutting and pasting sound files, applying effects and filters, and converting sound files between formats.

23.1 Manipulating Selections from Sound Files

Snd
  DEB: snd
  RPM: snd
  WWW: http://www-ccrma.stanford.edu/software/snd/

Snd is a sound-file editing environment for X, and it aims to be for sound what Emacs is to text. (It also uses Emacs-style key bindings.)

You'll find a complete manual for it in the /usr/doc/snd directory; this section explains how to use Snd to work with selections from sound files.

To open a sound file in Snd, give the name of the file to be opened as an argument to **snd**.

⇒ To open the sound file **mixdown.wav** in Snd, type:

    $ snd mixdown.wav ⟨RET⟩

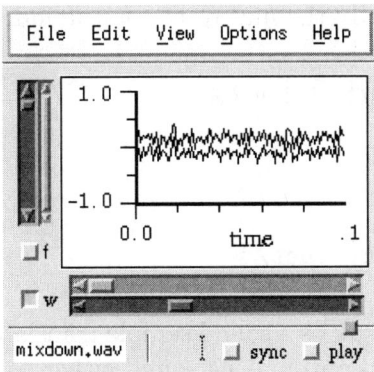

Figure 23-1. Snd with a file loaded.

This command starts Snd with a WAV file called **mixdown.wav**, as in Figure 23-1.

Selecting a section of a sound file in Snd is similar to selecting text in
Emacs; you can mark a section of a sound file or recording you've made in
Snd by left-clicking and dragging across the area with the mouse. The area
you drag across becomes shaded and is called the *selection*. Once you select a
portion of the sound, any effect you choose works on that selection. You can
also cut and paste selections of the sound you are editing into other sound
buffers.

The `xwave` tool (and many others, no doubt) have similar capabilities and
functions (see Recipe 23.4 [Using Other Sound Editors], page 496).

23.1.1 Cutting Out Part of a Sound File

To cut out a portion of a sound file you are editing in Snd, first select that
portion by left-clicking and dragging, and then choose `Cut` from the `Edit`
menu, somewhat like cropping an image file.

23.1.2 Pasting a Selection into a Sound File

Paste a cut sound selection into a different sound buffer in Snd by opening the
new buffer, left-clicking in the target buffer, and then choosing `Paste` from
the `Edit` menu. Your most recent selection will be pasted at the point where
you clicked in the sound buffer.

23.1.3 Mixing Sound Files Together

To mix different audio files together as multiple tracks in Snd, choose `Mix`
from the `File` menu and specify the files to use as the individual tracks.

23.2 Applying Sound Effects

SOund eXchange
  DEB: `sox`
  RPM: `sox`
  WWW: `http://sox.sourceforge.net/`

The "Sound eXchange" tool, `sox`, is a sound sample translator. It reads sound
as files or standard input, and outputs the sound either to a file or standard
output, while translating in between. You can use `sox` to convert sound files
from one format to another or to process sounds with special effects. This
section describes some of the special effects you can apply to sound files with
`sox`.

When applying an effect, the original file is never altered. You must specify an output file, or use a hyphen character (-) to indicate the standard output. Specify the output format as an argument to the -t option. You can only apply one effect with each **sox** command; thus, to add both echo and reverb to a sound file, you would need to issue two **sox** commands.

The amount and levels applied for each effect will vary with every situation. As such, consider the following recipes as guidelines only for using the options; you will probably end up experimenting a bit to achieve your intended effect for any particular sound file.

Almost all of the sound effects are applied by specifying the input and output file arguments, followed by the name of the effect to use and any options the effect takes (with notable exceptions, like the -v option for changing the amplitude of a file).

NOTES: For more information on the sound effects **sox** can apply, see the various files in /usr/doc/sox/, and read the **sox man** page (see Recipe 2.8.4 [Reading a Page from the System Manual], page 46).

23.2.1 Changing the Amplitude of a Sound File

To change the volume or amplitude of a sound file, use **sox** with the -v option, giving the volume level as an argument. Levels below 1.0 lower the amplitude, and higher numbers raise it.

⇒ Here are two ways to use this.

- To raise the volume of file **old.wav** twofold and write the output to **new.wav**, type:

      $ sox -v3 old.wav new.wav ⟨RET⟩

- To lower the volume of file **old.wav** by half and write the output to **new.wav**, type:

      $ sox -v.5 old.wav new.wav ⟨RET⟩

Use **sox** with the **stat** option and -v to determine the largest possible value that can be used before distortion or clipping occurs (it performs a statistical analysis on the file and outputs a numeric value). This value comes in handy when you want to raise a file's volume as high as possible without ruining its fidelity.

⇒ To raise the volume of the file `quiet.cdr` as high as possible without distortion, type:

```
$ sox quiet.cdr loud.cdr stat -v (RET)
3.125
$ sox -v 3.125 quiet.cdr loud.cdr (RET)
$
```

The preceding example writes a new file, `loud.cdr`.

23.2.2 Changing the Sampling Rate of a Sound File

To change the sampling rate of a sound file, use the `-r` option followed by the sample rate to use, in Hertz. Like the `-v` option, specify this option before giving the name of the output file.

⇒ To change the sampling rate of file `old.wav` to 7,000 Hz and write the output to `new.wav`, type:

```
$ sox old.wav -r 7000 new.wav (RET)
```

You can use this effect to raise or lower the pitch of a sound file. To do this, specify the desired pitch as the argument to the `-r` option, and give this option for the input file; then, specify the original sampling rate for the output file as an argument to `-r`.

⇒ To slow the pitch of the sound in `bell.wav`, sampled at 44,100 Hz, and write it to a new file called `slowbell.wav`, also at 44,100 Hz, type:

```
$ sox -r 30000 bell.wav -r 44100 slowbell.wav (RET)
```

In this example, the sound in `bell.wav`, sampled at 44,100 Hz, was played at the slower 30,000 Hz. This was then resampled to the output file back to the 44,100 Hz sampling rate, but the pitch now differs from the original.

23.2.3 Adding Reverb to a Sound File

To add reverb to a sound file, use the "`reverb`" effect. "`reverb`" takes three arguments: the volume of the output (its "gain-out"); the time (in milliseconds) of reverb; and the length (in milliseconds) of delay. You can specify more than one delay; the more you specify, the more of an overlapping echo the reverb will have.

⇒ Here are some ways to use this.

- To add a basic reverb to file `old.wav` and write the output to file `new.wav`, type:

    $ sox old.wav new.wav reverb .5 1000 100 〈RET〉

- To add a spacey, echoing reverb to file `old.wav` and write the output to `new.wav`, type:

    $ sox old.wav new.wav reverb 1 1000 333 333 333 333 〈RET〉

NOTES: This last example makes a sound similar to some of the recordings of the band Flying Saucer Attack. (You know who they are, don't you?)

23.2.4 Adding Echo to a Sound File

To add echo to a sound file, use the "`echo`" effect. It takes as arguments the "gain-in" and "gain-out" volume levels, as well as the delay and decay, both in milliseconds.

⇒ Here are some ways to use this.

- To add a 100-millisecond echo to the sound file `old.wav` and write output to `new.wav`, type:

    $ sox old.wav new.wav echo .5 .5 100 .5 〈RET〉

- To add a one-second echo to the sound file `old.wav` and write output to `new.wav`, type:

    $ sox old.wav new.wav echo .5 .5 1000 .5 〈RET〉

- To add a "tin-can" echo effect to `old.wav` and write the output to `new.wav`, type:

    $ sox old.wav new.wav echo 1 .5 5 .5 〈RET〉

NOTES: The "`echos`" effect works like "`echo`," but adds a *sequence* of echos to the sound file.

23.2.5 Adding Flange to a Sound File

The "`flanger`" effect adds flange to a sound file. It takes as arguments the "gain-in" and "gain-out" volume levels, as well as the delay and decay in milliseconds, and the speed of the flange in Hertz. Specify the type of modulation with either `-s` (for sinodial) or `-t` (for triangular).

⇒ Here are two ways to use this.

- To add an "underwater" flange to the file `old.wav` and write the output to `new.wav`, type:

  `$ sox old.wav new.wav flanger .5 .5 4 .5 1 -t` ⟨RET⟩

- To add flange that sounds somewhat like a "wah-wah" effects pedal to the file `old.wav` and write the output to `new.wav`, type:

  `$ sox old.wav new.wav flanger .5 .5 .5 1 2 -t` ⟨RET⟩

23.2.6 Adding Phase to a Sound File

The "`phaser`" effect adds phase to a sound file. It takes the same arguments as the "`flanger`" effect.

⇒ Here are two ways to use this.

- To add a heavy phase to the file `old.wav` and write the output to `new.wav`, type:

  `$ sox old.wav new.wav phaser 1 .5 4 .5 1 -s` ⟨RET⟩

- To add a phased "breathing" effect to the file `old.wav` and write the output to `new.wav`, type:

  `$ sox old.wav new.wav phaser .5 .5 .5 .9 .5 -t` ⟨RET⟩

NOTES: Using a decay greater than .5 may result in feedback.

23.2.7 Adding Chorus to a Sound File

To add a chorus effect to a sound file, use "`chorus`." Its options are the "gain-in" and "gain-out" of the volume, the delay and decay in milliseconds, the speed in Hertz, and the depth of the chorus in milliseconds. Specify either `-s` or `-t` for sinodial or triangular modulation.

⇒ Here are two ways to use this.

- To add a 100 millisecond chorus to the file `old.wav` and write the output to `new.wav`, type:

  `$ sox old.wav new.wav chorus 1 .5 100 1 1 1 -t` ⟨RET⟩

- To add a deep, "alien-sounding" chorus to the file `old.wav` and write the output to `new.wav`, type:

  `$ sox old.wav new.wav chorus 1 .5 100 1 5 9 -t` ⟨RET⟩

23.2.8 Adding Vibro-Champ Effects to a Sound File

The "vibro" effect imitates the effect of the old Fender Vibro-Champ amplifier. Give the speed in Hertz (30 maximum) as an option, and specify an optional depth value between 0 and 1 (the default is .5).

⇒ Here are some ways to use this.

- To add a subtle Vibro-Champ effect to the file old.wav and write the output to new.wav, type:

  $ sox old.wav new.wav vibro 1 ⟨RET⟩

- To add an effect of a maxed-out Vibro-Champ to the file old.wav and write the output to new.wav, type:

  $ sox old.wav new.wav vibro 30 1 ⟨RET⟩

23.2.9 Reversing the Audio in a Sound File

Use the "reverse" effect to reverse the sound in a sound file.

⇒ To reverse the sound in the file old.wav and write the output to new.wav, type:

  $ sox old.wav new.wav reverse ⟨RET⟩

23.3 Converting Sound Files

SOund eXchange
  DEB: sox
  RPM: sox
  WWW: http://sox.sourceforge.net/

Use sox for most sound-file conversions. Give as arguments the name of the input file and the name of the output file to write to; use a file name extension specifying the sound format for the output file (see Appendix B [Conventional File Name Extensions], page 723).

⇒ To convert the file new.wav to an audio CD format file, type:

  $ sox new.wav new.cdr ⟨RET⟩

This command writes a new file, new.cdr, in the audio CD format; the original file, new.wav, is not altered.

You may sometimes need to specify additional options, such as with raw audio files where the sampling rate and other properties must be specified.

⇒ To convert all of the raw audio files in the current directory to audio CD
   format files, type:

```
$ for i in *.raw (RET)
{ (RET)
sox -s -w -c2 -r 44100 $i -x $i.cdr (RET)
} (RET)
```

This command writes all of the `.raw` files to new files of the same name
but with a `.cdr` extension. You could then use **cdrecord** to burn an audio
CD with the `.cdr` files (see Recipe 22.3 [Writing an Audio CD-R], page 482).

To convert a file to a particular format without using the standard extension, specify the format to write to with the **-t** option.

⇒ To convert the file **new.wav** to the audio CD format and write output to
   a file named **cd-single**, type:

```
$ sox new.wav -t cdr cd-single (RET)
```

23.3.1 Converting an MP3 File

SOund eXchange
  DEB: sox
  RPM: sox
  WWW: http://sox.sourceforge.net/

Mpg123
  DEB: mpg321
  RPM: mpg321
  WWW: http://mpg321.sourceforge.net/

To convert an MP3 file to another format, use **mpg321** (or another command
line MP3 player) to play the file to the standard output, and then use **sox** to
read the resultant raw audio and write it to another file with a specified input
format.

⇒ To convert the MP3 file **remix.mp3** to a WAV file **remix.wav**, type (all on
   one line):

```
$ mpg321 -b 10000 -s remix.mp3 | sox -t raw -r 44100
-s -w -c 2 - remix.wav (RET)
```

NOTES: The process of making an MP3 file from a raw audio or WAV format
audio file is called *encoding* (or sometimes "ripping") an MP3 file; programs

that do this are MP3 *encoders*. This is not so much a recording process as it is a *conversion* process: Existing audio is converted to MPEG audio format. Unfortunately, the algorithm for encoding MP3s is patented, and all software that uses it must pay a license fee. This restriction means that it is against the law to write a software program to encode MP3 without licensing it. That is the main reason why MP3 is now losing its popularity in favor of the Ogg Vorbis audio format. As with many computing trends, this one has found its early adopters in the Linux world.

23.3.2 Encoding an Ogg File

Oggenc
  DEB: vorbis-tools
  RPM: vorbis-tools
  WWW: http://www.vorbis.com/

Use `oggenc` to encode an Ogg Vorbis audio file. It takes an audio file as an argument and writes a new file with the same base file name and an `.ogg` extension. To specify a different file name, give the name to use as an argument to the `-o` option.

⇒ To make an Ogg Vorbis file from the WAV file `interview.wav`, type:

> `$ oggenc interview.wav` (RET)

This command makes a new file, `interview.ogg`.

23.3.3 Converting Ogg to Another Format

To convert an Ogg Vorbis audio file to another format, use `ogg123` and specify the "`wav`" driver with the `-d` option. The Ogg Vorbis file you give as an argument to this command will be written to a WAV-format file (in the current directory) with the name of `output.wav`.

⇒ To convert the Ogg Vorbis file `bobhopehour.ogg` to WAV format, type:

> `$ ogg123 -d wav bobhopehour.ogg` (RET)

This command writes a new file, `output.wav`, in the current directory.

Specify the file to output by giving it as an argument to the `-o` option.

⇒ To convert the Ogg Vorbis file `bobhopehour.ogg` to WAV format, writing to a file named `hope1.wav`, type:

> `$ ogg123 -d wav -o hope1.wav bobhopehour.ogg` (RET)

NOTES: The WAV output can be further converted into other formats using the traditional methods (for examples, see the previous recipe).

If you want to listen to the file as it's being converted, you may do so by giving an additional -d option for the audio system driver you have.

23.4 Using Other Sound Editors

Sound software in Linux is a fast-moving target, and it is impossible for a printed volume to keep up with it; you can stay abreast of the latest developments by checking out Dave Phillips's "Sound & MIDI Software for Linux." It has the most comprehensive and up-to-date list of Linux-related sound software available (see Appendix D [References for Further Interest], page 731).

As with text editors, there are all manner of sound editors, ranging from simple editors to advanced environments. The following table lists a few of the most popular ones.

Audacity	Audio editor with spectrogram display. Known for its speed. DEB: `audacity` RPM: `audacity` WWW: `http://audacity.sourceforge.net/`
Brahms	Graphical music editor for KDE whose features include both score and piano-roll notation. DEB: `brahms` RPM: `brahms` WWW: `http://brahms.sourceforge.net/`
DAP	Graphical tool for editing sound files. RPM: `dap` WWW: `http://www.cee.hw.ac.uk/~richardk/`
Festival	Speech-synthesis system that reads English (British and American), Spanish, and Welsh plain text input, and outputs speech as sound. DEB: `festival` RPM: `festival` WWW: `http://www.cstr.ed.ac.uk/projects/festival/`

Freebirth

Sequencer, bass synthesizer, and sample player.
DEB: freebirth
RPM: freebirth
WWW: http://www.hitsquad.com/smm/programs/Freebirth/

GLAME

Audio editor described as "the GIMP of audio." GLAME is
an acronym for "GNU/Linux Audio Mechanics."
DEB: glame
RPM: glame
WWW: http://glame.sourceforge.net/

Pure Data

Powerful system for programming real-time audio.
DEB: pd
WWW: http://www-crca.ucsd.edu/~msp/software.html

Rosegarden

MIDI sequencer, music notation (score) editor, and music
composition editor.
DEB: rosegarden
RPM: rosegarden
WWW: http://www.rosegardenmusic.com/

Tapiir

Graphical, real-time audio effects processor inspired by old
magnetic-tape delay effects.
DEB: tapiir
WWW: http://www.iua.upf.es/~mdeboer/projects/tapiir/

XWave

A simple sound editor that performs the basic functions
you would expect in a WAV file editor.
DEB: xwave
WWW: http://www.ibiblio.org/pub/linux/apps/sound/editors/

VI. PRODUCTIVITY

Disk Storage

All files and directories on a Linux-based system are stored on a Linux *filesystem*, which is a disk device (such as a hard drive) that is formatted to store a directory tree (see Chapter 5 [Files and Directories], page 125).

There are two kinds of disk storage on a Linux system: fixed and removable. *Fixed storage* refers to a disk that is firmly attached to the computer system and is not intended for casual removal (except when upgrading). Your hard drive (sometimes called a "hard disk" or "fixed disk"), which stores the operating system, application software, and user data, is the prime example of fixed storage.

The second kind of disk storage is *removable storage*, which are disks that are intended to be removed for archiving or transfer to another system. Common examples of removable storage are floppy disks (or "diskettes") and CD-ROMs—you typically remove the storage media from its drive bay when you're done using it.

On Linux systems, disks are used by *mounting* them to a directory, which makes the directory tree the disk contains available at that given directory *mount point*. Disks can be mounted on any directory on the system, but any divisions between disks are transparent. This means that a system that has separate physical hard disks for the `/home`, `/usr`, and `/usr/local` directory trees will look and feel no different from a system that only has one physical hard disk.

System administrators often mount high-capacity drives on directory trees that will contain a lot of data (such as a `/home` directory tree on a system with a lot of users), and for purposes of fault tolerance, administrators often use several physical hard disks on one system—if there is a disk failure, only the data on that one disk is lost (though ideally it can be recovered from a backup).

This chapter describes tools and techniques for manipulating disks and storage media.

24.1 Listing a Disk's Free Space

To see how much free space is left on a disk, use `df`. Without any options, `df` outputs a list of all mounted filesystems. Six columns are output, displaying information about each disk: the name of its device file in `/dev`; the number of 1024-byte blocks the system uses; the number of blocks in use; the number of blocks available; the percent of the device used; and the name of the directory tree the device is mounted on.

⇒ To see how much free space is left on the system's disks, type:

```
$ df ⟨RET⟩
Filesystem          1024-blocks  Used Available Capacity Mounted on
/dev/hda1               195167   43405   141684    23%    /
/dev/hda2              2783807  688916  1950949    26%    /usr
/dev/hdb1              2039559 1675652   258472    87%    /home/webb
$
```

This example shows that three filesystems are mounted on the system—the filesystem mounted on / is at 23 percent capacity, the filesystem mounted on /usr is at 26 percent capacity, and the filesystem mounted on /home/webb, a home directory, is at 87 percent capacity.

24.2 Listing a File's Disk Usage

Use du to list the amount of space on a disk used by files. To specify a particular file name or directory tree, give it as an argument. With no arguments, du works on the current directory.

It outputs a line for each subdirectory in the tree, listing the space used and the subdirectory name; the last line lists the total amount of space used for the entire directory tree.

⇒ To output the disk usage for the directory tree whose root is the current directory, type:

```
$ du ⟨RET⟩
8          ./projects/documentation
12         ./projects/source
4          ./projects/etc
24         ./projects
3          ./tmp
27         .
$
```

This example shows two subdirectories in the directory tree: projects and tmp. The projects subdirectory contains three additional directories. The

amount of disk space used by the individual directories is the total on the last
line, 27 KB.

By default, output is in 1 KB blocks, but you can specify another unit to
use as an option: **-k** for kilobytes and **-m** for megabytes.

⇒ Here are two ways to use this.

- To output the disk usage, in kilobytes, of the **/usr/local** directory
  tree, type:

  $ du -k /usr/local (RET)

- To show the number of megabytes used by the file **/tmp/cache**, type:

  $ du -m /tmp/cache (RET)

Use the **-s** option ("summarize") to output only the last line containing the
total for the entire directory tree. This is useful when you are only interested
in the total disk usage of a directory tree.

⇒ Here are two ways to use this.

- To output *only* the total disk usage of the **/usr/local** directory tree,
  type:

  $ du -s /usr/local (RET)

- To output only the total disk usage, in kilobytes, of the **/usr/local**
  directory tree, type:

  $ du -s -k /usr/local (RET)

24.3 Using Floppy Disks

Before you can use a floppy disk for the first time, it must be *formatted*, which
creates an empty filesystem on the disk.

To read or write files to a formatted disk, you mount the floppy on an empty
directory, making its filesystem available in the specified directory. Usually,
Linux systems have an empty **/floppy** directory for this purpose. (Another
general-purpose directory for mounting filesystems is the **/mnt** directory.)

While you cannot mount a filesystem on a directory containing other files,
you can always create a new directory somewhere to mount a filesystem.

When you mount a disk on a directory, that directory contains all the files
and directories of the disk's filesystem; when you later *unmount* the disk, that
directory will be empty—all the files and directories on the disk are still on
the disk's filesystem, but the filesystem is no longer mounted.

When you're done using a floppy, you must unmount it before you remove
it from the drive. If you don't, you risk corrupting or deleting some of the

files on it—Linux may still be using the mounted files when you remove the disk (see Recipe 2.1.2 [Turning Off the System], page 27).

The following sections show you how to format, mount, and unmount floppies. On many systems, you need superuser privileges to do any of these actions.

NOTES: For recipes describing the use of MS-DOS (and Microsoft Windows) formatted disks under Linux, see Recipe 26.1 [Using DOS and Windows Disks], page 525.

24.3.1 Formatting a Floppy Disk

You can use `fdformat` to do a low-level format on a floppy disk device that you give as an argument. To format a 1.44 MB floppy in the first floppy drive, use the `/dev/fd0H1440` device as the argument to use.

⇒ To perform a low-level format on a 1.44 MB floppy disk in the first removable floppy drive, type:

    `$ fdformat /dev/fd0H1440` ⟨RET⟩

This will erase all the information on the disk.

Once a disk is formatted, you need to make a Linux filesystem on the disk.[1] Use `mke2fs` to do this. Give the name of the device file of the floppy drive as an argument—usually the first removable disk drive, `/dev/fd0`. The floppy disk must be in the drive when you give this command, and any data already on it will be lost.

⇒ To make a Linux filesystem on the floppy disk in the first removable floppy drive, type:

    `$ mke2fs /dev/fd0` ⟨RET⟩

NOTES: You can make 2 MB high-capacity formats with `superformat`. This formats a floppy disk beyond its normal carrying capacity; it is a lengthy process, but if you need to store extra data on your disk, you might consider it.

24.3.2 Mounting a Floppy Disk

To mount a floppy disk, use `mount` with the `/floppy` option.[2]

---

[1] Technically, this filesystem is a *second extended file system* (E2FS), the native filesystem currently used with Linux.

[2] This works if your administrator has set up the floppy drive filesystem for user access— see Recipe A.6.3 [Letting Users Access Hardware Peripherals], page 718.

⇒ To mount a floppy, type:

    $ `mount /floppy` (RET)

To mount a floppy disk to a specific directory, use **mount** and give as arguments the device name of the floppy drive (usually **/dev/fd0** for one-floppy systems) and the name of the directory to mount to.

⇒ To mount the floppy in the first floppy drive to **~/tmp**, type:

    $ `mount /dev/fd0 ~/tmp` (RET)

Once you have mounted a floppy, its contents appear in the directory you specify, and you can use any file command on them.

⇒ Here are two ways to use this.

- To list the contents of the base directory of the floppy mounted on **/floppy**, type:

       $ `ls /floppy` (RET)

- To list the contents of the entire directory tree on the floppy mounted on **/floppy**, type:

       $ `ls -lR /floppy` (RET)

NOTES: You can copy files to and from the directory tree that the floppy is mounted on, make and remove directories, and do anything else you could on any other directory tree. But remember, before you remove it, you must first unmount it.

24.3.3 Unmounting a Floppy Disk

Use **umount** to unmount a floppy disk, using the name of the directory it is mounted on as an argument.

⇒ To unmount the floppy that is mounted on **/floppy**, type:

    $ `umount /floppy` (RET)

NOTES: You can't unmount a disk if your current working directory, the directory you are in, is somewhere in that disk's directory tree.[3] In this case, trying to unmount the disk will give the error that the **/floppy** filesystem is in use; change to a different directory that isn't in the **/floppy** directory tree, and then you can unmount the disk.

Sometimes when you unmount a floppy, the light on the floppy drive will go on and remain on for a few seconds after it has been unmounted. This

---

[3] This is sometimes called being "under the mount point" of the disk.

is because Linux sometimes keeps changes to files in memory before it writes
them to disk; it's making sure that the files on the floppy are up-to-date.
Simply wait until the light goes off before you remove the floppy from the
drive.

24.4 Using Data CDs

As with a floppy disk, before you can use a data CD ("compact disc") on your
system, you must first mount it on an empty directory. You then unmount
it from the directory before you can eject the CD from the CD drive (you can
also eject the disc using software—see Recipe 22.1.6 [Ejecting an Audio CD],
page 480).

NOTES: To use audio CDs, see Chapter 22 [Audio Compact Discs], page 477.

24.4.1 Mounting a Data CD

To mount a data CD on the system, use **mount** with the **/cdrom** option.[4]

⇒ To mount a data CD on the system, type:

    `$ mount /cdrom` ⟨RET⟩

    This command makes the contents of the data CD available from the **/cdrom**
directory tree. You can use any Linux file command on the files and directories
on a data CD, but you can only write to one if it is a CDRW disc.

    Like the **/floppy** directory, the use of the **/cdrom** directory is a standard
practice and convenient, but not necessary—you can mount disks in whatever
empty directory you like. (You could even, for example, mount discs from
the CD drive to **/floppy** and mount floppy disks to **/cdrom**, but why would
anyone do that!)

    To mount a data CD to a specific directory, use **mount** and give as arguments
the name of the device file in **/dev** corresponding to the CD drive, and the
name of the directory to mount to. This directory must already exist on the
filesystem, and it must be empty. If it doesn't exist, use **mkdir** to create it
first (see Recipe 5.1.2 [Making a Directory], page 130).

    Most Linux systems are set up so that the device file of the first CD drive
is **/dev/cdrom**, but the name of the device file may be different, especially if
you have a SCSI CD-ROM drive.

---

[4] This works if your administrator has set up the CD drive filesystem for user access—see
    Recipe A.6.3 [Letting Users Access Hardware Peripherals], page 718.

⇒ To mount the disc in the CD drive to the /usr/local/share/clipart directory, type:

```
$ mount /dev/cdrom /usr/local/share/clipart (RET)
```

The contents of the disc in the CD drive will then be available in the /usr/local/share/clipart directory tree, and you can then use the files and directories on the data CD as you would any other files.

⇒ Here are some ways to use this.

- To peruse a directory tree graph of the data CD's contents, type:

```
$ tree /usr/local/share/clipart | less (RET)
```

- To change to the root directory on the data CD, type:

```
$ cd /usr/local/share/clipart (RET)
```

- To list the contents of the root directory on the data CD, type:

```
$ ls /usr/local/share/clipart (RET)
```

24.4.2 Unmounting a Data CD

Use **umount** to unmount a data CD; give as an argument the name of the directory it's mounted on.

⇒ To unmount the disc in the CD drive mounted on /cdrom, type:

```
$ umount /cdrom (RET)
```

NOTES: As with unmounting any kind of filesystem, make sure that none of the files on the disc are in use, or else you won't be able to unmount it. For example, if the current working directory in a shell is somewhere inside the /cdrom directory tree, you won't be able to unmount the data CD until you change to a different directory.

## CHAPTER 25

Printing

The usual way to print on a Linux system is to send a print job to the printer with `lpr`, as described in Recipe 25.1.1 [Sending a Print Job to the Printer], page 510.

But you won't always send a file straight to the printer—sometimes you may want to add special things to it before you print, such as headers or graphic trim. Or you might want to split a text file into pages and add a header to the top of each page containing the file name and page number; all of this is described in Chapter 13 [Formatting Text], page 305.

Sometimes you may need to convert or otherwise prepare a file so that it can be printed on your particular printer, since not all print hardware can print the same kinds of file formats. Recipes in this chapter show how to do this, such as how to convert PostScript files so that they will print properly on a non-PostScript printer (see Recipe 25.3 [Preparing Files for Printing], page 518).

This chapter also shows how to format PostScript files for printing. To convert plain text to PostScript and enhance it for printing, by adding fonts, graphic headers, and the like, see Recipe 15.2 [Outputting Text to PostScript], page 359.

This chapter isn't in the files section of the book because you can print things that aren't in a file—for example, you can pipe the output of another tool or series of tools to `lpr`, and it will spool that command output to the printer. This usage is actually very common.

25.1 Making and Managing Print Jobs

The traditional way to print on Linux-based systems is to send a *print job* for the file or data you want to print to the *spool queue* for the printer in question. The spool queue contains all of the print jobs sent to it by all users; these jobs are released in turn to the printer device as it becomes available. In this way, Linux can handle multiple print jobs going to the same printer at once.

The following recipes show how to make and manage print jobs. In practice, you will probably send print jobs all the time—since this is the way most printing is done in Linux—and use the tools for listing or canceling print jobs rarely. But sometimes things do go wrong, and it helps to know what to do when that happens.

25.1.1 Sending a Print Job to the Printer

Use `lpr` to send a print job to the printer—give the name of the file to print as an argument. (You can also pipe the output of a command to `lpr`.)

`lpr` writes a copy of the specified file or text to the spool queue of the specified printer, to be sent to the printer when the printer becomes available.

⇒ Here are some ways to use this.

- To print the file `invoice`, type:

    `$ lpr invoice` ⟨RET⟩

- To type a message with `banner` and send it to the printer, type:

    `$ banner "Bon voyage!" | lpr` ⟨RET⟩

- To print a verbose, recursive listing of the `/usr/doc/HOWTO` directory, type:

    `$ ls -lR /usr/doc/HOWTO | lpr` ⟨RET⟩

If you have more than one printer connected to your system, specify the printer to send to as an argument to the `-P` option. (Printers have names just as user accounts and hosts do, and it is the administrator's privilege to name them; the default printer is usually called `lp`, for "line printer.")

⇒ To send the file `nightly-report` to the printer called `statomatic`, type:

`$ lpr -P statomatic nightly-report` ⟨RET⟩

NOTES: The name of the `lpr` tool comes from "line printer," which was the kind of printer hardware in popular use back when this program was first developed.

25.1.2 Printing Multiple Copies of a Job

To print more than one copy of a print job, give the number of copies to print as an argument to the `-#` option of `lpr`.

⇒ To print a dozen copies of the file `nightly-report`, type:

`$ lpr -#12 nightly-report` ⟨RET⟩

25.1.3 Listing Your Print Jobs

To list your print jobs, use `lpq`, the "line printer queue" tool. It outputs a list of all print jobs currently in the default printer's spool queue, each on a line of its own, giving its rank in the queue, the username that sent the job, the print job number, the file names in the job, and the size of the data to be printed, in bytes.

⇒ To view the spool queue for the default printer, type:

```
$ lpq ⟨RET⟩
lp is ready and printing
Rank    Owner     Job  Files                         Total Size
active  groucho    83  cigar.ps                   1739030 bytes
1st     harpo      84  harp.ps                        499 bytes
2nd     chico      85  love.ps                      45576 bytes
$
```

In this example, there are three jobs queued for the default printer—one by user **groucho**, for the file **cigar.ps**, one by user **harpo**, for the file **harp.ps**, and one by user **chico**, who has printed a file called **love.ps**.

The job by user **groucho** is the *active job*; this is the job that is currently printing on the printer. The other jobs must wait until this file is finished printing, and then they print in rank order.

As with **lpr**, you can specify the name of a printer as an argument to the **-P** option.

⇒ To view the spool queue for the printer called **statomatic**, type:

    `$ lpq -P statomatic ⟨RET⟩`

To only list the jobs for a particular user, give the name of the user as an argument.

⇒ To list the print jobs for user **harpo**, type:

    `$ lpq harpo ⟨RET⟩`

NOTES: When there are no print jobs, **lpq** outputs the text "**no entries**."

25.1.4 Canceling a Print Job

To cancel a print job and remove it from the spool queue, use **lprm**, the "line printer remove" tool. If you accidentally sent something to the printer (or, in some application, accidentally hit a "print" button), you can stop it from printing by just running **lprm** with no options. This removes your active job.

⇒ To cancel your current print job, type:

    `$ lprm ⟨RET⟩`

When **lprm** cancels a job, it outputs the names of any print files that have been dequeued and removed (a single print job is usually listed in two lines). If you don't have a print job to cancel, **lprm** will report nothing.

You can also cancel a print job by its job number. To do this, give as an argument the number of the print job to remove.

⇒ To cancel print job 83, type:

    $ lprm 83 ⟨RET⟩

To cancel *all* of your print jobs in the spool queue, use a hyphen instead of the number of a print job. This is good for when you've sent several jobs to the printer but you want to cancel them.

⇒ To cancel all of your print jobs, type:

    $ lprm - ⟨RET⟩

NOTES: If you try to cancel an active job—one that has already been spooled to the printer—don't be alarmed if some pages still print; the printer probably has some of the job in its internal print buffer. To stop the printing in a case like this, take the printer offline, reset it, and then put it back online again (the printer will usually have buttons for these commands on its front control panel).

25.2 Other Things You Can Print

Another way of printing, besides making a print job, is to print from within an application.

Not all applications have print controls, but some of them do, including Emacs and LyX (see Recipe 15.4 [Using LyX], page 378). Their print commands essentially send the print job to the printer via `lpr`, after possibly formatting or otherwise preparing the data to print. If you are working in such an application and want to print your work, it can be more convenient to use the built-in print control than going to a shell to run `lpr`.

For example, to print the current document in the LyX document-processing application, choose **Print** from the **File** menu; it creates the proper output for your printer and makes a print job containing this output (see Recipe 15.4 [Using LyX], page 378).

Some tools, such as `dvips` and `enscript` (see Recipe 15.2 [Outputting Text to PostScript], page 359), are also configured to spool output to the printer.

You can view these print jobs in the spool queue and you can cancel them, just as you could any print job.

25.2.1 Printing a Printer Test Strip

It is sometimes useful to test your printer setup, both the configuration of the print system and the printer hardware itself. Use `lptest` to do this. It generates a traditional printer test pattern consisting of all 96 printable ASCII characters, on lines of 79 characters wide. The pattern is repeated over 200 lines, and in such a way so that the characters are staggered by one space from line to line. The effect is like a wave or banded ripple, and so it's called a *ripple pattern*.

By default, `lptest` outputs to the standard output. It's a good idea to run it once to see the output it generates, so you'll know what to expect from the printer.

⇒ Here are some ways to use this.

- To see the ripple pattern output by `lptest`, type:

    $ *lptest* ⟨RET⟩

- To send a test pattern to the default printer, type:

    $ *lptest | lpr* ⟨RET⟩

- To send a test pattern to the printer named **production**, type:

    $ *lptest | lpr -Pproduction* ⟨RET⟩

To specify the line width, give the new width as an argument.

⇒ To send a test pattern printing at 120 characters per line to the printer named **machine_room**, type:

    $ *lptest 120 | lpr -Pmachine_room* ⟨RET⟩

You can also specify the number of lines to output; do this by giving the new number as a second argument. This is useful for writing some "dummy" data to a file, when you need some.

⇒ To write a ripple pattern ten lines long, with 25 characters per line, to the file **testing**, type:

    $ *lptest 25 10 > testing* ⟨RET⟩

25.2.2 Printing Certain Pages of a PostScript File

PSUtils
 DEB: psutils
 RPM: psutils
 WWW: http://www.ctan.org/tex-archive/support/psutils/

To print only certain pages of a PostScript file, specify those pages with psselect and pipe the output to lpr (see Recipe 20.1.2 [Extracting Pages from a PostScript File], page 452). This is useful for when you have a very large file to print and you want to send it to the printer in sections.

⇒ Here are two ways to use this.

- To print pages 1 through 100 from the file input.ps, type:

  `$ psselect -p1-100 input.ps | lpr` (RET)

- To print four copies of pages 1 through 100 from the file input.ps, type:

  `$ psselect -p1-100 input.ps | lpr -#4` (RET)

25.2.3 Printing an Image

The most surefire way to print an image file is to view the file in the GIMP and select Print, an option on the File menu. This gives you the most control in printing: You can adjust the page size and orientation, brightness, and other options. You can also print it to a file (see Recipe 18.3 [Using the GIMP], page 434).

25.2.4 Printing a Web Page

There are a few nice methods for printing Web pages.

METHOD #1

Printing a Web page is usually done with Mozilla or another graphical Web browser.

In Mozilla, select Print from the File menu, or type (ALT)-(P) while Mozilla is displaying the page you want to print. You can choose paper size, color, page order, and margins; you can also select the printer device, or print the page to a PostScript file (see Recipe 33.1 [Using Mozilla], page 638).

This is the common method.

METHOD #2

To print the contents of a Web page with lpr, use lynx with the -dump option to pass the contents directly to lpr, or optionally through other filters or commands.

⇒ Here are some ways to use this.

- To print the URL `http://chem.example.edu/polymer99.ps`, which is a PostScript file, type:

    `$ lynx -dump http://chem.example.edu/polymer99.ps | lpr` (RET)

- To print the URL `http://chem.example.edu/info.txt`, which is a text file, type:

    `$ lynx -dump http://chem.example.edu/info.txt | lpr` (RET)

- To print URL `http://chem.example.edu/schedule.txt`, a text file, in Palatino bold text 20 points wide and ten points high, type (all on one line):

    `$ lynx -dump http://chem.example.edu/schedule.txt | enscript`
    `-B -f Palatino-Bold@20/10 -o - | lpr` (RET)

NOTES: This is also a good method for sending the contents of a Web page through any number of filters or pipelines in general.

METHOD #3

When in `lynx`, press (P) when on the page you want to print. This will bring up a new page, giving the URL of the page you were viewing and telling you the number of lines it contains and the number of physical pages it makes when printed. You will also be given four options: `Save to a local file`, `Mail the file`, `Print to the screen`, and `Print out on a printer attached to your vt100 terminal`. The last option will send it to the printer.

If you save to a local file, a plain text file will be written to the current directory with the name you specify. You can then process and print that file.

25.2.5 Printing a DVI File

DVIPS
 DEB: tetex-bin
 RPM: tetex-dvips
 WWW: http://www.radicaleye.com/dvips.html

You can print a DVI file directly with the `dvips` tool—omit the `-o` option that is used to specify an output file, and it will send the PostScript output directly to the spool queue of the default printer.

⇒ To print the DVI file `list.dvi`, type:

    `$ dvips list.dvi` (RET)

The following table lists some of dvips's options for controlling print output.

-A	Print only odd-numbered pages (DVI file must have been generated by TEX for this option).
-B	Print only even-numbered pages (DVI file must have been generated by TEX for this option).
-b *copies*	Specify the number of copies to print—useful for printing multiple copies of flyers, posters, signs, and the like.
-k	Print crop marks.
-l *last*	Specify the last page number to print.
-m	Use the manual feed tray.
-p *first*	Specify the first page to begin printing from.
-r	Reverse the order of the pages.
-t *format*	Specify paper size and format; valid options include "letter," "legal," "a4," and "landscape." (You can use this option twice, say to specify both "legal" and "landscape".)

Using the -m option, and specifying landscape as the paper format with the -t option, is very useful for printing on envelopes.

⇒ To print the file `envelope.dvi` on an envelope loaded in the manual feed tray of the default printer, type:

    $ dvips -m -t landscape envelope.dvi (RET)

NOTES: You can also print DVI files with `lpr` using the -d option.

25.2.6 Printing an Emacs Buffer

You can print a buffer from within Emacs, printing either the entire buffer or just the region. There are several methods.

METHOD #1

To print the current buffer in Emacs, choose **Print Buffer** from the **Print** submenu, found on the **Tools** menu on the menu bar. Another option on the print submenu is **Print Region**, which just prints the text between point and the mark (see Recipe 10.1.1 [Getting Acquainted with Emacs], page 232). Both commands print the hardcopy output separated into pages, with headers at the top of each page showing the file name and current page number.

METHOD #2

To generate and print a PostScript image of the buffer, use the **ps-print-buffer** function, which is also available on the **Print** submenu. A related function, **ps-print-region**, prints a PostScript image of the region. These commands are useful for sending the text of a buffer to a PostScript printer.

⇒ To send the current Emacs buffer to the default printer as a PostScript file, type:

⟨ALT⟩-⟨X⟩ *ps-print-buffer* ⟨RET⟩

METHOD #3

You can also run any of the aforementioned print functions by specifying them with the ⟨ALT⟩-⟨X⟩ command. Additionally, the **lpr-buffer** and **lpr-region** functions send the buffer and region to **lpr** without paginating the text or inserting headers.

⇒ Here are some ways to use this.

- To print the current buffer with page numbers and headers, type:

    ⟨ALT⟩-⟨X⟩ *print-buffer* ⟨RET⟩

- To print the current buffer with no additional print formatting done to the text, type:

    ⟨ALT⟩-⟨X⟩ *lpr-buffer* ⟨RET⟩

- To print a PostScript image of the current buffer, type:

    ⟨ALT⟩-⟨X⟩ *ps-print-buffer* ⟨RET⟩

25.2.7 Printing an Info Node

When you are running **info**, the hypertext Info viewer, you can print the current node by running the **print-node** function.

⇒ To print the current node in Info, type:

⟨ALT⟩-⟨X⟩ *print-node* ⟨RET⟩

25.2.8 Printing the Contents of a Terminal Window

To print the contents of an `xterm` window in X, press and hold ⟨CTRL⟩ and left-click anywhere inside the window, and then choose the `Print Window` option. This command will send a copy of all the text in the current window to the default printer.

25.3 Preparing Files for Printing

Strictly speaking, these are file conversions, but they are most often used for printing to certain devices. Not all printers recognize all output formats, so it's sometimes necessary to convert files before you print them.

Normally, you can print plain text on any printer. However, most graphics or image files must be converted to PostScript or EPS ("Encapsulated PostScript"). Some applications, such as TEX, produce DVI output; in this case, you should convert that to PostScript for printing.

If you have a PostScript printer, you can print PostScript files directly to it. If not, you'll need to convert the PostScript output to a format your printer uses. Filter programs like `magicfilter` make the conversion easier by doing this work for you, but they're not a panacea, since your system may use one of many print filters. Hence, the need for the following recipes.

25.3.1 Preparing a PostScript File for Printing

Ghostscript
  DEB: gs-common
       gs
  RPM: ghostscript
  WWW: http://www.cs.wisc.edu/~ghost/

If you don't have a PostScript printer, you can use Ghostscript, **gs**, to convert PostScript to an output format that your printer understands.

Use the `-?` option to list the printers that the version of **gs** installed on your system can write output for.

⇒ To list the available printer formats, type:

```
$ gs -? ⟨RET⟩
GNU Ghostscript 5.10 (1998-12-17)
...more output messages...
Input formats: PostScript PostScriptLevel1 PostScriptLevel2 PDF
Available devices:
   x11 x11alpha x11cmyk x11gray2 x11mono lvga256 vgalib
   t4693d8 tek4696 appledmp ccr lp2563 lbp8 lips3 m8510
   oki182 okiibm la50 la70 la75 la75plus sxlcrt deskjet
   djet500 laserjet ljetplus ljet2p ljet3 ljet4 declj250
   cdeskjet cdjcolor cdjmono cdj550 cdj500 djet500c
   hpdj uniprint epson eps9mid eps9high epsonc lq850
   ap3250 ibmpro bj10e bj200 bjc600 bjc800 ljet3d faxg3
   faxg32d faxg4 dfaxhigh dfaxlow pcxmono pcxgray pbm
   pbmraw pgm pgmraw pgnm pgnmraw pnm pnmraw ppm ppmraw
   pkm pkmraw tiffcrle tiffg3 tiffg32d tiffg4 psmono
   psgray jpeg
...more output messages...
$
```

A typical **gs** installation can write to more than 100 different print devices, including HP LaserJet 4 printers ("`ljet4`"), HP Color Deskjets ("`cdeskjet`"), and Group 4 fax ("`tiffg4`"). Newer versions of **gs** will have better support for newer printers, so make sure that you have a recent version installed if you have a new model printer.

gs takes the file to convert as an argument; give the device to write output for as an argument to the `-sDEVICE=` option, and give the name of the file to write to as an argument to the `-sOutputFile=` option.

Two additional options are commonly used: `-dSAFER`, which prevents the accidental deleting or overwriting of files, and `-dNOPAUSE`, which turns off the pause between pages.

When the conversion is complete, you will be at the **gs** prompt; type `quit` to exit.

⇒ To convert the file **tiger.ps** to a format suitable for printing on an HP Color Deskjet 500 printer, type (all on one line):

```
$ gs -sDEVICE=cdj500 -sOutputFile=tiger.dj -dSAFER
-dNOPAUSE tiger.ps < /dev/null ⟨RET⟩
```

This command writes the output to a file, `tiger.dj`, which you can spool as a print job with `lpr` to print it.

25.3.2 Preparing a DVI File for Printing

DVIPS
  DEB: `tetex-bin`
  RPM: `tetex-dvips`
  WWW: `http://www.radicaleye.com/dvips.html`

To convert a file from DVI format to PostScript, use `dvips`. It takes the file to convert as an argument; give the name of the PostScript file to write to as an argument to the `-o` option.

⇒ To convert the file `abstract.dvi` to PostScript, type:

> `$ dvips -o abstract.ps abstract.dvi` (RET)

This command reads the DVI file `abstract.dvi` and writes a PostScript version of it to the file `abstract.ps`; the original file is not altered.

To write only certain pages of a DVI file to the PostScript output, give the page or pages as arguments to the `-pp` option.

⇒ Here are some ways to use this.

- To output only pages 14 and 36 from file `abstract.dvi` to a PostScript file, 'codeabstract.ps, type:

  > `$ dvips -pp14,36 -o abstract.ps abstract.dvi` (RET)

- To output pages 2 through 100 from file `abstract.dvi` to a PostScript file, `abstract.ps`, type:

  > `$ dvips -pp2-100 -o abstract.ps abstract.dvi` (RET)

- To output page 1 and pages 5 through 20 from file `abstract.dvi` to a PostScript file, `abstract.ps`, type:

  > `$ dvips -pp1,5-20 -o abstract.ps abstract.dvi` (RET)

To specify an output paper size, give it as an argument to the `-t` option; if you have a PostScript printer, you can also send the output directly to the printer (see Recipe 25.2.5 [Printing a DVI File], page 515).

⇒ Here are two ways to use this.

- To output the file `abstract.dvi` as a PostScript file, `abstract.ps`, with a paper size of "`legal`," type:

  > `$ dvips -t legal -o abstract.ps abstract.dvi` (RET)

- To print the file **abstract.dvi** to the default printer in landscape mode, type:

  $ *dvips -t landscape abstract.dvi* ⟨RET⟩

Use the **-P** option with **dvips** to specify the printer name to write output to—use this option to make output for non-PostScript printers. For example, to convert TEX and LATEX files to PDF, use **dvips** and give "**pdf**" as an argument to the **-P** option.

⇒ To generate a PDF file from the DVI file **abstract.dvi**, type:

  $ *dvips -Ppdf -o abstract.pdf abstract.dvi* ⟨RET⟩

This command writes a new file, **abstract.pdf**, in PDF format.

NOTES: This type of conversion is not only useful for print preparation. Once the DVI file is converted to PostScript, you can then convert the PostScript to other formats, such as plain text or PDF—see Recipe 20.3 [Converting PostScript], page 459.

25.3.3 Preparing a PDF File for Printing

Xpdf
  DEB: xpdf-common
      xpdf-reader
  RPM: xpdf
  WWW: http://www.foolabs.com/xpdf/

Ghostscript
  DEB: gs-common
      gs
  RPM: ghostscript
  WWW: http://www.cs.wisc.edu/~ghost/

There are at least two ways to convert and print a file that's in Adobe's Portable Document Format (PDF), usually marked with a **.pdf** file name extension.

The first way is to view the file in **xpdf** (the PDF file viewer), and then left-click the printer icon. This won't actually send the file to the printer, but it writes a PostScript file in the same directory, with the same base file name as the PDF file but with a **.ps** extension. You can then print this file with **lpr** or convert it to another format (see Recipe 25.3.1 [Preparing a PostScript File for Printing], page 518).

The second way is to use **pdf2ps**, part of the **gs** package, to convert the PDF file to PostScript (to then print the PostScript output as described for **xpdf** above). **pdf2ps** takes two arguments: the name of the PDF file to convert, and the name of the PostScript file to write to.

⇒ To convert the PDF file `pricelist.pdf`, type:

> `$ pdf2ps pricelist.pdf pricelist.ps` ⟨RET⟩

This command writes a PostScript file `pricelist.ps` in the current directory.

25.3.4 Preparing a Manual Page for Printing

To convert a **man** page to output that is suitable for printing, use **man** with the **-T** option, giving "**ps**" as an argument to output PostScript. Either pipe the output to **lpr** (if you have a PostScript printer), or save it to a file that you can then convert for your printer.

⇒ Here are some ways to use this.

- To print the **man** page for **convert** to a PostScript printer, type:

  > `$ man -Tps convert | lpr` ⟨RET⟩

- To print the **man** page for **convert** to a PostScript printer, type:

  > `$ man -Tps convert | lpr` ⟨RET⟩

- To preview the **man** page for **convert** as PostScript, type:

  > `$ man -Tps convert | gv -` ⟨RET⟩

- To output the **man** page for **psbook** to the file **psbook.ps**, type:

  > `$ man -Tps psbook > psbook.ps` ⟨RET⟩

In the last example, you can then use **gs** to convert the file to a format your non-PostScript printer understands (see Recipe 25.3.1 [Preparing a PostScript File for Printing], page 518).

NOTES: A manual "page" can actually contain more than one physical page; the output will have as many pages as necessary to print it.

25.3.5 Preparing Text for Printing

There are many ways to prepare text for printing. You can paginate text and control other formatting, as described in Chapter 13 [Formatting Text], page 305. Then you can use **enscript** to convert the text to PostScript, and print that. This is good for printing text in a font; you can also select certain pages to print, including a range of pages or just even- or odd-numbered pages.

There are two methods worth noting for preparing etexts for printing.

METHOD #1

Etext filter
 WWW: `http://dsl.org/comp/enscript/`

Use the "**etext**" filter for **enscript** to convert an etext to PostScript. This takes a plain text file written with etext conventions, including etext-style italics (see Recipe 13.9 [Underlining Text], page 327), converts the italics, and writes a PostScript file as output.

⇒ To convert the etext `youth.txt` to PostScript, type:

```
$ enscript -Eetext -B -f "Times-Roman12" -o youth.ps youth.txt  (RET)
```

METHOD #2

Txt2html
 DEB: `txt2html`
 RPM: `txt2html`
 WWW: `http://txt2html.sourceforge.net/`

To convert plain text to PostScript for printing—whether the text is written with etext conventions or not—first use **txt2html** to convert the text to HTML, and then print the text from a Web browser, as described in Recipe 25.2.4 [Printing a Web Page], page 514.

⇒ To prepare the file **essays** for printing, type:

```
$ txt2html essays > essays.html  (RET)
```

This command writes a new file, **essays.html**, that you can then print with a Web browser.

NOTES: You could also convert the text to LaTeX with **txt2tex** (see Recipe 15.7 [Using Other Word Processors and Typesetting Systems], page 391).

## CHAPTER 26

Cross-Platform Conversions

Sometimes, it's inevitable—through no choice of your own, you must deal with a disk from another operating system, or a file with data stored in a proprietary format from one of those systems.

The recipes in this chapter are about converting data from other platforms—reading disks from DOS, Windows, and MacOS systems, and converting DOS text and Microsoft Word files.

To convert image files between formats, see Recipe 18.2 [Converting Image Files], page 432, and to convert audio files between formats, see Recipe 23.3 [Converting Sound Files], page 493.

26.1 Using DOS and Windows Disks

Mtools
  DEB: `mtools`
  RPM: `mtools`
  WWW: `http://mtools.linux.lu/`

The `mtools` package package provides a collection of tools to facilitate the manipulation of MS-DOS files. These tools allow you to use and manipulate MS-DOS disks (usually floppies, but Jaz and Zip drives are supported, too) without mounting them; they can handle the extensions to the MS-DOS format that are used by the different Microsoft Windows operating systems, including Windows NT.

The following recipes describe how to use some of the tools in this package to get directory listings of MS-DOS disks, copy files to and from them, delete files on them, and even format them. They're similar in use and syntax to the equivalent MS-DOS commands.

You can also mount DOS and Windows disks (see Recipe 26.3 [Mounting Windows and NT partitions], page 529).

26.1.1 Listing the Contents of a DOS Disk

Use `mdir` to get a directory listing of a DOS disk. Give as an argument the "drive letter" of the disk to read, as used by DOS. For example, to specify the primary floppy drive, use "A:" as the drive to read, and use "B:" to specify the secondary floppy drive.

⇒ To get a directory listing of the DOS disk currently in the primary floppy drive, type:

     `$ mdir a:` ⟨RET⟩

26.1.2 Copying Files to and from a DOS Disk

Use `mcopy` to copy files to and from a DOS disk.

     To copy a file *to* a DOS disk, give as arguments the name of the source file to copy and the "drive letter" of the disk to copy it to.

⇒ To copy the file **readme.txt** to the DOS disk in the primary floppy drive, type:

     `$ mcopy readme.txt a:` ⟨RET⟩

     To copy a file *from* a DOS disk, give the "drive letter" of the disk to copy from, followed by the file name to copy, and no other arguments; `mcopy` will copy the specified file to the current directory.

⇒ To copy the file **resume.doc** from the DOS disk in the secondary floppy drive to the current directory, type:

     `$ mcopy b:resume.doc` ⟨RET⟩

     To copy all files from a DOS disk, just give the "drive letter" without any file names.

⇒ To copy all of the files and directories from the DOS disk in the primary floppy drive to the current directory, type:

     `$ mcopy a:` ⟨RET⟩

26.1.3 Deleting Files on a DOS Disk

Use `mdel` to delete a file on a DOS disk. Give as an argument the name of the file to delete preceded by the "drive letter" of the disk to delete from.

⇒ To delete the file **resume.doc** on the DOS disk in the primary floppy drive, type:

     `$ mdel a:resume.doc` ⟨RET⟩

26.1.4 Formatting a DOS Disk

To format a floppy disk for DOS, writing an empty MS-DOS filesystem to the disk in the process, use `mformat`. Give as an argument the "drive letter" of the disk to format. (Remember, when you format a disk, any existing information contained on the disk is lost.)

⇒ To format the floppy disk in the primary floppy drive so that it can be
used with MS-DOS, type:

> $ mformat a: ⟨RET⟩

NOTES: If you want to use a floppy disk with your Linux system and don't
need DOS compatibility, don't bother using this MS-DOS format—the native
Linux format is much more efficient (see Recipe 24.3.1 [Formatting a Floppy
Disk], page 504). If you know how long a DOS format takes, you'll be amazed
at how much faster the Linux formatting is—it will be done so fast you'll think
it didn't even work!

26.2 Using Macintosh Disks

Hfsutils
  DEB: hfsutils
  RPM: hfsutils
  WWW: http://www.mars.org/home/rob/proj/hfs/

Apple Macintosh computers use a filesystem called the "Hierarchical File System," or HFS. If your kernel has support for the HFS filesystem, you can mount
disks from these systems by using **mount** and specifying "**hfs**" as an argument
to the **-t** option (see Recipe 24.3.2 [Mounting a Floppy Disk], page 504).

You can also use these disks with the **hfsutils** package, which contains
a set of tools for reading from and writing to HFS filesystems. The following
recipes describe the use of the individual tools in this package.

26.2.1 Specifying the Macintosh Disk to Use

To use a Macintosh disk with any of the **hfsutils** commands, you must first
use **hmount** to specify the location of the HFS filesystem. Give as an argument
the name of the Linux device file where the HFS filesystem exists; this virtually
"mounts" the disk for use with the other commands described in this section.

The device file for the first floppy drive is **/dev/fd0**, and for the second
drive, **/dev/fd1**. Any valid device name, such as a SCSI device or Zip disk,
may be given.

⇒ To introduce the floppy disk in the first floppy drive as an HFS volume
for the **hfsutils**, type:

> $ hmount /dev/fd0 ⟨RET⟩

After you run this command, the other tools in the **hfsutils** package will
work on the Macintosh disk in the first floppy drive.

26.2.2 Listing the Contents of a Macintosh Disk

Use `hls` to get a directory listing of the Macintosh disk currently specified with `hmount` (see the preceding recipe).

⇒ To get a directory listing of the currently specified Macintosh disk, type:

> `$ hls` (RET)

Give the name of a directory as a quoted argument to list just that directory.

⇒ To get a directory listing of the **Desktop Folder** directory in the currently specified Macintosh disk, type:

> `$ hls 'Desktop Folder'` (RET)

26.2.3 Copying Files to and from a Macintosh Disk

Use `hcopy` to copy files to and from the Macintosh disk currently specified with `hmount` (see Recipe 26.2.1 [Specifying the Macintosh Disk to Use], page 527).

To copy a file *to* a Macintosh disk, give as arguments the name of the source file to copy and the quoted name of the target directory on the Macintosh disk.

⇒ To copy the file **readme.txt** to the **Desktop Folder** directory in the current Macintosh disk, type:

> `$ hcopy readme.txt 'Desktop Folder'` (RET)

To copy a file *from* a Macintosh disk, give two arguments: the name of the directory and the file to copy as a quoted argument, and the name of the Linux target directory to copy to. Remember that MacOS uses the colon character (`:`) as the separator on the path.

⇒ To copy the file **Desktop Folder:Readme** from the current Mac disk to the current directory, type:

> `$ hcopy 'Desktop Folder:Readme' .` (RET)

26.2.4 Deleting Files on a Macintosh Disk

Use `hdel` to delete a file on the Macintosh disk currently specified with `hmount` (see Recipe 26.2.1 [Specifying the Macintosh Disk to Use], page 527). Give as a quoted argument the path name of the file to delete. It deletes both the resource fork and the data fork of the files you specify.

⇒ To delete the file **Desktop Folder:Readme** on the current Macintosh disk, type:

> `$ hdel 'Desktop Folder:Readme'` (RET)

26.2.5 Formatting a Macintosh Disk

To format a disk for the Macintosh, writing an empty HFS filesystem to the disk, use `hformat`. Give as an argument the Linux device file of the disk drive; for example, the device file for the first floppy drive is `/dev/fd0`, and the second drive is `/dev/fd1`.

⇒ To format the disk in the first floppy drive with a Macintosh HFS filesystem, type:

> `$ hformat /dev/fd0` (RET)

If the disk currently has a partition on it, this command won't work; use the `-f` option to *force* the format, thus erasing any existing partition and data the disk contains.

Give a label for the drive as a quoted argument to the `-l` option. The label name can't contain a colon character (`:`).

⇒ Here are two ways to use this.

- To format the disk in the first floppy drive with a Macintosh HFS filesystem, overwriting any existing Macintosh filesystem, type:

  > `$ hformat -f /dev/fd0` (RET)

- To format the disk in the second floppy drive with a Macintosh HFS filesystem, giving it a volume label of "`Work Disk`," type:

  > `$ hformat -l 'Work Disk' /dev/fd1` (RET)

When a disk has multiple partitions, give the number of the partition to format as an additional argument. To format the entire medium, give "0" as the partition to use.

⇒ Here are two ways to use this.

- To format the second partition of the SCSI disk at `/dev/sd2` with a Macintosh HFS filesystem, type:

  > `$ hformat /dev/sd2 2` (RET)

- To format the *entire* SCSI disk at `/dev/sd2` with a Macintosh HFS filesystem, overwriting any existing Macintosh filesystem and giving it a label of "`Joe's Work Disk`," type:

  > `$ hformat -f -l "Joe's Work Disk" /dev/sd2 0` (RET)

26.3 Mounting Windows and NT partitions

Windows partitions can be mounted if your Linux kernel has support for the VFAT filesystem, and NT partitions can be mounted (read-only) if your kernel has support for the NTFS filesystem.

⇒ To mount the Windows partition at the /dev/hdd1 device on /home/roger/mywin, type:

$ mount -t vfat /dev/hdd1 /home/roger/mywin ⟨RET⟩

The command in the preceding example makes the Windows partition at /dev/hdd1 available to Linux in the /home/roger/mywin directory.

⇒ To mount the Windows NT partition at the /dev/hea1 device on /mnt, type:

$ mount -t ntfs /dev/hea1 /mnt ⟨RET⟩

The command in the preceding example makes the Windows NT partition at /dev/hea1 available to Linux as a read-only filesystem in the /mnt directory.

26.4 Converting Text Files Between DOS and Linux

In all versions of DOS (and all subsequent versions of Microsoft Windows), text files are normally written with both a carriage return character and a newline, both "invisible" control characters, to signify the end of each line. In Linux and other unices, text files have only the newline character.

In either of these operating systems, text files that originated from the other may display irregularly—in DOS and Windows, the lines of a Linux text file may appear to run together; in Linux, a DOS or Windows text file may have "^M" carriage return characters at the end of each line.

There are several methods for converting text between these two systems.

METHOD #1

Tofrodos
  DEB: sysutils
  RPM: tofrodos
  WWW: http://www.uni-kassel.de/hrz/server/Software/dos2unix/

The fromdos and todos tools allow you to convert text files between DOS and Linux.

To convert a text file from DOS to Linux, removing the "^M" newline characters in the file, use fromdos. It converts the file you give as an argument, removing the newline characters from the ends of all its lines.

To convert a text file from Linux to the convention used by DOS and Windows, use todos. It adds newline characters to the ends of all lines in the file you give as an argument.

⇒ Here are two ways to use this.

- To remove the newline characters from the text file **autoexec.bat**, type:

      $ *fromdos autoexec.bat* ⟨RET⟩

- To add newline characters to all of the text files with a **.tex** extension in the current directory, type:

      $ *todos *.tex* ⟨RET⟩

NOTES: Both commands write directly to the files you specify. To make a backup of the original file, use the **-b** option; before the conversion, this writes a copy of each specified file with a **.bak** file name extension.

METHOD #2

Use the **col** filter to filter out carriage returns from text, as described in Recipe 13.1.9 [Removing Carriage Return Characters], page 310.

⇒ To filter out the carriage returns from the file **README.TXT**, writing to a new file called **readme.txt**, type:

      $ *col < README.TXT > readme.txt* ⟨RET⟩

METHOD #3

Another way to convert text from DOS is to use the **tr** filter to delete the carriage returns (see Recipe 13.4 [Transposing Characters in Text], page 316).

⇒ To filter out the carriage returns from the file **dos-version.txt**, writing to the new file **unix-version.txt**, type:

      $ *tr -d '\r' < dos-version.txt > unix-version.txt* ⟨RET⟩

NOTES: To do the reverse of this—to convert text from UNIX to DOS—I have been told that simply opening the file in the DOS text editor program called EDIT, and then saving the file and exiting, will work. This will automatically add the requisite carriage returns to the end of each line.

26.5 Converting Microsoft Word Files

word2x
  DEB: word2x
  RPM: word2x
  WWW: http://word2x.sourceforge.net/

Use `word2x` to convert Microsoft Word files to a format you can read. It can convert files to two different formats: LaTeX and plain text.

Convert to LaTeX when the *layout* of the original document, including its formatting and font characteristics, is important. When you just need the complete *text* of the document, convert it to plain text. `word2x` can send its output to the standard output, so the latter conversion is useful for adding to a pipeline.

Word files usually have a `.doc` or `.DOC` extension, which you don't have to specify. For example, if the Word file you want to convert is called `resume.doc`, you can simply give `resume` as the source file. (But if there exists another file named `resume` in the same directory, this trick won't work).

If you don't specify an output file, `word2x` writes its output to a file with the same base file name and an appropriate extension for the output format. This is useful for converting a lot of Word files in the same directory—specifying a wildcard such as `*.doc` as the input and giving no output name will convert them all.

You can also set the maximum line width to be used in the output file; specify the width as an argument to the `-w` option.

The following recipes describe how to use `word2x` to convert Word files to LaTeX and plain text format.

NOTES: While `word2x` does a pretty good job of conversion, it won't convert any pictures embedded in Word documents.

There are other ways to read or convert Word files; see Recipe 26.8 [Using Other Cross-Platform Conversion Tools], page 535, for a list of other tools you can use for this purpose.

26.5.1 Converting Word to LaTeX

To convert a Word file to LaTeX format, use `word2x` and give "`latex`" as an argument to the `-f` option.

⇒ To convert the Word file `resume.doc` to LaTeX, type:

```
$ word2x -f latex resume.doc RET
```

This command writes a new file, `resume.ltx`, in the LaTeX format. You can then view, print, or convert the file to other formats—see Recipe 15.3.3 [Processing a LaTeX File], page 374. The original `resume.doc` file is unaltered.

⇒ To convert all of the .DOC Word files in the current directory to LaTeX files with maximum line widths of 40 characters, type:

    $ word2x -f latex -w 40 *.DOC ⟨RET⟩

26.5.2 Converting Word to Plain Text

To convert a Word file to plain text, use **word2x** and give "**text**" as an argument to the **-format** option.

⇒ To convert the Word file **resume.doc** to a plain text file called **resume**, type:

    $ word2x -f text resume.doc resume ⟨RET⟩

To send a conversion to the standard output, give a hyphen character (-) as the output file to use. This is useful for piping the plain text conversion to other tools that work on text, such as **grep**, a tool for searching text (see Recipe 14.1 [Searching Text for a Word], page 333).

⇒ To search the text of the Word file **resume.doc** for the string "**linux**," regardless of case, type:

    $ word2x resume.doc - | grep -i linux ⟨RET⟩

These commands convert the Word file **resume.doc** to text and output all lines of that text, if any, that contain the string "**linux**" regardless of case. The original **resume.doc** file is unaltered.

26.6 Converting Text from Proprietary Formats

Use Recipe 9.3.6 [Listing Text in Binary Files], page 228, to output any text strings saved in a file with a proprietary format. This does not always work because not all proprietary formats keep text in ASCII strings, but it's usually worth trying.

⇒ To peruse all of the ASCII strings in the file **HCX1010A.BIN**, type:

    $ strings HCX1010A.BIN | less ⟨RET⟩

26.7 Managing ZIP Archives

Unzip
  DEB: unzip
  RPM: unzip
  WWW: http://www.info-zip.org/

ZIP file compression takes one or more files and compresses them into a single new file with a `.zip` extension. This is what most people new to Linux or UNIX in general think of when they think of "file archives." But in the UNIX world, file archives and compression are separate tools, even though they usually go hand in hand. We make compressed `tar` archives (see Recipe 8.5 [Managing File Archives], page 199). And then we can compress these archives, or any other file, with `gzip` or `bzip2` (see Recipe 8.4 [Using File Compression], page 196).

When sending and receiving groups of files with people who use other operating systems, the ZIP archive format is usually used. The `zip` and `unzip` tools make and extract ZIP archives as done by the popular PKZIP tools for other operating systems.

The following recipes show how to use these tools.

26.7.1 Zipping Files

Use `zip` to make a ZIP archive of a file or group of files. It takes as arguments the name of the ZIP archive to create and the filespec to put in the archive.

Giving the `.zip` extension for the archive name is optional; if the archive already exists, the given files will be added to the archive.

⇒ Here are two ways to use this.

- To make a ZIP archive file, `zippy.zip`, containing all of the `.png` files in the current directory, type:

      $ zip zippy *.png (RET)

- To add all of the `.tiff` files in the current directory to an existing ZIP archive file, `zippy.zip`, type:

      $ zip zippy *.tiff (RET)

When specifying a directory, if you give just the directory name, only that directory (and not its contents) will be included in the archive. Specifying a wildcard in a directory will include the files it contains and any subdirectory names, but it will not travel into those subdirectories to include any files that may be contained there. Use the `-r` option to travel *recursively* into any specified directories, thus including its entire contents.

⇒ To make a ZIP archive `zippy.zip` containing all files in the current directory, type:

      $ zip zippy * (RET)

If the current directory contains any directories, those directory names are included in the ZIP archive, but not any of their contents.

⇒ To make a ZIP archive **zippy.zip** containing all files in the current directory, as well as all files in the **addons** directory, type:

```
$ zip zippy * addons/* RET
```

This command puts all files in the current directory in an archive called **zippy.zip**, to which it also adds all files in the **addons** directory, but it does not add the contents of any subdirectories that **addons** may contain.

⇒ To make a ZIP archive **zippy.zip** containing the entire **addons** directory tree, type:

```
$ zip zippy -r addons/* RET
```

26.7.2 Unzipping Files

Use **unzip** to unzip files stored in ZIP archives. Given the name of an archive as an argument, it extracts all the files that archive contains. As with **zip**, giving the .zip extension is optional.

⇒ To unzip all the files in the ZIP archive **blueprints.zip**, type:

```
$ unzip blueprints.zip RET
```

It is sometimes a good idea to take a look inside the ZIP archive first, to see what you are getting into by unzipping—if a ZIP archive contains a hundred files and you are not expecting them, it could be inconvenient to just unzip it first.

That's where the **-t** option comes in handy, and I use it all the time before unzipping an archive for real. This just *tests* the files contained in the archive to make sure that the archive file has not become corrupt. As **unzip** runs through the tests, it lists each file in the archive. None of the files are unzipped with this command.

⇒ To test the ZIP archive **blueprints.zip** for errors, thus listing all the files it contains, type:

```
$ unzip -t blueprints.zip RET
```

26.8 Using Other Cross-Platform Conversion Tools

There are more tools for converting files from other platforms into formats that you can use on Linux; the following table describes some of them.

AbiWord	WYSIWYG-style word processor that can read, display, and convert files from proprietary word processors, including Microsoft Word. DEB: `abiword-common` RPM: `abiword` WWW: `http://www.abisource.com/`
Antiword	Converts Microsoft Word files into something usable. DEB: `antiword` RPM: `antiword` WWW: `http://www.winfield.demon.nl/`
catdoc	Outputs text from Microsoft Word files. Includes `xls2csv`, a tool to output data from Microsoft Excel spreadsheets as comma-delimited text. DEB: `catdoc` RPM: `catdoc` WWW: `http://www.45.free.net/~vitus/ice/catdoc/`
ppthtml	Converts Microsoft PowerPoint files to HTML. DEB: `ppthtml` RPM: `xlhtml`
GNU Unrtf	Converts Microsoft's Rich Text Format (RTF) to something usable. DEB: `unrtf` RPM: `unrtf` WWW: `http://www.gnu.org/software/unrtf/unrtf.html`
wp2x	Converts WordPerfect files to something usable. DEB: `wp2x` WWW: `http://tinyurl.com/2lzcq`
wvWare	Converts and previews Microsoft Word files. DEB: `wv` RPM: `wv` WWW: `http://sourceforge.net/projects/wvware`

## CHAPTER 27

Reminders

When you spend a lot of time working on the system, it can be very useful to be reminded when you should be doing something else. You can have the system do this for you, and this chapter tells you how. It describes software tools that provide reminders of various kinds—clocks, calendars, address books, and tools for tracking appointments.

27.1 Displaying the Date and Time

Use `date` to output the current system date and time.

⇒ To output the current system date and time, type:

```
$ date (RET)
Thu Jul  1 10:09:57 EDT 2004
$
```

The default format of the output is to display the day of the week; the month name; the day of the month; the 24-hour time in hours, minutes, and seconds; the time zone; and the year.

Use the -u option to output the current date and time in GMT ("Greenwich Mean Time," also known today as "Coordinated Universal Time", or UTC).

⇒ To output the current date and time in UTC, type:

```
$ date -u (RET)
Thu,  1 Jul 2004 10:09:57 -0400
$
```

Use the -R option to output the date in the format described in RFC822 (see Recipe 11.4 [Word Lists and Reference Files], page 289): day of week followed by day of month, month name, year, time, and time zone in numeric format. This is the date format used in email messages.

⇒ To output the current date and time in RFC822 format, type:

```
$ date -R (RET)
Fri, 11 May 2001 11:10:29 -0400
$
```

You can also use the -d option to specify the precise fields to output, and the order in which to output them. One useful example is given in the next recipe; for more information, consult the **date man** page (see Recipe 2.8.4 [Reading a Page from the System Manual], page 46).

The **date** tool has many parameters for formatting the output, all of which are preceded with **+**. They are sometimes useful for putting into scripts. The following recipes describe a few.

NOTES: To ensure that the time on your system clock remains as accurate as possible, your system administrator should install the **chrony** package; it periodically adjusts the time on the system clock according to measurements obtained from time service servers on the Internet via "Network Time Protocol."

27.1.1 Displaying the Day of the Year

Use **date** with the **%j** format parameter to output the day of the year.

⇒ To display the current day of the year, type:

    `$ date +'%j'` ⟨RET⟩

To output the number of days a particular date is into the year, use **-d** with "'*DD MMM*' **+%j**," where *DD* is the day of the month and *MMM* is the name of the month.

⇒ To output the numeric day of the year that 21 June falls on in the current year, type:

```
$ date -d '21 Jun' +%j ⟨RET⟩
172
$
```

This command outputs the number 172, which indicates that June 21st of the current year is the 172nd day of the current calendar year.

27.1.2 Displaying the Minute of the Hour

To output the minute of the hour, use **date** with the "%M" format parameter.

⇒ To output the minute of the hour, type:

    `$ date +'%M'` ⟨RET⟩

27.2 Playing an Audible Time Announcement

Saytime
  DEB: `saytime`
  WWW: `http://www.acme.com/software/saytime/`

Use the **saytime** command to output the current system time in an audible message in a male voice. You must have a sound card installed on your system, and it must be set up with speakers or some other output mechanism at an appropriate volume level in order for you to hear it (see Recipe 21.1 [Adjusting the Audio Controls], page 463).

⇒ To hear the current system time, type:

    $ saytime ⟨RET⟩

NOTES: If you're feeling adventurous, you can record another voice—like your own—and use that voice instead of the default voice; the sound files used are Sun `.au` files, and they are kept in the **/usr/share/saytime** directory.

27.3 Using Calendars

The following recipes describe a few of the basic tools for displaying calendars in Linux.

27.3.1 Displaying a Calendar

The `cal` tool outputs a calendar to the standard output. By default, it outputs a calendar of the current month.

⇒ To output a calendar for the current month, type:

    $ cal ⟨RET⟩

Use the `-y` option to output a calendar for the current year.

⇒ Here are two ways to use this.

   • To output a calendar for the current year, type:

        $ cal -y ⟨RET⟩

   • To print a calendar for the current year to the default printer, type:

        cal -y | lpr ⟨RET⟩

To output a calendar for a specific year, give just the year as an option.

⇒ To output a calendar for the year 2012, type:

```
$ cal 2012 RET
                              2012

        January                February               March
Su Mo Tu We Th Fr Sa   Su Mo Tu We Th Fr Sa   Su Mo Tu We Th Fr Sa
 1  2  3  4  5  6  7             1  2  3  4                   1  2  3
 8  9 10 11 12 13 14    5  6  7  8  9 10 11    4  5  6  7  8  9 10
15 16 17 18 19 20 21   12 13 14 15 16 17 18   11 12 13 14 15 16 17
22 23 24 25 26 27 28   19 20 21 22 23 24 25   18 19 20 21 22 23 24
29 30 31               26 27 28 29            25 26 27 28 29 30 31

         April                  May                   June
Su Mo Tu We Th Fr Sa   Su Mo Tu We Th Fr Sa   Su Mo Tu We Th Fr Sa
 1  2  3  4  5  6  7          1  2  3  4  5                      1  2
 8  9 10 11 12 13 14    6  7  8  9 10 11 12    3  4  5  6  7  8  9
15 16 17 18 19 20 21   13 14 15 16 17 18 19   10 11 12 13 14 15 16
22 23 24 25 26 27 28   20 21 22 23 24 25 26   17 18 19 20 21 22 23
29 30                  27 28 29 30 31         24 25 26 27 28 29 30

          July                August              September
Su Mo Tu We Th Fr Sa   Su Mo Tu We Th Fr Sa   Su Mo Tu We Th Fr Sa
 1  2  3  4  5  6  7             1  2  3  4                         1
 8  9 10 11 12 13 14    5  6  7  8  9 10 11    2  3  4  5  6  7  8
15 16 17 18 19 20 21   12 13 14 15 16 17 18    9 10 11 12 13 14 15
22 23 24 25 26 27 28   19 20 21 22 23 24 25   16 17 18 19 20 21 22
29 30 31               26 27 28 29 30 31      23 24 25 26 27 28 29
                                              30
        October               November              December
Su Mo Tu We Th Fr Sa   Su Mo Tu We Th Fr Sa   Su Mo Tu We Th Fr Sa
    1  2  3  4  5  6             1  2  3                         1
 7  8  9 10 11 12 13    4  5  6  7  8  9 10    2  3  4  5  6  7  8
14 15 16 17 18 19 20   11 12 13 14 15 16 17    9 10 11 12 13 14 15
21 22 23 24 25 26 27   18 19 20 21 22 23 24   16 17 18 19 20 21 22
28 29 30 31            25 26 27 28 29 30      23 24 25 26 27 28 29
                                              30 31
$
```

The -j option displays Julian dates, numbered consecutively though the year, from January 1.

⇒ To output a calendar for the current month with Julian dates, type:

    $ `cal -j` ⟨RET⟩

To output a calendar for a specific month, give both the numeric month and year as arguments.

⇒ To output a calendar for the month of April 1945, type:

```
$ cal 04 1945 ⟨RET⟩
      April 1945
Su Mo Tu We Th Fr Sa
 1  2  3  4  5  6  7
 8  9 10 11 12 13 14
15 16 17 18 19 20 21
22 23 24 25 26 27 28
29 30

$
```

27.3.2 Displaying a Calendar in Emacs

Emacs comes with its own calendar service. The `calendar` function displays a three-month calendar in a new buffer—it gives the current, previous, and next months, and it puts point on the current date. To select the month and year to display, preface the `calendar` function with the `universal-argument` command, ⟨CTRL⟩-⟨U⟩.

⇒ Here are two ways to use this.

- While in Emacs, to display a three-month calendar for the current month and year, type:

    $ ⟨ALT⟩-⟨X⟩ `calendar` ⟨RET⟩

- While in Emacs, to display a three-month calendar for the month of August 2000, type:

```
⟨CTRL⟩-⟨U⟩ ⟨ALT⟩-⟨X⟩ calendar ⟨RET⟩

Year (>0): 2010 ⟨BKSP⟩ ⟨BKSP⟩ 00 ⟨RET⟩

Month name: Aug ⟨RET⟩
```

NOTES: When you display a calendar for a specific month and year, Emacs fills in the current year in the minibuffer. In the previous example, the current year was 2010, and (BKSP) was typed twice to erase the last two digits, which were replaced with "00" to make it the year 2000.

27.4 Managing Appointments

The `calendar` tool is a reminder service that you can use to manage your appointments. It reads a *calendar file*, which is a text file in the current directory containing a list of appointments and reminders; then it outputs those entries from the file that have today's or tomorrow's date. (On a Friday, it outputs entries for that weekend and for the following Monday.)

For example, if today is Friday, June 16, and you run `calendar` in the same directory as your calendar file, typical output might look like Figure 27-1.

```
$ calendar (RET)
6/16    Finish draft of book
        Party at Jack's
Fri     Lunch with Kim and Jim, 12:30
Mon     Book manuscript due
$
```

Figure 27-1. Typical `calendar` output.

The following are recipes for writing your calendar files, including other calendar files in your own calendar file, and for automating the delivery of your reminders.

NOTES: The `calendar` tool was a one-time staple of UNIX systems, and reportedly first appeared in Version 7 of AT&T UNIX. It was rewritten early on for the BSD family of UNIX. Although this BSD derivative is a standard inclusion on Debian systems, `calendar` isn't yet standard on all Linux distributions, and a source or binary of the tool can be difficult for users of other distributions to locate. I advise those users to download the source files for the Debian `bsdmainutils` package and to install `calendar` from there.

Emacs has its own equivalent to this tool, which it calls the "Diary." For more information on this feature, see the Emacs Info documentation (see Recipe 2.8.5 [Reading an Info Manual], page 48).

27.4.1 Making an Appointment File

To begin using `calendar`, you need to make a "calendar file" where you can enter your appointments. It's just a plain text file, and it can be called either `calendar` or `.calendar`; the latter makes it a "hidden" file, as described in Recipe 5.3.4 [Listing Hidden Files], page 138.

Write each appointment or calendar entry on a line by itself; blank lines in the file are ignored. When an appointment is over, remove its entry from this file. The format of a calendar entry is as follows:

> *date*   *tab or spaces*   *text of reminder itself*

Just about every common date style is recognized. For example, Figure 27-2 shows a listing of valid dates for the fourth of July.

```
7/4
July 4
4 July
Jul. 4
Jul 4
4 Jul.
4 Jul
```

Figure 27-2. Valid dates for the fourth of July.

Entries aren't constrained to a single day, either; you can have entries for a day of the week or for a certain month—"**Mon**" or "**Monday**" for every Monday; "**Jun**" or "**June**" for the first day of every June. You can use an asterisk as a wildcard: "***/13**" reminds you of something on the 13th of every month. When the date is omitted on a line, the date of the preceding appointment is assumed.

For example, suppose you have a file called `calendar` in your home directory that looks like Figure 27-3.

```
6/16    Finish draft of book
        Party at Jack's
6/20    Gallery reading
Fri     Lunch with Kim and Jim, 12:30
Mon     Book manuscript due
```

Figure 27-3. Typical `calendar` file.

If the current date is 16 June, a Friday, and you run `calendar` in your home directory, you'll get the same output as in Figure 27-1.

NOTES: In the preceding example, the entry for the party doesn't have a date on it—it used the date of the preceding entry, "6/16."

27.4.2 Including Holidays in Your Reminders

The `calendar` package comes with a collection of prepared calendar files for many kinds of holidays and other occasions, which you can reference in your own calendar file to include their entries in your own reminders. These prepared files are stored in **/usr/share/calendar**. The following table gives the name of each calendar file and describes its contents.

`calendar.birthday`	Births and deaths of famous people
`calendar.christian`	Christian holidays
`calendar.computer`	Significant dates in the history of computing
`calendar.history`	Dates of U.S. historical events
`calendar.holiday`	Standard and obscure holidays
`calendar.judaic`	Jewish holidays
`calendar.music`	Dates related to music, almost entirely rock and roll of the Baby Boomer generation
`calendar.usholiday`	U.S. holidays
`calendar.hindu`	Hindu holidays

To have `calendar` output dates from one of these files along with your usual appointments, put the following line in your calendar file, where *file* is the name of the particular calendar file you want to include:

```
#include <file>
```

These are called *includes*.

```
#include <calendar.usholiday>
#include <calendar.birthday>
```

Figure 27-4. Includes for `calendar`.

For example, to output both U.S. holidays and famous births and deaths when you run `calendar`, your calendar file would include the two lines given in Figure 27-4.

NOTES: You can, of course, share your own calendar files with other users; this is useful for making special calendars for a group or organization. If the calendar file is in the current directory or `/usr/share/calendar`, you can just give the file name; otherwise, give its full path name in the `include` statement.

27.4.3 Automatic Appointment Delivery

You can automate your appointment service so that your appointments and reminders are delivered each time you log in or start a new shell, or you can have the day's reminders emailed to you each morning.

Add `calendar` to your `.bashrc` file to output the day's appointments and reminders every time you log in or start a new shell (see Recipe 3.7.3 [Using Shell Startup Files], page 86).

If you keep your calendar file in a directory other than your home directory, make sure that `calendar` (the tool) is called from that directory. For example, if your calendar file is in your `~/doc/etc` directory, you'd put the following line in your `.bashrc` file:

```
cd ~/doc/etc; calendar; cd
```

To have the system send you the day's appointments in email, use `crontab` to schedule a daily CRON job that runs `calendar` and, if there is any output, mails it to you with `mail` (see Recipe 28.3 [Scheduling Commands], page 557).

To do this, add the following line to your `crontab` file (if you don't have one, just put this line in a text file called `crontab` somewhere in your home directory tree):

```
45 05 * * 1-5 calendar | mail -s 'Your Appointments' joe@example.org
```

The "45 05 * * 1-5" specifies that these commands be run at 5:45 a.m. on every weekday. The rest of the line is the series of actual commands that are run: The `calendar` tool is run on your personal calendar file, and if there is any output, it's mailed to joe@example.org (replace that with your actual email address, or with your username on your local system if you check mail there).

Add this new entry to the schedule by running the `crontab` tool with the name of your `crontab` file as an argument.

⇒ To add to the CRON schedule any new entries that are in the file `crontab`, type:

    $ crontab crontab (RET)

NOTES: The name of the command, `crontab`, is the same as the file it uses, `crontab`.

27.5 Using Contact Managers

Loosely put, a *contact manager* is a piece of software that helps you keep track of information about people you may need to contact in the future. In the past, people often called the physical embodiment of these things a "rolodex," which incidentally is a trademarked brand name for the Cadillac of such contact managers, the circular Rolodex that sat atop the desk of every successful 20th century businessman. I hear that many people use them even today.

There are many contact manager programs available; the following recipes show two of the best and easiest methods of managing contact information with Linux.

27.5.1 Keeping a Free-Form Address List

The simplest way to keep names and addresses in Linux is to keep them in a text file as a free-form address list; to find an entry, use the search capabilities of tools like `grep`, `less`, and Emacs.

This method is useful when you need to keep track of name and address information for many parties, but you don't always keep the same kind of information for each—maybe sometimes a name and phone number, sometimes just a mailing address, sometimes a name and email address. With a free-form address list, each entry contains whatever information you have in the format you want. Separate the entries with a delimiter line of your preference. I happen to use "###," but you can use whatever characters you're comfortable with—just make it a combination that won't appear in the text for any of the entries themselves.

For example, suppose you have a text file, `rolo`, containing three entries, as in Figure 27-5.

Notice that each entry contains varied information, and is in no particular format. That's the benefit of a free-form list—you don't have to type the entries in any particular order, and you're not bound by a particular set of "fields"; you can even cut and paste text into it from email, the Web, or other windows (see Recipe 10.3 [Manipulating Selections of Text], page 253).

```
Mary Smith
14 Elm St
Centerville, New York


###


Susan Jones - 602 555 1803
(don't call after eight)


###


Prof. Jenkins, 25 College St, Uptown, New York
555-2011 jenkins@example.edu
```

Figure 27-5. The rolo file.

There are several ways to find text in such a file. Suppose, for example, you want to contact your friend Susan, and you need her telephone number.

⇒ To output the line in the file containing the text "susan," regardless of case, type:

```
$ grep -i susan rolo (RET)
Susan Jones - 602 555 1803
$
```

This works nicely when the information you need is on the same line as the information you search for—here, the name Susan is on the same line as the telephone number; however, the output did not show the warning that appears on the next line in the file. And what about when the term you search for and the information you need are on adjacent lines?

Use the -C option with grep to output several lines of context before and after matched lines.

⇒ To output the several lines around the line matching the text "`Jenkins`,"
 type:

```
$ grep -C Jenkins rolo ⟨RET⟩

Prof. Jenkins, 25 College St, Uptown, New York
(914) 555-2011 jenkins@example.edu
$
```

Another way to search such a file is to open it as a buffer in Emacs and
use any of the Emacs searches. The Emacs `incremental-search` function,
⟨CTRL⟩-⟨S⟩, is very useful for such files—even for very large ones. If you do such
a search on a large file, and the first result doesn't turn up the right record,
just keep typing ⟨CTRL⟩-⟨S⟩ until the right one appears. If you type the letters
to search for in all lowercase, Emacs matches those letters regardless of case.

⇒ Here are two ways to use this.

  • To search through the current buffer in Emacs for the first entry
    containing the text "`New York`," regardless of case, type:
    ⟨CTRL⟩-⟨S⟩ `new york`

  • To search for the next entry containing the text "`New York`," regard-
    less of case, type:
    ⟨CTRL⟩-⟨S⟩

You can repeat this keystroke as many times as you wish to show all entries
in the entire buffer with the text "`New York`" in them. Once you reach the
end of the buffer, type ⟨CTRL⟩-⟨S⟩ again to loop around to the beginning of the
buffer and continue the search from there. (The minibuffer will tell you when
you've reached the end of the buffer, and will remind you to type this if you
want to loop the search.)

NOTES: It's also useful to peruse and search through these kinds of files with
`less`—see Recipe 14.11 [Searching the Text You're Perusing], page 355.

27.5.2 Keeping a Contact Manager Database

BBDb
  DEB: bbdb
  RPM: bbdb
  WWW: http://bbdb.sourceforge.net/

The Insidious Big Brother Database is a contact manager tool for use with Emacs. You can use it with Emacs email and news readers; it stores contact information in *records* and allows you to search for records that match a regular expression, as well as records whose particular *fields* match a regular expression (see Recipe 14.3 [Matching Patterns of Text], page 335).

There are several ways to add a record to the database. Use the **bbdb-create** function to manually add a record. (When you run this command, **bbdb** prompts you to enter the relevant information for each field.) When in a mail reader inside Emacs, type a colon (:) to display the record for the author of the current message; if there is none, **bbdb** asks whether or not one should be created.

⇒ Here are two ways to use this.

- To create a new **bbdb** record from scratch, type:

  ⟨ALT⟩-⟨X⟩ *bbdb-create* ⟨RET⟩

- To add a new **bbdb** record for the author of the current email message, type:

  :

Use the **bbdb** function to search for records—it takes as an argument the pattern or regexp to search for.

⇒ To output records containing the text "**scott**" anywhere in the record, type:

  ⟨ALT⟩-⟨X⟩ *bbdb* ⟨RET⟩ *scott* ⟨RET⟩

There are additional functions that let you narrow your search to a particular field: **bbdb-name**, **bbdb-company**, **bbdb-net**, and **bbdb-notes**, which respectively search the name, company, email address, and notes fields.

⇒ To output records matching the regexp "***\.edu**" in the email address, type:

  ⟨ALT⟩-⟨X⟩ *bbdb-net* ⟨RET⟩ **\.edu* ⟨RET⟩

27.6 Reminding Yourself of Things

Sometimes it's useful to make a reminder for yourself that you'll see either later in your current login session, or the next time you log in. These recipes describe the best ways to do this.

NOTES: When you want to give yourself a reminder for a future appointment, use **calendar** (see Recipe 27.4 [Managing Appointments], page 542).

27.6.1 Reminding Yourself When You Have to Leave

Leave
  DEB: `leave`
  RPM: `leave`
  WWW: `ftp://ftp.netbsd.org/pub/NetBSD/NetBSD-current/src/usr.bin/`

Use the `leave` tool to remind yourself when you have to leave. Give as an
argument the time when you have to go, using the format of *hhmm*, where *hh*
is hours in 24-hour format and *mm* is minutes.

⇒ To remind yourself to leave at 8:05 p.m., type:

    $ leave 2005 〈RET〉

When you run `leave` with no arguments, it prompts you to enter a time;
if you just type 〈RET〉, `leave` exits without setting the reminder. This method
is good for adding `leave` to scripts or to your `.bashrc`, so that you can interactively give a time to leave, if desired, when the script runs (see Recipe 3.7.3
[Using Shell Startup Files], page 86).

NOTES: `leave` will output a reminder on the terminal screen five minutes
before the given time, one minute before the time, at the time itself, and then
every minute subsequently until the user logs off.

27.6.2 Sending Yourself Email Reminders

Sending yourself a short email message is often effective for reminding yourself
to do something during your next workday or next time you read mail; keeping
a message in your inbox works as a constant reminder to get something done—
provided you don't abuse it and fill your inbox with lots of these "urgent"
mails!

To quickly send an email reminder, give your email address (or just your
username on your local system, if you check mail there) as an argument to
the `mail` tool. You'll be prompted to give a subject for the message, and if
that isn't enough space for the reminder, you can write as many lines as you
need below it as the message body text. Type 〈CTRL〉-〈D〉 on a line by itself
to send the mail.

⇒ For example, if your username on your local system is `joe`, to send yourself an email reminder, you'd type:

```
$ mail joe ⟨RET⟩
Subject: Bring files to meeting ⟨RET⟩
⟨CTRL⟩-⟨D⟩
Cc: ⟨RET⟩
Null message body; hope that's ok
$
```

NOTES: For more about using the `mail` tool, see Recipe 32.1 [Sending Mail], page 612.

27.7 Telling Others You Are Away

If you are on a system that is connected directly to the Internet, you can set up an automatic reply message to incoming email when you are away, so that people know you are not around.

To do this, use the `vacation` tool. Write the message you want to send, complete with "From:" and "Subject:" lines, in a hidden file called `.vacation.msg` in your home directory. For example, if your email address is cpeterson@example.edu, your `~/vacation.msg` might contain something like Figure 27-6.

```
From: Dr. Constance Peterson <cpeterson@example.edu>
Subject: Regarding your message to Dr. Peterson
Precedence: bulk

I am away from the University for the first week of February. I will
return on February 8th and will address your mail then. If your business
is urgent, please address Dr. Edwards, at edwards@example.edu.
```

Figure 27-6. The `.vacation.msg` file.

Then, edit another hidden file in your home directory called `.forward`, and put the following line in it:

```
\cpeterson, "|/usr/bin/vacation cpeterson"
```

This will save a copy of all incoming mail in your inbox, and it will use `vacation` to reply to any mails addressed to the username `cpeterson`; the reply mail will be the one you wrote in `.vacation.msg`.

Then, when you return from vacation, just move the `.forward` file to something else.

⇒ To move your `.forward` to `.forward.not`, type

```
$ mv .forward .forward.not (RET)
```

NOTES: You can leave the `.vacation.msg` file where it is, and edit it as needed next time you are about to go away.

If you run `vacation`, it is a good idea to unsubscribe yourself from any mailing lists before your absence. That way, you will avoid the embarrassment of sending your message out to all the subscribers of a list whenever someone posts a message to it.

27.8 Reviewing What You Did Today

To help remember what you've done recently, you can use `find` to get a list of files that you looked at and files that you modified in the past day (see Recipe 7.2 [Finding Files in a Directory Tree], page 172).

⇒ Here are two ways to use this.

- To list all the files in your home directory tree, excluding directories, that were accessed today, type:

  ```
  $ find ~ -daystart -atime -1 \! -type d (RET)
  ```

- To list all the files in your home directory tree, excluding directories, that were modified today, type:

  ```
  $ find ~ -daystart -mtime -1 \! -type d (RET)
  ```

You can make variations on this recipe to see what you did at other times.

⇒ Here are two ways to use this.

- To list all the files in your home directory tree, excluding directories, that were accessed between now and two days ago, type:

  ```
  $ find ~ -daystart -atime -2 \! -type d (RET)
  ```

- To list all the files in your home directory tree, excluding directories, that were modified exactly two days ago, type:

  ```
  $ find ~ -daystart -mtime 2 \! -type d (RET)
  ```

To measure not by numbers of days ago, but to find files accessed or changed on a specific date, use `touch` to touch two temporary files: one with the date you are looking for, and one with the day after. Then use `find` to find files newer than the first, but not newer than the second.

⇒ To find out what you did on September 11, 2001, type:

```
$ touch -d "Sep 11 2001" /tmp/911 (RET)
$ touch -d "Sep 12 2001" /tmp/912 (RET)
$ find ~ -daystart -newer /tmp/911 \! -daystart -newer /tmp/912 (RET)
```

This lists all the files that were last modified on September 11, 2001. Use
-anewer to list files were last accessed that day, and **-cnewer** to list files
that were last changed that day. Two temporary files are made with special
timestamps, /tmp/911 and /tmp/912.

27.9 Using Other Reminder Tools

The following table lists additional tools that can be used to generate reminders, including calendars and appointment managers.

Ccal	Replacement for `cal` that outputs calendars in color. DEB: `ccal`
Evolution	"Groupware" suite that includes calendar and address facilities. DEB: `evolution` RPM: `evolution` WWW: `http://ximian.com/products/evolution/`
Gcal	Outputs many types of calendars, including astronomical ones. DEB: `gcal` RPM: `gcal` WWW: `http://www.gnu.org/software/gcal/gcal.html`
KOrganizer	Appointment manager for KDE, with built-in calendar and scheduler; uses `vCalendar` file format. DEB: `korganizer` RPM: `korganizer` WWW: `http://www.kde.org/`

Jpilot	Keeps names and addresses on a Palm desktop, and includes date book, address book, to-do list, and a facility for making memorandums; extensive plug-ins have been developed for it. DEB: `jpilot` RPM: `jpilot` WWW: `http://jpilot.org/`
ouR CLOCK	Analog clock for X that inverses its colors when you have new mail waiting; has built-in appointment facility. DEB: `rxvt` RPM: `rxvt` WWW: `http://sourceforge.net/projects/rxvt/`
Plan	Graphical schedule planner. DEB: `plan` RPM: `plan` WWW: `http://me.in-berlin.de/~bitrot/plan.html`
QuickList	Keep track of any sort of thing you can put in a list. DEB: `quicklist` RPM: `quicklist` WWW: `http://tinyurl.com/2a9d5`
Remind	Reminder service with www facilities. DEB: `remind`
Wmdate	Prints calendar in the "docking bar" of window managers, such as Window Maker. DEB: `wmdate` RPM: `wmdate`
Xwrits	Reminds you to take a break from typing. DEB: `xwrits`
Xcal	The original graphical calendar for X. Has programmable alarms and an appointment and memo facility. DEB: `xcal`

## CHAPTER 28

Scheduling

Sometimes it is useful to specify a command or set of commands so that they run not immediately, but at some other time. This chapter describes techniques for handling this sort of function, as well as techniques for monitoring commands that are currently running.

28.1 Running a Command on a Delay

The `sleep` tool does nothing but wait (or "sleep") for the number of seconds specified as an argument. This is useful for ringing the system bell, playing a sound file, or running some other command at your terminal after a short delay.

To do this, give the number of seconds to "sleep" as an argument to `sleep`, followed by a semicolon character (`;`)[1] and the commands to run. This runs the given commands only after `sleep` waits for the given number of seconds.

Since the shell where you type this command will be unusable until the commands you give are executed (or until you interrupt the whole thing), type this command in an `xterm` or virtual console window (see Recipe 2.3 [Using Consoles and Terminals], page 32) other than the one you are working in.

⇒ Here are two ways to use this.

- To ring the bell in five seconds, type:

      $ sleep 5; echo -e '\a' ⟨RET⟩

- To announce the time in 30 seconds, type:

      $ sleep 30; saytime ⟨RET⟩

You can also give the time in minutes, hours, or days. To do this, follow the argument with a unit, as listed in the following table.

s	Seconds
m	Minutes
h	Hours
d	Days

⇒ To announce the time in exactly five minutes, type:

      $ sleep 5m; saytime & ⟨RET⟩

---

[1] The shell command separator; see Recipe 3.1.7 [Running a List of Commands], page 63.

28.2 Running a Command on a Timer

Use **at** to run commands on a timer. It takes as an argument the exact time
you want to run a command, and then it reads commands from the standard
input, starting from the "at>" prompt and ending when you type ⟨CTRL⟩-⟨D⟩
on a line by itself. It schedules a job for the commands you give, and it runs
them at the specified time (see Recipe 3.3 [Managing Jobs], page 70). The
commands are executed by **/bin/sh**, the default shell; as a reminder, **at** warns
you about this fact when you specify the commands.

⇒ To mail yourself a reminder at five minutes after 5 p.m. today, type:

```
$ at 17:05 ⟨RET⟩
warning: commands will be executed using /bin/sh
at> mail chuck -s "IT'S TIME TO GO!" < /dev/null ⟨RET⟩
at> ⟨CTRL⟩-⟨D⟩ <EOT>
job 5 at 2003-08-09 17:05
$
```

   In this example, the username is **chuck** and the job number scheduled by
at is 5.

   The **at** tool understands many time formats, from the month, day, and
year to the hour and minute (optionally given in military time, or followed
by "AM" or "PM"), and the special words "**midnight**," "**noon**," and "**teatime**"
(the last of which translates to 4 p.m.). You can use the suffixes "**today**"
or "**tomorrow**," and you can use a "+" after a time followed by a number of
minutes, hours, days, or weeks—for example, "**8pm + 2 days**" means to run
two days from 8 p.m. tonight. So to run a command at a week from midnight,
use "**midnight + 1 week**."

⇒ To schedule ~/bin/clean and ~/bin/tidy to run at 9 p.m. tomorrow,
    type:

```
$ at 9pm tomorrow ⟨RET⟩
warning: commands will be executed using /bin/sh
at> ~/bin/clean ⟨RET⟩
at> ~/bin/tidy ⟨RET⟩
at> ⟨CTRL⟩-⟨D⟩ <EOT>
job 6 at 2003-08-09 17:10
$
```

Instead of giving the commands from the standard input, you can specify a list of commands to run from a file. To do this, give the name of the file as an argument to the -f option.

⇒ To have the system run the commands in the file `extra.work` at midnight tonight, type:

```
$ at -f extra.work midnight (RET)
```

NOTES: This method is not for running a command in your current shell, or running a command at your terminal; to do either of these, see Recipe 28.1 [Delay Command], page 555.

If you want to run a job at some regular interval, use **cron** instead (see Recipe 28.3 [Scheduling Commands], below).

28.2.1 Listing the Jobs Scheduled to Run

To list the jobs in the **at** queue, type **atq**. For each job, it gives the job number, date, hour, and job class.

⇒ To list all pending jobs, type:

```
$ atq (RET)
```

28.2.2 Deleting a Job Scheduled to Run

To delete a job that's scheduled to run, use **atrm**, giving the job number as an argument.

⇒ To delete job number 3, type:

```
atrm 3 (RET)
```

28.3 Scheduling Commands

You can schedule commands to run at regular intervals with the system CRON facility ("Command Run On").

Each command that you have scheduled to run is called a *cron job*. A listing of all of your CRON jobs is kept in your "CRON table," which in turn is read from your *crontab file*; this is a plain text file, often named **crontab**, containing all of your CRON jobs, one per line, arranged in the following format:

minute   hour   day of month   month   day of week   command

Hours are given in military time; months and days of week are given either numerically or with their three-letter abbreviations. The time and date fields may contain the value of an asterisk character (*), which means the first possible value to the last possible value of the field, inclusive. Time and date fields may also contain ranges of numbers, and individual numbers may be given separated by commas.

To write comments in your crontab file, begin a lines with a hash sign (#); the line will be ignored by the system. Blank lines are also ignored.

For example, a simple crontab file might look like Figure 28-1.

```
# This is my sample crontab file.

# Runs the 'foo' command at noon every single day.
0 12 * * * foo

# Runs the 'bar' command at 1:23 in the morning on every day in June.
23 1 * Jun * bar

# Runs the 'foobar' command at half-past four and five p.m. every Monday
# through Wednesday whose day of the month is between 1 and 14.
30 16,17 1-14 * Mon-Wed foobar
```

Figure 28-1. A simple `crontab` *file.*

The following recipes show how to manage CRON jobs.

28.3.1 Adding a CRON Job

To add or change a CRON job, make the appropriate changes to your `crontab` file, and then run `crontab` with the name of this file as an argument. This command replaces your existing CRON table with the one contained in your `crontab` file.

⇒ To add a new CRON job contained in your `crontab` file `cron.txt`, type:

     $ *crontab cron.txt* (RET)

28.3.2 Removing a CRON Job

You remove jobs from CRON by removing your CRON table. Do this by running `crontab` with the -r option.

⇒ To remove your CRON table, type:

     $ *crontab -r* (RET)

NOTES: To remove only some of your CRON jobs, or to change your CRON jobs, just revise your crontab file, deleting or revising the entries you want to, and then add your CRON table (as described in the previous recipe).

28.3.3 Listing Your CRON Jobs

To list all of the CRON jobs you have scheduled, use `crontab` with the `-l` option.

⇒ To list your CRON jobs, type:

```
$ crontab -l RET
```

28.4 Watching a Command from Time to Time

Use `watch` to observe the output of a command and watch it run from time to time. It runs the command you give as an argument, repeatedly, every two seconds, until it is interrupted. Each time the command is run, the display is updated with the new results. This is particularly useful for when you want to closely watch some files in a directory and note the changes as they occur.

⇒ To watch the detailed contents of the current directory, type:

```
$ watch ls -l RET
```

This command will display the contents of the current directory in the terminal you run it in, and it will continually update every two seconds. To change the interval, give it as an argument to the `-n` option.

⇒ To watch the detailed contents of the current directory, updating by the second, type:

```
$ watch -n 1 ls -l RET
```

Use the `-d` flag to highlight the differences in the updates.

⇒ To watch the detailed contents of the current directory, updating every ten seconds, and highlighting all the differences, type:

```
$ watch -d -n 10 ls -l RET
```

NOTES: Sometimes you might find it nice to run your `watch` session in a little `xterm` of its own. If you're not in X, you might want to devote a console terminal to it.

## CHAPTER 29

Mathematics

Tools and techniques for dealing with numbers are the subject of this chapter: listing them in sequence or randomly, calculating arithmetic, cryptography, and converting between units. Larger applications, such as spreadsheets and plotting tools, are also mentioned.

29.1 Calculating Arithmetic

As you might expect, there are many tools for making arithmetic calculations in Linux. The following recipes describe how to use two of them for two common scenarios; a list of other calculator tools, including a visual calculator, appears at the end of this chapter (see Recipe 29.9 [Using Other Mathematics Tools], page 579).

29.1.1 Making a Quick Arithmetic Calculation

To do a quick calculation that requires only addition, subtraction, multiplication, or division, you can use Bash's built-in arithmetic evaluation feature to perform the calculation right at the shell prompt. It makes it even easier if you make a shell script named `calc`, as in Figure 29-1.

```
#!/bin/sh
echo $(( expression = $ ))
```

Figure 29-1. The `calc` script.

Once you install this script (see Recipe A.3.4 [Installing a Shell Script], page 708), you can use it at the shell prompt to get the results of any simple arithmetic calculation.

To do this, give the expression to evaluate as an argument to `calc`. Use an asterisk (`*`) for a multiplication sign and a forward slash (`/`) for division; to output the remainder, use a percent sign (`%`) instead of a slash. You can use parentheses to group expressions—but when you do, be sure to quote them (see Recipe 3.1.3 [Quoting Reserved Characters], page 56).

⇒ Here are some ways to use this.

  • To output the result of 50 times 10, type:

```
$ calc 50*10 (RET)
500
$
```

  • To output the result of 100 times the sum of 4 plus 420, type:

```
$ calc '100*(4+420)' (RET)
42400
$
```

  • To output the remainder of 10 divided by 3, type:

```
$ calc 10%3 (RET)
1
$
```

NOTES: This is a method for speed. It's useful for quickly computing a simple arithmetic equation at the shell prompt, but it has several drawbacks: It only outputs whole integers; its operators are limited; and complex expressions must be quoted. Still, if you're at a shell prompt and need to know the product of 12,342 and 587, I don't think there's a faster way. But for doing anything more than the very simplest operations, see the next recipe, which describes bc.

29.1.2 Using a Calculator

bc
  DEB: bc
  RPM: bc
  WWW: http://www.gnu.org/software/bc/

There are a great many calculators, for X or any terminal. One of the more venerable standbys is bc, a calculation language that supports arbitrary-precision numbers, scripts, variables, functions, and algebraic statements. Use it when you have a lot of calculations to make, or when you must compute numbers with decimals.

Type bc to start it; you can then perform arithmetic operations interactively, just as you would with a desktop calculator or adding machine.

When you are running bc, you type each statement to be evaluated on a line by itself, typing ⟨RET⟩ at the end of the statement; the evaluation of what you type is output on the following line. Each line you type will be evaluated by bc as an arithmetic expression. To exit, type *quit* on a line by itself.

⇒ To multiply 42 by 17 with bc, type:

```
$ bc ⟨RET⟩
bc 1.06
Copyright 1991, 1992, 1993, 1994, 1997, 1998, 2000 Free Software
Foundation, Inc.
This is free software with ABSOLUTELY NO WARRANTY.
For details type `warranty'.
42 * 17 ⟨RET⟩
714
quit ⟨RET⟩
$
```

In this example, bc output its version number and warranty information when it started; then, the statement "42 * 17" was typed by the user, bc output the result ("714"), and then the user typed *quit* to exit bc.

By default, digits to the right of the decimal point are truncated from the output—so dividing 10 by 3 would output "3" as a result, and outputting the remainder from this operation by typing "10%3" would output "1." But since bc is an arbitrary-precision calculator, you can give the number of digits to use after the decimal point. Do this by specifying the value of the scale variable; its default value is 0.

⇒ To use **bc** to compute the result of 10 divided by 3, using 20 digits after the decimal point, type:

```
$ bc (RET)
bc 1.06
Copyright 1991, 1992, 1993, 1994, 1997, 1998, 2000 Free Software
Foundation, Inc.
This is free software with ABSOLUTELY NO WARRANTY.
For details type `warranty'.
scale=20 (RET)
10 / 3 (RET)
3.33333333333333333333
quit (RET)
$
```

Use the **-l** option to start **bc** with a scale of 20, and with a number of math functions loaded, as described in the following table.

s (*x*)	Outputs sine of *x* (*x* is given in radians).
c (*x*)	Outputs cosine of *x* (*x* is given in radians).
a (*x*)	Outputs arctangent of *x*, in radians.
l (*x*)	Outputs the logarithm of *x*.
e (*x*)	Outputs the exponential function of **e** to the *x*th power.
j (*n*,*x*)	Outputs the Bessel function of integer order *n* of *x*.

The following table describes the symbols you can use to specify mathematical operations.

expression + *expression*	Add: Output the sum of the two expressions.
expression - *expression*	Subtract: Output the difference of the two expressions.
expression * *expression*	Multiply: Output the product of the two expressions.
expression / *expression*	Divide: Output the quotient of the two expressions.

expression % *expression*	Remainder: Output the remainder resulting from dividing the two expressions.
expression ^ *expression*	Power: Raise the first expression to the power of the second expression.
(*expressions*)	Group an expression or expressions together, altering the standard precedence of performing operations.
sqrt(*expression*)	Output the square root of *expression*.

The -q option is nice—it suppresses the copyright and warranty message at start-up. Starting bc with both this and the -l option is a good way to run it, and you might want to make an alias for bc with these two options (see Recipe 3.6 [Using Alias Words], page 82):

```
alias bc='/usr/bin/bc -ql'
```

29.2 Outputting a Random Number

To get a random number, display the contents of the RANDOM variable. It is a special shell variable that outputs a random integer between 0 and 32,767.

⇒ To output a random number, type:

```
$ echo $RANDOM (RET)
```

To output a random number in a range starting from zero but under a certain number, use RANDOM with the Bash arithmetic evaluation expression "$(($RANDOM % *number*))," where *number* is the integer that the output should be under.

⇒ To output a random number from 0 to 9, type:

```
$ echo $(( $RANDOM % 10 )) (RET)
```

29.3 Listing a Sequence of Numbers

Use seq to print a sequence of numbers. This is very useful for getting a listing of numbers to use as arguments, or for otherwise passing sequences of numbers to commands.

To output the sequence from 1 to any number, give that number as an argument.

⇒ Here are two ways to use this.

- To output the sequence of numbers from 1 to 7, type:

  ```
  $ seq 7 (RET)
  ```
- To output the sequence of numbers from 1 to -7, type:

  ```
  $ seq -7 (RET)
  ```

To output the sequence from any one number to another, give those numbers as arguments.

⇒ Here are two ways to use this.

- To output the sequence of numbers from 9 to 0, type:

  ```
  $ seq 9 0 (RET)
  ```
- To output the sequence of numbers from -1 to -20, type:

  ```
  $ seq -1 -20 (RET)
  ```

To specify an increment other than one, give it as the *second* argument, between the starting and ending number.

⇒ To output the sequence of numbers from -1 to 14, incrementing by 3, type:

  ```
  $ seq -1 3 14 (RET)
  ```

Use the -w option to pad numbers with leading zeros so that they're all output with the same width.

Specify a separator string to be output between numbers as an argument to the -s option; the default is a newline character, which outputs each number in the sequence on its own line.

⇒ Here are two ways to use this.

- To output the sequence of numbers from 9 to 999, incrementing by 23, with numbers padded with zeros so that they're all of equal width, type:

  ```
  $ seq -w 9 23 999 (RET)
  ```
- To output the sequence of numbers from 1 to 23, with a space character between each, type:

  ```
  $ seq -s ' ' 1 23 (RET)
  ```

To pass a sequence of numbers as arguments to a command, pipe the output of seq using a space character as a separator.

⇒ To concatenate all the files in the current directory, whose names are numbers from 25 through 75, into a new file called **selected-mail**, type:

  ```
  $ cat `seq -s " " 25 75` > selected-mail (RET)
  ```

The preceding example substitutes the output of `seq` as an argument to `cat` (see Recipe 3.1.11 [Specifying the Output of a Command as an Argument], page 65).

29.4 Finding Prime Factors

The `factor` tool calculates and outputs the prime factors of numbers passed as arguments.

⇒ To output the prime factors of 2000, type:

```
$ factor 2000 (RET)
2000: 2 2 2 2 5 5 5
$
```

NOTES: If no number is given, `factor` reads numbers from standard input; numbers should be separated by space, tab, or newline characters.

29.5 Converting Amounts and Numbers

The following recipes are for converting numbers in various ways.

29.5.1 Converting an Amount Between Units of Measurement

Units
  DEB: `units`
  RPM: `units`
  WWW: `http://www.gnu.org/software/units/`

Use the `units` tool to convert a measurement from one measurement scale to another. Give two quoted arguments: the value and the name of the units you have, and the name of the units to convert to. It outputs two values: the converted value in the new units, and how much of the original measurement is equivalent to one of the new units.

⇒ To output the number of ounces in 50 grams, type:

```
$ units '50 grams' 'ounces' (RET)
        * 1.7636981
        / 0.56699046
$
```

In this example, the output indicates that there are about 1.7636981 ounces in 50 grams, and that conversely, one ounce is about 0.56699046 times 50 grams.

The units tool understands a great many different kinds of units—from Celsius and Fahrenheit to pounds, hectares, the speed of light, and a "baker's dozen." All understood units are kept in a text file database; use the -V option to output the location of this database on your system, and then peruse or search through it to see which units your version supports.

⇒ To determine the location of the units database, type:

```
$ units -V (RET)
units version 1.55 with readline, units database in
/usr/share/misc/units.dat
$
```

In this example, the units database is located in the file /usr/share/misc/units.dat, which is the file to peruse to list all of the units data.

NOTES: With no arguments, units runs interactively, asking you first what you have, and then second what you want.

More units of measurement can be found in *A Dictionary of Units of Measurement* [http://www.unc.edu/~rowlett/units/].

29.5.2 Converting an Arabic Numeral to English

Bsd-games
  DEB: bsdgames
  RPM: bsd-games
  WWW: http://www.ibiblio.org/pub/Linux/games/

Use **number** to convert Arabic numerals to English text. Give a numeral as an argument; with no argument, **number** reads a numeral from the standard input.

⇒ To output the English text equivalent of 100,000, type:

    `$ number 100000` ⟨RET⟩

29.6 Using ROT13 Encryption

You may, from time to time, come across mention of ROT13. Or you may come across a message—especially on Usenet, or in old email archives—that ybbxf yvxr guvf.

This is text encoded in ROT13 encryption, so named because each letter in the alphabet is rotated thirteen places over, so that (in a 26-letter alphabet) the first thirteen letters are substituted for the last thirteen, and vice versa. Therefore, in ROT13, "A" (the first letter of the alphabet) becomes "N" (the 13th letter of the alphabet), "B" becomes "O," "C" becomes "P," and so on all the way through:

    A B C D E F G H I J K L M N O P Q R S T U V W X Y Z

becomes

    N O P Q R S T U V W X Y Z A B C D E F G H I J K L M

This type of cipher, where letters are substituted by rotating the entire alphabet according to some offset, is known today as *Julius Caesar's cipher*, named after its most famous adopter.[1]

There are two primary methods, both using filters, for encoding and decoding text in and out of ROT13. One, the traditional method, is to use **tr** to transpose the characters, giving a set of the first and last 13 letters to transpose from, and a set of the last and first 13 letters to transpose to.

The second method automates this process with a tool called **rot13**, part of the **bsd-games** package. This package also includes **caesar**, a tool for decoding Caesar ciphers in general via statistical analysis of input.

ROT13 is not intended as a method for general encryption—it's much too easy to figure out—but it's good for when you want to temporarily obscure some text, such as the punch line of a joke or the "spoiler" portion of a movie review. To encode some text, make it a selection in X and then send it through one of the two filters for encoding it, or just type it as input to either filter. To decode some lines of ROT13 in text, do the same thing: make a selection of the encoded text, and then pass it through either of the filters (see Recipe 10.3 [Manipulating Selections of Text], page 253); press ⟨CTRL⟩-⟨D⟩ to terminate and exit the filter.

---

[1] According to Suetonius, Caesar's cipher had an offset of 4.

29.6.1 Encoding Text in ROT13

There are a few good methods for encoding text in ROT13.

METHOD #1

Use `tr` to encode some text in ROT13, giving as arguments the set containing the first 13 letters, in both uppercase and lowercase, and then as the second set, the last 13 letters in both uppercase and lowercase.

⇒ Here are some ways to use this.

- To encode the contents of the file `script` in ROT13, and output it to the file `secret.script`, type:

  `$ tr [a-mn-zA-MN-Z] [n-za-mN-ZA-M] < script > secret.script` ⟨RET⟩

- To type some text and encode it in ROT13, type:

  ```
  $ tr [a-mn-zA-MN-Z] [n-za-mN-ZA-M] ⟨RET⟩
  Hello, world. ⟨RET⟩
  Uryyb, jbeyq.
  ⟨CTRL⟩-⟨D⟩
  ```

- To encode the current text selection using the keyboard, type:

  ```
  $ tr [a-mn-zA-MN-Z] [n-za-mN-ZA-M] ⟨RET⟩
  ⟨SHIFT⟩-⟨INS⟩ ⟨RET⟩
  This is a secret message. ⟨RET⟩
  Guvf vf n frperg zrffntr.
  ⟨CTRL⟩-⟨D⟩
  ```

In the last example above, the text "`This is a secret message.`" was the current text selection.

METHOD #2

Bsd-games
  DEB: bsdgames
  RPM: bsd-games
  WWW: http://www.ibiblio.org/pub/Linux/games/

Use the `rot13` filter to encode text in ROT13. It works in the same way as `tr`, described previously.

⇒ Here are some ways to use this.

- To encode the text in **message** in ROT13, and output it to a new file called **secret_message**, type:

  $ *rot13 < message > secret_message* ⟨RET⟩

- To type some text and encode it in ROT13, type:

  ```
  $ rot13 ⟨RET⟩
  Hello, world. ⟨RET⟩
  Uryyb, jbeyq.
  ⟨CTRL⟩-⟨D⟩
  ```

- To encode the current text selection in ROT13, type:

  ```
  $ rot13 ⟨RET⟩
  ⟨SHIFT⟩-⟨INS⟩ ⟨RET⟩
  This is a secret message. ⟨RET⟩
  Guvf vf n frperg zrffntr.
  ⟨CTRL⟩-⟨D⟩
  ```

NOTES: To insert the text selection with the mouse, press the middle mouse button instead of ⟨SHIFT⟩-⟨INS⟩.

29.6.2 Decoding Text in ROT13

The methods for decoding text in ROT13 are identical to the methods for encoding in it, for the transformation is exactly the same either way.

METHOD #1

Use the same **tr** filter method to decode text encoded in ROT13 that you would use to *encode* in ROT13.

⇒ Here are some ways to use this.

- To decode the ROT13-encoded text in **secret_message**, sending the decoded text to the standard output, type:

  $ *tr [a-mn-zA-MN-Z] [n-za-mN-ZA-M] < secret_message* ⟨RET⟩

- To decode the ROT13-encoded text in **secret.script**, writing the decoded text to a file named **script**, type:

  $ *tr [a-mn-zA-MN-Z] [n-za-mN-ZA-M] < secret.script > script* ⟨RET⟩

- To decode the ROT13-encoded text selection, type:

```
$ tr [a-mn-zA-MN-Z] [n-za-mN-ZA-M] (RET)
(SHIFT)-(INS) (RET)
Guvf vf n frperg zrffntr. (RET)
This is a secret message.
(CTRL)-(D)
```

METHOD #2

Bsd-games
  DEB: bsdgames
  RPM: bsd-games
  WWW: http://www.ibiblio.org/pub/Linux/games/

Use the **rot13** filter to decode text encoded in ROT13.

⇒ Here are some ways to use this.

- To decode the ROT13-encoded text in **secret_message**, sending the decoded text to the standard output, type:

    ```
    $ rot13 < secret_message (RET)
    ```

- To decode the ROT13-encoded text in **secret_message**, writing the decoded text to a file named **message**, type:

    ```
    $ rot13 < secret_message > message (RET)
    ```

- To decode the ROT13-encoded text selection, type:

```
$ rot13 (RET)
(SHIFT)-(INS) (RET)
Guvf vf n frperg zrffntr. (RET)
This is a secret message.
(CTRL)-(D)
```

29.7 Using GPG Encryption

GnuPG
  DEB: gnupg
  RPM: gnupg
  WWW: http://www.gnupg.org/

GNU Privacy Guard (GPG) is a public key encryption system. It is a free and open replacement for PGP, "Pretty Good Privacy,"[2] and is mostly compatible with newer PGP versions.

Public key encryption works like this. Everyone who uses it first runs the program in such a way as to get his own set of *keys*, which are strings of numbers generated by a particular mathematical function built into the public key encryption system. Two keys are made: a *public key*, which you make public to anyone you want to send your encrypted data to, and a *private key*, which only you have access to. Both are unique series of data, and they are generated by a passphrase that you type when making the keys.

When the public key is processed by the **gpg** tool, it will output a unique function and encode its input data in such a way that it cannot be decrypted, except when **gpg** is called with the private key. People who use GPG make their public keys available, so that anyone else who uses GPG can encrypt some data for a particular person by using that person's public key. Once encrypted, nobody but the recipient—not even the sender—can decrypt the data. Only by using the private key corresponding to a particular public key can the text be decrypted.

So to begin using GPG, you must first generate your own set of keys. Do this by running **gpg** with the special **--gen-key** option.

⇒ To generate your own set of keys, type:

    $ *gpg --gen-key* ⟨RET⟩

When you run this command, you will be asked to specify some things: the algorithm used (DSA/ElGamal is recommended), the key length (longer keys give more security at the expense of taking longer to compute; many recommend no fewer than 2,048 bits, while an older standard is 1,024 bits), some names and email addresses of individuals you would like to exchange encrypted data with (you can always add more later), and finally a special passphrase. This passphrase is what turns your private key in the encryption lock: You will use it every time you wish to unlock anything encrypted for you with your public key.

The passphrase ought to be at least 32 characters long, varied in its characters (using numerals, symbols, and both uppercase and lowercase letters), and it should be something that nobody else will be able to guess.

---

[2] PGP, popularized in the early 1990s Internet rush, uses patented algorithms and thus cannot be free software; GPG carries no such restrictions.

The keys will take some time to generate. To make your key available for others, export it to an ASCII file with both the -a and --export options.

⇒ To export your public key to a file named alice.key, type:

$ *gpg -a --export > alice.key* (RET)

You can make this data available to anyone you'd like to communicate with via GPG—you can send it to someone via email, put it on a Web site, and so on.

To begin to communicate securely with someone else via GPG, you will also need to import his public key. Do this by using **gpg** with the --import option, and giving as an argument a file containing his public key.

⇒ To import the public key for your friend Bill, which you have put in the file bill.key, type:

$ *gpg --import bill.key* (RET)

This command puts your friend Bill on your *keyring*, which is the list of recipients that **gpg** knows about and can encrypt for. Use the --list-keys option to list the people on your keyring.

⇒ To list the keys **gpg** knows about, type:

$ *gpg --list-keys* (RET)

29.7.1 Encrypting Data with GPG

To encrypt a file with **gpg**, give the email address of the recipient as an argument to the -e option, and send the contents of the file to its standard input.

⇒ To encrypt the contents of **mission** for your associate Bill, whose email is bill@example.net, type:

$ *gpg -e bill@example.net < mission* (RET)

This command writes an encrypted binary file named **mission.gpg**, which can be decrypted only by Bill.

Use the --armor option to make an *armored* file, or one that only uses 7-bit ASCII characters. The file will be longer in length, but it will be easy to transmit in the body of an email message, or via other means not possible for a binary file.

⇒ To encrypt the contents of **mission** for your associate Bill, and output an armored text file, type:

$ *gpg --armor -e bill@example.net < mission* (RET)

29.7.2 Decrypting Data with GPG

Use `gpg` with the `-d` option to decrypt data that was encrypted with your public key. Send the data to `gpg`'s standard input; the decryption is written to the standard output.

⇒ Here are two ways to use this.

- To decode the data in the file `secret.and.urgent` to the standard output, type:

    `$ gpg -d < secret.and.urgent` (RET)

- To decode the data in the file `message.gpg` and write it to a new file, `message.txt`, type:

    `$ gpg -d < message.gpg > message.txt` (RET)

29.8 Plotting Data

Gnuplot
  DEB: gnuplot
  RPM: gnuplot
  WWW: http://www.gnuplot.info/

The `gnuplot` tool is a versatile program that can be used for data visualization, making 2D and 3D graphs, and for plotting contours, surfaces, and functions. It takes input in the form of a set of commands, either in a file or typed at the `gnuplot` command prompt, and it outputs a plot for those commands. It can read data from external text files and either display output in a new window or write it to a PostScript file. Output styles are highly configurable.

This is a large program with many features that we won't get into; the following recipes will demonstrate a few ways to use `gnuplot` to plot simple graphs. For more information on using `gnuplot` to plot data, consult its Info documentation (see Recipe 2.8.5 [Reading an Info Manual], page 48).

29.8.1 Making Graphs with a Single Data Set

To plot a single data set as a graph, give the values of the X and Y axes in a data file, and run `gnuplot` with the `plot` command in this fashion:

    `plot "inputfile" using 1:2 with plotstyle`

where *inputfile* is the name of the input file, and *plotstyle* specifies the drawing style to be used for the plot. Preface the `plot` command with any number of `set` commands to change the default settings; these commands may be typed interactively after running **gnuplot**, or they may be written to a file and called as an argument.

For example, suppose you have a file **temperature.data** containing two columns of text, delimited by tab characters, as in Figure 29-2.

```
January     68.9
February    68.7
March       69.0
April       70.2
May         72.0
June        73.4
July        74.3
August      75.8
September   74.6
October     73.8
November    71.8
December    70.1
```

Figure 29-2. The **temperature.data** *file.*

```
set title "Mean Monthly Temperatures for Hawaii, 1905-1938"
set xlabel "Month"
set ylabel "Temperature"
set nokey
set xdata time
set timefmt "%B"
set format x "%b"
set nomxtics
set terminal postscript color
set output "temps.ps"
plot "temperature.data" using 1:2 with linespoints
```

Figure 29-3. The **temperature.gnuplot** *file.*

And suppose you also have a file **temperature.gnuplot**, as in Figure 29-3, containing a set of **gnuplot** commands to plot a graph. It contains several lines of settings that affect or change the default behavior, including setting the title of the graph and labels for the X and Y axes.

The last line in the file contains the command to do the actual plotting. It reads the plot data from the file **temperature.data**, using the first column as month data for the graph's X axis, and the second column as the data to plot along the Y axis, using the `linespoints` style.

⇒ To process the commands in `temperature.gnuplot`, type:

$ *gnuplot temperature.gnuplot* (RET)

This command starts **gnuplot** and runs the commands in the file `temperature.gnuplot`. A new PostScript file, `temps.ps`, is written, which looks like Figure 29-4. (While the printed illustration is in black and white, the actual image created from this command has a red plot.)

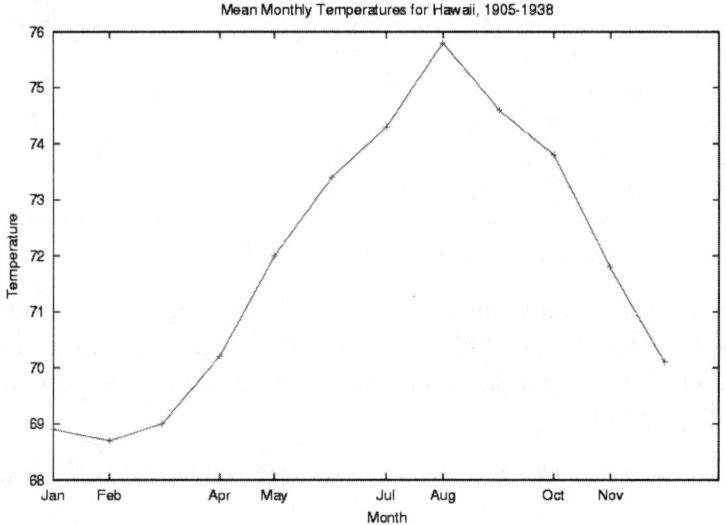

Figure 29-4. The `temps.ps` *file.*

29.8.2 Making Graphs with Multiple Data Sets

To plot multiple data sets on a graph, the method is the same as with the single data set, but for this exception: Give the values of the X axis and the multiple values of the plots along the Y axes in a data file, running **gnuplot** with the **plot** command in this fashion:

plot "*inputfile*" using 1:*plot* title *titlename* with *plotstyle*

where *inputfile* is the name of the input file and, for each plot, *plot* is the number of the column containing the plot, *titlename* is the name for its title in the key, and *plotstyle* is the drawing style to be used. Each **using** statement may be followed by a comma and the **using** statement for the next plot until all are specified.

For example, suppose you have a file `temperature2.data`, as in Figure 29-5.

```
#Month      Honolulu      Tampa      New York
January     73            60         32
February    73            61         33
March       74            66         41
April       76            72         53
May         78            77         62
June        79            81         71
July        80            82         77
August      81            82         75
September   81            81         68
October     80            74         58
November    77            67         47
December    74            61         36
```

Figure 29-5. The `temperature2.data` file.

This file contains four columns of text, delimited by tab characters. The first line is a comment—any lines beginning with a pound-sign character (#), in either input data or **gnuplot** command files, are considered comments and are ignored by **gnuplot**.

Now suppose you also have a file `temperature2.gnuplot`, as in Figure 29-6.

```
set title "Mean Monthly Temperatures for Company Locations"
set xlabel "Month"
set ylabel "Temperature"
set xdata time
set timefmt "%B"
set format x "%b"
set nomxtics
set terminal postscript landscape color
set output "temps2.ps"
plot "temperature2.data" using 1:2 title "Honolulu" with linespoints,
"" using 1:3 title "Tampa" with linespoints, "" using 1:4 title
"New York" with linespoints
```

Figure 29-6. The `temperature2.gnuplot` file.

This is very similar to the command file in the previous example, except for the following differences: The title is changed; the command to turn off the key is not printed; the name of the output file differs; and in the long last `plot` line, columns two through three are each plotted against the first column (the month names) in the input file, each with the `linespoints` style as before, but each with its own label for the key.

⇒ To process the commands in `temperature2.gnuplot`, type:

    $ gnuplot temperature.gnuplot ⟨RET⟩

This command starts **gnuplot** and runs the commands in the file `temperature2.gnuplot`. A new PostScript file, `temps2.ps`, is written, which looks like Figure 29-7. (While the printed illustration is in black and white, the actual image created from this command has colored plots.)

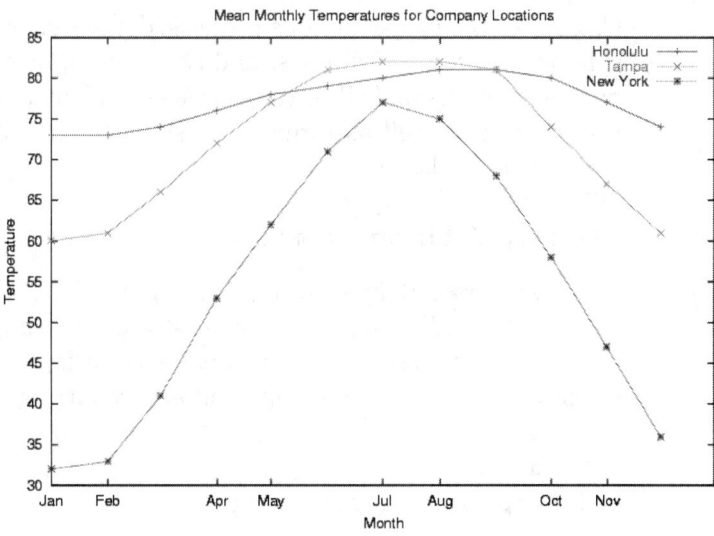

Figure 29-7. The `temps2.ps` file.

29.9 Using Other Mathematics Tools

The following table lists some of the other more popular mathematics-related tools available for Linux.

Calc

Scientific calculator tool for Emacs.
DEB: `calc`
RPM: `calc`
WWW: `http://www.isthe.com/chongo/tech/comp/calc/`

Desk Calculator

Arbitrary-precision calculator that reads from standard input and writes to standard output. DC is a *reverse-polish* calculator; that is, numbers are pushed on a last-in first-out (LIFO) list called a *stack*. When you give an arithmetic operation symbol, DC pops numbers off the stack for their operands, and then it pushes the evaluation on the stack. Very useful for getting evaluations in scripts and at the command line.
DEB: `dc`
WWW: `http://www.cypherspace.org/~adam/rsa/dc.html`

Dome

Calculates the properties of a geodesic dome—chord factors, spherical vertex coordinates, and so on. Supports "Buckyball" formations and elliptical geodesics, and generates plain text output as well as formats for spreadsheets, CAD, and ray-tracing tools.
DEB: `dome`
WWW: `http://tinyurl.com/2p5b4`

GnuCash

Intuitive personal finance application, used for managing finances (including bank accounts, stocks, income, and expenses); it's "based on professional accounting principles" to ensure accuracy in computation and reporting.
DEB: `gnucash`
RPM: `gnucash`
WWW: `http://www.gnucash.org/`

Gnumeric

Powerful spreadsheet application for GNOME that is somewhat reminiscent of Excel.
DEB: `gnumeric`
RPM: `gnumeric`
WWW: `http://www.gnome.org/projects/gnumeric/`

Oleo	Small GNU spreadsheet application that can run in both an X window and in terminals, has Emacs-like key bindings, and can generate PostScript output. DEB: `oleo` RPM: `oleo` WWW: `http://www.gnu.org/software/oleo/`
Piechart	Facilitates making graphical pie charts with the GNU plotting utilities (below). WWW: `http://tinyurl.com/jdi6`
Plotutils	Package of GNU programs for plotting data, including GNU replacements for the old UNIX standbys of **graph**, **plot**, and **spline**. DEB: `plotutils` RPM: `plotutils` WWW: `http://tinyurl.com/3eygd`
Sc	Spreadsheet tool that runs in the console; even smaller than Oleo, it provides formulas and other basic features you would expect from a minimal spreadsheet. DEB: `sc`
Sieb	Fast C program for computing prime numbers. WWW: `http://bytesex.org/misc.html`
Xcalc	Visual scientific calculator for the X Window System—it draws a calculator on the screen, and you can use the mouse or keyboard to use it. It is capable of emulating the TI-30 and HP-10C calculators. DEB: `xbase-clients` RPM: `XFree86-tools`
Xspread	X client front-end to `sc`. RPM: `xspread`

## CHAPTER 30

Amusements

What's productivity without a section on how to manage extra time?

The recipes in this chapter describe those classic games and whimsies that were traditionally found on UNIX systems, and are now available for Linux. It also includes recipes for solving word games with your system and other amusements sure to keep you occupied.

30.1 Playing Classic UNIX Games

Bsd-games
 DEB: bsdgames
 RPM: bsd-games
 WWW: ftp://metalab.unc.edu/pub/Linux/games/

This is a collection of venerable card games, action and adventure games, board games, and screen amusements.

By contemporary standards, they offer little in terms of sensory stimulation. But they are classics that in olden days were mainstays on college campuses and computer labs everywhere, and they can still be played on any terminal. They may amuse children and old-timers alike.

The following table lists the various games and programs included in this package, giving their system names and descriptions.

adventure	Text-based simulation game based on an actual cave in Kentucky called Colossal Cave. Written by William Crowther and Don Woods in the 1970s, it predates the PC era ZORK. More information on the history of this game is online at http://www.rickadams.org/adventure/.
arithmetic	Quizzes you on a set of elementary addition and subtraction problems and times your speed of answer.
atc	Air Traffic Controller simulation.
backgammon	One- or two-player backgammon game, with rules.

`banner`	Outputs text in a long vertical text font, good for printing large banners. (see Recipe 16.4.2 [Outputting Text Banners], page 402. On Debian systems, `banner` is included in the `bsdmainutils` package instead.)
`battlestar`	Text-based adventure game with a fantasy theme. Written by David Riggle in 1979.
`bcd`	Filters text into paper punch card output.
`boggle`	Popular word game.
`caesar`	Decrypts Julius Caesar's cipher (see Recipe 29.6 [Using ROT13 Encryption], page 569).
`canfield`	Variant of solitaire.
`cfscores`	Displays your canfield scores.
`countmail`	Tells you how much mail you have, but in a "rather obnoxious" manner.
`cribbage`	The card game of cribbage.
`fish`	The children's card game of Go Fish.
`gomoku`	Two-player game of Five in a Row.
`hangman`	The classic "guess the word" game.
`hunt`	Multi-player network game whose object is to hunt and kill all other players.
`mille`	Mille Bornes, a two-handed card game.
`monop`	Monopoly, a property management game similar to the famous board game.
`morse`	Filters text into Morse code. Writes the words "dit" and "daw" by default; use `-s` to output dots and dashes instead of words. To decode Morse code into plain text, use the `-d` option.

number	Converts Arabic numerals to English (see Recipe 29.5.2 [Converting an Arabic Numeral to English], page 568).
phantasia	A role-playing fantasy game.
pig	Filters text into Pig Latin. No reverse filter is currently available.
pom	Tells you the current phase of the Moon.
ppt	Filters text into paper tape ribbon output.
primes	Outputs prime numbers, beginning at 0 and stopping at 4,294,967,295 or a number given in standard input; you can also give start and stop values as arguments. For example, to output the prime numbers between one and ten, primes 1 10 is the command to run.
quiz	Quizzes you on facts and trivia from a variety of subjects.
rot13	Encrypts and decrypts ROT13 ciphers (see Recipe 29.6 [Using ROT13 Encryption], page 569).
rain	Displays an animation of raindrops falling on the screen. Control the delay by giving a value, in milliseconds, as an argument to the -d option. For example, rain -d 160 is a good setting to try.
random	Outputs random lines from its input.
robots	Shoot-'em-up game where you battle killer robots.
sail	Role-playing game of an old-fashioned sea battle.
snake	Avoid the snake while collecting money.
snscore	Displays the high scores of snake.
teachgammon	Instructions for the game of backgammon.
tetris-bsd	The famous Russian video game of Tetris.
trek	Space adventure game.

`wargames`	The game of Global Thermonuclear War, as inspired by the film *WarGames*: "Shall we play a game?"
`worm`	The "growing worm" game.
`worms`	Displays an animations of worms squirming over the display screen.
`wtf`	Explains acronyms used in online communication. It isn't very advanced (for instance, it doesn't even know what FAQs are), but it does know what LOL is. If it doesn't know the acronym, it looks to see if `whatis` can give any help (see Recipe 11.4.2 [Translating Common Acronyms], page 292).
`wump`	The adventure game of "Hunt the Wumpus," perhaps the most famous of classic computer games.

NOTES: In the DEB package, a list of original authors for all of the included programs is at `usr/share/doc/bsdgames/AUTHORS`.

30.2 Filtering Text Through a Dialect

Talk Filters
 DEB: filters
 WWW: `http://www.gnu.org/directory/games/GNUTalkFilters.html`

Generally speaking, a *filter* is a tool that works on standard input, changing it in some way, and then passing it to standard output.

There are all kinds of tools that work as filters on text; this recipe describes a specific group of filters—those that filter their standard input to give the text an accent or dialect and are intended to be humorous. They are collected in a package called the GNU Talk Filters.

⇒ To apply the `kraut` filter to the text in the file `/etc/motd`, type:

    $ kraut < /etc/motd ⟨RET⟩

This command passes the contents of the file `/etc/motd` to the `kraut` filter, whose output is then sent to standard output. The contents of `/etc/motd` are not changed.

NOTES: Some of the dialect filters available include `nyc`, which gives a "New Yawker" dialect to text, and `newspeak`, which translates what is really said into the approved, politically correct language of the thought police, as described in George Orwell's novel, *1984*. War Is Peace! Freedom Is Slavery!

Some sample text and the way it appears through the various filters is kept in the file `/usr/share/doc/filters/SAMPLES`.

While all of the given filters are humorous, it is possible to write your own filters to change patterns of text in its input for some serious purpose, such as filtering text for a publication's "house style."

30.3 Testing Your Typing Speed

You can test your typing speed by combining a few tools. To test your typing speed at the shell prompt, run `cat` and type some text, piping the output to `wc` to get the word count of what you type. Run `date` immediately before and after the test by running all of these commands in a list (see Recipe 3.1.7 [Running a List of Commands], page 63).

⇒ To test your typing speed, type:

```
$ date; cat | wc -w; date ⟨RET⟩
Mon Aug 11 15:14:06 EDT 2003
The quick brown fox jumped over the lazy dog. ⟨RET⟩
⟨CTRL⟩-⟨D⟩
        9
Mon Aug 11 15:14:12 EDT 2003
$
```

In this example, "9" was output indicating that the user typed nine words (in a real typing test, you want to type for longer than that—at least a few hundred words to get an accurate count). The dates listed before and after the typing show that it took the user six seconds to type these nine words.

Use `bc` or any other calculator to divide the number of words by the time in minutes (or seconds) it took to type them.

NOTES: You can test your typing in Emacs by running the `time` function before and after your typing; then select the text that was typed and send it to `wc` to get the number of words.

30.4 Displaying Random Quotations

There are at least two ways to get a random quotation in Linux.

METHOD #1

Fortune
  DEB: fortune-mod
       fortune-min
  RPM: fortune-mod
  WWW: http://www.ibiblio.org/pub/Linux/games/amusements/fortune/

Use `fortune` to output a "fortune cookie" to the standard output.

⇒ To get a fortune, type:

> $ *fortune* ⟨RET⟩

NOTES: This venerable program has been on UNIX systems for a long time, and several types of specialized `fortune` databases are available. You can even make your own `fortune` files, containing quotations of your own choosing—these are made with the `strfile` command.

METHOD #2

In Emacs, you can get random quotations from Zippy the Pinhead, the comic strip character. When you run the `yow` function, a Zippy quote is written to the minibuffer.

⇒ To get a line from Zippy, type:

> ⟨ALT⟩-⟨X⟩ *yow* ⟨RET⟩

30.5 Finding Matches for Word Games

The following recipes describe ways to use various tools for finding words you might use for word games: anagrams, palindromes, and words for crossword puzzles.

30.5.1 Finding Anagrams in Text

An
  DEB: an

An *anagram* is a word or phrase whose characters consist entirely of all the characters of another given word or phrase—for example, "stop" and "tops" are both anagrams of "pots."

Use **an** to find and output anagrams. Give as an argument the word or quoted phrase to use; **an** writes its results to the standard output.

⇒ Here are two ways to use this.

- To output all anagrams of the word "lake," type:

  `$ an lake` $\langle$RET$\rangle$

- To output all anagrams of the phrase "lakes and oceans," type:

  `$ an 'lakes and oceans'` $\langle$RET$\rangle$

To limit the anagrams that are output to those containing a given string, specify that string with the `-c` option.

⇒ To output only anagrams of the phrase "lakes and oceans" that contain the string "seas," type:

  `$ an -c seas 'lakes and oceans'` $\langle$RET$\rangle$

To print all of the words that can be made with some or all of the letters in a given word or phrase, use the `-w` option. This outputs words that are not anagrams, because anagrams must contain *all* of the letters of the other word or phrase.

⇒ To output all of the words that can be made from the letters of the word "seas," type:

  `$ an -w seas` $\langle$RET$\rangle$

This command outputs all of the words that can be formed from all or some of the characters in "seas," including "see" and "as."

NOTES: There are other tools for finding anagrams, but this one is the best. Unfortunately, it isn't widely available outside of the Debian distribution; if you can't locate a copy, you can always install the sources from the Debian package (see Recipe 1.1.2 [Preparation of Recipes], page 4).

30.5.2 Finding Palindromes in Text

A *palindrome* is a word or phrase that reads the same both forwards and backwards; for example, "Mom," "nun," and "Madam, I'm Adam" are all palindromes.

Here are a few PERL "one-liners" for finding palindromes.

METHOD #1

To output all lines in a file that are palindromes, use this simple PERL one-liner, and substitute the name of the file to check for *file*:

```
perl -lne 'map { print if $_ eq reverse } split' file
```

This outputs all lines in *file* that are palindromes. To check for palindromes in the standard input, specify - as the file name to check. This is useful at the end of a pipeline.

⇒ To output all of the palindromes in the system dictionary, type:

    $ perl -lne 'print if $_ eq reverse' /usr/dict/words (RET)

METHOD #2

To output all lines in a file that are palindromes, regardless of whitespace, punctuation, and case, use the following one-liner instead of the one given in Method #1:

    perl -lne '{ $_ = lc; $_ =~ s/\W//g; $_ = reverse; print if $_ eq
    reverse }' file

This outputs all lines in *file* that are palindromes (all whitespace and punctuation will be removed, and all letters will be converted to lowercase).

⇒ To output all of the lines in the file `riddles` that are palindromes regardless of whitespace, punctuation, and case, type (all on one line):

    $ perl -lne '{ $_ = lc; $_ =~ s/\W//g; $_ = reverse; print if $_
    eq reverse }' riddles (RET)

30.5.3 Finding Crossword Puzzle Words

There are a few things you can do with a Linux system to help solve a crossword puzzle.

METHOD #1

One method for finding crossword puzzle words is to peruse the system dictionary file, `/usr/dict/words`, for words you are looking for. Use `less` with the -p option to begin perusing at a certain point—such as a letter or a word prefix.

⇒ Here are two ways to use this.

   • To peruse the system dictionary, beginning at the first match for the pattern "dog," type:

       $ less -pdog /usr/dict/words (RET)

   • To peruse the system dictionary, starting at the word "cat," type:

       $ less -p"^cat" /usr/dict/words (RET)

In the last example, the system dictionary will load and begin at the word "cat," and that string will be highlighted in the text.

You can also use **look** to output all words that begin with a given string (see Recipe 11.2.1 [Listing Words That Match a Pattern], page 283).

⇒ To list all words that begin with "**anti**," type:

```
$ look anti ⟨RET⟩
```

METHOD #2

Another method you can try for finding crossword puzzle words is **grep** the dictionary for the pattern you need—if you know a word is so many characters long, or has characters in certain positions, you can search for all words that fit the pattern. Use the **-i** option to do a case-insensitive search.

⇒ Here are some ways to use this.

- To output all words in the system dictionary that are four characters long, begin with the letter "z," and end with an "a," regardless of case, type:

```
$ grep -i '^z..a$' /usr/dict/words ⟨RET⟩
```

- To output all words in the system dictionary that are six characters long, have the letter "e" in the second position, and have either an "s" or an "o" in the fourth position, type:

```
$ grep -i '^.e.[so]..$' /usr/dict/words ⟨RET⟩
```

NOTES: These methods are also good for Scrabble and other word games.

On some systems, **/usr/share/dict/words** is where the the system dictionary is kept.

30.6 Cuting Up Text

A *cut-up* is a random rearrangement of a physical layout of text, made with the intention of finding unique or interesting phrases in the rearrangement. Software for rearranging text in random ways has existed since the earliest text-processing tools; the popularity of these tools will never die.

The cut-up technique in literature was discovered by painter Brion Gysin and American writer William S. Burroughs in 1959; they believed it brought the montage technique of painting to the written word.

"All writing is in fact cut-ups," Burroughs wrote.[1] "A collage of words read heard overheard ... [u]se of scissors renders the process explicit and subject to extension and variation."

These recipes describe a few of the common ways to make text cut-ups.

---

[1] In *The Third Mind*, by William S. Burroughs and Brion Gysin (Viking Press, 1978).

30.6.1 Making Simple Text Cut-Ups

You can make a shell script to perform a simple cut-up of a text. It demonstrates the combined use of **head**, **tail**, and **paste**. Make a shell script called **cutup**, as in Figure 30-1 (see Recipe 3.7 [Using Shell Scripts], page 84).

```
#!/bin/sh
count=`wc -l < $1`
half=`expr $count / 2`
middle=`awk ' if (length($0) > max) max = length($0)
END  OFMT = "%.0f"
print max / 2' $1`
end=`expr $middle + 1`
head -$half $1|cut -b0-$middle  > $1.1
tail -$half $1|cut -b0-$middle  > $1.3
head -$half $1|cut -b$end-80 > $1.2
tail -$half $1|cut -b$end-80 > $1.4
paste -d "" $1.4 $1.3
paste -d "" $1.2 $1.1
rm $1.1 $1.2 $1.3 $1.4
```

Figure 30-1. The cutup *file.*

This script takes the name of a file as input and cuts it both horizontally and vertically along the middle, rearranges the four sections to their diagonally opposite corners, and then writes that cut-up to the standard output. The original file is not modified.

⇒ To make a cut-up from a file called **nova**, type:

$ *cutup nova* (RET)

30.6.2 Making Random Word Cut-Ups

Dadadodo
  DEB: dadadodo
  RPM: dadadodo
  WWW: http://www.jwz.org/dadadodo/

No simple cut-up filter, Jamie Zawinski's **dadadodo** uses the computer to go one step beyond—it generates passages of random text whose structure and characters are similar to the text input you give it. The program works better on larger texts, where more subtleties can be analyzed and hence more realistic-looking text is output.

Give as an argument the name of the text file to be used; by default, dadadodo outputs text to standard output until you interrupt it by typing ⟨CTRL⟩-⟨C⟩.

⇒ To output random text based on the text in the file **nova**, type:

        $ dadadodo nova ⟨RET⟩

This command will output passages of random text based on the text in the file **nova** until it is interrupted by the user.

You can analyze a text and save the analysis to a file of compiled data; this analysis can then be used to generate random text when the original input text is not present. The following table describes this and other **dadadodo** options.

-c *integer*	Generate *integer* sentences (default is 0, meaning "generate an infinite amount until interrupted").
-l *filename*	Load compiled data in *file* and use it to generate text.
-o *filename*	Output compiled data to *file* for later use.
-p *integer*	Pause for *integer* seconds between paragraphs.

30.6.3 Making Cut-Ups in Emacs

The **dissociated-press** function in Emacs makes random cut-ups of the current buffer in a new buffer called ***Dissociation***; the original buffer is not modified. The text in the new buffer is generated by combining random portions of the buffer by overlapping characters or words, thus (usually) creating plausible-sounding sentences. It pauses occasionally and asks whether or not you want to continue the dissociation.

⇒ To generate a Dissociated Press cut-up from the current buffer, type:

        ⟨ALT⟩-⟨X⟩ *dissociated-press* ⟨RET⟩

Give a positive argument to the **dissociated-press** function to specify the number of characters to use for overlap; give a negative argument to specify the number of *words* for overlap.

⇒ Here are two ways to use this.

- To generate a Dissociated Press cut-up from the current buffer, always overlapping by three characters, type:

        ⟨CTRL⟩-⟨U⟩ 3 ⟨ALT⟩-⟨X⟩ *dissociated-press* ⟨RET⟩

- To generate a Dissociated Press cut-up from the current buffer, always overlapping by one word, type:

  ⟨CTRL⟩-⟨U⟩ -1 ⟨ALT⟩-⟨X⟩ `dissociated-press` ⟨RET⟩

30.7 Undergoing Psychoanalysis

Emacs has a special mode called `doctor`, which is an implementation of the famous ELIZA program. As with "real" psychoanalysis, you talk out your troubles and the doctor asks you for more—only in this case it doesn't cost as much, and sessions last as long as you like. And since the "session" is an Emacs buffer, you can save it to a file for posterity.

⇒ To begin a session of psychoanalysis in Emacs, type:

   ⟨ALT⟩-⟨X⟩ `doctor` ⟨RET⟩

VII. NETWORKING

## CHAPTER 31

Communications

You will almost certainly want to go online or otherwise communicate with other computer systems. Most systems today are sold with the necessary hardware to connect to other systems, such as a modem or a network card. You connect this hardware to the outside world via a telephone line or network connection.

This chapter includes recipes for connecting your Linux system to the Internet with an ISP, using fax services, and making serial connections with a modem.

For more information on this subject, see the *Linux Network Administrators' Guide* [`http://metalab.unc.edu/mdw/LDP/nag/nag.html`].

31.1 Connecting to the Internet

PPP
  DEB: ppp
  RPM: ppp
  WWW: `ftp://cs.anu.edu.au/pub/software/ppp/`

There are several ways to connect a Linux box[1] to the Internet. Digital Subscriber Line (DSL) service, cable modems, and dial-up connections with ISDN or analog modems are currently the most popular methods. Each of these services has its own hardware and software requirements. Generally, you get these services by subscribing to them from an Internet Service Provider, or ISP.

For up-to-date, detailed instructions for using these services on Linux-based systems, the relevant HOWTOs published by the Linux Documentation Project [`http://xtldp.org/`] remain the definitive guides (see Recipe 2.8.6 [Reading System Documentation and Help Files], page 50):

- *ISP Hookup HOWTO*, by Egil Kvaleberg
  `http://tldp.org/HOWTO/ISP-Hookup-HOWTO.html`
- *DSL HOWTO for Linux*, by David Fannin et al.
  `http://en.tldp.org/HOWTO/DSL-HOWTO/`

---

[1] A computer is sometimes called a *box*, particularly when one aspect of it is being described; therefore when you hear talk about a "Linux box" you know it's just a computer that is running Linux. This slang is particularly popular among users of UNIX flavors, but people do talk of Windows boxes.

- *Cable Modem Providers HOWTO*, by Vladimir Vuksan
  http://en.tldp.org/HOWTO/Cable-Modem/

The following recipes show how to set up and use a PPP ("Point-to-Point Protocol") dial-up connection, long the *de facto* means of connecting a computer to the Internet over a dial-up line.

31.1.1 Setting Up PPP

To configure PPP for a regular dial-up connection, where your system is assigned a dynamic IP address (the norm for home Internet access), you need to be **root** (the superuser) to edit the PPP configuration files, and you'll need the standard connection information from your ISP: the dial-up number to use, the IP addresses for its nameservers, and a username and password.

Use this information to customize the file **/etc/chatscripts/provider**, as in Figure 31-1.

```
ABORT        BUSY
ABORT        "NO CARRIER"
ABORT        VOICE
ABORT        "NO DIALTONE"
""           "\p\p+++\p\p"
""           "at"
""           "at"
OK           "ath0"
""           atdt5551010,,
ost          ppp
ogin         smith
word         \qsecret\q
```

Figure 31-1. A sample /etc/chatscripts/provider file.

In Figure 31-1, after eight lines of modem initialization strings, the modem is instructed to dial the ISP dial-up number, 555-1010. Some systems need one or two commas after the number to signify pauses for the modem; only do this if you can't get a good connection with just the telephone number in this space.

Next come the lines which show the prompts your ISP is expected to send, and the strings to give in response to them. Traditionally, only partial strings are shown to match the prompts, in part because case for the various prompts differs between systems. This is why the file has "ost," "ogin," and "word," and not "`host:`," "`login:`," and "`Password:`," which are typically the full prompts you might expect.

The "`host:`" prompt is optional, and is used by some ISPs whose connection line contains a choice of services from which you must make a selection before entering your username and password (some ISPs offer SLIP and shell access along with the standard PPP, for example). Customize this and the following lines as instructed by your ISP. If your ISP does not have a "host" prompt, then remove this line.

In this example, the username `smith` is sent as a response to the "`login:`" prompt, and then the password of "`secret`" is sent for a password. The password appears between two "`\q`" strings in this file, which—for security purposes—instruct `ppp` to display question mark characters (`?`) instead of the actual password in system log files or other places where an intruder might see it.

Next, edit the file `/etc/ppp/peers/provider` so that it looks like Figure 31-2.

```
connect "/usr/sbin/chat -v -f /etc/chatscripts/provider"
defaultroute /dev/modem 115200 persist
```

Figure 31-2. The `/etc/ppp/peers/provider` file.

The last line in this file[2] should include the device name of the modem you are using and the maximum connect speed to try; Figure 31-2 uses `/dev/modem` as the device name of the modem, and 115,200 BPS as the maximum connect speed, which is a good value for a typical 56 K modem (a rule of thumb is to use the highest connect speed your modem supports; you can always go lower when a connection is made, but you can never raise the speed above what is given here).

Finally, edit the file `/etc/resolv.conf` so that it looks like Figure 31-3, using the two nameserver IP addresses given to you by your ISP.

```
search .
nameserver        nameserver address 1
nameserver        nameserver address 2
```

Figure 31-3. The `/etc/resolv.conf` file.

---

[2] On some newer PPP implementations, each of these words are not all on a single line, but are each given on a line of their own.

For the two *nameserver address* values, use the IP address of the nameserver machines, as given to you by your ISP. The second is optional—most ISPs have more than one designated nameserver as a backup in the event that the first system becomes unavailable.

Make sure that your user account has membership to the `dialout` group; otherwise, the superuser account will have to start and stop PPP, which is not recommended (see Recipe A.6.3 [Letting Users Access Hardware Peripherals], page 718).

Once you've done these things, you should be able to start and stop PPP connections to the Internet. Complete documentation for setting up PPP is in the `/usr/share/doc/ppp` directory.

31.1.2 Starting a PPP Connection

Once PPP has been installed and configured, use the `pon` tool to start a PPP connection to the Internet. It calls the number of your ISP with your modem, sends the appropriate login information, and starts the PPP connection.

After a PPP connection has been established, you can access the WWW or other network services, as described in the following chapters.

⇒ To start a PPP connection, type:

    $ pon ⟨RET⟩

NOTES: To make PPP automatically start when the system first boots, rename the file `/etc/ppp/no_ppp_on_boot` to `/etc/ppp/ppp_on_boot`. (You must be `root`, the superuser, to do this.)

31.1.3 Stopping a PPP Connection

Use the `poff` tool to stop a PPP connection. It disconnects your computer from your ISP and hangs up the modem.

⇒ To stop a PPP connection, type:

    $ poff ⟨RET⟩

If you ever accidentally run `pon` when a PPP connection is already established (it happens), `poff` will not work as expected because there are multiple PPP connections running. Use the `-a` option to stop all PPP connections.

⇒ To stop all PPP connections, type:

    $ poff -a ⟨RET⟩

31.1.4 Viewing the PPP Log

Use `plog` to output the last few lines of the PPP log file. This is useful for checking the progress of your PPP connection when it first dials.

⇒ To view the latest entries in the PPP log file, type:

  $ *plog* ⟨RET⟩

NOTES: You need to be a member of the `adm` group in order to view the log file (see Recipe A.6.3 [Letting Users Access Hardware Peripherals], page 718).

31.2 Faxing

Efax
  DEB: efax
  RPM: efax
  WWW: http://www.cce.com/efax/

If you have a Class 1 or 2 fax modem, you can send and receive fax ("facsimile") messages with your Linux system. The following recipes show how to do this with the `efax` package, which is designed for single user systems or relatively simple fax configurations (more complicated tools for faxing exist, but they are beyond the scope of this book).

To set up `efax` for faxing, edit the file `/etc/efax.rc` (you must be `root` to do this). The important things to specify in this file are the value for "DEV," which is the device name in `/dev` of the fax or modem device (this should almost always be "`modem`"), and the values for "FROM" and "NAME"—the fax number and organization name to appear on outgoing faxes.

NOTES: Unless you have membership to the `dialout` group, you must ask your system administrator for access to the modem hardware before you can use it (see Recipe A.6.3 [Letting Users Access Hardware Peripherals], page 718).

More information on faxing is contained in the *Fax Server mini-HOWTO* (see Recipe 2.8.6 [Reading System Documentation and Help Files], page 50).

31.2.1 Sending a Fax

Use `efax` to send a fax. It dials the telephone number you give and faxes the contents of the file or files you specify. You can send plain text files or files in TIFF Group 3 format as they are. You can also send files in other formats, but you must convert them to TIFFG3 format first—see Recipe 31.2.4 [Converting to and from Fax Format], page 604.

Use the -d option to specify the full path name of the fax device (usually /dev/modem if you are using the modem connected to your system), and use the -t option followed by a telephone number to specify the number to send the fax to. To specify DTMF tone dialing, precede the phone number with a "T"; specify pauses in the dialing sequence with a comma—particularly useful for dialing out from a PBX or office phone system.

⇒ To fax a copy of the file **resume.txt** to the number 555-9099, using DTMF tone dialing, type:

```
$ efax -d /dev/modem -t T555-9099 resume.txt ⟨RET⟩
```

To send more than one file, specify them as arguments in the order they are to be sent. You can also specify them with a wildcard character, but be careful—they are sent in the order in which the shell expands the file names, which is alphabetical order. If you have a lot of files that should be sent in a particular order, rename them so their file names begin with the number of the page they correspond to. But be sure to number them with the *same number of digits* for each file—for example, if you have 11 files to fax, don't name them 1.fax, 2.fax, and so on, to 10.fax and 11.fax, because the shell will expand them in the order of 1.fax, 10.fax, 11.fax, 2.fax, 3.fax, and so on up to 9.fax. In this case, you would number them as 01.fax, 02.fax, and so on, so that files 1 through 9 contain the same number of digits in their names as do 10.fax and 11.fax.

⇒ To fax all of the files with the .fax extension in the current directory to the number 555-9099, using DTMF tone dialing, type:

```
$ efax -d /dev/modem -t T555-9099 *.fax ⟨RET⟩
```

Another way to do this is to make a text file containing the list of files to fax, one file name per line, in the order you want them sent. If the files you want to send are not in the current directory, be sure to write the file names with path names relative to the current directory—so for example, if you want to send the file **header.fax**, which is in your home directory, and the current directory is ~/documents/faxes, the file should be specified as ~/header.fax.

⇒ To fax all of the files listed in the file **fax.list** to the number 555-9099, dialing a 9 first to obtain an outside line, and using DTMF tone dialing, type:

```
$ efax -d /dev/modem -t T9,555-9099 $(cat fax.list) ⟨RET⟩
```

NOTES: The **efax** tool doesn't delete the files it faxes.

31.2.2 Receiving a Fax

To receive a fax, use `efax` with the `-w` option. You may also have to use `-iSO=1` to send an SO=1 command to the modem to set it to auto answer, and use `-kZ` to send an "ATZ" reset request to the modem after `efax` exits.

As with sending a fax, specify the full path name of the device file to use with the `-d` option.

By default, `efax` outputs a "session log" to the standard error, containing information on the status of the fax messages received; use redirection to redirect it to a file (see Recipe 3.2.3 [Redirecting Error Messages to a File], page 68).

⇒ To set up `efax` to receive an incoming fax, saving the session log to a file, `faxlog`, type:

```
$ efax -d /dev/modem -kZ -w -iSO=1 2>&1 >> faxlog ⟨RET⟩
```

This command starts `efax` and sets up the modem to wait for an incoming fax. After a fax is received, `efax` exits. You can stop `efax` before it receives a fax by typing ⟨CTRL⟩-⟨C⟩ or by killing the `efax` job (see Recipe 3.3.5 [Stopping a Job], page 73).

When a fax is received, it is written to a file in the current directory whose base name consists of the current numeric date and a session number generated by `efax`; each page is written to a separate file whose three-digit file extension is the page number. The received fax files are in TIFF Group 3 fax format; use `display` to view them (see Recipe 17.1 [Viewing an Image in X], page 407), or convert them to PostScript or another format for printing (see Recipe 31.2.4 [Converting to and from Fax Format], page 604).

31.2.3 Receiving Faxes Automatically

The command described in the previous recipe can only receive one fax; once the fax is received, `efax` exits. To run `efax` so that you automatically receive all incoming fax messages, use a Bash `while` loop so that after a fax is received, `efax` is started again and continues until you interrupt it (see the Bash Info documentation for more information on this built-in).

⇒ To automatically receive any incoming fax messages, type:

```
$ while true ; do efax answer ; done (RET)
efax: Wed Feb 24 08:38:52 1999 efax v 0.8a (Debian release 08a-6)
Copyright 1996 Ed Casas
efax: 38:52 opened /dev/modem
efax: 38:53 waiting for activity
```

This command uses all of the default settings for the **efax** package, which you can configure. Old spool files are deleted and any recieved faxes are mailed to you.

If you need to set more switches on **efax** and don't wish to type this every time you want to set up the fax machine, you can write a shell script to do more and save it in a file called **faxon**, as in Figure 31-4. Put it in your personal **bin** directory (see Recipe C.1 [Using a Directory for Personal Binaries], page 727). Each time a fax is received and then saved, **efax** restarts, waiting for another fax. A session log is written to the file **faxlog** in your home directory.

```
#!/bin/sh
while :
    do
        trap break 2;
        efax -d /dev/modem -kZ -w -iS0=1 2>&1 >> ~/faxlog;
done
```

*Figure 31-4. The **faxon** file.*

Should an incoming facsimile message arrive, **efax** will receive it and write the message in files in the current directory, with a file name convention as described previously; then **efax** restarts, ready to receive another fax. Type ⟨CTRL⟩-⟨C⟩ to stop the script and exit **efax**.

31.2.4 Converting to and from Fax Format

In order to view or print a received fax, or to fax a file that you have, you must first convert the file to or from the TIFF Group 3 (TIFFG3) fax format, which is the standard format for sending fax files. (You can, however, view TIFFG3 files with the GIMP, or with **display**—see Recipe 17.1 [Viewing an Image in X], page 407). Consequently, files you receive via fax will be in this format, which you might want to convert to some other format.

There are several ways to do this.

METHOD #1

Use `efix` to convert (or "fix") files for faxing; it will convert a file you want to fax *to* the TIFFG3 format. You can also use it to convert received fax files to another format that you can view or print. The `efix` tool writes to the standard output, but you can redirect its output to a file to save it.

To convert a file for faxing, type `efix` followed by the name of the file to convert, and redirect standard output to the file you want to contain your fax image. `efix` can read plain text, PBM, and TIFF files.

⇒ To convert the file `chart.pbm` for faxing, type:

```
$ efix -i pbm chart.pbm > chart.fax ⟨RET⟩
```

This command converts a copy of the file `chart.pbm` to the TIFFG3 fax format, writing it to a file called `chart.fax`. The original PBM file is not altered.

METHOD #2

To convert a received fax file to a PostScript file that you can then preview (see Recipe 17.4.2 [Previewing a PostScript File], page 414) or print (see Recipe 25.1.1 [Sending a Print Job to the Printer], page 510), use `efix` with the `-o ps` option.

⇒ To convert `19990325.001`, a received fax file, to a PostScript file, type:

```
$ efix -o ps 19990325.001 > received.ps ⟨RET⟩
```

This command converts the fax file into PostScript, and writes the output to a file called `received.ps`. The original fax file is not altered.

METHOD #3

```
Ghostscript
  DEB: gs-common gs
  RPM: ghostscript
  WWW: http://www.cs.wisc.edu/~ghost/
```

To convert a PostScript file to fax format, use `gs` and specify "`tiffg3`" as the output device to write to.

⇒ To convert the PostScript file `resume.ps` to fax format, type (all on one line):

```
$ gs -q -sDEVICE=tiffg3 -dSAFER -dNOPAUSE
-sOutputFile=resume.fax resume.ps < /dev/null (RET)
```

This command writes a copy of the file `resume.ps` to the file `resume.fax` in TIFFG3 format, which you can then send as a fax. The original PostScript file is not altered.

NOTES: For more on using **gs**, see Recipe 25.3.1 [Preparing a PostScript File for Printing], page 518.

METHOD #4

teTeX
  DEB: `tetex-base`
       `tetex-bin`
       `tetex-doc`
       `tetex-extra`
  RPM: `tetex`
  WWW: `http://www.tug.org/teTeX/`

Use `dvi2fax` to convert a DVI file made from TeX into `tiffg3` format for faxing.

It takes as options either `-hi` for high resolution, outputting at 204x196 dpi (the default), or `-lo` for low resolution, outputting at 204x98 dpi.

Give as an argument the name of the DVI file to convert; giving the `.dvi` extension is optional.

⇒ To convert the file `proposal.let.dvi` to low resolution fax-format files, type:

```
$ dvi2fax -lo proposal.let (RET)
```

Each page of input is written to its own file, numbered in order and with a `.fax` extension.

31.3 Calling Out on a Modem

Minicom
  DEB: `minicom`
  RPM: `minicom`

Use Minicom to dial out with the modem and connect with another system, such as when you want to connect to a BBS ("Bulletin Board System"). It's a serial communications tool for X or the console; it resembles some of the communications tools of the DOS world, such as Telix and Procomm.

Type `minicom` to run Minicom. When Minicom starts, you will be given a connection screen, which looks like Figure 31-5.

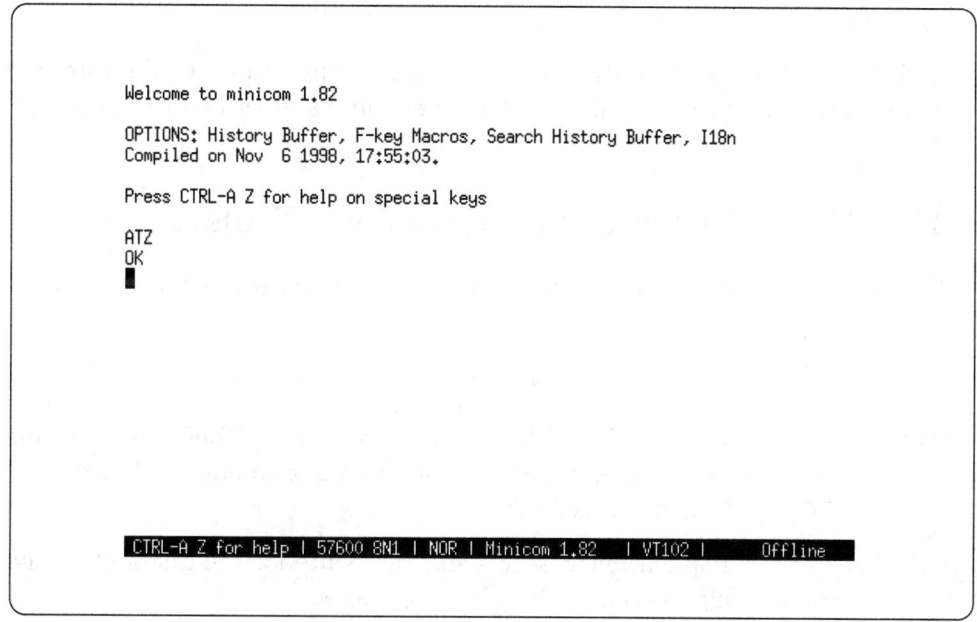

```
Welcome to minicom 1.82

OPTIONS: History Buffer, F-key Macros, Search History Buffer, I18n
Compiled on Nov  6 1998, 17:55:03.

Press CTRL-A Z for help on special keys

ATZ
OK
█




CTRL-A Z for help | 57600 8N1 | NOR | Minicom 1.82  | VT102 |     Offline
```

Figure 31-5. The `minicom` connection screen.

The bottom line contains a status bar showing a message describing how to get help, the current modem settings (in this case, 57,600 BPS, 8 data bits, no parity, one stop bit), whether or not cursor keys work (the mysterious "NOR" message), the version of the program ("1.82"), the kind of terminal emulation currently set ("VT102"), and whether or not an online connection is currently established.

To get a help menu, type ⟨CTRL⟩–⟨A⟩ z while in the connection screen; from the help menu, you can press ⟨P⟩ to set the communications parameters, ⟨T⟩ to set the terminal settings, ⟨O⟩ to configure `minicom`, or ⟨D⟩ to enter the dialing directory.

To dial a number from the connection screen, type `ATDT` followed by the number to dial.

⇒ To dial the number 368-2208,x type:

     ATDT3682208 ⟨RET⟩

When you type ⟨RET⟩, Minicom will begin dialing the number; type any key
to interrupt the dialing and hang up the line. Once connected, type ⟨CTRL⟩-⟨A⟩
h to hang up the line, or type ⟨CTRL⟩-⟨A⟩ x to hang up the line and exit the
program.

NOTES: Minicom isn't really a way to connect your system to the Internet;
to do that, you normally start a PPP connection, as described earlier in this
chapter.[3]

31.4 Using Other Communications Tools

The following table describes other tools for communications that you might
find handy.

DTMFdial
         Generates dual-tone multi-frequency ("Touch Tone"), and
         can be used for automatic dialing from address books.
         DEB: `dtmfdial`

HylaFAX
         Popular client-server software suite for sending and receiv-
         ing faxes as well as sending pages.
         DEB: `hylafax-client`
         DEB: `hylafax-server`
         DEB: `hylafax-doc`
         RPM: `hylafax`
         WWW: `http://www.hylafax.org/`

---

[3] Technically, you can use Minicom to dial a computer that *is* connected to the Internet,
like a local Free-Net system, but your access to the net will be restricted within this
Minicom window; with a traditional Internet connection such as PPP, your whole system
has direct access to the net, including your Web browsers, email software, and other
networking tools.

Lrzsz   Offers the Xmodem, Ymodem, and Zmodem protocols for file transfer over serial lines; based on the old **rzsz** package for UNIX systems.
DEB: lrzsz
RPM: lrzsz
WWW: http://www.ohse.de/uwe/software/lrzsz.html

Seyon   Old-time telecommunications tool for X, similar to Minicom, with Zmodem protocol support and scripting capabilities.
DEB: seyon
WWW: ftp://sipb.mit.edu/pub/seyon/

## CHAPTER 32

Email

The primary means of sending plain-text messages (or binaries in attachment files) between users across computer networks is called electronic mail, or *email* (and more often than not these days, just "mail").

Mail is sent and received in a special application called a *mail user agent*, or MUA.[1]

Most of them operate by the same general principle: When you start it, a list of all your incoming mail is displayed like a kind of stack, in the order in which they were received, with one numbered line representing each message, and on it is the author's name, the subject, and the date. Selecting a number will display its contents on the screen, and offer a means of replying to it with a mail of your own, as well as a facility to write new mail.

The number of these email applications available for Linux is large, and you could spend many hours exploring the details of all of them. Instead of beginning with such an exhibit, this chapter does three things: provide a brief introduction to using the default mail agent; show how you can use other tools on the system to manipulate your email, regardless of the MUA you use; and give an overview of the most popular and well-supported mail agents, with pointers on where to go for more information.

The default mail agent on Linux, as with other UNIX-based systems, is the `mail` tool.[2] This is the tool we will use in this chapter for showing how to send and receive mail.

It comes without many bells and whistles that are standard on most of the newer MUAs, and any user who sends and receives email more than occasionally will certainly want to learn a more advanced system (see Recipe 32.7 [Using Other Mail User Agents], page 631).

However, `mail` is available on almost all UNIX-based systems, it's capable of a few powerful tricks that you can't do with the other applications, and it always works in a pinch—by learning to use it, you can always send and receive email on any Linux- or UNIX-based system you ever encounter.

---

[1] Everyone outside of the UNIX world probably calls one of these an "email app" or email program.

[2] On many Linux systems, `Mail` is a synonymous name for this tool. And on some UNIX systems such as AIX, the name of the tool is `mailx`; Linux provides that name as an additional synonym.

32.1 Sending Mail

To send an email message with `mail`, give as arguments the email addresses to
which you are sending the message, and then type the subject and the body
of the message when prompted; type ⟨CTRL⟩-⟨D⟩ on a line by itself to signify
the end of the message body and send the message.

⇒ To send an email message to `lisa@example.com`, type:

```
$ mail lisa@example.com ⟨RET⟩
Subject: Hello ⟨RET⟩
Hi there, long time no talk! I'm just learning how to use ⟨RET⟩
Linux and thought I'd show you how easy it is to send email! ⟨RET⟩
⟨CTRL⟩-⟨D⟩
Cc: ⟨RET⟩
```

The text you type on the `Subject:` line is displayed as the subject of your
email message, and the lines of text you type after that are the body text
of the message. Various styles for sending email exist; some mimic paper
correspondence, with a salutation, closing, and signature, whole others give
just a signature, and still others omit all three. Email isn't always for proper
letters; sometimes it isn't elevated beyond the telegram or memo pad, used
only for the rapid transmission of brief informal messages.

Various commands available when composing email are described in
Recipe 32.1.5 [Composing a Mail], page 616.

Type ⟨CTRL⟩-⟨D⟩ on a line alone to end the message. Then, `mail` prompts
for `Cc:` addresses—a "carbon copy" of the email message is sent to any addresses you give here, if any. Separate multiple addresses with commas, or
just type ⟨RET⟩ if there are none.

When you type, `mail` just reads the standard input like any other command line tool, so there's little direct editing capability in this basic email
service—use ⟨CTRL⟩-⟨U⟩ to erase the current line, and ⟨CTRL⟩-⟨C⟩ ⟨CTRL⟩-⟨C⟩
(that is, ⟨CTRL⟩-⟨C⟩ pressed twice) to cancel your input and abort the message
altogether.

That's it! No bells, no whistles—but no time-wasting excess, either.

32.1.1 Mailing a User on the Same System

To send an email message to another user on the same system, give their username on the system instead of an email address.[3]

⇒ To send an email message to user `mrs` on your local system, type:

```
$ mail mrs ⟨RET⟩
Subject: Are you going to the party tonight? ⟨RET⟩
⟨CTRL⟩-⟨D⟩
Cc: ⟨RET⟩
Null message body; hope that's ok
$
```

This command sends an email message to the user `mrs` on the local system. The email message itself is empty, but the subject is a short note asking whether user `mrs` will be attending a party.

NOTES: Besides being good for sending mail to users that you might share your system with, `mail` is useful for sending *yourself* mail, as a way to give yourself a reminder at your terminal (see Recipe 27.6.2 [Sending Yourself Email Reminders], page 550).

32.1.2 Mailing a File or the Output of a Command

The `mail` tool is also useful for mailing the contents of a text file or the text output of a command. To do this, give the email addresses you want to send to as arguments to `mail`, and use the standard input redirection operators to redirect the text to use as the message body (see Recipe 3.2 [Redirecting Input and Output], page 67).

⇒ To mail the contents of the text file **traderoutes** to the email address **sofala@example.com**, type:

```
$ mail sofala@example.com < traderoutes ⟨RET⟩
```

32.1.3 Mailing a Directory

There are a few different methods for sending a directory of files in email.

---

[3] Technically, you still *are* giving the email address, since email addresses take the form of *username@hostname*; when *hostname* is omitted, the localhost is assumed.

METHOD #1

To send a directory of files with a MUA, you can put a copy of the directory in an archive (see Recipe 8.5 [Managing File Archives], page 199), `gzip` the archives, and then mail that compressed archive file as an attachment. This is how it's normally done.

METHOD #2

GNU Shar Utilities
DEB: sharutils
RPM: sharutils
WWW: http://www.gnu.org/software/sharutils/sharutils.html

You can also create a long pipeline to send the directory through the mail: Put a copy of the directory in a compressed archive with `tar`, and pipe the output of `tar` to uuencode, which encodes binary files into ASCII text that can be transmitted over mail in a plaintext message. Then, pipe that encoded text to `mail`.

⇒ To mail a copy of the `~/proj/latest` directory tree to `fred@example.org`, type (all on one line):

```
$ tar -czf - ~/proj/latest | uuencode latest.tar.gz |
mail -s "Here is the latest" fred@example.org (RET)
```

This command will mail the directory tree as a uuencoded compressed `tar` file in the body of the message. When it is received, `fred@example.org` should write the contents of the mail to a file, and run `uudecode` on it. It takes as an argument a uuencoded file, and it writes the decoded files to the current directory.

⇒ To decode the contents of `latest.uu`, type:

```
$ uudecode latest.uu (RET)
```

This command will write a compressed `tar` file, `latest.tar.gz`, in the current directory; to uncompress it, you would run `tar zxvf latest.tar.gz`.

32.1.4 Mailing a Web Page

A variation on the previous recipe is to use `mail` and shell redirection to send the output of some command to some address via email. The following methods show how to use this technique to mail a Web page as either rendered text or HTML source.

METHOD #1

Lynx
  DEB: lynx
  RPM: lynx
  WWW: http://lynx.browser.org/

To send a Web page as an annotated text file, pipe the output of the Lynx Web browser with the -dump option to mail (see Recipe 33.2 [Using Lynx], page 643). Since the output is plain text, you don't have to encode it before you mail it.

⇒ Here are two ways to use this.

- To send a mail to the address reader@example.com with the contents of http://gutenberg.net/etext98/rmnis10.txt, type (all on one line):

      $ *lynx -dump http://gutenberg.net/etext98/rmnis10.txt | mail reader@example.com* (RET)

- To send a mail to the address reader@example.com with the contents of http://gutenberg.net/etext98/rmnis10.txt and with a subject of "Some Reminiscences," type (all on one line):

      $ *lynx -dump http://gutenberg.net/etext98/rmnis10.txt | mail -s "Some Reminiscences" reader@example.com* (RET)

METHOD #2

Wget
  DEB: wget
  RPM: wget
  WWW: http://www.gnu.org/software/wget/wget.html

To send the HTML source of a Web page, use wget to retrieve the source, using the -q option to suppress messages and sending to the standard output by giving "-" as an argument to the -O option; pipe this to mail (see Recipe 33.5 [Getting Files from the Web], page 653).

⇒ Here are two ways to use this.

- To send a mail to the address reader@example.com with the contents of http://gutenberg.net/etext98/, type (all on one line):

      $ *wget -q -O - http://gutenberg.net/etext98/ | mail reader@example.com* (RET)

- To send a mail to the address `reader@example.com` with the contents of `http://gutenberg.net/etext98/` and with a subject of "Directory Listing," type (all on one line):

  $ *wget -q -O - http://gutenberg.net/etext98/* |
  mail -s "Directory Listing" reader@example.com ⟨RET⟩

32.1.5 Composing Mail

When composing a `mail` message, there are a number of special keystrokes available. The following table lists them, and describes their functions.

⟨CTRL⟩-⟨C⟩ ⟨CTRL⟩-⟨C⟩	Abort the current message and exit `mail` without sending it.
. ⟨RET⟩ *or* ⟨CTRL⟩-⟨D⟩	On a blank line, either of these commands will send the message and then exit `mail`.
⟨CTRL⟩-⟨U⟩	Erase the current line and move the cursor to the beginning of the line.

There are also a few special commands that you may use while composing the body of the message. They're known as *tilde escapes* because you specify them by typing a tilde character (~).

The following table lists some of these commands and describes their functions.

~!*command*	Run *command* in a shell.
~|*filter*	Pipe the body of the mail text through *filter*.
~b*address*	Send a blind carbon copy to the usernames or email addresses given, delimited by commas.
~d	Copy the file `dead.letter` from your home directory into the body of the message.
~e	Edit the message in the default text editor program. (When you exit the text editor, you are returned to `mail`.)

~f *number*	Insert copies of the specified received messages into the message body. Messages are specified by number or a range (for example, "2–4" inserts messages two through four inclusive); if no number is given, the current received message is inserted.
~F	Same as ~f, but reads in the messages with full headers.
~r *file*	Insert a copy of the file *file* into the message.
~w *file*	Write a copy of the body text into the file *file*.

These commands should each be typed on a line by itself.

⇒ To insert a copy of the current received message into the body of the message you are writing, and then open the message in the default text editor, type:

```
~f (RET)
~e (RET)
```

32.2 Receiving Mail

On Linux-based systems, the *inbox* is a text file on the system where your incoming mail is written to. Its location is always given by $MAIL, a special shell variable (see Recipe 3.5.6 [Changing the Shell Prompt], page 80).

⇒ To output the location of your inbox, type:

```
$ echo $MAIL (RET)
```

Usually, the inbox location is in the /var/spool/mail directory, and it has the same name as your username—so if your username is mrs, your inbox is likely /var/spool/mail/mrs. You shouldn't directly edit this file, because doing so can inadvertently cause you to lose incoming mail.

Run mail to read any new mail waiting in your inbox. If your inbox doesn't have any new mail, mail will indicate this and exit; if you *do* have new mail waiting, mail outputs a list of message headers, one line per message, each containing the status of the message ("N" for new messages, blank for previously read messages), the message number, the name of the sender, the date and time the message was received, and the number of lines and characters in the message.

⇒ To see if you have mail, type:

```
$ mail (RET)
Mail version 8.1 6/6/93.  Type ? for help.
"/var/spool/mail/m": 3 messages 3 new
>N  1 mrs          Mon Sep 6 17:29  13/345 "Re: A modest proposal"
 N  2 Ray          Tue Sep 7 04:20  15/694 "Latest news"
 N  3 lisa@example Tue Sep 7 09:35  19/869 "Re: Hello"
&
```

In this example, the user has three messages waiting—one from **mrs**, one from **Ray**, and one from **lisa@example.com**.

The **mail** prompt is an ampersand character (**&**); from there, you can read, delete, reply to, and save messages.

When you type (RET) at the "**&**" prompt, **mail** outputs the next unread message to the screen. You can also type a number to output that message.

⇒ Here are two ways to use this.

   • To read the next unread message in **mail**, type:

        & (RET)

   • To read message number three in **mail**, type:

        & 3 (RET)

There are two ways to exit **mail**: Type **q** to exit **mail** and apply the deletion commands you have given, if any, to your inbox; type **x** to exit **mail** and revert the state of your inbox to how it was before you ran **mail**.

⇒ To exit **mail** and revert your inbox to its state before you started **mail**, type:

        & x (RET)

You can always get help by typing **?** at the prompt; it gives a list of available **mail** commands. The following recipes describe some of them.

NOTES: By default, only you (and, as always, the superuser) have access to read your inbox. While there are tools available (such as **mail**, and the other MUAs) to read this file in special ways, you can also view this file like any other text file (see Chapter 9 [Viewing Text], page 211).

32.2.1 Showing a List of Mail Headers

Use the **headers** command (or just **h**) to output a list of headers of your mail messages. By default, it lists 18 messages, beginning with the current message.

You can specify a range of messages or the particular message number to start with; give – or + to display the previous or next 18 messages, respectively.

⇒ Here are some ways to use this.

- To list the headers of 18 messages, beginning with the current message, type:

    & headers ⟨RET⟩

- To list the headers of the next 18 messages, type:

    & h + ⟨RET⟩

- To list the headers of messages 101 through 200, type:

    & h 101-200 ⟨RET⟩

32.2.2 Deleting Mail

To delete a message in `mail`, use the `delete` command (or just `d` for short). With no arguments, it deletes the last message displayed; you can also specify a message by giving its number as an argument, or you can delete a range of messages.

⇒ Here are some ways to use this.

- To delete the message you just read, type:

    & d ⟨RET⟩

- To delete message three, type:

    & d 3 ⟨RET⟩

- To delete messages 10 through 14, type:

    & d 10-14 ⟨RET⟩

32.2.3 Undeleting Mail

Use the `undelete` (or just `u`) command to undelete a message that was previously marked for deletion. This will remove the deletion flag that is displayed when you list the message headers. Like `delete`, you can give a single number or a range to undelete specific messages; otherwise, it will work on the message you last read.

⇒ To undelete the last message read, type:

    u ⟨RET⟩

NOTES: This command only works for messages marked for deletion in the current `mail` session. Once you exit `mail`, any mail marked for deletion is permanently removed and cannot be undeleted.

32.2.4 Replying to Mail

Use `reply` (or just `r`) to reply to a message. This makes a new mail message, sent from you to the sender and all recipients of a mail in your inbox. With no arguments, it replies to the current message, such as the last message you read; you can also give a message number as an argument to reply to that message number.

⇒ Here are two ways to use this.

- To reply to the current message, type:

    `& reply` ⟨RET⟩

- To reply to message number 14, type:

    `& r 14` ⟨RET⟩

When you reply to a mail, use the keyboard commands for composing your message as described in Recipe 32.1.5 [Composing Mail], page 616.

32.2.5 Saving Mail to a File

Use `save` (or just `s`) to save a message to a file. By default, it works on the current message, but you can specify a number or a range, as well. Give the name of the file to save to as an argument; if the file exists, the mail will be appended.

⇒ Here are some ways to use this.

- To save the current message to a new file called **saved-mail**, type:

    `& s saved-mail` ⟨RET⟩

- To save messages 18 through 24 to a new file called **conference-reflections.2004**, type:

    `& save 18-24 conference-reflections.2004` ⟨RET⟩

- To save messages two through seven to a new file called **correspondence**, type:

    `& save 2-7 correspondence` ⟨RET⟩

- To save the current message to a new file called **conference-ideas**, type:

    `& save conference-ideas` ⟨RET⟩

- To append message 214 to an existing file called **saved-mail**, type:

    `& save 214 saved-mail` ⟨RET⟩

32.3 Using a Remote Mail Host

Most people with a home system are connected to the Internet via an ISP, and they use that system to send and receive personal mail.

If you have email via an ISP, you probably have a remote mail host. In this case, incoming mail isn't sent directly to your system, but to the ISP's mail host; your system, then, must be configured to retrieve mail from that host and store it in the expected place on your system.

This arrangement is called POP mail, which stands for "Post Office Protocol"; it is the protocol used to transfer your incoming mail, in bulk, from your ISP's mail host to your local machine. Your ISP will give you the information needed to configure your local system for POP mail: the name and IP address of its mail server and your username on that server, your ISP email address, and your ISP password.[4]

If you are using a system on a network, on the other hand—such as in an office, school, or some other organizational facility—you probably have a network administrator who has set up your Internet connection, and all of this happens "automagically."

The following recipes describe methods for using a remote mail host to read mail.

32.3.1 Using Mozilla for Mail

Mozilla
  DEB: `mozilla-browser`
  RPM: `mozilla`
  WWW: `http://www.mozilla.org/`

It is easy to set up Mozilla to retrieve email messages on a remote mail host. To do this, choose `Mail` from the `Tasks` menu bar, and give your ISP settings for your ISP email account and server. (There is an option for this, `Mail/News Account Settings`, on the `Edit` menu bar.)

Then, to get mail from your mail host, click the `Get` button in the main mail window. It will ask you to enter your ISP password, and then any messages waiting at the mail host will be downloaded.

---

[4] For *sending* mail through your ISP, you will also need to know the name or IP address of your ISP's SMTP server, which processes and sends all outgoing mail. This too is set up locally, either in your Web browser or via your local MTA (Mail Transport Agent), such as Sendmail.

32.3.2 Fetching POP Mail

Fetchmail
 DEB: `fetchmail`
      `fetchmail-common`
      `fetchmailconf`
 RPM: `fetchmail`
      `fetchmailconf`
 WWW: `http://catb.org/~esr/fetchmail/`

Rather than use a Web browser to read mail, if you'd like to run a MUA (including the `mail` tool) and use it to read Internet email, then you will want to run `fetchmail`. It fetches your mail from your ISP's POP server, and puts it where it belongs in your local mail spool directory, right in your inbox. Then you can read your mail from a local MUA.

Configuration is done via `.fetchmailrc`, a hidden file in your home directory. Then you just need to set up `fetchmail` so that it runs, with the proper options, whenever your Internet connection is started, and that it stops running whenever your Internet connection is stopped. (With PPP, this is facilitated by placing shell scripts in the `/etc/ppp/ip-up.d` and `/etc/ppp/ip-down.d` directories.)

You can use `fetchmailconf`, bundled in a separate package, to help configure your setup as described above.

⇒ To configure `fetchmail`, type:

> $ *fetchmailconf* (RET)

32.4 Managing Mail

The tools and techniques described in this section are useful for managing or otherwise manipulating your mail, no matter what your MUA. This is because a *mail folder* is simply a text file whose contents consist of saved mail messages; any tool that works on text can be used on a mail folder.

The following recipes describe some of the common ways to manage and otherwise modify your saved mail.

32.4.1 Viewing a Mail Folder

Aside from viewing a mail folder in your MUA, there are several other ways to view it and read its contents. Some methods allow for editing or otherwise altering it.

METHOD #1

You can view your mail folders in `less` or edit them in a text editor, although the folder will appear as one long scroll containing all of the messages the folder contains.

⇒ To view the mail folder ~/Mail/rachel in `less`, type:

> `$ less ~/Mail/rachel` (RET)

METHOD #2

You can view a mail folder in `mail` by specifying it as an argument to the `-f` option; it will appear the way your inbox would appear when running `mail` with no options.

⇒ To view the mail folder ~/Mail/rachel in `mail`, type:

> `$ mail -f ~/Mail/rachel` (RET)

METHOD #3

Elm
 RPM: elm
 WWW: http://www.instinct.org/elm/

You can view a mail folder in `elm` (see Recipe 32.7 [Using Other Mail User Agents], page 631) by giving its name as an argument to the `-f` option. As with `mail`, the folder will appear the usual way your inbox appears in `elm`.

⇒ To view the mail folder ~/Mail/rachel in `elm`, type:

> `$ elm -f ~/Mail/rachel` (RET)

If you save your mail messages in a lot of separate folders, you can view a sorted list of all messages from all files by using `cat` in conjunction with `elm`. Concatenate all the folders into one with `cat`, and then view that file in `elm` as you would view any folder.

⇒ To view the contents of all of the email folders in your ~/Mail directory, type:

> `$ cat ~/Mail/* > allmessages` (RET)
> `$ elm -f allmessages` (RET)

These commands write a new file, **allmessages**, in the current directory, containing the contents of all email folders in ~/Mail; then, that file is viewed in `elm`.

NOTES: To view a list showing who all the messages in a folder are from, use frm; see Recipe 32.4.4 [Seeing Who Your Mail Is From], page 626.

32.4.2 Setting Notification for New Mail

Biff
 DEB: biff
 RPM: biff
 WWW: ftp://ftp.uk.linux.org/pub/linux/Networking/mail/

The biff tool notifies you when new mail arrives by printing the header and first few lines of a mail message.

To turn biff on, use y as an option. To turn biff off, so that you stop being notified when new mail arrives, use n as an option. Unlike most tools, biff options don't take a hyphen.

⇒ To turn biff on, type:

    $ biff y ⟨RET⟩

Some people put the preceding line in their .bashrc file so that biff is always set on in all of their shells (see Recipe 3.5.6 [Changing the Shell Prompt], page 80).

Typing biff alone with no options will tell you whether biff is set to y or n.

⇒ To see what biff is set to, type:

    $ biff ⟨RET⟩

A companion tool, xbiff, works only in the X Window System (you can use the regular biff in X, too).

When you start xbiff, it draws a window containing a mailbox that looks like Figure 32-1. When mail arrives, xbiff rings the system bell, the window icon reverses color, and the mailbox flag goes up, as in Figure 32-2.[5]

NOTES: The original version of biff was named after a dog. In the early 1980s at a UC Berkeley computer lab, a girl would bring her dog, Biff, in with her when she went to use the computers. Biff was known for barking at the mailman whenever he came to deliver the day's mail. Biff was also very popular with all of the BSD UNIX hackers at Berkeley, and when one of them

---

[5] Noah Friedman has an alternate set of "Spam" images you can use, available from http://www.splode.com/~friedman/software/packages/index.html.

wrote a mail notification tool, he thought of Biff and the mailman—hence the
name. (Biff, the dog, died in August 1993.)

Figure 32-1. An xbiff *window.*

Figure 32-2. An xbiff *window when mail is waiting.*

32.4.3 Counting How Many Messages You Have

Elm
  DEB: `mailutils`
  RPM: `elm`
  WWW: `http://www.instinct.org/elm/`

Use the **messages** tool, distributed with Elm,[6] to count the number of mail
messages in a folder or file. Give the name of a mail folder as an argument;
with no arguments, it counts the mail you have waiting in your inbox.

---

[6] On Debian systems, **messages** comes with the GNU Mailutils package.

⇒ Here are two ways to use this.

- To see how many email messages you have waiting, type:

    $ *messages* (RET)

- To count the number of email messages in the mail folder `~/email/saved`, type:

    $ *messages ~/email/saved* (RET)

32.4.4 Seeing Who Your Mail Is From

There are two methods for seeing who mail is from, and they use two different tools of similar name.

METHOD #1

Elm
  DEB: `mailutils`
  RPM: `elm`
  WWW: `http://www.instinct.org/elm/`

Use **frm**, distributed with Elm,[7] to output a list of sender names and subjects for your mail. Give the name of a mail folder as an option; with no options, **frm** reads your inbox.

⇒ Here are two ways to use this.

- To output a list showing sender names and subjects of your incoming mail, type:

    $ *frm* (RET)

- To output a list showing sender names and subjects of the mail in the file `~/email/saved`, type:

    $ *frm ~/email/saved* (RET)

If you have no mail, **frm** tells you so.

METHOD #2

The **from** tool works in similar fashion to **frm**, but it does not output subject lines; instead, it outputs the names of senders and the time that messages were received.

---

[7] On Debian systems, **from** comes with the GNU Mailutils package.

⇒ To output a list of your incoming mail messages, showing sender names and the time and date received, type:

    $ *from* (RET)

If you have no mail, from outputs nothing.

32.4.5 Verifying an Email Address

vrfy
  DEB: `vrfy`
  RPM: `vrfy`

Use **vrfy** to determine whether or not a given email address works. This is useful when you are unsure of whether or not you have the right email address for someone. If the address works, **vrfy** outputs a message indicating that the recipient exists; if the address is not valid, **vrfy** outputs a message saying that the user is unknown.

⇒ To verify that the email address **user@example.edu** is valid, type:

    $ *vrfy user@example.edu* (RET)

Use the **-f** option to specify a text file containing email addresses; **vrfy** attempts to verify all email addresses contained in the file.

⇒ To verify all of the email addresses contained in the file **net-legends-faq**, type:

    $ *vrfy -f net-legends-faq* (RET)

NOTES: vrfy relies on the remote system to get this information; in these days of the heavily corporatized Internet, an increasing number of sites no longer supply this kind of information to the general public. However, it's still useful enough to be worth mentioning.

32.4.6 Searching Mail Archives

You can search the contents of a mail archive just like any text file: outputting lines matching a pattern with **grep**, or perusing the archive in a text viewer or editor and showing the searched-for text in context.

METHOD #1

To search the text of a mail archive, use **grep** in the usual way (see Chapter 14 [Searching Text], page 333).

⇒ To output all lines in ~/Mail/emily containing the text "password," regardless of case, type:

     $ *grep -i password ~/Mail/emily* ⟨RET⟩

METHOD #2

Use a text viewer or editor to peruse mail archives and search for text, as described in Chapter 9 [Viewing Text], page 211, and Chapter 10 [Editing Text], page 231.

A good way to search through mail archives is by subject; the **less** tool is particularly useful because search terms are highlighted.

⇒ To highlight all of the subject lines in the current file you are perusing in **less**, and move the cursor to the next one, type:

     /^Subject:.￼* ⟨RET⟩

32.5 Using Mail Attachments

MIME ("Multipurpose Internet Mail Extensions") is an Internet standard for encoding and attaching files to mail messages. It's used when sending image, audio, or other non-plain-text data via email.

Normally, you read and send MIME mail with your MUA. The following recipes, which show ways to send and receive MIME mail on the command line, are useful for when you just use the **mail** tool to read and send occasional mail with an attachment, but the built-in methods for manipulating MIME mail in any reasonable MUA will invariably be easier and more convenient than the techniques described here (see Recipe 32.7 [Using Other Mail User Agents], page 631).

32.5.1 Reading a Mail Attachment

There are two methods for reading attachments, outside of using your MUA.

METHOD #1

Metamail
  DEB: metamail
  RPM: metamail
  WWW: http://bmrc.berkeley.edu/~trey/emacs/metamail.html

To read a mail attachment, write the message to a file and then run **metamail** with the file name as an argument. `metamail` lists each attachment and prompts you to decide whether it should display the attachment, write it to a file, or skip it.

To read a mail attachment, type:

```
$ mail ⟨RET⟩
Mail version 8.1 6/6/93.  Type ? for help.
"/var/spool/mail/m": 1 messages 1 new
>N  1 Photo Dept.   Mon Feb 12 14:37   231/10980 "New Images"
& w1 image.mail ⟨RET⟩
"image.mail" [New file]
& x ⟨RET⟩
$ metamail image.mail ⟨RET⟩
```

In this example, the `mail` tool was used to open the inbox and write the message to a file called `image.mail`; then, `metamail` was run with the file name as an argument.

METHOD #2

Nmh
  DEB: nmh
  RPM: nmh
  WWW: http://www.nongnu.org/nmh/

Use `mhshow` to view the contents of an email message with MIME attachments. Give the name of the file containing the message as an argument to the `-file` option. This command shows first the headers of the mail, and then all remaining parts of the message in turn. For any portion that cannot be displayed on the screen, you will be given an option to write it to a file.

⇒ To view the contents of the multipart mail message stored in the file `~/Mail/inbox/1`, type:

```
$ mhshow -file ~/Mail/inbox/1 ⟨RET⟩
```

32.5.2 Sending a Mail Attachment

Metamail
  DEB: metamail
  RPM: metamail
  WWW: http://bmrc.berkeley.edu/~trey/emacs/metamail.html

To send a file as an email attachment, use `metasend`. It prompts for the values to use in the "`To:`," "`Subject:`," and "`CC:`" header fields, plus the following for each MIME attachment: its "`Content-type:`," which describes the kind of data the attachment contains; the file name; and the type of encoding to use, if any (usually one is recommended).

⇒ To mail the JPEG file `dream.jpeg` in the current directory to the address `dali@example.org`, type:

```
$ metasend ⟨RET⟩
To: dali@example.org ⟨RET⟩
Subject: The image you requested ⟨RET⟩
CC: ⟨RET⟩
Content-type: image/jpeg ⟨RET⟩
Name of file containing image/gif data: dream.jpeg ⟨RET⟩
Do you want to encode this data for sending through the mail?
 1 -- No, it is already in 7 bit ASCII
 2 -- Yes, encode in base64 (most efficient)
 3 -- Yes, encode in quoted-printable (less efficient, more readable)
 4 -- Yes, encode it using uuencode (not standard, being phased out)
2 ⟨RET⟩
Do you want to include another file too (y/n) [n] ? n ⟨RET⟩
Delivering mail, please wait...  Mail delivery apparently succeeded.
$
```

The following table lists values to use in the MIME `Content-type:` field for various kinds of files.

`application/gzip`	File compressed with `gzip`
`application/zip`	File compressed with `zip`
`application/postscript`	PostScript file
`image/jpeg`	JPEG image file
`image/png`	PNG image file
`audio/basic`	Audio file

audio/mpeg3	MP3 audio file
audio/ogg	Ogg Vorbis audio file
audio/wav	WAV audio file

32.6 Using an Email Signature

Sigrot
  DEB: `sigrot`
  WWW: `ftp://metalab.unc.edu/pub/Linux/system/mail/misc/`

A *signature file* (often pronounced "dot sig," and written as `.sig`) is a text file containing text that you want to appear at the end of email messages and other online postings. They are generally unfashionable now, but this will explain how to use one anyway.

Sometimes, people put their name, email address, and a small quote, or a piece of ASCII art (such as text written in a `figlet` font—see Recipe 16.4.1 [Outputting Horizontal Text Fonts], page 401) in the file. Once the World Wide Web became popular, many people started including the URL of their home page in their `.sig`.

You create your signature file in a text editor, just like any other text file. Name the file `.signature` or `.sig`, and keep it in your home directory.

Be sure to keep your `.sig` at most four lines in length—to use any more is considered very bad form. A first line consisting only of two hyphens and a space character ("`-- `") is sometimes used; many applications recognize this string as the beginning of a `.sig` when processing messages.

If you want to use more than one signature, use `sigrot` to "rotate" your various signatures—every time you run `sigrot`, it selects one of the signature files you keep in your `.sigrot` directory and writes it to `.signature`. To change your `.signature` every time you log in, you would run `sigrot` in your `.bash_login` file (see Chapter 3 [The Shell], page 53).

32.7 Using Other Mail User Agents

Some people use the built-in mail facility provided by a Web browser such as Mozilla, and leave it at that. Others may not send much mail, or have a need for anything beyond `mail`. But there are many MUAs to choose from.

The following table lists some of the more popular MUAs available for Linux, describing their special features.

Balsa
Graphical email client that works in X with GNOME installed; its interface is inspired somewhat by the proprietary Eudora.

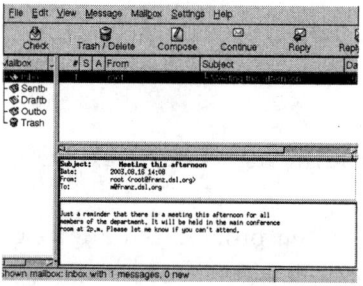

Figure 32-3. Balsa.

DEB: `balsa`
RPM: `balsa`
WWW: `http://www.balsa.net/`

Elm
Menu-driven MUA that was popular in the early 1990s among experienced users—it has some interesting features, including ways to send mail in batch mode to many addresses at once, and comes with a tool to send memorandums as email messages. Interest in Elm has waned considerably over the years, and most novices are advised to try Mutt instead.

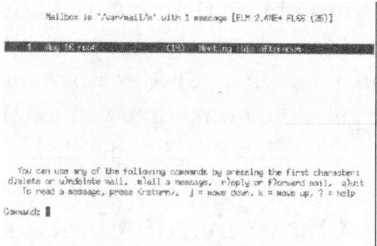

Figure 32-4. Elm.

RPM: `elm`
WWW: `http://www.instinct.org/elm/`

Gnus

Emacs newsreader (pre-installed with XEmacs) that can also be used to read and send mail. It has many features and should appeal to Emacs lovers—but a warning: Some find it daunting!

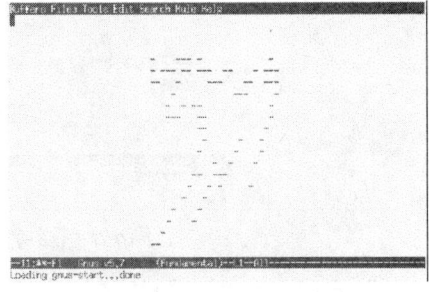

Figure 32-5. Gnus.

DEB: gnus
RPM: gnus
WWW: http://gnus.org/

MEW

Emacs mail and news facility developed in Japan, "Messaging in the Emacs World" has many features for handling mail in complex ways.

Figure 32-6. MEW.

DEB: mew
RPM: mew
WWW: http://www.mew.org/

MH-E   Emacs front-end to NMH. Powerful, yet easy to use.

Figure 32-7. MH-E.

DEB: `emacsen-common`
RPM: `emacs-21`
WWW: `http://www.emacs.org/`

Mozilla Mail Familiar email interface of this popular Web browser. Works
                  in the X Window System and is favored by newbies.

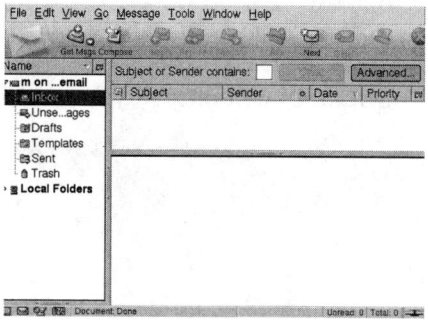

Figure 32-8. Mozilla Mail.

DEB: `mozilla-browser`
RPM: `mozilla`
WWW: `http://www.mozilla.org/`

Mutt   MUA currently in favor among many Vi users, and is one of
        the most popular MUAs for Linux today.

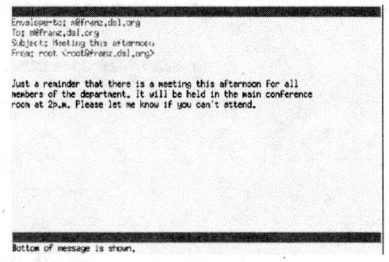

Figure 32-9. Mutt.

DEB: mutt
RPM: mutt
WWW: http://www.mutt.org/

Nmh   Rand Mail Handling system, MH; not a single application for
        mail, but a collection of small tools for manipulating mail
        folders and messages, installed in **/usr/bin/mh**. It should
        appeal to those who excel at building complex commands
        from combinations of simple tools and operators. NMH is
        the *new* "Mail Handling" system, containing rewrites and
        improved versions of the MH tools. Most Linux systems will
        install this over the old MH.

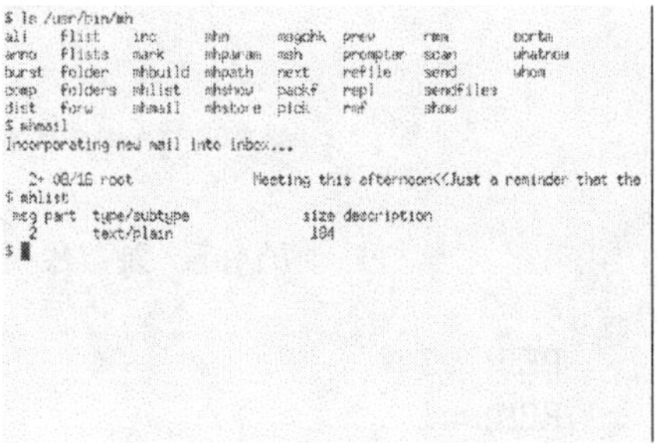

Figure 32-10. NMH.

DEB: nmh
RPM: nmh
WWW: http://www.nongnu.org/nmh/

VM   "View Mail" is an older MUA for Emacs that is very config-
                      urable.

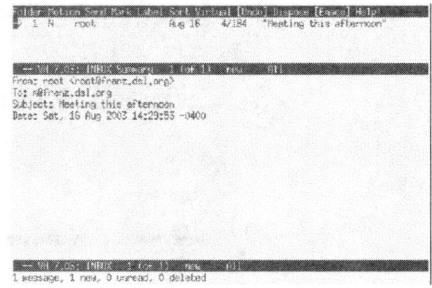

Figure 32-11. VM.

DEB: vm
RPM: vm
WWW: http://www.wonderworks.com/vm/

Wanderlust   MUA for Emacs designed to facilitate reading your mail on
                      multiple computers.

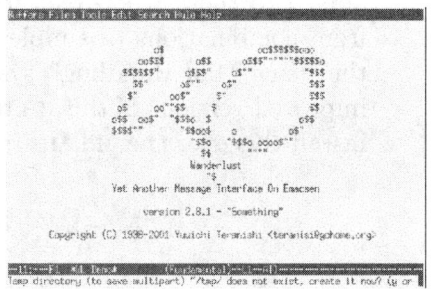

Figure 32-12. Wanderlust.

DEB: wl
RPM: wl
WWW: http://www.gohome.org/wl/

## CHAPTER 33

The World Wide Web

Next to email, the most useful service on the Internet is the *World Wide Web* (WWW, or most often just the "Web"). You certainly know about it; it is a giant network of hypertext documents and services, made available through the HyperText Transfer Protocol (HTTP). Anyone can publish to the Web, and anyone with an Internet-connected computer can read almost anything that's on the Web. For more than ten years, it has been growing by the instant. It is the new mass media, and it could well be the world's largest public repository of information.

What everybody does on the Web is "browse" it, which means to use a *Web browser* to access files published somewhere on the Web. Text files written in HTML ("HyperText Markup Language"), the native file format of the Web, are called *pages*; these Web pages have hypertext links in them that reference another file, Web page, or position in a Web page elsewhere on the Web; when you click a link, your browser will then retrieve and display the file it references. Some years ago the overused catchphrase du jour was to "surf" the Web, which means the same thing as browsing.

The unique address that specifies a particular document is called a *uniform resource locator*, or URL.[1] URLs can specify Web pages, local files, and documents available via other Internet services such as FTP.

When specifying a URL as an argument, unless the URL is very simple, be sure to quote it! URLs sometimes have characters in them that the shell reserves, such as ampersand characters (&). If the & is unquoted, Bash will interpret it as the end of the command, the & meaning to run the input line up to that point in the background; any text following the & will be run in the foreground as the next command—neither having the intended effect.

Of browsers, Mozilla is the most popular, and is arguably the "king" of them all. Lynx is a fast, text-only browser that is arguably the most powerful at the command line. This chapter shows how to use both of them, and then describes other handy tools for accessing and using the Web, including tools for writing Web pages in HTML.

---

[1] Some people pronounce it as "earl," while others insist that it can only be "yoo-are-ell."

33.1 Using Mozilla

Mozilla
 DEB: `mozilla-browser`
 RPM: `mozilla`
 WWW: `http://www.mozilla.org/`

When most people think of browsing or surfing the Web, they think of doing it graphically—and the mental image they conjure is usually that of the famous Netscape browser. Most Web sites today make heavy use of graphic images, and commercial Web sites are usually optimized for Netscape-compatible browsers—many of them are not even *accessible* with other browsers. That means you'll want to use this application for browsing this kind of Web site.

The version of Netscape's Navigator browser that was released as free, open source software in 1998 to much fanfare is called Mozilla.[2] It includes a browser (Mozilla Navigator), MUA and newsgroup reader (Mozilla Mail), Web page editor (Mozilla Composer), and contact manager (Mozilla Address Book). When first released, the Mozilla application was a "developer's only" release, but it has long reached a state where it is ready for general use.

The following recipes will help you get the most out of using Mozilla.

33.1.1 Getting Acquainted with Mozilla

Once Mozilla has been installed, run Mozilla Navigator in X either by typing `mozilla` in a shell, or by selecting it from a menu in the usual fashion, as dictated by your window manager.

You can, optionally, give a URL as an argument to start Mozilla with that URL; otherwise, Mozilla will load a pre-determined *start page*,[3] which you can also customize—see Recipe 33.7 [Setting Up a Start Page], page 658.

---

[2] Netscape's browsers, from its earliest Navigator release to its later Communicator series, were always referred to internally at the company as *Mozilla*; this was a slangy pun on the name Mosaic, which had been the first popular graphical Web browser in the early 1990s—Netscape's goal had been to make a "Mosaic killer."

[3] This term is mine. Mozilla calls it a *home page*, but this is confusing because that term chiefly refers to the main page of a person or organization's published Web site.

⇒ Here are some ways to use this.

- To start Mozilla with your default start page, type:

  `$ mozilla` $\widehat{\text{RET}}$

- To start Mozilla with the URL `http://gutenberg.net/`, type:

  `$ mozilla http://gutenberg.net/` $\widehat{\text{RET}}$

A typical Mozilla window looks like Figure 33-1, in which the home page of the Library of Congress [`http://www.loc.gov/`] is loaded.

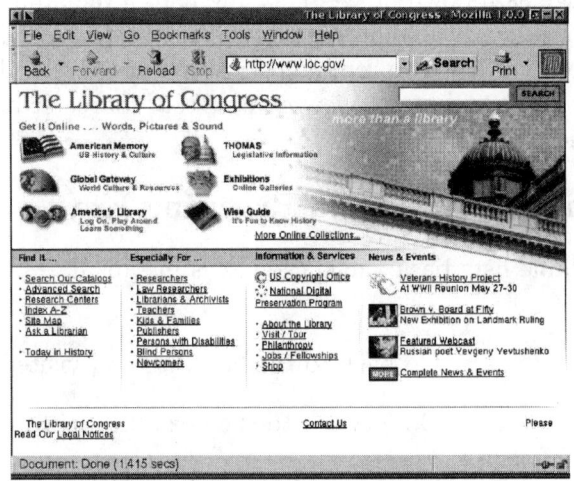

Figure 33-1. Mozilla.

The title of the Web page and the name Mozilla is written in the Mozilla window's title bar.

The top bar inside the Mozilla window is called the **Menu Bar**, and contains pull-down menus for accessing all of its major functions. The bar beneath that is called the **Navigation Bar**, and contains buttons for controlling page navigation. The **Location** box, in the middle of the **Navigation Bar**, contains the URL of the currently-loaded page. It also has buttons for searching, printing, and the stylized blue M, which takes you to the Mozilla home page [`http://www.mozilla.org/`].

Beneath that, the largest area of the window is for the Web page itself.

At the bottom is the **Status Bar**, which tells you (among other things), the status of the current Web page or document. In the example, the status is **Done**, meaning that the entire page has successfully loaded.

Like most graphical Web browsers, its use is fairly self-explanatory. Type a URL in the **Location** dialog box to open that URL, and left-click on a link to *follow* it, replacing the main contents of the browser window with the contents of that link.

The right mouse button opens a special options menu, whose contents depend on the context of the mouse pointer. If you right-click when the pointer is on a link, you will be presented with several options for handling the link, including opening it in a new window, bookmarking it, and displaying its properties. If you right-click when the pointer is on an image, you will be presented with options for handling the image, including viewing it (the browser display the image as its own "page"), saving it to a file, and bookmarking it. If you right-click when the pointer is on whitespace, plain text, or somewhere else on the page, you will be presented with options for handling the current page, including bookmarking it, viewing its HTML source or page information, reloading it, and saving it.

33.1.2 Using Basic Mozilla Browsing Keys

The following table lists basic navigation keys in Mozilla.

Navigation

⟨ALT⟩-⟨←⟩	Go back to the last URL you visited
⟨ALT⟩-⟨→⟩	Go forward to the next URL in your history.
⟨CTRL⟩-⟨H⟩	Open your browser history.
⟨ALT⟩-⟨HOME⟩	Go to your pre-defined Mozilla start (or "home") page.
⟨SHIFT⟩-⟨CTRL⟩-⟨L⟩	Open a URL.

Bookmarks

⟨CTRL⟩-⟨B⟩	Open your bookmarks file in a new window.
⟨CTRL⟩-⟨D⟩	Add page with current properties to the bottom of your bookmarks file.
⟨SHIFT⟩-⟨CTRL⟩-⟨D⟩	Add page to a particular place in your bookmarks file while optionally editing its properties.

Window Operations

⟨CTRL⟩-⟨N⟩	Open a new Mozilla window (see the following recipe).

(continued)
Window Operations

⟨CTRL⟩–⟨W⟩   Close current Mozilla window.

⟨CTRL⟩–⟨Q⟩   Quit and exit Mozilla.

Viewing Pages

⟨ESC⟩   Stop loading current page.

⟨CTRL⟩–⟨R⟩   Reload current page.

⟨CTRL⟩–⟨U⟩   View HTML source of current page.

⟨CTRL⟩–⟨I⟩   View file and server information of current page.

⟨CTRL⟩–⟨—⟩   Decrease size of text.

⟨CTRL⟩–⟨+⟩   Increase size of text.

⟨CTRL⟩–⟨E⟩   Edit current page.

⟨CTRL⟩–⟨P⟩   Print current page.

Text Selections

⟨CTRL⟩–⟨A⟩   Select all text on page.

⟨CTRL⟩–⟨X⟩   Cut text selection.

⟨CTRL⟩–⟨C⟩   Copy text selection.

⟨CTRL⟩–⟨V⟩   Paste text selection.

⟨DEL⟩   Delete text selection.

⟨CTRL⟩–⟨Z⟩   Undo last text operation.

⟨CTRL⟩–⟨Y⟩   Redo last text operation.

File Operations

⟨CTRL⟩–⟨O⟩   Open a file for viewing.

⟨CTRL⟩–⟨S⟩   Save current page as a file.

NOTES: These keys may not have the desired effect in some window managers; if they don't work for you, try using the ⟨CTRL⟩ key instead of the ⟨ALT⟩ key.

One nice feature for Emacs fans is that you can use Emacs-style keystrokes for cursor movement in Mozilla's dialog boxes (see Recipe 10.1.3 [Using Basic Emacs Editing Keys], page 237).

33.1.3 Making a New Mozilla Window

It's often useful to have several Mozilla windows open at once—this way, multiple Web pages can be displayed simultaneously. There are two methods for doing this: One makes a new window with the contents of a link, and another makes one with your Mozilla start page.

METHOD #1

To open a link in a new Mozilla window, middle-click the link. Opening multiple links in their own windows saves time when you are doing a lot of "power browsing."

METHOD #2

To open a new Mozilla window whose contents will be your Mozilla start page, type ⟨CTRL⟩-⟨N⟩.

33.1.4 Copying a Link to the Clipboard from Mozilla

To copy a link to the clipboard in Mozilla, right-click on the link and then select `Copy Link Location`.

Then you can paste the link somewhere else, including another X client window, by clicking the middle mouse button when the pointer is in the place you want to paste (see Recipe 10.3 [Manipulating Selections of Text], page 253).

NOTES: To copy a URL, such as the URL displayed in the `Location` dialog box, left-click on either side of the URL and drag the mouse across it. You can then paste the URL somewhere else.

33.1.5 Copying an Email Address to the Clipboard from Mozilla

To copy an email address to the clipboard in Mozilla, right-click on the address and choose `Copy Email Address`.

Then you can paste the email address somwhere else, including another X client window, by clicking the middle mouse button when the pointer is in the place you want to paste (see Recipe 10.3 [Manipulating Selections of Text], page 253).

33.1.6 Searching the Source of a Web Page in Mozilla

The `Find in This Page` command (see Recipe 33.1.2 [Using Basic Mozilla Browsing Keys], page 640) works on any page that is displayed in Mozilla, including HTML source views. This is useful for searching the HTML source for links or other text not visible in the rendered display.

⇒ To search the source of a Web page, do the following:

1. Type ⟨CTRL⟩-⟨U⟩ on the Web page to view its source.
2. Use the mouse pointer to move to the page source window.
3. Type ⟨CTRL⟩-⟨F⟩ to find text in the source.
4. Enter the text to search for and type ⟨RET⟩.
5. Type ⟨CTRL⟩-⟨G⟩ to repeat the search.

33.2 Using Lynx

Lynx
  DEB: lynx
  RPM: lynx
  WWW: http://lynx.browser.org/

As of this writing, the venerable Lynx is still the standard Web browser for use on many Linux systems; it was also one of the first Web browsers available for general use.[4] It doesn't display graphics, but it's a good interface for reading hypertext.

Type `lynx` to start it. If a start page is defined, it will load (see Recipe 33.7 [Setting Up a Start Page], page 658.

To open a URL, give it as an argument.

⇒ To view the contents of the URL `http://www.whitehouse.gov/`, type:

    $ lynx http://www.whitehouse.gov/ ⟨RET⟩

The following Lynx recipes include tips and hints for using Lynx in various ways.

33.2.1 Using Basic Lynx Browsing Keys

The following table describes some of the keyboard commands that work in Lynx.

---

[4] Like many of my generation, it was through Lynx that I had my first view of the Web.

Navigation within a Document

⟨↑⟩   Move up (backward) through links in the current document.

⟨↓⟩   Move down (forward) through links in the current document.

⟨CTRL⟩–⟨N⟩   Move down to the *next* line in the current document.

⟨CTRL⟩–⟨P⟩   Move up to the *previous* line in the current document.

⟨PgDn⟩ *or* ⟨CTRL⟩–⟨F⟩ *or*   Scroll down (*forward*) to the next screen in the cur-
⟨SPACEBAR⟩ *or* ⟨+⟩   rent document.

⟨PgUp⟩ *or* ⟨CTRL⟩–⟨B⟩ *or*   Scroll up (*backward*) to the previous screen in the
⟨−⟩   current document.

⟨CTRL⟩–⟨A⟩   Move to the head (top) of the current document.

⟨CTRL⟩–⟨E⟩   Move to the bottom (end) of the current document.

Navigation Between Documents

g   Go to a URL; Lynx will prompt you for the URL to go to. Type ⟨↑⟩ to insert on this line the last URL that was visited; once inserted, you can edit it.

G   Go to a URL, by editing the current URL; Lynx will display the current URL and let you edit it.

⟨→⟩ *or* ⟨RET⟩   Follow the hyperlink currently selected by the cursor.

⟨←⟩   Go back to the last document.

⟨DEL⟩   View a history of all documents visited during this session.

⟨Z⟩   Stop downloading current page.

(continued)
Information and Help

〈H〉 *or* ?   Display the Lynx help files.

〈K〉   Display a complete list of keystroke commands.

=   Display information about the current document
                             (like all documents displayed in Lynx, type 〈←〉 to
                             go back to the previous document).

\   Toggle between rendered HTML and source display
                             of current page.

〈BKSP〉   Display history of links visited in current session.

Exiting Lynx

!   Escape temporarily to a shell (〈CTRL〉-〈D〉 returns).

q   Quit browsing and exit the program; Lynx will ask
                             to verify this action.

Q *or* 〈CTRL〉-〈D〉   Quit browsing and exit the program without
                             verification.

33.2.2 Saving a Web Page from Lynx

Use the `Print to local file` option to save either the rendered content or
the HTML source file of a Web page in Lynx.

⇒ Here are two ways to use this.

- To save the rendered content of the Web page displayed in Lynx, do
  the following:

  1. Type 〈P〉 (the *print* option) to open the print options page.

  2. Select `Print to local file` and press 〈RET〉.

- To save the HTML source of the Web page displayed in Lynx, do the
  following:

  1. Type \ to view the source.

  2. Type *p* to open the print options page.

  3. Select `Print to local file`.

33.2.3 Listing All the Links in a Page

When you want to *browse* a hypertext list of all links a page contains, numbered and in HTML format so that each member of the list is a hotlink, use the `list references` command when viewing the page in Lynx.

⇒ To view a list of all links from the current page, press Ⓛ.

When you type this command, Lynx loads a new page containing a list of all links (called *references*) contained in the page you were viewing. This list, reminiscent of the old Internet Gopher service, is good for viewing the links on pages that contain "hidden" links, such as some image links. It's also good for making an HTML annotated list of links that a page contains; do this by saving the link page, as described in the previous recipe.

33.2.4 Sending Text from the Web to Standard Output

To output the rendered text of a URL, use `lynx` with the `-dump` option. This dumps the text of the given URL to the standard output, and you can pipe this to `less` for perusal or use redirection to save it to a file. This is good for many things, including perusing or formatting text from the Web.

⇒ To get the text of `http://sc.edu/fitzgerald/winterd/winter.html` and peruse it, type (all on one line):

```
$ lynx -dump http://www.sc.edu/fitzgerald/winterd/winter.html |
less ⟨RET⟩
```

It's an old net convention for italicized words to be displayed in an etext inside underscores like `_this_`; use the `-underscore` option to output any italicized text in this manner.

By default, `lynx` annotates all the hyperlinks and produces a list of footnoted links at the bottom of the screen.[5] If you don't want them, add the `-nolist` option and just the "pure text" will be returned.

⇒ To output the pure text of the previous URL, with underscores, and save it to the file `winter_dreams`, type (all on one line):

```
$ lynx -dump -nolist -underscore
http://sc.edu/fitzgerald/winterd/winter.html > winter_dreams ⟨RET⟩
```

To specify a line width for the dump, in characters, give it with the `-width=` option. The default is 80. You can do other things with the pure text, like pipe it to `enscript` for setting it in a font for printing.

---

[5] These links are controlled by the `-number_links` option; you can give this option to turn on annotations and footnotes in normal browsing too.

⇒ To print the pure text of the previous URL in a Times Roman font, with underscores translated into italics and a line width of 40 characters type (all on one line):

```
$ lynx -dump -width=40 -nolist -underscore
http://sc.edu/fitzgerald/winterd/winter.html | enscript -B
-Eetext -f "Times-Roman12" (RET)
```

NOTES: To peruse the plain text of a URL with its HTML tags removed and no formatting done to the text, see Recipe 33.9.2 [Converting HTML], page 663.

You can also use the **-dump** option to print a Web page (see Recipe 25.2.4 [Printing a Web Page], page 514), or to pass some file from the Web to another command, such as passing a WAV audio file to the **sox** audio processing tool.

33.2.5 Viewing a Site that Requires Authorization

To view a site or Web page that requires registration, use `lynx` with the -auth option, giving as arguments the username and password to use for authorization, separating them by a colon character (:).

⇒ To view the URL `http://www.example.com/archive/` with a username and password of "guest," type:

```
$ lynx -auth=guest:guest http://www.example.com/archive/ (RET)
```

It's common to combine this with the options for saving to a file, so that you can retrieve an annotated text copy of a file from a site that normally requires registration.

⇒ To save the URL `http://www.example.com/archive/` as an annotated text file, `mynews`, type (all on one line):

```
$ lynx -dump -number_links -auth=guest:guest
http://www.example.com/archive/ > mynews (RET)
```

NOTES: The username and password argument you give on the command line will be recorded in your shell history log (see Recipe 3.4 [Using Your Command History], page 74), and it will be visible to other users on the system should they look to see what processes you're running (see Recipe 2.7.2 [Listing All of a User's Processes], page 42).

33.2.6 Viewing an HTML Selection

To view a selection of HTML source code rendered in Lynx, select the source code and then use `lynx` with the -stdin option to read its start page from the standard input. Then, paste the selection to `lynx`'s standard input.

If you have friends who send you mail in HTML format that you cannot conveniently read with your MUA, this little-known tip will make you happy.

⇒ To view a selection of HTML source code as rendered text, do the following:

1. Select the source code to render by left-clicking and dragging the mouse pointer over it (see Recipe 10.3 [Manipulating Selections of Text], page 253).

2. Start Lynx in a terminal so that it reads from standard input:

   `$ lynx -stdin` ⟨RET⟩

3. Paste the text in the terminal that is running Lynx, by clicking the middle mouse button in that terminal.

4. End the input to Lynx by typing ⟨CTRL⟩-⟨D⟩ in that terminal.

When you do this, Lynx will render and display the HTML code.

NOTES: Lynx will still be running after it displays the code, and you will then have to type Q to quit and exit Lynx. Alternately, include the `-dump` option to have Lynx display the rendered HTML to its standard output and then immediately exit.

Whenever you have HTML code coming out of a stream, you can pipe it to `lynx -stdin -dump` to display the rendered code to the standard output.

This technique is also good for testing out arbitrary selections of HTML code.

33.2.7 Specifying Key Bindings in Lynx

You can specify special key bindings in Lynx, so that the movement commands work just like in your favorite editor: use the `-emacskeys` option to enable Emacs-style key bindings, and use the `-vikeys` option to enable Vi-style key bindings.

⇒ To start Lynx with the URL `http://nostarch.com/`, using Vi-style key bindings for movement, type:

   `$ lynx -vikeys http://nostarch.com/` ⟨RET⟩

33.2.8 Using Lynx with a Mouse

To use Lynx with the mouse, give the `-use_mouse` option to `lynx`. If your version of Lynx has mouse support enabled, giving this option will let you follow a link by just clicking on it with the left mouse button; right-click the mouse anywhere in the window to move back to the last page you visited.

⇒ To browse the files in the **/usr/share/doc** directory with **lynx**, using the mouse, type:

> `$ lynx -use_mouse /usr/share/doc` ⟨RET⟩

33.3 Accessing the Web in Emacs

W3
  DEB: w3-el-e21
  RPM: w3
  WWW: http://www.cs.indiana.edu/elisp/w3/docs.html

You can get the Web in Emacs. Currently it's quite slow, but it may have its uses. To do this, use **w3-mode**. Its features are many—just about the only things you may miss are SSL support (although this may be coming) and JavaScript and Java support (well, *you* may not miss it, but it will make some sites a bit hard to use). It can handle frames, tables, stylesheets, and many other HTML features.

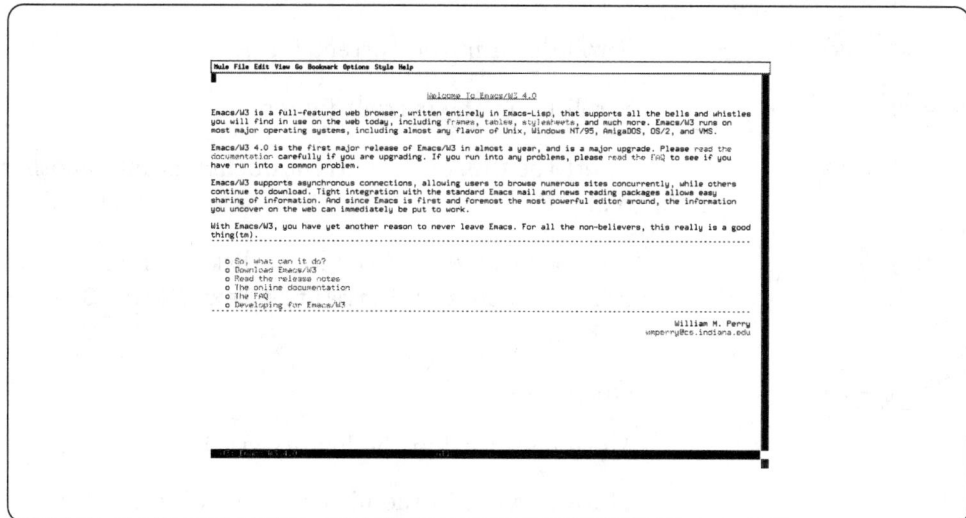

Figure 33-2. w3-mode *in Emacs.*

⇒ To load **w3-mode** in Emacs, type:

> ⟨ALT⟩-⟨X⟩ *w3* ⟨RET⟩

To open a URL in a new buffer, type ⟨CTRL⟩-⟨O⟩ and, in the minibuffer, give the URL to open (leaving this blank opens the **w3-mode** home page). Middle-click a link to follow it, opening the URL in a new buffer.

⇒ Here are two ways to use this.

- To open the URL `http://emacs.org/`, type:

  ⟨CTRL⟩-⟨O⟩ *http://emacs.org/* ⟨RET⟩

- To open the URL of the `w3-mode` home page, type:

  ⟨CTRL⟩-⟨O⟩ ⟨RET⟩

The last example opens the `w3-mode` home page in a buffer of its own, as in Figure 33-2.

The following table describes some of the special commands for use when in `w3-mode`.

⟨RET⟩	Follow the link at point.
⟨SPACEBAR⟩	Scroll down in the current buffer.
⟨BKSP⟩	Scroll up in the current buffer.
⟨ALT⟩-⟨TAB⟩	Insert the URL of the current document into another buffer.
⟨ALT⟩-⟨S⟩	Save a document to the local disk (you can choose from HTML Source, Formatted Text, LaTeX Source, or Binary).
⟨CTRL⟩-⟨O⟩	Open a URL.
B	Move backward in the history stack of visited URLs.
F	Move forward in the history stack of visited URLs.
i	View information about the document in the current buffer (the information opens in new buffer called Document Information).
I	View information about the link at point in the current buffer (the information opens in new buffer called Document Information).

k	Put the URL of the document in the current buffer in the kill ring, and make it the X selection (useful for copying and pasting the URL into another buffer or to another application; see Recipe 10.3 [Manipulating Selections of Text], page 253).
K	Put the URL of the link at point in the kill ring and make it the X selection (useful for copying and pasting the URL into another buffer or to another application; see Recipe 10.3 [Manipulating Selections of Text], page 253).
l	Move to the last visited buffer.
o	Open a local file.
q	Quit w3-mode, kill the current buffer, and go to the last visited buffer.
r	Reload the current document.
s	View the HTML source of the document in the current buffer (it opens in a new buffer with the URL as its name).
S	View the HTML source of the link at point in the current buffer (it opens in a new buffer with the URL as its name).
v	Show the URL of the current document (the URL is shown in the minibuffer).
V	Show the URL of the link at point in the current buffer (the URL is shown in the minibuffer).

33.4 Viewing an Image from the Web

Typically, you view images on the Web by opening them in the browser you are using, but you can view Web images without browsing, too—methods to do so follow.

METHOD #1

Lynx
  DEB: lynx
  RPM: lynx
  WWW: http://lynx.browser.org/

You can view an image on the Web by giving the URL of the image as an argument to `lynx` (see Recipe 33.2 [Using Lynx], page 643). The image will be displayed with whatever "helper" application is set up to show images via `lynx`.

⇒ To view the image at the URL ftp://garbo.uwasa.fi/garbo-gifs/garbo01.gif, type:

> $ `lynx ftp://garbo.uwasa.fi/garbo-gifs/garbo01.gif` (RET)

NOTES: This method only works in X.

You could also give the URL for the image as an argument in this way to some other browser, such as Mozilla (see Recipe 33.1 [Using Mozilla], page 638).

METHOD #2

ImageMagick
  DEB: imagemagick
  RPM: ImageMagick
  WWW: http://www.imagemagick.org/

Libwww-perl
  DEB: libwww-perl
  RPM: perl-libwww
  WWW: http://ftp.ics.uci.edu/pub/websoft/libwww-perl/

If you just want to view an image file from the Web, you don't have to use a Web browser at all—instead, you can use `display`, giving the URL you want to view as an argument. It uses GET (sometimes `get`), part of the `libwww-perl` package, to fetch the URL.

This method is especially nice for viewing your favorite webcam image, for viewing images on FTP sites, or for putting in scripts—you don't have to start a browser, log in, or type any other commands at all.

⇒ To view the image at the URL
http://waquarium.otted.hawaii.edu/coralcam/ccam.jpg, type:

$ *display http://waquarium.otted.hawaii.edu/coralcam/ccam.jpg* ⟨RET⟩

The **-remote** option opens the image in a **display** window that's already running; you can use this method to view an image that changes often—such as a webcam image—and automatically refresh the display with the latest image. To do this, first run **display** in the background, and then run **watch** (see Recipe 28.4 [Watching a Command from Time to Time], page 559). Give the number of seconds between reloads as an argument to the **-n** option, and give **display** with the **-remote** option and the image URL as a quoted argument as the command to be watched.

⇒ To view the image at the URL
http://waquarium.otted.hawaii.edu/coralcam/ccam.jpg, updating it with the latest image from the webcam every 30 seconds, type:

```
$ display http://waquarium.otted.hawaii.edu/coralcam/ccam.jpg & ⟨RET⟩
[3] 29621
$ watch -n 30 'display -remote
http://waquarium.otted.hawaii.edu/coralcam/ccam.jpg' ⟨RET⟩
```

In this example, the first **display** command was run in the background, as that shell's third job, with a process number of 29621. To stop viewing, type ⟨CTRL⟩-⟨C⟩ in the terminal that contains the **watch** command, and then kill the first **display** job (see Recipe 3.3.5 [Stopping a Job], page 73).

NOTES: When viewing the image, you can use all of the image-manipulation commands that **display** supports, including resizing and changing the magnification of the image. For more information about **display**, see Recipe 17.1 [Viewing an Image in X], page 407.

33.5 Getting Files from the Web

Wget
  DEB: wget
  RPM: wget
  WWW: http://www.gnu.org/software/wget/wget.html

Use **wget**, "Web get," to download files from the World Wide Web. It can retrieve files from HTTP or FTP urls. It keeps the file's original timestamp, it's

smaller and faster to use than a browser, and it shows a visual display of the
download progress.

To retrieve an HTML file from the Web and save it as rendered text, use
Lynx instead—see Recipe 33.2.4 [Sending Text from the Web to Standard
Output], page 646.

The following subsections contain recipes for using wget to retrieve information from the Web. For more examples of things you can do with wget,
consult its Info documentation (see Recipe 2.8.5 [Reading an Info Manual],
page 48).

33.5.1 Downloading a URL

To download a single file from the Web, give the URL of the file as an argument
to wget.

⇒ To download ftp://garbo.uwasa.fi/garbo-gifs/garbo20.gif to a
   file, type:

> $ wget ftp://garbo.uwasa.fi/garbo-gifs/garbo20.gif ⟨RET⟩

This command downloads a given URL, writing to a file in the current
working directory with the same name as the original URL, garbo20.gif.

If you interrupt a download before it's finished, the contents of the file you
were retrieving will contain only the portion of the file wget retrieved before
it was interrupted. Use wget with the -c option to resume the download from
the point it left off.

⇒ To resume a download of the URL from the previous example, type:

> $ wget -c ftp://garbo.uwasa.fi/garbo-gifs/garbo20.gif ⟨RET⟩

NOTES: In order for the -c option to have the desired effect, you should run
wget from the same directory as it was run previously, where that partially-
retrieved file should still exist.

33.5.2 Archiving an Entire Web Site

To archive a single Web site, use wget with the -m ("mirror") option, which
saves files with the exact timestamp of the original, if possible, and sets the
"recursive retrieval" option to download everything. To specify the number
of retries to use when an error occurs in retrieval, use the -t option with a
numeric argument—-t3 is usually good for safely retrieving across the net;
use -t0 to specify an infinite number of retries, good for when a network
connection is *really* bad but you *really* want to archive something, regardless

of how long it takes. Finally, use the -o option with a file name as an argument
to write a progress log to the file—examining it can be useful in the event
that something goes wrong during the archiving; once the archival process is
complete and you've determined that it was successful, you can delete the log
file.

⇒ To mirror the Web site at `http://www.example.org/`, giving up to three
   retries for retrieving files and putting error messages in a log file called
   `mirror.log`, type:

       $ *wget -m -t3 http://www.example.org/ -o mirror.log* (RET)

This command makes an archive of the Web site at
`http://www.example.org/` in a subdirectory called `www.example.org` in the
current directory. Log messages are written to a file in the current directory
called `mirror.log`.

To continue an archive that you've left off, use the -nc ("no clobber")
option; it doesn't retrieve files that have already been downloaded. For this
option to work the way you want it to, be sure that you are in the same
directory that you were in when you originally began archiving the site.

⇒ To continue an interrupted mirror of the Web site at
   `http://www.example.org/` and make sure that existing files are
   not downloaded, giving up to three retries for retrieval of files, and
   putting error messages in a log file called `mirror.log`, type:

       $ *wget -nc -m -t3 http://www.example.org/ -o mirror.log* (RET)

33.5.3 Archiving Part of a Web Site

To archive only part of a Web site—such as, say, a user's home page—use the
-I option followed by a list of the absolute path names of the directories to
archive; all other directories on the site are ignored.

⇒ To archive the Web site at `http://example.edu/~jim/`, only archiving
   the `/~jim` directory, and writing log messages to a file called `jim.log`,
   type:

       $ *wget -m -t3 -I /~jim http://example.edu/~jim/ -o jim.log* (RET)

This command archives all files on the `http://example.edu/~jim/` Web
site whose directory names begin with `/~jim`.

To only get files in a given directory, use the -r and -l options (the -l
option takes as an argument the number of levels to descend from the given
level). To only download files in a given directory, combine these options with
the --no-parent option, which specifies not to ascend to the parent directory.

Use the -A option to specify the exact file name extensions to accept—for example, use -A txt,text,tex to only download files whose names end with .txt, .text, and .tex extensions. The -R option works similarly, but specifies the file extensions to *reject* and not download.

⇒ To download only the files ending in a .gz extension and only in the given directory /~jim/papers/ at example.org, type (all on one line):

```
$ wget -m -r -l1 --no-parent -A.gz
http://www.example.org/~jim/papers/ ⟨RET⟩
```

33.5.4 Reading the Headers of a Web Page

All Web servers output special *headers* at the beginning of page requests, but you normally don't see them when you retrieve a URL with a Web browser. These headers contain information such as the current system date of the Web server host and the name and version of the Web server and operating system software.

Use the -S option with wget to output these headers when retrieving files; headers are output to standard output, or to the log file, if used.

⇒ To retrieve the file at http://google.com/ and output the headers, type:

```
$ wget -S http://google.com/ ⟨RET⟩
```

This command writes the server response headers to standard output and saves the contents of http://google.com/ to a file in the current directory whose name is the same as the original file.

33.6 Keeping a Browser History

browser-history
  DEB: browser-history
  RPM: browser-history
  WWW: http://www.inria.fr/koala/colas/browser-history/

Many Web browsers have a "history" function that keeps a listing of the sites you visit, and the time and date of your visit, but none are as good as the browser-history tool. If you presently keep a *weblog* (or "blog") in order to remember good links you find, you won't have to do that anymore, once you install this tool.

Use browser-history to maintain a history log of all the Web sites you visit.

You start it in the background, and each time you visit a URL in a Web browser (as of this writing, it works with the Netscape, Arena, and Amaya browsers, but not Mozilla), it writes the name and URL to its current history log, which you can view at any time.

⇒ To start `browser-history` every time you start X, put the following line in your `.xsession` file:

```
browser-history &
```

The following recipes show ways to use your history logs.

33.6.1 Viewing Your Browser History

The browser history logs are kept in a hidden directory called `.browser-history` inside your home directory. The history log for the current week is always called `history-log.html`; it's an HTML file that you can view in a Web browser.

⇒ To view the current history log with `lynx`, type:

```
$ lynx ~/.browser-history/history-log.html  ⟨RET⟩
```

Past history logs have the year, month, and week appended to their file name, and they are compressed (see Recipe 8.4 [Using File Compression], page 196). If you are viewing them in a browser, you should just be able to give the file name as an argument without uncompressing them—most browsers handle this automagically.

NOTES: If you have a start page, you'll find it useful to add a link on it to your current history log file, `~/.browser-history/history-log.html` (see Recipe 33.7 [Setting Up a Start Page], on the next page).

33.6.2 Searching Through Your Browser History

You can also use `zgrep` to search through your old browser history logs. The logs keep the URL and title of each site you visit, so you can search for either—then when someone asks, "Remember that good article about such-and-such?" you can do a `zgrep` on the files in your `~/.browser-history` directory to find it.

⇒ To find any URLs from the list of those you visited in the year 2000 whose titles contain the word "`Confessions`," type:

```
$ zgrep Confessions ~/.browser-history/history-log-2000*  ⟨RET⟩
```

This command searches all your logs from the year 2000 for the text "`Confessions`" in it, and outputs those lines.

NOTES: For more about `zgrep`, see Recipe 14.7.2 [Matching Lines in Compressed Files], page 349.

33.7 Setting Up a Start Page

A *start page* is the Web page that a browser automatically loads whenever it is started without a URL as an argument. It is also the page that loads when you click the browser's **Home** button, if it has one.

You can define your browser's start page. Some people set it to the URL of their favorite news source or publication, while other people even write their own start page with a list of frequently-visited links, forms for search engines, and whatnot.

To make your own, just write it as an HTML file; you can either keep it somewhere in your home directory and give its full path name or, if you are running a Web server on your local system, you can put it somewhere in the server's HTML directory tree and access it with an HTTP url instead.

The following are methods for defining a start page in Mozilla and Lynx.

METHOD #1

Mozilla
  DEB: `mozilla-browser`
  RPM: `mozilla`
  WWW: `http://www.mozilla.org/`

To define a start page in Mozilla, define the **Home Page** in the Mozilla **Preferences...** menu.

⇒ To change the default start page in Mozilla to your own start page at `http://localhost/start/`, do the following:

1. Choose **Preferences...** from the **Edit** menu on the menu bar.
2. Left-click in the **Location** box.
3. Replace its contents with the start page you want:

         http://localhost/start

4. Left-click the **OK** button.

NOTES: In Mozilla, the start page loads whenever you start it with no arguments, click on the **Home** button, or type ⟨ALT⟩-⟨HOME⟩.

METHOD #2

Lynx
  DEB: lynx
  RPM: lynx
  WWW: http://lynx.browser.org/

The Lynx start page is defined as STARTFILE in /etc/lynx.cfg, and it can
be any URL, including a file:// URL pointing to a local file on the system.
You need superuser privileges to edit this file.

- To change the Lynx start page to the url http://localhost/start/,
  edit /etc/lynx.cfg with a text editor so that it contains the following
  line:

    STARTFILE:http://localhost/start/

NOTES: Linux distributions often predefine the Lynx start page to the home
page of the distribution. On Debian systems, for example, the start file comes
defined as the Debian home page [http://www.debian.org/].

33.8 Listing the URLs in Text

Use one of these two methods to list the URLs in text—the HTML source of a
Web page, the text of a Web page, or any text file.

To list the URLs in some Web page source code, first use wget with the -q
and -O options to dump the source to the standard output (see Recipe 33.5
[Getting Files from the Web], page 653), and then pipe that to one of the
methods.

To list the URLs in the *text* of a Web page, and not its source, first use
lynx with the -dump option to dump the contents of the page to the standard
output, and then pipe that to one of the methods.

To make sure that no duplicate URLs are listed, pass the output to sort
to output only unique lines (see Method #2 in See Recipe 13.5 [Filtering Out
Duplicate Lines of Text], page 319).

One method uses grep and the other sed, both with the same regular
expression for finding a URL. This regexp is rather long, and it contains two
literal space and two literal tab characters; if you use either one of these
methods often, you will certainly want to put the command to run it in a
script (see Recipe 3.7 [Using Shell Scripts], page 84).

METHOD #1

To output a list of URLs in text, one per line, use **grep** with the -o option,[6] and give as an argument the regular expression to match URLs. To search a text file, give the name of the file as the second argument.

⇒ Here are some ways to use this.

- To output a list of all the URLs contained in the file **/etc/lynx.cfg**, type (all on one line):

  ```
  $ grep -o
  '\(\(\(http\(s\)\?\|ftp\|gopher\|telnet\|news\):\/\/\|mailto:\).[^
  ⟨SPACEBAR⟩ ,;⟨CTRL⟩-⟨V⟩ ⟨TAB⟩<">]*[^ ⟨SPACEBAR⟩
  .,;⟨CTRL⟩-⟨V⟩ ⟨TAB⟩<">]\)' /etc/lynx.cfg ⟨RET⟩
  ```

- To output a list of all the URLs contained in the text of the URL **http://news.example.com/**, type (all on one line):

  ```
  $ lynx -dump -nolist http://news.example.com/ | grep -o
  '\(\(\(http\(s\)\?\|ftp\|gopher\|telnet\|news\):\/\/\|mailto:\).[^
  ⟨SPACEBAR⟩ ,;⟨CTRL⟩-⟨V⟩ ⟨TAB⟩<">]*[^ ⟨SPACEBAR⟩
  .,;⟨CTRL⟩-⟨V⟩ ⟨TAB⟩<">]\)' ⟨RET⟩
  ```

- To output a list of the URLs contained in the HTML source file of **http://news.example.com/**, type (all on one line):

  ```
  $ wget -q -O - http://news.example.com/ | grep -o
  '\(\(\(http\(s\)\?\|ftp\|gopher\|telnet\|news\):\/\/\|mailto:\).[^
  ⟨SPACEBAR⟩ ,;⟨CTRL⟩-⟨V⟩ ⟨TAB⟩<">]*[^ ⟨SPACEBAR⟩
  .,;⟨CTRL⟩-⟨V⟩ ⟨TAB⟩<">]\)' ⟨RET⟩
  ```

METHOD #2

To output a list of URLs in text, one per line, use **sed** with the following command line. To search a text file, give the name of the file as an argument.

⇒ Here are some ways to use this.

- To output a list of all the URLs contained in the file **/etc/lynx.cfg**, type (all on one line):

  ```
  $ sed -n
  's/.*\(\(\(http\(s\)\?\|ftp\|gopher\|telnet\|news\):\/\/\|
  mailto:\).[^⟨SPACEBAR⟩ ,;⟨CTRL⟩-⟨V⟩ ⟨TAB⟩<">]*[^
  ⟨SPACEBAR⟩ .,;⟨CTRL⟩-⟨V⟩ ⟨TAB⟩<">]\).*/\1/p' /etc/lynx.cfg ⟨RET⟩
  ```

---

[6] Available in GNU **grep** version 2.5 and newer.

- To output a list of all the URLs contained in the text of the URL `http://news.example.com/`, type (all on one line):

  ```
  $ lynx -dump -nolist http://news.example.com/ | sed -n
  's/.*\(\(\(http\(s\)\?\|ftp\|gopher\|telnet\|news\):\/\/\|
  mailto:\).[^ SPACEBAR ,; CTRL - V  TAB <">]*[^
  SPACEBAR .,; CTRL - V  TAB <">]\).*/\1/p' RET
  ```

- To output a list of the URLs contained in the HTML source file of `http://news.example.com/`, type (all on one line):

  ```
  $ wget -q -O - http://news.example.com/ | sed -n
  's/.*\(\(\(http\(s\)\?\|ftp\|gopher\|telnet\|news\):\/\/\|
  mailto:\).[^ SPACEBAR ,; CTRL - V  TAB <">]*[^
  SPACEBAR .,; CTRL - V  TAB <">]\).*/\1/p' RET
  ```

NOTES: The regexp used in these methods, although complex, is not exhaustive—it won't find every possible URL, but it will do a perfect job in most instances.

The PERL regexp that *can* match all possible URLs is described in Regex for URLs [`http://www.foad.org/~abigail/Perl/url2.html`], and it can be seen here: `http://www.foad.org/~abigail/Perl/url.regexp`.

33.9 Writing HTML

HyperText Markup Language (HTML) is the markup language of the Web; HTML files are just plain text files written in this markup language. You can edit HTML files in any text editor, no different from other kinds of text files (see Chapter 10 [Editing Text], page 231).

The following are some special methods for this task.

METHOD #1

Mozilla
 DEB: `mozilla-browser`
 RPM: `mozilla`
 WWW: `http://www.mozilla.org/`

Use Mozilla Composer to write HTML. It is one of the most popular WYSIWYG HTML editors. You can launch Composer while in Mozilla by selecting it from the `Window` menu or by typing CTRL - 4.

⇒ To start Mozilla Composer, do the following:

1. Start Mozilla (see Recipe 33.1.1 [Getting Acquainted with Mozilla], page 638):

   $ `mozilla` ⟨RET⟩

2. Press ⟨CTRL⟩-⟨4⟩.

METHOD #2

Bluefish
 DEB: `bluefish`
 RPM: `bluefish`
 WWW: `http://bluefish.openoffice.nl/`

Many people swear by Bluefish, a full-featured, user-friendly HTML editor for X. It has syntax highlighting and can have over 500 documents open at a time.

⇒ To start Bluefish, type:

   $ `bluefish` ⟨RET⟩

METHOD #3

GNU Emacs
 DEB: `emacsen-common`
      `emacs21`
 RPM: `emacs`
 WWW: `http://www.emacs.org/`

Emacs (see Recipe 10.1 [Using Emacs], page 232) has a major mode to facilitate the editing of HTML files called `html-mode`.

⇒ To start `html-mode` in a buffer, type:

   ⟨ALT⟩-⟨X⟩ `html-mode` ⟨RET⟩

The features of `html-mode` include the insertion of "skeleton" constructs.

The Emacs help text for the `html-mode` function includes a very short `html` authoring tutorial—view the documentation on this function to display the tutorial.

⇒ To read a short HTML tutorial in Emacs, type:

   ⟨CTRL⟩-⟨H⟩ `f html-mode` ⟨RET⟩

NOTES: When you're editing an HTML file in an Emacs buffer, you can open the same file in a Web browser in another window—Web browsers only read and don't write the HTML files they open, so you can view the rendered document in the browser as you create it in Emacs. When you make and save a change in the Emacs buffer, reload the file in the browser to see your changes take effect immediately.

33.9.1 Adding Parameters to Image Tags

Imgsizer
  DEB: imgsizer
  WWW: http://www.catb.org/~esr/imgsizer/

For usability, HTML image source tags should have HEIGHT and WIDTH parameters, which specify the dimensions of the image the tag describes. By specifying these parameters in all the image tags on a page, the text in that page will display in the browser window *before the images are loaded*. Without them, the browser must load all the images before any of the text on the page is displayed.

Use `imgsizer` to automatically determine the proper values and insert them into an HTML file. Give the name of the HTML file to fix as an argument.

⇒ To add HEIGHT and WIDTH parameters to the file index.html, type:

$ *imgsizer index.html* ⟨RET⟩

33.9.2 Converting HTML

There are several ways to convert HTML files to other formats. You can convert the HTML to plain text for reading, processing, or conversion to still other formats; you can also convert the HTML to PostScript, which you can view, print, or also convert to other formats, including PDF.

METHOD #1

Unhtml
  DEB: unhtml
  WWW: http://linux.maruhn.com/sec/unhtml.html

To simply remove the HTML formatting from text, use `unhtml`. It reads from the standard input (or a specified file name), and it writes its output to standard output.

⇒ Here are two ways to use this.

- To peruse the file `index.html` with its HTML tags removed, type:

    ```
    $ unhtml index.html | less (RET)
    ```

- To remove the HTML tags from the file `index.html` and write the output to a file called `index.txt`, type:

    ```
    $ unhtml index.html > index.txt (RET)
    ```

NOTES: When you remove the HTML tags from a file with `unhtml`, no further formatting is done to the text. Furthermore, it only works on files, and not on URLs themselves.

METHOD #2

Lynx
  DEB: lynx
  RPM: lynx
  WWW: http://lynx.browser.org/

Use `lynx` to save an HTML file or a URL as a *formatted* text file, so that the resultant text looks like the original HTML when viewed in `lynx`. It can also preserve italics and hyperlink information in the original HTML. See Recipe 33.2.4 [Sending Text from the Web to Standard Output], page 646.

One thing you can do with this `lynx` output is pipe it to tools for spacing text, and then send that to `enscript` for setting in a font. This is useful for printing a Web page in typescript "manuscript" form, with images and graphics removed and text set double-spaced in a Courier font.

⇒ To print a copy of the URL `http://example.com/essay/` in typescript manuscript form, type (all on one line):

    ```
    $ lynx -dump -underscore -nolist http://example.com/essay/ | pr -d
    | enscript -B (RET)
    ```

NOTES: In some cases, you might want to edit the file before you print it, such as when a Web page contains text navigation bars or other text that you'd want to remove before you turn it into a manuscript. In such a case, you'd pipe the `lynx` output to a file, edit the file, and then use `pr` on the file and pipe *that* output to `enscript` for printing.

METHOD #3

Html2ps
  DEB: html2ps
  RPM: html2ps
  WWW: http://www.tdb.uu.se/~jan/html2ps.html

Use **html2ps** to convert an HTML file to PostScript; this is useful when you want to print a Web page with all its graphics and images, or when you want to convert all or part of a Web site into PDF. Give the URLs or file names of the HTML files to convert as options. Use the **-u** option to underline the anchor text of hypertext links; specify a file name to write to as an argument to the **-o** option. The defaults are to not underline links and to write to the standard output.

⇒ Here are two ways to use this.

- To print a PostScript copy of the document at the URL **http://example.com/essay/** to the default printer, type:

    $ *html2ps http://example.com/essay/ | lpr* ⟨RET⟩

- To write a copy of the document at the URL **http://example.com/essay/** to a PostScript file **submission.ps** with all hypertext links underlined, type:

    $ *html2ps -u -o submission.ps http://example.com/essay/* ⟨RET⟩

33.9.3 Validating HTML

Weblint
  DEB: weblint
  RPM: weblint
  WWW: http://www.webmaster.bham.ac.uk/weblint/

Use **weblint** to validate the basic structure and syntax of an HTML file. Give the name of the file to be checked as an argument, and **weblint** outputs any complaints it has about the file to standard output, such as whether or not **IMG** elements are missing **ALT** descriptions, or whether nested elements overlap.

⇒ To validate the HTML in the file **index.html**, type:

    $ *weblint index.html* ⟨RET⟩

33.10 Analyzing Your Web Traffic

If you have a Web site, you will undoubtedly have some interest in analyzing your Web traffic: knowing which pages are popular, who is looking at them, when they are looking and where they are coming from. Do this by retrieving the *Web logs* from the server that hosts your site—these are plain text files written by the server containing data for every access of your site, one per line. Tools exist to analyze these logs; here are the two easiest methods for doing this.

METHOD #1

Analog
  DEB: analog
  RPM: analog
  WWW: http://www.analog.cx/

The most popular tool in use for analyzing Web logs is **analog**, which produces a comprehensive set of reports, including the following:

- The top words people used in search engines to find your site.

- The *referrers*, which are pages with links that the requesting computers followed to get to your pages.

- The top organizations of the computers that requested your pages.

- The operating systems of the computers that requested your pages.

- The most popular directories on your site.

- The most popular files on your site.

Give the filespec for the log files to analyze as an argument to **analog**. This command reads the log file you give and it outputs the reports to the standard output. Output is in HTML format; either pipe it to the standard input of a Web browser to view it or redirect it to a file to save it. Log files have to be in a log format that **analog** can recognize, such as the format used by the popular Apache Web server; they can also be compressed.

⇒ Here are some ways to use this.

- To view an analysis of ~/web/logs/2005/www.20050408.gz, a Web log file, type:

      $ analog ~/web/logs/2005/www.20050408.gz | lynx -stdin ⟨RET⟩

- To save an analysis of all the Web log files in the `~/web/logs/2005/` directory to an HTML file in the current directory named `analog.html`, type:

```
$ analog ~/web/logs/2005/* > analog.html (RET)
```

METHOD #2

You can also **grep** your log files. If the log files follow a standard format, you can use **cut** to cut out fields you are not interested in, thus outputting the desired fields. This is useful in doing things like finding the number of unique domains that have visited a certain directory or page of yours, which you pass to **cut** via **grep**.

⇒ To list the number of unique domains that have visited your **reviews** page, based on your logs in the `~/private_html/logs/2006` directory, type (all on one line):

```
$ grep reviews ~/private_html/logs/2006/* | cut -f2 -d':' |
  cut -f1 -d' ' | sort -u | wc -l (RET)
```

NOTES: If any of the log files are compressed, use **zgrep** or use **grep** with the **-z** option.

33.11 Using Other Web Browsers

Surprisingly, there are not nearly as many Web browsers for Linux as there are text editors—or even text *viewers*. This is true for any operating system, and I have often pondered why this is; perhaps "browsing the Web," a fairly recent activity in itself, may soon be obsoleted by Web *readers* and other tools. In any event, the following table lists other browsers that are currently available for Linux systems.

Amaya	Developed by the World Wide Web Consortium; both a graphical Web browser and a WYSIWYG editor for writing HTML. DEB: amaya RPM: amaya WWW: http://www.w3.org/Amaya/

Arena	Developed by the World Wide Web Consortium; a very compact, HTML 3.0-compliant Web browser for X. RPM: `arena` WWW: `http://www.w3.org/Arena/`
Dillo	Very fast, and small, yet *graphical*, Web browser. DEB: `dillo` RPM: `dillo` WWW: `http://www.dillo.org/`
Express	Small browser that works in X with GNOME installed. WWW: `http://tinyurl.com/32p4d`
Galeon	GNOME browser based on Mozilla. DEB: `galeon-common` `galeon` RPM: `galeon` WWW: `http://galeon.sourceforge.net/`
Gzilla	Graphical browser for X, currently in an early stage of development. RPM: `gzilla` WWW: `http://www.levien.com/gzilla/`
Links	Newer, text-only browser that some prefer over Lynx. DEB: `links` RPM: `links` WWW: `http://artax.karlin.mff.cuni.cz/~mikulas/links/`
Skipstone	Graphical browser based on Mozilla, but with many excess components removed. RPM: `skipstone` WWW: `http://www.muhri.net/skipstone/`

W3m

Newer, text-only browser whose features include table support and an interesting free-form cursor control.
DEB: w3m
RPM: w3m
WWW: http://w3m.sourceforge.net/

CHAPTER 34

Other Internet Services

There are many Internet services other than email and the Web; this chapter
describes how to use many of the other popular (and less popular) services,
including `telnet`, `ftp`, and `finger`.

34.1 Connecting to a Remote Host

Use `telnet` to connect to a remote system. Give the name of the system to
connect to as an argument, specifying either its name or numeric IP address.
If that system is reachable, you will be connected to it and presented with
a `login:` or other connection prompt (the network is not exclusive to Linux
systems) just as if you were seated at a terminal connected to that system. If
you have an account on that system, you can then log in to it (see Recipe 2.2.1
[Logging In to the System], page 29).

⇒ To connect to the system `lab1.example.edu`, type:

```
$ telnet lab1.example.edu ⟨RET⟩
Trying 127.0.0.1...
Connected to lab1.example.edu.
Escape character is '^]'.


Welcome to the Chemistry Department Computer Lab!


login:
```

In this example, the user connected to the remote system at
`lab1.example.edu`; the `login:` prompt displayed is from that system.
At this point, entering a username and password that is valid for
`lab1.example.edu` will log you in to that system; you will be given a shell
prompt and you can run commands on that system through your terminal
just as if you were logged in at that system's console.[1]

---

[1] It's possible (although not often desirable) to "nest" multiple layers of `telnet` sessions
on top of each other by running `telnet` from one system to the next, to the next, and so
on, without disconnecting from the previous system. To avoid this, make sure you know
which host you're leaving when you're about to `telnet` off to another; the `hostname` tool
is useful for this (see Recipe 2.2.1 [Logging In to the System], page 29).

To disconnect from the system, follow the normal procedures for logging out from the system you are connected to (for how to do that on a Linux system, see Recipe 2.2.2 [Logging Out of the System], page 31).

⇒ To disconnect from a remote Linux system, type:

```
$ ⟨CTRL⟩-⟨D⟩
Connection closed.

$
```

In the preceding example, the first shell prompt was on the remote system, and the second prompt was on the local system; coincidentally, the prompts were the default on both systems—a dollar sign (**$**).

Once you are connected to a remote system with **telnet**, everything you type in the terminal is sent to the remote system until you are disconnected from that system. It is sometimes useful to temporarily escape back to the local shell on your local system, and you can do that by typing the *escape character*, which is a key sequence that is interpreted by **telnet** before it reaches the remote system. The default escape character is the sequence ⟨CTRL⟩-⟨[⟩.

When you type that, you are brought to the **telnet** command prompt, where you can do a number of useful things, including temporarily suspend the connection or terminate the connection entirely—both of which are described in the following recipes.

34.1.1 Suspending a Connection with a Remote Host

To suspend the connection with the remote host temporarily, type the escape character and then give the **z** command at the **telnet** command prompt.

⇒ To temporarily return to a local shell prompt, type:

```
faraway-system$ ⟨CTRL⟩-⟨[⟩
telnet> z ⟨RET⟩
[2]+ Stopped                    telnet
$
```

To return to the remote system, bring the **telnet** job back into the foreground (see Recipe 3.3.3 [Putting a Job in the Foreground], page 73).

⇒ To return to the remote system, type:

```
$ fg (RET)
faraway-system$
```

In the two preceding examples, the shell prompt of the remote system is "`faraway-system$`." (You don't have to type the escape character at a shell prompt, though; you can type it regardless of what program is running on the remote system.)

34.1.2 Terminating a Connection with a Remote Host

To terminate a connection with the remote host and exit `telnet`, type the escape character and then give the `q` command at the `telnet` command prompt. This is useful for when the remote host has stopped responding for one reason or another (bad network connection, the computer froze up, whatever) and you cannot terminate the connection normally.

⇒ To terminate a connection with a remote system, type:

```
faraway-system$ (CTRL)-([)
telnet> q (RET)
Connection closed.
$
```

34.2 Transferring Files to and from a Remote Host

File Transfer Protocol (FTP) is a way to exchange files across systems. Use the `ftp` tool to connect to another system using this protocol, giving the name or numeric IP address of the system you want to connect to as an argument. Once connected, you will be prompted to log in with a username and password (if you have one on that system).

Many systems are set up to accept *anonymous ftp* connections, where files are available for downloading by the general public. To access such repositories, log in with a username of **anonymous**, and give your email address for a password.

⇒ To make an anonymous `ftp` connection to `ftp.example.org`, type:

```
$ ftp ftp.example.org (RET)
Connected to ftp.example.org.
220-Welcome to EXAMPLE.ORG.
220-See file README for more information about this archive.
220-
220 FTP server example.org ready.
Name (ftp.example.org:tom): anonymous (RET)
331 Guest login ok, send your email address as password.
Password: tom@example.edu (RET)
230-
Remote system type is UNIX.
Using binary mode to transfer files.
ftp>
```

Once connected and logged in, use the `cd` and `ls` commands to change directories and to list files on the remote system.

It is standard practice for public systems to have a `/pub` directory on their FTP host that contains all the files and goodies available to the general public.

⇒ To change to the `/pub` directory on the remote system and look at the files that are there, type:

```
ftp> cd /pub (RET)
250 Directory changed to /pub.
ftp> ls (RET)
ftp> ls
200 PORT command successful.
150 Opening ASCII connection for file (918 bytes)
total 52048
-rw-rw-r--   1 ftpadmin ftpadmin 1095772 Sep 28 06:32 INDEX.gz
-rw-rw-r--   1 ftpadmin ftpadmin 9521446 Sep 28 06:42 ls-lR.gz
drwxr-xr-x   2 ftpadmin ftpadmin     512 Sep 17 18:23 rec
drwxr-xr-x   3 ftpadmin ftpadmin     512 Sep 17 18:23 sci
drwxr-xr-x   5 ftpadmin ftpadmin     512 Sep 17 18:23 text
226 Transfer completed with 918 Bytes/s.
ftp>
```

In this example, the `/pub` directory contained three subdirectories (`rec`, `sci`, and `text`) and two files (`INDEX.gz` and `ls-lR.gz`); many public systems have files similar to these in their `/pub` directories—`INDEX.gz` is a listing of all files on their `ftp` site, with descriptions, and `ls-lR.gz` is the output of the command `ls -lR` run on the directory tree of their `ftp` server.

The following subsections describe how to upload and download files. Use the `quit` command to exit `ftp` and close the connection to the remote system.

34.2.1 Uploading a File to a Remote Host

Use the `put` command to upload a file; give the name of the file as an argument. `put` takes that file in the current directory of the local system and puts a copy of it in the current directory of the remote system.

⇒ To upload a copy of the file `latest.rcp` from the current directory on the local system to the current directory of the remote system, type:

     `ftp>` *`put latest.rcp`* (RET)

The current directory of the *local* system is, by default, the directory where you ran the `ftp` command. To change directories on your local system, use `lcd`; it works just like the `cd` command, but it changes the *local* directory.

⇒ To change to the parent directory of the current directory on the local system, type:

```
ftp> lcd ..  (RET)
Local directory now /home/james/demos
ftp>
```

In this example, the local current directory is now `/home/james/demos`.

There are other important commands for downloading files—use `i` to specify that files be transferred as *binary*; normally, the transfer is set up for text files. When you want to transfer programs, archives, compressed files, or any other non-text file, set the transfer type to `i` first.

In recent years, most public systems have added a security measure forbidding the upload by anonymous users to anywhere but the `/incoming` or `/pub/incoming` directories.

The `mput` command works like `put`, but it allows you to specify wildcards. By default, `mput` asks you, for each file, whether to upload the file or not; to turn off this file prompting, type `prompt` before giving the `mput` command.

This command is a toggle—type **prompt** again to turn file prompting back on for your session.

34.2.2 Downloading a File from a Remote Host

The **get** command works like **put**, but in reverse—specify a file on the remote system, and **get** saves a copy to the current directory on the local system. Again, use **i** first when downloading non-text files. (You can also download text files with **i**, so it is good practice to *always* set it before you transfer files; most Linux systems are configured to set the type to **i** immediately upon connection).

⇒ To download the file **INDEX.gz** in the current directory on the remote system, saving it to your **~/tmp** directory, type:

```
ftp> lcd ~/tmp (RET)
Local directory now /home/james/tmp
ftp get INDEX.gz (RET)
local: INDEX.gz remote: INDEX.gz
Transferred 10942767 bytes
ftp>
```

NOTES: The **mget** command works like **get** but allows wildcards; as with **mput**, you will be prompted to verify each file unless you use the **prompt** command first to turn this off.

34.3 Using Secure Internet Services

OpenSSH
  DEB: ssh
  RPM: openssh
  WWW: http://www.openssh.com/

These newer methods involving secure, encrypted connections replace the older methods in the recipes described previously for connecting to a remote system and for transferring files to and from a remote system. Use them in place of **telnet** and **ftp** when enhanced security is desired, or required.

You can still use the old ways, and they may be fine for local networks, but on the Internet the secure variants have become the standard in most places—the Net is not the safe haven it was a decade ago, and in practice, few sites allow `telnet` access anymore.

The following recipes describe how to use the OpenSSH implementation of the famous SSH ("Secure Shell") protocol. OpenSSH includes the contemporary replacements for older `rlogin`, `rsh`, and `rcp` secure-connection tools.

NOTES: The first time you use one of these tools to connect with a remote system, you may get a message telling you that the "host key" was not found in the list of known hosts, and asking whether or not to continue with the connection—answer "yes."

34.3.1 Making a Secure Shell Connection to a Remote Host

Use `ssh` to connect securely to a remote system. It opens a login connection on a remote system whose hostname you give as an argument.

⇒ To open a secure connection to `arctic.example.org`, type:

```
$ ssh arctic.example.org ⟨RET⟩
ernie@arctic.example.org's password: snowshoe ⟨RET⟩
Last login: Wed Aug 13 11:39:29 EDT 2003

Welcome to arctic.example.org!

[ernie@arctic ~]
```

In this example, the username `ernie` made a SSH connection to the system `arctic.example.org`, on which his password is "`snowshoe`." The "`~ $`" is the shell prompt on that system, where he can run commands until he exits by either running the `exit` command or by typing ⟨CTRL⟩-⟨D⟩ at a shell prompt.

If your username on the remote system differs from your username on your local system, use the `-l` option to specify a different username.

⇒ To open a secure connection to `arctic.example.org` with a remote username of `scout`, type:

```
$ ssh -l scout arctic.example.org (RET)
scout@arctic.example.org's password: igloo (RET)
Last login: Wed Aug 13 13:14:53 EDT 2003

Welcome to arctic.example.org!

You have new mail.
[scout@arctic ~]
```

In this example, the user logged into `arctic.example.org` with a username on that system of `scout`, whose password was "igloo."

34.3.2 Making a Secure File Copy to a Remote Host

Use SCP to make secure file copies between your local system and a remote
host. It takes as arguments the name of the file to copy from and the name
of the file to copy to. For the file on the local system, just give the file name
as usual; specify the file name on the remote system in this format:

> `user@remote:filename`

For *user*, give the name of your username on the remote system (if it's the
same as the local system, omit both it and the trailing at sign (`@`). For *remote*,
give the hostname of the remote system to connect to, and for *filename* give
the name of the file as it should appear in the home directory of *user*.

⇒ To copy the file `index.html` from your `local_html` directory
   to the `public_html` directory in your account on the system
   `arctic.example.org`, type (all on one line):

```
$ scp local_html/index.html
arctic.example.com:public_html/index.html (RET)
ernie@arctic.example.org's password: snowshoe (RET)
index.html      100% |****************************|    2365    00:00
$
```

In this example, the user has a username of `ernie` on both systems; the
progress of the copy is displayed on the screen before `scp` exits.

Use the `-r` option to copy an entire directory tree.

$\Rightarrow$ Here are some ways to use this.

- To copy the `local_html` directory tree, making it the `public_html` directory in your account on the system `arctic.example.org`, type:

```
$ scp -r local_html arctic.example.com:public_html (RET)
ernie@arctic.example.org's password: snowshoe (RET)
public_html  100% |*****************************|  4096    00:00
$
```

- To copy the file `log.txt` from the user `scout`'s `public_html` directory on the system `arctic.example.org`, placing it in the current directory on your local system, type:

```
$ scp scout@arctic.example.org:public_html/log.txt log.txt (RET)
scout@arctic.example.org's password: igloo (RET)
access_log   100% |*****************************|  12655  00:00
$
```

In the last example, the user's local username on `arctic` differed from his username on `scout`.

NOTES: Use the `-v` option for a verbose display; this will display information about the file transfer process as it happens.

34.4 Reading Usenet

Usenet is a famous, vast collection of world-around discussion boards called *newsgroups*, where messages (called *articles*) can be posted, read, and publicly responded to.

With thousands of such newsgroups—on topics like home repair, cooking, collecting, home brewing, local jobs, and setting up hardware running on Linux—Usenet is always good for getting the answer to a technical question,[2] but expect few Platonic dialogues; the discussion rarely rises above water-cooler talk, and the seeker won't find much more than that. Searchable archives exist online,[3] containing most of it—20 years of chit-chat and opinion.

---

[2] Always be prepared to be *flamed*, or have your question or purposes mocked, by some bellicose individual who wishes to display his vast knowledge.

[3] http://groups.google.com/

Newsgroups are named and organized by hierarchies, which can have any number of branches. Each branch is delineated by a period character (`.`); for example, the `comp.os.linux` newsgroup is part of the `comp.os` branch of the `comp` hierarchy.

The following table lists the "Big Eight" Usenet hierarchies and gives examples of some newsgroups in each one.

`comp`	Computing
	`news:comp.os.linux.advocacy`,
	`news:comp.text.tex`
`humanities`	Humanities
	`news:humanities.music.composers.wagner`
`misc`	Miscellaneous
	`news:misc.consumers.frugal-living`
`news`	Newsgroups relating to Usenet itself
	`news.newusers.questions`
`rec`	Recreation
	`news:rec.music.marketplace.vinyl`,
	`news:rec.food.cooking`
`sci`	Science
	`news:sci.math`, `news:sci.cognitive`
`soc`	Social groups and cultures
	`news:soc.culture.usa`,
	`news:soc.college`
`talk`	Talk and chit-chat
	`news:talk.environment`,
	`news:talk.politics.guns`

There are many other hierarchies, but these eight are technically the only newsgroups considered to be part of Usenet proper. While *netnews* is the term for the collection of all newsgroups including those in Usenet, these terms are often used interchangeably.

The "alternative" hierarchy, `alt`, is perhaps the most popular hierarchy of all—just about every subject you might want to discuss (and a good deal that you probably wouldn't) has an appropriate newsgroup here. It even has a place for non sequiturs.

There are also hierarchies for topics concerning certain geographical areas: For example, the `cmh.` hierarchy is for topics pertaining to the greater Columbus, Ohio metropolitan area; `seattle` is for the city of Seattle, Washington. So, while `cmh.forsale` pertains to items posted for sale in the greater Columbus area, `seattle.forsale` is for items posted for sale in and around Seattle. Hierarchies can exist also for certain organizations; for example, the `gnu` hierarchy is for newsgroups concerning the GNU Project, and `bit` is for newsgroup redistributions of the popular Bitnet LISTSERV mailing lists.

The following recipes describe tools for reading and posting articles to netnews.

34.4.1 Choosing a Newsreader

An application that lets you read and post articles to newsgroups is called a *newsreader*. Here are some of the best newsreaders available for Linux-based systems.

Gnus   Very powerful and feature-full newsreader for use in Emacs; can be used to read mail, too.
DEB: gnus
RPM: gnus
WWW: http://gnus.org/

Knews   Graphical newsreader for use in X whose features include the display of article threads in a graphical tree and options for reading news over slow connections.
DEB: knews
RPM: knews
WWW: http://www.matematik.su.se/~kjj/

Mozilla News   Newsreader built into the Mozilla browser (historically, commercial Web browsers had mail and newsreaders built into them, and that capability remains in the Mozilla browser.)
DEB: mozilla-browser
RPM: mozilla
WWW: http://mozilla.org/

NN   Older (and very popular) newsreader that was designed for reading
             the most news in the minimal amount of time; its motto is "No
             News is good news, but NN is better."
             DEB: `nn`
             RPM: `nn`
             WWW: `http://www.nndev.org/`

PAN   GNOME newsreader designed for speed and is meant to be easy for
             beginners.
             DEB: `pan`
             RPM: `pan`
             WWW: `http://pan.rebelbase.com/`

News   Suite of small tools for use in X that facilitates the reading and com-
Peruser   posing of news articles when you're offline, by downloading batches
             of news when your system is online.
             DEB: `peruser`
             WWW: `http://ibiblio.org/pub/Linux/system/news/readers/`

SLRN   Optimized for use over slow connections (like home dial-up connec-
             tions). Based on RN, one of the oldest newsreaders.
             DEB: `slrn`
             RPM: `slrn`
             WWW: `http://www.slrn.org/`

34.4.2 Finding Newsgroups for a Topic

NN
  DEB: `nn`
  RPM: `nn`
  WWW: `http://www.nndev.org/`

Use **nngrep** to find newsgroup names that match a pattern. This is useful for
finding groups on a particular topic.

⇒ To output a list of all newsgroups that match the pattern "`society`,"
  type:

      $ *nngrep society* (RET)

   Use the `-u` option to only search through *unsubscribed* groups. This is
useful if you are subscribed to a number of groups, and you are looking only
for groups you aren't subscribed to yet.

⇒ To output a list of all unsubscribed-to newsgroups that match the pattern
   "society," type:

   $ *nngrep society* (RET)

   In the previous example, if you were already subscribed to the group
`alt.society.neutopia`, that group will not be displayed, but other groups
matching the pattern "society" that you are not subscribed to would be
listed.

NOTES: nngrep uses your `~/.newsrc` file to get the list of groups you are
subscribed to.

34.5 Displaying Information About Users

The following tools are used to list the activity of other users and systems on
the Internet, showing whether or not they are currently online and perhaps
displaying a little more information about them.

34.5.1 Checking Whether a User Is Online

Use **finger** to check whether or not a given user is online. Give as an argument
the username of the given user (if on the local system) or his email address
(if on a remote system).

   If the system he is using has **finger** enabled (most UNIX-based systems
should, but are often forced to turn it off today because of security concerns),
the command will tell you the following: the date and time when he last
logged in; whether or not he is currently logged in; his full name; his office
room and telephone number; the full path name of his home directory; what
shell he uses; whether or not he has mail waiting; the last time he read mail;
and, finally, his "plan," as described below.

⇒ To finger the user `joe@home.example.org`, type:

```
$ finger joe@home.example.org (RET)
[home.example.org]
Login: joe                              Name: Joe Smith
Directory: /sp1/joe                     Shell: /bin/tcsh
Last login Fri Jan 20 16:38 1989 (PST) on ttypb from work.example.com
No mail.
No plan.
$
```

In this example, the user `joe` on the system at `home.example.org` is not currently logged in, logged in last on January 20, and uses the `tsch` shell.

NOTES: On UNIX-based systems, you can put information in a hidden file in your home directory called `.plan`, and that text will be output when someone `finger`s you. Some people put elaborate information in their `.plan` files; in the early 1990s, it was very much in vogue to have long, rambling `.plan`s. Sometimes, people put information in their `.plan` file for special events—for example, someone who is having a party next weekend might put directions to his house in his `.plan` file.

34.5.2 Listing Who Is Logged In to a System

To get a listing of *all* users who are currently logged in to a given system, use `finger` and specify the name (or numeric IP address) of the system, preceded with an at sign (`@`).

This gives a listing of all the users who are currently logged in on that system. It doesn't give out each person's `.plan`s, but the output includes how long each user has been idle, where he is connected from, and (sometimes) what command he is running. (The particular information that is output depends on the operating system and configuration of the remote system.)

⇒ To output the users who are currently logged in to the system `ap.example.org`, type:

```
$ finger @ap.example.org (RET)
[ap.example.org]
Login     Name           Tty  Idle  Login Time    Office
joe       Joe Smith      *q2  16:23 Sep 27 17:22  (work.example.com)
gopherd   Gopher Client  *r4  1:01  Sep 28 08:29  (gopherd)
friday    Hildy Johnson  *r1  14    Sep 28 09:35  (ap.example.org)
sysop     Admin Account  t2   2     Sep 28 08:42  (console)
$
```

34.6 Displaying Information About a Host

These are all methods for displaying information about a host connected to the Internet.

34.6.1 Determining If a Host Is Online

Use **ping** to determine whether a particular system is currently connected to the Internet. It tells the time it takes for an IP packet to travel from your system to the other one, and back.

Type **ping** followed by the hostname or numeric IP address of the system you want to check; if your system is online and the system to be checked is also online, **ping** should continually output lines telling how long the latency, in milliseconds, is between the two systems. Type ⟨CTRL⟩-⟨C⟩ to interrupt it and stop **ping**ing.

⇒ To ping the host **bfi.org**, type:

```
$ ping bfi.org ⟨RET⟩
PING bfi.org (209.196.135.250): 56 data bytes
64 bytes from 209.196.135.250: icmp_seq=0 ttl=63 time=190.0 ms
64 bytes from 209.196.135.250: icmp_seq=1 ttl=63 time=159.9 ms
64 bytes from 209.196.135.250: icmp_seq=2 ttl=63 time=160.5 ms
⟨CTRL⟩-⟨C⟩
--- bfi.org ping statistics ---
3 packets transmitted, 3 packets received, 0% packet loss
round-trip min/avg/max = 159.9/170.1/190.0 ms
$
```

In this example, the host **bfi.org** was **ping**ed and a total of three **ping**s were sent and received before the user typed ⟨CTRL⟩-⟨C⟩ to interrupt it. As long as these **ping** lines are output, you know that the other machine is connected to the Internet (or at least to the same network that your localhost is connected to).

You really don't need to analyze the information on each line of a **ping** message—the only useful information is the number at the end of the line, which tells you how many milliseconds it took to go out to the Internet, touch or "ping" that host, and come back.[4] The quicker the better—**ping**s that are four or five digits long (or greater) mean a slow connection between the two machines. When you interrupt the **ping**, some statistics are output, including the minimum, average, and maximum number of milliseconds it took to **ping**

---

[4] "I named it after the sound that a sonar makes, inspired by the whole principle of echo-location," said the original author of **ping**, Mike Muss. He died in an automobile accident in November 2000.

the given host. In the previous example, the high was 190 and the low was 159.9 milliseconds, with an average of 170.1 milliseconds to make the trip.

NOTES: If your own system is not online, `ping` will report that either the network is unreachable or that the host isn't found.

34.6.2 Tracing the Path to Another Host

Use `traceroute` to trace the path from your host to another. Give the name of the remote host as an argument, and `traceroute` will show a list of all the systems connected between yours and that host. This is good for checking what ISP or type of connectivity a particular host has, for checking the route traveled between you and the host, and for seeing if a host is online at all.

⇒ To trace the path between your host and `whitehouse.gov`, type:

> `$ traceroute whitehouse.gov` (RET)

NOTES: On some systems, `traceroute` is kept in `/usr/sbin/`. When so, it's not on the path of regular users, although such users can still run it—just specify the full path name when you run it, such as `/usr/sbin/traceroute`.

34.6.3 Getting the IP Address of a Hostname

When you know the name of a particular host, and you want to find the IP address that corresponds to it, there are a few things you can do.

METHOD #1

To get the IP address of a host, `ping` the host in question; this will output the IP address of the host in parentheses (see Recipe 34.6.1 [Determining Whether a Host is Online], page 685).

METHOD #2

Use `host` to get the IP address of the host whose name you give as an argument.

⇒ To get the IP address of `linart.net`, type:

> `$ host linart.net` (RET)

NOTES: Depending on how the remote host is set up, this method may not work.

METHOD #3

Use `dig`, the "domain information groper" tool, to get the IP address of a host. Give a hostname as an argument to output information about that host, including its IP address, in a section labeled `ANSWER SECTION`.

⇒ To find the IP address of the host `linart.net`, type:

```
$ dig linart.net (RET)
...output messages...
;; ANSWER SECTION:
linart.net.              1D IN A          64.240.156.195
...output messages...
$
```

In this example, `dig` output the IP address of `64.240.156.195` as the IP address for the host `linart.net`.

34.6.4 Getting the Hostname of an IP Address

When you know the IP address of a system, you can determine its full network name, or FQDN ("fully qualified domain name"). There are a few methods for this.

METHOD #1

Use `host` to get the hostname of the system whose IP address you give as an argument.

⇒ To get the hostname of 127.0.0.1, type:

```
$ host 127.0.0.1 (RET)
```

NOTES: Depending on how the remote host is set up, this method may not work.

METHOD #2

To find the hostname for a given IP address, use `dig` with the `-x` option. Give an IP address as an argument to output information about that address, including its hostname in a section labeled `ANSWER SECTION`.

⇒ To find the hostname that corresponds to the IP address 152.2.210.81, type:

```
$ dig -x 152.2.210.81 (RET)
...output messages...
;; ANSWER SECTION:
81.210.2.152.in-addr.arpa.   1D IN PTR   metalab.unc.edu.
...output messages...
$
```

In this example, dig output that the FQDN corresponding to the given IP address was metalab.unc.edu.

34.6.5 Listing the Owner of a Domain Name

An Internet domain name's *domain record* contains contact information for the organization or individual that has registered that domain. Use the whois command to view the domain records for the common .com, .org, .net, and .edu top-level domains.

With only a domain name as an argument, whois outputs the name of the "Whois Server" that has that particular domain record. To output the domain record, specify the Whois Server to use as an argument to the -h option.

⇒ Here are two ways to use this.

- To output the name of the Whois Server for columbia.edu, type:

  ```
  $ whois columbia.edu (RET)
  ```

- To view the domain record for columbia.edu, using the whois.educause.net Whois Server, type:

  ```
  $ whois -h whois.educause.net columbia.edu (RET)
  ```

NOTES: This command also outputs the names of the nameservers that handle the given domain—this is useful to get an idea of where a particular Web site is hosted.

34.7 Chatting with Other Users

There are several ways to interactively chat with other users on the Internet, regardless of their platforms or operating systems. The following recipes describe the most popular tools and methods for doing this.

34.7.1 Sending a Message to Another User's Terminal

There are a few ways to do this, depending on whether you are sending to a particular user or to *all* users.

METHOD #1

Use **write** to write a message to the terminal of another user. Give the username you want to write to as an argument. This command writes the message you give, preceded with a header line indicating that the following is a message from you, and giving the current system time. It also rings the bell on the user's terminal.

⇒ To send the message "Wake up!" to the terminal where user **sleepy** is logged in, type:

```
$ write sleepy ⟨RET⟩
Wake up!
⟨CTRL⟩-⟨D⟩
$
```

The other user can reply to you by running **write** and giving your username as an argument. Traditionally, a user ended a **write** message with -o, which indicated that what he was saying was "over" and that it was now the other person's turn to talk. When a user believed that a conversation was completed, he would end a line with "oo," meaning that he was "over and out."

METHOD #2

A similar command, **wall**, writes a text message to all other users on the local system. It takes a text file as an argument and outputs the contents of that file; with no argument, it outputs what you type until you type ⟨CTRL⟩-⟨D⟩ on a line by itself. It precedes the message with the text "Broadcast message from *username*" (where *username* is your username) followed by the current system time, and it rings the bell on all terminals it broadcasts to.

⇒ Here are two ways to use this.

  • To output the contents of /etc/motd to all logged-in terminals, type:

   ```
   $ wall /etc/motd ⟨RET⟩
   ```

- To output the text "Who wants to go out for Chinese food?" to all
  logged-in terminals, type:

  ```
  $ wall ⟨RET⟩
  Who wants to go out for Chinese food? ⟨RET⟩
  ⟨CTRL⟩-⟨D⟩
  ```

34.7.2 Denying Messages to Your Terminal

You can control write access to your terminal for commands like write and
wall, so that you aren't interrupted. Do this with mesg. It works like biff
(see Recipe 32.4.2 [Setting Notification for New Mail], page 624): With no
arguments, it outputs whether or not it is set; with y as an argument, it
allows messages to be sent to your terminal; and with n as an argument, it
disallows them.

The default for all users is to allow messages to be written to their terminals; antisocial people usually put the line mesg n in their .bashrc file (see
Recipe 3.7.3 [Using Shell Startup Files], page 86).

⇒ Here are some ways to use this.

- To disallow messages to be written to your terminal, type:

  ```
  $ mesg n ⟨RET⟩
  ```

- To output the current access state of your terminal, type:

  ```
  $ mesg ⟨RET⟩
  is n
  $
  ```

In the preceding example, mesg indicated that messages are currently dis-
allowed to be written to your terminal.

34.7.3 Chatting Directly with a User

```
Ytalk
 DEB: ytalk
 RPM: ytalk
 WWW: http://www.iagora.com/~espel/ytalk/ytalk.html
```

Use talk to interactively chat in realtime with another user. Give the username (or email address) of the user you want to chat with as an argument;
a message will be sent to that user's terminal, indicating that a connection

is requested. If that person then runs **talk**, giving your username as an argument, you will both be connected in a **talk** session—the screen will clear, and then what you type will appear on the top of the screen; what the other user types will appear at the bottom of the screen.

⇒ To request a chat with the user **watson@example.edu**, type:

$ *talk watson@example.edu* ⟨RET⟩

This command sends a connection request to the user **watson@example.edu**. If the user is not logged on or is refusing messages, **talk** will output a message indicating such; but if that user is available, **talk** will send a message to that user asking to complete the connection, and it will tell you that it is ringing your party.

If that user isn't logged on, you will be told so and then **talk** will exit. If the user is logged on and then types *talk bell@myers.example.org* (if, in this example, that's what your email address is), the **talk** connection will be established between you. At this point, your screen will clear and look like Figure 34-1.

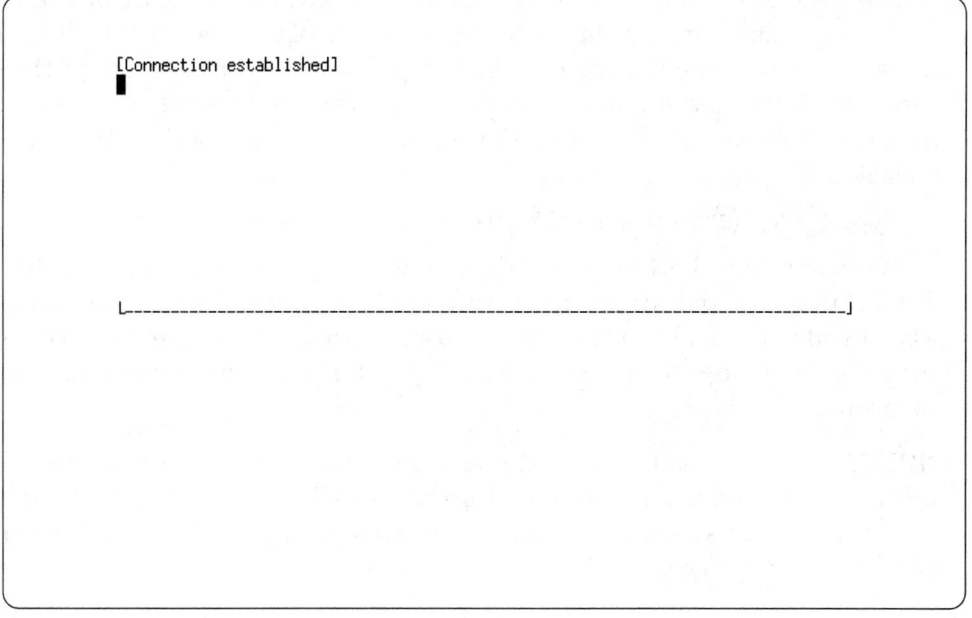

[Connection established]

*Figure 34-1. Beginning a **talk** session.*

You can then type, and what you type will appear on both your screen and that user's screen; that user, in turn, can *also* type—even while you are typing—and what that user types appears on the other half of both screens, as in Figure 34-2.

```
[Connection established]
Is that you, Watson?

I'd like to see you.
Can you make it over to the laboratory?

Excellent!
█

L_____J
Yes, it's me.

Sure, I'll be right over.
```

Figure 34-2. A `talk` *session in progress.*

It is convention to indicate that you are done saying something by typing ⟨RET⟩ ⟨RET⟩, thus bringing the cursor down past a blank line on your half of the screen. Some users, once they have typed down to the bottom of their part of the screen during the course of the conversation, type ⟨RET⟩ repeatedly to "clear" their half of the screen, thus bringing the cursor back to the top of a blank half.

Type ⟨CTRL⟩-⟨C⟩ to end a `talk` session.

When you type, both users see the characters appear in realtime; my first demonstration of the interactive nature of the Internet, back in 1991, was when I had a live, real-time chat with a user in Australia, on the other side of the globe from me—the magic felt that day still remains whenever I run this command!

NOTES: A similar command, `ytalk`, allows simultaneous connection between *multiple* users, and it contains other features as well; it is generally considered to be the superior successor of `talk`, but it is not yet available or standard on all UNIX-based systems.

34.7.4 Chatting on IRC

Internet Relay Chat (IRC) is a global chat system, probably the oldest and largest on the Internet. IRC is a great way to meet and talk to people, live on the Internet; it has historically been very popular with Linux users.

There are several IRC networks, each with its own servers and tens of thousands of users; to "go on" IRC, you use an IRC client program to connect with an IRC server. Like CB radio, IRC networks have *channels*, usually based on a particular topic, which you join to chat with other users in that channel (you can also send private messages to other users).

The following table lists some of the IRC clients available for Linux.

BitchX	IRC client whose features include ANSI color escapes, so it can display all of the character escape codes that are popularly used on IRC for special effects. Despite what you might gather from its name, it actually doesn't require X in order to run. DEB: `bitchx` RPM: `BitchX` WWW: `http://www.bitchx.org/`
EPIC	Large, feature-filled IRC client. DEB: `epic` RPM: `epic` WWW: `http://www.epicsol.org/`
Irssi	Modular IRC client; note that some versions can only be run in X with GNOME. DEB: `irssi-common` RPM: `irssi` WWW: `http://irssi.org/`
Xchat	Graphical IRC chat client for use in X. DEB: `xchat` RPM: `xchat` WWW: `http://www.xchat.org/`
ZenIRC	Minimalist and no-frills (yet fully extensible) IRC mode for Emacs. DEB: `zenirc` WWW: `http://www.zenirc.org/`

34.7.5 Chatting on ICQ

In the late 1990s, a company called Mirabilis released a proprietary program for PCs called ICQ ("I Seek You"), which was used to send text messages to other users in realtime. Since then, many free software chat tools have been written that use the ICQ protocol.

One nice feature of ICQ is that you can maintain a "buddy list" of email addresses, and when you have an ICQ client running, it will tell you whether or not any of your buddies are online. But unlike `talk`, you can't watch the other user type in realtime—messages are displayed in the other user's ICQ client only when you send them.

The following table lists some of the free software ICQ clients currently available.

LICQ   ICQ client for use in X.
                                DEB: `licq`
                                RPM: `licq`
                                WWW: `http://www.licq.org/`

MICQ   "Matt's ICQ clone," an easy-to-use ICQ client that
                                can be used in a shell.
                                DEB: `micq`
                                RPM: `micq`
                                WWW: `http://www.micq.org/`

ZICQ   MICQ with a modified user interface.
                                RPM: `zicq`

34.7.6 Using IM Services

AOL's Instant Messenger (AIM) is similar to `write`, made to work over the Internet—it sends a message to the terminal of a user, and with the "buddy list" feature, it tells you whether or not your friends are online. Initially, AIM and similar services had proprietary formats, but now there are various free software tools to use with AIM (though you still must register with AOL's AIM site to use them), and there other new IM services too.

The following table describes some of the various IM tools now available for Linux.

Everybuddy   IM client (now called "Ayttm") that recognizes the
                                protocols used with AIM, ICQ, Yahoo, and MSN.
                                DEB: everybuddy
                                RPM: everybuddy
                                WWW: http://ayttm.sourceforge.net/

Gaim   Popular message client that recognizes the protocols
                                used with many IM networks, including AIM, ICQ,
                                Yahoo, MSN, IRC, and Jabber.
                                DEB: gaim
                                RPM: gaim
                                WWW: http://gaim.sourceforge.net/

Jabber   Free IM system using an XML-based protocol, popu-
                                lar in the Linux world.
                                DEB: jabber
                                RPM: jabber
                                WWW: http://www.jabber.org/

Tik   TCL/TK client for AIM.
                                DEB: tik
                                RPM: tik
                                WWW: http://tik.sourceforge.net/

APPENDICES

APPENDICES

Administrative Issues

Every Linux system has an *administrator*—someone who installs the hardware and software, maintains the system, and generally keeps things running smoothly. A single-user home Linux system, once installed and running, needs little administration—but the occasional upgrade or maintenance task is necessary.

This appendix exists as a reference for those users who will also be performing the administrative duties on their systems. While a complete administrative guide is out of the scope of this book, the goal of this appendix is to point the new Linux administrator in the right direction, giving tips on how to choose the computer you'll use for Linux, install Linux on it, and get it ready for use.

Unlike the rest of this book, this chapter contains recipes describing commands to be run by `root`, the superuser account. Many of these commands *cannot* be run by an ordinary user. Instead of the normal "$" shell prompt used for examples throughout the rest of the book, the examples in these recipes use a pound sign (#), which is the default prompt for the `root` account.

If you're new to Linux administration, you may want to consult the help resources listed in Recipe 1.6 [If You Need More Help], page 13.

A.1 Setting Up Hardware

In days gone by, Linux enthusiasts had to piece together computer systems from individual components, since the salesmen at computer stores had never even *heard* of Linux or the free software movement. But no more. Today, many dealers sell complete systems with Linux pre-installed, including corporations like Dell Computers and IBM.[1]

A.1.1 Determining Which Hardware Is Compatible

Since Linux runs on many different computers and supports a wide range of hardware, and because everyone has different needs, I won't make too many recommendations as to which specific hardware to buy. (Systems change too fast for such a list to ever be useful, anyway.)

---

[1] For a complete list of such dealers, see `http://www.linux.org/hardware/`.

Before you make a hardware purchase, though, make sure that it's compatible with Linux—that bargain video-capture board will be worthless if it has a proprietary interface that only works with a certain non-free operating system.

To find out whether your hardware will work under Linux, try the following:

1. Read the *Linux Hardware Compatibility HOWTO* (see Recipe 2.8.6 [Reading System Documentation and Help Files], page 50), an up-to-date list of hardware that is compatible with Linux.

2. Search for it on the two sites that provide reviews and information about hardware that works with Linux, `http://www.linuxhardware.net/` and `http://www.linuxhardware.org/`.

3. Search the Internet—particularly Usenet news and the `linux.com` site—for information on the hardware you intend to buy. Read any trouble reports people may have written about getting it to work with Linux, so that *you* won't be writing the next one about it.

A.1.2 Setting the System Date and Time

There are a few methods for setting the system date and time. The first is simple and works on all systems, but it relies on the operator to input an accurate, correct time; if you need or want a greater degree of accuracy, use one of the tools described in the second method.

METHOD #1

Use `date` with the `-s` option to set the system date. Give as an argument the time and date to use—the system date is set to this date the moment the command is run. Quote long-format dates.

⇒ Here are two ways to use this.

- To set the system date to noon on March 4, 1994, type:

    ```
    # date -s "Mar 4 12:00 1994" (RET)
    ```

- To set the system date to 4:15 p.m., type:

    ```
    # date -s 16:15 (RET)
    ```

In the second example above, the day, month, and year are not set, and remain at the value they had before this command was run.

METHOD #2

Use one of the following tools to set the system date and time to that given by remote hosts on the Internet. This is good for keeping your time adjusted with various public time servers, such as the ones run by the United States Navy.

Chrony	Sets the date according to time servers available on the Internet, and adjusts for "drift" by periodically readjusting the system time from these servers. DEB: `chrony` RPM: `chrony` WWW: `http://chrony.sunsite.dk/index.php`
Rdate	Sets the system date to the time and date given by a remote host. DEB: `rdate` RPM: `rdate`

A.1.3 Specifying Mount Points for Certain Devices

It is sometimes nice to set up a special mount point for a device, such as a CD or floppy drive you use all the time, so that when you specify that mount point as an argument to `mount`, that device is automatically mounted.

To do this, edit `/etc/fstab` so that the particular mount point has an entry, and so the name of the device is given in the first column. For example, you might want to have a variation on the two lines given in Figure A-1 somewhere in your `/etc/inittab`.

```
/dev/fd0      /floppy    auto      defaults,user,noauto         0    0
/dev/cdrom    /cdrom     iso9660 defaults,ro,user,noauto        0    0
```

Figure A-1. User-mountable devices in `/etc/inittab`.

This would mean that whenever any user (since both of these mount points have **user** access) typed `mount /floppy`, the disk corresponding to the `/dev/fd0` device (the first floppy drive) would be mounted on `/floppy`, and its filesystem type would be detected automatically. If a user were to type `mount /cdrom`, the data CD in the drive corresponding to the `/dev/cdrom` device would be mounted on `/cdrom` as an ISO 9660 filesystem.

NOTES: If you do specify a particular mount point for a device already in your `/etc/fstab`, that device will be mounted at the point you specify—this method doesn't limit your mount point to only the device specified in the file.

A.1.4 Making a Boot Floppy

A *boot floppy* is a floppy disk with a bootable Linux kernel on it. It is useful to have a boot floppy in case your *root partition*—that is, the partition of your hard drive containing the bootable Linux kernel—should ever become corrupted. In an emergency, you can boot your system from the floppy, and then mount your other partitions. If you didn't have a boot floppy, you would be stuck. This is why a boot floppy is sometimes called a "rescue disk."

To make a boot floppy, you first need to find the file on your system containing the Linux kernel image that you want the floppy to have. Often there is a `vmlinuz` compressed kernel boot image file kept in `/boot`. You can also obtain a boot image from your distribution.

⇒ Here are two ways to use this.

- For Debian systems, you can always get a rescue image for the latest X86 release from the following URL (given all on one line):

  ```
  ftp://debian.crosslink.net/debian/dists/stable/
  main/disks-i386/current/images-1.44/rescue.bin
  ```

- For Red Hat systems, X86 boot images are available via FTP (see Recipe 34.2 [Transferring Files to and from a Remote Host], page 673), from the host `ftp.redhat.com`. It's kept in a directory named `/pub/redhat/linux/`*version*`/en/os/i386/images`, where *version* is your Red Hat version number, and the file is called either `boot.img` (on older versions) or `bootdisk.img`.

To make a boot floppy from a Linux kernel image, use `dd`, giving the name of the kernel image as the input file and the name of the floppy device as the output file.

⇒ To make the floppy in the first floppy drive a boot disk, containing the boot image file `bootdisk.img`, type:

```
# dd if=bootdisk.img of=/dev/fd0 (RET)
```

A.1.5 Removing a Master Boot Record

To remove the master boot record (MBR) of a disk, use `dd` to write the contents of `/dev/zero` over the first 512 bytes of the disk.

⇒ To remove the master boot record of `/dev/hda`, type:

```
# dd if=/dev/zero of=/dev/hda bs=512 count=1 (RET)
```

NOTES: Use caution with this command. If you erase the MBR on a disk that you rely on for booting, you won't be able to boot with it until you write a new, bootable image on that MBR.

A.1.6 Setting Up a Printer

Magicfilter
  DEB: `magicfilter`
  RPM: `magicfilter`
  WWW: `http://www.pell.portland.or.us/~orc/Code/magicfilter/`

When a printer is properly configured on Linux, it is a pleasure to use, but a misconfigured printer can lead to all kinds of trouble—including the dreaded "staircase effect," where a text file prints with each subsequent line of output offset to the right by the length of the previous line.

If print services haven't been configured yet on your system, I strongly recommend that the `magicfilter` package be installed; it includes filters for the automatic detection of file types—when you print a file, it automatically converts it to the proper format for your printer.

Comprehensive details on the setup of printer resources can be found in both the *Printing HOWTO* and the *Printing Usage HOWTO* (see Recipe 2.8.6 [Reading System Documentation and Help Files], page 50). More information on printing in Linux is available from the `http://linuxprinting.org/` site.

A.2 Shutting Down the System

The most proper way to shut down a system is to use `shutdown`, which only `root` can do. This command notifies all users and processes of the impending shutdown, blocks new logins, and brings the system down cleanly. Options allow you to halt the system upon shutdown, or reboot it and begin again.

To halt the system once the shutdown is complete, use the `-h` option; to reboot the system after shutdown, use `-r` instead.

The following recipes describe ways of using `shutdown` to do useful things.

NOTES: You can also bring the system down and then reboot it by typing ⟨CTRL⟩-⟨ALT⟩-⟨DEL⟩ from the console terminal; the shutdown process starts immediately when you press this key combination (see Recipe 2.1.2 [Turning Off the System], page 27).

A.2.1 Shutting Down Immediately

Normally, you order the system `shutdown` by giving the time to do it as an argument; use the special `now` argument to begin the process immediately.

⇒ Here are two ways to use this.

- To immediately shut down and halt the system, type:

    `# shutdown -h now` (RET)

- To immediately shut down the system, and then reboot, type:

    `# shutdown -r now` (RET)

You can follow the **now** argument with a quoted message that will be displayed on all terminals of all users currently logged in.

⇒ To immediately shut down and halt the system, and send a warning message to all users, type:

    `# shutdown -h now "The system is being shut down now!"` (RET)

A.2.2 Shutting Down at a Certain Time

To shut down the system at a certain time, give that time (in 24-hour format) as an argument.

⇒ Here are two ways to use this.

- To shut down and then reboot the system at 4:23 a.m., type:

    `# shutdown -r 4:23` (RET)

- To shut down and halt the system at 8:00 p.m., type:

    `# shutdown -h 20:00` (RET)

To shut down the system in a certain number of minutes, give that number of minutes prefaced by a plus sign (+).

⇒ To shut down and halt the system in five minutes, type:

    `# shutdown -h +5` (RET)

Follow the time with a quoted message to be displayed on the terminals of all logged-in users.

⇒ To shut down and halt the system at midnight, and give a warning message to all logged-in users, type (all on one line):

    `# shutdown -h 00:00 "The system is going down for maintenance at midnight"` (RET)

A.2.3 Canceling a Shutdown

If you have given **shutdown** orders and decide that you don't actually want to shut the system down after all, run **shutdown** again with the **-c** option. This command stops any **shutdown**s in progress.

⇒ To cancel any pending `shutdown`, type:

> `# shutdown -c` ⟨RET⟩

As with a normal system shutdown, you can send out an explanatory message with the cancel to be shown to all users.

⇒ To cancel any pending `shutdown` and send an explanatory message to all logged-in users, type:

> `# shutdown -c "Sorry, I hit the wrong key!"` ⟨RET⟩

This command cancels any pending system shutdown and displays the message, "`Sorry, I hit the wrong key!`" on all the terminals of anyone logged in.

NOTES: If the shutdown process has advanced to the point where all terminals are stopped, you won't be able to run this command.

A.2.4 Going into Maintenance Mode

Sometimes it is useful to go into single-user maintenance mode—maybe for running `e2fsck` on a hard drive partition or for performing some other system diagnostic. Do this by shutting the system down, and then give the `root` password to enter maintenance mode.

⇒ To go into maintenance mode, type:

```
# shutdown now ⟨RET⟩
... shutdown messages ...
Give root password for maintenance: abracadabra ⟨RET⟩
#
```

This command will put you in a root shell on the console, where you can run `e2fsck` or do whatever it is you intended to do. In the example, the `root` user has the simple password of "`abracadabra`."

To exit the shell, type ⟨CTRL⟩-⟨D⟩; depending on what you did, you may wish to reboot again with ⟨CTRL⟩-⟨ALT⟩-⟨DEL⟩.

A.3 Managing Software

All Linux distributions come with a multitude of software programs (also called *binaries*, because programs are usually contained in a binary file that is executable).

People are constantly contributing to the free software movement, publishing their work online. This means that new software programs are constantly being added to Linux distributions, and current software programs are continually being improved—new features to match new hardware, faster program execution, security updates, and so forth. A Linux system, therefore, needs to be kept up to date in order to reap the benefits of the latest free software. And sooner or later, you will want to install more programs, or you will want to upgrade your existing software when newer versions are available with some feature you desire.

The following recipes are for installing software on your system.

A.3.1 Getting and Installing a Linux Distribution

You can get a copy of Linux on CD-ROM from local or online vendors, or from a friend. Some distributions also allow for download off the Internet (recommended only if you have a fast Internet connection, of course). A list of Linux distributions is in Appendix D [References for Further Interest], page 731.

Wherever you get your copy of Linux, be sure you get the most recent version of a reputable distribution. If you are offered only an older version, you might pass on it: The software might not work with your brand-new hardware!

If you'd rather buy a copy online, a recommended source is Cheap*Bytes [http://www.cheapbytes.com/]. There you can find various Linux distributions on CD-ROM for sale at affordable prices.

Installation procedures vary from distribution to distribution, and the specifics for installing any one distribution and version is outside this book's scope. However, the process usually involves making a Linux "boot disk" from a tool provided on CD-ROM, or starting Linux on your system. The hard drives are partitioned and formatted, and the Linux software is loaded onto them. Many users then recompile a Linux kernel that is customized for their needs and hardware. If you find this difficult, or need assistance, you should find your local Linux User Group and bring your computer there—there are always some LUG members who are especially happy to help install Linux on a first-timer's computer, and many LUGs have regular "InstallFests" for this purpose, where participation is always free of charge (see Recipe 1.6 [If You Need More Help], page 13).

A.3.2 Installing Packages for Your Linux Distribution

Linux distributions place software programs in *packages*, which are single files, usually compressed, that contain an archive of all of the files necessary for that particular program. Distributions have a software management system for installing and maintaining packages; upon installation, a package is first checked for other packages it might depend on to function correctly (its *dependencies*). In this way, you can be assured that the software you have installed on your system will function correctly.

There are two primary package formats in the Linux world: the Debian DEB format, and Red Hat's Package Manager format, RPM. The former is used by the Debian and KNOPPIX distributions; the latter, by Red Hat, Mandrake-linux, SuSE, and others. Still other distributions may not use packages at all, or may use source packages (see the following recipe).

Most of the software that you need for your system will be in the package format of your distribution, but you are not limited to even that. You can always install source packages, and even software that is packaged in another distribution's format: Debian has long been able to read and install RPM packages through special software, and the distributions that default to RPM (including Fedora and Red Hat Enterprise) equally have tools to use DEB. I am a bit old-fashioned in that I don't like to mix packaging systems with distributions, but some people may need to do so.

Management of these package formats is described in later sections of this appendix: Recipe A.4 [Managing DEB Packages], page 709 and Recipe A.5 [Managing EPM Packages], page 714.

A.3.3 Installing a Source Package

Usually a source package is distributed in a compressed `tar` archive as a single file with a `.tar.gz` or `.tgz` file name extension.[2] This collection of files is often called the *sources* of a computer program.

These files are usually placed in `/usr/local/src` and are uncompressed into their own directories. If they are source distributions, the software will have to be compiled. Usually a file named `INSTALL` or `README` in the package directory will instruct you how to do that. Many source packages come with a script named `configure` that is run to configure the compilation routine for

---

[2] This is, like any file name, just convention. Nothing but convention (and common sense) is to stop you from giving a compressed `tar` file an `.EXE` extension, or a Debian DEB format file an `.rpm`, or from omitting file extensions altogether.

your system, and then `make` is run with either `install` or `all` as an argument, depending on what the package's particular documentation instructs.

⇒ To compile and install a software package from its source directory, you generally type:

```
# ./configure (RET)
... configuration messages ...
# make install (RET)
... compilation messages ...
... installation messages ...
#
```

When you install source packages on your system, you are said to be installing `local` software—the files are kept in the `/usr/local` directory tree. Binaries are placed in `/usr/local/bin`, libraries in `/usr/local/lib`, `man` pages in `/usr/local/man`, and documentation in either `/usr/local/doc` or `/usr/local/share/doc`.

A.3.4 Installing a Shell Script

When you have a shell script that you want to install on the system, you first make sure that the script file is executable (see Recipe 6.3.6 [Making a File Executable], page 170).

Generally, the administrator installs new shell scripts in the `/usr/local/bin` directory. If you are on a multi-user system and you are the only user liable to run a particular script, you can put it in a special directory in your home directory tree—the `~/bin` directory is the standard recommendation here—and then add that directory to your path (see Recipe 3.5.7 [Adding to Your Path], page 81).

Not all executable script files are *shell* scripts. The first line of a script contains the full path name of the shell or other program that is to interpret and execute the script; sometimes the path may differ on your system from the one the script was written on, so you may have to change this line.

For example, a script may start with the following line:

`#!/usr/local/bin/perl`

This line means that the script is written in the `perl` language; the text after the "`#!`" is the full path name of the `perl` program, which in this case is `/usr/local/bin/perl`. If the location for a tool here in the first line of the script is different from the location on your system, it will not work (see

Recipe 7.5 [Finding Where a Program Is Located], page 185). For example, if `perl` is located on your system at `/usr/bin/perl`, you will have to edit the first line in this script so that it matches that actual location.

If you try to execute this script, and the system reports an error finding the file, you'll have to change that first line to correspond to the location of the `perl` binary on your system. The `which` tool will output this location.

⇒ To find out where `perl` is installed on your system, type:

    # which perl ⟨RET⟩

If this command returns `/usr/bin/perl` or some path name other than `/usr/local/bin/perl`, you'll have to change the location in the first line of the script to the path name given:

    #!/usr/bin/perl

NOTES: If the output of the `which` command returns nothing, that means that the `perl` program is not installed on your system at all; in that case, you should install the `perl` software in order to run the script.

A.4 Managing DEB Packages

Dpkg
  DEB: dpkg

  or

Apt
  DEB: apt

DEB is the native package format on Debian systems. These packages are available on the Web from `http://packages.debian.org/`.

There are a number of tools available for DEB package management. Traditionally, `dselect`, where you select packages from a menu, was the tool for installing and removing software from the system. Its interface is unique, it so requires study. Proper usage is, unfortunately, an acquired skill.[3] Administrators who are installing a new system are urged to run through `dselect` and reboot at least a few times, so that all essential packages and their dependencies are installed.

The `dpkg` tool is Debian's primary command line package manager tool (in fact, `dselect` is just a front-end interface to it), and it can be used on

---

[3] Even its `man` page makes note of this: "The `dselect` package selection interface is confusing or even alarming to the new user."

its own at the command line. This is what will be described in the following recipes. Methods using the newer **apt-get** tool, part of Debian's "Advanced Package Tool" system, will also be described; **apt-get** is preferred by most experienced users.

NOTES: All of the following actions can also be done with the **dselect** application, but that method will not be described.

A.4.1 Listing DEB Packages

Use **dpkg** with the **-l** option to list installed DEB packages. Alone, it lists all packages presently installed on the system and describes their status; you can give a quoted glob expression as an argument to list packages that match that pattern (see Recipe 5.8 [Specifying File Names with Patterns], page 153).

⇒ Here are some ways to use this.

- To peruse all DEB packages on the system, type:

  # dpkg -l | less ⟨RET⟩

- To list all known DEB packages whose name begins with "**gimp**," type:

  # dpkg -l gimp* ⟨RET⟩

- To list all DEB packages on the system whose name has "**gimp**" anywhere in it, type:

  # dpkg -l '*gimp*' ⟨RET⟩

To list a particular package, give its name. To search for a pattern among installed packages, pipe the output of **dpkg -l** to **grep**.

⇒ Here are two ways to use this.

- To determine whether or not the **gimp** package is installed, type:

  # dpkg -l gimp ⟨RET⟩

- To list all installed DEB packages with "**gimp**" in their names, type:

  # dpkg -l | grep gimp ⟨RET⟩

You can also get a summary of a particular DEB package by giving it as an argument to **apt-cache** with the **show** option.

⇒ To get a summary of the **gimp** package, type:

  # apt-cache show gimp ⟨RET⟩

A.4.2 Installing a DEB Package

There are two methods for installing a DEB package.

METHOD #1

To install a DEB package with **dpkg**, give the name of the package file to install as an argument with the **-i** option.

⇒ To install the DEB file **gimp1.2_1.2.3-2_i386.deb**, type:

> `# dpkg -i gimp1.2_1.2.3-2_i386.deb` (RET)

NOTES: Any conflicts or dependencies will have to be resolved by you before the package is installed. If a problem is detected, **dpkg** will report it and exit without installing the package.

You can also combine **-i** with the **--no-act** flag, to test the installation. This will go through all the motions of installation, but will not actually install any files.

METHOD #2

To obtain and install a package with **apt-get**, use the **install** option and give the base name of the package as an argument.

Make sure your Debian distribution is ready when you run this command. If you are installing from CD-ROM, put the first Debian CD-ROM disc in your CD drive; if installing via Internet, make sure that your system is online.

⇒ To obtain and install the proper file for the **hello** DEB package, type:

> `# apt-get install hello` (RET)

NOTES: Should there be any dependences, or should the package conflict with others already installed, an action will be presented to fix this, and you will be prompted to confirm or abort the operation.

A.4.3 Upgrading a DEB Package

To upgrade a DEB package, just install the newer package file. There are two methods for doing this, based on the package tool you use.

METHOD #1

To upgrade a DEB package with **dpkg**, just install it again with the **-i** option; if the package file you are installing is newer, Debian will automatically upgrade; if it is older, it will automatically downgrade.

⇒ To upgrade the `gimp1.2` package with the DEB file `gimp1.2_1.2.4_`
   `i386.deb`, type:

> `# dpkg -i gimp1.2_1.2.4_i386.deb` ⟨RET⟩

METHOD #2

Use `apt-get` to upgrade either single packages or the entire system.

To upgrade a single package with `apt-get`, just install it again with the
`install` option, and follow that with the name of the package to upgrade.

⇒ To upgrade the `hello` package, type:

> `# apt-get install hello` ⟨RET⟩

This command will upgrade the `hello` package to the most current version
available on your Debian distribution source, if there is one greater than the
version already installed on your system. If additional packages must be up-
graded first, in order for this new package upgrade to function properly, this
command will fetch and upgrade those packages, too. Before downloading
any packages, `apt-get` will show the list of packages that will be installed,
replaced, or otherwise changed, and it will wait for confirmation first.

To bring your entire Debian system up to date, use the `apt-get` tool with
the following command arguments. First, use the **update** argument to update
your system's list of available software packages. Then run **apt-get** again,
using either the **upgrade** argument to upgrade all of the installed packages
to their most recently available versions, or use the **dist-upgrade** argument
when a new version of the Debian system is announced, to upgrade to that
new version.

⇒ Here are two ways to use this.

- To upgrade all of the software on your system to their most recent
  versions, type:

```
# apt-get update ⟨RET⟩
...processing messages...
# apt-get upgrade ⟨RET⟩
...processing messages...
#
```

- To upgrade your Debian system to the most recent release, type:

```
# apt-get update (RET)
...processing messages...
# apt-get dist-upgrade (RET)
...processing messages...
#
```

A.4.4 Removing a DEB Package

To remove a DEB package, use **dpkg** with the **-r** option, and give the name of the package (not the package file) to remove.

⇒ To remove the **gimp1.2** package, type:

> # dpkg -r gimp1.2 (RET)

This removes the package but keeps any configuration files. Use the **--purge** option to completely eliminate everything related to a package, including all configuration and setup files.

⇒ To purge the **gimp1.2** package, type:

> # dpkg --purge gimp1.2 (RET)

NOTES: If purging a package will break dependencies, **dpkg** will not let you do it. You can force it, though; to get a list of "force" options, run **dpkg** with the **--force-help** option.

A.4.5 Getting the Status of a DEB Package

To get the status of a DEB package, use **dpkg** with the **-s** option, and give the name of the package (not its file name) as an argument.

This tells you the package name, installation status, Debian "priority" level, and section. If the package is installed, **dpkg** will also give a description and other information.

⇒ To output the status of the **gimp1.2** package, type:

> # dpkg -s gimp1.2 (RET)

A.4.6 Listing All Files in a DEB Package

Use **dpkg** with the **-L** option to list all of the files on the system that come with a particular package you have installed. Give the package name (not its file name) as an argument.

⇒ To peruse all of the files that are part of the **gimp1.2** package, type:

> # *dpkg -L gimp1.2* (RET)

NOTES: If a package is not installed, **dpkg** will say so.

A.4.7 Listing the DEB Package a File Is a Part Of

To determine which package a file belongs to, give the file as an argument to **dpkg** with the **-S** option.

⇒ To list the name of the package that the file **/bin/ls** belongs to, type:

> # *dpkg -S /bin/ls* (RET)

A.4.8 Listing Dependences for a DEB Package

To find out what dependencies a DEB package has, use **dpkg** with the **-s** option, and give the package name as an argument. Then use **grep** to show the line containing "**Depends.**" This will output a list of other packages that the given package depends on in order to work.

⇒ To list the dependencies for the **gimp-1.2** package, type:

> # *dpkg -s gimp-1.2 |grep Depends* (RET)

A.5 Managing RPM Packages

RPM Package Manager
 RPM: rpm
 WWW: http://www.rpm.org/

RPM, the RPM Package Manager,[4] is the native package format of the Red Hat distribution, as well as many other popular Linux distributions, including Mandrakelinux and SuSE.

You can obtain RPM packages on the Web from **http://rpmfind.net/** and **http://freshrpms.net/**, both searchable package databases.

Management of RPM packages is done with the command line **rpm** tool; the following recipes describe its use.

---

[4] Like GNU, this is a recursive acronym.

A.5.1 Listing RPM Packages

Use **rpm** with the **-qa** option to list all RPM packages installed on the system. You can pipe this output to **grep** to search for particular package names.

⇒ Here are two ways to use this.

- To peruse all RPM packages installed on the system, type:

    # *rpm -qa | less* ⟨RET⟩

- To list all RPM packages with the string "**gimp**" in their names, regardless of case, type:

    # *rpm -qa | grep -i gimp* ⟨RET⟩

To list a particular package, use **rpm** with the **-q** option, and give the package name.

⇒ To see if the **gimp** package is installed, type:

    # *rpm -q gimp* ⟨RET⟩

A.5.2 Installing an RPM Package

To install an RPM package, use **rpm** with the **-i** option, and give the name of the package to install.

⇒ To install the **gimp-1.2.3-9.i386.rpm** package, type:

    # *rpm -i gimp-1.2.3-9.i386.rpm* ⟨RET⟩

If a package has unmet dependencies, **rpm** will not install it; it also won't install a package if a current or newer version is installed. Use **-i** in conjunction with the **--nodeps** flag to install a package even if it has unmet dependencies.

⇒ To install the **gimp-1.2.3-9.i386.rpm** package, regardless of unmet dependencies, type:

    # *rpm -i --nodeps gimp-1.2.3-9.i386.rpm* ⟨RET⟩

A.5.3 Upgrading an RPM Package

To upgrade an RPM package, use the **-U** option, and give the name of the newer package file to install.

⇒ To upgrade to the **gimp-1.2.3-10.i386.rpm** package, type:

    # *rpm -U gimp-1.2.3-10.i386.rpm* ⟨RET⟩

A.5.4 Removing an RPM **Package**

To remove an RPM package that is currently installed, use the **-e** ("erase")
option, and give the name of the package (*not* the file name) as an argument.

⇒ To remove the **gimp** package, type:

    # rpm -e gimp ⟨RET⟩

If other packages depend on the package, **rpm** won't erase it; use **--nodeps**
to override this behavior.

⇒ To remove the **gimp** package, regardless of any dependencies, type:

    # rpm -e --nodeps gimp ⟨RET⟩

A.5.5 Getting the Status of an RPM **Package**

Use **rpm** with the **-q** option to see if an RPM package is installed. Give as
an argument the name of the package, not the file name. This displays the
version number of an installed package.

⇒ To determine whether or not the **gimp** package is installed, type:

    # rpm -q gimp ⟨RET⟩

To get some basic information about a package, including a brief description, use **rpm** with the **-qi** option, and give as an argument the package name.

⇒ To display some information about the **gimp** package, type:

    # rpm -qi gimp ⟨RET⟩

A.5.6 Listing All Files in an RPM **Package**

Use **rpm** with the **-ql** option to list the files that are part of an RPM package.
Give as an argument the package name.

⇒ To list all of the files contained in the **gimp** package, type:

    # rpm -ql gimp ⟨RET⟩

A.5.7 Listing the RPM **Package a File Is a Part Of**

To determine which package a particular file belongs to, give the file name as
an argument to **rpm** with the **-qf** option.

⇒ To list the package that the file **/bin/ls** belongs to, type:

    # rpm -qf /bin/ls ⟨RET⟩

A.5.8 Listing Dependences for an RPM Package

Use `rpm` with the `-qR` option to list the dependencies of a particular RPM package. Give the name of the package as an argument.

⇒ To list the dependencies of the `gimp` package, type:

```
# rpm -qR gimp (RET)
```

A.6 Administrating Users

This section describes some of the things the system administrator will have to do in administrating the system's users. All of these commands must be run by the superuser, using the `root` account—these commands edit system files.

A.6.1 Making a User Account

To make a new user account, use `adduser`. It takes as an argument the username to use for the new account. It will prompt for default setup information, including the user's full name and an initial password to use.

⇒ To create a new user with a username of `mary`, type:

```
# adduser mary (RET)
```

NOTES: By default, the name of the user's home directory will be the same as the username. So, for example, the user `mary` will have a home directory of `/home/mary`.

A.6.2 Seeing Which Users Exist on the System

The `/etc/passwd` file contains a list of all users on the system, including "special" users such as *daemons*, which are system programs that run as a background process and don't correspond to normal login accounts.

The information in this file is written with one user per line, and each line consists of several fields delimited by a colon character (`:`). The fields are as follows: the username; the encrypted password (or, more often than not, an "x" to indicate that a *shadow password* file is used on the system for added security); the user ID (UID); the group ID (GID); the full user name; the home directory; and the shell or interpreter that runs at login.

To output just the list of usernames, filter it through `cut`, giving the colon character as a field delimiter, and specifying that only the first field be output.

⇒ Here are some ways to use this.

- To get a list of all usernames on the system, type:

    `# cut -d: -f1 /etc/passwd` (RET)

- To get a list of all full user names on the system, type:

    `# cut -d: -f5 /etc/passwd` (RET)

- To output your own full user name, type:

    `grep `id -u` /etc/passwd | cut -d ':' -f5 | cut -d "," -f1` (RET)

NOTES: These examples are good to use in shell scripts.

A.6.3 Letting Users Access Hardware Peripherals

Certain hardware peripherals, like CD drives and sound cards, normally require superuser privileges in order to access them. These devices also have *groups* of their own, so a regular user can also access them by having membership in their groups (see Recipe 6.1 [Working in Groups], page 163).

The groups that regular users might want to be part of include `floppy` (the floppy disk drive), `audio` (the sound card), and `dialout` and `dip` (modem dial-out privileges).

Use `addgroup` to add a user to the group associated with a hardware device. Give as arguments the username to add and the name of the group to add to.

⇒ To add the user `doug` to the `audio` group, type:

    `# addgroup doug audio` (RET)

A.6.4 Letting Users Mount Drives

The `/etc/fstab` file specifies the details about the filesystems in use on a system, including those that may be mounted by floppy or CD drive. In order to let users mount disks on these drives, make sure that there is a line in `/etc/fstab` for both the floppy and CD drives, each containing the `user` flag, as in Figure A-1 (see Recipe A.1.3 [Specifying Mount Points for Certain Devices], page 701).

A.7 Displaying Information About Your System

The following recipes describe ways of displaying information about the system you are running.

A.7.1 Displaying How Long the System Has Been Up

To find out how long the system has been running, use the uptime tool. When you run it as a command, it outputs the current time, how long the system has been running, how many users are logged on, and what the system "load averages" have been for the past 1, 5, and 15 minutes.

⇒ To find out how long the system has been up, type:

```
# uptime ⟨RET⟩
3:34pm  up  4:31,  4 users,  load average: 0.01, 0.05, 0.07
#
```

To get a list of the times and dates when the system was recently rebooted, give "reboot" as an argument to last (see Recipe 2.6.4 [Listing the Last Time a User Logged In], page 41).

⇒ To output a list of times when the system was rebooted, type:

```
# last reboot ⟨RET⟩
```

NOTES: An operating system capable of running constantly for a long time without crashes or freeze-ups is a good one, so having a high uptime value is a matter of pride for many Linux users. It is not uncommon to hear of systems that have been running for months and sometimes even *years* non-stop—one Linux administrator reported on the Internet about one of his work systems, which had been running continuously without reboot for three years!

A.7.2 Displaying CPU Type

There are a few methods for displaying the CPU type.

METHOD #1

The file /proc/cpuinfo contains information about the central processing unit of the system, including its make and model, and its speed in MHz. Use cat to output the contents of this file.

⇒ To display information about the system's CPU, type:

```
# cat /proc/cpuinfo ⟨RET⟩
```

NOTES: This requires that the special /proc filesystem is installed, but this has been a Linux standard for some time.

METHOD #2

You can also use GNU **uname** to output the CPU processor type of the system (such as I686, PowerPC, etc.); specify this with the -m option.

⇒ To output the CPU processor type of the system, type:

    # uname -m ⟨RET⟩

A.7.3 Displaying Memory Usage

Use **free** to display system memory usage. It displays both physical memory and swap memory, giving values for total memory available on the system, amount used, and amount free. The output is displayed in kilobytes; use -b to display in bytes, and -m to display in megabytes. The -t switch will also display a list of totals for all of the types of memory on the system.

⇒ To output a report on current system memory usage, in megabytes, and with a line of calculated total values, type:

    # free -m -t ⟨RET⟩

A.7.4 Displaying the Linux Version

Use the GNU **uname** tool to see what version of Linux you are running. By default, it outputs the name of the operating system.

⇒ To output the name of the operating system, type:

    # uname ⟨RET⟩

Use the -r option to output the operating system release number.

⇒ To output the release number of the operating system, type:

    # uname -r ⟨RET⟩

The -a option is useful; it outputs *all* information about the system that it can, including OS name and release number, CPU type, plus the version date and number of the operating system and the machine's hostname.

⇒ To output all of the **uname** information for the system you are on, type:

    # uname -a ⟨RET⟩

A.7.5 Displaying the Distribution Version

The version of the installed distribution is kept in a particular file in /etc, whose name depends on the distribution. These are listed in the following table. Use **cat** to display the contents of this file.

`/etc/debian-version`	Debian
`/etc/fedora-release`	Fedora
`/etc/mandrake-release`	Mandrakelinux
`/etc/redhat-release`	Red Hat
`/etc/SuSE-release`	SuSE
`/etc/slackware-version`	Slackware

⇒ To output the distribution version on a Fedora system, type:

> # *cat /etc/fedora-release* (RET)

Conventional File Name Extensions

File types indicate the type of data in the file, generally one of text, image, audio, or binary. You can always use `file` to determine what kind of data a file contains (see Recipe 8.1.1 [Determining a File's Type and Format], page 187).

The following table lists typical *file name extensions* (the part of the file name following the last dot) used for certain file types, identifies what type of file the extension is used for, and describes the particular format.

`.aiff`	AUDIO	Apple Macintosh audio file.
`.au`	AUDIO	Sun Microsystems audio file (8,000 Hz, u-law compression).
`.bmp`	IMAGE	Microsoft Windows bitmap image.
`.bz`	BINARY	A file compressed with (obsolete) `bzip` compression.
`.bz2`	BINARY	A file compressed with `bzip2` compression.
`.cdda` `.cdr`	AUDIO	Audio compact disc format, used for burning audio CD-RS and CD-RWS (44.1 KHz raw stereo).
`.cgm`	IMAGE	Computer Graphics Metafile format.
`.cmyk`	IMAGE	Raw cyan, magenta, yellow, and black bytes.
`.eps`	IMAGE	Adobe Encapsulated PostScript.
`.fax`	IMAGE	Group 3 fax format.
`.fig`	IMAGE	TransFig image format.
`.flc` `.fli`	IMAGE	ASCII art animation.
`.fpx`	IMAGE	FlashPix format.
`.gif`	IMAGE	CompuServe Graphics Interchange Format, version GIF89A (usually pronounced "giff," rhyming with "biff").
`.gpg`	DATA	GNU Privacy Guard encrypted data.
`.gray`	IMAGE	Raw gray bytes.

.gsm	AUDIO	Global System for Mobile Communications (GSM) speech file format, used in some voice-mail applications.
.gz	BINARY	A file compressed with gzip compression.
.htm .html	TEXT	HTML ("HyperText Markup Language") format.
.it	AUDIO	Impulse Tracker MOD file.
.jpeg .jpg	IMAGE	Joint Photographic Experts Group (JPEG) File Interchange Format (JFIF) format (usually pronounced "jay-peg").
.latex .ltx	TEXT	LaTeX document.
.me	TEXT	Troff input file.
.mid .midi	AUDIO	Standard extensions for MIDI files.
.miff	IMAGE	ImageMagick MIFF (Magick Image Format File) format.
.mod	AUDIO	MOD (tracker "module") file.
.mp3	AUDIO	MPEG-1 or -2, layer 3 file.
.ms	TEXT	Troff input file.
.mtm	AUDIO	MOD file.
.ogg	AUDIO	Ogg Vorbis file.
.pbm	IMAGE	Black and white portable bitmap format.
.pcd	IMAGE	Kodak PhotoCD format, 512x768 pixels maximum resolution.
.pcl	IMAGE	Page Control Language format.
.pcx	IMAGE	ZSoft IBM PC Paintbrush format.
.pdf	IMAGE	Adobe Portable Document Format.

`.pict`	IMAGE	Apple Macintosh QuickDraw format.
`.png`	IMAGE	Portable Network Graphics format (usually pronounced "ping").
`.pnm`	IMAGE	Portable "anymap" format.
`.ppm`	IMAGE	Color portable pixmap format.
`.ps`	IMAGE	Adobe PostScript format.
`.ra`	AUDIO	RealAudio file.
`.raw`	AUDIO	Raw audio data.
`.rgb`	IMAGE	Raw red, green, and blue bytes.
`.s3m`	AUDIO	MOD file.
`.sf`	AUDIO	IRCAM SoundFile format, used by some music composition software, such as CSound and MiXViews.
`.sgml`	TEXT	SGML ("Standardized General Markup Language") format.
`.stm`	AUDIO	MOD file.
`.tex`	TEXT	TEX or LATEX document.
`.text`	TEXT	Plain, unformatted text.
`.tga`	IMAGE	TrueVision Targa image format.
`.tif` `.tiff`	IMAGE	Tagged Image File Format.
`.txt`	TEXT	Plain, unformatted text.
`.ult`	AUDIO	MOD file.
`.uni`	AUDIO	MOD file.
`.voc`	AUDIO	SoundBlaster VOC file.
`.wav`	AUDIO	Microsoft RIFF format (aka WAV).
`.xbm`	IMAGE	X Window System bitmap format.

`.xm`	AUDIO	MOD file.
`.xml`	TEXT	XML ("Extended Markup Language") format.
`.xpm`	IMAGE	Color X Window System pixmap format.
`.xwd`	IMAGE	Color X Window System window "dump" file format.

Setting Up Your Home Directory

Your home directory is the place where you keep your own files. Good organizational skills and some foresight will help keep your "home" in order. This appendix is all about giving hints for organizing your home directory.

You'll find that the home directory as outlined here mirrors, in many ways, the /usr/local directory tree, which itself somewhat mirrors the system root directory, /; this is no coincidence. The Linux directory tree structure is well-organized and lends itself to this purpose; I've found that the home directory, and directories for any particular project or "thing," usually have some similar directories and files: bin, doc, etc, src, tmp, THANKS, passwd, and so on.

You can configure your home directory any way you like, and you can change it at any time, of course. There is no rule that says, "You must store this kind of file in a directory here," "You must have an etc," or anything like that. Here is what I do.

C.1 Using a Directory for Personal Binaries

A directory for binaries is simply a directory where you store executable files. To make the shell recognize it, add this directory to your PATH variable, as defined in your ~/.bashrc file. The directory can have any name. I prefer sticking with the bin convention and putting it right in the home directory: ~/bin.

⇒ To make your own bin directory and add it to your path, do the following:

1. Use mkdir to make a bin directory in your home directory:

   $ *mkdir ~/bin* (RET)

2. Use a text editor to edit your .bashrc, and change the path to include ~/bin (see Recipe 3.5.7 [Adding to Your Path], page 81). It is a quoted, comma-delimited list. For example:

   PATH="/usr/local/bin:/usr/bin:/bin:/usr/bin/X11:/usr/games:~/bin:."

In your own bin, you can put scripts and tools of your own devising. They will be executable by you, but by no other users on the system. To make a file executable by all users, the superuser will have to put the file in /usr/local/bin, the system-wide local directory for binaries.

NOTES: The current shell won't recognize any changes you make in your .bashrc; you'll have to run it by hand the first time, or just exit and start a new shell.

C.2 Using a Directory for Personal Lists and Data

Everybody has his own set of personal files containing lists, data, and other "configurations," such as passwords, accounts and pass-phrases, account information, addresses, and so on. These are good things to put in a directory named `etc`. Some people might like using `personal` or `per` for this instead, but regardless of the name, I find that having a directory for expressly this purpose is very handy.

This is a good place to keep the kinds of files listed in the following table.

`address` *or* `addr` *or* `contacts`	Address book (see Recipe 27.5.1 [Keeping a Free-Form Address List], page 546).
`appointments` *or* `todo` *or* `TODO`	To-do list. Uppercase file names are sorted first in directory listings.
`birthdays`	List of birthdays.
`calendar`	Personal calendar file. You can keep specialized calendars for your interests, such as `calendar.birthdays` or `calendar.wwii`.
`crontab`	Personal `cron` table file (see Recipe 28.3 [Scheduling Commands], page 557).
`passwd` *or* `passwords`	Personal password file. Be sure to change its permissions so that nobody else can look at it (see Recipe 6.3.4 [Making a File Private], page 169).
`quotes`	Favorite quotations.

C.3 Using a Directory for Mail

You will probably want a directory to keep all your email correspondence, including both incoming and outgoing mail. Most people use either `Mail` or `mail` as the name of this directory; many email applications use one name or the other as the default for storing messages. You can build subdirectories in here to store messages away in neater folders, such as `outgoing` for outgoing mail, `family` for family correspondence, and `projects` for project mail.

C.4 Using a Directory for Projects

It is sometimes desirable to keep a group of files together when working on a project of some sort. Depending on your work and enterprise, you might like to make a directory for your projects—say, `jobs`, `projects`, `work`, `drafts`, or `research`, depending on what you do, and make subdirectories in it for any particular project or job you are working on.

Programmers usually have a `src` directory for computer program source code; other common directories for special work that you may want to consider include `photos` or `photographs`, `art` or `images`, `books`, and `music` or `recordings`. Hobbyists might keep `scrapbook` or `craft` directories.

These main categories may, in turn, contain directories for particular projects, and those project directories may contain their own `src` directory for source files, `doc` for documentation, a `THANKS` file for acknowledgements, and so on.

C.5 Using a Directory for Temporary Files

You might like to have a directory that you use as a kind of "holding pen" to bring in new files that perhaps should be processed soon, but not right at the moment. I don't like to clutter up my home directory, so having a `~/tmp` directory to put these things in keeps it clean and tidy.

You can, of course, save files in the system-wide temporary directory, `/tmp`, but that directory is cleared out periodically by the system, and if you are on a multi-user system, you might want to have a private temp directory anyway (all users normally have read and write access to `/tmp`).

References for Further Interest

This appendix lists important sources of Linux software and information that you should know about.

D.1 Sources of Linux Software and Hardware

These are sources for obtaining software, including entire Linux distributions, as well as information on hardware that works with Linux.

D.1.1 Linux Distributions

The following are among the most popular Linux distributions. A larger list may be found online at DistroWatch [http://www.distrowatch.com/], which has a chart that compares their features.

Debian Gnu/Linux is developed by volunteers committed to the idea of free software. [http://debian.org/]

Fedora Core is one of two contemporary descendants of the old Red Hat Linux distribution (the other is Red Hat Enterprise Linux). [http://fedora.redhat.com/]

Gentoo Linux, unlike other distributions, is distributed only in source form— all binaries are compiled for the host system, affording the highest possible efficiency. [http://www.gentoo.org/]

KNOPPIX is a German distribution on bootable CD-ROM. It uses DEB as a package format. [http://www.knoppix.com/]

Mandrakelinux boasts a simple installation and lets you keep your pre-existing OS on a partition of the hard disk. [http://www.mandrakelinux.com/en/]

muLinux is a small distribution, designed for old computers. [http://mulinux.sunsite.dk/]

Red Hat Enterprise Linux is Red Hat, Inc.'s successor to its popular and well-established distribution. [http://redhat.com/]

Run Up to date Linux Everywhere (RULE) is designed for users who need modern Linux, but cannot afford a modern computer. It is based on the very latest Fedora Core, but it can run on systems with low memory and small CPUs. [http://www.rule-project.org/]

Slackware Linux is the oldest Linux distribution still publishing. [http://slackware.com/]

SuSE Linux is German-designed, is now owned by Novell, and is popular in Europe. [`http://suse.com/`]

Turbolinux, a variation on the UnitedLinux distribution, is the most popular distribution in China. [`http://www.turbolinux.com/`]

Yellow Dog Linux is made specially for PowerPC computers, such as some Apple Macintoshes (Debian and other distributions have such versions too). [`http://www.yellowdoglinux.com/`]

D.1.2 Archives of Linux and Related Software

These are online sources of free software for Linux, and entire Linux distributions.

Freshmeat contains searchable descriptions and links to thousands of free software packages. It includes a repository of GUI "themes" for your desktop. [`http://freshmeat.net/` and `http://themes.freshmeat.net/`]

FSF/UNESCO Free Software Directory is a large directory of packages, sorted by category. [`http://www.gnu.org/directory/`]

Ibiblio Linux Archive (formerly SUNsite) is a very large archive of Linux software, and it may be the oldest in continuous operation. It includes a public archive of complete distributions for download. [`http://www.ibiblio.org/pub/Linux/`]

Savannah hosts software packages that are not part of the GNU Project, yet are still free software. [`http://savannah.nongnu.org/`]

Scientific Applications on Linux (SAL) is an authoritative listing of scientific software that runs on Linux-based systems. [`http://ftp.llp.fu-berlin.de/lsoft/`]

Sound and MIDI Software for Linux is a comprehensive guide to sound and audio for Linux-based systems. [`http://linux-sound.org/`]

SourceForge is the Internet's largest community for developers of free software; it gives free resources to developers of free software. [`http://sourceforge.net/`]

Sweetcode tracks free software that is *innovative*—not just the latest free clone of some old proprietary application that wasn't all that interesting to begin with. [`http://sweetcode.org/`]

D.1.3 Hardware for Linux

These online resources will help you pick out and obtain hardware that works with Linux.

LinuxHardware.net is a user-contributed database of hardware that works with Linux. [http://www.linuxhardware.net/]

LinuxHardware.org has hardware news and reviews components that work with Linux. [http://linuxhardware.org/]

Linux on Laptops has an up-to-date database of laptop and notebook computer models and the extent of their support for Linux. [http://www.linux-laptop.net/]

ResellerRatings is a consumer database of hardware resellers, with ratings and comments. [http://resellerratings.com/]

Price Watch is an up-to-the-minute database of reseller stock and their prices. Search by component or brand to get current listings for sale. [http://pricewatch.com/]

D.2 Linux Books and Guides

These are complete guides to a particular subject, often full-length books.

D.2.1 General Linux Guides and Instruction

These books and online resources are for learning about using the Linux system in general.

Kirch, Olaf, and Terry Dawson, Linux Network Administrators' Guide, Second Edition, Linux Documentation Project, 2000. A classic early-90s text on administrating a Linux network, revised by O'Reilly & Associates in 2000. [http://tldp.org/LDP/nag2/]

Linux Gazette. A monthly webzine devoted to "making Linux just a little more fun," it has been published by ssc for years. Its "More 2-Cent Tips" column is famous. [http://linuxgazette.com/]

Linux HOWTOs and mini-HOWTOs, The Linux Documentation Project. A collection of famous documents on every aspect of using Linux. The LDP also hosts a number of larger, book-length Guides. [http://tldp.org/HOWTO/HOWTO-INDEX/]

Merrill, David C., The Linux FAQ, 2003. Contains the answers to the most frequently-asked questions about Linux.
[http://tldp.org/FAQ/Linux-FAQ/]

Sheer, Paul, Linux: Rute Users Tutorial and Exposition, Prentice Hall PTR, 2001. A complete guide to Linux, including much technical material on programming and networking. Like the Cook-

BOOK, it is typeset with TEX on a Linux system (CD-ROM included). [http://rute.sourceforge.net/]

Wirzenius, Lars, et al., LINUX SYSTEM ADMINISTRATOR'S GUIDE, Linux Documentation Project, 1993. A classic text on administrating a Linux system. [http://tldp.org/LDP/sag/]

D.2.2 Linux Tool and Application Guides

These documents describe particular software programs.

AWK

Robbins, Arnold D., THE GNU AWK USER'S GUIDE, Free Software Foundation, 1997. [http://gnu.org/software/gawk/manual/]

Dselect

Bortzmeyer, Stéphane, DSELECT DOCUMENTATION FOR BEGINNERS, Debian Documentation Project, 1999. Recommended for first-time users of dselect.
[http://debian.org/releases/2.1/i386/dselect-beginner.en.html]

GROFF

MY GROFF RESOURCES, Web site, 2002. A collection of documents and links. [http://www.neverland.ch/groff/]

Corderoy, Ralph, THE TEXT PROCESSOR FOR TYPESETTERS, Web site, 2001. [http://troff.org/]

Collver, Ben, ONLINE GROFF RESOURCES, Web site, undated. A large list of documentation.
[http://tylx.tripod.com/groff-resources.html]

Lesk, M.E., TBL—A PROGRAM TO FORMAT TABLES, Bell Laboratories, 1976. An invaluable introduction to using tbl.
[http://www.neverland.ch/groff/tbl.ps.gz]

Provins, Dean Allen, THE GROFF AND FRIENDS HOWTO. An introduction to using GROFF. [http://www.neverland.ch/groff/TheGroffFriendsHowto.ps.gz]

IRC

Caraballo, David, and Joseph Lo, THE IRC PRELUDE, Web site, 2000. Excellent introduction to IRC for first-timers. [http://irchelp.org/irchelp/new2irc.html]

PERL

Kuhn, Bradley M., PICKING UP PERL, Web site, 2002. A good but unfinished PERL tutorial. [http://www.ebb.org/PickingUpPerl/]

PostScript

Capella Archive Publications, CAPELLA ARCHIVE, Web site, 2001. Hands-on tutorials and reference library for programming in PostScript. [http://www.cappella.demon.co.uk/]

SED

Bonzini, Paolo, THE SEDER'S GRAB-BAG, Web site, 2002. A useful collection of SED information including a FAQ and many example scripts. [http://sed.sourceforge.net/grabbag/]

Pement, Eric, HANDY ONE-LINERS FOR SED, Web site, 2003. A single page listing many useful commands for editing and processing text. [http://www.student.northpark.edu/pemente/sed/sed1line.txt]

Pizzini, Ken, SED, A STREAM EDITOR, Free Software Foundation, 1998. [http://www.gnu.org/software/sed/manual/sed.html]

TEX and Friends

Doob, Michael, A GENTLE INTRODUCTION TO TEX, Web page, 1993. A recommended introduction to using plain TEX. [ftp://ctan.tug.org/tex-archive/documentation/gentle/]

Grandsire, Christophe, THE METAFONT AND TEX/LATEX RESOURCE PAGE, Web site, 2003. Gives an introductory tutorial to using META-FONT. [http://metafont.latex.free.fr/]

Hahn, Jane, LATEX FOR EVERYONE, PTR Prentice-Hall Inc., 1993. A wonderful book for those who want to use the power of TEX for typesetting correspondence, papers, articles, and reports.

Knuth, Donald E., THE TEXBOOK, Addison-Wesley, 1984. The original TEX book, written by the author of TEX.

Oetiker, Tobias, et al., THE NOT SO SHORT INTRODUCTION TO LATEX, Web site, 1999. A recommended introduction to using LATEX.
[ftp://ctan.tug.org/tex-archive/documentation/lshort/]

Robbins, Arnold, "What's GNU: Texinfo," LINUX JOURNAL, issue 6, October 1994. An introductory tutorial.
[http://www.linuxjournal.com/article.php?sid=2840]

Underwood, Rebecca, et al., LATEX AND BIBTEX TUTORIALS AND ASSIGNMENT, Web site, 1996. A good LATEX tutorial that shows how to typeset an article. Available online in DVI format.
[http://www.soe.ucsc.edu/~karplus/80k/latex-tutorial-new.dvi]

D.2.3 UNIX and Linux History Books

These are books about the history of the system and its software.

Finseth, Craig A., THE CRAFT OF TEXT EDITING, Springer-Verlag and Co., 1991. The theory of text editing; a technical description of the technology of text editors.
[http://www.finseth.com/~fin/craft]

Hauben, Michael and Ronda Hauben, NETIZENS: ON THE HISTORY AND IMPACT OF THE NET, IEEE Computer Society Press, 1997. A thorough social history of the net, with much material on UNIX history throughout.
[http://www.columbia.edu/~hauben/netbook/]

Kernighan, Brian W. and Rob Pike, THE UNIX PROGRAMMING ENVIRONMENT, Prentice Hall Computer Books, 1984. Describes the tools philosophy of UNIX and what it affords programmers.
[http://cm.bell-labs.com/cm/cs/upe/]

Salus, Peter H., A QUARTER CENTURY OF UNIX, Addison-Wesley, 1994. A complete history of the UNIX operating system.

Walker, A.N., THE UNIX ENVIRONMENT, John Wiley and Sons Ltd., 1984. A pleasant tour of the system; the fact that it is taken on such dated equipment only demonstrates the tenacity of the tools.

D.3 Linux News and Commentary

These are the essential sources of news and opinion on Linux and free software.

The **Free Software Foundation**'s Web site is a source for both philosophical readings and news about the GNU Project, its free software operating system. [http://gnu.org/]

Linux.Com provides feature stories, links, and a database of Linux User Groups (LUGs). [http://linux.com/]

Linux Journal is the oldest print magazine devoted to Linux.   Monthly. [http://linuxjournal.com/]

Linux Today aggregates and publishes "Linux News on Internet Time." [http://linuxtoday.com/]

Linux Weekly News has covered Linux and the free software movement since 1998. [http://lwn.net/]

Slashdot is a popular news and discussion site for enthusiasts of Linux and free software; newshounds usually check Slashdot several times daily. [http://slashdot.org/]

Program Index

Concept Index

I

Q

R